THE SOURCES OF
CHRISTIAN ETHICS

Servais Pinckaers, O.P.

THE SOURCES OF CHRISTIAN ETHICS

Translated from the third edition by
Sr. Mary Thomas Noble, O.P.

The Catholic University of America Press
Washington, D.C.

First published as Servais Pinckaers, *Les sources de la morale chrétienne,*
copyright © University Press Fribourg, 1985, 1990, 1993. The
translation was funded in part by a grant from the Council of
the University of Fribourg.

The original French edition won the 1985 Lichtenstein Prize awarded by
the University of Fribourg, Switzerland.

LIBRARY OF CONGRESS CATALOGING-IN-PUBLICATION DATA
Pinckaers, Servais.
    [Sources de la morale chrétienne. English]
    The sources of Christian ethics / Servais
Pinckaers : translated by Mary Thomas Noble.
        p.   cm.
    Includes bibliographical references and index.
        1. Christian ethics—Catholic authors.   2. Christian
ethics—History.   I. Title.
    BJ1249.P5613   1995
    241—dc20
    94-28663
    ISBN 0-8132-0834-3 (alk. paper)
    ISBN 0-8132-0818-1 (pbk. : alk. paper)

Dedicated in faithful love
to Our Lady of La Sarte*
and to my parents

*For readers unfamiliar with this title of Our Lady, the author's dedication refers to a shrine of Our Lady in La Sarte, a town near Huy in Belgium. Since the seventeenth century, La Sarte has been an important center for Marian pilgrimages. Until 1967 it was also the site of the Dominican Novitiate and House of Studies where Father Pinckaers taught. La Sarte evokes too the memory of Father Dominique Pire, O.P., one-time pastor there, founder of the organization "Aid for Displaced Persons" in the wake of World War II. Because of his outstanding work with the "hard core refugees," Father Pire was awarded the Nobel Peace Prize in 1958.

Contents

Foreword to the English Edition

ROMANUS CESSARIO, O.P.

A Recovery of Moral Teaching in the Church

The Sources of Christian Ethics reaches its English-speaking readership at a particularly opportune moment. Dominican Father Servais Pinckaers provides both professional theologians and educated readers with an invaluable compendium for practicing and studying moral theology in the aftermath of *Veritatis splendor*. As one who has benefited immensely from Father Pinckaers's learning, I am honored to introduce this edition of his book published through the good services of The Catholic Unversity of America Press.

The 1993 encyclical *Veritatis splendor* represents a new initiative in the history of magisterial teaching. It undertakes to expound "fundamental questions of the Church's moral teaching" and so provides authoritative norms for establishing the morality of particular human actions of all kinds. In other words, the encyclical takes up the challenge of helping each believer answer what Pope John Paul II calls "the primordial question: What is good and evil? What must be done to have eternal life?" (no. 111). The encyclical gives technical precision to the moral teaching of the *Catechism of the Catholic Church,* which presents Christian moral teaching as an instruction about living in Christ. The present volume offers precious commentary on these two documents of the Magisterium and thereby helps the reader develop his or her own response to the question concerning moral conduct and Christian salvation.

Prudence, working through the moral virtues, disposes a person to good actions. In *Veritatis Splendor,* Pope John Paul II appropriates this central thesis of Thomist moral theology for the common teaching of the Church: "It is the 'heart' converted to the Lord and to the love of what is good which is really the source of true judgments of conscience. Indeed, in order to 'prove what is the will of God, what is good and acceptable and perfect' (Rom 12:2), knowledge of God's law in general is certainly necessary, but it is not sufficient: what is essential is a sort of 'connaturality' between man and the true good" (no. 64).

The connaturality between man and the true good is one of the major underlying themes in Father Pinckaers's book. When he explains why the moral condition of the person affects the judgment of prudence, he is showing us how connaturality works. In brief, upright living supports prudence, whereas vicious *habitus* impair and can even destroy it. Unfortunately, however, the truth of connaturality has long been eclipsed in moral theology. Father Pinckaers provides a masterful account of how, in the sixteenth century, the development of legalistic casuistry suppressed the classical moral understanding of the virtues as expressions of a graced connaturality between man and the true good. The casuist systems controlled the moral context of the Church for roughly four centuries, from the mid-sixteenth century through the first half of the twentieth century. Because casuistry constituted a kind of ecclesiastical jurisprudence, its practitioners paid little attention to connaturality. In this book, Father Pinckaers strives to recover this important classical theme.

One of the ways in which the present volume executes this recovery is by rooting moral theology more firmly in its source, the Gospel of Christ. Father Pinckaers begins with revelation and mines the theological works that helped to articulate the moral message of the Gospel. The focus of Father Pinckaers's work thus comes to center on the person of Christ. Indeed, the heart of this book lies in chapters 5 and 6, which consider the Sermon on the Mount and St. Paul. Here the Gospel message is central: in the same way that Christ, because he remains the Eternal Word of Truth, exercises his authentic human freedom so that it always embodies the greatest charity or love, so the one who remains united to Christ enjoys the assurance that his or her actions embody the full measure of moral truth.

This Christological portrayal of the moral life reveals the deepest strains of the thought of Thomas Aquinas. In his moral treatises, Aquinas demonstrates with utter clarity the role of theology and the centrality of the New Law. Basing his thesis on Paul's Letter to the Romans, on Matthew's Gospel, and on certain texts of St. Augustine, Aquinas describes the moral life as flowing from the grace of the Holy Spirit received by faith in Christ; he shows how it operates in charity and finds its truest expression in Scripture, particularly in the Sermon on the

Mount. For St. Thomas, the Spirit and the Gospel are the primary sources of theology and Christian morality. His voluminous work in the *Summa* flows directly from the Word of God. It is a commentary on Scripture, on the Fathers, and on the Church's teaching and experience, enriched by his own philosophical insights.

Father Pinckaers has argued consistently, before and since the Second Vatican Council, that St. Thomas must be read and interpreted anew. He must be seen not through the eyes of his commentators but from the vantage point of his forebears in the history of thought. We must know Aquinas's sources. In this book, Father Pinckaers illuminates those sources. He invites us to go even further back than the Fathers of the Church—back to the Gospel itself, with its whole moral context. This sacred instruction, Father Pinckaers contends, will supply the basis for our theological reflection. There is a common tendency to view St. Thomas's moral teaching exclusively in terms of its Aristotelian sources. But this perspective ignores or neglects the deeply evangelical character of Aquinas's moral thought as embodied in his discussions of the New Law, especially as expressed in the theological virtues and the gifts of the Holy Spirit, of divine grace, which is the root source of these gifts, and of beatitude (including the Gospel Beatitudes), which is the end-term of the New Law. Father Pinckaers presents Thomas Aquinas as a man of the Gospel, heir and herald of the good news preached by Saints Dominic and Francis.

But Father Pinckaers's esteem for the Angelic Doctor is neither exclusive nor blind. Aquinas himself repeatedly invites us to return to the Word of God, that Word expressive beyond all words, and to explore every available resource of theology, philosophy, and science. He encourages dialogue with a variety of traditions, within the Church and outside of it. Far from inducing a fortress mentality in which one would seek refuge in a Thomistic system, an authentic engagement with Aquinas fosters the solidity and openness needed for ongoing theological enterprise. Finally, Father Pinckaers considers that a genuine esteem for St. Thomas will deepen our appreciation of the Fathers of the Church and of the authentic theologians of any age.

Our Contemporary Circumstances

In this book, Father Pinckaers takes on several disputed questions in contemporary Christian ethics. Three issues stand out. First, he addresses the methodological question of the proper relation between the Scriptures and moral theology. Indeed, his own work exemplifies the correct way to develop a moral theology fully grounded in its biblical sources. Second, Father Pinckaers investigates the link between Christian ethics and the life sciences. He renders us an invaluable service by pointing up the significant differences in the competencies of the two sets of disciplines. Finally, Father Pinckaers raises important questions in the field of theological anthropology, giving full consideration to the pre-ethical dimension of moral action. In contrast to prevailing views of ethics influenced by Enlightenment thinkers, Father Pinckaers underscores the positive role that natural inclinations play in the moral life. Let us consider these three issues in turn.

The return of moral theology to Scripture, as encouraged by the Second Vatican Council, must be supported by a recovery of lost theological memory. The return, therefore, should not occur in a historical or systematic vacuum. Historical studies reveal the great difference between two alternative visions of moral theory that emerged in the wake of late medieval nominalism. On the one hand, a shrinking process began to affect moral teaching—a process that resulted in the gradual distancing of moral teaching from Scripture, faith, the virtues, and other elements of a complete moral instruction. But we can also observe a moral teaching, such as that reflected in the Thomist commentator John Capreolus (+ 1444), that remained more faithful to the spirit of the Gospel and refused to surrender the science of morals into the hands of jurists. Father Pinckaers points up the defects of both Ockham and the authors of the later casuist manuals, but his criticism is always positive and acknowledges the truth contained in any given work or school. Still, he maintains that a renewal of casuistry, however attractive such an option might appear as a way to solve difficult moral cases, would entail a return to legalism, and so he calls instead for a return to the Scriptures as words of "spirit and life" (Jn 6:63).

Father Pinckaers's discussion of the relation between Christian ethics and science concerns only essentials. He distinguishes the two according to their basic methods of procedure: observation for science, self-awareness and reflection for Christian ethics. This distinction, of course, provides the necessary condition for real dialogue between two different but complementary types of knowledge and understanding. But Christian ethics, and the anthropology that undergirds it, must not, even for the sake of such dialogue, ape the methods and contributions of the behavioral sciences. Christian ethics is characterized by and presupposes a spiritual interiority. As *Veritatis splendor* affirms, "what is essential is a sort of 'connaturality' between man and the true good" (no. 64). Only God's grace can bestow this wisdom "from on high" (Lk 1:78).

Finally, Father Pinckaers develops the anthropology that unfolds in the encyclical as well as in the *Catechism*. His success in setting forth a moral teaching that both upholds moral truth and takes full account of human freedom is due, at least in part, to his familiarity with modern philosophy, especially modern theories of ethics and anthropology. His helpful commentary on the place of natural inclinations in discussions of moral theology is a case in point. Prevailing modern views of natural inclinations cannot contribute much to an authentic moral theology. For some ethicists, these inclinations are merely biological mechanisms or psychic impulses, instinctive and inferior, blind and compelling, with no useful place in moral theology. In contrast, Father Pinckaers shows that natural, human inclinations actually belong to the spiritual order. Inclinations to truth, goodness, and life in society are at the heart of our freedom. They are its dynamic, life-giving source. We are not required to confront and dominate our natural inclinations so as to subjugate them. Inclinations, he argues, make the man. They provide the first principles of moral action, principles articulated in natural law. This realist anthropology offers a refreshing contrast to accounts influenced by Ockham or Kant.

To be sure, Father Pinckaers does not neglect human freedom and moral absolutes. His argument echoes *Veritatis splendor* in urging us to confront the false voices of freedom crying out in "many different 'areopagi,'" as the West becomes estranged from its Christian roots (*Tertio millennio adveniente*, no. 57). Father Pinckaers's book discusses *Veritatis splendor*'s "exceptionless moral norms" (no. 82) without recapitulating the legalism of the old casuistry. Instead, Father Pinckaers describes how the Christian develops connaturality with the true Good. This occurs only within a communion of persons where individuals are shaped by the truth of the divine and evangelical law. Father Pinckaers adopts a virtue-centered approach to moral theology, one that relies on the cardinal virtue of prudence, alongside the canons of moral jurisprudence. His work represents an expansive commentary on a central claim of *Veritatis splendor*, namely, that "man's genuine moral autonomy in no way means the rejection but rather means the acceptance of the moral law, of God's command . . ." (no. 41). In other words, the prudent man or woman is able to embrace the full truth-value of Catholic moral teaching and at the same time exercise a full measure of personal freedom.

The theology of the moral life found in *The Sources of Christian Ethics* emerges most clearly in the author's discussion of freedom. Special discernment is required to distinguish the authentic meaning of freedom—

a freedom that always leads to excellence—from freedom that is false. As *Veritatis splendor* expresses it, in a false freedom the person's choices are not "in harmony with the true good of the person" (no. 72). The true good of the person must never be compromised for reasons of expediency. Even one bad choice, so the Holy Father affirms, puts "us in conflict with our ultimate end, the supreme good, God himself" (ibid.). As the Christian believer acts under the influence of infused prudence and with the aid of its gift of the Holy Spirit, counsel, he or she already possesses the Good. "Genuine freedom is an outstanding manifestation of the divine image in man. For God willed to leave man 'in the power of his own counsel' (see Sir 15:14), so that he would seek his Creator of his own accord and would freely arrive at full and blessed perfection by cleaving to God" (no. 34). Freedom understood in this way Father Pinckaers calls "freedom for excellence" (liberté de qualité). Those who want to fathom his thought and the contribution that it makes to contemporary theological discussion will need to discover the meaning of this phrase in the New Testament account of Christ's own freedom. For as the "concrete norm" of the moral life, Christ himself alone makes it possible for the human person to achieve his or her most high calling through the exercise of both the theological virtues and the infused moral virtues.

Acknowledgments

Father Pinckaers wants to acknowledge several persons who helped to make *The Sources of Christian Ethics* available to the English-speaking world. Father Thomas Donlan, O.P., a longstanding and devoted promoter of Dominican publications, was actively involved in the early stages of the translation. Sister Mary E. Ingham, C.S.J., labored extensively on a first draft and the notes. The Benedictine nuns who staff St. Bede's Publications began work on publishing the book and, later, generously handed the project over to The Catholic University of America Press. There a large debt of gratitude is owed to David McGonagle and his staff, especially to Susan Needham, who worked closely with the translator, Sister Mary Thomas Noble, O.P., in order to bring this important enterprise to a successful completion. Finally, grateful acknowledgment is made to the Homeland Foundation for a grant that helped to support work on this edition.

Dominican Cardinal Jerôme Hamer, who once taught Father Pinckaers at La Sartre in Belgium, expressed a sentiment shared by all those who had the privilege of working on this edition of *Les sources de la morale chrétienne*: "Father Pinckaers has specialized in moral theology for a long time. Today he is its undisputed master."

28 January 1995
Feast of Saint Thomas Aquinas
Dominican House of Studies
Washington, D.C.

Introduction

Vatican Council II, expressing its concern for the renewal of Christian morality, noted that "its scientific exposition should be more thoroughly nourished by scriptural teaching." The Council further urged the re-establishment of moral theology's links with dogma and the teaching of the Church Fathers. It reaffirmed the connectedness of moral theology with spirituality, pastoral practice, philosophy, and the behavioral sciences.[1] These directives confirm certain strong currents that have been developing within the Church over the last decades, initiatives of renewal in the fields of Scripture, patristics, liturgy, and ecumenism.

One of the principal changes introduced by the Council has been, for the People of God, a new, full access to Scripture and to the liturgy, which is the Word of God prayed by his people. But obviously, no decree or document, however enlightened, can bring about the proposed reforms unaided. What is needed is revision in depth. The theologian, for example, cannot be content with merely multiplying references to Scripture or to extensive patristic sources, but must penetrate and grasp theology's deepest foundations and principles.

Most importantly, Christian morality cannot be a mere "given." The riches of its vast heritage have not yet been tapped as have those of Scripture and dogma. Christian moral teaching is far more than a catalogue of precepts concerning behavior, classified and more or less determined by particular situations. It must convey a systematic overview of its field, provide basic criteria for judgment, and come to terms with the entire domain of human activity. In the course of the ages, moreover, it has developed its own language and technical procedures. The reform of moral theology, urged because of a certain narrowness of vision and

---

1. See *Decree on the Training of Priests*, in *Vatican Council II. The Conciliar and Post Conciliar Documents*. Ed. Austin Flannery. Northport, NY: Costello, 1975. See also the document issued by the Sacred Congregation for Catholic Education, *The Formation of Future Priests*, February 22, 1976.

notable gaps observed in the recent past, must deal with this entire range, beginning with what is known as fundamental moral theology.[2] For an authentic restoration, foundations must first be laid bare, assessed, and renewed.

This is by no means easy. Although most of us can make moral judgments in concrete cases, it is extremely hard to reflect on the criteria determining our values and to explain the various concepts implicit in them. We are inclined to take for granted the truths we learned in early childhood or at school without close scrutiny. While this may well lead us to the truth, it can also place impoverishing limitations and narrowness on our grasp of that same truth. For clear vision we must look more closely, ponder more deeply.

It would be all too easy to oppose traditional moral principles simply because they are traditional, on the pretext of furthering the renewal and openness the Council has asked for. Simplistic, too, to say we are so broad-minded that we prefer liberty to law. This would be tantamount to setting out on that broad road of which the Gospel speaks, reviving a host of ancient errors, and getting nowhere. It would mean turning away from the narrow path that moral theology has followed fruitfully for over two thousand years—the only path that bears the footprints of Christ and leads to God. We have to beware of trendy expressions and ideas that only touch the surface. We need to plunge into the reality of the moral life, where we will find depth and solidity. In the field of Christian ethics, as elsewhere, we must earn our bread by the sweat of our brow.

In my opinion the chief task for today's moral theologians is to reopen the lines of communication between Christian ethics and the Word of God. We must seize upon the grace offered by the Council. Doubtless most Catholic ethicists would agree with this in theory, but we have not yet made it happen. We can even identify a strong contemporary current of thought that would posit an ethical system so rational and so autonomous as to be quite independent of Scripture. Our undertaking is more difficult than we realize. It is not enough, for example, for moral theologians to proliferate their contacts with exegetes, plying them for documents they can use as source material in their attempted renewal. It is all too obvious that we no longer speak the same language. The roadblocks to encounter seem endless. It may even be that a certain concept of moral theology current today has, by an internal logic, greatly diminished our contact with Scripture.

---

2. Council document on "The Formation of Future Priests," n. 96.

I would go still further. Is the mere text of the Bible sufficient for the renewal of Christian moral theory? It is hardly enough to lace our presentations with biblical quotations. This kind of dependence on the letter cannot give life. Surely the decisive issue is rather the rediscovery of that point at the heart of Christian morality and of the Christian personality where the Spirit dwells. Finding this, we must throw aside the encumbering clods of earth so that the Source may well up once more in all its fulness.

This is no trifling project. There are enormous obstacles, particularly on the intellectual plane. Christian ethics, by concentrating over the last few centuries on obligations, has become hard as rock. It blocks the life that would spring up in new growth. True, subjectivity and human passions did need to be put in their place. Yet how can we ignore the existence of another kind of spontaneity, the spiritual? How can we eliminate mystical spirituality from the domain of Christian ethics?

Why was Scripture given to us? Clearly, to quench our thirst with the torrents of the Holy Spirit, to feed us with the bread of the Word. Scripture is the primary source of all theology, and we need to return to it if we wish to make any kind of worthwhile contribution to the work of renewal in the field of Christian ethics. Hence my title, *The Source of Christian Ethics.*

This problem is not the exclusive preserve of moral theologians. Any Christian can see that morality is in crisis; we know this from peoples' reactions at large. A professor of moral theology notes a wide spectrum of attitudes in his class. "Good heavens, this is no laughing matter!" A priest may challenge: "Do you really think Christian ethics is still valid?" Moral problems of all kinds are the order of the day, and experts in the most specialized studies are bound to take them into consideration. There is endless work ahead for moral theologians, but the field has become so muddied with agitation and conflict that the inconclusive answers and casuistic solutions of former times no longer serve. Once more we must explore the world and the human person in depth.

The scope of Christian ethics is vast, especially in its relationship to Scripture, dogma, spirituality, and the sciences. To become entangled in the discussions and problems escalating in all directions is to get lost in a forest thick with brambles and thorns and seemingly endless. We cannot follow every path or bark up every tree. Once we have clarified our goal and our initial orientation, we have to choose one single path and keep to it. It is imperative to find the one that will bring us to our goal.

I have been guided in my undertaking primarily by the subject matter itself rather than by current disputes between moral theologians. I have tried to dig deep enough to uncover and follow the logical threads woven by history and by systematic reflection, somewhat as a miner or a quarrier might trace the veins in coal or rock. I have tried, too, to set up my own "order of procedure" or "order of precedence," rather than chase after all the questions and opinions that have ranged so far afield and bypassed some of the most essential and neglected problems.

Also, confronted by the countless roads carving up the moral terrain, I have had to make some deliberate choices. I have opted for the roads that lead most directly to my main goal, and this goal has become progressively clearer to me. I have tried, in a word, to clear the way, all too often obstructed or even condemned, that leads to a rebonding of Christian ethics and spiritual spontaneity within the human heart, under the action of the Holy Spirit, through faith in Christ. This has been a priority for me. It has led me to bypass some very interesting problems, so as to keep this book within realistic limits.

My readers—my public—fill my mental foreground. A book is a word that needs to be adapted, shaped, for its readers. This book is addressed primarily to theology students; it is the fruit of many years of teaching. I have never thought of my students as potential technical experts in the field of Christian ethics, but rather as persons called to help other Christians in their response to the deep questions in life, which lie at the heart of moral theology. I have known that they would work out of their own personal experience and ideas, and from the vantage point of the doctrinal heritage they were receiving.

While fully aware of the need for a thoroughly serious treatment of the material, I have opted for the simplest and clearest presentation possible, since I am convinced that this is the best way to promote growth and discovery and to make my ideas more generally accessible. It has often struck me that an understanding of moral principles is essentially the fruit of human experience and maturity; it calls for more than study and skill in juggling ideas. This is another reason for leaving aside problematics requiring a good deal of technical knowledge, which might only result in frustrating and discouraging readers. For the same reason I have tried to relate even the most abstract questions to everyday experience, and to talk about them in ordinary language. As a matter of fact, the material at hand corresponds rather neatly with my experience in moral matters and with the need for order and clarity in teaching. In view of this, my book is not meant to be another manual but rather a guide, opening up roadways and horizons.

I am under no illusions. When the last page of a book is written, the adventure is just beginning. There are inevitable risks, but the seed that is planted holds new hope. This is all the more true when the book is about Christian realities. Here, nothing is achieved without the workings of grace. This remark is not meant to add a touch of piety to my introduction but to point to a truth underlying the very substance of the whole enterprise. Particularly in the field of Christian ethics, I am convinced that work is useless unless it flows from faith and prayer. This applies equally to intellectual work, study, and daily effort. Theology is ecclesial work, and no one, whether concerned with minor details or with the entire building, can build without the Holy Spirit.

At the outset of this book, therefore, it seems fitting that we should ask in all confidence for a share in the gift of filial fear, which St. Thomas relates to the virtue of hope, and which finds direct expression in the invocation "Our Father." May this Name be glorified in our words, our thoughts, our actions. It is not without significance that the beatitude of the poor in spirit has been associated with hope, for this beatitude is about the humble, the little ones to whom the mysteries of God's Wisdom are revealed. Why should we not include among these everyone who is interested in theology, who yearns for a deeper understanding of Christian ethics?

This book is divided into three parts. After defining Christian ethics and giving a brief overview of its scope, I have dwelt on two principal aspects: its human dimension, as related to the behavioral sciences, and its Christian dimension, as found in St. Paul and in the Sermon on the Mount as interpreted by St. Augustine and St. Thomas. The second part traces the history of Christian ethics, principally from the viewpoint of the systematization imposed upon it from the time of the Church Fathers to our own day. Finally, in the third section, I examine the deepest foundations of the human moral edifice: freedom and law. Throughout the book, my aim has been to return Christian ethics to its sources: Scripture, the Holy Spirit, the Gospel law, and natural law, which is rooted in freedom itself.

I

———

What Is Christian Ethics? The Search
for a Definition

I. VARIOUS DEFINITIONS AND CONCEPTS

What is Christian ethics? The simplest questions, things a child might ask, are often the deepest and most difficult. For scholastic authors, definitions had to come first. A definition told you the nature of the subject you were going to study, its essential elements and in general the material it would cover. It determined your point of view and the method you would use; the scholastics called this the formal object. Their first concern, on embarking on the study of some branch of theology, was to answer the natural question, What is it?

But when we ask moral theologians, ancient or modern, traditional or innovative, for a definition of their science, we get a surprise. There are many answers to the question, some quite divergent, others lengthy and vague. Father Prümmer, a classic moralist familiar with nearly all the works of moral theologians up to his own day, put it this way: "It is very hard to get a real definition of moral theology from the ancients. As for the moderns, their definitions are often obscure or incomplete."[1]

---

1. "Vix reperitur apud antiquos definitio realis Theologiae Moralis. Definitiones autem a modernis datae non raro sunt obscurae vel incompletae." D. Prümmer, *Manuale Theologiae Moralis,* I, n. 1

After studying a score of manuals of the last two centuries, I can attest that they present

By "ancients" he meant the Fathers of the Church and medieval theologians; "moderns" were the authors of the manuals of moral theology written in the past four centuries. As for the post-conciliar moral theologians—beyond Father Prümmer's horizon—their often critical reactions to traditional moral theology and their propensity for reworking it have left them in a perpetual state of uncertainty and research, so that their chances of framing a generic definition are slim indeed.

---

a fairly common definition of moral theology, corresponding to Father Prümmer's and containing four main elements:

1. A branch of theology. In regard to the first element, authors differ. Some hold that it is a branch of theology (e.g., Scavini, Marc, Génicot, Merkelbach), while others call it a science (Nüssle, Lehmkuhl, Noldin, Vermeesch, Vittrant). Father Prümmer uses both terms, referring to it as a branch of theological science.

2. Directing human actions. In all the manuals, human actions or activities are mentioned as the subject matter of moral theology, but there are different terms for expressing the bearing that morality has on them: "directing" (Marc, Haine, Sebastiani), "regulating" (Vermeesch), "ordering" (Merkelbach), or vaguer still, "looking into" (D'Annibale, Bucceroni), "regarding" (Lehmkuhl, Van Kol), "considering" (Génicot). Prümmer is clearer: "judges and directs."

3. Reference to the light of revelation appears in various forms: "according to the principles of Christian revelation" (Lehmkuhl); "according to revealed principles" (Merkelbach and Prümmer); "according to the norms of divine revelation" (Nüssle). But there is some hesitation here. Others are less explicit, and say only "according to the law of God" (Marc); "what is licit and illicit as indicated by divine law" (Bucceroni). Some additionally mention reason (H. Jone), and others say nothing of revelation (D'Annibale, Noldin, Vittrant, Van Kol), thinking perhaps that the next part of the definition suffices to include it.

4. Almost all the authors of the manuals conclude their definitions with the ordering of actions to their ultimate end, either without further elaboration (D'Annibale, Lehmkuhl, Merkelbach) or with the qualification "supernatural" (Noldin, Prümmer, Jone, Vittrant) or some similar expression such as *eternal life* (Marc, Haine, Bucceroni). Only Génicot mentions supernatural beatitude.

From this rapid rundown we can draw a few conclusions:

1. If no definition of moral theology can be found among the "earlier theologians," as Father Prümmer puts it, the simple reason is that they did not think it necessary; they thought it was enough to speak of speculative and practical theology. The need for a definition arose when moral theology set itself up as an independent science, separate from dogma and asceticism, in the modern era. This indicated a change in the concept of morality.

2. Finding no definition authorized by the scholastic school, modern ethicists created one they thought would satisfy everyone, basing it mainly on St. Thomas's *prima secundae*. There were variations in the way it was articulated, but its principal elements were fairly generally accepted.

3. In my opinion, these definitions are flawed in being more verbal than real. They do not bring out the formal element of morality at work in the composition of the manuals, which is its connection with law, the source of obligations, and they allay suspicion by introducing the idea of the ordering to a supernatural end. Yet this end plays only a minor role, subordinate to law. This is why I shall propose a little further on some definitions of moral theology that better express the formal element characterizing the varying concepts.

The difficulty is genuine but not insuperable. In fact on closer scrutiny we see that it throws light on the whole question. At the very least it alerts us to the fact that the original question, apparently so innocent, contains implications we never suspected, implications that are quite important.

Modern sciences also experience difficulty in marking off their areas of competence and in defining their objects and methods, but this does not prevent their continual development. In the same way, the work of theologians and the moral reflections of ordinary people can grow and develop even before they reach a common agreement about definitions. Whereas the logical order requires definitions at the outset of a properly scientific exposition, the order of discovery operates inversely. Only after thorough research and reflection on the methods followed and the results obtained do we arrive at a well-formulated definition.

Still, we need some adequate definition if we are going to explain Christian ethics to students or readers who are encountering this "sacred science" for the first time. And the definition must be something more than a glib formula. A definition is something like an airport: some people are landing after a long flight—these are the researchers; others are taking off, and for them the airport is a point of departure. Every definition carries within it a choice of direction; it is important to clarify this.

Moral theologians differ widely in defining their science, but this is no reason for dismay. It simply reminds us that in this field there are no easy answers. In order to discern the firm foundations, rules, and limitations of moral action, deep reflection is needed. Moral action is not merely a matter of practical obedience; the mind's role is essential. Nor is it the exclusive preserve of specialists; the wise and learned may fall into error while the simple are given understanding and go straight to the heart of things. Christian ethics bonds people perhaps more successfully than any other science: the great and the insignificant, the learned and the simple meet on common ground. In our searching we each need all the others and can be enriched by the fruits of their experience. This is why the hunt for a good definition involves everyone.

I shall, in the following pages, discuss a number of typical definitions and show how they answer to different concepts and divisions of this science. I will not quote these definitions verbatim, but simply summarize them as honestly as I can, so as to include the chief moral positions held throughout the history of Christian theology, and perduring even to our own day. With the help of such a survey, we should be in a position to make an informed choice of our own definition.

Various Definitions

In all definitions of Christian ethics there are certain elements included by all moralists but interpreted differently. We can begin by saying that Christian ethics is a branch of theology that studies human acts in the light of revelation. Differences emerge in the middle of this definition, where rules for right moral action have to be spelled out. This is where the determining element of the definition and of the concept of right moral action lies. As Schopenhauer wrote, "It is easy enough to preach about the right way of acting, but how hard it is to give reasons." This is the point on which definitions and systems of Christian ethics differ: the fundamental basis of moral principles.

First Definition

Christian ethics is the branch of theology that studies human acts insofar as they are subject to the moral law, to its imperatives and the obligations determined by these, in the light of revelation.

The central concept underlying this definition is law, seen as an expression of God's will and of reason. It is the idea of freedom overlaid with obligation. Morality becomes a matter of obligations, classified according to the commands issued.

This idea of morality was disseminated, particularly from the seventeenth century onward, by way of the manuals of moral theology. Such manuals divided their material roughly into two parts, one devoted to the basics, the other to particulars. The first part was dominated by the concept of law in general, while the second focused on the Ten Commandments seen as an expression of natural law. To these were added the precepts of the Church and some prescriptions of canon law.

This view of Christian ethics has become classic over the past four centuries, to the point of being identified, often, with Catholic moral theology. It is the viewpoint of "the moderns" of whom Father Prümmer speaks, and it characterizes casuistry. Its influence has been powerful; from the manuals, destined for the formation of priests, it passed into the pulpits and, finally, the catechisms.

Second Definition

Christian ethics is that branch of theology that studies human acts in order to conform them to duty and to the norms imposed on us by reason and by the will of God, in the light of revelation.

The central idea here is duty, linked doubtless to the idea of obligations but connoting a greater interiority. The basic orientation is to reason and personal conscience. Obviously we are moving into the tradition of Kant and his categorical imperative. The expression *norms* begins to supersede *law,* which has the ring of an authority external to ourselves.

This far more philosophical concept of Christian ethics has also slipped into the manuals of moral theology, no distinction being made between obligation and duty, even though this conception creates a different presentation of moral theory. This definition favors the older division of duties to God, to neighbor, and to oneself, and we find this, too, in catechisms and examinations of conscience.

Third Definition

Christian ethics is that branch of theology that studies human acts in order to direct them to the attainment of true happiness and to the ultimate end of the person by means of the virtues, and this in the light of revelation.

In this view, a person's true happiness or personal good, seen as an ultimate goal, becomes the be all and end all of Christian ethics, outweighing any consideration of obligations, precepts, or norms. Here we are dealing with a theory of morality based on an attraction for the true and the good, rather than an orientation to commands and obligations.

In this instance Christian ethics is divided according to the virtues, theological or moral, considered as interior principles of action, to which are joined particular laws and grace, by their origin exterior principles. Here we recognize a concept of St. Thomas Aquinas, who begins his moral theology not with a definition but with the treatise on beatitude and our final end. As we shall see further on, this viewpoint is basically in harmony with the Fathers of the Church. There is a difference, however, which emerges later in the very heart of the Thomistic teaching on moral theology:

a. Despite their concern to follow St. Thomas, many have actually salvaged, from his treatise on beatitude, only the idea of the human person in relation to a final goal. Prümmer defines Christian ethics as "the branch of theological science that judges human actions and directs them to a supernatural end in the light of revealed principles."[2] E. Dublanchy writes in his article on ethics in the *Dictionnaire de Théologie Catholique*: "According to the definition of St. Thomas Aquinas, moral theology has as its object the study of human acts considered in their relationship of harmony or disharmony with the ultimate supernatural end willed by God as obligatory for all people."[3] This last quotation shows clearly why beatitude was eliminated from the third definition. Being ordered to a final end established by the divine will implied an objective obligation, and so harmonized with the theory of moral obligation. On the other hand, the desire for happiness seemed too subjective, and would always be countered, as we shall see, by moral codes based on obligation or duty.

These would-be expressions of the Thomistic concept of obedience belong actually to the modern school of obligation. In theory they generally prefer to divide their subject matter according to the virtues as St. Thomas did, but in practice their treatment of the virtues focuses principally on the obligations arising from them.

b. For St. Thomas, in the mainstream tradition of Aristotle and the Fathers of the Church, the question of happiness is incontestably the first consideration in Christian moral theory. It is natural to everyone. It points to the question of our last end, which presupposes a certain amount of reflection, as can be seen from the more abstract way in which it is formulated. The question of true happiness is essential to St. Thomas's definition of Christian ethics. It expresses the fundamental human thrust toward the true and the good. This in turn is strengthened by the exercise of virtue and the resulting experience gained in all areas of human activity.

For St. Thomas as for his forerunners, it was the most obvious thing in the world to divide the subject matter of Christian ethics according to the virtues. The question of precepts and obligations was secondary, at the service of the virtues.

---

2. Prümmer, *Manuale*, n. 2: "Theologia moralis est scientiae illa pars, quae dijudicat atque dirigit actus humanos in ordine ad finem supernaturalem iuxta principia revelata."
3. "Suivant la définition de saint Thomas, la théologie morale a pour objet l'étude des actes humains, considérés selon leur relation de convenance ou de disconvenance avec la fin dernière surnaturelle voulue par Dieu comme obligatoire pour tous les hommes."

Fourth Definition

Christian ethics is a branch of theology that studies human acts in order to conform them to the values contributing to human enrichment, and this in the light of revelation.

This definition is inspired by the modern value theory, represented notably by Max Scheler, and is much in vogue among Catholic writers. It divides moral theory according to a value system arranged in ascending order. Thus we have: vital values, such as health, ecology, and all that contributes to our vital well-being; sense values, such as pleasure; ascetical values, found in the arts; social, moral, religious, spiritual, and mystical values. The moral dimension, even if it is only one type of value among others, ought to take all the other values into account if it is going to judge and direct human activity.

This concept of morality seems more positive than that of obligations, which is in fact more concerned with sin than with virtue.

Contemporary Theories

We can characterize these by their new emphases and reactions to traditional morality rather than by any particular definition. Freedom and personal conscience override law; love and interconnectedness outweigh relationships of duty. Responsibility, creativity, and dialogue are seen as more important than obedience to authority, and a personal, individual way of acting yields to social projects. The accent is on criticism and questioning, on flexibility and marginality, rather than on speculative reflection and whatever is traditional. Modern ethicists prefer the image of explorers who proceed by way of questions and critiques, who blaze trails and leave landmarks rather than formulate definitions that might hamper the free movement of the spirit.

II. MY PROPOSAL OF A DEFINITION OF CHRISTIAN ETHICS AND MY REASONS FOR IT

Constructing a system of moral theology is like building a house. We have to begin with a solid foundation. Far from being a hindrance, this task is indispensable. In the same way, a clear, precise definition is no obstacle to the moral theologian; it undergirds his thinking and gives him a working basis.

The definition might be compared to the roof of a house. It covers and encloses the area and provides security for those within. It shields the hearth, from which the family moves outward to various activities. In the same way, the definition of a science like Christian ethics safeguards and shapes the thinking of those who pursue it and provides a springboard for action.

At this point it seems only fair and responsible to give my own definition of Christian ethics together with my reasons for it. I shall choose from among the various concepts I have described, explaining my choices as I go along. My position lies squarely within the great theological tradition reaching from the Fathers of the Church to St. Thomas. I shall be at pains to show how this traditional concept addresses the aspirations and moral problems of our time.

My Own Definition of Christian Ethics

Christian ethics is the branch of theology that studies human acts so as to direct them to a loving vision of God seen as our true, complete happiness and our final end. This vision is attained by means of grace, the virtues, and the gifts, in the light of revelation and reason.

My Reasons

1. "Christian ethics is a branch of theology . . ."

Everyone admits this. It seems obvious. Yet it raises some serious problems. In recent centuries Christian ethics has been sharply distinguished from dogma, exegesis, and spirituality. A look at the division of courses in a faculty of theology shows this clearly. This sort of division, useful enough for pedagogical purposes, could of course remain purely theoretical, a simple measure for achieving some clarity among burgeoning theological disciplines. But in actual fact it does more than translate into specialization among professors. At bottom, this division is based on a certain idea that has gradually separated Christian ethics from the other branches of sacred science. Ethicists have staked off for themselves a special area where they are autonomous. They use methods, technical terms, and categories specific to themselves and obscure to the uninitiated. Since specialists in other fields have done the same thing, dialogue between ethicists and dogmatic and biblical experts has tended to break down, with loss on both sides. In this context, theology risks being a single science in name only, and in actual fact a tangle of disconnected parts.

One of the principal tasks of theology today is to restore its own unity. Christian ethicists need to work out a concept and a definition of their science that will favor a rebonding in depth with the other branches of theology. If the object of Christian ethics is to lead us, by our actions, to the God of revelation who is our true happiness, then it is bound to maintain a deep interest in the Trinity and in the Christ who reveals this end to us and shows us how to achieve it. It will recognize in Scripture the wellspring of such knowledge.

The dogmatic theologian, on the other hand, must bear in mind that the Gospel was intended primarily not for doctrinal teaching but for preaching and for personal growth in grace. Reopening the lines of communication with the other branches of "sacred science" is vital to Christian ethics. In a very real, we could almost say a biological, sense, Christian ethics deserves to be called a part of theology. Did not St. Thomas claim that theology, with all its branches, possessed a more intrinsic unity than philosophy, since the latter admits the innate duality of metaphysics and ethics?

2. *". . . which studies human acts . . ."*

Obviously, by human acts we mean free, voluntary acts. I shall return to this later.

Once again everyone seems to be in agreement, but on closer scrutiny divergencies come to light. The casuist, for example, concentrates largely on individual acts and cases of conscience, thus narrowing the field to a multitude of separate, distinct actions. Such actions orient an entire life according to a particular intention (which goes on increasing in strength if one is faithful to it) toward an end that profoundly determines the daily choices made under its influence. Examples are a priestly or religious vocation, or a conversion. The orientation of an entire life can depend on such actions. Faithfulness to a certain intention can lead a person to a goal with a decisiveness that affects daily choices in depth.

The subject matter of Christian ethics includes, therefore, in addition to individual actions, all those orientations that determine a person's future and merge in many interrelated actions.

In recent centuries Catholic morality has been accused of concentrating too exclusively on individual actions, which is another way of fostering singularity. The accusation is well founded, yet we need not go to the opposite extreme of communitarianism and the collective, jeopardizing the personal. It is important to see that one and the same action can be profoundly personal and yet still possess a very real communitarian dimension. A priestly vocation, for example, has to be first of all highly personal, yet it gives rise to a wide involvement in ecclesial ministry, reaching far beyond the pale of believers at times. We can discover the same richness in every human vocation when it is authentic and is lived to the full. A political career might be an example. Every truly human act possesses this twofold dimension, personal and communitarian, which ought to be reflected in morality.

I propose another helpful distinction. Human acts have both an interior and an external dimension. We speak of interior acts such as knowing, willing, loving, choosing, praying, and of external acts such as vocal prayer, theft, restitution. During recent centuries moral theory, when dealing with cases of conscience, has been overly concerned with works to be done and external actions required by law, to the detriment of interiority. The latter has been reduced to a subjective intention. I should like to clarify this point in my definition. In referring to human actions, I include all the free, personal, interior actions of a person as well as the external acts we tend to think of when moral issues are raised. I might add here that I am talking about free acts, issuing from a human will in a personal and responsible way. I shall return to this, particularly in my treatment of freedom.

3. ". . . to direct them to a loving vision of God . . ."

This expresses the Christian response to the question of human destiny: we are made for the vision of God. Theologians give us a number of scriptural texts on this. We read in 1 Corinthians 13:12: "For now we see in a mirror dimly, but then face to face . . . ; then I shall understand fully, even as I have been fully understood." Again, in 1 John 3:2: ". . . we know that when he appears we shall be like him, for we shall see him as he is." And in Matthew 5:8, the sixth beatitude: "Blessed are the pure in heart, for they shall see God."

The search for God is a major biblical theme. We can find other expressions in Scripture for the fulfillment of the divine call, such as the kingdom of heaven and eternal life. They reveal different aspects of a reality that is unique and beyond words. Theology attempts to show how they converge.

I speak of a "loving" vision so as to complement the intellectual overtones of the word *vision* or *knowledge* and to savor the full meaning of biblical language. On the text of John 10:14, "I am the good shepherd; I know my own and my own know me," the Jerusalem Bible notes: "In biblical language 'knowledge' is not merely the conclusion of an intellectual process, but the fruit of an 'experience', a personal contact; when it matures, it is love." Knowledge, and the vision it brings, must be understood as happening at the heart of a personal relationship. It engages the entire person: the mind, where wisdom dwells; the will, which desires and loves; the imagination, the sensibilities, even the body. In Scripture we are dealing with a concrete, overall perception expressed in rich language and always traceable to an experience. Christian theology preserved this powerful language in large measure up to the end of the Middle Ages, at which point abstraction and analysis took over.

By "loving vision," therefore, I mean a vision that gives rise to love, and a love that seeks to know and to see. In the thirteenth century, the Dominican school stressed understanding and vision; the Franciscan school, love. These are the two main orientations of theology, and there has been a regrettable rift. I would unite them in the expression "a loving vision of God."

4. "... seen as our true, complete happiness ..."

The loving vision of God is revelation's true, complete answer to the spontaneous question raised in every human heart. I use the expression *beatitude* because it calls to mind the Gospel Beatitudes, principal sources of theological reflection on happiness. This term also adds a further refinement to the concept of happiness. We move away from just any kind of happiness and fix our attention on true, rightful happiness, which deserves our choice and the pursuit of an entire lifetime. *Beatitude* also connotes the fulness of happiness, the perfection that alone can satisfy our human yearning.

Words have their limitations. *Beatitude* is a bit abstract, less forceful and concrete than *happiness*. I shall use both terms, in order that a question so crucial in the study of Christian ethics will not become too intellectual or disappear in the mist of discussions about ideas.

In defining Christian ethics as the ordering of human actions to beatitude, I have clearly opted for a certain concept held traditionally by the Fathers of the Church and St. Thomas. For them the question of happiness was the gateway to moral theology. I believe that for our contemporary world, too, this viewpoint opens up possibilities of real progress, since it is closer to sacred Scripture and resonates the most profound of human experiences.

Like the human actions discussed above, beatitude can be at one and the same time intensely personal and communitarian in orientation. God's beatitude, or bliss, is precisely what we mean by the kingdom of heaven, the communion of saints, the Church. Through love, if it is pure, we can share in this bliss with others. We need to determine at this point what kind of happiness is capable of generating such communion. For each individual it will include both Church and world.

5. "... and our final end ..."

By final end I mean that supreme goal toward which our whole life and all our actions are oriented, the goal we envisage through all our successive choices. It corresponds to the first commandment, to love God above all things with our whole heart and to direct all our actions to him.

When we move toward a final end, a hierarchy of lesser ends is set up. This means that our actions will be assessed according to the intentions inspiring them and the particular areas of life they reflect.

Within the context of this concept of morality, finality, like the desire for happiness, is an essential dimension of our actions. It is not extrinsic to them but rather penetrates to their core, which is the willed intention. Our actions are no longer isolated; finality draws them into a dynamic whole.

Our end, and particularly our final end, need not be viewed as a kind of finish line bringing us to a full stop. It is more like an outcome, perfecting our actions and bringing our capacities to full performance. St. Augustine gives us an apt simile, telling us not to think of our end as we think of the end of the piece of bread we have eaten, but rather as a fulfillment, in the sense in which we "finish" a dress or suit and are now ready to put it on.

In considering finality we find both a personal and a communitarian dimension. Every community of persons must have a final goal: it is the common end of their activities and desires that draws people together and brings societies into being. The same finality, on the level of internal acts of faith, hope and love, and on the exterior plane of prayer, common life and the apostolate, has formed the Christian community from the earliest days of the Church and transcends all isolated activities and individuals.

6. "... by means of grace, the virtues, and the gifts ..."

A system of morality in which considerations of beatitude, interior acts, and finality predominate will naturally be divided according to the virtues—those qualities of heart and soul that are the interior, lasting principles of action—rather than according to external commandments, which determine obligations. The theological and moral virtues will be seen as the principal means for attaining to the loving vision of God.

For the grasp of such an end and such beatitude, human powers are totally inadequate. Only God himself, through the sheer gift of grace, can reveal himself to us and bring us to possess him. According to Scripture, this grace is the special work of the Holy Spirit. This is why St. Paul describes the Christian life as life in the Spirit. The treatise on grace, therefore, laid aside during the age of casuistry, needs to be reinstated in moral theology, for it is the crowning glory of Christian ethics. We must at the same time reintroduce the study of the gifts, which express theologically the Spirit's action at the level of interior dispositions and virtues.

These are the essential elements of a system of morality based on the Gospel. This is why I include them in my definition. I shall return to them again.

7. "... in the light of revelation and reason."

The closing phrase in my definition appears to be acceptable to all theologians and does not seem to raise any difficulties. Yet within it lurks one of the most serious problems confronting Catholic morality today: its relationship to revelation. Should ethics, understood in a theological context, claim autonomy as a science based exclusively on rational norms? In this case, revelation's role would be simply one of confirmation and external inspiration. Or rather, should Christian ethics consider revelation as its principal and direct source?

Without a moment's hesitation I choose the second alternative. I hold that the priority given to Scripture and faith in no way fetters the use of reason in theology, but rather supports it. Reason has its rightful place in my definition. But this faculty must not be viewed according to the rationalistic concept, which would separate it radically from faith. It should be viewed rather as the power of a human intelligence simultaneously open to spiritual enlightenment and faithful to the rigorous discipline of thought. This is how the Fathers saw it.

2

———

Overview of Christian Ethics:
Some Basic Questions

As we embark on the study of any new subject, a good definition is certainly a help, but it is not enough. Those few words can never really give us an adequate idea of where we are going. I should like therefore to touch briefly on some of the basic questions Christian ethics addresses, so as to convey a general idea of the ground we will be covering.

This chapter will be neither systematic nor exhaustive. It is meant only to give an overall picture. We are fellow travelers. A hiker on a hilltop, looking out over the countryside stretching away in all directions beneath his gaze, is in a good position to describe to a friend some of the characteristic features of the terrain they plan to explore.

I. MORAL OBLIGATION

This is the first question that comes to mind about ethics: What may I do, what not? What is allowed, what is forbidden, where do I draw the line? What is obligatory, what sinful? Or simply, in Kant's words, What should I do? What is the moral imperative? All these questions hinge upon the idea and sense of obligations imposed by laws, commandments, and norms. They express the commonest contemporary notions about morality.

A. Janssen puts it pithily: "If there is one point on which moralists seem to achieve a rare unanimity, it is the decisive, fundamental role assigned to obligation. True, this unanimity disappears when writers try to formulate their ideas of moral obligation, and notably when they attempt to describe its justification, or, as they say, its foundation."[1]

A look at the works of moralists verifies this statement. Their books are usually divided into two main sections:

1. The treatment of moral obligations from the point of view of the laws, commandments, or norms that determine them.

2. The application of these laws to specific actions, with special attention to difficult cases where the dividing line between the permissible and the forbidden is not clearly discernible. These are cases of conscience.

The manual by Fathers Génicot and Salsmans is typical. In the first part fundamental morality and the commandments are discussed; the second part deals with cases of conscience.[2] We find the same division among secular ethicists. Here is Littré's definition: "Ethics is concerned with the rules that ought to direct free human action, and is divided into two parts: the fact that we have duties and obligations, and a description of them."

The concept of obligation is obviously an important one in moral theory, and in Christian theology it would be unthinkable to attempt the construction of any kind of moral system emptied of obligations and duties. However, the problem I want to emphasize here, at the very heart of Catholic morality, is this: Is the idea of obligation, as viewed almost unanimously by all the moralists cited by Janssen, really all that central and basic? For many, actually, the notion of obligation is so primary and decisive that it sets the boundaries of the whole field of morality. From this viewpoint, moral theology is about human actions that are obligatory, regulated by law. Actions transcending obligation are referred to other sciences such as asceticism or spirituality. In this context, ethics is reduced in practice to the question of obligation.

Certain problems discussed by ethicists are revealing, by the very fact of their predominant, even excessive, emphasis on obligation. There is, for example, the question of how many times a Christian is obliged to make an explicit act of charity in the course of a lifetime. In the article "Charity" in the *Dictionnaire de Théologie Catholique* E. Dublanchy

---

1. A. Janssen, review of J. Tonneau's book, *Absolu et obligation en morale,* in *Ephem. Theol. Louvain* 41 (1965): 617.

2. E. Génicot and J. Salsmans, *Institutiones theologiae moralis,* vols. 1–3, 17th ed. (Brussels, 1951). Vol. 3, studies, 1339, individual cases of conscience.

writes: "The Carmelites of Salamanca, in their 'Treatise on Moral Theology' (tr. XXI. c. VI. NB. 12), compare the precept of charity to those
concerning the sacraments of reconciliation and the Eucharist, and state
that we are obliged to make an explicit act of love at least once a year.
St. Alphonsus (*Theologia moralis*, 1.2.8) prefers the opinion that this
act should be performed at least once a month, an opinion based on the
difficulty involved in observing God's precepts without the help of frequent acts of love."[3]

The same problem arises in regard to prayer, as A. Fonck shows in
the article "Prayer": "Yes, but can we decide more explicitly how often
we should pray? Given their frequent exhortation to prayer, it is surprising to see how theologians downplay the requirements of the divine
law on this point. 'I think,' says Suarez, 'that prayer is so necessary for
upright living that we ought to have recourse to it every year, or perhaps
even every month. . . .' Yet they hesitate to call this obligation to pray
every month, or every two months, a grave one."[4]

We need to remember, of course, the background of these questions:
the obligation to confess grave sins in the sacrament of reconciliation.
Still, they witness to the dangers inherent in a concept of morality that
focuses excessively on obligation. We could miss what lies beyond and
above obligation, could overlook the life-giving principles of the Gospel
such as the power of love to animate all of a Christian's actions, or the
Savior's advice to "pray always," which is the origin of the development
of Christian prayer, liturgical as well as personal. Thus the core of Gospel teaching could be overlaid by an ethics of obligation.

This emphasis on obligation crops up in philosophical thought as well,
but it is expressed in different terms. Renouvier defined man as "a law-
oriented animal." The expression encapsulates the priority given to justice over love. "In a state of ideal justice, not charity but justice should
reign. This is the perfection of justice, whose beauty outshines all the
glory of the saints." Justice obliges us to respect the inviolable dignity
of every person, whereas the passion of love, even at its best, ends by
using force to gain its worthy end.[5] The primacy of justice over love,
seen as a passion, is characteristic of moral systems based on obligation
or duty. Dictionaries typically reflect this concept of morality. Webster
defines ethics as "the discipline dealing with what is good and bad and
with moral duty and obligation . . . a set of moral principles or values."

3. *Dictionnaire de Théologie Catholique*, vol. 2, cols. 2255–2256.
4. Ibid., 13, col. 212.
5. Cited by J. Lacroix, *Vocation personelle et tradition nationale* (Paris, 1942).

The dictionary of philosophy calls it "a system of norms of conduct having absolute and universal value."

In this view of morality, the question of obligation is not simply one among others; it is *the* question, even the only question. Morality becomes exclusively the science of obligations or duties. The moralist is, then, the guardian of law, the interpreter of commands, the judge of obligations.

Originating in manuals intended for the education of the clergy, this idea of morality spread to the people during recent centuries through homilies and catechisms. It created an image of the priest as one who taught what we should and should not do, with the accent on sins to be avoided. This was its outstanding feature.

To avoid all misunderstanding, I should like to affirm that a sense of moral obligation and duty can produce high moral quality when it is lived out in a personal way and seen as an ideal capable of carrying us far beyond the legal minimum. Great Christians and saints were able to live with this concept of morality. But they were always driven by a certain spiritual impulse, which carried them far beyond mere obligation.

This being said, we need to determine now whether the question of obligation holds a unique place in moral theology, from which all else flows, or whether there are other equally important questions in the field.

II. THE QUESTION OF HAPPINESS

We can open this question with a continuation of A. Janssen's remark quoted above: "Thomists do not fail to note that their master does not give, at least apparently, such importance to the idea of obligation, and that he is singularly laconic on the subject. Father Tonneau takes this as his starting point. He wants to know how St. Thomas could, inadvertently as it were, deny the primary role of obligation in morality."

All we have to do is run through the contents of the *prima secundae* of the *Summa theologiae,* in which St. Thomas discusses the principal elements of the moral world, to see that there was no "question" about obligation. This is why A. Janssen could speak of "inadvertence." Admittedly, in treating the virtues St. Thomas does deal with laws and their precepts. But for him law is, by its very nature, closer to the mind than to the will. In determining the morality of actions, law does not play the same role as it does for modern moralists.

In any case, something else is abundantly clear: St. Thomas gives priority to the question of happiness in his treatise on beatitude. This treatise is in no sense a preamble: it is the keystone of the whole moral edifice; it determines its ultimate end and general orientation. The entire structure of the second part of the *Summa* depends directly on the answer to the question of happiness discussed in this first treatise.

The stress on happiness over obligation is confirmed when we look at St. Thomas's sources, the currents of thought preceding him. For earlier thinkers, whether they were philosophers with Aristotle as their principal mentor or theologians following the Greek and Latin Fathers (notably St. Augustine), the question of happiness or "the good life" was beyond any doubt the principal concern of morality. Aristotle devotes the first and last books of his *Nicomachean Ethics* to the study of happiness. St. Augustine, countering Manichean heresy, did not hesitate for an instant about the reasonableness of his opening thesis: "Everyone wants to be happy. There is no one who will not agree with me on this almost before the words are out of my mouth."[6] He then went on to show how the Gospel offers the true answer to what is our highest happiness (*hominis optimum*), the leitmotif of morality. Later, in the brief treatise on prayer addressed to Proba, St. Augustine in three words answered the difficult question about what we should ask of God: "*Ora beatam vitam*"—"Ask for the happy life." This is how he related prayer to the desire for happiness; prayer utters the desire to God. There is no point in multiplying quotations; we need only reflect.

To anyone with an open mind, one huge fact stands out in the history of morality: for the ancients, Christians and pagans alike, the question of happiness was primary. As they saw it, morality in its totality was simply the answer to this question. The thing was obvious; it never occurred to them to talk about it. St. Augustine even thought that the question of happiness was at the root of philosophy: "A person engages in philosophy only in order to be happy," he wrote in *The City of God*.[7]

This massive historical evidence stands out in bold relief against the kind of morality conceived by modern philosophers and theologians. Concentration on obligations does away completely with the question of happiness, perhaps "inadvertently."[8] We can accurately point to two

---

6. *De moribus ecclesiae catholicae*, 3.4. Bibliothèque Augustinienne, vol. 1, trans. B. Roland (Paris: Gosselin, 1936).

7. *De civitate Dei*, 19.1

8. For example, in J. B. Vittrant's *Théologie morale*, formerly used in French seminaries, there is no reference to "happiness" or "beatitude" in the topical index, still less in the table of contents. This is true of most manuals not following the Thomistic tradition.

main periods in the history of morality, the first dominated by the question of happiness and the second by the question of obligation.

Two great models of moral thought are therefore open to us. The question of happiness leads to a different organization of the subject matter, according to virtues rather than commandments. Ethics becomes the science of ways leading to true happiness, those qualities of soul and heart that we call virtues.

Have we come upon one more area of conflict between ancients and moderns? Must we follow the ancients in order to restore the concept of happiness to morality? This dilemma is simplistic, the option superficial. A sense of happiness and a knowledge of its importance for the moral quality of life are not lost upon our times. What would life be worth without happiness? And what purpose would a system of morality serve if it gave no hope of attaining it? Even Kant could not do without it, but only deferred the happiness to another world. Whatever we may think about morality, we know instinctively that the question of happiness is a basic one. It is the primordial longing of every human being. Nothing can snuff it out.

Whether we decide to approach ethics by way of the question of happiness or by way of the question of obligation is going to have some unexpected consequences. Simply to highlight the problem, I shall point out two.

1. Several important themes in ancient moral thought have disappeared from modern ethics precisely because of the latter's emphasis on the concept of obligation. First there is the theme of beatitude, which we are presently considering. Then there is the theme of friendship, discussed by Aristotle in Books 8 and 9 of the *Nicomachean Ethics*. This is how he introduces it: "[Friendship] is absolutely indispensable: even though possessed of every other good thing, without friends a person would have no desire to live." According to him, the whole point of law and the political life, over and above justice, was to provide for friendship among citizens.

The theme of friendship was prominent among the Greek Fathers, even those who lived in the desert, as Cassian attests in his sixteenth conference. It reached its climax in St. Thomas, who defined charity as friendship with God (IIaIIae, q 23) and who described the work of the Holy Spirit in the world as a work of friendship (*Summa contra gentiles* 1.21–22.)

This theme has completely disappeared from modern books on morality. The reason is obvious: friendship, being essentially free, could hardly be considered an obligation. Friendship can create obligations, but the inverse is not true. As a result, friendship has been excluded from the field of morality as an indifferent sentiment—mistrusted by moral theologians, moreover, because of "particular friendships."

Likewise, we will look in vain for a simple allusion, still less for a full treatment, of the virtue of courage in many of the manuals. Courage is not a matter of obligation. Yet it is numbered among the four cardinal virtues. St. Thomas associated it with the ideal of martyrdom, the inspiration of the early centuries of Christianity. Everyone knows from experience how great is the need for courage throughout our moral life.

It is easy to reinstate friendship and courage in moral theology if we begin with the question of happiness. Can a person be happy without the harmonious relationship we call friendship? It is a concrete form of charity. Again, how can we be happy without the courage that strengthens us in the face of difficulties and keeps us steady in the day-to-day grind? This is all the more true when our goal surpasses human power and calls for an audacious faith and trust in the Word of God.

2. Another consequence for moral theology has to do with its relationship to sacred Scripture. A moral system that addresses the question of happiness easily finds answers in Scripture. Texts abound: the Beatitudes with their corresponding promises, the teaching of the Gospels and St. Paul on the virtues, the Wisdom literature. The moral tracts of the Fathers of the Church, too, are interwoven with quotations revealing a continual pondering on Scripture.

Adherents of the emphasis on obligation quote Scripture rarely. Their commonest reference is to the Decalogue, seen as an expression of the natural law and a code of basic rules. For the rest, they manage to find very few texts imperative enough and strict enough to suit their purpose, which is the framing of their particular moral structure. They pay no attention whatsoever to the sapiential books, or to exhortatory passages, although these occupy a fair amount of space in St. Paul's descriptions of the Christian life. It seems as if the Apostle and the other sacred authors have little relevance for moral theology, at least in the modern sense.

This is a serious question for ethics. To approach it solely from the standpoint of obligation leads logically, inevitably, to a minimal use of Scripture. Surely this is a sign that the sacred authors held a different view, closer to that of the Fathers, who began with the question of happiness. Much is at stake: the scriptural, evangelical, and Christian dimension of morality.

It is well worth our while to raise the question of happiness openly, even though we may meet with resistance. Especially since Kant, any moral system viewing human happiness as a goal has been suspected of hedonism; a theory of morality based on happiness must be self-serving.

This is the opinion of Father Bernard Häring, for example. He suggests that personal perfection and individual salvation are the ultimate end of Aristotelian ethics, "as if loving dialogue with God were no more than a necessary means for attaining our final end: self-perfection, the soul's salvation, and beatitude." For Häring, adaptations of Aristotelian ethics for Christian purposes opposes Gospel morality and values, which are based on the preaching of the Commandments and the law. These ought to remain the central concepts of Christian moral teaching, he believes, since they guarantee God's sovereignty and provide the only basis for any discussion of the subject.[9]

We need to return to the fundamental problem of hedonism, which calls into question the entire moral system of the ancients. Here I shall simply give a partial answer, to show us a way out. The quality of our desire for happiness depends on the love that inspires it and on our concept of the human person. If the love is selfish, and still more if the human person is seen as a being with needs craving satisfaction, then the desire for happiness is bound to be self-centered. Only a utilitarian moral theory could be constructed on such a foundation, one directly contrary to Gospel teaching.

If, on the other hand, a person is capable of true, unselfish love for God and neighbor—the love of friendship of which St. Thomas speaks—then the desire for happiness can lead that person to be open to God and neighbor and to become generous. Can we love others truly without wanting their happiness? In the same sense St. Thomas, in defining charity as friendship, sees a sharing in God's beatitude as charity's foundation. As St. Paul reports the Lord's words, "It is more blessed to give than to receive."

The discovery that giving is the path to true happiness is a decisive experience. It transforms our desire and reveals to us the most authentic moral values. This was the kind of desire for happiness that the Fathers envisioned when they shaped their moral theology: the open, generous desire that characterizes friendship. They had no problem in reconciling this with the Gospels and their teaching on charity.

The question of obligation and the question of happiness: these are so fundamental that they give rise to two different conceptions of moral theology. They have often been felt to be in opposition, as if either one

9. Bernard Häring, *The Law of Christ*, trans. Kaiser (Paramus, N.J.: Newman Press, 1961), vol. 1, 41–42: ". . . as though the living friendship with God was only an essential means for the full attainment of the moral purpose—it is evident that the concept of self-perfection or external happiness and salvation cannot be the sound and appropriate foundation for a religious moral system."

would have to cancel out the other. But I am convinced that the moral theory of beatitude, if properly understood, can perfectly well include the question of obligation and accord the Commandments a fitting role within its structure.

This would be to place Christian ethics in a very different context. It would be seen as the science of happiness and of the ways that lead thereto. Far more attractive, it would draw everyone because of its positive and dynamic aspect, and this would harmonize well with the perspectives of Scripture. In Scripture, God always approaches us with promises of happiness before speaking of precepts. Inspired by the desire for happiness, the movements of the human heart and all its actions, even on the level of emotion, can work together to foster moral growth, as St. Thomas teaches in his treatise on the passions.

As a result of this, the roles of the ethicist, the priest, and the Christian educator are transformed. Their first responsibility is to teach the Beatitudes, the Kingdom of God, and the paths that lead to it, including all of Christ's radical demands. It becomes each Christian's mission to give to others Christ's answer to the great question of happiness.

But the question of happiness does not stand alone. To exhaust its possibilities or present all its aspects does not suffice; the question of happiness opens up further questions for us to explore.

III. LIFE'S MEANING AND GOAL

Alfred Adler was right when he recognized the importance, in a person's psychic life, of orientation to a goal. "The first thing we can discover in the psychic trends is that the movements are directed toward a goal. . . . The psychic life of man is determined by his goal. No human being can think, feel, will, dream, without all these activities being determined, continued, modified and directed toward an ever-present objective. . . . We cannot conceive of psychic evolution except within the pattern of an ever-present objective." And further on: "Because of this possibility of many meanings, we can never judge the expressions of psychic life as single isolated phenomena; on the contrary, we must evaluate them according to the unit goal toward which they are directed. The essential meaning can be learned only when we know what value a phenomenon has in the entire context of a person's life."[10]

10. A. Adler, *Understanding Human Nature*, trans. Wolfe (New York: Greenberg, 1946), 19–20 and 82.

Though not always articulated, the problem of life's meaning and goal is primordial. It matures within us through experience and reflection. Yet it is already present, in germ, in the multiple activities in which we become involved. We dread emptiness and seek a great variety of things to fill up our time and lives: wealth, work, pleasure, knowledge, politics, love. Each of these gives a sense of purpose and meaning to our lives. The hardest thing for us to endure is a sense of emptiness or a conviction that all our hopes and plans are doomed to stillbirth. When one failure follows another we see a void opening before us, the chasm of meaninglessness.

The question of life's meaning and goal is one aspect of the question of happiness. Philosophy, and then theology, came to define happiness as our ultimate end. Giving purpose to all lesser ends, happiness is always desired for its own sake and for no other; it is the sum of all goods and the goal of all goals. It is the final object of all we do, though we do not always advert to this consciously. We may deceive ourselves about it, or hide from it, like the miser for whom money is everything.

The question of our goal or final end is, as it were, the backbone, essential to the question of happiness. This is why St. Thomas began with it in his treatise on happiness.

Modern ethicists do not address our ultimate end, believing it too speculative for practical moral teaching. Actually, they have lost the sense of finality and of its importance. Their main objective—I might almost say their final end—has become the study of individual actions in relation to law, the study of cases of conscience. Their field is the morality of actions, and finality is accorded only a secondary value.

To give an example, consider the difference between a miser's attendance at Mass and that of a religious sister. The miser believes his presence in church is going to further the business transactions of his day; prayer matters little or nothing. The religious on the other hand draws strength from the Eucharist to devote herself wholeheartedly to her nursing or teaching. Considered from the point of view of the law of attendance at Sunday Mass, the actions of both are equally praiseworthy, but they differ profoundly because of the final ends that motivate them. One honors God with his lips but dishonors him by making money his ultimate goal. The other, finding all her happiness in God, is giving him sincere love which is the only true worship.

Since the question of life's goal or ultimate end is so important, we might define Christian ethics as the science that teaches us the meaning of life. It shows us the supreme end toward which all our actions should be directed, the end that gives them meaning, value, and wholeness.

Within this perspective, the work of the ethicist and the priest will be to help every Christian, indeed all whose lives they touch, to respond personally to the question of the real meaning of life. Their task will be to point out the highest good in the light of the Gospel and to show how all lesser goods can lead to it.

IV. SUFFERING

The manuals of moral theology have little to say about suffering. In his book *The Law of Christ,* Father Bernard Häring approaches it only by way of particular questions about sickness, anesthesia, childbirth, the difficulties of marriage, repentance. Reading these works gives us the impression that suffering has no particular relevance or purpose in moral theory. True, it can be seen as an occasion of merit, but by preference it is relegated to dogmatic theology.

As we read Scripture however, and especially the Gospels and the letters of St. Paul, it becomes clear that suffering holds a central position in the life and Passion of Christ, and in the lives of his disciples, who are called to carry their crosses and follow him. Without this central role of suffering, the Gospel message would be incomprehensible, and there would be no way of explaining the Christian life. Even the Beatitudes turn upon various forms of suffering. Paradoxically, they are described as approaches to the Kingdom: poverty, affliction, and mourning; hunger and thirst, persecution and calumny.

To a certain extent, human experience corroborates the Gospel on this point. It is suffering, whether physical, emotional, moral, or spiritual, that brings us in the last analysis to confront the problem of the meaning of our life and to question ourselves about our moral and religious values. The just man overwhelmed with misfortune is scandalized by the success of the rich:

> "Look at them: these are the wicked,
> well-off and still getting richer!"
> After all, why should I keep my own heart pure,
> and wash my hands in innocence,
> if you plague me all day long
> and discipline me every morning?
>
> . . . .
>
> Instead, I tried to analyse the problem,
> hard though I found it—
>
> (Ps 73:12–16)

We remember Job, too, and his debate with his friends and with God: the entire moral universe was being weighed in the balance.

The problem of suffering has a metaphysical dimension as well. It leads us to question God's goodness and, in the end, even his very existence. For us, suffering is the concrete shape of the problem of evil. St. Thomas's first objection to the existence of God is the fact of suffering (Ia q 2, a 3). The experience of suffering can overturn the moral values of a lifetime, penetrating deeper than our habitual ideas and emotions. By the thrust of its ambiguity, it challenges us to a decisive existential choice: either suffering will destroy the roots of hope in us and bring us to a more or less articulate despair, or we will discover in it and beyond it new, strong values, notably Gospel values, which will engraft in us a "hope against hope" and give us "the courage to be."

Think of a person who has never known suffering. Is this person real? Or even happy? It seems that solid moral values cannot exist without the experience of suffering, and that suffering is the only gateway to them. The problem of suffering, of sorrow, is one of the major themes of ancient philosophy, to which all schools of thought contributed, as is shown in Book 3 of Cicero's *Tusculanae disputationes*. It is the point of departure for Buddhist moral thought as well.

How is it that many ethicists have not grasped the importance of suffering and have built up moral systems that bypass it? The explanation is simple enough: once the idea of obligation becomes dominant and determines the scope of morality, the consideration of suffering becomes marginal, since it is not a matter of obligation.

On the other hand, if the idea of happiness is the initial consideration in moral theology, the place of suffering will be obvious, for it is precisely the reverse of happiness. Suffering will then be an element of moral theology from the very start. Moreover, the question of happiness does not arise for us until we experience trial. Without suffering, the idea of happiness would be too romantic, too much a thing of the imagination; happiness becomes real only when we are confronted with suffering over the long haul. This is the indispensable experience that lends genuine authenticity to any moral theory based on happiness.

The moral theory of the Beatitudes bears this out. St. Thomas, too, gave an important place to suffering, but we do not find his theories in the manuals. In the treatise on the passions he devoted twenty-five articles to sorrow and pain (IaIIae qq 35–39). Further on he analyzed courage, with its attendant virtues, and the gift of fortitude. The culminating point was Christian martyrdom, where courage was directly related to the Passion of Christ (IIaIIae qq 123–40).

Those who stress a moral theory of obligation would probably maintain that they in no way downplay the importance of suffering in the Christian life, but that they simply situate it within the framework of asceticism or, better still, pastoral theology for the sake of those who suffer.

This is exactly what I have been describing: a moral theory that excludes the question of suffering, and happiness as well, relegating them to a related science as if they were merely material for specialists, while in reality they are fundamental human experiences. Actually, this banishment of the consideration of suffering from ethics is an outgrowth of a rationalistic conception of the human person. Its thesis is that our interior world is divided into two areas: on the higher plane are reason and will, which constitute the proper field of morality, established by law and its imperatives; somewhere below this lies the area of affectivity, which includes desires, love and suffering. The second plane, a realm of sentiments often in disagreement with reason, is only indirectly related to morality and must be dominated by it.

In setting up this dichotomy between reason and appetite, rationalism misunderstands the existence of what might be termed spiritual sensibility, which supersedes reason and the will's imperative. Spiritual sensibility is associated with direct perception—a kind of instinct or connatural knowledge—and with the unique movement of selfless love which is the love of friendship, a far cry from sensible love. It is in this sense that St. Thomas spoke of "reason's instinct." And delightedly he called the gifts of the Holy Spirit "instincts of the Holy Spirit" in both intellect and will (IaIIae q 68). Are we transcending moral theology here and entering the field of mysticism? But what kind of moral theology would it be that first assumed superiority to all sentiment, even spiritual, and then became too lowly even to approach such heights? This is a serious problem rooted in the anthropology of modern rationalism. It appears even in theologians most strongly convinced of their faith.

I shall close with a quotation from René Le Senne. "Our moral life takes its rise from an awareness of suffering and failure. The first conclusion reached from our self-examination is that we cannot pretend that suffering does not exist, because everything begins there historically. . . . Either such a theory will succeed in doing away with suffering, which is quite incredible, or it will fail, and its failure will be its finish."[11]

To the question of suffering we must add that of death, the reverse

11. R. Le Senne, Le devoir (Paris, 1931).

side of the question of life's meaning. The question of death is keenly present in our society with its problems of suicide, capital punishment, euthanasia, war, the afterlife. Death is in our midst despite all efforts to ignore it. We cannot reduce this question to difficult cases of conscience or to theoretical or sentimental stances. Everyone has to face death sooner or later; we must dare to face it openly. Moral theology needs to deal with it frankly; all life's strands are caught up in it. This applies above all to Christian ethics, which must transmit the Gospel message of Christ's death—for believers, the source of a new life.

V. LOVE

All Christian ethicists recognize the prime place of love in Christian morality. They all repeat the classic theological formula: charity is the form of the virtues. New Testament texts establishing the primacy of charity or *agape* are so explicit that no one would dream of denying them. To quote from St. Paul's Letter to the Romans, "All the commandments . . . are summed up in this single command: *You must love your neighbor as yourself.* . . . [T]hat is why it is the answer to every one of the commandments" (Rom 13:9–10). Again, consider the celebrated hymn to charity (1 Cor 13).

The theme of the primacy of charity has been developed by Christian theology since the age of the Fathers. In his *De moribus ecclesiae* St. Augustine redefined the classical four cardinal virtues as forms of charity: "If virtue leads us to the happy life, I daresay virtue is nothing other than supreme love. For in describing virtue as fourfold, as I see it, we are talking about different movements of the one love" ("ex ipsius amoris vario quodam affectu"—15.25). This new interpretation of the nature of virtue led to a profound transformation of classical moral theory, which, in harmony with the Gospel teaching, came to be seen as rooted in charity.

We can discern some hesitancy in the development of the thought of the Fathers regarding the relation between charity and other forms of love. This is clear from variations of expression among the Greek Fathers, ranging from *agape* or *philia* to Pseudo-Dionysius's use of *eros* in the sixth century. Among the Latins we find *dilectio* or *caritas* and finally *amor* in St. Augustine. In both the Greek and the Latin tradition, however, charity always ranked first among the virtues, as the foundation of moral theology, with consistent references to the great texts of the New Testament.

St. Thomas analyzed love in the introduction to his treatise on charity (IaIIae qq 26–28). He considered the act of loving as the first movement of the will, at the origin of all others. He characterized it as a love of friendship in its integral form, that is, love of an object for its own sake, whether the object be God, others, or self. This love was perfected by the virtue of charity, which he defined as friendship, and was elicited by the grace of the Holy Spirit. Without charity no other virtue, faith included, was truly alive. If St. Thomas did not affirm that the nature of the other virtues was transformed by charity, he did recognize that it enlivened them all through its inspiration and conformed them to itself so that they became ways of loving, each within its own context. Charity was the first movement in Christian life, as love was the first sentiment of the human heart and will.

Modern Catholic ethicists are careful not to oppose such authorities, and they try to transmit this heritage. However, when we study the presentation of charity in modern manuals, we immediately note a change in perspective and a diminishment. The writers are interested mainly in the obligations to God and neighbor imposed by charity. We observe the same tendency in treatises on the other virtues. In studies of the Ten Commandments—preferred subject matter for courses in ethics—the primacy of charity becomes more or less theoretical. Practical primacy is given to obedience to the law, ever present and all-determining. Obedience to legal obligations is now seen as the true form of the virtues and the chief inspiration of our actions. This new perspective, dominated by obligation, is revealed typically in the question mentioned above: How many acts of charity must be made in the course of a lifetime?

Here we are getting into a fundamental question found also in philosophy and notably in Kant: How do we interpret the first two commandments on love? Are they precepts, obligations, duties to God and neighbor? This is how Kant saw them, as would any moralist of the school of obligation. Or do we start with love, an upright and authentic love, and so explain the two commandments and lay the foundation, cause, and end of every law and obligation, as the Fathers did? Briefly, do we love out of obedience or obey out of love? Once more we encounter that inner spiritual and natural spontaneity that impels us, through love, toward truth, uprightness, and goodness. Can love be upright only when it is constrained by obligation? Or does it possess a natural sense of truth and goodness directed by light under the influence of grace?

It would be unfair to say that the authors of the manuals did not realize the depth and riches of charity. Some of them were saints and wrote beautifully of charity. But since they identified the field of Christian ethics with obligations, they diminished charity's scope. They discussed duties in moral theology but left to ascetical and mystical theology the full development of charity.

It was in this context that Father Gilleman felt the need—urgency even—to write a book restablishing "the primacy of charity in moral theology."[12] The problem is very real, and this book was a step in the right direction. The question is central for Christian ethics. In my opinion a moral system based on obligation or duty could never give charity its rightful place. On the other hand, if we begin with the question of happiness—linked of course with that of suffering or evil—the question of love and its truth come to the fore at once. Love is seen as the root of desire, for how can we hope to be happy if our love is not authentic? Charity thus addresses the question of hope as well.

Despite efforts for renewal in recent years, the problem is still with us. On the one hand, traditional ethicists find it hard to set aside their instinctive mistrust of love and passion, which seem too close to sex for comfort. They discuss love mainly in terms of faults to be avoided. They are prepared to accuse or absolve, rather than to promote love's growth and development. Their mistrust is leveled even against spiritual and mystical love; they suspect pride here and believe that it will lead to dangerous moral and psychic imbalance. This territory they consider as reserved for the chosen few and in no sense necessary for salvation.

Today an opposite reaction can be observed among ethicists and Christians. There is a strong attraction for love and spontaneity, without due regard for the demands of integrity and truth. For some, love has become the "Open, Sesame," the cure for all problems. They misapply St. Augustine's magnificent expression, "Love, and do what you will," as if warmth of emotion liberates a person from all commandments and restraints. For St. Augustine, however, the greater the love the greater the adherence to commandments, for they are the expression of God's love. Without the rectitude ensured by the commandments, love will not be true, will not survive.

We are faced, therefore, with a kind of sickness induced by the morality of obligation. The symptom is allergy to all obligation or authority in the name of the primacy of a naive and confused love. This exaggeration of love's role in the moral sphere leads to the rejection of one of the conditions for authentic love: love is extolled on all sides, but any

12. G. Gilleman, *The Primacy of Charity in Moral Theology* (Westminster, 1959).

reference to sacrifice and renunciation is unacceptable. Yet Scripture and experience send another message: there is no true love without the willingness to sacrifice. Human love is built on sacrifice. As we read in Genesis, and again in the Gospel, "This is why a man must leave father and mother, and cling to his wife, and the two become one body" (Mt 19:5). Such detachment is not easy. How many homes have been broken because one partner could not endure sacrifice. Gospel love demands even more: "If any man comes to me without hating his father, mother, wife, children, brothers, sisters, yes and his own life too, he cannot be my disciple. Anyone who does not carry his cross and come after me cannot be my disciple" (Lk 14:26–27). However this text may be nuanced by exegetes, radical self-renunciation is a necessary condition for love of Christ. There is no real charity without detachment and self-renunciation. As love deepens through trial, so its capacity for sacrifice grows stronger. This is the realism, the power of love.

The place given to charity in Christian ethics has vast repercussions. It determines our concept of God. A moral theory of obligation depicts God as an all-powerful legislator issuing his law in the midst of thunder and lightning. This is a God to inspire fear and trembling, a sovereign Judge. The contemporary reaction to such a picture has the advantage of highlighting the goodness of God. Yet there is a risk of devaluation. In removing from God all power of judgment and punishment, and in focusing exclusively on his universal pardon, we are left with a soft and spineless God. Here we encounter one of the major problems of Christian ethics today: how to reconcile God's love and justice. Both stand at the very heart of morality.

I shall return to this point later. For the present I should simply like to mention the close connection between the primary role of charity in the moral life of Christians and their idea of God. Christ shows us the Father's love at work in the world through his mercy, which is greater than all sin.

Beauty

The inclusion of the question of love in Christian moral teaching brings up a great theme that has completely disappeared from it: beauty. Beauty is in fact the first and specific cause of love, according to St. Thomas. The beautiful differs from the good only in its notion (IaIIae, q 27 a 1 ad 3), implying a special relation to our faculties of knowledge within the modalities of seeing and hearing. Yet this affirmation does not account entirely for the importance of the theme for the Fathers. We remember St. Augustine's cry: "Too late have I loved you, O Beauty ever ancient and ever new, too late have I loved you!" (*Confessions*, 10.27). It was through beauty that God drew St. Augustine from his youth to the time of his first loss, and captivated him. "And I marveled that now I loved you, and not a phantom in your stead. . . . I was borne up to you by your beauty, then borne away from you by my own weight" (*Confessions* 7.17).

St. Basil also tells us that the beauty of God is the first cause of our love: "In receiving God's commandment of love, we immediately, from the first moment of our existence, possess the ability to love. The command does not come from outside of us . . . , it is a part of our nature to seek what is beautiful, though ideas of it differ from one person to another. Now, what could be more lovable than divine beauty?" (*Moralia*, q 2).

Scripture does not hesitate to ascribe beauty to God, to those who love him, and to all his works. Of Wisdom it is written: "She it was I loved and searched for from my youth; I resolved to have her as my bride, I fell in love with her beauty" (Wis 8:2).

Clearly the Fathers did not consider beauty only from an aesthetic viewpoint in the modern sense of the word. Beyond visible forms, this beauty radiated from the inmost being of persons and their actions and qualified their very substance. This is why good actions were at the same time beautiful. And this is why the invisible God could draw us by his beauty even as he attracted us by his goodness and truth, so that we might love him in charity. The love, goodness, and beauty of God, shining through Jesus Christ: these were the wellsprings of the dynamism of the Christian life for the Fathers.

It is surprising that modern ethicists have lost the sense of beauty to such a point that they no longer attribute a moral dimension to it. As for love, they are suspicious of it, pausing, among other things, on the problems that artists pose. It is always for the same reason: they do not see how to include beauty among obligations, nor how the latter may flow from the divine beauty. In connection with this I am led to wonder if the frequent loss of the sense of beauty in religious art in recent centuries is the sign of a profound, very regrettable rift between the life of faith and beauty, between charity and artistic sensibility, for which theologians may be in part responsible. Surely in our times theirs is a special call to rediscover with us the beauty of God and creation.

Charity and the Mystical

The role assigned to love also determines the relation of morality to mysticism. If we understand the word "mystical" in its original sense we will see that all love is by its very nature mystical. The Greek word *mysterion* means something hidden, secret. It is a property of love to enter into the secret depths of the beloved, to establish a certain communication between persons on the plane of the mysterious and unfathomable. The preoccupation of Christian mysticism has always been love, its growth, and the different stages leading to its perfection, as well as its most concrete manifestations. Unfortunately, mysticism has been excluded from Christian ethics, as if it were intended only for the elite and as if morality could forego this dimension without cutting itself off from the very strength and dynamism of charity.

Charity and Violence

Finally we note that the question of love, like that of happiness, has also its shadow side: the problem of violence. Even the ancients saw love and hate as two contrary principles explaining the actions of human beings. Among modern thinkers there is a certain idea of human nature that has destroyed the concept of friendship as a natural thing. Human beings are now viewed as totally selfish and pleasure-seeking, determined to satisfy their own needs and regarding others as enemies. The attempt has been made to prove violence the source of all relationships, whether in the evolution of the species with the fight for survival, in society with its class wars, or in the history of peoples with the initial murder of the father or scapegoat.[13] Everything takes its rise from opposition, the class struggle, violence. There is no place in this theory for friendship or love, even though these sentiments are alive in every human heart.

The question of love and violence is tremendously important therefore. To answer it from a Christian viewpoint, it is not enough to introduce a merely sentimental love. A love is needed that dares to confront violence, and knows how to uproot it. We need to overcome it first in our own hearts, then in the hearts of others, and finally in society. This calls

13. Cf. R. Girard, *La violence et le sacré* (Paris, 1972), and *Des choses cachées depuis la fondation du monde* (Paris, 1978); also my review, "La violence, le sacré et le christianisme" in *Nova et Vetera* 54 (1979): 292–305.

for a genuine rediscovery of charity and friendship, our weapons for the combat.

VI. TRUTH

The question of truth is equally fundamental in Christian ethics. It is closely linked with the preceding questions, since without truth there can be no lasting happiness or love. The bond is reciprocal: truth without love is dessicating and ultimately leads a person astray. The theme of truth thus has broad application; it touches upon all the virtues and through them affects the entire scope of morality.

The question of truth cannot be reduced to the question of lying. As the casuist puts it, do we always have to tell the truth? Is lying intrinsically evil? Isn't it sometimes permissable? These are real problems when it is a case of secrets to be kept, an illness to be concealed, victims to be protected. Yet the love of truth has its exigencies, which reach far beyond particular cases, and ethicists have too often lost sight of this. We are speaking here of the truth about God, oneself, others, life, the truth about our thoughts, emotions, and actions, our entire personality. Furthermore, rationalism has bequeathed to us an impoverished notion of truth. It has become an abstraction, separating our hearts from our heads. Thus, in theology truth will fall under dogma; in ethics it will apply only where there is an obligation to believe certain truths taught by our faith.

Scripture gives a much richer, more concrete meaning to the word "truth." Truth is often associated with love, like two aspects of the same reality. In Psalm 25:10 we read: "All Yahweh's paths are love and truth for those who keep his covenant and his decrees." And again, "Loyalty reaches up from earth and righteousness leans down from heaven" (Ps 85:11). Or, "Your love is high as heaven, your faithfulness as the clouds" (Ps 57:10). We know, too, what depth of meaning St. John gives to the words *truth* and *knowledge*. The Jerusalem Bible attempts to explain this in its notes, in the weak language of today. Commenting on 1 John 3:19, Father Braun explains: "In the Old Testament 'truth' (as contrasted with injustice, evil) often designates the moral rectitude of a life lived in accordance with the divine will (fidelity to God). This is the way John uses the word. In harmony with the double commandment of faith and love, people who believe and love are 'of the truth'; they 'walk [live] in the truth', they 'do the truth' (as opposed to 'doing evil')." On

John 10:14 Father Mollat notes: "In the Bible 'knowledge' comes not from purely intellectual activity but rather from 'an experience', a presence . . . ; it flowers in love."

In contrast to Descartes' methodical procedure by way of doubt, which involved only a clear idea, this loving knowledge grows out of a concrete, total experience engaging the entire person in encounter with the other. This is a description of our relationship to God.

We might apply here the classical definition of truth—"the mind's grasp of the thing"—but with a new interpretation. The "thing" is not now something material we think about but a personal reality—God or neighbor. This personal reality reveals itself in all its nature and mystery, as light, goodness, beauty, energy, life. "Mind" is not now abstract reason but intelligence united to will, love and desire, informing and directing them. It is understanding joined to sensitivity and imagination, guiding and regulating them.

This kind of intelligence is active, because it leads to action in truth. In this sense we can talk about doing the truth. Truth is beneficial; through upright love it creates a profound harmony between our various faculties and between persons. It is penetrating, and in this it corresponds to St. Thomas's definition of the human intellect as a power that "reads into" reality (IIaIIae, q 8, a 1). It penetrates beyond the outward show of words, gestures, the literal text, to the very depths of a person, a thought, a life, and it understands. This understanding, flowing from active experience and profound contact, gives us a unique kind of knowledge that is universal, constructive, concrete, somewhat intuitive. It is very sure in its judgments because it is founded on a connaturality acquired through doing the truth in love. It fosters and develops a taste for truth and goodness. Its name is wisdom. It culminates in the gift of wisdom, which perfects charity, and the gift of understanding, which perfects faith.

Theology, at least for the Fathers and the great Scholastics, was the work of such wisdom, both practical and contemplative. It was what St. Paul asked for his Christians. "May the God of our Lord Jesus Christ, the Father of glory, give you a spirit of wisdom and perception of what is revealed, to bring you to full knowledge of him. May he enlighten the eyes of your mind so that you can see what hope his call holds for you" (Eph 1:17–18). This is the kind of knowledge and truth appropriate for those who want to "live by the Spirit."

Finally, the expression *grasp* is not about anything static or frozen. It implies a direct, continuous advance: the more we know, the stronger our desire and taste for knowledge. The "grasp" thus directs the ongoing movement of loving knowledge.

Clearly it is no small task to rediscover truth's riches and reintegrate them in moral theology. There are novelists who can help in this. Bernanos, for example, shows us the determined will to lie, as it flickers for an instant in the liar's eye. Love of truth or of lying is primordial, basic to a person, and will affect his actions decisively so that they will be rich or empty. "You prefer evil to good, lying to honest speech," the Psalmist says to the wicked one (52:3). Russian dissidents, too, with their oath "never to lie" alert us to the importance of this question of truth. We realize the gravity of lying when it drags us into a system where words and conversation are no more than ideological tactics in the service of politics. Thus the question of truth takes us to the heart of reality in our modern world, East and West.

Love for "the fulness of truth," as St. John puts it, or the search for wisdom, is therefore essential in Christian ethics. We might define the ethicist's task as a search for "the fulness of truth," so that it may throw light on all human actions. To sum up, the contemplative dimension must be restored to Christian ethics, which has become profoundly voluntaristic in recent centuries.

VII. JUSTICE

The question of justice is so vast that we can touch here only briefly on some aspects of it relating to our subject.

Ethicists of recent centuries can certainly not be accused of having slighted the importance of justice's role. A glance at the table of contents in any of the manuals shows a generous amount of space allotted to it. Vittrant, for example, devotes 25 numbers to the theological virtues in his *Moral Theology* and 306 to justice. If any fault were to be found with these ethicists it would be that they give exaggerated emphasis to the study of justice, resulting in an overly juridical presentation of morality.

In any case we owe a debt of gratitude to the great Spanish theologians of the sixteenth century, such as Vitoria, for their studies on justice, which are the foundation of modern international law. But their profound insights were lost to succeeding manuals. The latter are far less impressive and seem to have limited themselves to the examination of cases of conscience. Their primary concern was commutative justice, which regulated relations between individuals and imposed strict obligations. General justice, dealing with social relations, was passed over, and this precisely when philosophers were elaborating new structures for the modern state.

Today Christians are in the process of rediscovering the social and political dimensions of Christian life, in the light of papal encyclicals from Leo XIII to John Paul II, or under the pressure of new and urgent circumstances such as the evolution of liberation theology. In the course of this research it might be very enlightening to study the theologians who lived at the time when the modern world was coming into being, as well as their sources in the Middle Ages. In the latter there are unexpectedly broad and rich insights on justice.

Variations on the Theme of Justice

If we want to return to the origins of Christian teaching on justice, found in Scripture itself, we have to consider the profound variations in the concept as it evolved through the course of history. There have been modifications so subtle no dictionary could capture them: the changes happen behind the words and definitions. I shall indicate briefly the principal stages of this evolution of the concept of justice.

1. Justice in Scripture

In Scripture, justice has none of the impersonal, juridical, and legal overtones we associate with it today. It is found at the heart of direct relationships between God and his people or between believers, and is spelled out in words and actions. It indicates the rightness of these relationships, in the spirit of Covenant and Law. It runs as deep as love, since the first two commandments, love of God and love of neighbor, are at its origin and source. Justice and love form one unique entity: justice emphasizes the righteousness of love, while love stresses the profound spontaneity that attracts people to one another. Seen in this light, justice becomes the supreme moral quality in Scripture, as wisdom is for the Greeks. It is totally desirable and worthy of the prolonged hymn of praise given it in the 119th psalm.

It would be a great mistake to accuse St. Matthew of legalism when he describes the new justice in the Sermon on the Mount and declares that not one jot or tittle of the law will pass away and that the least precept is to be observed. Justice lies not in the observance of an external, obligatory law but in the interior need of the heart's love to expand. Matthew throws still more light on this love. It is characterized by a superabundance in giving and forgiving, in imitation of the Father's generosity. It will not do to take the word about the jot and tittle out of context; it tells us, in its own way, about the perfection to which evangelical love aspires. This should be the justice of Jesus' disciples: an overflowing justice of the heart that longs to do the Father's will down to the smallest detail.

This justice was Isaiah's joy:

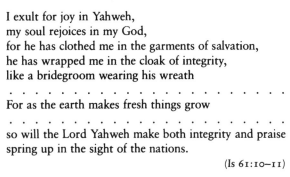

> I exult for joy in Yahweh,
> my soul rejoices in my God,
> for he has clothed me in the garments of salvation,
> he has wrapped me in the cloak of integrity,
> like a bridegroom wearing his wreath
>
> . . . .
> For as the earth makes fresh things grow
>
> . . . .
> so will the Lord Yahweh make both integrity and praise
> spring up in the sight of the nations.
>
> (Is 61:10–11)

2. Justice in St. Thomas

The thirteenth century—in its revival, on a theological level, of the debate between Plato and Aristotle—marked an important stage in the evolution of the concept of justice.

Beginning with interior justice, Plato defined it as harmony among a person's faculties: reason and the irascible and concupiscible appetites, which were perfected by prudence, courage, and temperance. He then extended the image to society, as a kind of harmony among the corresponding classes of people: judges, warriors, and farmers (*Laws*, Book 9).

St. Augustine took up the same theme but cast it in the more religious, dramatic perspective provided by Scripture, notably in Genesis and St. Paul. He saw justice as an active sort of harmony in which the submission of a person's rational powers to God became the condition for mastery over the senses. This personal justice was lost through sin, committed because of the attraction of external goods; it was regained under the attraction of grace and the interior return to God (*City of God*, 1.13). Despite some differences, justice for Plato and Augustine was primarily and principally interior.

For Aristotle, on the contrary, the proper setting for justice was society; it was concerned with relations between citizens. It was first of all politic, therefore external to the individual because of its object. Only by extension and analogy could we speak of justice within a person's powers and faculties (*Nicomachean Ethics*, 1.5.1138b5).

St. Thomas adopted the Aristotelian notion of justice. Justice properly so-called was about relationships between people and was determined according to the rule of equality. Law would be its objective measure. One could indeed talk about justice in terms of reason's mastery over the irascible and concupiscible appetites, but in a derived, metaphorical sense (IIaIIae, q 58 a 2). Also in a metaphorical sense St. Paul used the word *justice* to designate justification by faith, which restores harmony within the soul (IIaIIae, ad 1 m).

Obviously St. Thomas had no wish to reject the Augustinian and Pauline teaching on justice. But he gave theological thought an important orientation. From his time onward, justice was to designate the virtue that regulates relationships between persons within society. Classified as a moral virtue, it would be clearly distinguished from the theological virtues, which effect justification. Since it directly concerns law, justice does not escape a juridical dimension. To be impartial, it would have to discriminate on the basis of person and would inevitably lose warmth through its concern for objectivity.

Yet for all these authors, from antiquity to the thirteenth century, justice was a virtue, a quality of the soul or, as Cicero said, the constant will to give to all their due. Justice was therefore an inclination to give freely to others. Grafted onto the natural human desire for the social life, it brought this desire to growth and fruition. It was akin to friendship, the highest end of all law, according to Aristotle, and in Christian morality it culminated in charity. St. Thomas saw justice as a necessary stage in the development of charity, but it was not as closely linked to charity in his view as it was for St. Augustine. In becoming more juridical and external, justice forfeited some of its personal character.

3. Modern Justice and Subjective Rights

The modern era is characterized by its subjective conception of rights, as formulated by fourteenth-century nominalism. From that time on, rights refer not to what I owe others, but to what others, and society, owe me. Rights have changed hands: I think now in terms of my own rights, not those of others. The fundamental orientation of justice has been reversed: the burden of the debt falls on others, not on me. Justice no longer implies a quality of soul, a movement outward toward others;

it concentrates on the defense of external rights. In this sense it is a matter of taking rather than giving.

The change accelerated with a new conception of the person's relation to society. This was no longer based on a natural human inclination but became instead an artificial creation, set up to meet human needs and to prevent destructive rivalry.

In this context, justice hardened and assumed two contrary aspects: defense of subjective rights on the one hand and, on the other, societal pressure in the name of the law, with the force of obligation and the threat of constraint. These were quickly resented as forms of oppression.

Under these conditions the relation between justice and charity degenerated, with consequent serious problems. Since the two were now moving in opposite directions, the one giving and the other taking, these virtues could no longer operate harmoniously. Justice, with its stronger, more immediate claims, left little to charity but a supplementary generosity, which could easily be included among the duties of justice as far as the law allowed. As a result, Christian terms such as charity, bounty, mercy, benevolence, and almsgiving were considerably devalued.

It is the great merit of the encyclical *Dives in misericordia* that it attempts to reconcile justice and mercy by showing that, without attentive mercy to real people, justice inevitably gives rise to injustice, at both personal and social levels.

We need to understand this evolution of justice in the modern era if we wish to restore justice to its rightful place in Christian morality, or reestablish its bonds with Scripture, or even understand the Gospels rightly ourselves.

4. *The Sources of Justice*

There is still the basic problem of justice's relationship to Christian ethics. One thing is certain: moral theory must give up the individualism that has locked it in and reevaluate its political and social dimensions. The pressure of current events and the new openness to modern thought have given a strong push in this direction but have not as yet achieved a balance.

Within crises and current unrest, in the midst of theological explorations on the political and social scene, one fundamental question emerges: What is the origin and core of justice? The question is important. If justice is a product of political society, then morality and even theology risk being subordinated to the imperatives of state, party, or special interest groups. They could become the tools of a system or an ideology. Yet the autonomy of political and social fields cannot be denied; on the contrary, it should be safeguarded and promoted.

I should like to single out three related sources of justice:

1. The ultimate source of justice is God, who created and governs the universe and who redeemed us in Christ Jesus. He alone is the sole Just One, capable of restoring justice and love to us in our relationships—first with him and then with individuals, society, and all of creation. This is the center, the divine core of justice of which Scripture speaks. Out of it flows theology.

2. The second source of justice is the human heart, which receives God's justice as the earth enfolds the seed. Out of the human heart come the thoughts and deeds that make us pure or impure, just or unjust, as we choose to follow or reject the divine precepts. On this personal level, justice becomes a quality of the soul, a virtue.

3. Civil society is the third source of justice. It develops through laws and rights. It belongs to everyone and depends upon everyone but is usually concentrated in the hands of rulers and lawmakers. These are responsible for establishing the most just relations possible between individuals, within and between communities, and finally on the international level.

For the theologian these three sources meet and mesh. The contemporary concern for human rights within states and governments flows from the primacy of the person and of human conscience, the priority of the moral over the social and political. But for the theologian, morality itself is based upon each person's relationship to God, our ultimate end. Moral justice is rooted in theological justice.

VIII. SIN

The question of sin has always been a preoccupation of Christian ethicists. Manuals of recent centuries have given it increasing space because their main objective, since the Council of Trent, has been to provide priests with adequate knowledge for the administration of the sacrament of reconciliation. Sin therefore has pride of place in these books. This explains why the study of sin has been included among the four treatises on basic Christian ethics and replaces the one on the virtues. This concentration on sin lends a negative tone to the teaching in the manuals, which might be called the morality of sin or of prohibitions.

In recent years this approach has come under fire, especially in the name of psychology. It has been felt to encourage scruples and a morbid guilt feeling, owing to the fear of sin it engenders. Reacting to this, some have tried to set up a morality without sin, eliminating even the word "sin" from the moral vocabulary. The sacrament of reconciliation has been widely contested, indeed abandoned. Yet to all appearances, the reality of sin has not notably lessened in our world. There seems no dearth of injustices, wars, violence, theft, fraud. . . . Whatever name we give it, sin takes center stage in the media. If in the last century people thought that we were all basically good and that the progress of human sciences would ensure the solution of most of our moral problems, today we are more inclined to think that with the collapse of scientific optimism no one can avoid a guilt complex. Sin is indeed a daily human reality for individuals and for society. So the ethicist must take it seriously. But it is another matter to make sin the chief subject matter of moral theology and the dominant theme in teaching.

The Gospel devotes a large place to sin. The life of Christ is described as a struggle against sin and its consequences, suffering and death. The very name of Jesus means "the one who is to save his people from their sins" (Mt 1:21). During his Passion in particular, Jesus appeared, in the eyes of the early Christians, as a warrior who conquered evil and brought sin low, after allowing it to wreak all its violence upon his person. Yet it is never sin, but always grace, the proclamation of God's mercy, that predominates. The Gospel is the good news of the victory of grace over sin, in Jesus and in all who believe in him, through the power of the Spirit.

In contrast to the pessimistic interpretations of the sixteenth and seventeenth centuries, St. Paul in his Letter to the Romans speaks of Adam's original sin only to emphasize the salvation Jesus won for us. By its very enormity, sin points to the superabundance of grace. By the same token, as grace increases, sin becomes more visible, down to its very roots. The theologian who pays more attention to sin than to grace is like someone who puts out the light in order to peer into a dark recess. Christian ethics therefore should have a care to show the predominance of grace over sin, bringing out in strong relief the action of the Holy Spirit in the lives of believers.

We need to clarify, too, our approach to sin, for this has many aspects. Casuistry studied sins as individual actions, distinguished by their relation to different commandments, and classified them as mortal or venial. This viewpoint, determined by the material act as it related to an external law, slighted another dimension of sin brought out by the Gospels: its unity as rooted in the human person. Behind sins stands Sin. Rather than talk of the "remission of sins," St. John preferred to speak of Christ, who "takes away the sin of the world" (Jn 1:29). Beyond individual actions, he was showing us the mysterious reality that engenders them: rejection of the light, lying, envy, surrender to Satan.

St. Matthew also invites us to search the human heart more deeply to find sin's core: "But the things that come out of the mouth come from the heart, and it is these that make a man unclean. For from the heart come evil intentions: murder, adultery, fornication, theft, perjury, slander. These are the things that make a man unclean" (Mt 15:18–20). It is in the depths of the human heart, the seat of personal freedom, that sin is conceived and impurity brought forth.

Christian thought has endeavored to penetrate these secret places whence come good and evil. In the tradition of St. Augustine we can begin with the choice between two loves, which generate two freedoms. There is an open and generous freedom bent on loving God above all things and our neighbor as ourself, to the point of total self-forgetfulness. And there is a closed freedom, turned in on itself, loving self supremely to the point of despising God and neighbor. Sin's root lies in turning in upon oneself, or in self-love as spiritual writers call it. This kind of love is not necessarily always turned inward, however. It can become extremely active and move out to conquer the universe. But in the end it sucks everything into itself. Its supreme goal is domination, the utilization of all things for its own advantage. Being diametrically opposed to charity, its ultimate end is always its own interest, pleasure, pride of place. Self-love is self-centered even when it looks generous. Pascal said of it: "The ego is hateful." Thus the radical sin is linked to our initial choice between open and closed freedom, between supreme love of God and of self.

We need to distinguish, however, in Christian ethics, between two kinds of self-love: natural love of self and egoism. Deep within each person there is a natural, spontaneous love of self, which is good like all God's works (Genesis). This underlies love of neighbor; we are told to love our neighbor "as ourself." This spontaneous love is expressed in the pronoun *I,* which we use to conjugate verbs and to describe our most personal actions: I love, I believe, I hope, I wish. St. Thomas tells us that this natural love of self is the foundation of friendship and charity.

Unfortunately, this initial love never retains its original purity. As soon as it springs up it is muddied, so to speak, by a self-directed glance, which almost inevitably engenders egoism. We might explain this by saying that the pristine "I," in an immediate and very hidden movement, turns into a "me," which bespeaks interested self-love. This subtle twist isolates us from other people and at the same time incites us to affirm ourselves. Pride is born.

The transition from "I" to "me," from a good, natural love of self to egoism, happens before we are aware of it. Extremely delicate, the movement often escapes us altogether. The fetters it creates go so deep that we can scarcely break them without a real death to self.

This is the renunciation of self, the dying to self of which the Gospel speaks. Egoism is the most natural of all parasites, because it feeds on the spontaneous love that images God. In directing this love toward the "me," it empties it of all substance and corrupts it. Such was the desire "to become like gods" that tempted Adam and Eve in the Genesis account. Such is the "will to power" that Nietzsche claimed to predict, and such the virile egoism described by Montherlant in "Pitié pour les Femmes." Whatever its form, egoism always exalts itself, and this very exaltation can lead to its destruction, since it claims the power to dispose of itself ultimately.

Egoism also has the power to vitiate and twist the answers to all the questions we have been examining. "I love" becomes, beneath the surface, "I love myself" or "I love to be loved" by God or neighbor. "I seek happiness" is transformed into "I seek my happiness" or "I seek happiness for myself." "I look for the truth" becomes "I look for my truth, the truth that suits me" or indeed "I make my own truth." "I want justice" means "I want my justice, my rights," or "I do justice to myself." The distinctions are very subtle, because egoism uses the terms of love so as to give the appearance of it. We can discern the difference only by observing actions closely.

The crowning activity of egoism is to assume the garb of justice and religion and to gain control of their best projects so as to deflect them from God and use them for its own glory and honor. This was the attitude of the Pharisees so strongly attacked by Jesus. It is the gravest of sins to attempt to deceive God himself and wax fat upon his gifts. Jesus contrasted these apparently "just" ones with public sinners, prostitutes and publicans who were fully aware of their sin. They at least did not dream of exalting themselves, either in their own hearts or before God and others.

Only the truth of humility, working through renunciation to the point of self-contempt and "hating [one's] life" (Lk 14:26) can rid us of egoism and reestablish the purity of natural self-love which flowers in charity.

It is important to distinguish between a natural love of self and egoism if we want to understand the spiritual classics, and even the Gospels, when they talk about "death to self." Prescinding from moral experience, these authors sometimes use very strong, almost violent expressions in their desire to engage and break the resistance of egoism. They use the language of warfare. But in the more ontological language and perspective of theology, used by St. Thomas, "death to self" never means the destruction of the primitive "I" or of the natural love of self that God has placed in us. On the contrary, by destroying the "me," renunciation frees the "I" from its parasite and opens it to growth in true love.

The sin that should be considered first in Christian ethics is the interior sin that engenders all other sins and can vitiate even our best actions.

Conclusion

I have touched on only some of the main questions arising in Christian ethics. There are many others. It may cause surprise, for example, that I have not mentioned sexuality, over which ethicists generally linger. The sixth commandment is a special area of moral action best linked with the question of love. My intention has been simply to give an overview of the whole field of morality, beginning with the more general questions, so as to broaden an outlook that is often limited by a concentration on obligations.

We are now in a position to gather together all the strands of our discussion in one comprehensive definition of Christian ethics: Christian ethics is that branch of theological wisdom that studies human actions so as to direct them to the loving vision of God, which is complete happiness and our final end. This is done under the impulse of the theological and moral virtues, especially charity and justice, with the gifts of the Holy Spirit. It is effected through experiences of the human condition such as suffering and sin, and is implemented by laws of behavior and commandments, which reveal God's ways to us.

PART ONE

ETHICS, HUMAN AND CHRISTIAN

3

―――

The Human Aspect of Christian Ethics

Having formed our definition of Christian ethics, we now need to determine its subject matter more precisely, and its relationship to other sciences and techniques that also deal with human action.

At this point we can formulate two questions. First, how does Christian ethics differ from the behavioral sciences, arts and techniques, in their approach to human action? And following from this, how can all these disciplines collaborate? As we search for the answers to these questions, the human aspect of Christian ethics will begin to emerge.

I. CHRISTIAN ETHICS DEALS WITH ALL HUMAN ACTS INSOFAR AS THEY ARE VOLUNTARY

Ethicists agree that their study is concerned with human action, carried out deliberately and freely. But when we examine the theories of obligation, it becomes evident that they are too narrow to include this entire range. They divide human acts into two groups, obligatory and free; the first of these is their exclusive concern.

This distinction is rarely perceived but constantly applied; the consequences are serious. Some of the richest, most interesting human actions, where personal involvement is deepest, are withdrawn from the moral realm. Consider, for example, the choice of a vocation, the achievement of a lifelong project, or the search for perfection. All of these spring dynamically from freedom and love and contribute on a

47

spiritual and human level to a very fruitful creativity. Exclusive concentration on legal obligations, by contrast, is obviously limiting and leads to impoverishment.

I believe with St. Thomas that human acts belong to the moral sphere precisely because they are deliberate and free and not obligatory. In fact, the freer an act is in its thrust toward perfection, the richer its human quality, since this is the ultimate purpose of law and its crowning glory. Here we have an important shift in perspective, and we will do well to keep it in mind when we describe the limits of the moral domain and compare morality with other sciences also dealing with human actions.

This does not make our task easier. We cannot agree that ethics is distinguished from the other sciences simply because it is concerned only with obligatory human actions enjoined by law, to the exclusion of all others. Nor can the distinction be purely material. We need to find a formal distinction that exposes the difference and shows, moreover, the way to collaboration between ethics and these sciences by throwing light on the nature of human action and directing it.

II. THE DIFFERENCE BETWEEN MORAL THEOLOGY AND THE BEHAVIORAL SCIENCES

This is the problem: If moral theology includes all human acts in its subject matter, how does it differ from other sciences that do the same?

The classic response, already formulated by Aristotle, runs thus: Generally speaking, sciences have as their direct object the acquisition of truth, knowledge, and growth in knowledge. These are theoretical. Ethics also pursues knowledge, but of a practical kind. Its aim is the production of a work, namely human action. Hence it is directive or normative.

This distinction is very sound, but I prefer to approach the problem from a slightly different angle. The extraordinary development of science and technology in our day has modified the entire notion of science. For many people, positive sciences have become models of knowledge in general, and their techniques seem to affect the entire practical field of study. Therefore, in order to avoid regrettable confusion, we need to make some clear distinctions between the kinds of knowledge envisaged in moral theory and the kinds envisaged in the positive sciences.

To do this, let us take another look at the methods that characterize and determine these two types of knowledge. We will consider first the method proper to ethics in its treatment of human acts, and then the method followed by the positive sciences and its relation to moral knowledge. Finally we will make a distinction between ethics and technical expertise.

A. Knowledge in the Moral Context

To describe this type of knowledge, its development and method of procedure, is a challenging proposition. Let me quote Newman on the subject. "The longer anyone has persevered in the practice of virtue, the less likely is he to recollect how he began it; what were his difficulties on starting and how surmounted; by what process one truth led to another; and the less likely to elicit justly the real reasons latent in his mind for particular observances or opinions. . . . Hence it is that some of the most deeply exercised and variously gifted Christians, when they proceed to write or speak upon Religion, either fail altogether or cannot be understood except on attentive study." And in a later passage, "It is considered the highest of gifts to possess an intuitive knowledge of the beautiful in art, or the effective in action, without reasoning or investigating; that this, in fact, is genius and that they who have a corresponding insight into moral truth (as far as they have it) have reached that especial perfection in the spiritual part of their nature, which is so rarely found and so greatly prized among the intellectual endowments of the soul."[1]

A long quotation, perhaps, but it is rich, and throws light on many aspects of our subject. Moral awareness presents us with a paradox: the longer we live the more powerful is its hold upon us, and the harder it is for us to put into words, to explain or justify it to other people. Think, for instance, of the most crucial decisions in life. Why did this husband and wife, so deeply in love, choose each other? What inspired conversions like those of Augustine and Newman? What is the deepest motive underlying a vocation? What happens in these decisions of lifelong consequence takes place on a small scale in our everyday moral choices. We are well aware of our personal involvement, but when we try to explain what moved us to make these choices, it escapes us. We have to stop and think about it. Only with luck may we succeed, but the result is always less than perfect.

1. Sermon, "Personal Influence, the Means of Propagating the Truth," in Newman, *Fifteen Sermons Preached before the University of Oxford* (London, 1906), 83–84.

This is the task we face, in all its difficulty. If ethics is the science that considers human acts from the point of view of the responsible person, then the heart of the moral question and the basis of its method will be the knowledge that generates human acts, forms them, brings them to the light of day and joins them to the human will. To reach this goal, ethicists must engage in patient reflection upon human action, pursuing it from its outward show to its inner sources, to its ultimate origin in conscience and personal will. All the dimensions of the human act, all its elements in their harmonious ordering, can be surveyed only from this central point.

This kind of searching corresponds perfectly to the famous Socratic saying, "Know thyself!" Tracing the causes of action through reflection results in self-questioning: "Who am I, who did that? What prompted me from within?" As St. Paul says: "I cannot understand my own behavior. I fail to carry out the things I want to do, and I find myself doing the very things I hate" (Rom 7:15). This is the most fundamental moral question. Here then is the way we can describe the development of moral consciousness, beginning with the deepest level whence it springs forth as a source of light and action.

1. "Fontal" or Causal Knowledge

At the origin of every human act, at the moment of its conception and coming forth, there is a unique kind of knowledge. This knowledge is the very source of the act, so I shall call it "fontal." It is too rich to be adequately described. It is a direct, intuitive, total perception, often instantaneous and dynamic, of all the elements of an action. These elements include the cause of the action—the self—as well as a variety of parts forming a new composite whole. Fontal knowledge grasps self and the other, the act and its object. It perceives these in a new relationship, an interplay of truth, goodness, happiness, and the moral dimension. It is both light and impulse, yet has a shadowed, resisting quality also. It runs so deep that we are not fully aware of it at times and might be tempted to think of it as part of our subconscious, but it would be truer to recognize it as superconscious, at the source and origin of awareness.

Fontal knowledge usually results from a more or less lengthy searching and deliberating process, as happens in the case of a difficult and important decision. Yet it transcends the search by the keenness of its perception and leads to an active, personal commitment.

To get a clearer idea of this kind of knowledge, it may be helpful to consider preaching, an art that combines oratorical skill and moral commitment. We are told that Lacordaire could never prepare his homilies in advance. His main preparation consisted in meditation on the subject matter. Only when he was in direct contact with his listeners did his words pour forth, his ideas develop in ordered harmony; still later it became possible to put them in writing. This is an example of the oratorical art. In the very act of preaching, fontal knowledge springs up and takes shape even as the discourse it inspires is developing. It is direct, intuitive, dynamic, creative, inexhaustible as a wellspring. Words can never adequately express it, even though they are its necessary instruments.

It is this fontal knowledge or awareness that we all possess at the moment of action, even though we may perceive it only in a confused way and cannot put it into words. On the moral plane, as contrasted with other ambiences, everyone possesses a little spark in the depths of his consciousness that lights up the good for him and disposes him for this direct and constructive knowledge in his personal life.

Fontal knowledge is situated at the soul's center, in the deepest, most hidden part of us. As St. Paul says, "After all, the depths of a man can only be known by his own spirit, not by any other man" (1 Cor 2:11). And again, "The Spirit himself and our spirit bear united witness" (Rom 8:16). It is on the level of this interior activity that the Holy Spirit acts within us.

Fontal knowledge may also be envisioned as originating in the heart, understood in the Gospel sense. Out of the heart come good or evil deeds, rendering a person pure or impure. Intentions, the roots of our actions, are formed there. Again, fontal knowledge resides in the "inmost I," which Laval called "the sole reality in a world that is essentially active." It springs up powerfully in creativity, making us truly be.

Finally we think of the "soul's spark" of which St. Jerome spoke, that flame which becomes for theologians a synthesis, an intuition of the first principles of moral action, destined to be translated by fontal knowledge into action.

We have seen that fontal knowledge cannot be fully described, because it anticipates ideas and words, even as the spring precedes the brook that flows from it. Yet it is present and active in every person, regardless of degrees of culture, and in every personal action, as a light shining out of our depths. It is a part of our spiritual nature.

2. *Reflex or Instinctive Knowledge*

Fontal knowledge is not the only kind of knowledge we possess. In the act of observing ourselves, another kind of knowledge emerges, which we call reflex or instinctive: a reflection of action in our consciousness. It creates a split in fontal knowledge. Characteristically it operates in the order of vision, not action. We might call it "speculative," in the sense of something that looks and observes. When we act or speak, even when we think, we are looking at ourselves as if in an interior mirror.

This self-regard can jeopardize fontal knowledge and even the quality of our actions. It gives rise to timidity, vanity, the egoism we spoke of above, self-centeredness, and pride. The orator who listens to himself speaking loses his naturalness. The preacher who admires himself is apt to lose the train of his thought. Reflex knowledge can thus compromise the simplicity of fontal knowledge and cause ambivalence, ambiguity in our actions.[2]

Yet reflex knowledge can also play a positive role, because it is owing to it that we can control our actions, feelings, and thoughts. This interior glance can help us master our actions and carry them through to the finish. To achieve this, we need to collaborate constantly with our fontal knowledge, placing ourselves at its service.

It is through reflex knowledge that conscience is awakened in us, conscience in the etymological sense in which St. Thomas understands it: "knowledge with another," or "accompanying knowledge." Thus conscience unites fontal and reflex knowledge at the source of all moral knowledge.

Here we have returned to the origins of language. The word is like the double of the reality it names. It corresponds to the twofold relationship of reflex knowledge to fontal knowledge and to action. It, too, is bound to be ambivalent: either it will serve as a faithful, apt sign to convey and manifest a profound reality, or it will block our access to it, like a screen substituting itself for the reality.

Whatever the harmony between fontal and reflex knowledge, they will always be distanced from each other, and this will cause our thought processes to shift back and forth between them. Reflex knowledge can never adequately express its fontal counterpart, any more than discourse can exhaust inspiration or genius; nor can it reveal all that is in the human heart. A simple examination of conscience is enough to demonstrate this: the attempt to penetrate our deepest motives.

3. Reflective Knowledge

Reflex knowledge becomes reflective when we try to engage in reflection, which usually happens when people ask us "why" and "how."

---

2. This danger can be illustrated by Sartre's admission in *Les carnets de la drôle de guerre*: "Whenever I feel anything, even before I feel it, I know that I feel it. And then I am so busy defining it and thinking about it that I only half feel it."

Reflection tries to grasp the motives for an action and its unfolding, so as to explain, justify, critique, or improve it. From past experience it draws lessons, resolutions, practical advice, and directives for living. This type of knowledge will be expressed in instructive or wisdom literature and in maxims, proverbs, precepts, and ultimately in laws. Linked closely with experience, it sets up a process of generalization and subsequent communication, while maintaining a strictly practical orientation.

The sapiential and moral teaching in Scripture may be attributed to reflective knowledge, even though a certain systemization can already be traced here. Spiritual and mystical works may also be included, for they are written in concrete, ordinary language and use examples, images, and symbols drawn from everyday life. Works dealing with oratorical skills discussed above will fall under the same category.

4. Theoretic, Systematic Knowledge

When reasoning and logical thought come into play, they transform reflective knowledge into more theoretic and general thought patterns. Theoretic knowledge attempts to gather together the strands of moral knowledge and organize them into a universal system on a scientific plane.

This process, already begun in the New Testament, was to be developed by the Fathers and later especially in medieval scholasticism, thanks to the study of Greek philosophy. Morality then became a science of happiness, the virtues being drawn from revelation. In modern times a science of obligations was developed and shaped into a fairly rigorous system that endowed it with theological status. This science maintains the practical orientation inherent in moral theory, but it is worked out with the help of rational processes and uses a technical vocabulary special to it. Consequently, as a theory it is somewhat distanced from experience. The moralist, however learned, is not necessarily a virtuous or experienced person.

At this point, Christian ethics comes to the fore, in works such as St. Thomas's *Summa theologiae* and manuals of moral theology.

Systematic knowledge can no more exhaust the content of fontal knowledge than could the reflective type, nor does it reveal all the richness of moral experience. By the same token it does not take into account all the teachings of revelation. Perfect though they be, moral systems will always remain incomplete. In fact, this is the very condition of their fidelity to moral reality. We should not be surprised, therefore, to see that Church history presents us with a variety of moral systems corresponding to changes in periods and intellectual currents. Nonetheless, this work of systemization is the indispensable guarantee of the solidity and progress of our moral knowledge.

We need to see the difference between the systemization of ethics and its Christian content. Gospel teaching, which takes place on the level of reflective knowledge but has its origin in the interior action of the Holy Spirit, is transmitted by the Church from one generation to the next as an integral part of revelation. Theology's function is to analyze and present this heritage, but the heritage cannot be substantially changed by a variety and succession of ethical systems. It is precisely through their fidelity to the evangelical source that the various systems and different schools of theology can enjoy fruitful collaboration.

5. A Return to Fontal Knowledge and Action

In order to distinguish the stages of moral knowledge, we have had to insist on their differences, but we can never forget the dynamic continuity that unites them. Fontal knowledge is the source of all moral knowledge, even the most theoretical, and the latter, no matter how scientific, would fall short of its natural end if it did not return to this original knowledge to collaborate with it in producing action. Even in its theoretical stage, moral theory is a type of knowledge oriented to action as to its proper goal and fulfillment. It is through action, especially upright action, that the authenticity of a moral system is put to the test and can grow by experience.

Thus a vast circular movement is set up at the heart of moral knowledge, beginning with fontal knowledge and returning to it after passing through the stages we have described. It could be compared to the circulation of the blood beginning from the heart. The comparison is all the more striking if we think of the heart in the scriptural sense as the seat of mind and emotion, forming our actions as a tree brings forth its fruit.

The Connections among the Different Forms of Moral Knowledge

This presentation of the circular movement of moral knowledge allows us to situate its principal forms very precisely and to show their necessary relationships. Knowledge may be personal or prudential, sapiential or spiritual, scientific or theological. Fontal knowledge tends to develop into sapiential and then scientific forms. The process may extend over centuries, as we can see from the history of theology. But this growth is continually nurtured by a return to concrete action and experience. Theological knowledge, for its part, comes at the end of this development, with the exercise of reason. Because of its quality of abstraction and universality, it stands at the opposite pole from fontal knowledge. Yet it can never be separated from it without cutting itself off from its source and failing to reach its goal.

We can see now how the various types of moral knowledge, as expressed in the works of inspired authors, sages and theologians, preachers and spiritual leaders, are connected by a vital bond, which gives them unity in diversity. The section on moral theology in St. Thomas's *Summa theologiae,* therefore, is not so alien to apostolic or patristic preaching, to the witness of the mystics, or to accounts of personal experience as we might think. This last, the personal aspect, containing fontal knowledge, opens out to all the other forms of moral knowledge and is indeed their final end.

Critique of the Classic Categories of Moral Knowledge

My description of moral theology differs somewhat from the classic categories of recent centuries. These posit two stages: first come abstract, universal principles, expressed in general laws; then follows individual, concrete action, modified by circumstances and situations. The ethicist's task is to apply the principles or universal laws to individual actions as faithfully as possible.

It is not possible to give an exhaustive critique of this schema here. I can only compare it with my own. Insofar as it applies the processes of speculative reason to practical reason, the schema is good and has value. It corresponds to the legislative and theological work that I have placed at the end of my third stage and in my fourth. It describes law as returning to concrete action, in the final stage, by way of a normative application.

However, this presentation, as utilized by modern obligation-driven ethicists, is too narrow and can become quite inadequate. Seen from the viewpoint of the distinction between the universal and the individual, which sets law and freedom in opposition to each other, there will always be tension between abstract and concrete moral knowledge.

In the context of this theory, it is hard to see how principles and moral science flow from an experience of reality, human or divine, and lead back to it. They seem to emerge arbitrarily from the sphere of ideas, being worked out to the last detail in the imperative mood. We can no longer find in them the sources of light contained in active, upright experience. Principles and laws are applied to actions by deductions of pure reason, while the agent remains overly passive. Moral knowledge loses its dynamism and life. Its horizon shrinks to the measure of legal formulas and its activity is reduced to the eternal debate between law and freedom as applied to cases of conscience.

Fortunately there is another way of applying principles to individual actions. We can share St. Thomas's outlook, remembering his concept of the totality of moral theory. For him, practical reason has a clear function. Its role, however practical, is achieved through concrete, personal knowledge supplied by virtues such as wisdom, knowledge, and above all prudence, combined with the virtues related to the appetites. Practical reason goes hand in hand with the connatural knowledge of which the Angelic Doctor so often speaks. Thus, by means of the virtues, vital connections are forged, in the dynamic inner depths of the person who is performing an action, between the universal and the individual, between principles and action. Such is the living movement of moral knowledge I have tried to describe in detailing the traditional schema.

Although it is not immediately obvious, it is quite simple to show how St. Thomas's moral theology relates closely to experience. He richly exploited Aristotle's profound analyses of human moral standards. His greatest strength was drawn from his contemplative study of the Scriptures, particularly St. Paul and St. John; his debt to the spiritual experience of St. Augustine and the Fathers is well known. We are aware too that many of St. Thomas's treatises were written in response to contemporary problems, which could at times be very heated. His work may be described, further, as a theological expression of the powerful Gospel preaching recorded in the early days of the mendicant orders.

Finally, we may be sure that St. Thomas could never have have produced so original and innovative a work had his reflection not been fed by a personal experience of the virtues he spoke of so finely and the gifts of the Holy Spirit he described so luminously. On close examination, St. Thomas's teaching points to an intimate bond with human, Christian experience.

To sum up, we can characterize moral knowledge by the method it follows. It comes into being through dynamic reflection on human actions. Starting with the acts themselves, it goes back to their source and origin in the human person. Not content with hindsight, it would capture the interior movement that produces the action, so as to direct it to its fulfillment. This method is similar to that of philosophy, but becomes theological when the light of revelation and the impulse of the Spirit penetrate to the inner depths of the believer.

B. Positivist Knowledge

How do the behavioral sciences envisage human acts? How do they study them, what is their chief source of light?

I do not propose to analyze the various sciences with their individual methods here. What interests me, as a moral theologian, is to identify the general method of the behavioral sciences, especially their attitudes toward the human person and human activity. This, I hope, will enable us to see how their approach differs from that of Christian ethics.

To go straight to the point, since the last century modern sciences have been dominated by the positivist method. This was introduced by Bacon and spread by Comte, who made it into a philosophical system.

We might define positivist knowledge as knowledge that proceeds by way of rigorous observation of facts perceptible to the senses (and to instruments that in turn perfect the senses), or phenomena. It observes these things as far as they are quantitatively measurable and reducible to invariable laws expressing precise formulas. Comte wrote: "All sound thinkers since Bacon hold that the only authentic knowledge is that based on observable facts."

What interests me particularly is the human behavior of the scientist in the face of "observable facts"—and I am thinking here of human actions—which this method calls for and which will characterize it. The ideal stance of such a person would be that of a pure and simple spectator, who remains outside the action and refrains from any intervention in its unfolding. This would ensure complete objectivity of outlook and scientific rigor in formulating laws connecting the phenomena. This is the attitude of the chemist peering through a microscope or the astronomer gazing through a telescope: they merely observe. So too with the psychoanalyst seated behind the patient: sheer listening.

It has been demonstrated that this type of pure and simple observation cannot continue indefinitely. Vision requires light and light will modify the phenomena under observation, since the psychologist or sociologist cannot completely bracket personal feelings and ideas.

These critical remarks do not, however, affect the validity of the method. They merely indicate its limitations. They have been made before, in the desire to correct errors and insure science's progress towards its ideal of objectivity.

I think we need to recognize openly the value of the positivist method and the contribution made by the sciences which use it. Yet we must be aware of its limits, and guard against a certain danger inherent in it: we cannot make it an absolute, conferring upon it philosophical status, nor can we conclude that there can be no other genuine kind of science or knowledge.

In this connection, Auguste Comte's remark is highly significant. According to him, the test of a sound thinker is that he endorses this principle: There is no authentic knowledge except that which is based on the observation of facts according to the positivist method. Every other kind of knowledge is rejected as unrealistic and undemonstrable, and every other method is seen as illusory and wrong. Only positivist knowledge is authentic: this is the tenet of positivism, a science turned philosophy, perhaps even turned religion.

Prescinding from this absolutism and exclusivism, attractive to some contemporary thinkers despite the obvious errors and illusions, I should like to retain for our own purposes all that is valid in positivist methods and sciences as they are applied to human phenomena. I am particularly interested in their attitude of rigorous observation, an ever-present ideal.

I should like to compare the distinctive features of moral knowledge and the positivist sciences point by point, beginning with their characteristic methods: the one, reflection, the other, observation. My object is not to depict one as preferable to the other, but simply to distinguish them clearly so as to discern possibilities for their collaboration.

C. A Comparison between Methods: Reflective and Positivist

1. The Reflective Moral Method Studies Actions from Within, the Positivist Sciences from Without

a. Moral Knowledge.   I have described the method used in Christian ethics as reflective and dynamic. Returning to the source of action within the person, moral knowledge tries to grasp and understand the action from an interior viewpoint. This is its perspective as it examines the elements of an action so as to shape it and bring it into actuality. This is how St. Thomas analyzed human action, beginning with the interior act of the will, which he saw as the principal cause of morality. Moral knowledge seeks at the same time to penetrate to the inmost significance of the actions proposed for its consideration. This enables it to understand and explain them from the point of view of the person whose ideas and qualities they reflect. The substance of an action interests the moralist more than its outward shape.

This interiority is dynamic. It consists in the knowledge and the willing impulse that give rise to action, forming it as efficient and final causes. As to the efficient cause, moral knowledge establishes a person's responsibility in acting. Operating as final cause, it insures a certain mastery in the choice of means and end. This twofold dimension, to which we add formal causality in the reason's grasp of the object, is what characterizes moral knowledge.

A concrete expression of these typical dimensions can be found in the Sermon on the Mount and the Decalogue. "Anyone who is angry with his brother will answer for it before the court" (Mt 5:22): efficient causality. "How happy are the poor in spirit; theirs is the kingdom of heaven" (Mt 5:3): final causality, in the form of a promise. Thus St. Thomas saw in the Gospel Beatitudes the revelation of the true happiness and ultimate end to which God calls us.

Similarly, the Decalogue is at the heart of the great promises made to Abraham and Moses. Establishing the covenant and laws, it determines the responsibility of the chosen people before God.

b. Positivist Knowledge.   In keeping with its preferred method, positivist knowledge begins with a consideration of human actions from the point of view of their external appearances. It considers the human action first as a fact to be observed, then as something "done" rather than "to be done." The same attention to the external can be seen in the laws established to relate actions to other observable factors that condition and explain them.

Positivist sciences use the relationships of succession and simultaneity as an essential foundation for their laws. They abstract from efficient or final causality, so characteristic of moral consciousness. As Comte observed so categorically: "The fundamental characteristic of positivist philosophy is to consider all phenomena as subject to invariable natural laws. The end of all our efforts is to discover these and reduce them to the smallest possible number. The search for so-called first or final causes strikes us as absolutely impossible and meaningless."

There is no doubt that in actual scientific research it is practically impossible to ignore efficient and final causality entirely. Comte himself, in the above quotation, speaks of the end of all his efforts. Still, it is true that positivist science by its very method gives priority to material causality, since its starting point is the succession and simultaneity of phenomena. It sets out to establish coordination by means of invariable laws, or a causality that might be called efficient, if you will, but is determined and not free. This is something quite other than moral causality. The latter operates from within, while the former determines a person from without, as if he were a robot. This is verified in psychic phenomena, which may be considered either from the point of view of a person's dynamic interiority, in moral theory, or from the vantage point of an observer who uses evaluative instruments and tests in positivist psychology.

There is no reason to fear clarifying this difference in methods and outlook, even if in concrete research the two views may blend to a certain extent. It helps us to see both the validity of the positivist sciences as applied to the human person and their limitations. To quote Jean Fourastié in a review of his *Le long chemin des hommes*: "For a long time it was thought, in the tradition of Renan, that science could take the place of religion [we could say of ethics] in explaining the human mystery. The great ones among scientists are returning to this theory today. . . . The information that science provides is sure and practical and is increasing in quality and quantity, yet is rarely sufficient for the making of a decision. It explains the *how* of many things, but not the *why*, and is silent about our ultimate end."

My distinction between moral and positivist knowledge rests upon a fundamental difference in attitude toward the human person and the relation of thought to action. Actions may be viewed on the one hand as issuing from within, performed by the agent. On the other hand they may be studied from observation, as exterior to the person, and so merely phenomena of the outer world in which they take place.

2. Moral Knowledge Is Dynamic, Directive, Normative; Positivist Knowledge Is "Neutral," Nondirective, Nonnormative

a. Moral Knowledge.   Moral knowledge is dynamic in its origin— which is fontal knowledge—and in its goal, the thing to be done, which will bring it to term. It accompanies the action throughout its development: in the deliberation and judgment that form the choice and in all the efforts, repetitions, and adjustments required for its execution. Establishing a relationship between the person who is acting and the end in view with the necessary truthfulness and rectitude, this knowledge is essentially directive, regulative, normative. Typically it speaks in the imperative mood, by way of commands that extend, thanks to prudence, to the level of the individual action: "Do this, do that."

We should note, however, that the command may be sapiential in nature, charged with a light and spontaneity that distinguish it clearly from the purely voluntary imperative of the morality of obligation. Such are the precepts at the peak of the "new" justice of the Sermon on the Mount. "Offer the wicked man no resistance. On the contrary, if anyone hits you on the right cheek, offer him the other as well. . . . I say this to you: love your enemies and pray for those who persecute you. . . . You must therefore be perfect just as your heavenly Father is perfect" (Mt 5:39, 44, 48). These commands have the power of the love they inspire and even of the threats they evoke: "If you do not forgive others, your Father will not forgive your failings either" (Mt 6:15).

These are actually the commands found in the Decalogue, but permeated and empowered by the commandments of love of God and neighbor. For St. Thomas, even the expressions *command* and *precept* are seen as acts of reason, human or divine, charged with a voluntary impulse, as are acts of efficacious wisdom. Being dynamic, moral knowledge will be by nature rather synthetic. In order to produce action, it has to build out of the elements at hand a new synthesis, much as one builds a house. Like wisdom, it is architechtonic, and thus leads to a unified knowledge, such as the connatural knowledge that the virtues develop by dint of practice and experience.

Under all these aspects, moral knowledge can be called "committed." The person who acquires it cannot remain indifferent, since it directly concerns the quality of the one who acts. Nor can moral knowledge truly grow and develop without being involved effectively in a person's good actions and the experience resulting from them.

b. Positivist Knowledge. Positivist knowledge is quite another thing. As compared with the dynamism of moral knowledge, it could be called "static," in the sense that it places the scientist at some fixed, stable point from which he both observes and measures phenomena as they unfold. These phenomena are considered as a succession of accomplished facts, fixed and stable, even though observed in the actual process of taking place.

Abstracting from efficient and final causality—and the efficient cause is essentially free—the positivist, according to his chosen method, makes no attempt to address the question of responsibility in the actions he observes. Nor is he concerned to use the data provided for subsequent action. The knowledge he acquires is neither directive nor normative in itself. It is simply a statement of fact about the present or past.

For example, a sociologist assessing a religious situation in a diocese may offer a very useful analysis to those who have employed him, but he will make no attempt to evaluate the events that have created the situation, make decisions that will alter it, or determine the ends that will orientate ultimate procedures. Such things are beyond his competence. Concern for rigorous, objective observation keeps the scientist in a state of "neutrality" in regard to the facts and actions he is studying. He has to remove himself as far as possible from personal feelings and opinions, so as to become like a mirror, faithfully reflecting whatever is before him. He will look for no other laws and apply no other criteria of judgment apart from those inherent in the facts. Positivist knowledge thus differs profoundly from moral knowledge. Because of the requirements of its method, it is uncommitted or detached.

When studying the same documents—such as the Beatitudes or the Decalogue—the strictly positivist exegete will have a different attitude and reaction from that of the ethicist or the Christian. The positivist will see only historical texts; the ethicist will recognize the principle sources of morality, and the Christian will experience the texts as the Word of God, having a highly personal impact. One holds the text at a distance so as not to be touched by it; the others are interested in the text precisely because it does touch them and concern them as responsible persons.

In spite of their differences, the two attitudes toward the same writings can coexist and be coordinated within a single person. This will produce a fruitful alliance between scientist and ethicist.

It has been made sufficiently clear, moreover, that the supposed perfect neutrality is really an illusion, especially in the behavioral sciences. One person cannot remain totally abstracted and withdrawn from another. If this were possible, there would be no understanding, but only destruction. Here in particular, one's attitude conditions one's very vision and, consequently, the object being observed.

As noted above, this critical remark does not lessen the validity of the positivist sciences or their method; it simply invites us to estimate their scope and limitations better. Nor should we go to the opposite extreme, abandoning our regard for objectivity and for the truth that undergirds all the sciences, including moral theory.

We should note finally that positivist knowledge stresses analysis above all else, since its main object is to break down phenomena into their simplest elements, so as to discover the laws determining them. In comparison with moral theory, philosophy, and theology, which move from multiplicity toward unity, the positivist sciences have created a growing division and specialization, which lessen our hope for synthesis.

This results in a moral system conceived as a science of morals or a technique of acting, such as Levy-Bruhl's project at the beginning of this century.

3. Moral Knowledge Is Personal, Positivist Knowledge Apersonal

a. Moral Knowledge. The human person is the ethicist's chief consideration, since the person is the source and responsible cause of actions. Recognition of personality, therefore, constitutes a fundamental premise of moral science.

Moreover, if, in the moral world, everything originates in the person, so too does it return to the same source, ultimately qualifying the person as good or evil according to the intervening actions.

This is why the moral law is preferably expressed in the second person: "You must not kill, you must not commit adultery. . . . Love your enemies and pray for those who persecute you" (Mt 5:21, 27, 44). Even when the third person is used, it easily slips into the second: "I say this to you: anyone who is angry with his brother will answer for it before the court. . . . So then, if you are bringing your offering to the altar and there remember that your brother has something against you . . ." (Mt 5:22–23).

We need to go still further and say that moral knowledge requires a personal commitment even from the moralist, since adequate understanding of moral realities is impossible without a certain degree of personal experience. Hence Aristotle thought young people unsuited for moral science, as they lacked sufficient human experience. Virtues, for example, do not attract those who do not practice them; they turn them off with their unbearable demands. The unvirtuous cannot understand and esteem virtue, since they have never learned to love it.

The human person is at the heart of moral knowledge, thanks to free will which empowers human action. Freedom too, like personality, is a basic premise of moral science. As we shall see, our image of the moral world depends directly on our concept of the freedom of our actions.

b. Positivist Knowledge. Because of its method, positive knowledge rejects the consideration of personal and subjective factors, either on the part of the observer or in what is being observed. It focuses its attention on outward facts and the connections between them, so as to deduce, if possible, determining laws. The purpose of this research is to reconstitute a certain "mechanism" which can explain phenomena and produce facts.

Positivist knowledge is based, therefore, not on personal experience but on the experience of facts observable by everyone. Either this experience may be produced at will or the documents recording it may enjoy a perfect scientific guarantee open to anyone's examination.

In reality, personal experience gained by the practice of science, and the intuition of even the most positivistic of scientists, play an important role in scientific progress. Yet these factors are excluded from positivist consideration and act upon it only indirectly, since they cannot be faced outright. Only a reflection on scientific activity can discern them; this pertains to an entirely different philosophical method.

When the positivist method is set up as the universal principle of a science, as in positivism, it leads to a determinism that affects even the human person. Personality and freedom disappear behind the mechanisms that regulate the phenomena observed in people and their actions. They are related to these phenomena and ultimately denied. Emotions, moral decisions, and spiritual aspirations are interpreted from the viewpoint of material data, reduced to their physiological, biological, or psychic components, and dismissed with the remark: that's all there is to it!

"Person" becomes an inappropriate term, something prescientific, signifying the organized body of elements and movements unfolding in an individual's psychic world or social relationships. In this situation, the free personality and scientific determinism are radically opposed to each other.

This is not to say that the application of the positivist method to the human person is not perfectly legitimate and valuable, as long as we recognize that some part of human personality and activity necessarily eludes it. The positivist sciences that study the human person are and should be apersonal, in the sense we have discussed. Precisely for this reason, they need to be complemented by knowledge of another kind, acquired by a reflective and personalistic method.

4. Objectivity in Positivist and Moral Knowledge

a. Objectivity in Positivist Knowledge.   Sciences have imposed upon us their own concept of objectivity to such an extent that it is difficult for us to imagine any other. So perhaps we ought to talk first of all about the objectivity that positivist knowledge seeks.

Positivist objectivity is characterized by the distance, opposition even, that it sets up between object and subject. The scientific observer has to be detached from himself as subject (his ideas, feelings, reactions) so as to ensure an unprejudiced look at the facts. In this sense, scientific objectivity is essentially asubjective; we might call it cold and bare.

This objectivity will be material. It enters the fields of psychology and ethics only through the mediation of perceptible facts, documents, and texts reflecting them. There is a danger of reducing these human dimensions to their material substratum in the name of science, without realizing that the constitutive principle of the object being researched, which in this case is in the spiritual order, will be lost.

Positive objectivity confers on sciences a universality proper to them. The results of scientific research are accessible and communicable to everyone having the requisite intellectual formation. Their universality is wholly a thing of reason, independent of other human factors such as sentiment, race, nation, class, etc. This facilitates communication and widens its scope, at least in theory.

In reality, scientific objectivity can be achieved only partially. Despite all efforts, the scientist can never prescind totally from his subjectivity, which includes, for example, the desire to know, to master his material, to surpass his rivals, etc., all of which may be motives for the research itself. Nor can he, especially if he is studying the human person, avoid problems in the moral order that are raised by his discoveries and their utilization, on the political level among others. Thus the scientist comes to realize that the positivist method and the objectivity demanded by science have their limitations. Their universality is more quantitative than qualitative, for in itself science cannot extend to all human dimensions and aspects of the human act.

b. Moral Objectivity. In moral theory there is an objectivity every bit as real and demanding as scientific objectivity, but it is of a different kind. I shall call it "trans-subjective" because it goes beyond the subjects themselves.

I call it "subjective," not in the sense of its being arbitrarily controlled by the subject, for this would negate even objectivity, but because it takes place at the precise point where the person begins to act. It is manifested as an exigency of truth, which informs and governs the desire for good, at the source of the action, in choice and decision. It is at the very heart of personal action that our guiding light touches us, especially on the level of prudential judgment. This objectivity will be the work of the practical reason penetrating our free will. It will be the truth of goodness. Such objectivity can be called "trans-subjective," for truth and goodness move moral persons to go beyond themselves and overcome the singularities that stand in their way. They provide the only solid basis for moral communion and collaboration.

There is therefore in moral theory an objectivity that can be qualified as "personal." It is expressed in the wisdom that responds to life's deepest questions and thus engenders moral science. Without doubt, this objectivity never reaches full perfection in us, because of the complexity of human nature. But it impels us powerfully, and with an even deeper attraction than the truth and objectivity of the other sciences. Consequently moral theory will enjoy a kind of "personal" universality. This is illustrated in the formulation of moral precepts expressed in the second person: "You must not kill, you must not lie," etc. These precepts possess a universal value that cannot be contested, even if their application allows for discussion in some instances. We should not be afraid to emphasize this characteristic of moral laws. Far from endangering their universality, it roots it in their nature. Quite different is the universality of sciences, or the universality of abstract rational propositions, to which moral laws have too often been reduced. Different, too, is the universality of moral theory, which touches the most intimate part of the human personality, free will. This kind of universality may seem paradoxical: it is none the less real and demonstrable.

When we consider the works of the great artists, we note that the more personal they are, the more deeply they touch us, drawing a vast audience throughout the world and over the centuries. How deeply the *Confessions* of St. Augustine, for example, which trace one man's personal, inward journey to his own depths, have influenced readers up to our own day, throwing light on the great questions of life and faith. The same is true of many other accounts of conversions, such as Newman's, and of the best biographies. From this we can deduce the following principle: the more profound the personal truth expressed in such works, the deeper their resonance and the wider their audience.

It is this basically personal universality that we find in the Decalogue, given to Moses in the solitude of Sinai. The same universality is found in the Sermon on the Mount and in the teachings of St. Paul or St. John, a Word echoing in the intimacy of faith and love and laying the very foundations of ecclesial universality.

Communicating moral knowledge, and thus insuring its universality, is done in a language other than that of science. Concepts, formulas and statistics are not enough. The experience of the reader or the listener and a faithful response to truth's appeal enter into the process as indispensable conditions for understanding and revealing universality.

c. Different Meanings of the Term Object.   From the above it is clear that the term *object* can mean different things when used in the sciences and in moral theory. In the positivist sciences, "object" denotes facts under observation. As such, it is opposed to "subject" and favors the commonly accepted idea of identifying "object" with material reality. We cannot qualify a person as an object in this context without compromising the proper note of personality. In moral theory the case is quite different. It is true that some ethicists have been called "objectivists" because they locate the chief moral criterion in the object of the human act conceived as a physical reality. In this regard they approximate rationalist concepts that oppose object to subject. In moral theory the object stands over against the acting subject (*obiectum,* placed in front of) as a determining element of the subject's knowledge and action. The object, being known, awakens love and desire, elicits respect, wins friendship, and initiates relationships of justice and truth. Thus understood, the object can obviously be a person, recognized as such. I can talk about the object of my love, my hope, or my faith. This is what Christ is for Christians, married spouses for each other. In fact, human persons are the chief object of moral theory, for only in the context of persons can we conceive of morality at all.

It is in this rich sense that St. Thomas uses the term *object* when he makes it the first criterion for the goodness or badness of actions. He sees the object at the level of the interior act (knowing, loving, willing) where action originates, as well as at the level of exterior action. The object possesses the same human quality as the intention and choice it expresses. In this way the object can become the principle determining the quality of moral acts as well as the seat of the faculties and habits that engender them.

5. *Experience in Positivist and Moral Knowledge*

a. Experiments Basic to the Sciences.   Recourse to experiment is basic in the positivist or experimental method, which undergirds modern sciences. It has had such great success that many identify experimentation with the use of this method. We need to study its nature, however, so as to assess the scope of the sciences it has founded. This is all the more necessary since, in common parlance, the real and the experienced are interchangeable. Should reality merge with the findings of scientific experimentation?

The positivist experiment begins with sense perception as applied to the observation of phenomena, the procedure being facilitated by instruments that increase its power. The experiment is external on two counts. The material under observation can be perceived by the senses, and the scientific observer, faithful to the method, considers only the external aspect of what is experienced, so as to guarantee objectivity. This kind of experiment can, in theory, be reproduced by an indefinite number of people. All that is needed is to bring together the same components and supply the identical conditions. In this context we would be talking about scientific experiments, in the plural.

It should be noted that an experiment conducted by the senses is not wholly confined to positivist observation. Reason carries it beyond sense to dimensions of time and space, and these are open to precise measurements formulated mathematically. Now we are dealing with an experiment in the area of quantity and number. The remaining element of the sensible experiment, quality, is ignored since it cannot be assimilated.

To give a simple example, take the contemplation of the moon. This night luminary has aroused many emotions in human beings, many religious, poetic, and philosophical thoughts. They spring from a sensible experience resonating more or less profoundly in mind and heart. Yet none of these things will be of the slightest help in scientific preparations for a trip to the moon or in the creation of computer programs.

Scientific experimentation has its strengths, therefore, and its limitations. Its power lies in its close relation to sensible experience. Because of this it can deduce measurements and laws to be verified later by technical expertise. From this viewpoint its potential knows no bounds. But there are limits, inherent to the method itself, since it is centered on external objectivity. Scientific observation cannot reveal to us the nature of living things. Most especially, it cannot penetrate the moral and spiritual dimensions of the human soul. To plumb the depths of human inwardness, we must seek another kind of experience. This too will be closely linked with sense perception, but in a different modality.

b. Moral or Interior Experience.   Each of us, and this includes the most convinced scientist, will admit to a kind of personal experience totally different from the scientific variety. It is a composite of the numberless trauma that make up human existence: affection, suffering, love, struggle, effort, sin, failure and success, even the passage of time at various stages of life. Experience is the very pith of life at the heart of the human person. It is made up of events lived through, shocks sustained, the impact of emotions, decisions made and carried out. We become most aware of this when, with the perspective of age, we can look back over our life and trace the lines of growth, the ruptures, the healings, and the overall impact of the years upon our inmost being. Here is our true self.

We are speaking about interior experience. It is interior on two counts: first, because it takes place at the core of our personality and second, because we can grasp this kind of experience and understand it only by studying it from within. Self-perception is the one indispensable approach. In the case of others, sympathy, enabling us to share their experiences and feel them as our own, will have the same effect. This is assuming, of course, that our own personal experience is sufficiently mature.

This perception of interiority is so delicate that it can vanish like a mirage if we pause for an instant to look at ourselves from the outside, through the eyes of others—a sociologist, an historian, a psychologist. Yet the interiority perdures within us, no matter what happens; it is the very texture of our being. The work of interior experience is to reveal to us our deepest self, with its genesis, growth, or diminishment in the course of our life. It lets us perceive—like the immediate data of consciousness, as Bergson would say—our spirit, heart, and soul, as well as the inner freedom no science or technique can reach. Now the whole world of personal interiority lies open to us, our actions as solid and undeniable as is any material fact to the clear, unclouded eye. Out of all this a true science can be constructed, but it will not resemble the positivist sciences. Moral theory, for example, will give rise to a wisdom deeper than science.

The obvious objection to this will be that interior experience, being personal, is incommunicable and it therefore cannot enjoy the status of general knowledge required by science. The answer is paradoxical, but it is based on actual experience. The more authentically personal an experience is, the greater its resonance in the human audience. St. Augustine's *Confessions* bears this out; so do the works of Rousseau. By the same token, the more deeply we enter into our own solitude, the more clearly we will be able to perceive what is in the heart of others and the more we will be able to relate to them in depth. Thus solitude opens us to the truest, vastest communication. Upon these experiences, when they are lived, a philosophical or theological science can be constructed. Clearly, though, it will have its own proper methods.

We might compare these two types of experience with our own bodily perception, in health and in sickness, and the knowledge a doctor acquires in examining us. The doctor knows our body from the outside, through the "experiments" he makes with the use of his instruments.

He gathers precise data, partial but objective, and can relate this to the laws he already knows about the human mechanism. If he is keen on objectivity he will instinctively mistrust what we have to say, considering it as merely subjective. In our day, medecine has advanced so rapidly and succeeded so well that we easily believe it to be the only sure, practical knowledge available about the human body.

Yet all of us, including doctors, have an interior awareness of our own bodies, their organs and conditions. It provides us with a knowledge we could perfectly well call objective, since through it we use our bodies, move about, and can even cure ourselves, if need be. Medicine, we need to remember, always presupposes nature's work, which it aids. The effectiveness of our personal experience of our own bodies demonstrates the reality and richness of interior awareness. Without it, we simply could not live. If we depended completely on acquired scientific knowledge in order to move, even if we possessed all the knowledge in existence, we would not be able to take a single step without falling, or raise a finger, for the slightest gesture involves the entire body.

Interior awareness differs vastly from scientific data about the body. It is so natural to us that ordinarily we do not avert to it, and we are hard put to formulate it. It is all-inclusive and synthetic, grasping the body in its organic unity. Consequently, in the analysis of symptoms it may appear confused and imprecise. It rests, however, on a foundation of truth necessary for synthesis. Notably, this kind of experience is profound, because it is not limited to the materiality of phenomena but includes all the dimensions of personal interiority, ranging from sensibility to spirituality.

From this point of view, illness has an essentially psychological dimension; it can also trigger moral and spiritual problems. We pass easily from one plane to another in reaching the heart of the experience. The connections here are perfectly real, even should the imaginary intervene. These relationships are not apparent to one who observes from the outside, but this type of experience is common to all human beings, whether recognized or not.

As to moral experience, it has its own characteristic features. Firstly, it is the most interior and the most personal of all experiences, being formed by our free actions. These are linked as a succession of living deeds and ordered to the fulfillment of some project or vocation, which determines us most intimately. Our moral action gradually forms us in the solitude of our interiority and in the unfolding events of life. At the same time we discover, in a surprising way, that moral experience stems from the most radical exteriority. At the very heart of the "fontal" knowledge we discussed above, we perceive with the utmost clarity, in decisive moments, that we ourselves are neither the measure of truth nor the source of good. We recognize a light beyond, which calls and transforms us, which commands if need be, and which judges us. This was the light St. Augustine addressed when he said, "You were closer to me than my inmost self, higher than my loftiest height." This is the light of which the Gospel speaks when urging us to act so as to be seen not by men but by the Father, who sees in secret. This, the very heart of moral and spiritual experience, can be reached only through inwardness.

At the close of this study, before turning to the chart that sums up my comparison between moral and positivist knowledge, I should like to quote a great historian who knew how to reflect upon the science he had developed throughout his life and the human experience he had acquired. At the close of his famous conferences *What Is Christianity?* Adolph Harnack bequeathes to us his intellectual legacy. What he says about religion can be applied to moral science as the answer to the great questions of life. I have italicized phrases that are most significant in relation to our discussion.

Gentlemen! It is religion, *the love of God and neighbour, which gives life a meaning;* knowledge cannot do it. Let me, if you please, speak of my own experience, as one who for thirty years has taken an earnest interest in these things. Pure knowledge is a glorious thing, and woe to the man who holds it light or blunts his sense of it. But to the question, Whence, whither, and to what purpose? it gives an answer today as little as it did two or three thousand years ago. It does, indeed, instruct us in facts; it detects inconsistencies; it links phenomena; it corrects the deceptions of sense and thought. But where and how the curve of the world and the curve of our own life begin—that curve of which it shows us only a section—and whither this curve leads, knowledge does not tell us. But if *with a steady will we affirm the forces and the standards which on the summits of our inner life shine out as our highest good, nay, as our real self;* if we are earnest and courageous enough *to accept them as the great Reality and direct our lives by them;* and if we then look at the course of mankind's history, follow its upward development, and search, in strenuous and patient services for the communion of minds in it, we shall not faint in weariness and despair, but become certain of God, of the God whom Jesus Christ called his Father and who is also our Father.[3]

---

3. A. von Harnack, *What Is Christianity? Lectures delivered in the University of Berlin during the winter-term 1899–1900,* trans. Thomas Bailey Suanders (New York: Putnam's Sons, 1903), 321–22.

COMPARATIVE TABLE

Moral Knowledge	Positivist Knowledge
1. Grasps the act from the point of view of the subject's dynamic *interiority,* through efficient causality (responsibility) and final causality (intention).	1. Grasps the human act from the point of view of *external observation,* according to relationships of simultaneity and succession of events.
2. *Dynamic:* produces action through practical judgment and by directing effort. This knowledge is committed, directive, normative. It is concerned with the action *to be performed.*	2. *"Neutral," "static,"* to insure pure observation. Knowledge that is "detached," not directive, not normative. Concerned with an action that *has been completed.*
3. *Personal:* There is an essential reference to the person as the freely willing cause and end of the action. It is linked to personal experience.	3. *Apersonal:* brackets the person and subjective factors, to concentrate on completed actions and their interconnection through necessary laws. Depends on the experience of facts. Danger of determinism and mechanicalism.
4. *"Trans-subjective" objectivity:* search for the truth, which concerns, transcends, and unites "subjects" or persons. Committed to truth and goodness. Interpersonal and concrete *universality.* *The object:* reality that confronts the subject, calling forth and qualifying the action. This could be a person as well as some material thing.	4. *Asubjective objectivity:* proper to actions observed apart from the subject. Materialistic, cold. Apersonal and abstract *universality.* *The object:* the material fact as opposed to the subject, the person.
5. *Interior experience,* which is personal, formed by the events of life, grasped by reflection. At once unique, and open to all humanity.	5. *External experiences,* dealing with sensible matter, which can be measured and calculated mathematically. Can be repeated indefinitely.

Conclusion: Toward Collaboration between Science and Moral Theory

The above analysis of the contrast between moral theory and the positivist sciences dealing with the human person can be summed up as follows. Moral theory considers human acts from the viewpoint of the person's dynamic interiority by means of reflection; the point of departure for positivist sciences is external, in keeping with their proper method.

The two stand at opposite poles in their methods of studying human persons and action. Yet they are not contraries. Once we discern the difference in their methods and viewpoints, we can see the relationship between them and the possibility of their collaboration.

The behavioral sciences need moral theory because they deal only with the visible, external aspect of human actions. The richest, most decisive human actions, such as love and hatred, intention and free choice, reactions to suffering and evil, truth and duty, and faith as well—in a word, all the movements of human interiority, which alone can adequately explain what we do, escape them by and large. Nor can they offer practical, satisfactory conclusions in this regard. It is becoming increasingly clear that the positivist sciences cannot treat of the human person comprehensively, cannot solve human problems or answer life's deepest questions. The myth of the science that will explain everything tomorrow has fortunately faded out, though it still lingers in some ideologies.

Moral theory, in turn, needs the positivist sciences. They promote a better understanding of the many social, psychological, historical, and cultural factors involved in any concrete action. These must be taken into consideration as far as possible if an adequate moral judgment is to be formed. Moral values and laws are translated into action in the outer world, but they cannot shape that world to human needs and aspirations without sufficient knowledge. Here science offers the ethicist an indispensable possibility for collaboration, obviously of great value today.

In spite of their differing viewpoints, therefore, moral theory and the positivist sciences can complement each other in fruitful collaboration. The condition for this is that their differences are clearly recognized and sincerely respected—a thing that takes more than mere mutual good will. It is not easy to reconcile two such different mindsets. Where, by its very method, scientific observation excludes the "me," moral reflection views it as central. Great breadth and flexibility is needed and can be acquired only over time, in patient search for a truth too rich to be grasped by any one method or type of science.

One area where the collaboration we are discussing will be particularly important for Christian ethics is the interpretation of Scripture since the development of exegesis. We cannot reaffirm Scripture's role as the main source of Christian ethics without considering its relation to positivist exegesis.

This whole debate seems to turn upon two different kinds of truth, sought principally by positivist science and theology, notably moral theology. The positivist method points exegesis toward the truth of "facts" about historical documents: authorship, authentic text, the writer's intent. The important question is whether the author really thought and wrote in this or that vein. Furthermore, when authors report the words and actions of another person, as the evangelists writing of Jesus for example, the question will be, how much of this is authentically Jesus and how much is simply a reflection of the writer or the primitive community? This is the kind of truth we might call historical, factual, or positivist.

There is another kind of truth, which can be overlooked when the positivist method is used excessively and uncritically. This is the truthfulness of the text itself. Is what the text affirms, what the author teaches, true? To establish the authenticity of the text of the first beatitude and reconstruct the history of its formation is one thing. It is quite another thing to ask whether it is true that the poor are happy, that they possess the Kingdom, and how this can be. The question is, in fact, put to the reader by the very text itself, by the paradox of the happiness of the poor that it affirms. Here we are talking about the "real" or substantial truth of the text.

This is the truth that chiefly interests the theologian and the ethicist. It is the meat of all their reflection. We can least afford to ignore the substantial truth of a scriptural text when it is directly intended by the authors of the New Testament and of Christ himself in his teaching. This is precisely what they want to transmit, the light they desire to communicate to us. The entire exegesis of the Fathers of the Church focused on the discovery and communication of this kind of truth. It is at the very wellspring of theology.

These two kinds of truth, if we know how to distinguish and discern their precise range, are neither contradictory nor mutually exclusive. Actually, they call forth and complement each other, like a sign and the reality it points to, or a container and its contents. It is extremely important that neither one is allowed to absorb or destroy the other.

D. Three Dangers to Be Encountered in the Relation between Moral Theology and the Behavioral Sciences

1. The Abdication of Ethicists

Catholic ethicists have fallen upon hard times in recent years. Formerly their role in the Church was a very formative one in regard to the faithful. They were commissioned to teach moral law, weigh obligations with precision, apply them concretely, and solve difficult cases of conscience. In this way they shared, to a certain extent, the authority of the law and magisterium. As teachers and judges they understandably felt a certain sense of superiority, tinged with authoritarianism, and all of this was reinforced by the prevailing concept of morality. As a result, they were inclined to be suspicious of the behavioral sciences, which impinged upon their territory and introduced innovative ways of dealing with human persons and actions.

Vatican II was the occasion of a real reversal of outlook and a profound crisis among ethicists. Many of them, urged by a sudden desire to be "open to the world," discovered new horizons and methods in psychology, sociology, and even politics. These captivated them and shook their confidence in the moral theory they had previously learned. Their former assurance gave place to an inferiority complex. It was now their duty, they felt, to study the behavioral sciences in order to construct a new theory of morality. They would adopt the new procedures and use the new categories—all this with the intention of building a moral system adapted to our times.

Undertaking such an enterprise, however, requires recognition of the specific, irreducible character of moral knowledge. Otherwise, ethicists will inevitably end up by abdicating. Carried away by the success of the behavioral sciences, they will be limited to a "shifting morality" adapted to the prevailing opinions of a given time or milieu. Yet the principle task of ethics is to affirm profound, unshakable human values that will be the measure of contemporary currents, and to oppose these currents when necessary, heading them off in better directions.

Ethics can certainly profit, for example, from the Freudian theory of psychic evolution: narcissism, maternal fixation, aggressiveness toward the father, finally fraternity. But this analysis does not take into consideration the decisive moral question posed in the conscience of every human being from childhood: what is my personal stand with regard to truth and goodness? This question emerges differently at different stages of life. This is a strictly moral factor, present at all stages of human life, exercising its influence interiorly and going beyond phenomena observable to the psychologist. Our moral life has its own evolution and progress, and these are linked to our psychic life, but they cannot be reduced to the limitations of the latter.

Likewise, sociological research and investigation can shed much light on human behavior in society and on the conditioning produced by various social milieux. The ethicist, like the legislator, needs to take these into account in view of the social dimension of the study of human actions.

Yet the ethicist cannot afford to make indiscriminate use of the contributions of sociologists. Sociological studies are concerned only with external behavior patterns of predetermined social groups. No sociological investigation can access those interior desires and emotions that constitute the chief subject matter of moral theory. Sociology, as its name implies, studies people from the point of view of the society in which they live. It cannot access the individuality of persons, which is at the origin of moral action.

Indeed, if sociology keeps to its own proper methods and avoids philosophical involvement, it has no directly normative function. As for morality, and notably Christian ethics, it operates on a different level. Its function is to throw light on our inner being and dignity as human persons and the claims made on our spiritual nature by God, other people, and the world. It envisages a universality in time and space that transcends the particularity of a social milieu or an era that might be covered by sociological research. This is why moral laws outlive whole civilizations and their histories.

Despite the shocks of recent years and the continuing crisis, ethicists should be aware of the service to the human family and to the Church entrusted to them. They are called to help all who are looking for answers to the great questions of life, in dialogue with the sciences and with Christian revelation.

2. The High-handedness of the Scientist

Would this be an illustration of St. Paul's phrase about knowledge puffing up? Every science carries with it, for its practitioners, the temptation to take over the controls and to explain everything from its own viewpoint, as if it were absolute. This is true of theologians and philosophers as well as scientists, but it has been very noticeable in the case of the latter in recent years, in light of the extraordinary advances science has made. We cannot blame science, but there seems to be a sort of evil genius lurking in the back of the scientist's mind, sowing the illusion that science will one day be able to explain absolutely everything, including the human personality.

The human person will then be for the biologist a complex conglomeration of molecules. The psychologist will be studying a mechanism compounded of compulsions and desires, and the sociologist, a puppet caught in the interplay of social trends. For the historian, the human person will be a bit of straw, bobbing about on the surface of the sea, then disappearing into the vast waves of history.

True scientists, thanks to their human experience and sense of reality, are fully aware of the limitations of their knowledge. In fact, the further they go in their discoveries, the humbler they are apt to become. But the temptation to pride takes on new vigor when it comes to philosophers who reflect upon science. I can say in truth that there are currents of thought in contemporary philosophy that actually lead to the destruction of the human person and the negation of the very qualities that make the person a moral subject. I quote: "The destruction of the subject is not just one theme among others in contemporary philosophy. It is what defines this philosophy; it has become its main task."[4]

This philosophical leap, whether implicit or explicit, cannot be laid at the door of science itself. It emerges from a kind of act of faith in science and in scientific reasoning. Here is what Jung says: "Science is certainly not a perfect instrument, but it is excellent and invaluable. It does no harm unless it makes itself out to be an end in itself. Science is meant to serve; when it lays claim to power it is on the wrong track. It is even meant to serve the other sciences, for each of them, being insufficient in itself, needs all the others. Science . . . contributes to our understanding. It dims our comprehension only when it considers its message to us to be an absolute."[5]

We could well ponder the advice Jung gave to a young colleague. It may sound a bit exaggerated but it demonstrates psychology's crying need for human experience.

The man who wants to understand the human soul will learn practically nothing from experimental psychology. He should put away his textbooks, stop acting like a scholar, get up from his desk and go out into the world with a heart of flesh and blood. Let him feel the terror that stalks the prisons, refugee camps and hospitals, plunge into the squalor of inner cities, houses of prostitution and dives. Let him visit the rich in their mansions and go down to the stock markets. Then let him attend socialist meetings and religious revivals, go into the churches and watch the sects at their orgies. Once he has experienced in his own body love, hatred and every form of passion, he will come home with a richer knowledge than any textbook could give him; for those who are ill he will be a physician, a man who truly understands the human soul.

3. Creating a One-Dimensional World; Interiority

Because their research extends to an entire universe open to the senses, scientists ultimately form a certain image of the world, which is filtered

4. G. Granel, "The Obliteration of the Subject in Contemporary Philosophy."
5. L'âme et la vie, ed. Buchet/Chastel, Paris, 256–257.

from the minds of the learned into the realm of public opinion, heir to their discoveries and inventions. When this image predominates and becomes exclusive, a world-view is born that might be called one dimensional. It concentrates on phenomena, whatever can be perceived by the senses or scientific instruments. Everything else is rejected as unknowable, imaginary, or unreal. We are given a flat picture of the world that lacks depth and interiority. A symbol of this might be the movie or television screen. It reproduces images of life and even simulates depth but is not real. There is nothing behind the screen. The watcher is confused by the phenomena recorded by human ingenuity, confused by all the images formed and received in the course of communication. Life becomes merely the interplay of appearances, reflections, and masks.

In such a world, morality has no role to play. With its rules and requirements it looks like a suspect reality coming from another world, an unmanageable phenomenon, or a vestige of the past. Scientists will attempt to explain it from the point of view of history or social pressure.

Life and Interiority

We would do well to consider briefly the nature of the human person's interiority, which gives life its moral dimension.

a. Moral Interiority.   This is not to be confused with the psychological interiority of persons engrossed in the rise and fall of their own emotions. Nor is it a refuge for the timid who fear the outer world with its struggles and problems.

Interiority can exist on several levels. First, there is spatial interiority, and here we refer to the physical space occupied by the body's internal organs. We can measure the human body like any other object, and we can also open it to examine its contents. True interiority comes only with life. On the biological level the lungs and the stomach, for example, form an active interiority where air and food are received and transformed so as to enter into the body's substance. This is due to a continual exchange between exterior and interior that enables the person to act upon the world.

Sensible interiority is the result of a certain openness to sense impressions from the outer world. It converts them into reactions and movements corresponding to needs and appetites.

Moral interiority goes deepest. It is essentially linked with personhood and gives us the radical ability to receive and experience within ourselves in a vital manner all truth and goodness, which render us fruitful and enable us to bring forth, in all the power of our free will, actions and works capable of transforming both ourselves and the world. Producing a free action is comparable to human generation, but the interiority or matrix where it takes place escapes scientific investigation in the same degree to which it is a free capacity to express our form and existence in action—a capacity which is by nature spiritual.

We can discern a deepening of interiority within our Christian experience. When our inner being is opened to the action of the Holy Spirit through faith and love, we as believers enter into communication with the deeps of God and acquire a new, unfathomable depth. This is the "secret place," which the Father alone sees and to which he calls us, the "inner man" St. Paul speaks of, who is capable of producing works pleasing to God and bringing forth the fruits of the Holy Spirit.

It is important to note that none of these levels of human interiority is normally watertight. On the contrary, the deeper the interiority, the greater will be its power to produce action. We belittle human nature when we oppose the interior and exterior in a superficial way or downgrade the interior life in favor of personal or Christian commitment to the world. Human life implies, rather, the creation of a dynamic interiority capable of transforming the world through ongoing interaction with it. Personal interiority is the matrix where the finest human actions are formed. We know, too, that the greatest masterpieces, whether on the moral, literary, or scientific plane, have generally been the fruit of a period of lengthy gestation, matured in personal solitude and trial.

b. Depth. Interiority includes several dimensions observable in moral action. Depth refers to seeing beneath the surface of impressions, emotions, ideas, and superficial images and penetrating to the heart of human realities and moral questions through reflection and active experience. This brings to mind Origen's symbol for meditation on Scripture: he likens it to Jacob's servants digging wells in the desert to find living water. The deepening of moral consciousness is obviously personal; it is related to the "fontal" knowledge we discussed above and to life in the Spirit. It fosters the formation of a sapiential type of knowledge.

c. Height. Height refers to the long, progressive effort required for attaining moral stature and can be compared with mountain climbing. It implies transcending what is morally base and resisting laziness and apathy. We speak of lofty sentiments and greatness of soul. Symbols of this are Mount Sinai, which Moses climbed to receive the tables of the Law, and the Mount of the Beatitudes, where Jesus proclaimed a justice higher than that of the scribes and Pharisees.

In harmony with Christian experience, this height should always be joined to the depths where humility lays its solid foundations—a humility that encounters reality and the Word of God. This will check the false exaltation of pride.

d. Solidity.   This results from patiently storing up in mind and heart our reflections, experiences, and efforts. All that is acquired from thinking and living, the richness of ideas and actions, is gradually assimilated and brought into focus. Solidity connotes a certain capacity for reverence and calls for ongoing fidelity to moral qualities or virtues.

A book is solid when it lends itself to re-reading, study, and pondering. Such are the biblical texts set before us in the liturgical cycle of the years as an inexhaustible source of nourishment.

e. Breadth.   Advance in depth, height, and solidity contribute to the broadening of mind and heart. Openness to ideas and emotions, and the capacity to understand them and perceive their interrelationships, grows and is strengthened. Interior horizons widen. One of the signs of this breadth of vision is the ability, through reflection, to grasp and harmonize many varying points of view, sometimes even opposing ones, and draw from them complementary truths that result in spiritual progress. There is also a growing ability to see at a glance and understand the thought of other eras in history, so as to trace the living continuity of a spiritual tradition.

A Life of Exteriority

Lack of interiority leads to a view of the world, life, and the human person that could be described by characteristics contrasting with the ones we have just discussed, and could be summed up as one-dimensional.

a. Exteriority.   Life is dominated by external influences—the seen and the felt—and prevalent public opinion. There is a flight from inwardness with its accompaniment of reflection, effort, silence, and solitude. Noise, external contacts, novelty, and access to quick information are sought. Appearance is substituted for reality, the attraction of forms for interest in essentials.

b. Superficiality.   This results from slavish acceptance of popular opinion and shifting surface impressions. Thought becomes like rainwater in the gutters of a thoroughfare, splashed underfoot. Superficiality prefers pictures to the written word and feeds on insatiable curiosity rather than reflection.

c. Triteness.   Mediocrity stamps the inclination to follow the line of least resistance, go with the flow, ape the fashions, or even to look for a cheap originality. It makes for a flat life, banal, boring, "like everyone else."

d. Dissipation.   This is produced by a rapid succession of varying impressions and reactions unrelated to any kind of reflection or deep meaning. Life is at the beck and call of circumstance and whim. Actions are weak, often contradictory, like a stream of idle chatter devoid of relevance, hollow to the ear.

e. Narrowness.   All these deficiencies restrict the mind and heart. They may not altogether prevent insights or sudden bursts of generosity, but these cannot flourish and become a part of human reality so as to transform and expand it. Thought is merely the outcropping of impressions and the prisoner of opinion. It may try to assert itself through the fragmentary truths it has grasped, but tolerance for the general opinion is mistaken for authentic broad-mindedness. The result is a growing indifference to truth with its demands.

Conclusion

Interiority is an essential dimension of morality. This statement is not sheer theory. It is eminently practical in a world like ours, dominated by science and technology. It shows us the indispensable antidote and counterpoise to the positivist view of the world and of life that is increasingly prevalent. The ethicist, like any other Christian, is called to defend the human person and the moral interiority that is an essential human quality, so that we can escape from the one-dimensional image of the world that threatens to rob us of our noblest possessions, our sense of moral values, and our personal dignity. The struggle is with us daily, for the change in the material conditions of life effected by technology constitutes a constant temptation to opt for convenience and superficiality.

Science, with its discoveries and inventions, is certainly good in itself; it discovers truths and values we should openly welcome. Unfortunately, it seems impossible to pursue science with complete, serene objectivity. It is difficult not to turn to it for answers to our innate questionings; in the end, we tend to see it as the means for achieving our own salvation. When this happens, science becomes in reality an object of faith; inevitably it goes counter to our Christian faith and concept of morality. Science is thus caught up in a huge debate beyond its powers, for it can never comprehend the whole person, nor does it touch on the noblest qualities of human nature. We might even conjecture that, were the human person to be totally subjected to the power of science, inevitable destruction would soon follow. Only by recognizing our moral dimension and by honoring our rightful claim to interiority will this danger be averted.

In completing this study of the differences and relations between moral theory and the sciences, it is appropriate to recall a notable debate that has been carried on for three centuries as part of modernity's fascination with scientific inquiry. But I shall conclude this chapter with a quotation from St. Paul; my discussion of interiority has simply been a commentary on it. St. Paul expresses far better the richness of the interiority proposed for the study of moral theologians: "Out of his infinite glory may [the Father] give you the power through his Spirit for your hidden self to grow strong, so that Christ may live in your hearts through faith, and then, planted in love and built on love, you will with all the saints have strength to grasp the breadth and the length, the height and the depth; until, knowing the love of Christ, which is beyond all knowledge, you are filled with the utter fullness of God" (Eph 3:16–19). Chapters 4 and 5 of Ephesians describe moral Christianity as St. Paul conceived it, including the spiritual combat with the powers of this world, who use science to establish their kingdom.

III. THE DISTINCTION BETWEEN MORALITY, ART, AND TECHNIQUE

A. The Problem: Vocabulary

Morality differs from science in that it is practical and ordered to the production of human acts, while science is theoretical, having for its direct object knowledge of the truth. It is important at this point to distinguish morality from art and technique, both of which have practical ends: the production of certain works and the transforming of various materials through human activity.

First, a clarification of terms is called for. I use the word *art* in its oldest and broadest sense, to designate any production requiring special knowledge and aptitude. In this sense we may speak of the military, veterinary, or culinary arts. Again, there are the fine arts, and we often reserve the terms *art* and *artist* for them. *Artisan* is a throwback to former times, but it currently refers to manual labor.

A frequent modern substitute for the term *art* is *technique*, deriving from the Greek *techne*, translated into the Latin *ars* and appearing in the mid-eighteenth century. Technique has become closely associated with modern sciences and designates the entire field of practical applications based on scientific discoveries, notably instruments and machines. Thus science has given rise to the technical, and our era has been called the scientific or technological age.

There is a further distinction. Technique traditionally meant a number of procedures combined to produce a determined result. Thus there was the technique of the dance or the theater. In our day *technical* has taken on the character of a number of methodical procedures performed with machines and perfected mechanisms, based on knowledge that is scientific and no longer empirical. So techniques are scientific applications, but their object is production. The term *technique* has generated several others such as *technician* and *technocrat*. The idea of art is more directly connected with human qualities than is that of technique.

Whatever may be their differences, we can associate art and technique in comparing them with morality.

The problem is not purely theoretical. It is not simply a matter of definition or of formal object, as the scholastics say. The extraordinary development of science and technology in this century has raised a question. In the scientific era to which we have advanced, might it not be appropriate to envisage a progressive transformation of morality into a human technique, worked out from our knowledge of the individual and society? This is the concept of morality as a science of customs developing into a relevant technique, such as was put forward by L. Levy-Bruhl at the turn of the century.

B. Differences between Ethics and Art or Technique

Here we would do well to look at some fine, penetrating distinctions made by Aristotle and St. Thomas.

1. Art and technique are independent of personal dispositions and the intentions of the agent, while these latter are the direct object of mo-

rality. A person can be an excellent technician, a famous engineer, or a great writer and still be thoroughly dishonest. By the same token, a very upright, even holy person could be totally lacking in technical or artistic talent. Morality qualifies a person comprehensively: this individual is a just, courageous person. Art and technique qualify a person only partially, in the context of external activity: this individual is a good surgeon, a clever worker, a great musician.

2. In the order of art and technique, it is preferable to make mistakes knowingly, while in the moral order errors of ignorance are better. We have no problem with the English teacher who deliberately uses an ungrammatical construction to attract the students' attention. The students realize the mistake is intentional; the teacher's knowledge is not depreciated. But in *moral* matters it is better to err through ignorance—for example, to take someone else's book or pencil thinking it is one's own rather than to take it in full awareness that it belongs to another. The reason for this is that the direct object of art is knowledge, rather than the use made of it, while morality is concerned with our use of knowledge, with voluntary acts which can be excused by ignorance.

3. Morality determines not only the right way of acting but also the right thing to do. St. Thomas does not limit the crowning virtue of prudence to deliberation and counsel. Its principle function is "command": it makes decisions and orders action. The prudent person is not the one who merely gives good advice but the one who knows when and how to act rightly. The courage to take action is a necessary part of true prudence. Art and technique, on the other hand, prepare the way for action but do not necessarily implement it. An architect can draw up fine plans for a building but need not execute them. He is nonetheless an artist. We should note, however, that an art cannot be acquired without practice. Still, the connection between prudence and action is more direct and compelling.

4. Further, arts and techniques, even though they may be our main occupation, are practiced only by a segment of society, for a limited time, and are channeled into many specialized fields. Morality is the concern of every person and extends to all actions. Regardless of the multiplicity of actions engaged in, morality remains one.

5. We may also say that technique transforms the material conditions of human action but remains detached from the moral, spiritual, or cultural content (which attracts the attention of art to a greater degree). Communications techniques have developed incredibly in little less than a century. Yet we have to admit that what is being communicated does not always reach a particularly high intellectual level. Technology can

transmit the best and the worst indifferently. Actually many of the most beautiful things it manages to portray for us had already been produced before the technical era came into being, and through extremely simple methods.

Definitions of Art and Ethics

In view of the contrasts enumerated above, we can formulate a distinction between ethics and art or technique. For the sake of clarity I will use a classical distinction as a foundation and will retain the Latin formula.

Ethics is defined as *recta ratio agibilium*, right reason or the science of human action. Art or technique is *recta ratio factibilium*. The word *factibilia* is difficult to translate. We could render the definition as "right reason or the science of work," or "the products of human work," or again, "the science of making." The definition of work as the coordination of human activities for the sake of production or a contribution to production throws interesting light on the Latin definitions above.

These definitions can be further refined by a distinction between two levels or components of human action: immanent and transitive action. Immanent action takes place within the agent. Examples are knowledge, love, willing, intention. Its effect is to transform or qualify the person who acts. Transitive action transforms material outside of the agent and could be called production or fabrication.[6]

Morality does not affect human action in the same way as do art and technique. Morality begins with the active willing that is the principle source of the action and that, being immanent, develops within the person. Art and technique deal directly with the external work produced by human action.

This distinction corresponds well to something John Paul II proposed in his encyclical *Laborem exercens* about the difference between objective and subjective work. The encyclical is the basis for his analysis of modern society from the moral viewpoint. "Objective" work refers to the activity of dominating and transforming the earth through technology and other methods of production. "Subjective" designates this same activity insofar as it proceeds from a human subject or person for whom

---

6. According to St. Thomas, "Ars est recta ratio factibilium; prudentia vero est recta ratio agibilium. Dicitur autem agere et facere quia, ut dicitur in IX Metaph., factio est actio transiens in exteriorem materiam, sicut aedificare, secare et huiusmodi; agere autem est actio permanens in ipso agente, sicut videre, velle et huiusmodi" (IaIIae q 17, a 4). See also *De veritate*, q 8 a 6.

it is intended. "Objective" work is distanced from the moral dimension and is governed by various technical and economic laws. "Subjective" work introduces the moral dimension into the work world and postulates the primacy of the person over technology, because the person is both origin and end of the work. The main criterion of judgment about work, therefore, becomes respect for and the promotion of human dignity.

Note. The distinction we have described is analytic and theoretical. In the concrete, morality, arts, and techniques mesh. There is no human, technological work that excludes the moral dimension. The engineer, no matter how specialized his work, is necessarily involved with an employer and other workers. By this very fact, he or she enters into relationships of justice, thus introducing the moral dimension. Even in the case of a solitary worker, the need for a purpose to inspire the activity confers a moral quality upon it, which will affect the worker personally. On the human level, work may done out of sheer interest, constraint, pleasure, devotion, or for the glory of God.

On the other hand, once the work is done, once it becomes a part of the external world, the moral action inevitably leads to procedures related to art and technique.

Moral actions and the activity of arts and techniques cannot therefore be entirely separated. Yet we need to make a careful distinction between them if we want to avoid misleading confusion and to understand clearly the differences between the contributions they make to human action.

C. High-handedness among Technicians

Like science, technical skill tempts its adepts to be cavalier, because of the control it gives them over the world. The technical mentality tends to analyze and solve all problems technically, according to its own method. People speak of a technique for a perfect marriage, techniques for relaxation, meditation, even contemplation. They would like to treat moral problems in the same way, applying tried and true methods, as they say, without realizing that the most specifically human element has escaped them.

The difficulty becomes very apparent in the case of the engineer who would like to consign the problems of his children's education or of his marriage to technical data, similar to that used in the factory. He will soon run into trouble and, feeling frustrated, will back off, terming such matters emotional and irrational. And yet the highest human values are at stake here. The same is true for religious questions.

The technical problem is not limited to individuals. It is as broad as modern civilization itself, as John Paul II has noted several times. From his first encyclical, the pope has questioned and expressed uneasiness about the technical progress that has become prevalent. "The development of technology and the development of contemporary civilization, marked by the ascendancy of technology, demand a proportionate development of morals and ethics. Unfortunately this latter always seems to lag behind. The first reason for disquiet concerns the essential and fundamental question: Does this progress which has man for its author and promoter, make human life on earth 'more human' in every aspect of that life? Does it make it 'more worthy of man'?" (*Redemptor hominis,* n. 15).

He returns to the subject in *Laborem exercens* and shows the danger when priority is given to "objective" rather than "subjective" work, that is, when economic and technical laws prevail over the human person. The latter is then seen to be expendable, an anonymous cog in production, a mere tool. Thus technology, when it takes over the controls, enslaves the human person through a lack of understanding of his moral dimension, to the detriment of human dignity. The key question is how to reaffirm the primacy of the person over work, of morality over technique. Is the person made for work or is work, including technology, meant to serve the person?

For ethicists, technical conquests give rise to the same temptation we saw earlier in regard to science: infatuation and then abdication at the very moment when researchers are in the greatest need of the kind of moral reflection science cannot give them. Some ethicists have even spoken of a future shaped by a symbiotic union between the human person and the machine.[7]

The answer to the problem of the relation between morality and technical science certainly does not lie in a romantic or fearful rejection of technology, which could not in any case be sustained, nor in unrestrained enthusiasm or resigned abandonment to technical progress. It takes constant effort and struggle, first of all in our own lives, to guarantee the primacy of the human person and the supremacy and permanence of moral values, faced as we are with technology's invasion of our world. Technology left to itself will turn on us to enslave us and destroy our best qualities. We have to fight to maintain it as a perfected instrument in our service. In this confrontation ethicists are called to play a decisive role; they need clear vision, courage, and audacity.

7. A. Gibson, "Visions of the Future," in *Concilium,* no. 86 (June 1973): 118–26.

Bergson, reflecting on the relation between the mechanical and the mystical, spoke of infusing into the world "a bit more soul." This would hardly be enough if the "bit more" were added only after the damage was done. What is at stake is the soul itself, the very essence of the human reality, together with those personal qualities which must be safeguarded and fostered as priorities. Technical resources should be used only where appropriate. The soul is both the inspiration and the goal determining the order of means to be used. Technology and its use are among the means.

IV. IN SEARCH OF THE HUMAN DIMENSION

The human element of moral theory is brought out in bold relief by comparing it with the sciences and arts. We might say that ethics is the most human of all sciences because its concern is with the human person as a free, competent, and responsible agent. It deals directly with the most human of actions: willing, loving, intending, choosing.

This characteristic of ethics goes beyond mere theory. The ethicist must defend the human person against dangers that threaten the very essence of humanity, must ward off the invasion of certain scientific and technical procedures. These are indeed human, both in origin and in the knowledge they provide about humanity, but they do not approach the inmost center of the individual nor affirm the human personality.

A. The Human Is More Than Human

It should be added, however, that moral theory can never truly grasp the full meaning of the human itself, unless it realizes, at the very instant of perceiving it, that the human is always greater than our idea of it. In rational research, above all, we need to mistrust our propensity for thinking that we can confine reality within the limits of concepts and theories. This is particularly true of the human person: whatever is human always exceeds our ideas about it. Moral science can never form itself into a closed, definitive system, for this would be to betray its true end. No concept of humanity, no anthropology can adequately grasp the best and noblest qualities of the human person. The source lies in actions and thoughts; it is these that make the person. The individual escapes the limitations of our moral systems as a horizon extends beyond the roads, villages, fields, and forests that make up the countryside. We need, therefore, to keep our minds open to growth and expansion if we would be faithful to the human in ethics.

This is not to say that moral teaching, with its precepts and judgments, is provisory and shifting, but this view of person helps us to see these things as pathways. With the help of determining limitations, moral precepts give us direction and solid, even hard, ground at times to walk on, precisely so as to lead us to what is beyond. We cannot attain to the human without the help of clear ideas and attitudes and without conforming to precepts. Yet we should not confuse these ways with the end to which they lead.

Clearly it takes experience to understand this. The human dimension is revealed particularly in times of trial and suffering, which touch us intimately and show us true reality. It also makes us sensitive to the suffering of others and teaches us that goodness of heart that we describe as "humane." The human is also revealed in love and hatred, hope and discouragement, sadness, fear, and joy, in all the stirrings of the human heart, which open to us life's secrets. Again, there is the experience of interior conflict, when a person becomes confused in the face of good and evil. We experience weakness and fear, out of which that most human of virtues, courage, is forged. These are the experiences that, far better than any book, teach us what is truly human.

The humanity of Jesus in the Gospels is an enlightening example. Jesus had a far keener understanding of human nature than did the legalistic Pharisees. This is revealed in his way of treating the sick, whom he cured even on the Sabbath, in his attitude toward sinners (for whose sake he risked his reputation) and toward the children who were being brushed aside by his disciples. He went so far as to identify himself with the little people. In each one—in the rich Zacchaeus as in the thief on the cross— Jesus sought what we might call the primordial human being, even as he had come forth from the hands of the Creator, an image to be restored. Surely it was this pristine humanity that Jesus compared to the stray sheep, the lost drachma. He would have us understand what we too easily forget—the innate nobility of ourselves and of others.

Ethicists, in order to be faithful to this Gospel view of humanity, should beware of treating people simply as the subject matter of the rational application of abstract principles, general laws, or theoretical ideas. The adjustment of moral laws to individual actions calls for tact and discernment in order to regain the individual, to whom the Gospels are addressed, with kindness and clear-sightedness, the person in whom weaknesses and sin are countered by divine potentialities. This is precisely the work of prudence.

B. The Human as It Opens onto the Divine

The foregoing belies the common opinion that the human is opposed to the divine as to a contrary. Since the Renaissance we have been victimized by a supposed dichotomy, a conflict between man and God, freedom and grace, the natural and the supernatural. It is as if giving to one required taking from the other. This has created a practical opposition between the human and the divine. In the ensuing confrontation, theologians, eager to defend revelation, have often shown a preference for the supernatural, to the occasional neglect of the human. Today, in reaction to this "supernaturalism," attention centers on the human person and human values. The basis for everything, even in religion, is now purely human experience, and all forms of the supernatural are rejected as if they had suddenly become a scandal, a sin against the person and the world.

This opposition set up between the human and divine cannot be resolved on a rational, abstract plane. We need to look to Christian experience. This would not be the first time that the human experience of trial has opened people to something beyond the human. In time of trial we look for something nobler than ourselves; we are ready to be docile.

But most importantly, the experience of the life of faith teaches us that the more we hand ourselves over to God, yielding to his grace and the workings of his Spirit, the more fully human we become and the more sensitive to others and to the whole of created reality. It is in this sense that the Greek Fathers spoke of God's "philanthropy." Enlightened by God through faith, we learn true love for others.

Above and beyond the corruption caused by sin, there is a certain harmony between the human and divine, which is the very work of God: the image of God in us, restored by grace. This is the reason for St. Thomas's principle that grace does not destroy nature, but perfects it (Ia, q 62 a 5). This means that the human being cannot be fully a person without the grace of God; it also means that this grace leads us toward what is most concretely and truly human, to be discovered and lived out in charity.

C. A Note on the Role of Experience in Moral Theory

Experience has a very important function in moral theory. Human action is always linked to a concrete experience within the life that produces it. Aristotle affirmed that lack of experience makes a person unsuited for the science of ethics, since it is an obstacle to the understanding of moral realities. This experience is not limited to the affective order: impressions, emotions, accumulated memories. It also throws light on the intelligence and reaches the level of theory. In moral science, our thought corresponds to our conduct. Moral knowledge comes to birth in the heart of an experience, which is its deepest source, and tends to reflect back on the experience as a guide for action.

Influenced by the rationalistic ambience separating reason from affectivity, ethicists in recent centuries have neglected experience in favor of a rational study of moral laws. In keeping with the general, abstract formation they received in Scholastic theology, they saw moral laws as a priori principles. Today, in contrast, they are beginning to question moral laws and their application in the name of concrete experience. They prefer to propose nothing in the moral domain that does not proceed from lived experience; the discernment of various experiences is not considered important. Formerly, moral theory was based on ideas; now it is experience that matters. The rationalistic dichotomy continues, but in the opposite direction.

It is important, therefore, to clarify what kind of human experience will foster moral knowledge, or at least to point out its essential traits. The subject is too complex to be handled in depth here.

1. Experience Gained from the Practice of Virtue

Not every experience is enlightening and fruitful. Some experiences can blind us to moral values and render our actions sterile. Experience should first of all penetrate to a moral and personal level. Superficial experiences, no matter how many and varied, result only in dissipation. They prevent us from being ourselves and acting responsibly, and they hinder the formation of an authentically moral experience.

In light of moral theory, the most fruitful experience is that of a morally virtuous act springing from the choice of truth and goodness. Admittedly, such a statement is sure to meet with ridicule today. The idea of virtue has been so downgraded that it seems sheer paradox to say that the experience of it is more interesting and enlightening than the experience of sin or any other activity we might engage in. Most of the literature of recent centuries portrays virtue as a bore. The phenomenon is startling: our cultural milieu has created a huge gap between literature, which sparks imagination, emotions, and ideas, and the reality of a moral experience that can continue to hold its own notwithstanding. And this moral experience, when it is lived courageously, can come across as something very different from its usual caricature. This fact underscores the need of lived experience if we are to understand the quality of virtuous action and explore the moral universe to which it leads.

A simple study of the ancient moralists, pagan as well as Christian, will convince us that virtue can be more interesting than we might suppose. Some of their most beautiful works were written on the subject of virtue and under its inspiration.[8] We can discard the image of the virtuous person as prim, submissive and restrained, a slave to law, without animation or human appeal. Once experienced, virtue breaks through this stereotype and, for those who dare to believe in it, is revealed as brimming over with life and light and an amazing abundance of gifts.

Let us look at some specific virtues. Who knows more about life, the courageous person or the coward? The one who accepts the monotony of the daily round in loyalty to a generous, often hidden, commitment or the one whose clever boasting camouflages total abandon to whim and self-interest? There is a hidden strength in courage, a keen insight, which words cannot convey. These radiate on encounter. People with courage inspire confidence.

St. Paul often speaks of meekness. This virtue has nothing to do with weakness, as many suppose. It is the fruit of a rare, little-known victory over the fear and aggressiveness that rise from the depths of the soul. True meekness presupposes tremendous inner strength and perfect mastery over the emotions. According to Scripture the meek man is stronger than the one who captures cities. Meekness goes hand in hand with a penetrating self-knowledge and awareness of the unruly passions that can toss us about like boats in a storm.

---

8. A passage from Cicero's *Disputationes Tusculanes* illustrates this: "What is nobler in man than a penetrating, virtuous spirit? We should use this gift if we wish to be happy. Now since the mind's highest good is virtue, this is where happiness is to be found. All that is beautiful, lofty, striking—I have already spoken about this, but I think it needs more emphasis—provides us with abundant cause for joy. Since joy, plenteous and continuing, is what makes for a happy life, it follows that a happy life is the result of virtue [precisely the 'honestas' which for Cicero describes the moral quality resulting from all the virtues together]" (5.23.67).

Chastity is not the virtue of the childish and timid, who fear to look things and people in the face, a weak virtue compounded of deprivation and frustration. If it is true that we can take the measure of an adversary best after having fought him and laid bare his ruses, it is also true that chastity is not as ignorant as we might think. Because its glance is pure, chastity can explore the hidden recesses of the human heart and penetrate its passions far more easily than the unchaste glance, which is caught in their toils.

Similarly, for a true understanding of the faith, a Christian needs the experience of being committed to it. Commitment enables a person to see by the unique light of faith and to discern new horizons opening out upon God and humanity, to perceive the world of sin and even of unbelief. We cannot grow in faith without combatting in our own heart and mind all that would hold us back from the leap of faith and the detachment demanded by love.

To sum it all up in a single question: Who knows whether the saint, practiced in the exercise of many virtues stemming from faith and charity, does not understand sin and unbelief far better than the sinner? This kind of experience is not as simple as it seems; it includes knowledge of all the vices that have had to be overcome and all the roots of sin that grace has had to tear out to make way for God's light. As St. Paul says, "The night is almost over, it will be daylight soon—let us give up all the things we prefer to do under cover of the dark; let us arm ourselves and appear in the light" (Rom 13:12). Could the experience of light reveal less than darkness does?

The experience we need, therefore, in order to develop moral knowledge is that of virtue, because of the special light it throws on the subject matter of morality. We include here the sins and vices along the way, which clamor for our attention. Virtue engenders this knowledge by a connaturality that St. Thomas attributes to the virtuous person. This person is the best connoisseur and the best judge of concrete actions.

2. The Use of Experience

There is no great gain from experience as such. Experience is the raw material; we need to study it and learn how to handle it for our greater knowledge. A person can have many experiences with little profit. On the other hand, there are those who can gain wide, rich knowledge from a single experience. For this, keenness of mind is needed.

Experience cannot produce its fruits without our reflection. This incites reciprocal currents of life and thought, ideas and action. We are then able to profit from works in which others have expressed their own experiences. The Wisdom literature offers condensed experiences for our meditation that relate to our lives. This wisdom is like the womb in which moral science is formed and to which it should continually return.

Material for experience is lacking to no one. It includes the basic human responses: love, suffering, effort, weakness, the struggle with evil, confrontation with others, the question of God, openness to his Word; the experience of time, too, and the patience and perseverance needed for all growth. We could explore the entire scope of the moral universe, the world of humanity and spiritual values, and gain the kindly understanding of others which leads to a very precious communication with them. No one experiences everything, but whatever our differences we can reach what might be called the human core of another's experience through sympathy of soul, which is the fruit of our own personal experience.

To know the human, it is not necessary to indulge in an unlimited number of experiences. In fact, too many would scatter our attention, exhaust our capacities, and risk confusing us. It is enough to sound the depths of the human experiences that come our way, particularly the most common ones, with an attentive mind and open heart. In this way we will discover beneath outward actions the essence of the human person and the hidden source of actions and behavior. We will reach the very origin of good and evil, out of which the entire moral life flows.

We are not, therefore, locked up within our own individual experience. A certain communication of experiences is possible on the moral plane. Each person can form, within, "the human sap" to be transmitted to others. This is wisdom. Here again we discover the need for virtue. Without it, the "sap" may soon be corrupted and become poison rather than delightful nourishment.

4

Christian Ethics: Its Distinctive Character

The Problem, and a Contemporary Solution

We come now to the question of Christian ethics: that it is, and what it is. In this chapter we shall discuss the problem and examine one response characteristic of our times.

We shall put the question about Christian ethics to some of the great theologians who have born witness to it from the beginning. From the New Testament I have chosen St. Paul; we will trace in his letters the main lines of Christian ethics. Next we will explore the Sermon on the Mount with St. Augustine, who considered it the epitome of Christian moral teaching. Doing this will initiate our rediscovery of one of the key texts on Christian ethics. Finally, we will put our question to St. Thomas, one of the great architects of Western theology, focusing on his treatise on the New Law.[1] Thus conceived, our research may have its limitations, but it will put us in touch with a great, rich tradition in full harmony with the teaching of the Greek Fathers. We will thus prepare the way for our answer to the question about Christian ethics, and this will serve us well in subsequent reflections.

---

1. Translator's note: Following standard practice among the Thomist commentators, Father Pinckaers uses the term *treatise* to refer to sections of the *Summa theologiae* where Aquinas treats specific topics, such as *habitus* (IaIIae qq 49–54), the notion of virtue (IaIIae qq 55–67), the New Law of grace (IaIIae qq 106–14), the virtue of charity (IIaIIae qq 23–46).

I. THE PROBLEM: WHETHER THERE IS A SPECIFICALLY CHRISTIAN ETHICS, AND, IF SO, WHAT ARE ITS CHARACTERISTIC FEATURES

To question the existence of a Christian ethical system would have been, thirty years ago, unimaginable to many—scandalous even. Today the question underlies all the debates that have arisen among Christian ethicists.

Formerly it was taken for granted within the Church that Christianity had its own moral system, more firmly established and far more precise in its regulations than philosophical or lay moral systems, and nobler than other systems of religious inspiration. The bond between Christian religion and morality was so strong that historians, who were known to take liberties with dogmas, thought Christianity could be reduced to the teaching of morality, which they considered to be its true essence. Even to nonbelievers, morality seemed the most characteristic feature of Catholicism, and they were eager to profit by it, especially in the education of their children. Since this was the case, to touch Christian ethics would have been to threaten the very foundations, in fact the essence, of Christianity.

For Christians, morality was obviously an essential part of religion. It was the principal subject matter of their teaching. In the old days the complaint was frequently made that, in preaching, dogma was neglected in favor of morality. For the faithful Christian, morality was not something speculative, a body of ideas that might change with changing eras, localities, or theological schools. It was the mainstay of life, a firm doctrine based on revelation, which guided one's conduct, attitudes, and personal choices.

The questioning of moral teaching therefore touched the Christian people profoundly. By and large they felt that to challenge the existence of a Christian moral system was to threaten Christianity itself. What would be the use of a religion that did not give true answers to the great questions in life and its practical problems? Theologians would do well to reflect on these spontaneous reactions of the Christian faithful. They should be alerted to the fact that moral problems cannot be treated in the same way in which ideas are manipulated or hypotheses worked out in books. They should become increasingly aware of the richly human and Christian dimension of moral questions.

It must be added, however, that the questioning of Christian ethics is not necessarily subversive. It can be done in a positive way. The great scholastic theologians did not hesitate to draw out points of Christian doctrine by way of questioning. St. Thomas, asking whether God existed, began by offering the strongest possible objections, such as the existence of evil in the world. Yet these theologians approached such problems in a wholly constructive spirit. They wanted, in all lucidity and clarity, to foster the growth of the Christian mind in the knowledge of the truths presented by faith. Also, they sought to defend Christian thinking against the attacks and errors that would inevitably arise.

Questioning Christian moral theory can therefore be positive and fruitful—necessary, actually, if we would discern its characteristic features and its relation to other systems. This type of research is particularly useful today, when philosophical and religious teachings the world over are seen to be in conflict with one another. Confronted by vast ideological confusion, we need to learn how to grasp the distinguishing notes of Christian ethics as well as those elements that will make for its bonding and eventual collaboration with other systems without yielding to dangerous compromise.

The question of the Christian character of morality is basic for theology. If Christian ethics is confused with purely human ethics, the theologian will have no reason to function in this field and will simply become a philosopher. It is necessary, therefore, that the theologian demonstrate how the sources, foundations, and principal expressions of the moral theory he teaches are specifically Christian and possess an authentically theological character.

How the Question of the Existence of Christian Morality Is Framed

This question has been raised among theologians since the Second Vatican Council. It is one of the results of the attitude of openness to the world and to other religions that was inaugurated at that time. Rather than work along traditional lines and maintain as a starting principle the superiority of Christian morality, theologians have begun to compare it with other moral systems and to search for its unique characteristics, not found elsewhere. To put it more succinctly, the direct cause of the problem has been the emergence of the phenomenon of secularization in the modern world together with a current of thought in the Church that might be called secular Christianity. No one has wished to deny that Christianity includes moral teaching. The question is, rather, whether this teaching is not the equivalent to natural morality and the dictates of reason, which rest on human values accessible to everyone of good will.

The question has become particularly acute in the discussion of concrete moral problems presented to public opinion in a pluralistic society. Christians have been struggling to establish renewed bases for friendly collaboration with those who do not share their faith. Faced with the difficult problems of contraception, abortion, euthanasia, homosexuality, violence, etc., which call for legislation that applies to everyone, may Christians follow their own lights, norms, and criteria implying special stands, or should they remain on the same level with others and form their judgments according to merely rational criteria, with the help of philosophy and the behavioral sciences? If the second alternative were preferable, could they go still further and reinterpret Christian morality in its entirety according to purely human values?

In a more theoretical context, other ethicists, particularly in Germanic countries, have wished to promote the autonomy of morality in relation to revelation, basing their position on the originally Kantian opposition between autonomy and the divine rule. Do moral norms originate outside of the human person, namely in the will of God—which subjects morality to the divine rule, as in classic theology—or do they arise within the human person, where reason and conscience determine obligations? The latter case would insure the autonomy of ethics. It seems the time has come, since the Council, to promote the autonomy of rational morality in judging concrete problems. This will free it from theological and ecclesiastical tutelage so as to assure its better collaboration with other sciences. This claim for an autonomous morality occasions criticism of any hierarchical intervention in moral questions, even when made in the name of natural law and reason.

Clearly the question of Christian ethics is at the center of a huge debate involving all moral thought at the level of principles and as well as practice. We should add that ethicists who reduce Christian morality to something merely human and rational do not deny the special inspiration contributed by revelation, faith in Christ, and charity. But in their opinion this changes nothing as far as norms for action are concerned; the inspiration has no direct bearing, and cannot intervene, at the moral level.

Behind the Scenes

If it is true that the change of viewpoint inaugurated by the Council triggered the crisis concerning Christian ethics, we have to admit that the stage had long been set. As far back as the end of the sixteenth century, Suarez (a fair representative of "moderns," according to Bossuet), using his own interpretation of a certain text of St. Thomas, taught that Christ in the New Law added no positive moral precept to what was already contained in the Old Law—that is, in the Decalogue or in natural law—and that precepts concerning faith in Christ, the Eucharist, etc., could be reduced to natural obligations.[2]

Since moral theory was understood, at the time of Suarez, to be a compendium of obligatory precepts, it followed that Christian ethics was equivalent to natural ethics and had no distinguishing characteristics of its own. The thought of Suarez tended entirely toward natural ethics in a treatise where St. Thomas's thought was used in the opposite sense to show the differences and point out the specific notes of the New Law, but on the level of virtues and interior acts rather than precepts.[3] Suarez even succeeded in finding an expedient for reducing to the natural plane the precept of confession of the faith, cited by St. Thomas as specifically Christian. Suarez's position can be found in the manuals even in our own day.[4]

This viewpoint harmonizes with the humanistic trend predominating in post-Tridentine Catholic moral theory, where the insistence upon natural law has had the advantage, admittedly, of demonstrating the rational character and universal thrust of Catholic moral teaching. However, the neglect of Christian sources and foundations paved the way for the present conflict and the reduction of Christian ethics to merely rational moral theory.

There is a difference that intensifies the problem today. Classical ethicists could tolerate considerable diversity among ethical opinions, as we can see from the lengthy quarrel over probabilism. Yet they accepted the existence of natural law as a firm basis for moral theory and respected the decisive authority of the Church. The present trend carries the point further. In its defense of moral autonomy, it contests the legitimacy of the Church's interventions at the level of natural ethics. Furthermore,

---

2. Suarez, *Opera*, 6.10.2 (ed. Vivès; Paris, 1856).

3. IIaIIae q 108 a 1 and 2.

4. For example in the manual of Genicot (Salsmans [Louvain, 1931], vol. 1, n. 90, p. 74), we find: "Praecepta moralia nulla Christus addidit eis quae iure naturali omnes astringebant. Verum quidem est praecepta virtutum theologalium se extendere ad quaedam obiecta nova ex. gr. ad credendum explicite Incarnationis mysterium, ad sperandam remissionem peccatorum explicite per Christum. Sed ista extensio, supposita horum obiectorum propositione a Christo facta, ex ipsa lege naturali sequitur. Proposuit insuper divinus Legislator altiorem prorsus perfectionem, sed per modum consilii, non praecepti." See also Ph. Delhaye, "La mise en cause de la spécificité de la morale chrétienne," in *Revue Th. Louv.* 4 (1973): 308–39.

the motive at work in this tendency is that of modern philosophies and behavioral sciences, which, for the most part, are ignorant of the existence of natural law in the human person and favor relativism and a constant shift in ideas and theories. When Church authority and natural law are jettisoned, there is a risk that incertitude and relativity will prevail throughout the entire field of moral thought, from concrete cases to principles. It would then be quite useless to appeal to any Christian inspiration whatsoever for support.

II. A CONTEMPORARY RESPONSE TO THE QUESTION OF CHRISTIAN ETHICS

We begin our research on Christian ethics with an examination of one response to this question. Most significant in my opinion is the theory of Father J. Fuchs, put forward in his book *Is There a Christian Ethics?*[5] I shall not give a detailed description of the author's position here, with his many nuanced theories. I only wish to draw out the main lines of his response, which have found a sympathetic hearing among modern ethicists.

Father Fuchs distinguishes two areas or levels of Christian ethics, clearly differentiated but lending themselves to interaction.

1. The *categorical* level comprises behavior, norms, and various categories of virtues and values such as justice, chastity, fidelity, etc.

2. The *transcendent* level comprises attitudes and norms that transcend yet penetrate the various moral categories. These take a general view of human beings as persons. They are virtuous attitudes such as faith, love, acceptance of redemption, life seen as sacramental, the imitation of Christ, etc.

If we consider Christian ethics at the transcendent level, we see that Scripture expresses itself fully and without ambiguity on such matters as faith, charity, etc., and that they appear as specifically Christian.

On the other hand, the indications of Scripture on behavior of the categorical order, such as social problems regarding marriage, etc., are less frequent and less clear in their significance and relevance to varying periods of human history.

5. In *The Distinctiveness of Christian Ethics,* ed. Curran and McCormick (New York: Paulist Press, 1980), 3–19.

The question of Christian ethics is most pressing on the categorical level. Does it differ from simple human moral teaching? Are there specifically Christian ways of behaving at this level?

In substance Father Fuch's response runs as follows:

> This is the fundamental question: Are there specifically Christian categories of behavior, or are genuinely human attitudes and life styles in the various areas of life not also those of Christians? . . . My answer is as follows: If we set aside the decisive, essential element of Christian ethics, Christian intentionality (as a transcendent aspect), then Christian ethics is fundamentally and essentially human in its categorical determination and materiality. It is therefore a morality of authentic humanness. In other words, truthfulness, honesty, and fidelity, considered materially, are not specifically Christian values but universal, human ones. This in no way denies the existence of an irreducibly Christian element within Christian ethics, but rather affirms it. (*Is There a Christian Ethics?* 5–8)

To sum up: Christian ethics has its own specific characteristics on the transcendent level, but on the categorical level its norms, values, virtues, and behavior patterns, considered materially, are simply human. They add nothing specifically Christian unless it be atmosphere and inspiration.

This is in substance Father Fuch's response. His book is, however, exceedingly nuanced. One even has the impression at times that he retracts with one hand what he has conceded with the other—for example, when he admits the specifically Christian character of consecrated virginity. But whatever the author's legitimate distinctions, what interests us here is the response as it has been understood by his readers, among them, Catholic ethicists. We need, therefore, to examine its most pronounced features, for in these lie its originality and the key to its success.

To summarize the position: Is there a specifically Christian ethics? Response: On the level of transcendent attitudes, yes; as for categorical behavior, no; on this level there is simply human morality.[6]

---

6. The distinction between transcendent and categorical used by Father Fuchs seems to have been borrowed from Karl Rahner, who applied it to Christianity in general in his book *Do You Believe in God?* trans. R. Strachen (New York: Newman Press, 1969). It is reminiscent of both Aristotle and Kant. For Aristotle, categories designate different classes of being and of predicates, whereas the transcendentals are the attributes that apply to all beings: existence, truth, goodness. For Kant the transcendental is opposed to the empirical as an a priori condition for knowledge independent of experience, whereas categories belong to the realm of possible experience, as a priori forms that represent essential forms of knowledge: quantity, quality, relation, etc. Father Fuchs makes a broad use of the distinction between the transcendent and categorical orders; nevertheless, the Kantian influence, with its separation between transcendent and concrete experience, is clearly perceptible in his work.

A Critique of This Response

Advantages

Father Fuchs's response is nuanced and takes into account all the elements of Christian moral teaching. It has the merit of highlighting the role of faith, charity, and the imitation of Christ in the moral life, while ethicists of recent centuries have fragmented these according to divisions determined by the commandments.

The distinction he makes is also useful in locating the source of the problem of Christian ethics at the categorical level, where Christian and human moral systems meet and where concrete problems of sexuality, justice, etc. (so widely discussed today), arise.

Disadvantages

1. The distinction made by Father Fuchs is admittedly clever, I think a bit too clever. It enables both sides to be right: the traditional opinion, which affirms the existence of a Christian ethics—valid on the transcendent level—and the new opinion, which reduces Christian ethics to human ethics—verified at the categorical level. Actually the advantage is clearly given to the second opinion. Father Fuchs opens the door wide to it, for it operates in the area of concrete action, which is the setting of most of the moral problems currently debated. Invoking the Christian inspiration of faith and love may protect the ethicist from the point of view of tradition and the magisterium, but it leaves him free in his judgment of practical problems and cases of conscience.

2. The principal fault I have to find with this concept of Christian morality is the distinction it makes between the transcendent and categorical levels, which results in their practical separation, despite all Father Fuchs's efforts to avoid this in his book. The distinction, as commonly understood, precludes the possibility of showing how what is specifically Christian penetrates and operates in concrete actions, in areas regulated by virtues and particular norms, or how faith and charity, notably, are practical virtues, capable of assuming and transforming both virtues and human values. The overriding concern seems to be to guarantee their autonomy in relation to Christian data. A Christian spirituality may be accepted, even recommended, but it cannot intervene in regard to norms of concrete, categorical action.

Furthermore, the impact of specific kinds of behavior on the moral character is severely underestimated, even though it is argued that categorical actions are to be distinguished from a transcendental relationship on the basis that only the latter engages the entire person's freedom. But do categorical choices engage us only partially? If the action is a voluntary one, a person is capable of really committing a serious injustice. Such an action, moreover, will also directly affect the virtue of charity, inasmuch as, for the Christian, a disordered relationship with the neighbor implies a disordered relationship with God. Furthermore, unjust actions easily lead to both a twisted heart and a disordered life, which constitute the essence of grave sin. A similar consideration holds for the theory of fundamental choice, which, according to the view of some theorists, can easily be disengaged from the choice to commit individual actions.

The question then, is how to reestablish an active and effective relationship between properly Christian virtues and human virtues or concrete norms. This could be done by returning to the classic distinction between the theological and the moral or human virtues, as St. Thomas does. This is not too far a cry from Father Fuchs's proposed distinction. It would make for a better demonstration, however, of how the theological virtues assume the human virtues, integrating them into a new moral structure or organism and perfecting and transforming them, while modifying them according to the greatest and deepest needs of the individual. But in doing this, we enter the field of the moral theory of virtues, which is very different, as we shall see, from that of norms or obligations. This is the crux of the problem.

5

———

Christian Ethics according to St. Paul

In studying the nature and special characteristics of Christian ethics, it seems that the obvious thing to do is to consult the primary documents of revelation. We shall begin, therefore, with St. Paul, who provides us with a well-rounded teaching on moral theory. How does he formulate the question of the specific characteristics of Christian ethics, and how does he address it?

Surprisingly, the majority of modern ethicists who deal with this question rarely go back to Scripture. The entire discussion seems to unfold in a theological ambience with specialized vocabulary and categories. The need to refer to the New Testament as a primary source, as the Fathers did, seems not to be felt.

An underlying problem in the relation between morality and Scripture emerges. Is it really possible to discuss the question of Christian ethics without reference to the very sources of revelation? When this is done it suggests a hidden agenda, some deep-rooted obstacle. In my opinion this problem affects even the way in which modern ethicists read Scripture. I shall try to demonstrate this point first, in order to clear the ground and to be able to approach St. Paul without being hindered by difficulties alien to his text and thought.

I. A CLARIFICATION OF THE QUESTION, IS THERE SUCH A THING AS CHRISTIAN ETHICS?

How do the authors of the New Testament present Christian ethics? To answer this, all we need do is read them attentively with the help of a good exegete. In fact, when we look with a little perspicacity at the manner in which ethicists consult Scripture, we notice that their methods raise important problems in regard to the very presentation of the moral question. If it is true that a question rightly phrased contains half its answer, then reflection should tell us that the results of our scriptural interrogation depend heavily upon what questions are asked. If the conclusions reached through certain inquiries are in the end so very slight, so very deceptive even, this may be because of our approach, our way of putting the question about morality relative to the sacred authors.

The Usual Method

In broad outline the usual method is this. We look for any commandments, laws, or imperatives in the New Testament that cannot be found in the Old Testament, in Greek philosophy, or in other religions. These we call specific. The procedure seems to consist in formulating what is proper to Christianity by eliminating whatever it may have in common with other teachings.

We have to admit that any results obtained through this method are quite sketchy. It is possible to find Old Testament or Jewish texts to match all the moral precepts contained in the New Testament. We shall also find them in other religious or philosophical moral systems. In the end we will be left with nothing but the new commandment of love for one another in St. John and the forgiveness of our enemies in the Sermon on the Mount. Again, interpretations differ. Some exegetes have even opposed the inclusion of these two great texts, and they fault St. John because, unlike St. Matthew, he limited agapé to the community of disciples. As for the precept of forgiveness, texts bearing the same sense can be cited from the Old Testament, even if the application is not as universal; they also resemble certain points in pagan moral systems such as Buddhism.

Again, we may ask if the precept of love is a command in the strict sense of the word. If it is, we are going to run head on into the further question: Can love be commanded? And then, does this precept have a valid place in the context of morality? Perhaps it falls under spirituality and should be classified as an exhortation rather than a moral imperative. Or, if we prefer, we may call it a transcendent attitude rather than one of those concrete, categorical norms that alone provide precise, practical moral criteria.

Clearly, a denial of the existence of specifically Christian morality will have no problem with eliminating New Testament texts that would support it. At the very least, they could be so closely related to non-Christian texts as to lose all relevance.

A Critique of the Usual Method

This way of framing the question of the relation of Christian ethics to the authors of the New Testament has two outstanding flaws. I shall simply indicate them here, with the clarifications needed to set us on the way to our study of St. Paul.

1. Our Original Categories

The first flaw leads to all the rest, but is so embedded in our thinking and so widespread that it takes a good deal of courage to challenge it. The error consists in projecting an interpretation upon St. Paul that is alien to his thought: the concept of morality as the realm of obligations, imperatives, and commands. This concept leads to a rift between dogma and morality, and a further rift between morality and what we might call exhortation. These rifts and separations are so taken for granted today that they have been used as the basis for the division of St. Paul's letters in several editions of the Bible. They have become habitual in exegesis.[1]

Such categories were totally foreign to St. Paul and to the ancients. For them, the leitmotif of morality was happiness and salvation; its chief

1. The division between dogma and morality goes back to ancient times but has been strongly emphasized in our day, when ethics has been set up as autonomous and focuses on obligation. Parenesis is a didactic term not much used, according to Littré. It designates moral exhortation as distinguished from dogmatic preaching, and is concerned with rulings and practical counsel rather than moral principles. In exegesis, parenesis is distinguished from kerygma and the catechesis that preceded it. Parenesis is therefore considered a moral genre, but it has actually been relegated to a secondary position in modern thought, which defines morality as dealing with imperatives. Because of this, exhortation, which is proper to parenesis, has become a rider, a bit of spiritual encouragement. Parenesis is no longer a part of ethics; it pertains rather to spirituality.

concern, the teaching of the virtues and those qualities of heart and mind that lead to God. When we superimpose our moral distinctions upon the New Testament, we become guilty of an anachronism that vitiates our question and falsifies our research from the start.

The chief drawback to such a modern reading is its narrowing of the field of morality in Scripture, which it limits to strictly imperative texts. Exhortation, and anything relating to faith or wisdom, tend to be ignored when morality is discussed.

It seems obvious to me that for St. Paul, among others, moral doctrine as such consisted in the teaching of the virtues, which he discussed at length in his exhortatory passages. While it is true that he only once used the term "virtue" (Phil 4:8), he continually mentioned virtues—principally faith, charity, wisdom, and humility—when describing the Christian life.

If we wish to know St. Paul's view of the existence and nature of Christian morality, we will have to set aside the moral categories we learned in school and simply let ourselves be guided by him, following his text and teaching and keeping our preconceived ideas firmly under control. In this way we can better discover how St. Paul addressed the question of Christian ethics, in what terms and according to what problematics. We will then be more likely to get an adequate answer, fuller and richer than what the question of obligatory commands and imperatives can yield.

This intellectual discipline will help us to understand better the numerous interpreters, Fathers and theologians, who read St. Paul in this way and progressively built up moral theology on the solid foundation of his teaching.

2. Two Methods: "Fragmented" and "Total"

The second flaw I should like to point out concerns the method of procedure, which we might call residual or fragmented. In order to discover what is unique in Christian morality, the New Testament texts that are thought to express it are compared with similar texts from the Old Testament, philosophy, or other religions. Whatever these latter duplicate will be eliminated, and what remains will be specifically Christian. This method involves cutting up the New Testament texts and reducing them to small fragments and units according to their supposed meaning, origin, and chronology. The texts are then successively compared.

Actually this procedure is clumsy and too materialistic. It is doomed to failure almost from the start. It is like attempting to compare one person's face with another's by eliminating all the features they have in common; this process would disfigure them both. The originality of a face stands out only when it is compared with another face as a whole, with its general composition and features and all its other distinguishing traits. Similarly, we need to compare Christian ethics with other moral systems as an organic and structured whole, contrasting the totality of its features with theirs instead of fragmenting it. This is what I mean by the "total" method.

Exegesis provides significant examples here. It has been maintained that there is nothing specifically Christian about the "Our Father." True, if we take each of the petitions singly we can find them among Jewish prayers. The "Our Father" would then be merely a collection of earlier prayers. But the perspective changes completely when we consider the "Our Father" as a whole, as in reality it is. It is original; nowhere in the Old Testament or in Judaism can a like composition be found, with the same structure and precision of expression. The unique quality of this prayer is again brought out when we consider its place in the wider context of the Sermon on the Mount and again in the overall setting of St. Matthew's Gospel. When the Lord's Prayer is seen against this background, not as a dead text but as a living organism, so to speak, its features stand out in bold relief. The invocation of the Father, for example, already unique in its Aramaic expression "Abba!" which is proper to Jesus, takes on a new dimension since "no one knows the Father except the Son and those to whom the Son chooses to reveal him" (Mt 11:27). Each one of the petitions that follow shares in this thrust toward the Father. They thus carry eschatalogical overtones.

We need to use the "total" method, therefore, in order to discern what is unique about Christian ethics: to compare it with other total entities such as Jewish moral teaching and Greek philosophical teaching. Indeed, this is the historical sequence, as I shall show further on.

I should like to add a special note on the particular relation between the Old and New Testament documents, in order to point up the error of the "fragmented" method. Due to the intention and perspective of the authors, it was inevitable that the texts of the New Testament should contain many features found in the Old. Far from wanting to reject the Old, the New Testament writers were generally at pains to show, even in their choice of words, how Christian teaching not only fulfilled but transcended the Old. In the same vein, as we shall see, St. Paul did not hesitate to integrate in his specifically Christian message all the good and useful elements he found in the Greek philosophy of his day. The New Testament continued to use the language of the Old even as it used

Greek. This is equally true of ideas. We could say it is the condition for the incarnation of Christian ethics. Yet this does not prevent the communication of a specific message that renews moral teaching in its entirety.

The fragmented method, which proceeds by way of the elimination of common texts is, in this sense, completely contrary to the work of integration and assimilation carried on by primitive Christianity. In our present situation its result is the elimination of Christian ethics itself.

As we explore the question, "What is unique about Christian ethics?" modern problematics and a priori assumptions intervene and modulate our reading of the New Testament. There is, for example, the humanist presupposition that our philosophical or cultural heritage precedes Christian data historically and causally and that the latter should therefore be identified through differentiation and separation. There is, too, the Protestant idea that evangelical teaching cannot succeed until it is radically purified of the Old Law and philosophy. Here I can only briefly note these questions and assumptions, which prejudice the mind's docility and transparency in reading the sacred authors.

The failure of modern ethicists in regard to Christian morality in their study of the New Testament is explained by the combination of the two flaws I have exposed: the reduction of moral texts to those dealing with commandments, obligations, and imperatives, and their overly materialistic interpretation through the "fragmented" method. The result is inevitable: we get nearer and nearer to the zero point. The inadequacy of the response clearly alerts us to the fact that the question has not been well put. It would be wholly astonishing if this were all the New Testament had to teach us about morality.

We will study St. Paul in this connection so as to discover at the outset how he views Christian ethics, its context and terms of reference. Next, we will trace the broad features that, in his eyes, characterized it in its totality and in relation to other moral concepts. We will make every effort to be as faithful as possible to the great Pauline texts, prescinding from the projection of modern problematics and categories, which are so difficult to avoid.

Our reading will obviously be that of an ethicist rather than a biblicist, but it will be animated by the desire to help fill in the gap that separates theology from exegesis today. It will provide a preliminary outline destined to orient other readings and to generate reflection on one of the most basic theological problems of our times: to reestablish the relation between Scripture and moral theory, so that the latter may become once more truly Christian.

II. ST. PAUL'S RESPONSE TO THE QUESTION OF
CHRISTIAN ETHICS

A. The Confrontation between Gospel Preaching, Jewish Justice, and Greek Wisdom

If we view morality as the answer to the great question of human happiness and salvation, in the tradition of the Fathers of the Church, it will not be difficult to see how the problem of Christian ethics was viewed by St. Paul. In his preaching of the Gospel he encountered two chief concepts of morality, the Jewish, based on the Law and the quest for justice, and the Greek, characterized by the teaching of wisdom and the great classical virtues. The confrontation of evangelical preaching with these two moral theories occurs particularly in the two major letters with which we shall begin our study: the First Letter to the Corinthians, which may be assigned to Easter of the year 57, and the Letter to the Romans, written in the winter of 57–58.[2]

Before taking up the study of this confrontation, we should note the circumstances in which it arose for St. Paul. It was not in the setting of a calm, peaceful theological reflection that the Apostle undertook to compare Greek and Jewish thought with the Gospel, but rather in the full tumult of preaching in the teeth of the rejection of the most cultured Jews and Greeks. The Gospel Paul proclaimed with a convert's zeal was rejected by the Jews, for whom it was first destined, and that in the name of the Law. Turning next to the Gentiles, he was ridiculed in Athens in the name of wisdom. The fire of the Gospel message, striking against Jewish and pagan incredulity, flashes through Paul's response.

Quite apart from all this, the question was a personal one; Paul had lived it in depth. He had from his youth been a follower of the Law, but had been led by his zeal to persecute the disciples of Jesus. Once converted, he in turn was being pursued by the Law and its observances. He was wholly committed to the preaching of the Gospel to the Gentiles and saw himself treated as a fool by their philosophers.

It is highly probable, therefore, that we shall get from St. Paul a vigorous, powerfully framed response to the question about the existence of a Gospel morality and its difference from Jewish and Greek systems.[3]

---

2. As a parallel to our study, see L. Cerfaux, *Le Christ dans la théologie de saint Paul,* especially Book 2, *Le don du Christ,* with its chapters: "Le Christ, notre justice"; "Le Christ, notre sagesse"; "Le Christ selon l'Esprit"; "Le Christ, notre vie"; "Le Christ et l'Eglise."

3. Some wonder whether the themes of justice in Romans and wisdom in 1 Corinthians

Jewish and Greek Moral Theories

Turning to the main features of Jewish and Greek moral theory according to St. Paul, we see that Jewish morality was dominated by the search for justice in the eyes of God. It was determined by the Law of Moses with its commandments and numerous prescriptions, customs, and observances, such as circumcision, that implemented it. Animated by hope in the divine promises, which the divine power will fulfill for those who observe the Law faithfully, Jewish morality was based on the covenant established by God with his chosen people and guaranteed by the divine fidelity. In all this we recognize the principal traits commonly associated with a moral system: the ideal of justice through conformity of one's actions to a law, joined to promises of happiness in return for merit and fidelity.

Greek moral theory can be likened to a temple raised to wisdom. It rested upon the beautifully carved columns of the intellectual and moral virtues depicted in Plato's *Dialogues,* Aristotle's *Ethics,* and (coming nearer to St. Paul's time) the discussions and teachings on the virtues among the Stoics. Under the aegis of this wisdom, inspired by the attraction of "the good and the beautiful" and sustained by the organism of the virtues, all human activities were harmoniously ordered to the perfection of action and human happiness. Wisdom, the virtues, happiness—these foundations of morality dominated the Mediterranean world in the time of St. Paul. Together with the Decalogue they later provided for Christian theology the axes and principal categories of its moral system.

We can add to this picture another ethical concept equally well known to St. Paul, although he did not refer to it. Roman moral theory, which prized beyond all else political honesty and a sense of justice, order and courage, was not shaped into a unique system but found its full expression in Roman law. St. Luke revealed his admiration for Roman justice in the Acts of the Apostles.

Finally we note that these ancient moral theories—Jewish justice,

---

really pertain to morality. This question arises from the concept of moral categories we have discussed. Justice considered in itself, in conformity with the Decalogue, clearly pertains to and constitutes revealed morality, while for the Greeks wisdom was the supreme moral virtue. But in the course of recent centuries the study of justification and grace has been removed from moral teaching. As for wisdom, it is no longer mentioned, since no commandment can be found to cover it, nor does it carry any special obligation. Modern moralists are not particularly interested in the wisdom texts of either Old or New Testament. St. Paul, apparently, felt otherwise. He begins his discourse on Gospel morality with justice and wisdom.

Greek wisdom, and Roman honesty and courage—are not really alien to us. They are direct sources of our own culture; we continue to live by the same heritage. All the renaissances of the West, notably those of the thirteenth and sixteenth centuries, were the fruits of a certain return to Greco-Roman antiquity. Scholastic theology was built with the aid of Aristotle. The ancient humanities have transmitted Greco-Latin culture to us, while the Protestant crisis began as a reaction to Renaissance humanism in the name of the Gospel. Finally, Roman law remains the foundation of our civil and ecclesiastical legislation. As for Judaism, it is present to us in the Decalogue and in all that the New Testament has taken from the Old.

The question of Christian ethics, as it arose for St. Paul, is still with us despite the passage of the centuries. The problem of humanism and the Gospel was a part of his era as it has been in each outstanding age in the Church's history.

The Attack on Greek Wisdom and Jewish Justice

The Gospel's confrontation with Greek wisdom and Jewish justice began with a direct attack. St. Paul knew that foundations were at stake; his word was an unsheathed sword piercing to the heart of the problem. Their pretended wisdom had led the Greeks to folly and the vilest corruption. The hypocritical justice of the Jews brought worldwide blasphemy upon the name of God. "They knew God and yet refused to honor him as God or to thank him; instead, they made nonsense out of logic and their empty minds were darkened. The more they called themselves philosophers, the stupider they grew, until they exchanged the glory of the immortal God for a worthless imitation, for the image of mortal man, of birds, of quadrupeds and reptiles. That is why God left them to their filthy enjoyments and the practices with which they dishonor their own bodies" (Rom 1:21ff).[4] There follows an enumeration of the sins of the pagans so harsh that we might think the picture exaggerated were it not for the exactitude with which it is verified in descriptions of the customs of the time by Roman historians, the *Annals* of Tacitus or Suetonius's *Lives of the Caesars*. With brutal realism St. Paul exposes the corruption behind the façade of wisdom in the Greco-Roman world.

The pride of the Jews received no kinder treatment: "If you call yourself a Jew, if you really trust in the Law and are proud of your God, if

4. I shall use the Jerusalem Bible translation, with some modifications.

you know God's will through the Law and can tell what is right, if you
are convinced you can guide the blind and be a beacon to those in the
dark, if you can teach the ignorant and instruct the unlearned because
your Law embodies all knowledge and truth, then why not teach yourself
as well as the others? You preach against stealing, yet you steal; you
forbid adultery, yet you commit adultery; you despise idols, yet you rob
their temples. By boasting about the Law and then disobeying it, you
bring God into contempt. As Scripture says: It is your fault that the name
of God is blasphemed among the pagans" (Rom 2:17–24). Here was
the proof of the radical failure of Jewish justice: it ended in blasphemy
against God. The merciless rigor of the attack explained the Jews' hatred
of Paul. Yet at bottom these reproaches were addressed first of all to
himself, to that man he once was in his youth, so zealous for the law.

This diatribe, which demolished the pretensions of Greek and Jewish
morality, was only the first stage in Pauline preaching. It paved the way
for the proclamation of Gospel morality, by showing the great need for
it and shocking the hearers into a desire for the message. It beat upon
the inward ear, the conscience of the listener: sin calls forth the anger
of God.

The Moral Teaching of the Gospel

In the face of Jewish and Greek morality, how did Paul describe Christian morality? What would he consider as its central, decisive trait? At
this point a reading of First Corinthians and the Letter to the Romans
is called for.

The passage that introduces the diatribe holds the answer to our question: "For I am not ashamed of the Good News: it is the power of God
saving all who have faith—Jews first, but Greeks as well—since this is
what reveals the justice of God to us: it shows how faith leads to faith,
or as scripture says, The upright man finds life through faith" (Rom
1:16–17). And this is the development: "While the Jews demand miracles and the Greeks look for wisdom, here are we preaching a crucified
Christ; to the Jews an obstacle that they cannot get over, to the pagans
madness, but to those who have been called, whether they are Jews or
Greeks, a Christ who is the power and the wisdom of God. For God's
foolishness is wiser than human wisdom, and God's weakness is
stronger than human strength. . . . During my stay with you, the only
knowledge I claimed to have was about Jesus, and only about him as
the crucified Christ . . . so that your faith should not depend on human
philosophy but on the power of God. But still we have a wisdom to offer

those who have reached maturity: . . . the hidden wisdom of God. . . . These are the very things that God has revealed to us through the Spirit" (1 Cor 1:22–25; 2:2, 5–6, 7, 10).

"God's justice that was made known through the Law and the Prophets has now been revealed outside the Law, since it is the same justice of God that comes through faith to everyone, Jew and pagan alike, who believes in Jesus Christ. Both Jew and pagan sinned and forfeited God's glory, and both are justified through the free gift of his grace by being redeemed in Christ Jesus who was appointed by God to sacrifice his life so as to win reconciliation through faith. In this way God makes his justice known; first, for the past, when sins went unpunished because he held his hand, then, for the present age, by showing positively that he is just, and that he justifies everyone who believes in Jesus. . . . There is only one God, and he is the one who will justify the circumcised because of their faith and justify the uncircumcised through their faith" (Rom 3:21–26, 30; see also Gal 2:16).

To add the personal witness of St. Paul: "As for the Law, I was a Pharisee; as for working for religion, I was a persecutor of the Church; as far as the Law can make you perfect, I was faultless. But because of Christ, I have come to consider all these advantages that I had as disadvantages. Not only that, but I believe nothing can happen that will outweigh the supreme advantage of knowing Christ Jesus my Lord. For him I have accepted the loss of everything, and I look on everything as so much rubbish if only I can have Christ and be given a place in him. I am no longer trying for perfection by my own efforts, the perfection that comes from the Law, but I want only the perfection that comes through faith in Christ, and is from God and based on faith. All I want is to know Christ and the power of his resurrection and to share his sufferings by reproducing the pattern of his death" (Phil 3:6–11).

Paul's response was delightfully clear and vigorous. In the face of Jewish justice and Greek wisdom he proclaimed a new virtue: faith in Jesus, crucified and risen and become for all the source of God's justice and wisdom. He was laying the foundation stone of morality, a virtue the Greeks did not know and the Jews misunderstood: faith, and faith in Jesus. He did not reject the desire for justice and wisdom but gave them a new source: no longer human virtue, but what might be called the virtue of God acting through Jesus Christ. He did not hide the fact that the exchange was traumatic: this faith seemed a scandal to the Jews and folly to the Greeks; but he had convicted Jewish justice of causing scandal and Greek wisdom of breeding folly.

In doing this, St. Paul laid bare the condition for all Christian ethics:

its unique foundation was to be faith in Jesus Christ. In embracing it, one could not avoid a clash with human wisdom and justice, cloaking sin as they did. Christian ethics would have to meet this challenge and come to terms with it. Every believer would experience it personally.

I shall rapidly trace the original elements of this response and the focus of Christian ethics on faith in Jesus.

Human Pride and Faith's Humility

Paul's eagle eye penetrated beyond the specious appearances of Jewish justice and Greek wisdom to the hidden flaw that vitiated them, led to their failure, and caused them to reject the Gospel: human pride, feeding on its own merits and virtues. Pride led the Jew to hypocrisy and the Greek to the most shameful vices. In the depths of the human heart, which no philosophy had been able to sound, beneath all virtues and laws, St. Paul discovered the principle of sin. Here he proposed to sow the seed of faith in Jesus: faith, the unsought virtue. Faith is humility before the truth of a humble word telling us of the One who humbled himself even to the obedience of the cross. In faith we move beyond ourselves, trust ourselves to another in all that most deeply concerns us, our justice, our wisdom, our sin, our happiness, our entire moral life. Faith breaks the human heart even in the avowal of its sinfulness, and opens it to the power of the Spirit and the pure grace of the Risen One.

Pride or faith, self-confidence or trust in Jesus, closing in upon oneself or a humble, docile opening to the Spirit: this is the decisive choice St. Paul places at the frontier of all human moral systems. In doing this, the Apostle changes the source, the tenor, and the quality of moral thought and action. For human wisdom and power he substitutes humility and the truth of faith which allows the light and power of the Spirit to enter. The Spirit brings forth a justice, a virtue, a holiness that come from God through Jesus Christ. In this way morality will be transformed in its entirety, in its inspiration, elements, structure, and applications, as we shall see.

The Person of Jesus

Another profoundly original characteristic of Paul is that he places at the heart of Christian morality a person, Jesus—he and no other, the center for everyone. For Paul, Jesus is not merely the preacher of the loftiest morality given by God, like another Moses. Nor is he a perfect model for the imitation of believers, as the Greeks might admire Socrates. Jesus, in his historical individuality—that is, in his body, which suffered and was raised from death—becomes the source and cause of the new holiness and wisdom offered to us by God. No human moral system could do that. Eager though they were to shed light along the way, Jewish and Greek moral theories left their adherents to face the law alone, to strive unaided for the virtues with their demands. But by a loving faith, the Christian, to use St. Paul's frequent expression, remains always "in Christ" through the grace of the Holy Spirit.

A New World

Personal union with Christ through faith and love has a direct and general effect on the moral life of the Christian. The center and goal of life—to which desires tend and the heart stretches forward—moves beyond visible horizons, beyond suffering and death, to where the risen Christ is seated with the Father. "You must look for the things that are in heaven, where Christ is, sitting at God's right hand. . . . The life you have is hidden with Christ in God" (Col 3:1–3). This hope, even now, creates a new dimension, even a new world within the human heart, where the moral life unfolds. Henceforth each virtue, each action of the believer will be modified from within, hiddenly, by this relation of faith and of life with the risen Christ. The very understanding of reality, formed through active experience, will be transformed, carried beyond the realm of emotions and ideas.

Power for Action

Finally, faith, transcending the realm of teaching, precepts, and models, responds to a difficulty that left Greek and Jewish moral systems powerless: the question of how to apply moral theory in the practical sphere and to carry it out courageously. The whole problem turns upon the inescapable distance separating our ideas and actions, our intentions and what we actually do. Faith delivers us from the secret despair born of the knowledge of our weakness and faults. It assures us that Christ has taken upon himself our miseries and even our sins and makes us experience his mercy crowning all his works in our everyday lives. It wins for us the the gracious strength of the Spirit which slowly, like a rising, pervading sap, produces works in us that are ours and done by us yet come from another source, nobler and more powerful than we.

B. Faith, the Source of Pauline Morality

Faith is for St. Paul an active, operative, practical virtue. We tend to forget this. Subsequent theological method separates dogma (consecrated to truths to be believed), from morality (which deals with the following of the commandments). This separation is reinforced by the Protestant separation of faith and works. Reading the Letter to the Romans in its entirety we see clearly that faith in Christ influences all aspects of the Christian personality, from its inmost depths to external actions and the concrete problems they entail. Here I shall describe in broad outline the major elements of St. Paul's moral teaching, founded on faith, as they emerge from his writings. I shall consider them in their totality, avoiding fragmentation, so as to give an overview of the Apostle's thought. Faith in Jesus will then be seen as penetrating the entire life of the believer.

1. Faith Gives Birth to a New Being

Faith joins the believer so intimately to Christ that it transforms his inmost being, producing in him through baptism a death whence springs a new source of life. "When we were baptised we went into the tomb with him and joined him in death, so that as Christ was raised from the dead by the Father's glory, we too might live a new life" (Rom 6:4). It is like a new creation: "And for anyone who is in Christ there is a new creation; the old creation [*ta archaia*] is gone, and now the new one [*kaina*] is here" (2 Cor 5:17). We cannot overemphasize the term "new being" used by the Jerusalem Bible. It refers to the level where the transformation takes place: there where the passage from death to life takes place in us, our coming to being by a new birth. Thus the believer is called *symphytos,* since he shares being, nature, and life with Christ (Rom 6:5).

These are not simply dogmatic, abstract statements; for St. Paul they are directly operative and effect a profound change in the personality and life of the Christian. Death to self and life with Christ are sown in us, engrafted upon us.

The change is not in the purely ontological order, escaping our perception. True, it transcends ordinary thought and emotion, but it accesses them at their source at the spiritual level through a perception proper to faith enlightened by the wisdom of God. "We have received the Spirit that comes from God, to teach us to understand the gifts that he has given us" (1 Cor 2:12).[5]

2. The Transformation of Personality

Faith sows in the believer the seed of a true change in personality which St. Paul describes in terms of the opposition between "the old man" and "the new man": "We must realize that our former selves have been crucified with him to destroy this sinful body and to free us from the slavery of sin. . . . You must not let any part of your body turn into an unholy weapon fighting on the side of sin; you should, instead, offer yourselves to God" (Rom 6:6, 13). This passage affirms the opposition between life according to the flesh and life according to the Spirit; it also affirms the spiritual worship animating the moral life of the Christian, which he will develop in the remainder of the letter.

The Letter to the Ephesians takes up the theme in the middle of the teaching on the new life of Christians: "You must give up your old way

---

5. It may be helpful in understanding the reality and solidity of St. Paul's affirmations to consider the Christian experience as reported by some converts. The account of Paul Claudel in particular has a remarkable affinity with the language of St. Paul and illustrates it well. It is well worth rereading.

"This was the wretched child who, on December 25, 1886, betook himself to Notre-Dame in Paris for the Christmas liturgy.

"I was standing in the crowd, near the second pillar at the entrance to the choir, to the right of the sacristy. And it was there that the thing happened that has dominated my entire life. In an instant, my heart was touched and I believed. [This faith was a thing of the heart, not the head. It was an event in time and space, like a birth, and happened precisely on the feast of the Lord's birth.]

"I believed, with such a force of adherence, such a lightening of my whole being, with so powerful a conviction and a certitude leaving no room for any kind of doubt, that ever since then all the books, reasonings, hazards of a tumultuous life, nothing has been able to shake my faith, nor, to tell the truth, to even touch it. [It is his being that is touched here, lifted up by a higher power, the spiritual being invaded by certitude, definitively.]

"I suddenly had a heart-rending sense of the innocence, the eternal childhood of God, an ineffable revelation [this, before the new-born babe in the crib]. In trying, as I have often done, to recapture the moments that followed this extraordinary incident, I find the following elements, which seem to blend in a single light, like an arm stretched out by Providence to touch, to open at last the heart of a poor, desperate child: How happy believers are! but what if this were true? It is true! God exists, he is there. He is someone, a being as personal as I am. He loves me, he calls me . . ." [This is a dialogue being-to-being, person to person, corresponding to the most personal vital questions: the yearning for goodness, the truth of being, for the presence, the personhood of God, the call to love.]

"A new and formidable being with terrifying demands to make to the young man, the artist that I was, had revealed himself to me. I could never reconcile him with any of my surroundings." [This is the new being with its moral demands, the transformation of life evolving slowly through interior struggles.] (Translator's version) (*Oeuvre en prose* [Paris: Pleiade, 1965], 1010).

of life; you must put aside your old self, which gets corrupted by following illusory desires. Your mind must be renewed by a spiritual revolution so that you can put on the new self that has been created in God's way, in the goodness and holiness of the truth" (4:22–24).[6]

This theme will be related to that of the inner and outer man, originally a Greek concept: "May he give you the power through his Spirit for your hidden self to grow strong, so that Christ may live in your hearts through faith . . ." (Eph 3:16–17 and, similarly, Rom 7:22).

Whatever the nuances in expression, faith does indeed engender a new person or a new, developing personality in the life of the Christian.

Unquestionably we have here the most profound, realistic response to the question of suffering and death, too little considered by ethicists. The question of being and life initiates Christian action. Christ's Passion and death take up our suffering and sin and instill in us, through faith, a life principle emanating from his Resurrection. Through the active presence of Christ, suffering and death are, as it were, driven back, already vanquished, and they become the instruments of a new hope. Even though they can still cause us injury and terror, they can no longer overcome us.

3. Conversion: Life according to the Spirit

The direct result of faith in Christ and union with him is a total transformation, which provides St. Paul with a background for his discussion of virtues and vices. On the one hand there is life according to the flesh, dominated by evil carnal desires, which lead to death. On the other is life according to the Spirit, led under the impulse of the Holy Spirit and animated by an attraction for the spiritual, which gives life and peace (Rom 8:5–11).

In the Letter to the Galatians, St. Paul describes in detail the two lines of conduct, which we might call the morality of the flesh or of the old man and that of the Spirit, which forms the new person. The apostle had ample opportunity to observe the fruits of the flesh in the Greek cities: fornication, impurity, debauchery . . . hatred, discord, jealousy, anger, quarrels, etc. The fruits of the Spirit are quite different and wholly desirable: charity, joy, peace, patience, kindness, goodness, trust, sweetness, self-mastery.

The picture might seem idealistic were it not for the mention of our

6. On the subject of the new creation see note f of the Jerusalem Bible for 2 Cor 5:17, which explains: "The central figure of this 'new creation' . . . is the 'new man' created in Christ, to lead a new life of virtue and holiness. Cf. the 'new birth' of baptism."

daily moral combat: ". . . self-indulgence is the opposite of the Spirit, the Spirit is totally against such a thing, and it is precisely because the two are so opposed that you do not always carry out your good intentions" (Gal 5:17). "In my inmost self I dearly love God's law, but I can see that my body follows a different law that battles against the law which my reason dictates. This is what makes me a prisoner of that law of sin which lives inside my body" (Rom 7:22–23).

The work of the Holy Spirit is in no way limited to proposing virtues and good qualities for us to acquire. The Spirit is actually a new life principle acting within us and producing in those who believe and are united with the Resurrection of Jesus the same fruits he has promised in Paul's words. "You cannot belong to Christ Jesus unless you crucify all self-indulgent passions and desires. Since the Spirit is our life, let us be directed by the Spirit" (Gal 5:24–25). "If you do live in that way you are doomed to die; but if by the Spirit you put an end to the misdeeds of the body you will live" (Rom 8:13).

Thus the Christian life becomes truly life according to the Spirit. We can use all of St. Paul's accounts of Christian behavior to describe the works of the Spirit. Chapters 5 and 6 of Galatians and chapters 8 and 12–15 of Romans present Christian behavior as spiritual ("reasonable") worship. Chapters 3 and 4 of Colossians describe a life hidden in Christ, while chapters 4–6 of Ephesians depict the behavior of the new person. A moral system cannot therefore be called fully Christian, or at least not Pauline, unless it gives a preponderant place to the action of the Holy Spirit. This was fully understood later by St. Augustine and St. Thomas.

4. Life in Christ and the Imitation of Christ

The power of the Holy Spirit communicates to Christians the new life issuing from the resurrection. It recreates them, changes them in the depths of their being, producing in them a presence that causes them to live "in Christ" and forms them in the image of Christ.

The expressions of St. Paul presenting the Christian life as life in Christ are many and powerful. "I live now not with my own life but with the life of Christ who lives in me. The life I now live in this body I live in faith: faith in the Son of God who loved me and who sacrificed himself for my sake" (Gal 2, 20–21). "Life to me, of course, is Christ" (Phil 1:21). "When he died, he died, once for all, to sin, so his life now is life with God; and in that way, you too must consider yourselves to be dead to sin but alive for God in Christ Jesus" (Rom 6:11). "If we live, we live for the Lord; and if we die, we die for the Lord" (Rom

14:8).[7] It is the same life of the risen Christ, which transforms believers and conforms them to his image.

Beginning with the Letters to the Thessalonians, the theme of imitation of Christ brings out the intimate bond formed with Christ through faith. "You were led to become imitators [*mimetai*] of us, and of the Lord; and it was with the joy of the Holy Spirit that you took to the gospel, in spite of the great opposition all round you. This has made you the great example [*typos*] to all believers in Macedonia and Achaia" (1 Thes 1:6–7). On this text the Jerusalem Bible notes that, in imitating Paul, the faithful will be imitating Christ, whom Paul imitates. Finally, they must imitate God (Eph 5:1) and each other. The same idea is expressed in the Letter to the Philippians: "Be united in following [*symmimetai*] my rule of life" (3:17). Thus the theme of imitation runs through the letters.

In St. Paul this theme is richer and more composite than the idea of simply copying a model, which is the usual interpretation of it. Role models such as the heroes or philosophers of antiquity, great historical characters or even popular figures of our own day leave us to our own devices as we try to imitate what we admire in them. Imitation rooted in faith operates at a deeper level, for it is the work of the Holy Spirit. He conforms us interiorly to the image of Christ and engraves "the sentiments of Christ Jesus" so profoundly upon our souls that we can ourselves become models for others, the model always being in the end the image of Christ, who is all in all. Thus the theme of imitation relates to the theme of the image of God within each person, restored by Christ, the Image of the Father.

This rich concept of the imitation of Christ answers an objection that quickly comes to mind when Paul proposes himself as a model for his readers. We wonder if this is secret pride. It all depends on what we are imitating and by whose power.

St. Paul imitates the Christ who "was humbler yet, even to accepting death, death on a cross" (Phil 2:8), becoming the servant of his disciples. With this in mind St. Paul saw himself, too, as the servant of all and called himself "a servant of Christ Jesus" (Rom 1:1). The reason for imitation, and the shape it takes, will be humility, obedience, service to one another.

Humility is surer when rooted in awareness of the sin from which Christ freed us, and a perception of the Spirit as the principle source of

7. See the study of the formula "in Christ Jesus" by L. Cerfaux. *La théologie de l'Eglise suivant saint Paul,* 2d ed. (Paris, 1965), 179–94, which shows clearly that the reference is to Jesus personally.

our imitation of Christ and sanctification. This is a far cry from the kind of imitation that would feed human pride, or a *"mimesis"* achieved by force. For St. Paul, the theme of imitation is meaningless except in the context of faith, which unites us to Christ, and the Spirit, who brings about this conformity in us. It leads the Christian to see life as a service to Christ and devotion to neighbor. All Gospel imitation focuses on Jesus and on his image reproduced in the conduct of believers.

5. Charity, the Holy Spirit's Greatest Gift

St. Paul's moral theory, based on faith and proceeding from the Holy Spirit and union with Christ, centers on charity, according to the teaching of the First Letter to the Corinthians. Charity surpasses all charisms and other virtues and is the bond of perfection.

A Unique Kind of Love.   Charity or *agape* is new and unique, a love that surpasses all human sentiments. Its source is God: it is the love of the Father manifested in the gift of the Son and communicated by the Holy Spirit.[8]

"The love of God has been poured into our hearts by the Holy Spirit which has been given us. . . . What proves that God loves us is that Christ died for us while we were still sinners" (Rom 5:5–8). "With God on our side, who can be against us? Since God did not spare his own Son, but gave him up to benefit us all, we may be certain, after such a gift, that he will not refuse anything he can give. . . . Nothing therefore can come between us and the love of Christ . . . neither death nor life

---

8. See the beautiful note in the Jerusalem Bible on 1 Cor 13:1, which associates St. Paul's teaching with St. John's: "The supreme charity is God's love for us, that made him give his Son so that sinners might be reconciled, and become not only God's chosen ones, but God's sons. This love is attributed to God (the Father), but as it is identical with God's nature it is found in the Son, so the Son loves the Father as the Son is loved by the Father, and as the Father loves us, so the Son loves the human race, which he was sent to save. This is the same love that the Holy Spirit gives Christians, to help them to carry out the essential commandment of the Law, which is love of God and neighbor. To love friends and enemies is not only the necessary consequence of God's love for us, but actually proves that God loves us, and it is the new commandment laid down by Christ and constantly emphasized by his disciples. . . . Love presupposes sincerity, humility, selflessness and self-sacrifice, service, mutual help. Love shows itself in the way we behave, and the way we obey the Lord's commands, and gives effect to our faith. Love holds the community together. . . . Nor can we be charitable without truth, and it is this that enables us to make moral judgments, and gives us spiritual understanding of the divine mystery, and spiritual knowledge of the otherwise unknowable love of Christ. Since Christ, and the whole Trinity, live in the soul that has this love, it fosters the theological virtues in any person where it is the dominant characteristic. Love is the only eternal virtue, and will only be perfect in the vision, when God gives his lovers the gifts he has promised."

. . . nor any created thing can ever come between us and the love of God made visible in Christ Jesus our Lord" (Rom 8:31–39).

For St. Paul, charity does not mean a general sort of love, assuming different forms according to different affective relationships between persons: married love, family love, friendship, brotherhood, benevolence or any of the many affections which might be oriented to God. It is not the spontaneous or voluntary sympathy for others that is due to everyone, nor even a desire for the common good.

The charity St. Paul proposes cannot be understood nor can it exist without that faith in Jesus which is its forerunner and which opens the door to the heart. This is why the Apostle speaks of hope and charity immediately after his exposition of justification by faith. In his eyes these virtues are inseparable. "So far then we have seen that, through our Lord Jesus Christ, by faith we are judged righteous and at peace with God, since it is by faith and through Jesus that we have entered this state of grace in which we can boast about looking forward to God's glory. . . . and this hope is not deceptive, because the love of God has been poured into our hearts by the Holy Spirit which has been given us" (Rom 5, 1–5). In the Letter to the Galatians, St. Paul expresses in a single sentence the essence of Christian morality: "I live in faith; faith in the Son of God who loved me and who sacrificed himself for my sake" (2:20).

Rising from this new source of love, charity fills the life of believers and takes over even the humblest human virtues and emotions. If moral theology wishes to give charity its preponderant place, it should begin with faith in Christ, as the love which comes from him and proceeds from the Holy Spirit. This in no way precludes an interest in human forms of love, for far from destroying these, charity purifies, deepens, and strengthens them, even enhancing them with a divine dimension. We could say that charity is enfleshed in human affections. The language of human love is used in Scripture and spiritual writings to express it. Nevertheless, charity springs from another source than human emotions, claims another essence.[9]

Personal and Communal Love.   The dimensions of charity are vast. It is at once very personal and broadly communal. Although he praised

---

9. Even the terms used by Christians show their awareness of the uniqueness and oneness of this love. The authors of the New Testament chose the little-used word *agape* in preference to *philia* and above all *eros*. This last would be reinstated only in the fifth century by Pseudo-Dionysius in a totally Christian setting. Latin authors, too, preferred *dilectio*, then *caritas*, and were reluctant to use *amor* until St. Augustine reintroduced it in Christian parlance, deepening its philosophical meaning.

it as the highest charism and the queen of virtues, St. Paul chose to describe it in terms of very humble dailiness, so concrete that translators have difficulty in presenting it: "Love is always patient and kind; it is never jealous; love is never boastful or conceited; it is never rude or selfish; it does not take offence, and is not resentful. Love takes no pleasure in other people's sins but delights in the truth; it is always ready to excuse, to trust, to hope, and to endure whatever comes" (1 Cor 13:4–7). Such also is the fruit of the Spirit: ". . . love, joy, peace, patience, kindness, goodness, trustfulness, gentleness and self-control" (Gal 5:22).

To read these texts, one might suppose that charity is found only in the private life of the Christian. Yet it is charity, with the one same movement, that forms the Church to make it the Body of Christ, passing all frontiers and extending to all nations. This teaching is found again in 1 Corinthians 12, where St. Paul compares the work of the Spirit through charity to the body's relationship to its members.

Here again we need to transcend the human viewpoint. The classic analogy of the body and its members takes on a new, specifically Christian significance under the pen of St. Paul. The concept of the Church as the Body of Christ stems from faith in Christ, who suffered and arose in his body. It is to the Body of Jesus that Christians are united in their own bodies, through the sacraments of baptism and the Eucharist. Through this personal relationship, animated by faith and love, Christians become members of "the Body of Christ." This profoundly realistic teaching was to be still further developed in the captivity letters, where Christ is presented as "the head of the Church, which is his Body" (Eph 1:22–23).[10]

Thus ruled by charity, St. Paul's moral teaching would be dominated by the call to unity, to the breaking down of divisions among Christians such as existed in the church at Corinth, where even charisms became an occasion for discord, and to the building up of the Church, of the brethren and the pagans themselves, which is the proper work of charity (1 Cor 14:12 and 22–25).

The power of faith and charity would be great enough to overcome the deepest divisions existing between persons, even those arising from the encounter between Gospel and ancient morality: "All baptized in Christ, you have all clothed yourselves in Christ, and there are no more distinctions between Jew and Greek, slave and free, male and female, but all of you are one in Christ Jesus" (Gal 3:27, 28). The idea is taken

10. See note j in the Jerusalem Bible on 1 Cor 12:12.

up again in the Letter to the Colossians (3:11), and here an exposition of Christian morality centered on charity is introduced: "Over all these clothes, to keep them together and complete them, put on love" (14).

Charity is the sovereign virtue because it unites the opposite extremes of the Christian life. It delights in the smallest virtues, which bring humility into ordinary life; supported by these, it includes all dimensions of the Church, transcending purely human views and obstacles.

6. Assimilating the Human Virtues

Faith and charity cannot actually be exercised without making use of the human virtues discussed by the Greek philosophers and sapiential literature. Again, but from a different point of view, we are confronted with the relation between Pauline and Greek morality. Actually we come across terms, ideas, and lists of virtues in St. Paul's moral teaching that are borrowed from Stoic philosophy in particular and that could be found in the popular culture of Greek cities. How exactly did Paul view these human virtues? After having upheld faith in Jesus Christ so vigorously in opposition to Greek wisdom and Jewish justice, had he now yielded to the subtle temptation to return to Greek virtues? Or, on the other hand, where did he fit them in and how did he include them in the context of Christian ethics?

This question is vastly important for subsequent moral theology, which has made broad use of philosophy to reinforce its position, among both Greek and Latin Fathers of the Church. Does the use of Plato, Aristotle, Cicero, Seneca, or Plotinus find legitimate justification in St. Paul?

We cannot answer this question with a simple yes or no. Once again we must beware of projecting onto St. Paul our modern problematics. We could give a categorical no to the use of Greek philosophy and Protestant thought, with the object of safeguarding purity of faith and the Gospel. Or we could say yes, in keeping with the Christian humanism of recent centuries, which chooses to stand upon reason and human virtues and from there rise up to faith. Perhaps an open-minded reading of St. Paul's Letters viewed as a whole will help us to rectify the theological categories which separate us and which function as a priori schemas in both exegesis and theology.

Two Stages in Pauline Moral Theory.   If we wish to do justice to all of St. Paul's texts and maintain the unity of his doctrine, we must choose a dialectical response to the question. I would therefore distinguish two essential stages in the thought of the Apostle and the formation of the Gospel morality he proposes.

1. The first stage in the encounter between the Gospel and Greek wisdom consists in a confrontation and a rupture regarding the heart of morality and the source of wisdom and justice. Before proud humanity, the would-be center and source of virtue, St. Paul holds up the humiliated Christ, obedient, crucified, risen. To human wisdom and virtue he opposes faith in God through Jesus Christ. The question is decisive. The choice is radical, painful, necessary, and leaves no room for compromise. As far as Gospel morality is concerned, it is all or nothing. It means the inevitable passage through the cross of Christ and death to self, "the old man," even if the latter appears as the figure of humanity itself, or of a given society.

2. Once this foundation is solidly laid, St. Paul, undertaking to describe Christian conduct in daily life, does not hesitate to include the virtues recognized by contemporary Greek culture and to integrate them in his teaching in the light of faith, recommending them to the study and efforts of believers. The clearest text on this is in the Letter to the Philippians and is of prime importance: "Finally, brothers, fill your minds with everything that is true, everything that is noble, everything that is good and pure, everything that we love and honor, and everything that can be thought virtuous [*arete*] or worthy of praise [*epainos*]" (4:8). St. Paul might have chosen these terms expressly for the Greeks, especially *arete,* which evokes all the classic virtues.

We should note in this connection that although this text is unique in its clarity it is nevertheless related to numerous passages where St. Paul recommends particular virtues. It cannot be isolated from the rest. Moreover, the context of Philippians is entirely Christian. The verses enclosing the text illustrate this: "The Lord is very near. There is no need to worry; but if there is anything you need, pray for it, asking God for it with prayer and thanksgiving. . . . Keep doing all the things that you learnt from me and have been taught by me and have heard or seen that I do. Then the God of peace will be with you" (5–7, 9).

Obviously, the practice of virtue was an integral part of Paul's teaching and life as a model for the Philippians. We cannot separate verse 8 from its context, from the specifically Christian moral doctrine of St. Paul.

The two stages we have just observed are in no way a pairing of contraries, set in opposition and then reconciled. In my opinion they constitute two aspects in the movement of faith in the formation of Christian morality. Its point of departure is a new center, a unique foundation, the "cornerstone" so firmly laid. The acceptance of the Greek virtues, following upon faith, brings with it something new. Faith has worked a transformation in depth and modified these virtues from within. After having laid the foundation of faith and charity St. Paul retrieves, if you will, the Greek virtues and inserts them into the new moral organism. I shall try to explain this.

The Organicity of the Virtues.   In order to understand how St. Paul salvages human virtues, we first need to look at a common error of perspective, which envisages the virtues as concepts enjoying an independent existence. If this were the case, we could join or separate them at will, attribute them to one or another philosopher or shuttle them between authors as circumstances might suggest. Some have thought that St. Paul, in including lists of virtues of Stoic origin, more or less consciously introduced a foreign element into his moral preaching, which marred its purity.

In reality the virtues have no independent existence of their own. They are always part of a dynamic organism, which unites them and orders them in relation to a dominant virtue, an ideal of life, or a basic sentiment, giving them precise value and measure. As a virtue passes from one moral system to another, it is integrated into the new organism. We cannot compare justice as viewed by Plato and Aristotle, for example, with the justice of Kant or Marx or the Bible, without taking into account the particular moral synthesis in which this virtue resides. It might be worlds away.

When St. Paul accepted the virtues taught by the Greeks he did not leave them intact. He inserted them into a moral and spiritual organism very different from Greek wisdom. There they were deepened considerably and given new modalities of operating. In order, therefore, to find an answer to our question, we need to rise to the level of Christian virtues.

St. Paul obviously did not construct an organized moral system like that of St. Thomas Aquinas. However, it is clear that for him the organism of charisms and virtues possessed an entirely Christian head, formed by three virtues of which the philosophers were ignorant. Faith, hope, and charity guaranteed a direct bond with the source of Christian life, Christ and his Spirit. These virtues were unique in their dependence on the initiative of divine grace. They governed all of Christian action and gave to the other virtues, working in harmony with them, an incomparable value, measure, dynamism, and finality.

7. The Transformation of the Virtues

Relation to Christ in Cases of Conscience. The relation the human virtues have to faith and charity, when practiced by believers, changes their mode of existence. It transforms them from within, by putting them in touch with Christ. We can therefore describe St. Paul's moral theory as a theory of action-with-Christ, or again, action-in-Christ. This deep bond was manifested explicitly whenever the Apostle made an extensive study of a moral question submitted to him. His answers in the First Letter to the Corinthians were very significant in this regard. Each time, after making some observations based on reason and common sense, his thought leapt beyond the limitations of circumstance and human views as he related the problem to Christ and drew from this relationship a decisive answer.

Take the case of fornication (1 Cor 6:12–20). St. Paul begins by saying: " 'For me there are no forbidden things'; maybe, but not everything does good. . . . Food is only meant for the stomach, and the stomach for food. . . . But the body—this is not meant for fornication;" and he continues, "it is for the Lord, and the Lord for the body. . . . You know, surely, that your bodies are members making up the body of Christ? . . . Your body, you know, is the temple of the Holy Spirit, who is in you since you received him from God. You are not your own property; you have been bought and paid for. That is why you should use your body for the glory of God." It is clear that the demand for purity becomes all the stronger, and more attractive as well, for the Christian. Concerning meat offered to idols, the decisive argument is based on charity and union with Christ: "By sinning in this way against your brothers, and injuring their weak consciences, it would be Christ against whom you sinned" (8:12).

This approach was a constant with St. Paul. The bond with Christ was his guiding principal in studying concrete situations. This may surprise us, for we are not used to dealing with cases of conscience in this way. Perhaps this is the effect of our myopia in regard to things Christian, of our narrowing the sphere of morality and so distancing it from the Gospel. How are we going to understand the Christian dimension of morality if we prescind from its relationship to Christ and let ourselves be guided by so-called scientific assumptions?

Morality within the Family. The discussions about family relationships that we find in the letters to the Colossians (3:18–4:1) and Ephesians (5:21–6.9) confirm this central thrust of Pauline teaching and express it with important nuances.[11] At first glance, these texts seem to affirm and corroborate customary relationships between husband and wife, master and slave, in contemporary society: "As the church submits to Christ, so should wives to their husbands, in everything. . . . Slaves, be obedient to the men who are called your masters in this world, with deep respect and sincere loyalty."

St. Paul had no problem with family customs and slavery at the societal level. He was not aware of having been given authority or a mission in this regard. It was not his main concern. Yet his opening phrase, as the statement of a principle applicable to everyone, already dealt a staggering blow to Roman society, where the father of the family had power of life and death over his wife, children, and slaves: "Give way to one another in obedience to Christ." The Christian faith was adding a new dimension to family relationships, to be expanded later, thanks to the personal bond with Christ that it engendered: "Wives should regard their husbands as they regard the Lord. . . . Husbands should love their wives just as Christ loved the Church. . . . Slaves . . . , work hard and willingly, but do it for the sake of the Lord and not for the sake of men."

These precepts were not meant to reinforce existing authority by the authority of Christ, rendering it sacred, as some have thought. They conveyed a transformation in depth, ordered to the equality all persons enjoy before Christ and before God. This was the meaning of St. Paul's insistence on reciprocal duties, nonexistent in the Roman family: "Each one of you must love his wife as he loves himself; and let every wife respect her husband. . . . And those of you who are employers, treat your slaves in the same spirit . . . remembering that they and you have the same Master in heaven and he is not impressed by one person more than by another."

These texts touch on different levels of Christian life and reveal the nuances needed for any response to a concrete question. They bring to the fore a new, higher dimension and are oriented to the morally revolutionary affirmation launched by the Letter to the Galatians and echoed by that found in Colossians: "All baptised in Christ, you have all clothed yourselves in Christ, and there are no more distinctions between Jew and Greek, slave and free, male and female, but all of you are one in Christ Jesus" (Gal 3:27–28). Aware from experience of the sharpness of divisions between people, and knowing well that faith could not put an end to them by magic, St. Paul proclaimed that a moral yeast had

11. Cf. the interpretation of E. Fuchs, *Le désir et la tendresse* (Geneva, 1982), 72–76.

come into the world capable of creating new relationships, but at a deeper level than that of their differences. Its effects would eventually permeate the social plane and would take the form of more humanitarian customs, and a recognition of the basic dignity and equality of persons, with special emphasis on the humblest, who most closely imaged the humbled, suffering Christ.

8. Restructuring

St. Paul restructured the organicity of the virtues, making them all depend on the faith, hope, and charity that bound the believer to Christ. The order of virtues was thus transformed; this was evident notably in the special place given to humility and the insistence upon chastity.

The Role of Humility.   In the Letter to the Philippians the exhortation to "always consider the other person to be better than yourself" (2:3) inspired the celebrated hymn depicting the humility of Christ: "He emptied himself . . . he was humbler yet, even to accepting death . . . ." Humility was a dominant trait in the soul of Jesus, which his disciples were to reproduce. It was not seen as isolated but rather as joined with his love—which the divine glory would crown—and as the extreme expression of that love. It was the irrefutable sign of its authenticity and depth. Humility would lead the disciples to acts of fraternal love, which gave glory to God. Thanks to it, they would learn how to love concretely and practically through mutual service, in gentleness and patience, putting aside all thought of vain glory, self-interest, and party spirit. There could be no true charity without humility.

Humility was opposed to the pride underlying Greek wisdom and Jewish justice. Paul rebuked the Greeks and Jews in his letters to the Corinthians and Romans because they rejected the Gospel. Although the Apostle did not refer to humility directly in these places, we gather that humility before the Word of God is what leads to faith. It was clearly evident in those who welcomed the Gospel: "those whom the world thinks common and contemptible are the ones that God has chosen" (1 Cor 1:28). Also consider Paul's own experience in preaching: "I came among you in great 'fear and trembling'" (2:3). Humility was indispensible for receiving the Word of God in faith. It was truth that rebuked and called to conversion and a new way of life. It was the threshold of the Christian life. Upon it any purely human morality was sure to stumble. The Fathers of the Church and Christian spiritual writers would see it as the foundation of the spiritual life.

Insistence upon Chastity.   St. Paul also gave pride of place to chastity in his teaching. His insistence upon it was due not merely to circumstances or to the difficulties encountered by Christians living in the midst of pagans whom God had delivered over to "degrading passions" (Rom 1:26). His teaching was forthright, open, addressed to all. He deepened the dimensions of this virtue by giving it a new foundation, which strengthened it wonderfully: the unchaste person sinned not only against his own body but against the Lord who redeemed us and joined us to himself as his members; sinned, too, against the Holy Spirit, for our bodies had become his temples. This teaching clearly referred to all forms of impurity, and in no way stemmed from a depreciation of the body.

St. Paul's recommendation of virginity and his praise of it bring to light the fact that chastity receives a new dimension and scope from the Gospel. The fruits of this teaching in the primitive Church would confirm its importance and originality. Still, it was not a personal counsel, but would nourish the ideal of virginity that was to flower in the early Church together with that of martyrdom.

Chastity, too, should not be isolated. It was closely linked with charity. Its demand for purity emanates from charity and the Holy Spirit. The choice of virginity would flow from love for Christ whom St. Paul presented as the Spouse to whom he wished to give his disciples (2 Cor 11:1–2). Chastity was a characteristic trait of life in the Spirit, as opposed to life according to the flesh (Gal 5:16ff).

We could continue to study various human virtues cited and recommended by St. Paul. If we take care to place them in their new literary and doctrinal setting, I think it can easily be shown how the influence of faith and charity transforms them. This is eminently true of courage, the virtue the Greeks considered was exercised mainly in warfare. The love of Christ increased St. Paul's courage enormously: "Nothing therefore can come between us and the love of Christ, even if we are troubled or worried, or being persecuted, or lacking food or clothes, or being threatened or even attacked. . . . These are the trials through which we daily triumph, by the power of him who loved us" (Rom 8:35–39). Here we already have the ideal of martyrdom, which inspired Christians in the first centuries and would define Christian courage for later theology.

Joy and Peace.   At the close of this research I should mention two sentiments that give Pauline morality, and the soul of the primitive Christian, their characteristic tone: joy and peace. The Apostle mentioned them constantly together with the virtues: "What the Spirit brings is very different: love, joy, peace" (Gal 5:22). They are the dominant theme of the Letter to the Philippians: "I want you to be happy, always happy in the Lord; I repeat, what I want is your happiness . . . and that the peace of God, which is so much greater than we can understand, will guard your hearts and your thoughts, in Christ Jesus" (4:4–7). They were linked with faith and hope: "May the God of hope bring you such joy and peace in your faith that the power of the Holy Spirit will remove all bounds to hope" (Rom 15:13). This exhortation—we could almost say commandment—to rejoice was all the more remarkable for being given in the midst of persecutions and all the difficulties encountered in Christian preaching. It is something ethicists could well reflect upon. It was clearly understood by the Church Fathers. St. Thomas affirmed that joy and peace are the direct effect of charity. He also considered joy as one of the signs of a virtuous action. Is joy still mentioned in modern moral theory? Rather, virtue seems to have become a tiresome bore.

Conclusion

St. Paul gives us a clear, rich answer to the question of Christian ethics if we consider it from his viewpoint and accept it on his terms—the confrontation of Christian preaching with Jewish justice and Greek wisdom—and move beyond the too-narrow limits of a morality of obligation. The comparison begins with a radical opposition—folly and scandal—that brings out the first specific element of Christian ethics: faith in Jesus Christ, who through his humility and obedience became for us the justice and wisdom of God, as opposed to pride and sin, which are the downfall of these too-human virtues. Then, once the foundation of faith was laid in the heart of the Christian, St. Paul did not hesitate—he seemed to have no problem with this—to incorporate these human virtues in his teaching and encourage their practice. In so doing, he built a new moral organism headed by new virtues, faith, hope and charity. These assimilated as far as possible all the truth and goodness of the Old Law and of philosophic wisdom. The human virtues were thus transformed from within and received a new dimension and scope. Certain virtues, such as humility and chastity, were given special importance, in view of their privileged bond with the love of Christ and the action of the Spirit.

I should like to stress once more the christological character of Pauline morality. The person of Christ, including his body which suffered and was raised, was truly the center around which all moral life revolved. "We are preaching a crucified Christ . . ." Relationship to Christ became the principle criterion for Christian morality: "In your minds you must be the same as Christ Jesus" (Phil 2:5).

St. Paul's moral teaching can equally well be described as Trinitarian. Christ is the manifestion of the love and mercy of the Father, who, through the gift of the Son, forgave the sins of both Jews and Greeks, giving them justice and wisdom through faith (1 Cor 2:7). Through Christ, seated at his right hand, Christian morality was directed to the Father: "Since you have been brought back to true life with Christ, you must look for the things that are in heaven, where Christ is, sitting at God's right hand" (Col 3:1). Finally, Christian morality was life in the Holy Spirit, enlightened and inspired by him, as the major letters show clearly (Gal 5; Rom 8; 1 Cor 1:10ff).

St. Paul's answer to the question of whether a specifically Christian ethics exists leaves us in no doubt. I think he would be amazed to hear theologians asking such a question. We could even say that, for him, no other kind of morality would have any value, for, when left to themselves, moral systems, Jewish as well as Greek, ended in sin and corruption, because of the human pride that fed on them and vitiated them from within.

Christian ethics, based on faith in Christ and on humility, manifests the power it receives from the Holy Spirit by accepting and fulfilling beyond all human hope the profound truths and aspirations contained in these teachings on justice and wisdom. Initiated by St. Paul, this process of rectifying and integrating human virtues was continued in the theological studies of the Fathers of the Church and the great scholastics. Yet the work will always need to be begun anew, because it rests on an ongoing dialectical debate between the human and the divine. The conflict is sparked by the question of faith in Jesus Christ and the call to conversion and a new life.

To conclude, St. Paul's moral teaching united dogma and morality closely and made no distinction between morality and spirituality, or even exhortation. Nor did it endorse the separation of transcendent and categorical levels. These distinctions, as we know them, stem from a concept of morality focusing on obligations—a concept that had never occurred to St. Paul.

6

The Sermon on the Mount and Christian Ethics

I. THE SERMON ON THE MOUNT—
VARIOUS INTERPRETATIONS

The Sermon on the Mount is a Gospel text of prime importance for Christian ethics. This seems to have been St. Matthew's intention in writing his Gospel. In this first of the five great discourses that form the body of his work, the Evangelist clearly wished to gather together the teachings on the sort of justice that Jesus proposed to his listeners, "higher than that of the Pharisees." These were to distinguish the conduct and moral standards of his followers. In this section we have a summary of Gospel morality as it came from the lips of the Lord himself. It is one of the chief documents used in primitive Christian catechesis and stands out as a principal source for Christian moral teaching, in both homiletics and theological reflection.

There is ample opportunity to find in the Sermon on the Mount an answer to our question on the specificity of Christian ethics. Jesus contrasts the principles of the Mosaic Law with the justice he preaches, and he asserts his authority: "But I tell you. . . ." He declares that his followers cannot be content to act as the pagans do. The concrete terms of Christ's preaching undeniably address the question of the specific nature of Christian ethics, as it differs from the morality of the Jews and pagans.

The Fathers of the Church and the great scholastics understood well the importance of the Sermon on the Mount. St. Augustine in particular—and we shall return to him later—saw in it the perfect model for the Christian life. In the thirteenth century, Franciscan theologians as well as St. Thomas were to see in the Sermon on the Mount the distinctive text of the New Law, as contrasted with the Decalogue and the Old Law. For them, as for the Greek Fathers, the Sermon was one of the most characteristic texts of Christian moral doctrine.

I should add that the Sermon on the Mount has been one of the chief sources of spiritual renewal known to the Church through the ages. Its fruitfulness is amply attested by its constant reappearance. There are few passages in Scripture that touch the Christian heart more surely and deeply, or that have a greater appeal for nonbelievers. The Sermon on the Mount was one of Ghandi's favorite texts; he reproached Christians for their neglect of it. Bergson saw in it the very expression of "open morality."

The Modern Problem with the Sermon on the Mount

In our times, however, the interpretation of the Sermon on the Mount has caused considerable concern to theologians as well as exegetes. It is not only the classic problems raised by this or that verse that trouble them—problems that are often due to Jesus' language of imagery, which does not lend itself easily to translation. Rather, there is a major difficulty that plagues interpreters, dividing them into opposite camps and occasioning many attempts at explanations. It even leads some to back off cautiously from the Sermon.

The difficulty is this. The moral teaching contained in the Sermon on the Mount appears to be so sublime and so demanding that no one can follow it in concrete reality, at least not the majority of people. Isn't it challenging us to impossible heights? This is a serious objection to a moral teaching that purports to be addressed to everyone. If it is impracticable, it falls short of its goal, which is to shape human action, and so it becomes useless. In the face of the Sermon, a person might say: "Isn't it enough to refrain from murder and injustice to my neighbor, to avoid adultery and keep my promises? Is anger a sin, that I should be called into court over it? Can I be forbidden to have impure thoughts? And how can it be decreed as a law of our society that we should not resist evil, that we should turn the other cheek?" In a word, does not the Sermon on the Mount preach impossible behavior, impossible, that is, for the generality of people?

The problem is seen at its most serious when morality is defined as the sum of obligations imposed on us by the will of God. If the Sermon on the Mount is this kind of law, if each of its prescriptions—and, they are stringent—expresses a binding command, as modern ethicists understand it, we can certainly ask if it is not laying on the shoulders of the disciples an intolerable legal burden, a yoke harsher even than that of the Old Law.

The problem has evoked many answers. Warren S. Kissinger counts thirty-four in his history of interpretations of the Sermon.[1] For the purposes of our research, we shall consider those that have a theological bearing upon the question.

1. The "Catholic" Interpretation

First let us look at what is still called the "Catholic" position, the one of immediate interest to us. It rests on a distinction between a moral code designed for all Christians, expressed primarily in the Decalogue, and a more spiritual and exacting doctrine reserved for an elite group such as religious, who have freely chosen to strive for evangelical perfection. The Sermon on the Mount therefore is not the concern of all Christians and does not oblige them. It falls under the classification of counsels, not commands. This distinction bypasses an exegetical problem: for whom was the Sermon intended? Christ was speaking not to the crowd, but to a group of disciples and apostles whom he called to himself.

This interpretation, which has become classic within recent centuries, has an initial flaw. In restricting the Sermon on the Mount to a select group, it opposes patristic tradition, to say nothing of the Evangelist's intention. St. John Chrysostom, in explaining the Sermon to his people, foresaw this danger and took care to explain: "Because it is said that Jesus Christ was teaching his apostles, we do not have to think he was speaking only to them. In teaching them, he was teaching all of us" (Homily XV on St. Matthew, N. 1). St. Augustine chose the Sermon on the Mount as the subject of his first homily to the people of Hippo because "this Sermon contains all the precepts needed for our guidance in the Christian life." In the view of the Fathers, the Sermon was intended for all people, even though the apostles were called to play the role of intermediaries.

The second drawback to this interpretation is that it has led to the

1. W. S. Kissinger, *The Sermon on the Mount* (Metuchen, N.J., 1975).

omission of the Sermon on the Mount in moral teaching, at all levels. Moral theology is based chiefly, according to the manuals, on the ten commandments; the Sermon is viewed as a bit of spirituality. This explains its relative neglect by Catholic authors: the Sermon is not essential to ethics, nor, strictly speaking, to salvation. Its message, however beautiful, is optional.

Finally, it does not seem that the distinction between a form of morality destined for all and a morality reserved to a religious elite responds adequately to the difficulty experienced in living out the Sermon. Can we be sure that the observances proper to the religious life—including the support of a community that seeks to live the Gospel—are sufficient to enable religious to put the Sermon on the Mount into practice any better than simple Christian folk? Can these observances give them the ability to do the "impossible"? Experience of religious life gives this the lie and shows rather the need for other intervening factors such as faith and grace, which, far from separating religious from other Christians, unite them profoundly.

2. An Idealistic Moral Theory

The teaching in the Sermon on the Mount has also been viewed as the expression of an ideal—unworkable no doubt, but still useful on the practical level, since we need to ask a great deal of people in order to obtain even a little effort and progress. The impossible is proposed so as to goad each into doing as much as he can.

We can hardly accept an explanation that places the Sermon on the Mount in the category of an imaginary ideal rather than a concrete reality where the action is. The perception of ourselves as unable to follow a moral teaching makes the teaching quite ineffective. We will soon abandon an ideal too far beyond us.

We can include here the interpretation of liberal theologians inspired by Kant and nineteenth-century idealism. In contrast to Judaism's obsession with works, the Sermon presents us, they would say, with a new morality of sentiment, where benevolence and one's personal intentions are central. This morality is altogether interior, in contrast to the external morality of law.

Beyond all doubt, the Sermon on the Mount brings a deepening of interiority on the level of the "heart," but Protestant exegetes themselves are becoming more and more convinced today of the need for the effective action demanded by the Sermon. The exterior dimension, in the sense of concrete action in our neighbor's behalf, is as essential to the

Sermon on the Mount as the interior dimension, in the sense of the "heart" and the "hidden place" where only the Father sees us. The teaching of the Sermon cannot be turned into a morality of sentiment or intention, any more than it can be considered as a purely formal morality consisting exclusively of universal principles, separated from experience and practice. The problem of realization, or of the "impossible," remains unsolved.

3. An Interim Morality

Early in this century, Albert Schweitzer, among others, proposed a new interpretation of the Sermon along eschatalogical lines, basing it on the belief of Jesus and the first disciples that the end of the world was near. The Sermon on the Mount proclaimed a very demanding doctrine approaching heroism, but it was valid only for the short space of time before the imminent return of Christ. It was an interim legislation, in preparation for a unique upcoming event. It could not be applied to a lengthy period of time or to life in the normal times that Christians knew as the Parousia delayed its coming.

Once again the Sermon was being excluded from Christian ethics. Its teaching was meant only for a heroic era; it could not serve as the basis of moral theory for ordinary Christian life. It remained a morality of "the impossible."

It is true that we need to take the historical context into account when interpreting the Sermon. The expectation of the end time, the urging of the Spirit, and the threat of persecution certainly contributed a special vitality and forcefulness to the Gospel precepts. Yet nowhere in the Sermon itself do we find any textual reference to a time limit for the fulfillment of its injunctions. The preaching of love for neighbor and even for enemies, for example, sets no limit as to time or persons; its thrust seems quite the opposite. So our problem is still with us.

4. The Sermon, A Social Program

It seems appropriate to mention Tolstoy's interpretation of the Sermon here, even though it is not directly theological. According to him, the Sermon was a blueprint for a new society ruled by love and enjoying peace; it would be the Kingdom of Christ on earth. The Sermon was to be accepted and carried out literally, notably the phrase "Offer the wicked man no resistance." Tolstoy saw as the logical result of the Sermon the abolition of armies, courtrooms, and oaths. His interpretation was directly social and political; he missed its distinctly spiritual level. For him the Kingdom of Heaven would come in this world if we followed the Sermon. We simply wonder if Tolstoy's nonviolent interpretation perhaps prepared the way for the violent methods of communism, by helping to weaken the resistance of the Russian people.

5. The Lutheran Interpretation

Luther read the Sermon on the Mount in light of the Letter to the Romans and its critique of the Law. He recognized that the Sermon confronts us with the impossible, but this was in order to make us aware of our sins and lead us through this revelation to repentance and faith. According to Luther, Christ alone fulfilled the precepts of the Sermon, as a substitute for us all. He alone possessed the necessary justice, and could clothe us with it through faith. But this justice remained extrinsic to us, and there could be no question of requiring Christians to do the works indicated in the Sermon. This would be to fall back into the error of seeking justification through works. Luther also rejected the "third use of the law," which sees in the Law an indication of God's will for those who have faith and want to conform their lives to it.

Luther's interpretation of the Sermon was merely an application of his teaching on justification and the Law. The Sermon was treated as the Old Law. It played the same role of prosecutor, with still stronger demands. This stress on justification by faith without works produced a break, an opposition in fact, between the Letter to the Romans and the Sermon and between St. Paul and St. Matthew, in the heart of the entire Protestant tradition. The Sermon was viewed as a law that promised justice in return for works. No matter how excellent, such a text would be considered inferior to the Pauline doctrine of justification by faith and would be interpreted in its light. Even if it were not suspect, it would remain subordinate.

To our surprise, we thus find Protestant thought in agreement with post-Tridentine Catholic tradition, at least on this point: the relegation of the Sermon on the Mount to a marginal position with respect to the central teachings. The Decalogue now claimed first place in Catholic moral teaching and in Protestant morality, particularly that inspired by Calvinism. On both sides we note a separation, too, between faith and morality as the measure of conduct.

The Question of the Relation between the Sermon on the Mount and Christian Ethics

Our study of various interpretations of the Sermon on the Mount raises a fundamental problem. How is it that this text, attributed to the Lord himself and for long the privileged source for Christian moral teaching, has been brusquely set aside and largely ignored by ethicists, both Catholic and Protestant? Furthermore, the difficulty in interpretation persists in spite of all the explanations proposed: Does not the Sermon challenge us to the impossible? Is it not impracticable? How then can it to be included in a moral system?

To help us clarify these problems, I believe it would be useful to consult one of the great architects of Christian ethics, St. Augustine, and particularly his commentary on the Sermon of the Lord, as he loves to call it.

St. Augustine is one of the principal witnesses to the patristic tradition and is in the best position to teach us how the Sermon was interpreted in the early Church. He can show us how to read the Sermon and will throw light on our problems. St. Augustine has the advantage of having been at the same time a theologian and an exegete, like the Church Fathers, a preacher and a man of experience. His exegesis was wholly the fruit of study, prayer and life, both his own and that of his people.

St. Augustine's commentary on the Sermon of the Lord has a particular interest for us. In my opinion it has unfortunately been eclipsed, doubtless because it was considered a minor work in comparison to the masterpieces that followed it. When we study it at close hand, however, we see that it contains a preliminary sketch for a presentation of Christian ethics in immediate contact with the Gospel, and some fruitful intuitions, which were to create a rich tradition. Almost all the medieval commentaries on the Sermon go back to Augustine's. St. Thomas, when he was about to compose his *Summa theologiae,* re-read the commentary of Augustine and drew from it (more successfully than his predecessors) the main ideas he would integrate into his own moral structure. Rarely has any preaching had such resonance or brought such influence to bear on theology.

II. FIVE MAJOR INTUITIONS OF ST. AUGUSTINE IN HIS COMMENTARY ON THE SERMON ON THE MOUNT

The commentary on the Sermon on the Mount was St. Augustine's first pastoral work. Scarcely had he been ordained a priest, at the beginning of the year 391, when his bishop, Valerius, put him in charge of preaching in Hippo. Augustine was thus the first African priest to assume this function, and his example served to spread the Western custom of having priests preach.

In order to prepare himself, Augustine asked his bishop for a few months of freedom. He spent this time in prayerful, reflective study of the Bible. He also set himself to commit the Scripture to memory, as he had learned to do in the schools of rhetoric. It was a living process, designed for meditation and the communication of the faith, and in harmony with the style of the Gospel itself, composed as it is of brief sayings easily memorized. Thus Augustine's preaching, particularly in his first work, would be sown with biblical quotations.

We are dealing therefore with a "novice" at preaching. Augustine wrote out his first homilies and learned them by heart, then revised the text for publication. His commentary thus combined two genres, being written in book form and also delivered as a homily. It does not have the spontaneity of the later homilies on the Psalms and on John. Since it was not a spontaneous work, we find in it the repetitions of the preacher and digressions designed to satisfy the topical interests of his hearers.

I should add at once, however, that these homilies are the work of a first-class rhetorician and one of the geniuses of Christian thought, who reached full maturity before the age of forty. The commentary contains some very rich ideas, which created a tradition and exerted an influence for centuries.

Augustine's commentary on the Sermon on the Mount possesses, in fact, more than one dimension. It is obviously pastoral in aim, which places it in the ambience of the Lord's Sermon, addressed by Jesus to the people. It is also personal, for Augustine applied the teaching of the Sermon to himself and tried to live by it. It is his own experience that he communicates in his preaching. As A. G. Hamman writes, "In filagree, the personal experience of Augustine is revealed; he is shaken by the overwhelming discourse, the charter he has made his own. The conversion he preaches is the story of his own life; the hunger for happiness that devoured him has been appeased with the Beatitudes, beyond the measure of his quest, beyond his thirst." The *Confessions,* which re-count this experience for us, were written some years later.

Because of Augustine's genius, the commentary on the Sermon also possessed a specifically theological dimension. Its structure was formed by several major concepts, which marked a preliminary organization of evangelical moral teaching and would pass into theological tradition.

Obviously, the commentary had its exegetical dimension. It was one of the earliest examples of Augustinian exegesis; the method would be described in his *De doctrina christiana* several years later. Here Augus-tine's first principle of theological thought was clearly explained: Scrip-ture was the wellspring, the direct source of Christian teaching, preach-ing, catechesis, and theology as well, a hearth of light and life for all Christians. From these perspectives, the Sermon on the Mount held a privileged place for Augustine.

We shall consider here the five major theological intuitions that in-spired St. Augustine's commentary on the Sermon. They will provide the principal features of the model we are trying to discover: a Christian ethics based on the Sermon on the Mount.

1. The Sermon on the Mount, A Charter for Christian Living

St. Augustine's first intuition was that the Sermon on the Mount is the perfect model of Christian life, a summary of the Lord's teachings on fitting conduct for his disciples. This perception determined his choice of the Sermon as the subject of his first preaching.

His choice was an original one; St. Augustine was the only Church Father to make his own commentary on the Sermon, apart from general commentaries on St. Matthew. Augustine realized he was departing from the common way. He felt the need to excuse his audacity on the grounds of the Lord's authority: "This affirmation [that the Sermon is the perfect model for Christian living] is not really rash; it is based on the Lord's own words."

His choice was guided, clearly, by pastoral considerations. Augustine wanted to speak with the people of Hippo about what would be of the greatest interest and value to them. The Gospel teaching on right con-duct brought them Christ's answer to their deepest questions about hap-piness, a way of life, virtues, and precepts that would lead them to God and help them to solve their daily problems. It was a moral catechesis he planned for his hearers, in perfect harmony with the Evangelist's own purposes.

But Augustine's viewpoint was also theological. He saw in the Sermon a complete, perfect teaching on Christian morality. In his introductory paragraph he returned to this idea of perfection three times: "I think that whoever meditates in earnest love upon the Lord's Sermon on the Mount, found in St. Matthew's Gospel, will find there a perfect model for Christian living [*perfectum vitae christianae modum*], in respect to the most fitting way to act." He then added: "At the close of the Sermon we see that it has brought together all the precepts we need for our guidance in life [*quae ad informandam vitam pertinent*]." And in his conclusion he affirmed: "I have made these observations to show that this Sermon is perfect, since it gives us all the precepts needed for Christian living [*quibus christiana vita informatur*]."

The moral perfection of the Sermon was the unifying theme of his discourse, found first of all in its content: it assembled all the necessary precepts with a kind of amplitude. We need to note here that the term *precept* was used in a broad sense, for it designated not only the Beatitudes but also the precepts of the new justice that followed them, such as the prescriptions on fasting, prayer, and forgiveness.

Augustine found further perfection in the sevenfold form the Sermon takes. For him, as for patristic tradition, the number seven was a symbol of perfection and plenitude. This was not Augustine's invention. He drew it from Scripture, from Psalm 11, as he remarked at the end of his commentary: "The words of the Lord are chaste words, silver mined from the earth, purified by fire, seven times refined. This number has inspired me to relate these precepts [the entire Sermon on the Mount] to the seven Beatitudes, which the Lord places at the beginning of the Sermon, and also to the seven works of the Holy Spirit mentioned by the prophet Isaiah." The idea was not new to St. Augustine, for in his commentary on Psalm 11 he had said, "There are seven degrees of blessedness noted by the Lord in his Sermon on the Mount as reported in St. Matthew: 'Blessed are the poor in spirit, etc. . . . blessed are the peacemakers.' You can see that the whole Sermon flows from these seven sayings. Because the eighth one, where it says, 'Blessed are they who suffer persecution for justice's sake,' refers to the fire in which the silver is seven times refined."

Augustine's appeal to the symbolism of the number seven was not as artificial from the exegetical point of view as we might be tempted to think. In connection with the seven petitions of the Our Father, the Jerusalem Bible notes: "The Lord's Prayer in its Matthaean form has seven petitions. The number is a favorite of Matthew's: 2 x 7 generations in the Genealogy (1:17); 7 beatitudes (5:4ff); 7 parables (13:3ff); forgiveness not 7 but 77 times (18:22); 7 woes for the Pharisees (23:13ff);

7 sections into which the Gospel is divided. Matthew may have added to the basic text (Lk 11:2–4) the third and seventh petitions in order to get the number 7" (Mt 6:9, note b).

Augustine's intuition was clear and firm: the Sermon on the Mount was the perfect rule of life for Christians. It could be called the charter of the Christian life. To gauge the value of this intuition we need to see that Augustine did not isolate the Sermon from the rest of Scripture but saw it as a summit upon which all revealed moral teachings converged. The Sermon was said to be the perfection of this teaching, in the sense that it contained and fulfilled all its precepts. We can say of it what Augustine was to say of the Lord's Prayer in his letter to Proba, where he remarked that every Christian prayer should flow from and harmonize with it.

Augustine had a very strong sense of this living concentration of Scripture within certain texts of the New Testament, texts that emphasized Scripture's immediate orientation to Christ, to his Word, his actions, his person. Augustine's art consisted in showing us Scripture as it stood out in bold relief against its background. Thus we see the Sermon on the Mount as the culminating point of evangelical moral teaching.

Here we are sounding the depths of Augustine's thought. The Sermon on the Mount had such import and resonance for him because it was the Word of the Lord, as the Our Father was the prayer of the Lord. Augustine took up the theme of the Evangelist when he reported that Jesus spoke with an authority that struck the crowds, and gave us the characteristic expression, "You have heard . . . but I say to you." The Sermon was the word of Christ who elicits our faith and enlightens it. Augustine's teaching was also an expression of his own faith seeking to understand and then communicate the word of Jesus as one plays a searchlight over a darkened terrain. His preaching was but a prolongation of the Lord's. The Sermon on the Mount thus became the basis for preaching and the wellspring of Christian ethics. We are at the source of Augustinian evangelism, which was to continue through the Middle Ages.

I should like to mention briefly its historical prolongation in theology. St. Thomas grasped the significance of Augustine's intuition more clearly than all the theologians who preceded him. He referred to it explicitly when he declared that the Sermon on the Mount was definitively the representative text of the New Law (IaIIae, 108 a 3).[2]

---

2. He was preceded in this by the summa of Alexander of Hales, but he reestablished in a new way the connection with St. Augustine's commentary.

Studying the content of the New Law, he started with a summary of a quotation from the beginning of Augustine's commentary on the Sermon: "We should notice that when [the Lord] said 'He that hears these my words,' his words signify that the Lord's discourse is perfect [because it contains] all the precepts that make up the Christian life." In his response he continued, "As Augustine shows, the Sermon which the Lord gave on the Mount contained everything pertaining to the Christian life [*totam informationem vitae christianae continet*]. It sets in order perfectly all the interior movements of the human person." We recognize in these terms the guiding thought of Augustine, notably in the word *informationem*, which designates formation or the orientation of life and activity to perfection.

Regarding this Father Guindon wrote: "It was not enough for St. Thomas to quote this rich Augustinian intuition. He made it his own, and in assimilating it gave it an even loftier interpretation than St. Augustine. . . ." I would simply say that in this concept of the Sermon as the perfect charter for the Christian life, St. Thomas met St. Augustine on a personal level as a disciple, at once faithful and creative.

2. The Beatitudes, Seven Stages in the Christian Life

Augustine's second intuition was his interpretation of the Beatitudes as representing seven degrees or stages leading the Christian from humility or poverty in spirit to wisdom and the vision of God.

St. Ambrose had preceded him, between 388 and 392, in expressing this view in his commentary on St. Luke (PL 15, 5.1734–39). He there interpreted the eight beatitudes of St. Matthew as the progressive ascent of the Christian from detachment from the goods of this world to the crown of martyrdom, with each stage or virtue leading to the next. At the same time St. Ambrose connected the four beatitudes in St. Luke with the four classic virtues of prudence, justice, temperance, and fortitude.

St. Augustine took up St. Ambrose's idea but developed it in his own personal way.[3] He first considered the beatitudes as a group of seven;

3. Cf P. Rollero, commentary on the *Expositio in Lucam* in *Augustinus Magister,* vol. 1 (Paris, 1954), 211–21. Also, the *Expositio evangelii secundam Lucam* of Ambrose as the source of Augustinian exegesis (University of Turin; published by the Faculty of Letters and Philosophy, Oct. 4, 1958). A. Mutzenbecher gives as Ambrose's source for the interpretation of the eight beatitudes according to the stages of the ascent to God, St. Gregory of Nyssa's commentary, dated 387. Did this have a direct influence on Augustine? There are similarities between the two commentaries, but the dependence is not certain. Cf. Gregory of Nyssa, *The Beatitudes* (Westminster, Md.: Newman Press, 1954).

in his mind the eighth was a summation of all the others and fulfilled them by returning to the initial promise of the Kingdom. This clearly fits in with his penchant for the number seven. In Augustine's view it was in no way a lessening, but rather an indication of plenitude, since these seven beatitudes affected the entire life of a Christian, from conversion to the vision of God, where they reached their fulfillment. They had their place throughout the whole life of the Christian.

In his interpretation of each beatitude and their mutual relations, St. Augustine was equally original, for here he made use of his wealth of personal experience, described in the *Confessions* a few years later. The connection between the explanation of the Beatitudes and Augustine's first masterpiece is so close that we could almost propose a division within the *Confessions*, beginning with the journey of the soul described in the commentary on the Beatitudes.[4] The discussion of certain beatitudes clearly evokes Augustine's experience—for example, the relation he notes between the beatitude of meekness and the reading of Scripture. For Augustine also, the Beatitudes describe his own journey following his conversion. The road was leading him toward the wisdom of God, for which he longed with all his heart and which he discussed in the closing books of the *Confessions*.

Yet we need not think that Augustine's personal experience slanted his reading of the Beatitudes. Actually it was reciprocal: for Augustine the Beatitudes came first; they were the words of Christ that lit up his whole life and named his experience; they taught him how to read and understand his own story. The Gospel words direct practical life, and putting them into practice deepens our understanding of them. This give and take characterized Augustine's interpretation of the Sermon and made it also an interpretation of experience. The practical aspect was essential, as Augustine himself reminds us at the end of his commentary: "Whether a person accepts this division [of the Sermon according to the seven beatitudes, as I have suggested] or some other, the important thing is to act upon what we have heard from the Lord, if we would build upon rock."

Because it found resonance in the words of the Beatitudes, St. Augustine's experience transcended the unique, personal sphere of his individual circumstances. It possessed a broad, general value, a significance for all believers whom he addressed, and it thus shared in the spiritual universality of the Sermon on the Mount.

4. U. Durchow, "Der Aufbau von Augustinus Schriften Confessiones und De Trinitate," in *Zeitschrift für Theologie und Kirche* 62 (1965): 338–67.

The Stages of Christian Life Portrayed in the Beatitudes

The action opens with the conflict between humility and pride. Humility, moved by the fear that is the beginning of wisdom (Sir 1:16), humbly submits to divine authority, while pride opens the door to every sin (Sir 10:15). Augustine turned aside from the pride of the philosophers to follow the way of humility traced by Christ (*Confessions*, 7.18.24, 20.26–21.27). His choice was made concrete in his attitude toward Scripture and in his docility and openness to the Word of God, which consisted in his readiness to be judged by it rather than to judge it himself, when it appeared difficult or obscure. Augustine had been "a blind brute, barking fiercely at holy writ," until he discovered, under Ambrose's influence, that it was "sweet with the honey of heaven and luminous with God's light" (*Confessions*, 9.4.8–12).

The light of Scriptures shows us our sins and makes us weep for them, accepting whatever correction we need, especially the giving up of those "old friends," which clung so to the young Augustine (*Confessions*, 8.9.21, 8.9.26). At the same time Scripture fills us with a hunger and thirst for justice, spurring us on to great efforts and courageous work. The evil allure of the passions is replaced by an attraction for the sweetness of God (*Confessions*, 9.1.1).

But we cannot reap the fruit of our moral undertakings without the help of a higher power, the mercy of God. The surest way to receive it is to show mercy to those who are weaker than ourselves. The heart of the Christian is purified by openness to Scripture, repentance and renunciation, personal effort and the mercy of God. We understand "through experience . . . that it is only normal for weak eyes to shun the same light that healthy eyes find delightful" (*Confessions*, 7.16.22). We grow in the ability to look upon God's light and to welcome his wisdom. This establishes us in a peaceful submission of ourselves and our emotions to God. Such was the wisdom Augustine longed for. He saw it symbolized by the highest heaven in the Book of Genesis, identified it with the heavenly Jerusalem, city of peace (*Confessions*, 12.15.20–17.24).

The beatitude of the persecuted, listed outside of the series, sums up all the Beatitudes as they are ordered to the Kingdom and shows their united strength, which no attack can overcome.

If we consider the interpretation of the Beatitudes as a whole, we see that it follows Augustine's own progressive experience in his conversion and life as a Christian, yet it is summarized in a few bold strokes to serve as a guide for all Christians. Two major experiences are coordinated here: conversion first, found in the first three beatitudes, then the search for wisdom, from the fourth to the seventh.

This recalls the division of the first two parts of the *Confessions*: the confession of faults, of what Augustine has been (Books I–IX); and then the confession of what he is at present, of his search for wisdom (Book X). Another underlying theme is the division between the active life, dealt with in the first five beatitudes, and the contemplative life, in the last two.[5]

This is a model for the spiritual journey. Its stages are not isolated, but bring out in ordered progression the principle elements of a Christian's personal life. Whether or not our hypothesis of a division of the *Confessions* according to the series of beatitudes is accurate, we can still find in it a preliminary sketch and general outline for the later work.

We should note, too, that the way of the Beatitudes is also a way of virtues. It introduces a series of virtues appropriate to this interpretation and different from the classical list of theological and moral virtues: humility, docility, repentance, hunger for justice, purity of heart, peace, and wisdom. This less systematic series harmonizes well with the description of Christian progress.

Carried on through History

We find the explanation of the Beatitudes as seven stages of the Christian life throughout the Middle Ages, up to the advent of scholasticism. In the ninth century there were, for example, Raban Maur and Paschase Radbert, in the eleventh St. Peter Damian, and in the twelfth St. Anselm, Hugh of St. Victor, and John of Salisbury, all of whom reveal their dependence upon St. Augustine. Scholasticism, which organized morality in the context of the theological and moral virtues, was to replace this genetic and psychological interpretation with a more speculative perception. St. Thomas saw in the Beatitudes the culmination of a succession of human responses to the question of happiness. Yet in his own way he took up Augustine's concept by associating with each beatitude a virtue attained through the corresponding gift. For him, too, the Beatitudes applied to the entire Christian life.

---

5. Cf. A. Multzenbecher, ed. Brépols, Introduction, pp. xii–xiii, *De consensu evangelistarum*, 1.5.8: two virtues are proposed, one active and the other contemplative.

3. Interpreting the Sermon in the Light of the Beatitudes

"The Lord described seven stages of happiness in his Sermon on the Mount recorded by St. Matthew. . . . The entire Sermon grows out of these" (Homily on Psalm 11). "The number seven has inspired me to relate all these precepts to the seven beatitudes with which the Lord began his Sermon" (conclusion of the commentary on the Sermon).

The third great intuition of St. Augustine was his interpretation and division of the entire Sermon, beginning with the Beatitudes. The Beatitudes are not simply an introduction to the Sermon, as has sometimes been thought, but a sort of keystone which dominates and divides it.

Some interpreters hesitate to create this division in the Sermon as the commentary does. A. G. Hamman writes: "Some editors, such as A. Mutzenbecher, go so far as to discern in the two books that make up the Commentary a redistribution of the material to fit the eight (seven) beatitudes. This is pushing the author's systemization a bit too far. From their viewpoint, the first book corresponds to the first five beatitudes and the active life; the second to the last two and the contemplative life, culminating in the vision of God. Accordingly, Augustine comes up with a numerical structure, to the delight of the Middle Ages." Father Hamman is unduly sceptical here, for a simple reading of the commentary shows the division of the Sermon according to the Beatitudes; it is done in broad outline but is nonetheless quite apparent. Father Hamman himself gives the division in a note: Book I: first beatitude, 5.13–10.28; second beatitude, 11.29–32; third beatitude, 12.33–36; fourth beatitude, 13.37–18.54; fifth beatitude, 18.55–23.80; sixth beatitude, Book II, 1.1–22.76; seventh beatitude, 23.77–25.86.[6] Actually the material division of the Sermon is less important than the precept. The Beatitudes pervade the whole Sermon as does the moral teaching it dispenses.

Augustine did not give us in his text the reason for this division. The number *seven* in Psalm 11 gave him the idea of relating all the precepts of the Sermon to the seven beatitudes. In reality, this ordering was determined by a basic idea: the Beatitudes give us Christ's answer to the primary human question about happiness, which is at the origin of the search for wisdom. Also, Augustine saw the Beatitudes as the principal part of the Sermon, just as the question of happiness dominates philosophy and morality.

St. Augustine expressed this view on numerous occasions. I shall sim-

---

6. *Explication du Sermon, Introduction* (Paris, 1978), 15–16.

ply quote from *De moribus Ecclesiae catholicae* (387–88), where he explains the moral teaching of the Church against the Manichaeans. "Let us inquire reasonably, then, how man ought to live. Indeed, we all want to be happy; there is not a person who would not agree with this even before the words are uttered" (3.4). In *The City of God* he wrote: "Since I must now discuss the appointed ends of the heavenly and earthly cities, I ought first to explain . . . the arguments men use to create happiness for themselves in the midst of the sorrows of this life, and the vast distance between their hollow pleasures and the hope held out to us by God, whose object is that blessed bliss he will one day grant us. This can be illustrated not only by revelation but also by the light of reason, for the sake of those who do not share our faith" (1.19.1).

In many of his works addressed in part to unbelievers, Augustine treated the question of happiness from the point of view of reason. He gave, in the *De moribus* for example, the Christian answer based on the charity that unites us to God and on the four classic virtues of prudence, justice, fortitude, and temperance. He showed how these acquire a higher excellence in Christians and become forms of charity.

In his preaching at Hippo, Augustine felt freer to speak as a Christian. Explaining the Gospel to the faithful, he could begin with the Beatitudes as the perfect answer to the question of happiness and make them the framework of his moral teaching. This perspective had, among other advantages, the possibility of throwing light on typically Christian virtues such as humility, penitence, mercy, and purity of heart, which do not stand out so clearly in the classifications of virtues found in Greek philosophy.[7]

Such was the basic idea, still in the outline stage, that makes division of the Sermon effective and fruitful. The symbolic use of the number seven was merely a way of expressing it.

St. Thomas adopted this idea. He made it the principle of his interpretation of the Beatitudes, and especially of his plan of moral theology in the Summa. Here again St. Augustine and St. Thomas have profound rapport: the Beatitudes are Christ's answer to the question of happiness and thus, together with the whole Sermon on the Mount, dominate Christian ethics. St. Thomas was undoubtedly the first scholastic theologian to have adopted this intuition of Augustine, giving it, in his treatise on the Beatitudes, the place of honor in Christian moral teaching.

---

7. For St. Thomas, in IIaIIae for example, humility is related to modesty, a virtue falling under temperance (q 161); penitence is not included among the virtues of IIaIIae, and is discussed with the sacrament of penance (IIIa q 85); mercy is an interior effect of charity (q 30).

4. The Beatitudes and the Gifts of the Holy Spirit

The most original note in St. Augustine's commentary on the Sermon was the connection he made between the Beatitudes in St. Matthew and the gifts of the Holy Spirit in Isaiah 11 according to the Septuagint. This prophetic text had already been used frequently by the Greek Fathers, but they, in line with the same text, attributed the gifts to Christ, the shoot from Jesse's stock. Augustine was the first to have linked the texts of Matthew and Isaiah, and consequently to have attributed the gifts of the Holy Spirit to the very Christians to whom the Beatitudes were addressed. That Augustine was fully aware he was being innovative is suggested by his discreet "It seems to me, therefore . . ." (4.11).

The connection between the Beatitudes and gifts might seem contrived if we read only St. Matthew's text, for he makes no obvious reference to the passage from Isaiah, but rather to chapter 61, which speaks of the Spirit resting upon the Anointed One of Yahweh and sending him to "bring good news to the poor . . . to console the afflicted." This fact does not detract from Augustine's profoundly scriptural intuition, rich and fruitful.

What is the point of this connection, if not to show that the Christian cannot follow the way of the Beatitudes without the grace of the Holy Spirit accompanying each stage of the journey? Augustine's idea, original in its form, was actually a development of the thought of St. Paul, frequently commented on by the Greek Fathers, that the Christian life is a life in the Holy Spirit.[8] In his preparatory retreat Augustine had meditated much on St. Paul, whose words (Rm 13:13) had occasioned his conversion. His very numerous quotations of St. Paul show how he concentrated on the Apostle's description of life in the Spirit, especially in Romans 8 and Galatians 5. Thus, in pondering the text of Isaiah, Augustine linked Paul with St. Matthew. According to him, the Beatitudes described the stages of the Christian life through which the Holy Spirit guides us progressively. Concerning the need for the Holy Spirit's help, we should ponder the lengthy meditation in Book 13 of the *Confessions* on the verse in Genesis depicting the Holy Spirit as moving over the waters. It is through charity and through his gifts that the Holy Spirit

---

8. St. Irenaeus had already, in the second century, represented the Holy Spirit as a ladder whereby we ascend to God: "Spiritus Sanctus, arrha incorruptelae et confirmatio fidei nostrae et scala ascensionis ad Deum" (*Adv. Haereses,* 3.24.1). The first rung was fear of the Lord according to Sir 1:16. In his *De Sacramentis,* St. Ambrose calls the Holy Spirit the guide to perfection (3.2.8).

leads us to rest and peace in God. Without him, charity cannot overcome the languor caused by earthly cares and the impurity of our thoughts.[9]

In every sense the overriding theme of Augustine was indeed Christian and notably Pauline: the Christian's life is a life according to the Beatitudes and the Holy Spirit. Augustine developed this theme by comparing the way of the Beatitudes and the way of the gifts in detail. He thus used his intuition in an interpretation at once exegetical, theological, artistic, and poetic. Augustine truly offered us "a new song," in the sense of Psalm 149, whose first verse he commented on so finely, showing how such a song is born of love and given by the Holy Spirit. It is small wonder if in this song of Beatitudes and gifts, St. Augustine's thought took liberties with staid reason or textual logic. If he was upheld by the Holy Spirit, who could prevent him from displaying the riches he had discovered in his meditation on the Scriptures?

We should note in passing how easily St. Augustine passed over the chasm later created by Protestant thought between the Sermon on the Mount and the Letter to the Romans. The relation between Beatitudes and gifts unites Matthew and Paul closely through Isaiah. We shall come upon the same seamless convergence in St. Thomas's teaching on the Gospel Law: he defined it by citing chapter 3 of Romans, which speaks of the law of faith, and chapter 8, which tells us of the law of the Spirit. Further on, he assigned the Sermon on the Mount as the proper text of this law (IaIIae, q 108, a 1 and 3). Far from seeing opposition between these great texts, these doctors experience the need to unite them, interpreting them by means of each other.

The Beatitudes and the Gifts

Let us look briefly at the relations of the Beatitudes to the gifts. Our understanding of them depends far more on experience and meditation than on textual study. The first thing St. Augustine saw was that in order to establish a correspondence he had to reverse the order of gifts, which

---

9. Let me quote this marvelous passage: "In this gift of yourself [the Holy Spirit] we find repose. Here we rejoice in you, we dwell in rest. Love lifts us up, your good Spirit lifts our lowliness above the gates of death. . . . My love is my weight; this it is that bears me aloft, wherever I am borne. The gift of yourself sets us on fire and carries us aloft. It enkindles us and we ascend. We mount the steps within our heart and we sing the gradual psalm. Your fire, your good fire inflames us and we mount, for we are going up to the peace of Jerusalem . . ." (13.9.10). In this beautiful text we can perceive the interpretation of the Beatitudes as tracing the gradual ascent from humility to peace under the guidance of God's word, seven times purified in the fire of the Spirit.

begin in Isaiah with wisdom, the highest, and end with fear of the Lord, which corresponds to poverty and humility. He returned to this parallelism on two occasions: in *De doctrina christiana* 2.7.9–11, that is, in his first years as a bishop; then in sermon 347, undated. Each time there are variants, for Augustine's thought was too vital to be simply repetitive.

The gift of fear corresponds to poverty and humility because it makes the heart humble and contrite. It also alerts us to our human condition, so that we will accept the challenge of the cross.

Filial piety is associated with an attitude of docility to Scripture. It inspires us to follow God's will as revealed in his Word and in all the happenings of life, even when they go against the grain, as they so often do, since they fall under his Providence.

The blessedness of those who weep is paired with the gift of knowledge, which reminds us that we are sinners before God and shows us how we are to love God for his own sake and to love our neighbor in God. This knowledge inspires us to do penance but shields us, too, from despair.

The gift of fortitude sustains the efforts of those who hunger and thirst for justice. The world is crucified to them and they to the world. Their love leads them toward eternal goods, toward the Holy Trinity.

The association of the gift of counsel with the blessedness of the merciful is unexpected, but in the light of experience it is a happy choice. The best advice the Lord gives us is that if we want his help in our weakness we must be merciful ourselves and forgive others. This advice is based on the typically evangelical connection between love of God and love of neighbor, which we meet again in the petition for forgiveness in the Lord's Prayer.

The gift of understanding befits the pure of heart, for their clear gaze penetrates the mysterious wisdom of God, "the things that no eye has seen and no ear has heard" (1 Cor 2:9). In his *De doctrina christiana*, Augustine makes it clear that this perception remains imperfect, "as in a mirror," for we walk more by faith than by sight (2 Cor 5:6–7). This purification consists in preferring truth to one's self and to all attachment to neighbor.

The goal of this progressive pilgrimage is attained through the gift of wisdom which corresponds to the beatitude of peacemakers. Wisdom is appropriate for those who are interiorly at peace, as far as is possible in this life. Sermon 347 adds: "And what is this goal, if not Jesus Christ? What is the wisdom of God, if not Jesus Christ? Who is the Son of God, if not Jesus Christ? It is in him, therefore, that we attain wisdom and become children of God when we receive this grace; and herein is perfect and eternal peace."

Notice here how three great themes in Augustinian thought are evoked and converge: wisdom, which is truth and charity; peace and repose in God, on which Augustine dwelt at the close of the *Confessions* and *The City of God*; justice, described in the Sermon on the Mount but already present in the commentaries on Genesis, where it is seen as a human quality in Paradise. The seventh beatitude and the gift of wisdom gather up all the yearnings of Augustine's heart and all the divine promises, which shall fulfill them.

To complete his exposition, Augustine explained the rewards attributed to each beatitude. He saw them as different names given to the one, unique reward that is the Kingdom of heaven, names appropriate to each stage of the journey. The Kingdom was identified with wisdom; fear was its beginning, the peace of God its culmination. It was also presented as an inheritance, consolation, replenishment, mercy, and the vision of God.

The eighth beatitude included and confirmed all the others. It represented humanity in all its perfection. Augustine, using the symbolic figure of fifty days, related it to the feast of Pentecost. This is the final achievement of the work undertaken and brought to completion by the Holy Spirit.

Throughout this schema, full of life and spiritual sensitivity, the main intuition is developed like a musical theme: the ongoing action of the Holy Spirit as the Christian pursues his course from beginning to end along the way of the Beatitudes. I should add that to speak of a spiritual journey as if it were something external to the moral life would be a betrayal of Augustine. His text does not give the slightest evidence of any distinction between morality and spirituality. The moral life is in continual need of the Holy Spirit's help and grace, as St. Augustine later affirmed so forcefully in his writings against the Pelagians.

The parallel between St. Matthew's Beatitudes and the gifts of the Holy Spirit in Isaiah 11 was St. Augustine's own concept and illustrates his influence on the numerous medieval writers who would comment on the Beatitudes. Scholastic theologians were to retain the idea, giving it a new form. Taking as their moral foundation the theological and cardinal virtues, they would relate them to the gifts and Beatitudes in the manner of St. Augustine. St. Thomas, notably, would introduce this concept of morality into the very structure of his *Summa*. He would base morality on the connections among the virtues, gifts, and Beatitudes, adding to them the fruits of the Holy Spirit mentioned in the Letter to the Galatians. He would work out precise definitions of the gifts and Beatitudes, which became classic and, in the *secunda secundae* he would have one beatitude correspond to each virtue, adopting the relationships established by St. Augustine. We could never understand these connections in the *Summa* without some knowledge of St. Augustine's commentary on the Sermon.

Once again we witness the encounter of the two great theological geniuses of the Western church. It is true that some historians, such as Dom Lottin, have thought that St. Thomas's teaching on the gifts of the Holy Spirit was determined by the weight of tradition. However, the Angelic Doctor was hardly passive in his use of Augustine's ideas. In the *Summa* his discussion of the commentary on the Sermon is highly personal, far more so than that of any of his forerunners or of his own earlier works.

5. The Seven Petitions of the Our Father

St. Augustine's fifth intuition was to establish the connections (2.11. 38) among the seven Beatitudes, the gifts, and the petitions of the Our Father. This idea, too, was introduced with the words "It seems to me . . . ," suggesting that Augustine once more saw himself as an innovator. In his division of the Our Father, St. Augustine had already shown his originality. As Mutzenbecher observes (op. cit. P. XII), he was the first to have spoken of seven petitions. The Greek Fathers saw only six, for they combined the last two on temptation and evil. As with the Beatitudes, St. Augustine's interpretation inclined to the number seven. He maintained this division of the Our Father in his later works (except for Sermon 58.10.10 and his *De dono perseverantiae* 5.9). Here again the sevenfold stands for plenitude. The Our Father is the perfect prayer and should accompany the Christian throughout life.

Even if St. Augustine did not say so explicitly, we can easily guess the source of his inspiration. The Christian cannot follow the way of the Beatitudes and virtues without the help of the Holy Spirit, and we cannot obtain this help without continual prayer, the model for which is the Lord's Prayer.

This, then, is the profound import of the parallel Augustine established: the need for prayer at each stage of the Christian's journey. This being said, we can no longer be so brash as to accuse him of artificiality or ingenuousness.[10]

10. Cf. Father Buzy's article "Beatitudes" in the *Dictionnaire de Spiritualité*, col. 1309:

In the letter to Proba (*Letters*, 130) we have Augustine's entire thinking on the importance of the Our Father: "Whatever words we use (in prayer) . . . there is nothing we can say that is not found in the Lord's Prayer, as long as we pray fittingly. But if anyone says something not in accord with this prayer, even if there is nothing intrinsically wrong with his prayer, it will be somewhat carnal. For I don't know how you could call it good, since all who are reborn in the Spirit ought to pray only according to the Spirit." The Our Father was therefore the prayer of the Lord inspired by the Spirit; this is why all Christian prayer should be in accord with it. It could be called a universal prayer.

To develop this idea, Augustine related each petition of the Our Father to a beatitude and a gift. We note that he moved from the gift to the petition, doubtless because of the direct link between the Holy Spirit and prayer. (The accompanying chart illustrates his plan.)

St. Augustine concluded by drawing attention to the Lord's fifth petition, for mercy, which is our only escape from misfortune.

It is obvious—and Augustine was fully aware of this—that this is not a hard and fast arrangement. It is comparable to the development of a musical theme, which is not necessarily the only possible one. The important thing is that an arrangement should be balanced and expressive, meaningful for meditation and action.

We should also note that Augustine was not speaking here of a succession by stages. The petitions of the Our Father form, rather, an accompaniment to all the gifts and Beatitudes taken together.

Prolongation in History

Later tradition, up to the seventeenth century, adopted the parallelism of the Our Father with the gifts and Beatitudes. We find it in Raban Maur (PL 107, col. 822) and in St. Peter Damian (PL 144, col. 814).

But with Paschase Radbert (PL 120, col. 220ff.) there was a surprising reversal of the order of petitions, so that the beatitude of the poor in spirit and the gift of fear were made to correspond with the final petition for deliverance from evil, and so forth. This new order reappeared in a homily of St. Anselm (PL 158, cols. 595–97), as well as the commentary on St. Matthew by Godfrey of Angers, attributed to Anselm of Laon. This interpretation had the advantage of beginning with the humblest

---

"This time, with the interweaving of exegesis and theology, we have reached an apex of cleverness. Let us say that this [system] has succeeded in pleasing those who love intricate combinations; but it is so artificial that there would be little point in trying to include it in the current spirituality of Holy Church."

Gifts and Beatitudes	Petitions of the Lord's Prayer
1. Fear of the Lord gives happiness to the poor through the promise of the Kingdom.	1. Hallowing of the divine name through chaste fear.
2. Piety gladdens the humble of heart, who will inherit the earth.	2. That God's kingdom may come.
3. Knowledge gives joy to those who mourn, through the consolation it brings.	3. That God's will may be done in our souls and bodies, so that we may be established in peace and comforted in our inner struggles.
4. Fortitude gives happiness to those who hunger and thirst, and satisfies them.	4. Request for daily bread to sustain us with sufficient nourishment.
5. Counsel gives joy to the merciful.	5. Forgiveness of others' debts to us and of our own by God.
6. Understanding delights the pure of heart with vision.	6. Avoidance of temptations which create duplicity of heart; the simplicity of a heart fixed on God.
7. Wisdom brings happiness to the peacemakers, the children of God.	7. Deliverance from evil frees us to be God's children, crying out: Abba, Father!

petition, deliverance from evil, and leading up to the highest, the hallowing of God's name. We can see from this how much liberty can be taken with a tradition that is truly living. In this instance, St. Augustine perhaps hesitated to reverse the Lord's Prayer, as he had done with Isaiah 11, since it was the prayer of the Lord himself.

Scholastic theologians knew the parallelism of the Lord's Prayer and classified it as one of the numerical symbolizations so dear to the twelfth century. But they could not fit it into their own structures, which followed a different logic, more rationally rigorous but perhaps more distanced from the experience of the Christian life.

St. Thomas, for example, did not add the petitions of the Our Father to the virtues, gifts, and Beatitudes discussed in the plan of the Second Part. The Augustinian interpretation of the Our Father is found in his study of prayer, connected with the virtue of religion (q 83 a 9).

In III *Sentences,* dist. 34, q 1 a 6) where he discussed the gifts, the Beatitudes, and the petitions of the Lord's Prayer, St. Thomas adopted the Augustinian interpretation but followed a descending order. He began with the first petition and related it to the gift of wisdom, according to the order inaugurated by Paschase Radbert, and he ended it with the seventh petition, corresponding to the beatitude of the poor in spirit. He then added the relation between the active and the contemplative life, with a few other considerations.

In the *Summa,* St. Thomas repeated the affirmation in the letter to Proba, that all Christian prayer, which expresses our desires, should be in harmony with the Our Father. The latter teaches us not only what we ought to ask for but also in what order. Thus the Our Father is the prayer that forms all our affections (*informativa totius nostri affectus*). It governs the whole realm of affectivity and desire. The order of the petitions follows the structure of the *prima secundae*: the relation between God's ultimate end and all that is ordered thereto. The same kind of interpretation was used for the question of happiness as for the Beatitudes (IaIIae, q 69, a 3). The Lord's Prayer expresses the desire that impels us toward the divine beatitude as our ultimate end. It dominates our entire moral life.

In this article the correspondence of petitions with gifts and Beatitudes appears only in the ad 3 (q 83 a 9), where St. Thomas deemed it sufficient to cite St. Augustine's text in the commentary on the Sermon, following Augustine's order this time: first beatitude, first petition, and so forth. Contrary to the opinion of Father Buzy ("Beatitudes," in the *Dictionnaire de spiritualité*), St. Thomas truly adopted the Augustinian parallelism of the petitions of the Lord's Prayer with the gifts and used the original text. However, in the more rigorous ordering in the *Summa*, which follows its own logic, he could not accord it primary consideration.

Nonetheless when St. Thomas preached on the Our Father in Naples, toward the end of his life, he explained each petition in the Lord's Prayer in the light of the gifts of the Holy Spirit and followed the exact order used by Augustine in his preaching in Hippo, thus showing his deep esteem for it. Yet it is surprising that he mentioned the gifts only after the second petition. This is due to the fact that the first part of the text in our possession, up to the first petition, is not authentic.[11]

---

11. Cf. B. G. Guyot, "Aldobrandinus de Toscanella: source de la Ia Petitio des éditions de S. Thomas sur le Pater," *Archivum Fratrum Praedicatorum* 53 (1983): 175–201.

Summary

Our study has shown the fruitfulness of Augustine's commentary on the Sermon on the Mount. Rarely has any preaching had such resonance. This commentary was to be the principle source of numerous explanations of the Sermon, from the sixth to the thirteenth century. Its dominant concepts would be adopted by scholasticism and introduced, with variations, into the new theological structures. The utilization of this work was particularly important for St. Thomas in the composition of the *Summa theologiae*. Augustine's intuitions contributed to the determination of the New Law's place in the Sermon on the Mount and to the basing of Christian morality on the foundation of the treatise on beatitude. They inspired the arrangement of the Second Part according to the parallelism of virtues, gifts, and Beatitudes, and reappeared in the interpretation of the Lord's Prayer as the "form" of every prayer together with the virtues and the gifts of the Holy Spirit.

History has proved the richness of Augustine's commentary on the Sermon through facts, which a simple reading of the text does not yield. It is a valuable source for preaching, exegesis, and theology, and can be considered as a model for Christian meditation on Scripture.

The Role of the Commentary Today

What was the ultimate destiny of St. Augustine's commentary on the Sermon? It continued to be read, certainly, and is still cited today as a classic commentary. Nevertheless, it hardly produces the same fruits in our time that it did in the Middle Ages. The advent of nominalism and the concentration of moral teaching on obligation have made this impossible. After morality became mainly a matter of commands and prohibitions—without any consideration, among its basic elements, of the Beatitudes and the action of the Holy Spirit, and finally with the separation of morality from spirituality—the full theological and moral significance of St. Augustine's commentary was no longer understood. Ethicists saw in it merely a work of spirituality with some interesting interpretations of problems such as divorce. What they did not realize, however, was that this attitude marginalized the Sermon on the Mount itself as something extrinsic to morality. This was in direct opposition to Augustine's initial affirmation that the Sermon of the Lord was the perfect model or charter for the Christian life. Moral teaching would once more center around the Decalogue. No one seemed to realize that such a conception carried with it a serious risk of regressing to the level of Old Testament justice.

The Augustinian Response to the Question of the Impracticality of the Sermon on the Mount

In this context, the difficulty that obstructs and divides modern exegetes in regard to the Sermon carries greater weight than ever. With all its precepts, surely the Sermon commands the impossible? We can surmise how St. Augustine would have answered this question, if today's scholars had put it to him.

He would certainly have begun by clarifying the origin of ethics: it originates with the question of happiness, not with obligations. This has a direct bearing on the relation between ethics and the Sermon. If ethics is a matter of obligations, it cannot possibly assimilate the Sermon. The Lord's teaching penetrates the depths of human nature far too intimately to be viewed as a body of strict commands imposed by an external law.

On the other hand the question of happiness gives rise to an ethical system based on the attraction to truth and goodness, which readily harmonizes with the promises of the Beatitudes and the paths traced out by the Gospel precepts. Linked with the desire for happiness, the teaching of the Sermon penetrates to our inmost souls and responds to our deepest aspirations, purifying them and directing them to God. The inner logic of the two systems is born out by history. The Sermon played a major role in the happiness-based morality of the great Christian tradition. Later moral constructs of obligation, whether Catholic or Protestant, have been incapable of adopting or adequately explaining the teaching of the Sermon.

To the question of how the precepts in the Sermon could possibly be carried out, St. Augustine would answer in the words of Jesus: "For men, this is impossible; for God everything is possible" (Mt 19:26)—by recourse to the gift of Christ's grace, which is proper to the New Testament, as the entire patristic tradition teaches. In our commentary, grace refers specifically to the action of the Holy Spirit working through the Beatitudes and gifts. Thus we could say that the main lesson of the Sermon is about the works the Holy Spirit wishes to accomplish in us through the power of his grace, with our humble and docile cooperation, as described in the Beatitudes. The Sermon gives us the Spirit's promises and calls us to hope before telling us what we must do. Through the work of the Spirit, the precepts prompt us first to the inner obedience of love. By removing the study of grace and the gifts of the Spirit from moral theology, today's ethicists lose the specifically Christian principle that should enable them to answer the question about the practicability of the Sermon.

In his answer, Augustine united St. Paul's teaching on life in the Spirit and St. Matthew's on true justice so closely that they became inseparable. His association of the two concepts flowed from his meditation on Scripture and tradition and on his personal experience. This is what we might call experiential exegesis, in which understanding is acquired by living the faith and reflecting upon it.

Again, it is significant that modern theology has eliminated the patristic tradition in separating St. Matthew and St. Paul, either by the Protestant split between faith and works or by the Catholic concentration on obligation. The result is the same for both: Christian ethics loses the Sermon on the Mount and has no way of answering the difficulty about putting it into practice. Yet the Lord's word could hardly be more explicit and imperative: "Everyone who listens to these words of mine and does not act on them will be like a stupid man who built his house on sand" (Mt 7:26). Does this not apply to ethicists and theologians?

A Specifically Christian Ethics

St. Augustine's answer to the question of whether or not there is a specifically Christian ethics was very clear. He gave a preliminary outline drawn straight from the Gospel and based on a few dominant ideas. It was concentrated in three textual blocks: the Beatitudes, followed by the precepts or ways leading to them; the gifts of the Holy Spirit according to Isaiah; and the Lord's Prayer. It is wholly remarkable that St. Thomas, having personally re-read the commentary on the Sermon, used precisely these "intuitions" of Augustine to shape the Second Part of his *Summa*. It can be proven historically, moreover, that Augustine's text on the Beatitudes was the principal and most profound source for his own treatise on happiness, even before Aristotle's *Ethics*. St. Thomas always read the Sermon on the Mount looking over Augustine's shoulder. If he occasionally took liberties in his interpretation, he still shared the principal themes and gave them their entire theological weight.

Toward a Renewal of Christian Ethics

By way of conclusion, we can draw a few lessons from the teachings of St. Augustine that may contribute to the contemporary elaboration of an ethical system that is Christian.

1. The Sermon of the Lord is a perfect model or charter for Christian living.   The Sermon must once again become a basic text and primary source of moral theology, ahead of the Decalogue, natural law, or an assemblage of norms or rights established by pure reason. In the face of the rationalism of our times, this demands of us an audacious faith in the solidity of the Gospel, both at the intellectual and at the moral level. This is our only real chance to shore up today's moral edifice, shaken as it is to its very foundations by the winds, storms, and floods of our age.

It is less a matter of returning to Augustine and St. Thomas than of going back to the actual Word of God, the Gospel text inspired by the Holy Spirit in faith. In doing this we shall be following those two masters who made themselves servants of the Lord's Sermon. Their words are no substitutes for the Gospel, but they lead us to it. This is how we ought to read and exploit them.

Neither is it a question of reshaping moral theology in the material form of the Sermon on the Mount. These are two distinct literary genres, different types of teaching. Theology should express in its own language the dominant ideas of the Sermon, which convey the new justice. Moral theology would thus become the fruit of the Sermon on the Mount.

2. Interpretation of the Sermon and consequent shaping of moral theology in light of the Beatitudes.   Reintegrating the study of happiness in moral theology and giving it the primary role in light of the Beatitudes implies a veritable revolution for contemporary ethics. Duty-driven, compelled by obligations and commands, modern ethics is faced with a dilemma: either conform to morality and give up the idea of happiness, or seek happiness and abandon morality. The choice is crucial.

The Sermon, and St. Augustine's and St. Thomas's interpretations of it, can help us to reconcile morality with the desire for happiness. The reconciliation will not be easy, for it postulates an in-depth reshaping of morality. The concept of duty will no longer be central, but will be subordinated to that of virtue, and virtue's vitality and dynamism will have to be rediscovered.

3. The interpretation of the Beatitudes as seven stages of the Christian life.   St. Augustine's interpretation is one of many. Its advantage is that it shows the historic dimension of the Beatitudes, their integration in Christian history and in the history of the pilgrim Church. It harmonizes therefore with salvation history and lived experience. It also alerts us to the fact that we need to practice the Gospel virtues, from humility to purity of heart, if we are to acquire a vital understanding of the Sermon and to build up theology.

4. The correlation of Beatitudes to gifts. This leads us to abandon the separation between morality and spirituality (ascetical and mystical), in order to give morality a truly spiritual dimension, as "life in the Spirit." It is through the gifts, in fact, that the Holy Spirit inspires Christian life, giving believers interior light and impulse. The gifts are far more important for Christian living than all the charisms we hear so much about in the Church today.

5. The relation between the Lord's Prayer, the gifts, and the Beatitudes. There must be a link between personal and liturgical prayer— where the Our Father was placed—and theology. Today we realize more and more the need for prayer in theological reflection. Under the influence of rationalism, we have too long believed that theology was a work of pure reason and prayer a matter of emotion. We have forgotten that the theologian cannot acquire an experiential, accurate understanding of what he teaches without the light of grace and therefore of prayer, without his share in the gifts of wisdom, understanding, knowledge, and counsel.

Actually, whether or not we integrate prayer in the process of theological reflection is going to affect the essence of theology itself and its insertion into the current of faith. The principle underlying St. Augustine's own research convinces us of this. His assertion, "Unless you believe, you will not understand," can easily translate into: "Unless you pray, you will not understand."

As a final remark, let me say that we have no need to fear presenting the Sermon on the Mount to nonbelievers, on the pretext that only a natural ethic is appropriate for them. Experience shows, and the reading of commentaries confirms it: the Sermon touches non-Christians more deeply and has far greater appeal than any moral theory based on natural law in the name of reason. It is as if the Sermon strikes a human chord more "natural" and universal than reason by itself can ever do.

However this may be, we can never stop preaching the Sermon on the Mount to everyone. Theology is at the service of this kind of preaching. It is, in its own way, a commentary on the Gospel, designed to show us how to apply it in all the dimensions of life. And it is here that the works of St. Augustine and St. Thomas can be our models. This is precisely why they were written.

III. TOWARD A REDISCOVERY OF PRIMITIVE
MORAL CATECHESIS

The two studies we have just made, on St. Matthew and St. Paul, put us on the way to a rediscovery of primitive moral catechesis. Once we realize that morality is not limited to the narrow confines of obligations and commands but includes as its best part the study of happiness and the virtues, the moral teaching in the New Testament stands out in all its rich fulness. Biblical texts abound to illustrate this and have pride of place in the Scriptures, as the necessary supplement to the preaching of the faith. Obviously we are dealing here, as the Fathers of the Church saw clearly, with the earliest authentic sources of catechesis and Christian moral theology. We need to return to these again and again, to enrich our thought and our lives. A summary of the main texts of catechesis in apostolic times follows.

The Primary Text: The Sermon on the Mount

The primary text is none other than the Sermon on the Mount, proposed by St. Matthew as a summary of Jesus' teaching on justice and the moral precepts appropriate for his disciples. We have in this a clearly defined catechesis, which has been called a charter of the Christian life. The Sermon is unique in its authority; it enjoys the authority of the Lord himself, expressed in the clearest terms: "I have come not to abolish but to complete. . . . It was said . . . but I say this to you. . . ." "His teaching made a deep impression on the people because he taught them with authority" (Mt 5:17, 21–22; 7:28). Clearly in the mind of the apostolic community this was a primary source of moral teaching. It would have to be included in any theology fully faithful to the Gospel.

We should note that the Sermon, like the entire Gospel, is addressed to all, beginning with the poor and humble. St. John Chrysostom and St. Augustine knew this well and said it to the people. It can hardly be viewed therefore simply as a counsel reserved for the chosen few. The teaching is unequivocal: if you wish to enter the Kingdom of heaven, you must practice Gospel "justice." If you do this you are building on rock; if not, on sand.

The Sermon of the Lord is a model of the moral teaching of the primitive Church. It begins with the gift of the Beatitudes, which fulfill the promises of the Old Testament. With St. Thomas, we see them as

Christ's answer to the search for happiness. This teaching deepens the precepts of the Decalogue, penetrating to the "heart," where actions are conceived in the depths of a person and where virtues are formed, ranging from humility and gentleness to love for enemies.

The style of the Sermon is typical of a catechesis with its short sentences summing up the doctrine and its carefully worked-out composition, easily memorized and passed on to others.

Apostolic Exhortation or Paraclesis

Moral teaching was expanded with apostolic exhortation, called paraclesis rather than parenesis. We have to admit that the kind of apostolic exhortation found in the Sermon of the Lord is almost entirely rejected by modern ethicists. It is now considered as a minor, unimportant genre useful only for people who are aiming at perfection. It is sharply distinguished from a duty-driven morality or ethic, and is given the name *paranesis* to indicate that it is optional.

Once again, the mistake is a serious one, for exhortation seems to have been the characteristic mode of apostolic moral teaching. If we are faithful to the primitive Christian vocabulary, we will replace *paranesis,* a term very rarely used, (three times only: in Luke 3:18 and in Acts 27:2 and 22) with *paraclesis,* which designates an earnest exhortation. We might think of it as a technical term in St. Paul, for he often uses it to introduce moral teaching in his letters. For example, "Think of God's mercy, my brothers, and worship him, I beg you" (Rom 12:1. See also Phil 2:1; Eph 4:1 and I Peter 2:11). Paraclesis puts us in a relationship with God that has passed beyond legal justice to mercy. It is the most appropriate mode for the apostle when he is transmitting the doctrine of the Lord's mercy to his disciples, who have become his brothers and whom he addresses with the tenderness of a father. He does not give them orders as if they were servants, for he has already opened their hearts to love. He exhorts them by word and example, as his brothers and friends.

Pauline paraclesis is therefore definitely a part of moral teaching. It is catechesis similar to the Sermon of the Lord, but given in a manner suited to the apostle, whose authority is delegated. It is phrased in a chiseled style to insure its being passed on. The sentences are short and rhythmic and make use of assonance, as for example in Romans 12:9–13.

We have here a principal source of moral theology, constantly adopted by the Fathers of the Church in their teaching. The liturgy too provides this regularly.

It is important not to separate these moral passages from the dogmatic ones preceding them; for example, the paraclesis of Romans, chapters 12 to 15, should not be separated from the earlier chapters on the faith that justifies. This kind of separation is an arbitrary cutting, due usually to some later theological problematic, Catholic or Protestant. The virtues taught by the Apostle in his paraclesis are the direct and necessary result of the faith that justifies and the love of Christ poured into our hearts by the Holy Spirit. They are always related, often in an explicit and profound way, to the mystery of Christ: "In your minds you must be the same as Christ Jesus" (Phil 2:5).

A listing of the principle passages containing moral catechesis found in the letters of the apostles, in biblical order, follows.

Romans 12–15. The Christian life is presented as a liturgy, a spiritual worship we give to God by offering him our bodies and our persons within the Body of Christ. We have become Christ's members through baptism, and his charity animates us.

1 Corinthians. After having discussed a series of "cases of conscience" solved mainly in their relation to Christ and having to do with incest, appeal to pagan courts, fornication, etc., chapters 12 and 13 give us the hierarchy of the gifts of the Spirit. These are ruled by charity, which binds together the Body of Christ, the Church, and inspires all the other virtues, ministries, and charisms.

Galatians 5. A description of the spiritual combat, in which the flesh is opposed to the fruits of the Spirit, of which charity is the first.

Ephesians 4–5. An exhortation to unity in one Body and one Spirit and to the putting off of the old man to be reclothed in the New Man, "created in God's way, in the goodness and holiness of the truth."

Philippians 2:1–17 and 3:1–4, 9. An exhortation to imitate the sentiments of Christ in the humility and obedience of the cross in order to share in his glory, and to become imitators of St. Paul, stretching forward on his course to win the prize of the knowledge of Christ Jesus.

Colossians 3:1–4, 10. An exhortation to live a life hidden in Christ, to put on the new man, "a new self which will progress towards true knowledge the more it is renewed in the image of its creator." (Notice too, in Colossians and Ephesians, the two great initial hymns describing the mystery of Christ, given for Christian hope and contemplation: they show us our destiny in the divine plan.)

1 Thessalonians 4–5. An exhortation to holiness and vigilance while

awaiting the Day of the Lord, as children of the light, in imitation of Christ, who lives anew in our fraternal imitation of him.

We should also note in their entirety: The Letter of James and his sapiential teaching, so delightfully concrete; The First Letter of Peter, which is a real gem of moral exhortation (its teaching is often reminiscent of St. Paul and the Sermon on the Mount); The First Letter of John, with its great themes of light, sin and the world, charity and faith.

In my opinion, there can be no renewal of moral theology today without the rediscovery and exploitation of these Gospel sources. They alone can restore to moral theology its true dimension and spiritual vitality.

Finally, we should not overlook the riches of moral experience found in the Old Testament, notably in the sapiential books. These are frequently used by the authors of the New Testament.

7

Is St. Thomas's Moral Teaching Christian?

Is St. Thomas's moral teaching Christian? The question might seem odd, offensive even, in its reference to one of the highest theological authorities in the Church. Nevertheless, it is not new. It was expressed in the thirteenth century by the Franciscans in their criticism of the theology of the Dominican Master. They considered his teachings "innovations," and a number of his theses were condemned in Paris. The question was put forward once again in the attacks of Luther and Protestantism against scholasticism. In our own time the same question surfaces in accusations brought against expositions of Catholic moral teaching inspired by the *Summa theologiae.*

The Problem

The main criticism is that St. Thomas's moral teaching gives so much space to Aristotle's *Ethics* and the work of reason that it ought to be called Aristotelian rather than Christian. This recalls St. Jerome's dream, in which Christ treats him as a Ciceronian rather than a Christian. Aristotle's influence is so significant in Thomistic theology that we meet it everywhere, even in the study of eminently Christian realities such as grace and the theological virtues. It is almost like a pagan, Hellenistic intrusion, affecting all branches of theology, even to the vital centers that determine its structure and direct its orientations.

Furthermore, ethicists who consult the *Summa* are amazed to see that in St. Thomas's chief treatises on morality, such as those on happiness, actions, virtues and vices, law, and so forth, he never mentions Christ, nor does he show how these actions should be directed to the God of the Gospels, Father, Son, and Holy Spirit. Perhaps St. Augustine, reading the moral section of the *Summa,* might express the same regret he did in regard to Cicero's *Hortensius*: "Only one thing dampened my enthusiasm for it; there was never a mention of Christ." St. Thomas's moral teaching is not christological or trinitarian enough. It is too rational and Aristotelian. This is the problem.

These are serious criticisms. If they are true, if St. Thomas's moral teaching is not authentically Christian, or at least too little to be completely faithful to the Gospel, we shall have to say that the angelic Doctor helped to paganize Christian morality, that his influence vitiated all later theological tradition that still appeals to him as its source.

It is possible, however, to approach the question from a less polemical, more constructive angle. Scholastic authors generally seek to establish the truth by way of questions, by weighing the pros and cons. We in our turn can ask whether St. Thomas's moral teaching is Christian, not in order to throw suspicion on his teaching but to understand it better. We can make a loyal study of his work and of the criticisms leveled against it, so as to discern the specific notes of Christian moral teaching in his thought. St. Thomas's moral teaching is classic. We need to study it if we would acquire an authentic understanding of Christian ethics.

I. TWO PITFALLS

We shall respond to the questions raised above first by mentioning two possibilities in regard to the reading of St. Thomas. All reading and all interpretation depend partially upon the reader's attitude, of which he may not be fully aware. There are two traps into which the reader of St. Thomas can fall. These have had a part to play, as a matter of fact, in the criticisms already mentioned. It is absolutely necessary to correct certain propensities if we are to perceive the Christian character of St. Thomas's moral teaching.

Myopia

The first obstacle to a true reading of the *Summa theologiae* is myopia. Many readers are content to read questions on some subject that has attracted their interest: war, suicide, marriage, etc. They would not think of looking any further, or of studying the general plan of this work, which reveals the structure of the theological material being presented. The *Summa* can be compared to a cathedral. Each separate part, self-contained though it may seem, is so closely related to the whole that it cannot be understood or·interpreted correctly unless we are aware of where it fits In the overall plan.

This is why the second part seems so scantily christological and trin-itarian. It is the third part, centering on Christ as our one way to God, that gives to the entire *Summa,* and especially to the virtues and gifts, their christological dimension. Similarly, the trinitarian dimension of the *Summa* is provided by the study of the divine Persons in the first part. In order to undertake a study of charity according to St. Thomas, we would need to consider the questions devoted to the Holy Spirit seen as love and as gift, in the first part, and the grace of Christ formed in the Passion and communicated through the sacraments, especially the Eu-charist, in the third part.

It is no cause for surprise to find that the Blessed Sacrament is located in only one place in a cathedral: we know that It radiates throughout the whole edifice. In the same way, the *Summa,* a well-planned work, treats of Christ, the Trinity, and the Eucharist in specific sections de-signed to stand out in eminence for those who know how to take an overall view of the theological construction in its entirety.

The study of the *Summa theologiae* requires an effort on our part to keep the entire plan in mind, the vast expanse of the scene. We need keenness, too, to discern the background against which the various re-lationships between the material discussed unfold. This viewpoint, which develops as we continue to read the *Summa* regularly, enables us to per-ceive very clearly the Christian character of St. Thomas's moral teaching and to pick out the treatises where this dimension is most apparent.

Double Vision

By this I mean a way of reading through the lenses, so to speak, of preconceived categories that are not in the text and were never in the author's mind. Double vision is not an illness like schizophrenia, the split personality. It can affect perfectly sound minds, and deceive even the learned. It has the effect of bifocals, which give two levels of vision.

The preconceived categories that produce double vision in the modern reader of St. Thomas are the divisions between dogma and morality,

morality and spirituality (formerly asceticism and mysticism), and philosophy and theology. These categories are easily associated. Let us look at the effect they produce in the reading of the outline of the Prima Secunda. We will don our bifocals and peruse the text.

The treatise on happiness seems to be completely philosophical. Furthermore, we wonder if it has anything at all to do with morality, for modern texts of fundamental moral teaching no longer include it. Shouldn't it be classified as a kind of spirituality or as a philosophical exhortation leading on to the moral life?

The treatise on human acts is obviously a bit of ethics, basically philosophical. The section on the passions is marginal to moral teaching. Passions are reduced to a very minor role, ranked among obstacles to freedom. Besides this, there are some articles here, on love, for example, that really belong to the mystical order.

When we come to the treatise on virtues, we find it extremely philosophical, except for the theological virtues. As for the gifts, Beatitudes, and fruits of the Holy Spirit, they have nothing to do with morality properly speaking; they are about spirituality. The theological virtues themselves relate to morality only because of the obligations they impose. Naturally speaking, faith pertains to dogma and charity to spirituality, along with hope.

The treatise on sin is perhaps the most spontaneous one in moral theology. As for the treatise on law, we need to distinguish between natural law (the basic rationale for morality), human law (which is partly moral), the Old Law (with the Decalogue falling under natural law), and the law of the Gospel (which is much closer to spirituality). Finally, the treatise on grace belongs no longer to moral teaching but to dogmatics.

Clearly these distinctions, usually lodged incognito in the reader's head, have so dissected St. Thomas's moral teaching that there is hardly anything left but human acts, a smattering of passion, and a small sampling of virtue. The place in the sun is turned over to natural law and sin. We also note that the most explicitly Christian treatises have been removed from moral theory proper.

We have witnessed the decapitation of St. Thomas. This is literally true of the treatise on happiness, which dominates the entire edifice of Thomistic moral theory. It is equally true of the banishment of the action of the Holy Spirit and the New Law. Practically the entire Gospel capstone of St. Thomas's moral teaching has likewise been suppressed. Is it any wonder that the Christian dimension of his teaching is no longer seen?

It is obvious, however, that for St. Thomas the entire *prima secundae,* from happiness to grace, belongs properly to moral teaching and sets forth its basic, indispensable elements. There is nothing in the plan of the second part, carefully arranged as it is, to warrant the divisions and distinctions we have mentioned. On the contrary, the entire structure of this work moves from diversity to unity. Moral teaching is oriented to the contemplation of the divine realities treated in dogmatics. Philosophic reflection is integrated in a theological understanding that fulfills its desire for truth and happiness. As for the current separation between morality and spirituality, this was something totally unknown to St. Thomas and the Fathers of the Church.

If we want St. Thomas's answer, therefore, to the question of Christian moral teaching, we need to read the second part as a whole, with due attention to the layout and interconnectedness of the treatises, as indicated by the author himself. This done, we will be able to answer the question put to us, which can be formulated in these terms: What is the essence of St. Thomas's moral teaching? Is it inspired by Aristotelian ethics or by the Christian, Gospel tradition? Are we dealing with a moral philosophy passing for theology, or a theology so powerful that it could assimilate the moral message of Aristotle?

II. THE TREATISE ON THE EVANGELICAL LAW, HIGH POINT OF ST. THOMAS'S MORAL TEACHING

When we look at the treatises in the *prima secundae* dealing with specifically Christian topics and examine their emphases and interrelationships, what gradually emerges from the shadows is the treatise on the evangelical Law, also called the New Law.

In St. Thomas's moral teaching there are three towering peaks, which almost seem to touch the heavens: our journey in search of happiness, which culminates in the vision of God; the way of the theological virtues, which render God present to us; and finally the evangelical Law, which is the high point of all legislation issuing from the wisdom of God and communicated to human beings. It should be noted that these summits are found in the very treatises that have been removed from moral teaching by the "double vision" described above. By far the most neglected is undoubtedly the treatise on evangelical Law. Yet this is the treatise that demonstrates most clearly the fundamentally Christian character of St. Thomas's moral teaching.

The History of the Treatise on the Evangelical Law

St. Thomas's treatise on the evangelical Law (IaIIae, qq 106–8) was admittedly never a success in the schools. Most commentators completely ignored it. Cajetan (1469–1534), the prince among the schoolmen, made two brief comments on question 106 and was content to suggest that the reader memorize the two following questions, so that they might understand and explain the evangelical Law. He himself had no more to say on the subject.[1]

Billuart (1685–1757), who was the guide for so many manuals written "according to the mind of St. Thomas," after commenting at length on natural law, saw no reason to add what St. Thomas had said about the Old and New Laws. Besides, he remarked, they do not speak of this much in the schools.[2]

Suarez (1548–1617) had previously spent a good deal of time on the treatise on the New Law, but he simply accommodated it to the legalistic ideas of his time. As far as he was concerned, Christ was a new Moses and the Sermon on the Mount a new text of the Law, promulgated on the day of Pentecost. In any case, moral law, in his opinion, was contained in natural law. The majority of Catholic ethicists followed his lead in this.

We note in passing the original commentary of Patuzzi, O.P. (1700–1769; the adversary of St. Alphonsus), who was particularly interested in the New Law and held that the Sermon on the Mount was addressed to all Christians and not just to religious. But his opinion, which on this point follows that of St. Thomas and the Fathers, was not taken up.

Yet the study of the historical context of the thirteenth century shows us that the treatise on the evangelical Law was in large measure a product of its time. It was the theological expression of the powerful evangelism of the Franciscans and Dominicans. The *Summa* of Alexander of Hales contained a detailed study of the evangelical Law, much longer than that of St. Thomas.[3] But St. Thomas, while taking advantage of Alexander's work, still produced his own original work by condensing

---

1. "In qq 107–108 nihil scribendum occurrit, nisi ut mandes eas memoriae, ut intelligas Evangelii legem, et reddere scias rationem christianae legis."

2. "De lege veteri et nova, nemo melius fusius quam noster Doctor Angelicus, ideo, et quia de utroque pauce disseritur in scholis, lectorem ad eumdem S. Doctorem remitto." *De legibus*, dist. 5 a 4, last sentence.

3. Alexander of Hales, *Summa theologica*, 3.2 q 4.

this vast quantity of material into three questions and, especially, by working out a new definition of the evangelical Law, which made it the true foundation stone of moral teaching. St. Thomas's study was the fruit of a re-reading of the Letter to the Romans together with Augustine's *De spiritu et littera* and commentary on the Sermon on the Mount. His work brought out far more clearly the spiritual dimension of this Law.

In the three questions in the *Summa* (IaIIae, qq 106–8) we find a small masterpiece, which expresses in a most explicit way the specifically Christian character of Thomistic morality. It is all the more interesting to see how in recent years the treatise on the evangelical Law has finally emerged from the shadows of theological history and once again attracts the attention of ethicists both Catholic and Protestant.

Definition of the Evangelical Law

The definition of the evangelical Law is altogether remarkable. It is at once original, even audacious, and yet a return to the richest scriptural and patristic tradition.

The definition was new, and valuable for its distinction between the principal and the secondary elements of the evangelical Law. This distinction allowed for an accurate assessment of the various parts of the law and their functions. It was audacious in emphasizing the action of the Holy Spirit, which was so important that it determined the very nature of this law and made it chiefly interior, inscribed upon the heart.

Let us take a quick look at the text: "According to Aristotle, in the tenth Book of the *Ethics*, 'The essence of a thing seems to be determined by whatever predominates in it.' But what predominates in the New Testament Law, the source of its strength, is the grace of the Holy Spirit given through faith in Christ. Thus the New Law consists principally in the grace of the Holy Spirit given to the Christian faithful."

In a discussion of the new or evangelical Law, we would expect to see the Gospel text placed alongside the Decalogue, especially passages from the Sermon on the Mount which could be compared with the Mosaic Law. But this was not what happened. St. Thomas would even remark further on that the letter of the Gospel can "kill," if it is not animated by the grace of faith (art. 2). The essence of the evangelical Law was something other: it was formed by the grace of the Holy Spirit, given in response to faith in Christ. Here we are in perfect accord with St. Paul when he defines Christian action as life in the Spirit and when he places faith in Christ, rather than Jewish justice and Greek wisdom, at the beginning of the moral life. Further on, St. Thomas would refine this by pointing out that faith works through charity (q 108, a 1).

The names of the authorities or sources from which St. Thomas drew his inspiration follow. These are not quotations, however. Each presupposes a personal reading of the authors and evokes a rich background: "This is clear from what the Apostle says to the Romans (3:27): 'So what becomes of our boasts? There is no room for them. What sort of law excludes them? The sort of law that tells us what to do? On the contrary, it is the law of faith.' He says still more explicitly (Rom 8:2): 'The law of the spirit of life in Christ Jesus has set you free from the law of sin and death.' This caused St. Augustine to say in his work *De spiritu et littera* (chap. XXIV, 41): 'As the law of works was written on tablets of stone, so the law of faith was written in the hearts of the faithful.' And elsewhere in the same work (chap. XXI, 36): 'What are these laws of God written by God himself in our hearts, if not the very presence of the Holy Spirit?' "

Paralleling his work in the *Summa*, St. Thomas composed a new commentary on the Letter to the Romans. It contained the same elements but there was a certain hesitancy as to the definition. St. Thomas proposes two explanations of the expression "the law of the Spirit": "Firstly, it may mean the law that is the Spirit, for the Holy Spirit, dwelling in the souls of believers, does not limit himself to teaching them and enlightening their minds as to what they ought to do, but he moves their hearts to take action. Secondly, it may mean the law that is the effect or work of the Spirit, that is, faith operating through love, which teaches the believer interiorly and urges the heart to action" (*In Rom,* 8.11).[4]

In his study of St. Paul, St. Thomas was in agreement with St. Augustine, whose *De spiritu et littera,* Augustinianism in miniature, was a meditation on the texts of Romans and 2 Corinthians (chaps. 3 and 4). These describe the action of the Holy Spirit as lawgiver dwelling in the depths of human hearts, according to the promises of Jeremiah (31:33): "Deep within them I will plant my Law, writing it on their

---

4. ". . . hoc est ergo quod dicit: 'Lex enim spiritus, etc., quae quidem lex potest dici uno modo Spiritus Sanctus, ut sit sensus: Lex spiritus, id est, lex quae est spiritus; lex enim ad hoc datur, ut per eam homines inducantur ad bonum. . . . Alio modo lex spiritus potest dici proprie effectus Spiritus Sancti, sc. fides per dilectionem operans, quae quidem et docet interius de agendis, secundum illud I Jn 2: 'Unctio docebit vos de omnibus,' et inclinat affectum ad agendum, secundum illud II Cor 5: 'Caritas Christi urget nos.' Et haec quidem lex spiritus dicitur lex nova, quae vel est ipse Spiritus Sanctus, vel eam in cordibus nostris Spiritus Sanctus facit. 'Dabo legem meam in visceribus eorum, et in corde eorum superscribam eam.' "

hearts," and Ezekiel (36:26): "I shall give you a new heart, and put a new spirit in you; I shall remove the heart of stone from your bodies and give you a heart of flesh instead. I shall put my spirit in you. . . ." These texts proclaim a new covenant in the Spirit.

Clearly the definition of the evangelical Law was in the mainstream of the most authentic spiritual tradition: Jeremiah, St. Paul, and St. Augustine. It brought together prophets, apostles, and Church Fathers, putting their thought in the precise, theological terms of early scholasticism.

The last part of the definition contained a very important addition, even though it was referred to as secondary in relation to the action of the Holy Spirit: "The New Law also includes certain elements that dispose us to receive the grace of the Holy Spirit, or are related to the use of this grace, such as sayings or writings about what the faithful ought to believe or do, and in which they need instruction. This is a second group of elements of the New Law."

Among these second (and not secondary) elements ordered to the action of the Holy Spirit through faith and charity St. Thomas considered first the Gospel text and then the Sacraments, which communicate to us the grace of Christ. All that is institutional and visible in the Church can be included here. These are the instruments formed by the Holy Spirit for the work of grace, justification, and sanctification which he wishes to accomplish.

The conclusion was brief: "Consequently we must say that the New Law is principally an interior law and secondarily a written law." The translation "interior law" is approximate. It is difficult to find an apt term for the Latin *indita*. The verb *indere* means "put into" or "inspire," as we might say "inspire fear." Thus it means "to place within," which corresponds to Jeremiah's "writing it on their hearts." Only the Holy Spirit can act in this way within the human heart. And thus the New Law is wholly unique.

We can put it this way: the principle of the New Law, and consequently of Christian ethics, is not the Gospel viewed as a text or an external word, comparable to a physical body, but rather the life principle, the breath of God which animates this body. Without it would have only an inert material object. We hasten to add, however, that the body formed by the Gospel texts is indispensable if we are to receive the breath of the Spirit, for it was formed by him and is perfectly adapted to his action. The Spirit could not animate a body of doctrine that was not conformed to the Gospel.

The definition of the evangelical Law as an interior law, dependent upon the Spirit's action, was novel in the explicit, clear form given it by

St. Thomas. "In the scholastic tradition, the general opinion was that in the New Law the help of sufficient, fitting, divine grace was given so that we might carry out the divine commands—but that the New Law was properly speaking a *lex indita,* an interior law, was not stated by Peter Lombard or the Franciscans or St. Albert the Great; we do not even find it in St. Thomas's *Commentary on the Sentences.*"[5] Still less do we find, prior to the *Summa,* a complete definition of the evangelical Law, with the distinction between its principal and second elements, which allows us to show the connections between this treatise and every other part of the *Summa.*

III. THE EVANGELICAL LAW, CORNERSTONE OF THEOLOGY

The definition of the evangelical Law is extraordinarily precise and concise. All we need do is consider each of the words composing it, to perceive the relations that, like arches of a vault, join the New Law to the other treatises of the *Summa theologiae.*

The evangelical Law, St. Thomas wrote, is a "grace." This established a link with the treatise on grace and justification, which immediately followed and was continued in the study of Christ, Head of the Church, and the instruments of grace, in the third part.

The evangelical Law is the grace "of the Holy Spirit." Here we are referred to the study of the Holy Spirit as love and as gift in the heart of the Trinity, in the first part (qq 37 and 38), and then to the study of the gifts, Beatitudes and fruits of the Holy Spirit in the *prima secunda* (qq 68–70), and to the association of gifts with virtues throughout the *secunda secundae.*

This grace is given "through faith in Christ." The mention of faith, refined further on by the operation of charity, points to the head of the organism of virtues that governs the moral realm and determines its division. The reference to Christ leads us to the third part, consecrated to Christ seen as our unique way to God, but it leads us also to the study of the Word of God in the first part. We are clearly in the tradition of St. Paul.

5. U. Kühn *Via caritatis,* p. 194: "Es war zwar allgemeine Meinung in der scholastischen Tradition, dass in neuen Gesetz zur Erfüllung der Gebote auch die entsprechende zureichende göttliche Gnadenhilfe gewärt würde—dass aber der neue Gesetz eigenlich Franziskanern noch auch bei Albertus Magnus gesagt und ist selbst in SK des Thomas noch nicht zu finden."

Among the second elements, Scripture constituted the material proper to theology. Its study began with the first question of the *Summa*, and was developed by the consideration of the Gospel, its fulfillment and highest point. The sacraments, too, had a place in the definition (q 108, a 1), and the study of them is found in the third part.

Clearly, not only ethics but the whole of theology converges in the treatise on the evangelical Law, from the moment of its definition.

The Evangelical Law as the Head of the Body of Moral Teaching

The relationships we have just established are based upon a few words. But it is a simple matter to flesh them out and to show how the grace of the Holy Spirit, acting through faith and charity, is truly the head of the organism of virtues that shapes the structure of St. Thomas's moral teaching. We can picture this in the form of two circles, one above the other. The first begins with the grace of the Holy Spirit, whence the evangelical or supernatural virtues proceed. The second is joined to the first by reason and will, which receive the theological virtues and engender the human or natural virtues to form the second circle. These two circles function in the Christian moral organism as a circulatory system (see diagram).

Let me explain the diagram. The grace of the Holy Spirit engenders faith, hope, and charity in the human intellect and will. These take over the natural virtues ruled by reason: first prudence and justice, then fortitude or courage, and temperance. The last-named moderates sensitivity. In this way, a new moral organism is formed, which is specifically Christian.

The action of the Holy Spirit goes still further. Not limited to forming within us personal capacities for action, or virtues, it also engenders dispositions for receiving the spiritual inspirations and impulses needed for producing perfect works. This is why St. Thomas, following St. Augustine, added to each of the virtues a gift that perfects it. The gifts of understanding and knowledge correspond to faith, fear of the Lord to hope, and wisdom to charity. With prudence goes the gift of counsel; with justice, piety; with courage, the gift of fortitude. Temperance shares the gift of fear of the Lord with hope.[6]

---

6. Here we note a slight anomaly, due to St. Thomas's adaptation of the Augustinian teaching on the correspondence of the gifts with particular beatitudes. In his commentary

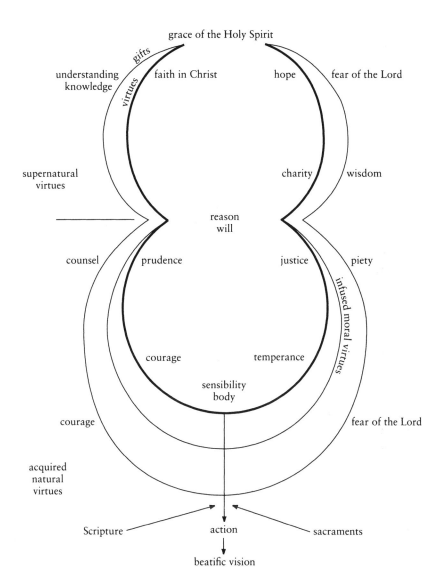

grace of the Holy Spirit

gifts

virtues

understanding
knowledge   faith in Christ   hope   fear of the Lord

supernatural
virtues

charity   wisdom

reason
will

counsel   prudence   justice   piety

infused moral virtues

courage   temperance

sensibility
body

courage   fear of the Lord

acquired
natural
virtues

Scripture   action   sacraments

beatific vision

It is clear, therefore, that the gifts of the Holy Spirit perfect the moral virtues themselves. This shows the integration of the moral virtues within the organism of the theological virtues and within the life in the Spirit which they produce.

The ordering toward supernatural happiness, which is brought about by the virtues and gifts, led St. Thomas to elaborate his theory of infused moral virtues. These are added to the acquired virtues to fit them for a supernatural end surpassing human powers.[7] These qualities penetrate the interior of the natural virtues, enabling them to act in view of supernatural happiness. When this happens, they are given a new criterion of judgment and proportion. The temperance that strives to preserve health reasonably becomes the temperance that, like St. Paul, "chastises the body and reduces it to servitude" for the love and service of Christ. The measure of Christian asceticism will differ from the requirements of simple reason. Similarly, infused chastity engenders the ideal of virginity, and infused fortitude that of martyrdom. Thus the infused moral virtues contribute to trace specific lines of Christian morality even at the level of the natural virtues or, as Father Fuchs would say, at the categorical level.

Not all theological schools have accepted the theory of infused moral virtues—far from it. Yet the theory shows us that, for St. Thomas, the theological virtues, which point us to divine happiness, work a profound transformation even at the level of the moral virtues, so as to engage the whole person, sensitivity included, in the action performed for this supernatural end. Thus Christian moral teaching extends even to the natural virtues, to give them a more perfect, characteristic mode of concrete action.

The diagram shows clearly how the evangelical Law is truly the head or soul of St. Thomas's moral teaching, penetrating all the members and acting within them, including even the least virtues, so as to regulate concrete actions and order them toward the promised happiness.

Within this moral theory we can easily distinguish the level of the

---

on the Sermon, St. Augustine began with the Beatitudes. Taking as the basis for his moral teaching the sevenfold theological and moral virtues, St. Thomas first established their correspondence with the gifts. Later, discussing each gift, he showed its relationship to one of the Beatitudes. The relationship is not a perfect fit, however, for the gifts of understanding and knowledge are joined to faith. This leaves only five gifts for the remaining six virtues. The treatise on temperance does not contain a study of a gift. St. Thomas was quite aware of this anomaly. He explained it in his consideration of the gifts (IaIIae q 68 a 4 ad 1) and relative to temperance (IIaIIae q 141 a 1 ad 3). This slight dissonance, which comes about more from the movement of life than from abstract logic, should not blind us to the profound truth inherent in the coordination of virtues, gifts, and Beatitudes.

7. Cf. IaIIae 63 a 3 and 4.

Gospel, with its revealed Christian teaching on the theological virtues and gifts, from the philosophical level of Aristotelian ethics and the moral virtues. But, despite the opinion of modern authors, there is no separation or opposition between the two. On the contrary, Aristotelian teaching is placed at the service of Christian ethics to the greatest degree possible and in all loyalty. The idea is supported that Aristotle, as a witness to humanity and reason, helps us to understand human nature as created by God. Yet it is the light of the Holy Spirit, given to us through faith in Christ and the gift of wisdom, that dominates the entire enterprise. St. Thomas's moral teaching is therefore primarily evangelical and only secondarily Aristotelian. Aristotle's teaching, together with the natural virtues, is lifted up into a new moral organism. It is assimilated and transformed. In St. Thomas's teaching we are not dealing with an Aristotle of the past, reconstituted historically, but with an Aristotle of the present, revitalized and actualized within a specifically Christian moral setting, where the principal role is played by the evangelical Law.

The Evangelical Law, High Point of Divine Revelation

In order to show more clearly the superiority that the evangelical Law enjoys in St. Thomas's moral teaching, a word should be added on its place in the treatise on law. Modern ethicists have conceived of moral law as an expression of the divine will and have centered it in natural law, expressed in the Ten Commandments, to such a point that the evangelical Law has for all practical purposes been set aside.

St. Thomas's view was very different. For him, law was a work of wisdom, first engaging the intelligence, and only then the will. His study of law was far more nuanced and dynamic. He distinguished five kinds of law: the eternal law, divine source of all legislation; natural law, which is the human heart's direct participation in this; then human law, which derives from natural law. Revelation further added the Old Law, centered in the Decalogue and relating to natural law, and the evangelical Law of the New Testament. These different laws were dynamically interconnected, beginning with the eternal law, descending through natural law to civil law, and ascending again toward God to reach their summit in the evangelical Law, the most perfect possible participation in the eternal law that can be found on earth and the closest approximation to our final goal (IaIIae q 106, a 4).

St. Thomas gave primacy to the evangelical Law. It prevailed over natural law and the Decalogue, obviously not destroying them but rather bringing them to perfection. In Christian moral teaching, all laws were ordered to the evangelical Law as to their perfection and earthly culmination, and were caught up in it.

We see once more, therefore, that all of moral teaching, directed by the various kinds of laws, is oriented to the evangelical Law. The questions that St. Thomas devoted to this subject are indeed a high point in the second part of the *Summa*, assuring its Christian dimension.

IV. THE SERMON ON THE MOUNT, TEXT OF THE EVANGELICAL LAW

Among the second elements of the evangelical Law, St. Thomas cited first of all the Gospel text, summit of Scripture. He clarified his teaching in question 108, where he discussed the content of this Law. Making explicit use of St. Augustine's idea and terms, he declared that "the Lord's Sermon on the Mount contains all teaching on the Christian life."[8] The Sermon on the Mount was a summary of Christ's teaching on Christian conduct. As such, and because of the authority of Christ himself, it was a privileged source of Christian moral teaching. It could therefore be considered the proper, typical text of the evangelical Law, even as the Decalogue was for the Old Law.

This endorsement of St. Augustine's view of the Sermon presupposes, as we have said, a personal re-reading of the commentary on the Sermon. What we might call St. Thomas's faithful originality comes to the fore in the way he used Augustine's idea and its interpretation of the teaching contained in the Sermon in order to integrate it with his own moral construct.

His explanation of the Sermon was extremely concise, in the manner of the *Summa*. Yet it is eminently clear for one who knows how to grasp the implications.

The exegetical interpretation of the Sermon was determined by the distinction between interior and external actions, which applies to all moral teaching and which was taken up in the treatise on human acts. St. Thomas first examined the Sermon's bearing at the level of external actions (art. 2) and concluded that there were no new teachings at this

8. "Sicut ex inducta auctoritate Augustini apparet, sermo quem Dominus in montem proposuit, totam informationem christianae vitae continet." Here he is obviously referring to Augustine's commentary on the Sermon discussed in the previous chapter of this book.

level. We shall return to this point later. The entire teaching of the Sermon centered, in his eyes, on the regulation of interior acts, of the will, intention, love, desire, etc. We need to understand clearly that the distinction between interior and exterior acts does not posit two completely different acts, but rather indicates the interior and exterior aspects of one concrete act. The act of the will is interior to the concrete action; it is its cause, the principle that animates and orders it. For St. Thomas morality operates principally or formally at the level of the interior act, and secondarily or materially at the level of the external act. This division would be found again in connection with principles of action, or virtues, seen as interior principles, and the law, with its precepts, as an external principle. The evangelical Law, however, had its own unique nature. As law, it had an external origin, superior to human nature, which was Christ's divine revelation. As the grace of the Holy Spirit, it penetrated to the interior of the human person and became the very source of the virtues, which were therefore called "infused." The Sermon on the Mount, in regulating interior acts, touched the Christian at the very sources of the morality of his actions. Its teachings had an essential bearing on the virtues that make up justice, in the biblical sense of the term— that justice around which morality is ordered.

Within this perspective, the plan for the explanation of the Sermon took its inspiration from the *Summa*. First came the teaching about happiness, then the relationships of the person with self and others, which evoked charity, the form of all the virtues.

The reference to happiness was quite brief. In literal translation it reads: "Having stated the end, which is happiness . . ." The Beatitudes were seen as Christ's answer to the question of happiness and our final end. In his commentary on St. Matthew, St. Thomas had interpreted the Beatitudes in this way: Christ considered all the human answers proposed to the question of happiness according to those things that were humanly most attractive; he then set aside faulty or insufficient answers relating to exterior and interior goods, in order to bring out beatitude in all its fulness. We rediscover the need for detachment from these goods in the course of the Sermon and of our article. The teaching on the Gospel Beatitudes was thus the primary source for St. Thomas's treatise on our ultimate end and happiness. The principal intention inspiring Christian action would be the following of the way traced out by Christ.

The remainder of the Sermon was divided in light of a twofold relationship. There was our relation to self, as we are oriented to our last end; this was regulated by detachment from other goods and leads us to love God supremely. Then there was our interior relationship to others, the area of fraternal charity. The end of the Sermon showed us how to carry out the Gospel teaching.

To understand this explanation of the Sermon, we need to remember the difference between Jesus' teaching, presented in concrete, popular language, and the terminology of a theological work like that of St. Thomas. We cannot expect to find identical divisions and structures. The thought patterns and expressions are too different. Nevertheless, St. Thomas's thesis is clear: the Sermon is the primary and highest source of moral theology. It vitalizes moral theology's inmost depths and works outward to regulate all of Christian morality. In his second part he translated the Sermon, so to speak, into theological and rational language, so that it might become available to all, believers and nonbelievers alike.

It should be made clear that the interiority where St. Thomas situated the teaching of the Sermon was not limited to the order of intentions and sentiments, as opposed to the order of external, concrete actions, as certain modern interpretations would have it. For St. Thomas the intention is directed to the external act and needs it for its own fulfillment. The external act, through its matter and circumstances, communicates to the intention a certain moral quality, and can help to develop the very quality that belongs properly to the intention (q 20 a 4). The intention and the act unite as soul and body to form the complete action.

The Evangelical Law and Moral Precepts

We need one final, important clarification regarding St. Thomas's statement that the New Law added no new moral precept to those of the Old Law as far as external action is concerned (q 108 a 2). Some interpreters have taken this to mean that, since Christian ethics has no unique precepts, it adds nothing essential to the natural morality expressed in the Decalogue. From here it is only a step to the conclusion that there is no such thing as a specifically Christian ethics.

Any interpretation will depend upon one's concept of the ethical dimension. If ethics consists essentially of obligations and prohibitions that determine precepts, it would obviously be easy to conclude from St. Thomas's statement that Christian ethics adds nothing new to natural morality and that it merely contributes a certain inspirational value, which does not modify its criteria for concrete judgment.

But St. Thomas's concept of ethics was quite different. For him, ethics consisted mainly in virtues and only secondarily in precepts, whose function was to determine what was necessary to make virtuous action possible. Virtues regulated moral action, beginning with a person's interior acts; precepts were directly concerned with external actions. This is why each treatise on a virtue closes, in the *secunda secundae*, with a study of the precept involved.

Therefore it is at the level of virtues that we must, according to St. Thomas, pose the problem of Christian ethics. It is quite clear that some virtues, such as the theological ones, are specifically Christian. These, together with the natural virtues and precepts, orient all moral action to the happiness revealed notably in the Sermon. What St. Thomas has given us is a new moral organism, properly Christian. In it, the virtues outstrip the precepts so effectively that, as the former increase, the need for the latter decreases. This is precisely why the New Law is called "the law of freedom": the action of the Spirit through the virtues creates within us a spontaneous, personal movement toward good acts. This in turn allows for a reduction of precepts to the minimum, so as to open up a wider field for freedom's initiative. But we need to understand very clearly that inspired by charity this spontaneity, far from acting against the precepts, tends to bring to perfection the moral qualities they would safeguard.

It would be a serious error, therefore, to interpret the limitation of precepts in the New Law to a reduction of Christian ethics to natural law or the Decalogue. St. Thomas would not see such a reduction as constituting a specifically Christian morality, which in his view lies principally in virtues and interior acts, as described in the Sermon on the Mount.

V. THE EVANGELICAL LAW, "THE LAW OF FREEDOM"

We have only to add a few words on a special note that, according to St. Thomas, is proper to the evangelical Law and that it shares with Christian ethics: it is a law of freedom. This sounds like a paradox to the modern ear, because we tend to oppose law and liberty, especially in the context of duty-driven moral systems. This was not the case for St. Thomas, because he saw law as a tutor, needed to guide moral freedom to maturity through training in virtue. For him, the expression designated the evangelical Law proper to Christians who had reached maturity through the action of the Holy Spirit, as described in Romans and in 2 Corinthians 3:17: "This Lord is the Spirit, and where the Spirit of the Lord is, there is freedom" (cited in q 108, a 1, arg 2). Curiously enough, the actual expression *law of freedom* is found only in the Letter of James, "the law of perfect liberty," cited in the response to this argument, which also explains the text from Corinthians as well as James 2:12. Apparently no opposition between St. Paul and St. James even occurred to St. Thomas.

The Evangelical Law and Free Spontaneity

Whatever may be the origin of the expression *law of freedom,* St. Thomas adopted it fully and gave three reasons for it. We have already mentioned the first: the reduction of precepts to what is necessary for salvation, leaving a wider scope for freedom informed by virtue.

The second reason had to do with the very nature of freedom. The person who acts of his own accord following a natural instinct that has been perfected by virtue can be said to act with full freedom. This is what Christian action is like when it emanates from the instinct of grace and the charity infused in us by the Holy Spirit. Let me note that the word "instinct" is a favorite one of St. Thomas when he is speaking about the gifts of the Holy Spirit: in question 68, which is devoted to this topic, he used it sixteen times. He was evidently referring to a spiritual instinct, which corresponded to the actual definition of the voluntary as a movement originating within a person who acts in awareness of a goal.[9]

This spiritual spontaneity, perfected by the virtues, characterizes the evangelical Law and causes it to be called a law of freedom. It animates all of Christian morality. For St. Thomas there was absolutely no question of a separation between this inspiration, which is the very perfection of freedom, and morality. Christian morality was spiritual in the Pauline sense of the word or it was nothing. Here we are at the opposite pole from legalism. Legalism is characterized by the external quality of the law as opposed to freedom and spontaneity, and by the tension set

9. Translator's note: *Instinctus* (the root of our English *instigate*) is a very general term for what prompts an action from a living being. Animals as well as human beings are subject to *instinctus,* which may come from natural drives within, which in rational creatures appear as natural inclinations, as well as from an exterior agent. Thus, Aquinas analogically applies this term to the movement of the Holy Spirit that produces what Latin theology has come to designate as the gifts. For further information, see Edward D. O'Connor, C.S.C., *The Gifts of the Holy Spirit,* vol. 24, *Summa theologiae* (New York: McGraw-Hill, 1973), appendix 5, pp. 131–41.

up between the two. When law is seen from this standpoint, it drags morality along in its wake and hinders it from exercising its free spontaneity. "Law of liberty" becomes a contradiction in terms and loses all meaning. Moral life is adrift, separated from the Gospel and St. Paul.

The rediscovery of spiritual spontaneity at the heart of morality, and an appreciation of its value, are beyond doubt the chief conditions for the rebuilding of a specifically Christian ethics.

The Evangelical Law and the Counsels

The evangelical law is a law of freedom for a third reason, particularly dear to the heart of St. Thomas. We might say he invented it as a specific expression of the religious message of his times, both Dominican and Franciscan. He devoted the last article in his treatise on the New Law to this.

The evangelical Law includes an innovation that makes it unique among all laws. It is not composed exclusively of precepts, like other laws; it adds counsels, invaluable indications of ways to advance more smoothly and speedily along the path to the perfection of charity and the promised beatitude. These counsels, drawn from the Gospel, have been refined by the Church, thanks to all those who have striven through the course of the ages to live according to the New Law. They are poverty, chastity, and obedience, which disengage the Christian from the preoccupations of the world and clear the way for a single-minded concern with the Gospel. They are the foundation of the religious state.

Here we must be explicit. St. Thomas did not separate the religious state from the common condition of Christians in the heart of the Church, as has been done subsequently. All his moral teaching, centered on the theological virtues, the evangelical Law, and the Sermon on the Mount, was addressed to the entire body of Christians through the grace of the Holy Spirit. The religious state was situated within this context and had for its end the end proposed for all: life according to the Gospel, and the perfection of charity. Nonetheless, this state became a special sign of adherence to the Gospel, because its way of life was more directly oriented to it through the chief counsels it implemented. The evangelical counsels were indeed addressed to everyone, but not all could practice them in the same way, for vocations differ and lead to distinct patterns of living. The special practice of the counsels by some was intended for the good of all in charity. We cannot without detriment to all concerned separate religious from other Christians in the following of the evangelical Law. If lifestyles differ in some measure, the end, and the virtues leading to it, are the same for all.

This clarification is needed because subsequently attitudes toward morality and the religious life underwent considerable changes. The concentration of common moral teaching on the Decalogue, and its separation from spirituality, led to the idea that life according to the Gospel and the search for perfection applied only to religious. St. Thomas's distinction between the precepts and counsels was used as grounds for this division; yet in reality his distinction was being mistakenly applied, since the context had been basically modified. The context had become a matter of a morality of laws and obligations, quite incapable of being integrated in St. Thomas's treatise on the evangelical Law, since the latter was a "law of freedom" in the three senses we have discussed.

Christian moral teaching was for St. Thomas "a morality of freedom," since it was enhanced by spiritual spontaneity in line with the virtues and gifts; because it limited external precepts to the necessary, placing them at the service of the virtues; and finally, because it included counsels designed to favor free initiative in regard to the perfection of charity. In this way, the widest possible field of activity was opened up for the freedom of the children of God.

Conclusion: St. Thomas, the Gospel, and Aristotle

Is St. Thomas's moral teaching Christian? The answer cannot be in doubt when we consider the *Summa theologiae* as a whole, when we follow the plan and structure St. Thomas gave to his moral teaching in the second part, and when we learn to avoid the pitfalls of perspective which we have discussed, which would unduly separate his work into moral, spiritual, philosophical and theological sections. The treatise on the New Law, in particular, gives an evangelical and Christian character to St. Thomas's moral teaching, and this penetrates the structure in all its parts.

As for Aristotle's *Ethics,* so widely used by St. Thomas, he intended to place it at the service of Gospel morality, which he interpreted as a theologian. In so doing he was following the tradition of St. Paul himself, who wrote in his Letter to the Philippians, "Fill your minds with everything that is true, everything that is noble, everything that is good and pure, everything that we love and honor, and everything that can be thought virtuous or worthy of praise" (4:8). He was also within the tradition of the Greek and Latin Fathers, notably St. Augustine, when they included in their works the virtues and wisdom of the Greeks in the service of the Gospel. Yet along with the Fathers, St. Thomas was fully conscious of the irreducible newness of the Gospel, its difference, indeed its opposition to secular morality, as proclaimed in Romans and Corinthians.

It seems to me, however, that in his *Summa theologiae* St. Thomas brought out in an overall perspective the harmony existing between evangelical faith and philosophical reason. Like his Dominican brethren, St. Thomas preached the Gospel in a Christian world, which knew an extraordinary spiritual and intellectual renewal, and at the same time confronted pagan culture in a new way. St. Thomas undertook to demonstrate as far as possible to both Christians and pagans the Gospel's higher harmony with reason, whose best interpreter, in his view, was Aristotle. He gave a reason for his evangelical hope to all who asked, in accordance with St. Peter's urging (1 Peter 3:15).·

His vibrant confidence in the agreement between faith and reason, which St. Thomas shared with his century, led him to a maximum use of Aristotle's arguments. These would serve as a common ground in his discussion with pagans, with anyone in fact, and an introduction to the Gospel as far as this lay within human power.

Thus, for example, St. Thomas demonstrated through reason that eternal happiness alone could satisfy our natural desire for happiness (which is an expression of our longing for the true and the good), and that in consequence, this desire, which Aristotle says is oriented to contemplation, by its very existence witnesses to our capacity to be lifted up by the power of grace to the vision of God. This is the famous argument from natural desire, which modern theologians so greatly fear and which was central for St. Thomas. Here, then, in the treatise on beatitude, Aristotle is put into the service of demonstrating our call to the vision of God. Likewise, throughout his moral teaching, St. Thomas drew unhesitatingly upon the Stagirite.

This free, broad use of Aristotle has deceived modern readers, because of the shift in perspective since the Renaissance. Once we begin, with Luther, to separate faith and reason, theology and philosophy, or the Gospel and humanism, and to set up an opposition between them, we are no longer able to understand the harmonies portrayed by St. Thomas and his demonstration of the agreement between the Gospel and Aristotle. The question then becomes, Shall we follow the Gospel or Aristotle? St. Thomas almost inevitably begins to look more like an Aristotelian than a Christian. The Angelic Doctor wanted moral teaching to be both Christian and human, each dimension supporting the other. Now we think we have to choose between a Christian and a human morality, between the natural and the supernatural. St. Thomas's confidence in Aristotle's natural contribution only accredits the idea that his teaching was primarily philosophical; it conceals its Christian dimension.

It is high time to rediscover the basically evangelical character of St. Thomas's moral teaching. This will contribute to the rebuilding of a moral system that is both authentically Christian and human, transcending the current crisis caused by the excessive influence of rationalism in recent centuries.

PART TWO

A BRIEF HISTORY OF MORAL THEOLOGY

Introduction: The Advantage of a History of Moral Theology or Christian Ethics, and the Difficulties Involved

Our knowledge of the history of moral theology is sketchy. In recent centuries, historians of Christianity have focused their research chiefly upon Scripture and the development of dogma. Their interest in moral theology has been slight; only incidentally have they touched upon it at all. Separated from dogmatics in the modern era, moral theology plays an insignificant role in theological and historical research. At the present moment, when ethical problems are vociferously claiming the attention of a self-alienated world, and when the very existence of Christian morality is at stake, the time has come to fill in the lacuna. Moral theology needs to take advantage of the historical method used with such profit in the other branches of theology.

Ethicists themselves are partly to blame for this neglect. The lack can, to some extent, be laid at the door of a certain concept of moral theology. It is not immediately obvious that historical research might offer a substantial contribution to the working out of Christian ethics. The latter is viewed as a firm and solid block, standing rocklike above the moving tides of history. What would be the point of tracing the history of something that has always resisted history? Such a study might lead to relativism, which could threaten morality's stability and norms. Then, too, the scholastic method as it has been practiced in recent centuries would hardly seem to favor openness to the historical perspective, because of its rational, logical, and abstract character.

In spite of this, I believe that an historical study is indispensable for the renewal of Christian ethics. It would have to be accompanied by a deepened theological reflection, in accord with the demands of such material.[1] In examining past studies closely, we soon realize that moral theology has undergone changes far more significant than might be supposed, through the systemizations that have been established over the ages. The principal precepts of moral doctrine and the discipline of the Church have remained firm through the centuries, but the ways in which theologians have organized this teaching reveals considerable variety. This, expressed in catechesis and preaching, has in turn had a strong influence on the ideas of the faithful.

Just as it is impossible to know a person without some awareness of his past, so knowledge of the history of moral theology can be very enlightening for us. The genesis of concepts and systems, traced by historical study, gives a new dimension to their content, bringing them into relief with a new clarity. We are then enabled to make verifications and rectifications. These renew the material and actually benefit speculative research.

History also helps us to discern the most fruitful sources of theology—those capable of nourishing an authentic renewal—and to dispense with additions useful at one time but no longer relevant. Thanks to history, we can better grasp the great heritage of Christian ethics, verifying its foundations by a return to the sources and following its evolution from stage to stage up to our own times. In this way we can lay claim to all its accumulated riches, making them as fruitful as possible for our own times.

In the course of these reflections it is not my intention to trace the entire history of moral theology with its array of authors, writings, and debates. What I should like to do, rather, is to go beyond external events and bring out the basic lines and trends of this history, showing the elements that have formed the structure of moral theology and have determined its organization in different periods. I propose to sketch the history of fundamental moral theory in broad outline.

My study will cover five stages, a division that seems to be indicated by the historical development itself:

1. The patristic period, extending to the twelfth century
2. Thirteenth-century scholasticism

1. See my book, The Renewal of Morality (Paris, 1964 and 1979), Ch. III: "The Value of the Historical Method in the Study of Thomistic Moral Theology," 44–60.

3. *The advent of nominalism with Ockham in the fourteenth century*

4. *The post-Tridentine period; modern manuals of moral theology and the Protestant crisis*

5. *The contemporary period, up to Vatican II*

Like the solution of problems of fundamental morality, the writing of a history of moral theology is a difficult undertaking because of the ideas and moral convictions so deeply rooted in our minds and hearts. As Schopenhauer remarked, it is easy to preach morality but very hard to instill it.

Before beginning my exposition, I must clarify one important point. The chief difficulty encountered in an historical study of ethical systems comes less from the subject matter itself than from the attitude we bring to it. We all have in our minds—and this could be compared to contact lenses for reading—certain ideas and moral categories learned in school, which seem quite obvious to us. We apply these to texts such as the ancient documents, which in fact do not contain these categories, and which arrange the material of moral theory in quite a different way.

I have already mentioned this hazard in connection with the way we read St. Thomas, but I mention it again as we enter upon the patristic period and the Middle Ages. I shall indicate four modern categories that could deeply flaw our understanding of the most productive periods of theology. Historical research itself will best show up this danger and its disadvantages.

The crucial point is the modern ethicist's concentration on the idea and feeling of obligation, which gives rise to the organization of moral theology around laws, commandments, and norms. The moral world thus becomes a world of obligations and duties, precepts and prohibitions. From this there follows a separation between properly so-called ethics, dealing with obligations imposed upon everyone, and what has been called asceticism, mysticism, and finally spirituality, forming a special area of perfection, supplementary and freely chosen. A further result is an even greater separation—between dogmatic theology, which has become more speculative in its study of the documents of faith, and moral theology, totally practical in its examination of laws and their application in individual cases of conscience. Finally I should mention the sharp distinction made by the modern authors between philosophy and theology. This is so clearly defined that when we come upon something in philosophy such as the teaching of a pagan author, we feel that it is necessarily alien to theology, even though a theologian *may have incorporated it into his system. Thus philosophy and theology are constantly in conflict in our minds, stealing ideas from each other, and this inevitably works to the detriment of theology.*

The Church Fathers and the great scholastics were unaware of these distinctions, separations, and oppositions. For them, as for the Greek philosophers, ethics addressed the question of happiness and was organized around the principle virtues, and first the theological virtues. In their eyes, precepts and obligations played the tutor's role, guiding us to life in the Spirit. Aware of the dangers of philosophy, and maintaining their loyalty, they tried to make use of its advantageous features and integrated them harmoniously in their theology. Their moral and theological world was quite different from ours therefore. Awareness of this is indispensable if we are to understand them and derive profit from their works.

happiness
virtues

8

The Patristic Period

~ 12th C.

In the West the patristic period ran roughly to the middle of the twelfth century, or to the rise of scholasticism, which introduced a new method in theological study.

Authors tend to consider this period as the infancy of moral theology, for it had not yet been established as a distinct science at the heart of theology, nor had it received a systematic form and organization, as would be the case from the thirteenth century onward. We may wonder, however, if this way of seeing things does justice to the moral teaching of the Church Fathers, or if it is perhaps unduly influenced by a certain modern conception of morality.

It would indeed be surprising if the patristic period, so fruitful above all in its first six centuries and meriting the name of the Golden Age of the Church in its dogmatic theology and liturgy, had been able to produce in the field of moral theology only the babbling of babes and a few rough outlines. We may be viewing the Fathers at too great a distance, through a microscope as it were. Let us get a little closer to them, to find out their views on morality. These may be richer than we think.

I. MATERIAL ON MORAL THEOLOGY IN THE WRITINGS OF THE FATHERS

There are three types of patristic work that treat of moral theology: homilies and commentaries on Scripture, collections of personal compositions, and works dealing with particular moral problems.

1. Scriptural Commentaries

As the Fathers saw it, the bishops' chief task was to proclaim and explain the Scriptures. This was done through preaching and catechesis, particularly in a liturgical context. The scriptural commentaries of bishops, whether spoken or written, were the primary source of their moral teaching. Here they exposed the moral teaching of the Scriptures, beginning with its principal texts, and used their wealth of experience to apply it to the lives of their Christian audience.

St. John Chrysostom, for example (344–407), delivered ninety homilies on St. Matthew, eighty-eight on St. John, two hundred and fifty on St. Paul's letters, and sermons on nearly sixty psalms and several other books of both Old and New Testaments. St. John Chrysostom merits consideration as *the* moralist among the Fathers because of the richness of his teaching and the pastoral orientation of his oratorical genius.

Before him, St. Basil (330–79) had composed a work entitled *Moralia,* a collection of extracts chiefly from the Gospels and Epistles, arranged in chapters with a brief introduction.

In the West we have St. Augustine's commentaries: his preaching on the Sermon on the Mount, one hundred and twenty-four homilies on the Gospel of John, ten treatises on the First Letter of John, and his celebrated meditations on the Psalms, a spiritual gem. His explanation of the Sermon on the Mount is of great significance, as we have seen. Augustine chose this as the subject of his first series of homilies after he became a priest, precisely because it contained a complete exposition of the Gospel teaching on Christian ethics.

Scriptural commentaries in their varying forms—homilies, occasional sermons, catechesis, or written works—made up the first and indeed the principal reference for patristic moral teaching, being closest to the inspired source.

2. Personal Documents

Onto the explications of Scripture were soon grafted works of a more personal nature, in which an author tried to rearrange his material so as to present an overall view.

Our first example would be the Didache (written at the end of the first century or the beginning of the second), which is considered the first manual of moral teaching, liturgy, and disciplinary rules. Morality was presented in the form of two ways open to the Christian's free choice: the way of life and the way of death. The way of life was inspired by charity, which extended even to the love of one's enemies. It called for a struggle against evil and was made concrete by precepts and counsels concerning the representatives of God, the poor, the education of children, and so forth.

Clement of Alexandria (150–211), in *The Teacher*, confronted pagan philosophy and morality with a systematic outline of Christian ethics, focusing on the virtues to be practiced by the faithful living in the world. For him the true teacher, the one who taught true morality and enabled us to practice it, was Christ, the Word made man.

We should also mention Origen (185–255), who was the major initiator of spiritual exegesis among the Fathers. He undertook to compile a *Summa theologiae* before the fact in his *Peri Archon*. Book III was devoted to morality. Here he dealt with freedom—which he established through reason and Scripture—the world and the flesh, and the definitive triumph of good at the end of time.

Among the Latin Fathers, St. Ambrose (333–97) gave a remarkable exposition in his *De officiis* of the virtues of clerics and Christians. The work was inspired by Cicero's work of the same title, but he drew his doctrine and examples from Scripture and Christian experience rather than from pagan sources.

It was with St. Augustine that the theological material began to take on its principal forms and to receive the categories and problematics that were transmitted to medieval scholasticism and have come down to our own times. St. Augustine devoted several works to an exposition of Christian morals. Already his *Commentary on the Sermon on the Mount* contained the fundamental concepts that were to guide St. Thomas himself.

Scarcely was he converted when St. Augustine wrote *The Christian Way of Life,* in which he attacked the Manicheans. The Gospel gave the only adequate answer to the question of happiness and transformed the classical virtues of prudence, justice, courage, and temperance into forms of the principal Christian virtue, charity.

His *De doctrina christiana* distinguished between useful and enjoyable goods (*quibus utendum, quibus fruendum*). The good that is God is solely to be enjoyed; there are other goods, which man may both use and enjoy. This distinction between goods, which determines the quality of the human heart and actions, dominates the Augustinian concept of morality and most especially of charity, which is an attachment to the good.

The *Enchiridion ad Laurentium* has been considered the manual of true Augustinanism. It follows the order of the theological virtues and culminates with hope and charity, the goal of all the commandments. We will find in the Lord's Prayer all we should hope for and love. Through this prayer, faith, hope and charity become praying virtues. In their train follow all the other virtues and the entire life which they inspire.

3. Works Dealing with Particular Ethical Problems

Very early on, in the tradition of the First Letter to the Corinthians, the Fathers preached and wrote about particular ethical problems confronting Christians living in a pagan world, or about the main points of the ideal life proposed by Christianity. Tertullian (150–240) was particularly interested in concrete problems. He wrote treatises on games, idolatry, feminine styles and the veil of virgins, on prayer, patience, fasting, chastity, and monogamy.

In the same vein, St. Augustine's pastoral concern called his attention to the problems of his people. On two occasions he wrote about lying (in 395 and 419), then about continence, the duties of married couples, virginity, widows; also about patience, the usefulness of fasting, and so forth. Nor should we forget his letters, in which he sometimes answered his correspondents at great length. His letter to Proba (*Letters,* 130) is actually a small treatise on prayer, much used in medieval theology.

Following the same tradition but with greater brevity, St. John Chrysostom wrote on the education of children, virginity, and the state of widowhood. Apparently the Greek Fathers tended to be more speculative in their interests and approach than the Latins, yet St. John's pastoral and practical orientations come out clearly in his sermons.

This brief survey of the works of the best-known Church Fathers shows us that they gave full attention and treatment to questions of morality, scattered though these might be throughout their scriptural commentaries and homilies. We have good reason to believe that their moral teaching, fed by the deepest sources of Scripture and culture, was every bit as rich spiritually as their dogmatic teaching. In order to understand this more clearly and learn from them more fully, we will now study the characteristic features of the moral teaching of the Fathers.

II. CHARACTERISTIC ASPECTS OF THE MORAL TEACHING OF THE FATHERS

1. The Primacy of Holy Scripture

In the patristic period, a dominant characteristic of Christian thought, which could even be called a first principle, was the acceptance of Scripture as the main, direct source of sacred science in all its forms. The Christian continually fed on the Scriptures. Hence, the first works of the Fathers were commentaries on the Old and New Testaments. Even works that made most use of Greek philosophy rigorously upheld the primacy of Scripture. The most personal works, such as those of St. Augustine, were watered by the vivifying springs of Scripture to the point of saturation. The numerous citations so perfectly integrated in his texts, often from memory, bear witness to this. The entire moral teaching of the Church Fathers flowed from this recognized primacy of Scripture. It was not merely a doctrinal affirmation but a veritable methodological principle, constantly applied.

We should note, moreover, that where morality was concerned the Fathers read Scripture differently than we do. When a modern ethicist consults Scripture, he is looking for normative texts, laws, commands, and prohibitions in which the divine will expresses its authority. The results are rather meager; he usually falls back on the Decalogue.

The outlook of the Fathers was far broader. For them, all of Scripture possessed a moral dimension and significance. This explains their theory of the four senses of Scripture. One of the principal forms of interpretation was the moral sense, which led to the actualization of Scripture in the life and action of a Christian. This was St. Thomas's explanation in establishing the foundation of the sacred science (Ia, q 1 a 10). In the opinion of the Fathers, all Scripture was of concern to the ethicist. St. Ambrose, for example, took from the historical books of the Old Testament most of the examples of virtue he needed in order to Christianize Cicero's *De officiis*. St. Gregory's commentary on Job was entitled *Moralia in Job* and became a goldmine for medieval ethicists and spiritual writers. St. Thomas declared that every movement of the human heart could be found in it.[1]

The reason for this breadth of view regarding Scripture is not far to seek. The Fathers' vision embraced Scripture from beginning to end,

---

1. In his commentary on 1 Corinthians 14, lectio 5.

since for them the principal question for moral theology was happiness or salvation, and the ways leading thereto. As they pondered in the Scriptures God's response to this crucial question, each book brought them some teaching which would point humanity to the practice of the principal virtues. They also found in their faith in this Word, and their contemplation of it, a strength that no human teaching could have given them.

There were certain books or portions of Scripture, however, that the Fathers recognized as pertaining more directly to morality by reason of their content and intention. Among these were the wisdom literature of the Old Testament, the Sermon on the Mount in the Gospels, and the sections in St. Paul's letters that today are called paranetic but that he himself undoubtedly considered as carefully worked out expositions of Gospel morality.

Patristic Exegesis

It will be helpful to consider the manner in which the Fathers read the Scriptures, drawing from it their moral doctrine. They did not have at their disposal the resources of modern historical exegesis, but they did possess a method of interpretation that enabled them to discover the rich spiritual substance their works contain and that still nourishes us today.

Patristic exegesis might be described as a "real" reading of Scripture, as contrasted with a literary or positivist approach.[2] The main object of the Fathers was to penetrate beyond the signs, the words, to the reality signified, even to the mystery of Christ and God. They were aware that

---

2. See my article, "Lecture positive et lecture 'réelle' de la bible" in *Sources* 3 (1977): 108–18. The expression "real reading" corresponds to what Newman intended by "real" assent as distinct from notional assent. I quote here a relevant passage from *A Grammar of Assent*: "And what the experience of the world effects for the illustration of classical authors, that office the religious sense, carefully cultivated, fulfils towards Holy Scripture. To the devout and spiritual, the Divine Word speaks of things, not merely of notions. And again, to the disconsolate, the tempted, the perplexed, the suffering, there comes, by means of their very trials, an enlargment of thought, which enables them to see in it what they never saw before. Henceforth there is to them a reality in its teachings, which they recognize as an argument, and the best of arguments, for its divine origin. Hence the practice of meditation on the Sacred Text, so highly thought of by Catholics. Reading, as we do, the Gospels from our youth up, we are in danger of becoming so familiar with them as to be dead to their force, and to view them as a mere history. The purpose, then, of meditation, is to realize them; to make the facts which they relate stand out before our minds as objects, such as may be appropriated by a faith as living as the imagination which apprehends them" (John Henry Cardinal Newman, *Essay in Aid of a Grammar of Assent* [New York: Longmans, Green, 1906], 79).

they could reach this mystery only through faith in Christ and obedience to his word. Their reading was therefore directly related to their lives and was enlightened by a gradually formed experience of the reality and truth of what they believed. Their exegetical works expressed the penetration of their minds into the mysteries contained in Scripture, a penetration due to their active experience of the mysteries. They are properly speaking works of wisdom. Patristic exegesis was essentially linked to faith and practice. It included nonetheless some very fine literary analyses and carefully wrought intellectual reflections such as we find, for example, in St. Augustine's *De doctrina christiana*. Still, the main thing for them was an intellectual savoring of the divine realities communicated by the Holy Spirit, the principal Author of Scripture. In the work cited above, St. Augustine linked progress in knowledge of Scripture with moral progress under the action of the Holy Spirit (2.7.9–11).

So we are dealing with a special type of exegesis that has its own method. I call this kind of reading "real" for two reasons. First, it desires to attain the realities to which the words of Scripture point—it moves from signs and words to the *res* of which St. Augustine speaks. Second, it causes these realities to penetrate into the reality of our lives and our being, through practice. This kind of reading might also be called "interior," because it draws us to the inmost depths of Scripture, beyond the words proposed and the ideas evoked, while simultaneously introducing the Word into our inmost being, to be implemented by our conversion of heart and works of charity.

St. Augustine's explanation of the Beatitudes is a fine illustration of this type of exegesis. In his commentary on the Sermon on the Mount and in several subsequent works he described the Beatitudes as the Christian's journey, with seven stages ranging from humility to wisdom. He thus proposed a model for the Christian's moral pilgrimage in the light of the Gospel. Among other things, he interpreted the second beatitude as an attitude of docility to Scripture, preserving us from arrogant judgments concerning those texts that might puzzle or convict us. In this he was describing his own personal experience. As we saw above in Chapter 6, his explanation of the Beatitudes is closely related to his *Confessions*. This is what we might call experiential exegesis. We are not speaking of just any kind of experience, but of what proceeds from obedience to the Gospel Word and gives a renewed understanding of this Word. A current is established between the Word, which comes first, and the life conformed to it in faith.

The Nourishing Bread of Scripture

The following image may be helpful in demonstrating the patristic method. The Church Fathers possessed the art of forming nourishing bread from the wheat of Scripture.[3] The comparison of scriptural texts to wheat is apt, for they are often made up of short sentences that enclose in a few words a theme or a rich doctrine containing a seed of life. Let us consider the stages of this spiritual work.

The first task was to strip off the husk covering the grain, to free the Word from its human coverings: language, literary genre, the particularities of the author, the setting, period and so forth. To get at the living grain in this way, faith was needed as much as dexterity, for faith alone opens our minds to the Word and allows it to penetrate to the depths of our hearts. By the same token, it is faith that enables us to penetrate this Word and so grasp and understand it.

Next, the grain was ground to produce flour; they needed to meditate on the Word and crush it, so to speak, through reflection and life, with the aid of memory and experience. Meditation led to practice, comparable to kneading, for the demands of action, with all its ardors, resistance, and delays, truly knead and mold us. This task could not succeed without the water of regular prayer. Finally the bread that had been shaped must be put in the oven; it passed through the fire of trial, like the gold of the Word, seven times purified, purified slowly. Only now was the bread ready to be offered as nourishment. The reader of the Scriptures could offer to others a substantial explanation of the Word of God: this the Fathers did in their commentaries.

The Scripture reading I have just described is in no way artificial. It corresponds exactly to the intention of the sacred authors, who wrote "from faith to faith," to stir up faith, to impart an understanding of divine realities, and to transform the lives of believers. This kind of reading is particularly appropriate for the ethicist. Like moral theory itself, it is directed toward practice and puts experience to work. It tends toward an active wisdom which is at once vast, profound and concrete—the perfection of moral proficiency. This is why I believe it is indispensable for us to relearn, in the school of the Fathers, the art of "baking the bread of the Word," which they possessed to so high a degree. This will not prevent us from profiting from the methods and discoveries of modern ethicists. I am convinced that it is the necessary condition for

---

3. Such will be, according to St. Thomas, the work of the gift of understanding: to penetrate to the heart of proposed truths, "penetratio ad intima eorum [quae proponuntur]" (IIaIIae q 8 a 6).

reestablishing close, vital bonds between current moral theology and Scripture.

2. The Integration of Greco-Roman Culture

If Scripture was incontestably the first and principal source of patristic thought, Greek wisdom was nonetheless an important element in the theology of the Fathers. Ancient moral theory centered around the four cardinal virtues of prudence, justice, courage and temperance, already mentioned in the Book of Wisdom. In this way philosophy, full of human experience but varying greatly according to schools, gave the classic answer to the great question of happiness.

The Fathers made considerable use of philosophy. Platonic thought in particular appeared to many of the Greek Fathers as closest to Christianity and most apt for expressing revealed truths because of its spiritual orientation and its transcendence of the sensible world in favor of the world of Ideas which it constructed. Here we should mention Dionysius the Areopagite (fifth century) whose mystical doctrine, of Neoplatonic inspiration, has played an often preponderant role in Western theology. St. Augustine for his part recounted in his *Confessions* that the reading of the Neoplatonists had turned his mind to God and had even made him understand the Word of God.

Stoic influence was equally pronounced, especially in regard to the teaching on the virtues of daily life. The works of Seneca, who has been compared to St. Paul, were influential up to the Middle Ages. St. Ambrose, as we have seen, did not hesitate to use Cicero's *De officiis* as the basis for his exposition of Christian morality. We might even say that the philosophical works of Cicero were the foundation of the thought of the Latin Fathers. Cicero's teachings were at times so favorable to Christians that his works were rejected by fourth-century pagans. We should also mention the influence of Roman law with its concept of justice which, through Tertullian the lawyer and Ambrose the great administrator, passed into the body of Christian teaching.

This brief listing of names shows the important part played by Greco-Roman thought in the formation of patristic theology, particularly moral theology. We can admit quite frankly that there would have been no Christian theology or "philosophy" were it not for the contribution of Greek wisdom.

At first sight, so broad and open a relationship between Gospel teaching and philosophical systems of non-Christian origin may give us moderns pause. We find it hard to understand and to interpret correctly, particularly because of the subjective divisions and distinctions we make, which were unknown to the Fathers. Protestant thought, dominated by a critical concern for the purity of the Gospel and by its opposition of faith to human works, always maintained a basic opposition between the Gospel and philosophy. Because of this, it could not credit the close connection the Fathers saw here. As for us Catholics, we have learned so well to separate theology and philosophy that we cannot conceive of their innocent collaboration. Historians attribute the strongest influence to philosophers, as if Christian thought were unable to make innovations regarding human reason.

Patristic theology, however, demonstrates historically that there can be a close, vital bond between Christian faith and human thought, which together form what was later to be called theology or a new, *sui generis* wisdom with its own laws and criteria. We have proof here also, after the fact, of the power of the believing mind to accept a philosophical system freely and to integrate it in a new intellectual organism which is at one and the same time specifically Christian and profoundly human.

A bit of docility in following the lead of the Fathers will convince us of this, if we are willing to revise some of our preconceived categories. In our day, so addicted to criticism, this critique of our own ideas merits our acceptance, because it can reopen for us horizons that have seemed forever closed.

Stages in the Assimilation of Greek Philosophy

In this theological enterprise St. Paul had already opened up the way and set the first boundaries. The Fathers had only to continue the work begun, following to the best of their ability the "model" and rules the Apostle had laid down. As we saw in Chapter 5, St. Paul made broad use of contemporary teaching on the virtues. In his last letters, he presented the mystery of Christ as knowledge, as true wisdom and understanding accessible to faith. Still, the encounter of apostolic preaching and Greek wisdom was complex and traumatic. It could not be concluded with a simple choice of *yes* or *no*. The initial opening, an appeal, met with a vigorous *no*; this in turn was transformed into a welcoming *yes.* We encounter this dialectical exchange once more in the Fathers. It provides the necessary key to an understanding of their relation to Greek philosophy and their theological undertaking.

To Hellenism and to the Gnostic temptation, then to Arianism, which
succeeded it; to the efforts of powerful thinkers to interpret Christianity
in the light of philosophy and within its framework—all of these the
Fathers answered with a resounding *no*. This was the condition for their
radical *yes* to the wisdom of God revealed in Jesus Christ. They refused
to reduce the Gospel to human ideas, however lofty or well meaning in
view of inculturation. They proclaimed vigorously, at times vehemently,
that the divine mystery transcended all human reason. The dogmatic
affirmations of the great councils could be said to have sundered and
overturned, one by one, each of the principal categories with which
Greek culture would have seized and interpreted Christianity. They ex-
alted far above all human thought the different aspects of the mystery
of Christ to which faith leads the human mind.

The same work went forward with less bombast in the field of morality. Faith in Christ, to the Greeks weakness and folly; hope in God's
promises and no longer in human power; and finally the charity that
comes from Christ and surpasses all other sentiments: these were ele-
vated far above the human virtues, including understanding and wisdom. The theological virtues led the soul to open itself to the mystery
transmitted by the Gospel and to live it. We become aware of this change
of perspective when we realize that, in patristic tradition, humility was
assigned the highest place, as opposed to the philosophic pride noted
by St. Augustine in his criticism of the Neoplatonists: in humility, to
follow the humble Christ.

Once the foundations of faith and mystery, charity and grace, were
firmly laid, the Fathers were able to turn again to the various philosophical systems and human virtues in an attitude of positive acceptance. This marked the beginning of an ongoing work of discernment,
assimilation, and construction and resulted in a new organism: Christian theology. In it could be found "everything that is true . . . everything
that can be thought virtuous or worthy of praise" (Phil 4:8).

In this delicate and demanding work, the Fathers were animated by
their consideration of the correspondence between the creative work of
God—the divine image inscribed in the human person—and the re-
demptive work accomplished by the Son, the Image of the Father, who
came to restore humanity in both mind and heart. They therefore did
not hesitate to make free use of whatever good they found in the works
of the philosophers, even the pagans, for they saw that, in spite of human
sinfulness, there was in them a human sense of truth coming from God.
So convinced were they of their rights in regard to the philosophers that,

when they borrowed from them, they saw it not as theft but as the lawful restitution of truths and goods formerly taken over from primitive revelation.

3. Spirituality, The Main Theme of Patristic Moral Teaching

One final point will complete our picture of Christian moral teaching in the first centuries. The Fathers were totally unaware of the distinction between morality and spirituality that became customary in later periods. It seems likely that they would have rejected it. For them, what we call spirituality was the high point of Christian ethics. It was the expression of the Gospel call to perfection and to a "justice higher than that of the scribes and pharisees." They believed that all Christians, regardless of their imperfections, ought to bend every moral effort and desire to its attainment.

If we want to understand the moral teaching of the patristic period we need to take into account the main spiritual currents that inspired Christian ethics. They are its better part. To prescind from them would be to do violence to both history and reality.

The letters of St. Paul and the Gospels provided the main texts that were to inspire and develop the ideal of virginity, so characteristic of the action of the Holy Spirit in a very carnal world that it could be viewed as specifically Christian. The spirituality of virginity or of consecrated chastity grew and was recognized in the Church from earliest times, and flowered eventually in religious life. It was one of the most active ferments in Christian life and found vigorous expression in the preaching of the fourth-century Fathers, being one of their favorite themes. We can cite the treatises on virginity of St. Gregory of Nyssa and St. John Chrysostom, several writings of St. Ambrose, and St. Augustine's *Book of Holy Virginity*.

The spirituality of martyrdom also had its source in the writings of the New Testament and developed at the same time. It proposed to all, without distinction of age, sex, social condition, or function within the Church, the ideal of the imitation of Christ unto the supreme witness of suffering and death for his sake. We find it in the letters of St. Ignatius of Antioch and in the authentic accounts of the martyrs: St. Polycarp, the Martyrs of Lyons, St. Cyprian, and so forth. These works were so powerfully moving that they gave rise to a particular literary genre, in which imagination had its part, as in our novels.

Beginning with the fourth century and the end of the persecutions, continuity was insured by the spirituality of the Desert Fathers and monks who developed religious life in the Church in its many forms, like a vigorous tree sending forth new shoots and branches through the centuries. Augustine exclaimed of Anthony, father of monks, and his disciples: "How can we endure it? The unlearned rise up and take heaven by storm, and we, with all our unfeeling erudition, can only wallow in flesh and blood!" (*Confessions,* 8.8.19).

Obviously, not all Christians were destined for martyrdom, nor were all called to remain virgins or become monks. St. Paul himself, referring to virginity, presented it as a counsel offered to personal initiative. Nevertheless, the ideal the Gospel presented in these three forms was important to all Christians, since it was one of the main themes of Christian moral teaching. It had particular revelance for some, but affected the lives of all living in the heart of the Church, according to their situations, charisms, and individual missions. Every Christian was invited to bear witness to Christ in life and death. The message came not only through exhortation and teaching but also through persons and examples. All were to live chastely and to imitate Christ to the best of their ability. There was no real separation, therefore, between the martyrs, virgins and monks, and the rest of the Church. Their ideal was the common ideal, even though not all could actualize it in the same way; it was an integral part of the Gospel teaching proposed to each one. We cannot perceive, much less understand the moral teaching of the Fathers unless we take into account its spiritual dimension.

Conclusion: The Golden Age of Moral Theology

In light of the truth of what we have been considering, it can hardly be claimed that the moral teaching of the patristic period was inferior, or that it was at an infantile stage. Patristic morality fed directly upon Scripture in all its fulness. It knew how to weigh and assess the riches of Greek and Latin culture. Ultimately it presented the spirituality of martyrdom, monasticism and virginity for the sake of Christ as the culmination and crowning peak of morality. The fruits of this spirituality have perdured to our own day. The patristic period was indeed a golden age for morality as it was for all theology. During it, the foundations of moral teaching and Christian living were carefully laid and fortified; these formed our noble tradition, which has been able to withstand the changing currents of the ages by means of continual renewals.

The moral teaching of the Fathers is, after Scripture, a primary source for the Christian ethicist. St. Thomas was convinced of this. The vast collection of patristic texts in his *Catena aurea* bears witness to the fact, as well as his extensive reading of the works of the Fathers, revealed in his *Summa theologiae*.

III. MORAL THEOLOGY IN ST. AUGUSTINE

In any discussion of moral theology, St. Augustine merits special attention. His work marks a decisive stage in the development of Western theology, indeed, of Western thought. Together with St. Thomas he can be considered one of the greatest moralists in the history of the Church. He has always been recognized by classical moralists as a major author.

It would obviously be impossible to cover St. Augustine's moral teaching here, even in summary. I can only note that for him, as for the philosophers and all the Fathers of the Church, the point of departure for Christian ethics is the question of happiness. Setting out to explain the Catholic way of life in contrast with that of the Manicheans, he proposes: "Let us inquire reasonably how we ought to live. Of course we all want to live a happy life; anyone would agree with this, even before the words are out of my mouth." He goes on to clarify: "A person can be happy only in the enjoyment of what is best for him" (*De moribus Ecclesiae catholicae, 3.4*).

Christian faith provides the answer: man's highest good is the enjoyment of the true God—Father, Son, and Holy Spirit, one God. Moral teaching will therefore be ordered according to three broad categories of goods: those which are to be used, and this refers to all creatures; those which are to be enjoyed because they answer sufficiently our desire for happiness and our inclination to love, and this refers to the Trinity alone.[4] As for man, he has a place apart: he both uses and enjoys, he desires and loves; he is the one for whom the good, happiness, and God are willed.

4. The Augustinian concept of "use" should not be understood in a modern sense, reduced to the relationship of means to end as an instrument. Rather it is understood within the context of love and its movement. Desire and love, when they attain a good, must conform themselves to its nature. In the case of a created good they cannot rest in it but must continue their search for the supreme good. It is as if they received a message through this limited good, so well expressed in the description of the vision at Ostia: "For if any man has ears to hear, all these things cry out to him, 'We did not make ourselves, but he who endures forever made us.' When they have uttered these words they then fall silent; they have opened his ear to him who made them" (*Confessions, 9.10.25*).

St. Augustine's moral teaching focuses on charity. The moral virtues he borrows from Greek philosophy—prudence, justice, temperance, and courage—are transformed and redefined as forms of charity. At the same time, St. Augustine restores the term *love*, which Christians had avoided as suspect, and by it he designates the radical inclination to love placed in the human heart by God and flowering in charity. For him two loves dominate history and the moral world: love of God above all things, to the point of forgetfulness of self, and love of self to the point of contempt for God, which results in pride. This counterpoint appears also in our relationships with our neighbors.

Love is not a purely subjective outpouring for St. Augustine. It poses objective demands. It can be authentic only when it is rightly related to the goods it seeks. Love calls for order and uprightness; these make it true and a thing of beauty. St. Augustine defines it in two words: "Here is a brief, true definition of virtue, I think: [it is] ordered love" (*The City of God*, 15.22).[5] This definition expresses the very essence of Augustinian morality: love and truth embrace, as we read in the psalm.

When with St. Augustine we view morality as Christ's answer to the question of happiness, we discover that each of his works makes its own distinct contribution to Christian moral teaching. There are, for example, his rich commentaries on Scripture, often preached, especially those on the Psalms and St. John. The *Confessions* give us Augustine's personal experience, his passionate search for truth and happiness, along the path of error and evil but under the guidance of sovereign light and grace. Augustine tells us, too, in his *De trinitate*, of his spiritual and mystical journey, his long-enduring contemplation of the Trinity as mirrored in man and reflected in creation.

Augustine's moral vision was also oriented to the Church and the world. In *The City of God* he describes the history of the Church in the midst of the world as a struggle between love of God and love of self. Pastorally concerned, he dealt with concrete problems in numerous brief works on marriage and virginity, on lying, patience, fasting. We need to keep in mind, too, his voluminous correspondence, in which he responded at length to problems submitted to him.

Augustine's penetrating mind was particularly interested in the foundations of Christian ethics. On several occasions he detailed its principal elements, notably in *De moribus Ecclesiae* and the *Enchiridion*.

5. "Nam et amor ipse ordinate amandus est, quo bene amatur quod amandum est, ut sit in nobis virtus qua vivitur bene. Unde mihi videtur, quod definitio brevis et vera virtutis ordo est amoris; propter quod in sancto cantico canticorum cantat sponsa Christi, civitas Dei: Ordinate in me caritatem." See the edition of his works in the Bibliothèque Augustinienne, vol. 36, note 8 by G. Bardy.

role of grace

We should mark well that one of the fundamental aspects of Augustine's concept of Christian ethics was the intervention and preponderant role of grace in the life and activity of the Christian. During the last three centuries, the majority of Catholic ethicists have left the study of grace to dogmatic theologians. Doubtless they were pushed into this position by the increasingly speculative character of the discussions on grace and free will during the sixteenth and seventeenth centuries, at a time when morality sought to be practical in light of the sacrament of penance. Yet they would not have abandoned the treatise on grace had they realized its importance for Christian ethics, even if it meant using simpler and more reasonable terms of reference.

As for St. Augustine, the further his thought progresses and matures the more clearly we can observe in his works the preeminent place of grace and its determining, even decisive, role (no word is too strong) in his concept of Christian conduct and moral theory. According to the witness of his experience and reflection, the essence of morality is formed by the relation of grace and freedom at the source of Christian life. He is deservedly called the doctor of grace. His works on grace, based principally on his reading of St. Paul and St. John, spearheaded his fierce battle against Pelagianism and became an integral part of his moral teaching. We can easily believe that, had St. Augustine learned that desert theologians were working out a moral theory that did not assign to grace its due priority, he would certainly have convoked a council much sooner in his province of Africa, to set thing right with the weight of his authority. St. Thomas was true to this ideal when he associated the study of moral law and grace, even defining the evangelical Law as the grace of the Holy Spirit.

Unity and Rhythm in Augustinian Thought

We cannot emphasize too strongly the importance of St. Augustine for Latin theology. He was the first Western thinker to have studied theology in depth, particularly moral theology. He was responsible for a new Christian terminology, an overview of morality, an original reassessment of the principles of ancient philosophy, and an extensive treatment of fundamental problems become practical issues. Obviously he did all this in his own highly personal manner, quite different from the Thomist synthesis to follow and the moral casuistry of the seventeenth century.

St. Augustine's thought is characterized by a strong tendency toward unity. There is unity of movement toward the one God who brings unity and harmony out of the diversity found in humankind and all creation. There is unity, too, in our constant return to inward, personal experience, centered in charity and self-knowledge.

Again, Augustinian thought rejects the separation between philosophy and theology that modern readers would impose, or between dogma and mystical and moral spirituality, or between metaphysics, psychology, and ethics. The works of St. Augustine are all this simultaneously. His thought moves from one level to another, as supple, casual and sure as life itself, creating a single work at a single thrust. Thus we can speak of a unique rhythm in St. Augustine's thought. An image of this might be a sphere, with each point on the surface connected to the hidden center so as to reveal its presence at all times. This makes it practically impossible to set forth St. Augustine's theology in a fixed synthesis with analytical divisions and linear progressions. We are accustomed to this way of doing since the time of St. Thomas, but such a method would only cramp and distort St. Augustine.

The fact that St. Augustine's thought remains forever in a state of incompletion is no weakness. His intellectual thrust is simply different from that of the medievals, somewhat as Plato differed from Aristotle.

St. Augustine and St. Thomas

We need to keep these characteristics in mind so as not to do an injustice to St. Augustine and fall into errors we might later regret. It does not seem quite accurate to say that St. Augustine was the first great builder of moral theology but that, as happens with pioneers, he had to leave the work unfinished like an open scaffolding, to be completed by the genius of St. Thomas. St. Augustine's theology was brought to as finished a state as was humanly possible, like any human work. Theology must always remain unfinished in this world, outstripped by the mystery of the God it seeks to grasp.

St. Augustine's major work *De trinitate* illustrates this point clearly. It is as spiritual and mystical as it is speculative; it was written at the height of an experience of love—concretely, love of neighbor (Book 8). As such it reaches the summit of Augustinian morality, the answer to the question of happiness. "Behold, 'God is love' [*dilectio*]). Why do we rush to the heights of heaven, the depths of the earth, in search of the One who is near to us, if we would be near to him? Let no one say, 'I don't know what to love.' Let him only love his brother, and he will be loving this same love [*dilectionem*]" (8.7.11–8.8.12).

Having depicted the highest and truest image of the Trinity in the human person, who cleaves to God in wisdom with memory, knowledge, and love, St. Augustine hastens to point out the weakness of such an image of the divine Trinity. It is on this humble, true note that he brings his theological masterpiece to a close.

St. Augustine teaches us a great lesson: theology must always remain humble before the mystery of God present in the least of believers. It must be lovingly aware of the imperfection of all its theories and systems in the face of the divine reality. Far from causing discouragement, this should spur us on to further research, so that we may advance toward the light, which illumines and attracts us through the darkness of faith. Like St. Paul, forgetting the past we should strain forward with our whole being to the goal of all our journeying (see *De trinitate*, 8.1.1).

Consequently, no theological or moral system should be viewed as absolutely complete or definitive, to the point of supplanting others or rendering them useless. Nor should any one system be seen as the center and measure of all others. When we compare St. Augustine's moral theology with that of St. Thomas, we naturally note that the latter marks a clear advance in the development and completion of the analysis and in the structural perfection of the system. But an Augustinian could well answer that St. Augustine's thought is superior in its sapiental character and its Christian and human solidarity, and that it is better suited to moral and spiritual progress.[6] On considering the theology of the two in their entirety, we cannot say one is better than the other. We need rather to see them as two magnificent expressions of the inexhaustible riches of the mystery of Christ, and try to profit from them both. Since they belonged to two different spiritual families, these theologians complement each other. It is useless to seek to interpret one through the other or to reduce them to a common denominator. St. Augustine cannot be contained within Thomistic categories, at least not those of the modern textbooks. To recognize this diversity in theology is a fine exercise in developing mental breadth and flexibility. Theology is diverse because of the richness of its object. We need to resist the temptation to judge everything according to our habitual conceptions and ideas.

St. Augustine, Fomenter of Heresies?

The criticism has sometimes been made about St. Augustine that he gave rise to heresies: Protestantism, Jansenism, and so forth. In asserting

6. Cf. J. Maritain, *The Degrees of Knowledge* (New York: Scribner, 1938).

this, his critics overlook the fact that in Western Christendom he was the father of theology, spirituality, and mystical theology from the high Middle Ages until the modern era, and that among his innumerable disciples are included St. Bernard, St. Bonaventure, St. Thomas, St. John of the Cross, Bossuet, and many others in our own day. The heresies he is accused of fomenting were accidental phenomena, as the scholastics say, withered, wild branches, which only prove the fertility of the parent tree with all its fruitfulness and life. Only sterile trunks produce evil outcroppings. The same criticism could be made of Scripture, with even more examples to support it.

IV. THE LESSON OF THE FATHERS

Before leaving the Fathers, let us cast a retrospective glance, taking care first to avoid a rather persistent optical illusion.

A person who has studied moral theology in modern textbooks, or even in the Thomistic school—a great school to which I belong—and who has become aware of a certain synthesis in this study, may sometimes begin to wonder: how did the Church manage for so many centuries without a complete, rational systym of morality? Was it not dangerously open to the shifting currents of the world, like a spineless jellyfish?

The answer is simple. The Church of the Fathers had something far more valuable than a rational system: Scripture, the Gospel contemplated and fulfilled, living tradition, and the help of the Holy Spirit. These form the permanent source of the Church's life and work through the centuries, and are one of the causes of the resurgence of theology and its systematization through the ages. Who would have the temerity to maintain that the rock of faith in Christ and in his word is less solid as a foundation for the upbuilding of the Church than a moral system?

Surely we can draw a lesson from this. In working toward the renewal of moral teaching, we may need to moderate our penchant for speculation and systematization a bit so as to open ourselves, in the manner of our Fathers in the faith, to the Gospel, the Holy Spirit, and the living Church. In so doing, we may become more aware of the limitations and narrowness of the rationalism we have breathed in and fed upon for the last few centuries. It has infiltrated at the intellectual level—where both logical, critical reasoning and an excessive adulation of sensible experience dominate—and at the level of the will, where a hard and suspicious voluntarism restrains the will's natural élan.

What we as ethicists can learn from the patristic period is vast indeed. The Fathers repeatedly invite us to read and meditate on the Scriptures. Our contemplation of them should be broadened and deepened so that the broken bonds between them and morality may be restored. The Fathers also teach us how to study the Scriptures: in faith and through practical experience, and with an eye to scientific research. We need to read Scripture in the context of the Church as well, becoming familiar with its authorized expressions of living tradition. We might add the setting of Christian prayer, liturgical and private, which was essential for the Fathers but mentioned here only in passing. The Fathers further serve us as models in the task of discernment, of assimilating philosophies and cultures so as to build a theology and morality both profoundly evangelical and broadly human. They open up new horizons to us, vaster than our own.

Thanks to the Fathers, we can take a broader view of the ideas and categories we have studied and get to know better their shapes, their limitations, weaknesses, and strengths. This will give our minds room to expand, and a new impetus. Thus empowered, we shall succeed in restoring to moral theology the riches of Gospel spirituality and grace, which have lately been overlooked or left untapped.

The men we call "Fathers in the faith" can become for us fathers in Christian ethics, brothers as well as companions in our meditation on the Gospel and our confrontation with the moral problems of our lives and times. How much we should lose, in losing them!

V. THE HIGH MIDDLE AGES

Since this does not purport to be a complete history of moral theory, we need not linger over the period extending from St. Gregory to St. Bernard. Theologically this era was not particularly creative; rather, it exploited the riches accumulated by the Fathers in the first six centuries. Nevertheless doctrine was not transmitted slavishly and in a materialistic way. It was living and often more original than we might suppose.

Unfortunately this period is little known and not greatly esteemed, partly because of our ignorance, as it was the most obscure period of the Middle Ages. To take but one example, Warren S. Kissinger published a very well documented, almost exhaustive history of interpretations of the Sermon on the Mount and a bibliography on the Sermon and the Beatitudes from the Fathers to the present day. Yet between St.

Gregory and Luther, for the medieval period the author mentions only Thomas Aquinas, to whom he gives three pages. Now a glance at Migne's Latin patrology reveals the existence of a dozen commentaries on Matthew and several treatises and homilies on the Beatitudes and the Sermon, composed notably by St. Bede the Venerable, St. Peter Damian, John of Salisbury, St. Anselm of Canterbury, Hugh of St. Victor, and St. Bernard, to mention only a few familiar names. In these we discover a tradition of interpretation that typically appealed to St. Augustine but included some rather surprising innovations and manifested the profound vitality of Christian thought at this period, constantly in touch as it was with Scripture and experience. It seems obvious that this period, which created Roman art, should evidence originality in the field of theological thought. Yet the history of it largely remains yet to be explored.

Touching moral theology, there are some men whose influence was marked and whose teachings were adopted by the scholastics. In the East, St. Maximin the Confessor (580–662) and St. John Damascene (675–749), whose analyses of human action would be utilized by St. Thomas. In the West we have Boethius (470–523) with his famous *Consolations of Philosophy* focusing on the search for true happiness; it was he who bequeathed the definition of happiness to scholasticism. Isidore of Seville (560–636) with his *Etymologies*" provided one of the basic sources used by scholasticism in their definitions. It is also important to note the pastoral effort influencing concrete moral teaching relative to the sacrament of Penance, which generated the penitentiaries.

With St. Anselm, Hugh of St. Victor, and St. Bernard we are on the threshold of scholasticism, which they anticipated or eventually attacked.

9

Moral Theology in the Period of
High Scholasticism

In the middle of the twelfth century, under the influence of Abelard's
dialectic and the *Sentences* of Peter Lombard, a profound transformation occurred in theological work, methods, and writings. During the
new period thus inaugurated, moral theology received increasingly precise treatment, until with St. Thomas's *Summa theologiae* it attained its
full development as one of the principal branches of theological science.

I. SCHOLASTIC THEOLOGY

The decisive and most characteristic element of this period was the
adoption and general use of the scholastic method. This meant a veritable revolution in intellectual research, in theology as in other sciences.
We can define the scholastic method by its two essential and complementary features:

1. the acceptance of "authorities," or major works of antiquity, as
sources of knowledge and bases for teaching;
2. the use of dialectic as reason's chief tool in the working out of
science.

Regarding the first point, we need to realize that "authority" was
understood in the context of teaching, in the relationship of disciple to

master. This did not imply pressure exerted upon the mind of the student, but rather the authoritative proposal of a truth to be grasped, and the offer of the help needed in intellectual formation.

As for dialectic, well represented by Abelard's *"sic et non,"* it became in the Middle Ages a precision tool for rational research. It consisted in the frank confrontation of contrary opinions in regard to a given question. Through answers to opposing arguments, a deeper, broader, and surer understanding of the truth was aimed at. Dialectic was equally in vogue in public disputations in the schools, in the new universities, and in personal research. This intellectual technique, which proceded by way of questions and articles, gave scholastic works their characteristic literary form, a form observable in the works of all thirteenth-century theologians.

Through a remarkable and fruitful association between listening faith and searching reason, scholasticism, in a single century, brought Western theology to its highest point and gave it a new technique, which has become classic. Theology became the work of faith, drawing largely from the sources of Scripture and patristic tradition and boldly training reason, logic, and dialectic upon the vast material offered by revelation, philosophy, and the other sciences.

Another feature of scholasticism was its corporate character. It lay at the origin of our universities, notably Paris. Once theology ceased to be the preserve of intellectual personalities such as the Fathers of the Church, great bishops and monks like St. Ambrose and the Victorines began to gather disciples around them, forming them into schools. Theology became a corporate enterprise grouped around the faculty of theology, which drew together numerous professors and students from all parts of the world. These enjoyed direct contact with other faculties devoted to different branches of human knowledge and with life in expanding mercantile cities. The goal of theology students was not exclusively spiritual progress or the upbuilding of the Christian populace through preaching. They proposed to form a vast and complete body of theological knowledge, which could address the problems of their times, and they were not indifferent to the scholastic degrees, which would provide access to positions of influence in Church and society. Scholasticism thus started a kind of revolution in the theological world, a close parallel to the social transformation effected by the rise of the great merchant cities and communes.

Finally, the new military and commercial growth of Western society put Christian thought in touch with the lost sources of Greek philosophy, notably Aristotelian, and with the Arabian and Jewish thinkers who transmitted them. Thanks to the strong bond between faith and reason, thirteenth-century scholasticism was to evidence an amazing openness and an enormous power of assimilation of teachings alien to Christianity. These endangered some scholars, but also contributed much material and many useful truths for the fashioning of a theological system at once fully human and authentically Christian.

II. THE DEVELOPMENT OF MORAL THEOLOGY FROM PETER LOMBARD TO THE TIME OF ST. THOMAS

The first scholastic theologians did not give much space to moral theology in their works. Peter Abelard (1079–1142) conceived the idea of a theological synthesis ordered around faith, hope, and charity, in which moral material would have pride of place under the aegis of this last virtue; but his work remained unfinished.

Peter Lombard, in the mid-twelfth century, gave no special place to moral questions in his *Sentences of the Fathers,* a work that later became the required text for theological teaching. He treated some of them, however, in connection with other subjects. The study of creation led him to speak of original sin, of sin in general, of merit, and of virtue. The study of the Incarnation raised the question of whether Christ possessed the virtues of faith, hope, and charity and the other virtues. The consideration of last ends occasioned a reflection on happiness.

Only in the thirteenth century do we see moral theology getting off the ground, with Philip the Chancellor's *Summa de bono* and his study on the virtues, and notably with the *Summa* of Alexander of Hales, which was actually the work of a Franciscan group working under the guidance of the first master of the Friars Minor. Morality is dealt with extensively in this work. The study of sin took up the entire second part of Book II. Beginning with evil in general and misconduct, the sin of the angels was discussed, then that of men; original sin first, then actual sins divided into eight classifications; venial and mortal sins, the seven capital sins, sins against God, neighbor and self, and so forth.

The second part of Book III was devoted to the study of law, grace, and the virtues. The author treated first of eternal and natural law, then lingered over the law of Moses and passed in review the commandments of the Decalogue, with further attention to judicial and cultural precepts. The *Summa* made a detailed study of the evangelical Law and its precepts, then went on to a discussion of grace and the virtues. Unfortunately, it came to a halt in the middle of the treatise on faith, at the point of explaining the Athanasian Creed.

The *Summa* of Alexander of Hales was divided into two large sections on sin and law. A consideration of the virtues was meant to follow, but it is perhaps significant that the Franciscan group never completed the drafting of this section.

The service rendered to thirteenth-century theology by this *Summa* was enormous, and St. Thomas was one of its beneficiaries. It is always helpful, too, to consult this work when studying the Angelic Doctor, to get an idea of contemporary theology and to put his own teaching and the originality of his thought into perspective. In arranging moral material, for example, St. Thomas, in contrast to the Alexandrine *Summa,* placed the virtues first and discussed sins and the precepts of the Decalogue later on (Prologue of IaIIae).

In any event, an attempt to relate Alexander's *Summa* to post-Tridentine ethicists should be made only with caution. While it is true that the latter also arranged their material according to law and sin, yet there is no explicit historical relationship. The ethicists of the seventeenth century did not know Alexander of Hales, who by their time had been wholly supplanted by St. Thomas. Furthermore, there were serious differences, such as the importance given to the evangelical Law and grace by Alexander, which indicated a different conception of law and its role. Nevertheless, the existence of these predominant themes, sin and law, in the earliest major work of the Franciscan school let us glimpse in outline the current of thought that was to lead to nominalism and later to the morality of the textbooks.

We should also mention St. Albert the Great. He was the principal protagonist for the introduction of Aristotle into the University of Paris and the most celebrated theologian of his time. As a professor in the Dominican Studium at Cologne he made a commentary on Aristotle's *Ethics* that was taken down by his student Thomas Aquinas and still exists in manuscript form. Albert thus put into the hands of his disciple the instrument Thomas needed for the future construction of the moral section of his theology. Albert also treated of moral theology in other works: his commentary on the *Sentences* and his summas, particularly the *Summa de bono.* In his work of organizing moral theology, however, he was to be far surpassed by his pupil.

III. ST. THOMAS'S MORAL THEOLOGY

It would not be possible to give a general review of St. Thomas's moral theology here. I prefer to indicate the essential features of its structure and organization. The modern reader, easily put off by the length of the work and deceived by its analytical character, does not usually succeed in grasping an overall view of the work and taking this into account in his interpretation. As we have already observed, however, the *Summa* is rightly compared to a Gothic cathedral because of the harmonious ordering of its main lines and the precision of its details. It is impossible to understand one section without seeing its relation to the others and its position in the general plan.

The structure of St. Thomas's moral theology has had a major historical bearing on the entire field, in retrospect and in what followed. For the first time in the history of Christian thought, we have in the *Summa theologiae* a complete organization of theological material, particularly of moral theology. It reaches a point of perfection that has never been equalled, in the establishment of basic principles and elements, in the analysis and coordination of factors entering into moral action, and in the rigorous logic and order prevailing from beginning to end of the work. The perfection of his analysis and the incomparable power of his synthesis result in a sheer masterpiece, equal to the architectural creations of the same century and the greatest philosophical systems. Historically his work is a phenomenon of capital importance. It is an extraordinary production, containing within itself the main themes of earlier traditions, enhanced by a new arrangement and the resolution of innumerable problems. It was to determine the theological tradition of the future.[1]

Unfortunately, this original Thomistic structure of moral theology was misunderstood and abandoned in the following century, and replaced by a very different organization of moral material, one far less satisfactory in my opinion. But the change thus introduced into Catholic moral thought was concealed by its adherence to most of the treatises, ideas, and positions that form the façade of St. Thomas's moral theory. The

---

1. Harnack's reflection on the Church could aptly be applied to St. Thomas: "How can we fail to see that this Church, despite her frequent toleration of moral laxity, has, by means of her great medieval theologians, applied the Gospel in most areas of life and truly created a Christian ethic? Here and elsewhere she has shown that she bears within herself evangelical themes, as a river sweeps along in its current bits of gold; but these themes and thoughts are one thing with her, fruitful with her own life" A. von Harnack, "What is Christianity?" (New York: Harper, 1957, 267).

changes were said to be only minor, but even the untrained eye can easily
see the upheaval and overturning of the moral structure that took place,
particularly in the seventeenth century. It is as obvious as the difference
between gothic and baroque architecture. In order to understand the
history of moral theology in a more than superficial way, we need to
trace the changes in its architectural structure that occurred from one
century to another.

A. The Structure of St. Thomas's Moral Theology

1. *The* Summa Theologiae

St. Thomas's *Summa theologiae* boasts a profound unity because in
it the very source of theological knowledge—awareness of God—is communicated to us through faith and the gifts of wisdom and knowledge.
The second part, devoted to moral theology, cannot be separated from
the first and third parts, which expound dogma. St. Thomas refused to
adopt the division made by Aristotle in philosophy between metaphysics
and ethics. He believed that the light of faith possessed a greater power
for unification than did human reason.

The unity of the *Summa* is not only logical and intellectual. We could
also call it ontological and dynamic, because it attempts to reproduce
the very movement of Wisdom and the divine action in the work of
creation—culminating in man, the image of God—and in the work of
government, which leads all creatures back to God, their ultimate goal
and happiness. Preeminently, man is so drawn, by means of his free will,
since he is master of his actions and capable of enjoying God. This work,
at once divine and human, cannot be achieved without Christ, who in
his humanity has become for all the way to the Father. The dynamic
unity of the divine Wisdom and work communicates itself to theology
and determines its plan.

The links of the second part with the other two parts are many and
essential. The first part studies the triune God, true bliss of man and the
only answer to the question of happiness, which introduces and dominates St. Thomas's moral teaching. Man's happiness is a participation
in that of God himself. The first part also deals with man the creature
and his faculties, particularly intellect and free will, as well as his sensitivity. These constitute the principles and sources of moral action. Furthermore, certain themes run through the entire *Summa* and are found
in each part, such as the study of goodness, happiness, and love as they

are found in God, angels, men, Christ. The third part treats of the road leading to true happiness: Christ and the aid of his grace, dispensed through the sacraments.

It is absolutely impossible, therefore, to separate the moral section of the *Summa* from the study of God in the first part, which stresses his trinitarian dimension, and from the third part, which gives us the christological and sacramental dimension.

We can, however, call the second part the moral section of the *Summa*, as St. Thomas himself did, but always with the consciousness of its integration in a profoundly theological and vitally unified whole. It belongs to the body of thought as a member; separation would mean death for it.

2. The Treatise on Beatitude

This treatise answers the first and central question of all preceding theological and philosophical tradition: What is man's true happiness? This is likewise the central question in St. Thomas's architectonic plan, for the answer to it is the keystone of his moral theory: According to revelation and in line with reason itself, man's true and complete happiness lies in the loving vision of God. This is the main theme of all his moral treatises: the ultimate end—and corresponding intentionality—which draws human acts together and forms them into a dynamic unity ordered to a single end. The same finality can merge the acts of numerous individuals within communities. St. Thomas even sees in the desire for happiness the beginning of a convergence of all men toward God and a basis of solidarity with the rest of creation, even that which is insentient.

The position of the treatise on beatitude at the beginning of the second part is not, for all this, an obvious choice. It will be recalled that Peter Lombard placed his discussion of beatitude at the end of the *Sentences* with the last ends of man. Aristotle treated of happiness in the first and last books of his *Ethics*. St. Thomas's decision to place his study of happiness at the beginning of his moral theology was therefore a deliberate one.

3. Free Will

The position that St. Thomas assigned to the study of the question of happiness presupposed the study of the human faculties, particularly free will, which was taken up in the first part and continued in the discussion of natural law and its inclinations.

For St. Thomas free will was rooted in the two spiritual faculties of intellect and will, which make the human person an image of God possessing freedom of action, particularly in regard to the natural inclination toward happiness and love and in the inclination to truth. It opened these faculties to the measure of divine infinity, beyond any created object and any created love. Thus the human person was free and in control of his actions, not in spite of, but because of this natural inclination to happiness and truth. The prime moral question, inscribed in our spiritual faculties was, then, what is true happiness? All moral theory was an answer to this question.

This concept of freedom was based on the harmonious interplay of mind and will. I name it freedom for excellence or perfection, since it tends spontaneously to the good and true, to what is of highest quality in view of human perfection. We shall return to this later.

4. The Organization of Moral Theology

The treatise on happiness demonstrated where true human happiness and our ultimate end were to be found. The chief goods that move us and tempt us to make them our final goal were reviewed: riches, honors, power, pleasure, and knowledge. The conclusion reached was that none of these goods could fully satisfy us, for there is within us a natural desire that surpasses them all and reaches out to the God of revelation, become accessible through the grace of Jesus Christ.

The subject matter of moral theology was arranged within this perspective. Since our end is the vision of God, human life was seen as a road leading to him and our actions the steps which would bring us to his presence. Consequently, moral theology quite naturally fell into two main sections. As a science, it first sought general, universal knowledge; as a practical science it regulated individual, particular actions. The *prima secundae* of the *Summa* considered elements common to all human acts. This was followed in the *secunda secundae* by a more specialized study of various virtues.

We will take a brief look at the two major divisions of St. Thomas's moral theory, with special attention to their structural arrangement.

5. An Outline of the Prima Secundae

—The study of *human actions*: analysis and structure, division into good and evil acts, followed by the study of the *passions*, which affect our actions.

—The study of the principles of human actions, which are of two sorts:

Interior principles: These are the *faculties*—intelligence, will, freedom, and sensibility, already studied in the first part. These work together to produce voluntary action. Next come the *virtues,* dynamic potentialities for carrying out noble actions. They are of two kinds: those infused or received from God and those acquired through practice. They are completed by the *gifts, Beatitudes,* and *fruits* of the Holy Spirit. After the virtues, their contraries by defect—the *vices* and *sins*—are studied.

Exterior principles: These originate outside of the person yet are capable of affecting interior action. They are *law,* issuing from divine wisdom through the eternal law and natural law, which culminate in the evangelical law, defined as the action of the Holy Spirit working through faith in Christ; and *grace,* which comes to us through the Passion and Resurrection, by way of the sacraments and which unites us to Christ and sets us upon the one way leading unfailingly to God, which is Christ himself.

I shall comment briefly on each of these points.

The treatise on human acts and the treatise on the passions are veritable works of genius. St. Thomas's analysis of the elements of a human act and its structure included countless borrowings from Aristotelian and Augustinian tradition, but he gave them a new, very precise order, which has become classical. This important account of human action, which deals notably with free will, was foundational for all subsequent analyses and definitions of virtue, law, and so forth. Its nature was structural, not chronological (consider the "twelve stages" of the human act), in contrast to the misinterpretation of those who followed Goudin and Billuart.[2]

Next came the study of the difference between good and bad acts, where St. Thomas introduced the distinction between the interior act, whose object is the end of the action, and the exterior act, whose object is the actual matter of the action. In this connection, he considered the dimensions of interiority and exteriority, found throughout his moral teaching. Modern ethicists are surprised that there is no treatise on conscience here; they do not understand that the role of conscience is filled more dynamically by the practical reason and the virtue of prudence.

The treatise on the passions is quite remarkable, in fact unique. St.

2. Cf. *Somme des Jeunes,* Actes humaines, vol. 1, 414–37 (Paris, 1962).

Thomas analyzed the different passions or emotions and showed how they could make a positive contribution to moral action under the guidance of the virtues. His analysis of love, desire, pleasure, and the rest was not conducted on the sensible level, but took into account what might be termed spiritual sensibility, at work in mystical experience as described by Christian writers.

Then followed the study of the *principles of human action*, which are of two kinds, interior and exterior. Among the *interior principles* we find the *faculties*—intellect, will, free will, sensibility, etc., already discussed in the first part—which work together to form a human action. Here is the basic anthropology that underlies all of St. Thomas's moral theory. Also among the interior principles are located the *habitus*, which received St. Thomas's special attention.[3] These are stable dispositions that develop the power of our faculties and render us capable of performing actions of high quality. They are not to be confused with our ordinary understanding of habits—psychological mechanisms that diminish the moral commitment to an action. The *habitus* as St. Thomas intended it is a principle of progress and resourcefulness through full commitment. It is through these *habitus* or stable dispositions that we acquire mastery over our actions and become entirely free. We might say that, on the level of human action, the *habitus* is proper to the human person. Unfortunately there is no word in our modern languages to convey the meaning of this characteristic reality, which we encounter in all human activity, at all levels.

As with actions, the *habitus* may be either good or evil, a virtue or a vice. *Virtues* were the mainstay of St. Thomas's moral teaching. He therefore studied them with care, drawing upon all the resources of philosophical and Christian tradition. For him, as for the ancients, virtue was the noblest of human, moral qualities; for moderns, on the contrary, the word connotes weakness, deformity, a kind of caricature. The virtues are multiple: intellectual, moral, theological. They are perfected by the gifts of the Holy Spirit, to which are added the Beatitudes and the fruits of the Holy Spirit. St. Thomas thus exploited all the riches of the Christian experience. He also investigated the causes, conditions, interrelationships and duration of the virtues.

The treatise on *vices* and *sins* has always provided ample material for

---

3. Translator's note: In order to signal that the author uses the term in its original Thomist sense, I have used the Latin form, *habitus*, instead of the English word *habit*, which unfortunately carries the connotations of automatic and repetitive behavior. For further discussion, see Romanus Cessario, *The Moral Virtues and Theological Ethics* (Notre Dame/London: University of Notre Dame Press, 1991), chap. 2.

ethicists, whether on original sin, generally discussed first in traditional theology, or on actual sins. St. Thomas covered this vast field in just under twenty questions (71–89). Vice and sin were presented in relation to the virtues, as their contraries. The principle that enabled him to organize the virtues and vices in such a simple yet comprehensive way, in contrast to the lengthy classifications that had preceded him, lies in their relation to a formal object. This object is not to be understood in a physical sense, as in our contemporary idea of the word, but as the reality placed before us. It may be something spiritual, such as goodness or truth, and it specifies the virtues and vices as also the actions and faculties.

law. The first *exterior principle* of our actions is *law.* St. Thomas gave a general definition of law at once precise and flexible. He affirmed that law proceeds from the practical reason and wisdom of the lawgiver, and he then worked out a harmonious scheme of various human and divine laws. Their source is the eternal law in God, reflected in the human heart by natural law, which in turn enables us to establish human laws. In revealed law, God comes to the aid of sinners and leads us to supernatural happiness by a path set out in two main stages. The first, the Old Law, was centered around the Decalogue; the evangelical or New Law was, like the natural law, inscribed in human hearts by the action of the Holy Spirit, and it claims as its privileged text the Sermon on the Mount.

As we see in the study of the virtues and gifts, the Christian life is lived according to the Spirit with the help of Gospel and sacraments. The New Law includes within itself the other laws and carries them to a higher perfection, for it governs even interior actions, those movements of the heart that generate good or evil deeds.

The study of *grace* necessarily followed that of the New Law. According to the Fathers, the specific character of Gospel preaching was that it gave us not only a law but also the help of grace to carry it out. Grace is the principal work of the Holy Spirit. Through it, the evangelical Law justifies us by faith and makes us holy through charity. The treatise on grace is essential to Christian moral teaching and cannot be separated from it. It is completed by the study of merit, the fruit of human acts done for the sake of eternal happiness.

6. An Outline of the Secunda Secundae

This portion of St. Thomas's *Summa* is devoted to particular moral teaching, the study of individual virtues. In each treatise we find the same structure with slight variations:

a. a study of each cardinal virtue and the virtues related to it;
b. a study of the corresponding gift of the Holy Spirit;
c. a study of the contrary vices and sins;
d. a study of the precepts related to the virtue, which support it.

St. Thomas's moral system was therefore one of virtues and gifts. It dealt with sin only as the negation of virtue and saw legal precepts and obligations as aids to virtue.

All his material was grouped around the major classical virtues provided by Christian tradition—faith, hope, and charity—and by those in the philosophical tradition—prudence, justice, temperance, and courage. To these, numerous other virtues were joined. All told, fifty-three virtues were discussed in individual questions or articles.

This classification was established according to the nature of each virtue, which was determined by its proper object. In this sense the classification was analytical and theoretical, each virtue being studied separately, somewhat as one studies the human body and its organs in an anatomical treatise.

In spite of this presentation we must not forget that the virtues form a living, structured organism. In actuality, the virtues always work together in concrete action, each contributing its part, just as the members of our bodies interact as we move about. When we act justly, for example, in the context of our professional work, prudential judgment plays a directive role; we need courage to make certain decisions and implement them, and a certain moderation to temper our desires. Charity, too, intervenes, according to our commitment to higher values. In this context, it would be ridiculous to attempt to acquire one virtue after another, following the listing in the *secunda secundae*. The virtues are all of a piece; they are interrelated, and they progress as a harmonious whole.

There was, therefore, a dynamic ordering of virtues different from their theoretic arrangement. St. Thomas dealt with this in special questions, where he described the coordination and connectedness between certain virtues in particular. He also compared the virtues to show their mutual influence. Thus, charity is the form of all the virtues, for it is charity that moves them toward the vision of God seen as our complete happiness and the ultimate end of all our actions. Justice, too, has a place in all actions relating to others and to society (cf. IaIIae q 65). This is extremely important when we move from the analytic, theoretical perspective of the *Summa* to a consideration of familiar virtues within our concrete experience in a pedagogical or pastoral setting, as spiritual writers habitually do.

The study of virtues provided in the *secunda secundae* was one of the major models of its kind and certainly the most complete in Christian tradition. Consequently, this monumental analysis has dominated Christian theology. In the Middle Ages it was read and utilized more than any other part of the *Summa*.

Nonetheless it poses certain problems for the theologian who attempts to take into full account Christian moral theory as expounded in the New Testament. In his study of the moral virtues, St. Thomas wished to follow faithfully the greatest witnesses to human experience. In his eyes, these were Aristotle and his Greek and Latin disciples and commentators. They provided him notably with lists of virtues annexed to the cardinal virtues. This method of procedure, perfectly legitimate though it was, still gave him some difficulty, since he wished to incorporate in his study certain virtues that were more properly Christian or accentuated in the New Testament and the Fathers and spiritual writers. One such was humility, a central virtue for St. Paul (cf. the hymn in Philippians), St. Augustine, the Desert Fathers and St. Benedict. They made humility the foundation of the entire moral and spiritual edifice. Yet, because he followed the lists of virtues of Cicero and Andronicus of Rhodes, St. Thomas gave humility a place that seemed quite modest. He joined it with modesty, which in turn depends upon temperance. We need to read what St. Thomas wrote about humility and pride (qq 161–62) in order to realize how fully he adopted the Christian teaching on humility.

The case of the virtue of penitence is still clearer. Penitence is an aspect of conversion, of evangelical metanoia, a turning away from sin toward God under the action of grace. It is therefore of paramount importance to the Christian, and Peter Lombard studied it in connection with grace. However, this virtue was not found in the pagan philosophers. Nor did St. Thomas include it among the virtues in his *secunda secundae*. We have to wait for the treatise on the sacrament of penance to see his exposition of it.

The moral teaching presented in this way was general in its intention. It applied to all insofar as they were endowed with reason and were following Christ's call, regardless of their state of life and condition. It needed however to be completed by *a special study of certain graces and particular conditions* within the Church. These were the charisms (the first of which was prophecy), the distinction between the active and the contemplative life, and the states of life, notably those of bishops and religious. These treatises, often exceedingly relevant to the times, as for instance the one on the religious life in the thirteenth century, were always original. They were placed in the ecclesial perspective of the Letters to the Corinthians and Ephesians concerning charisms and ministries. These latter were ordered to the good of the whole Church, and their diversity should remain at the service of its unity, under the inspiration of charity. In moral teaching and in the Church, these graces, states of life, and ministries did not give rise to separate classes with different moral standards. All were called to the perfection of charity through the practice of the virtues, by the Way of Christ, who was studied in the third part. These graces and special states of life were designed to facilitate the journey along the one unique way.

An Overall View

St. Thomas's *Summa*—we can well repeat—is in many ways comparable to the great architectural structures of his generation. This implies that not one of his sections or questions can be interpreted without an awareness of its place in the overall plan of the work and an examination of its many connections with other parts. In order to read the *Summa* we need to keep in mind the general plan which is explained in the prologues. In addition to being an in-depth analysis, this plan shows us the *Summa*'s synthetic dimension, which lends unity to the multiplicity of its questions. The three parts of the *Summa* are like three naves within a cathedral. They communicate and converge upon the same choir, the unique Beatitude.

We should also note here that the plan of the *Summa* was not static like the blueprint of a building or the table of contents of a book. Actually, it was profoundly dynamic. It flowed from the very dynamism of the divine action which creates and governs. It showed the unfolding of free will and human activity in its desire for the promised truth and happiness, and explained the way in which this would be achieved, and the instruments to be used. All of moral theology, down to its slightest details, was undergirded by this powerful movement, which emanates from God and penetrates the human person so as to draw him freely toward God, leading him to the loving vision that fulfills and surpasses every desire.

B. Comparison with Modern Ethicists

St. Thomas's moral theology rapidly became a classic. In the Middle Ages the parts were circulated separately. An unfortunate consequence of this was that the overall plan was lost to view, and the correspondence of the moral section with the study of God in the first part and of Christ in the third part obscured. The *secunda secundae* was the section most widely studied and exploited. It met the pastoral needs of the time most directly, particularly in the mendicant orders, because of its ample, precise, and detailed presentation of the virtues. Of all the "summas of virtues" it was considered the masterpiece.[4]

In the sixteenth century, the success of the *Summa theologiae* was confirmed with its adoption as the basic theological text, replacing Peter Lombard's *Sentences*. St. Thomas then became an authority of first rank, particularly among ethicists. The *prima secundae* served as a model for the earliest manuals of moral theology in the seventeenth century. One would have looked for a tremendous renewal of Thomistic moral theory at that time, but reading and interpretation followed contemporary concepts, categories, and preoccupations, a far cry from those of the Middle Ages.

As we leave our study of the Angelic Doctor, it may be of interest to note the principal areas in the second part where modern ethicists part company with him, often without averting to the fact. I shall indicate here only those differences that emerge from a simple material comparison with the arrangement of the second part. Certain structural changes, which result from current concepts of morality, explain these errors of interpretation and will be reviewed in a later chapter.

1. From the beginning of the seventeenth century, the treatise on *happiness* was passed over in silence. The earliest manuals actually excluded it from fundamental moral teaching. It was thought to be too speculative, but the fundamental reason was that at this time the question of obligation and law was substituted for that of happiness as the central theme of moral teaching. Then, too, the very writers who preserved a place for this treatise out of a sense of obedience to the Thomistic tradition failed to give it the determining and all-important role it filled in the *Summa*. They preferred to stress the study of our ultimate end, as though fearing to speak of happiness. It seems as if modern ethicists were becoming allergic to the question of happiness.

2. In the treatise on *human acts,* the distinction between interior and exterior action was for all practical purposes dropped. This obscured the dimension of interiority, which was of prime importance to St. Thomas, and left only an exterior objectivity in relation to law. At the

---

4. Cf. L. E. Boyle, *The Setting of the Summa theologiae of St. Thomas* (Toronto: Pontifical Institute of Mediaeval Studies, 1982), 23.

same time, finality was reduced to the status of a circumstance of human action. This meant that the intentional bond uniting our successive acts from within so as to form them into one integral whole disappeared also. From this time onward, each action was considered as an isolated entity, an independent case of conscience. The concept of finality shrank to the measure of the immediate intention behind the individual action.

The treatise on the *passions,* that brief masterpiece in which St. Thomas shows how all our sentiments can contribute to even the noblest of moral actions, was transformed into a study of the hindrances and obstacles to the freedom of voluntary acts and took on an entirely negative orientation.

On the other hand, a treatise on *conscience* was added to the study of human acts. It was quite lengthy, and no one has been able to justify its position here within the overall plan of the *Summa.* Actually the role assigned to conscience had been filled, in St. Thomas, by the practical reason aided by the virtue of prudence and the other moral virtues discussed in the *secunda secundae.* While any examination of prudence (whose true nature was never understood) was neglected, a new treatise was created that has since become the centerpiece of fundamental moral teaching.

3. The study of the *virtues* lost its pride of place in basic moral teaching and almost lost it in specialized morality as well, but there the theological virtues could hardly be passed over in complete silence. In place of the virtues, basic moral theory dealt with laws and sins, and it divided specialized moral theory according to the commandments. The study of the virtues, more extensive for those ethicists following the Thomist tradition, was in reality conceived as an examination of the obligations imposed by each virtue and of cases of conscience that might arise therefrom. It was no longer a matter of a moral theory of the virtues, but rather of legal obligations.

The *gifts* of the Holy Spirit, the *Beatitudes,* and the *fruits* of the Holy Spirit disappeared entirely from moral teaching. They were relegated to the field of asceticism and mysticism, as to a subordinate, optional science, although they had been for St. Thomas the evangelical summit to which all Christian life led.

The treatise on *sins* was given considerable space because of the overriding concern of modern ethicists to determine the matter for the sacrament of penance. This treatise took the place of the one on the virtues in basic moral theory. Preoccupation with sin outweighed any interest in the virtues and gave morality the negative aspect of a series of prohibitions.

4. The treatise on *law* held a predominant position in modern moral theory. Law became the unique source of morality, as opposed to freedom. Moreover, its nature changed. It was no longer the work of guiding wisdom addressing itself primarily to human reason; it was now simply the expression of the will of the divine legislator. Moral law was summed up in the natural law, articulated chiefly in the Decalogue and in the positive laws framed by the authority of church or state. The eternal law received only brief mention, and the evangelical Law was practically forgotten, even in the Thomist school. Because of the legalistic spirit prevailing in moral thinking, a definition of the New Law as the interior action of the Holy Spirit was no longer comprehensible, nor could the Sermon on the Mount be conceived as anything other than a collection of counsels.

5. The treatise on *grace* was simply removed from moral theory and relegated to dogma. It is true that it had become very speculative, but how can a Christian theory of morality be constructed without showing the intervention of grace? The links with the treatise on the Trinity and with Christology were weakened. A study of the sacraments was introduced into specialized moral theory, but it was viewed from the angle of the obligations governing their administration and reception.

6. In specialized moral theory, the *virtues* yielded their place to the commandments, and were given very slight importance. They were viewed merely as good habits, and were studied only in light of the obligations involved—hence the neglect of virtues such as hope and courage, which carried no obligations, but were in daily demand. Other virtues, on the contrary, came to the fore. Justice, for example, was closely connected with legal obligation because its object was the law. The treatise on justice became the longest of all, and we could even say that this virtue, seen as obedience to the law, took the place of charity in forming and inspiring moral action. The study of temperance, and especially of chastity, were also expanded.

7. St. Thomas, in his treatise on particular states of life, used the distinction between what is *obligatory* and what is a matter of *counsel* in order to show the scope for freedom that was opened up by the virtues and that extended beyond obligations. This distinction was now applied to moral teaching in its entirety. The moral field was cut in two. On the one hand there were strict obligations; these constituted morality properly so-called. On the other hand there were counsels; these went further than the commandments and pertained to asceticism and mysticism. They constituted a subordinate science, always marginal in moral teaching.

8. Finally, the *religious state* came under review by the ethicists. This, too, they considered from the aspect of the special obligations it imposed rather than the spiritual ideal that had inspired it. As for the *charisms,* such as prophecy, these were assigned either to dogmatic or to mystical theology.

9. I shall conclude this comparison with a rather significant fact. Out of the 303 questions and some 1542 articles which make up the second part, practically no study of a case of conscience can be found. This fact is all the more revealing in that St. Thomas affirms in the prologue to the *prima secundae*: "Since human actions have to do with individual realities, every practical science achieves its goal through particular considerations." Hence he divides his moral teaching into general and particular parts. The latter part is devoted to the study of virtues in particular, yet never moves to the level of cases of conscience. Only in his quodlibetal questions, whose subjects were freely proposed in public disputations, did St. Thomas take up concrete, difficult cases of conscience, such as the question as to whether a salesman was bound to point out the defects in his merchandise, or whether a religious is bound to reveal another's hidden fault to a superior who demands the information.

From the seventeenth century onward, moral teaching concentrated on the examination of cases of conscience. *The* question of the Middle Ages became the case of conscience, which henceforth constituted the chief and characteristic subject matter of modern ethics.

Clearly we are dealing with two different types of moral teaching: on the one hand, a morality of virtues, whose task is to educate to the practice of virtue, notably prudence and concrete discernment; on the other hand, a morality of cases of conscience, scrutinized in their relation to legal obligations.

This simple comparison between the subject matter of the two types of moral teaching shows the profound changes made between the century of St. Thomas and the era of the manuals. After the Council of Trent, a new concept of the organization of moral studies came into being, as we shall see further on. Despite its declared intentions, it could only in part approximate the work of the Angelic Doctor.

Conclusion

St. Thomas's *Summa theologiae* is the greatest masterpiece of medieval scholasticism, particularly in its moral section. It surpasses all the other works of this creative period in the various dimensions of the scholastic method it exploits: in the number of sources utilized—the Latin and Greek Fathers, Aristotle and his Greek, Arabic, and Jewish commentators—and in the profound unity conferred on this vast collection, which could easily have become an ill-assorted clutter; in the perfection and precision of his analysis of all the elements of the moral and theological world; and in the power of synthesis that combined them in a natural and logical order in which none was neglected and each had its part in the forming of a magnificent structure.

We should also mention the basically rational character of the Thomistic system. Moral theory is governed by practical reason, which is in its turn perfected by the infused and acquired virtues. The reference to reason constitutes the principal criterion for forming a moral judgment. Yet this reason is rooted in faith and receives from faith, as well as from the gifts of wisdom and counsel, a higher light. It is also closely linked with the concrete experience produced by the will and sensibility, and their inclinations and desires, rectified and strengthened by the moral virtues and their corresponding gifts. For St. Thomas, therefore, practical reason functions in coordination and harmony, in synergy with the world of faith and the integrated human person.

When, later on, reason became increasingly separated from faith on the one hand and from the will and sensibility on the other, scholasticism was in danger of turning into rationalism and intellectualism. Rationalism sought to explain everything in terms of laws, judgments, and rational criteria; intellectualism confounded reality with abstract concepts and logical reasoning. Scholastic moral theory was greatly impoverished by its loss of contact with human and spiritual experience.

To Counter an Optical Illusion

St. Thomas's power of synthesis and the perfection of his reasoning often led his disciples, we must admit, to a certain optical illusion regarding theology and its history. It was as if they said, "Since St. Thomas has gathered together in his work the best teachings and opinions of all his predecessors, and has arranged the material in such a superlative way, there is no need for us to read all those authors, be they Fathers of the Church or philosophers." And without daring to articulate it, they would apply the same reasoning to Scripture itself. Was it not all there, at a level of heightened rationality, in the work of the Angelic Doctor?

This attitude was supported by the basically rational character of scholasticism, which gave it a timeless perspective. Unaware of the relevance of history, unfamiliar with St. Thomas's predecessors and contemporaries, they came to see him as a kind of theological Himalaya: nothing before his time but preparations and approximations, and after him only anticlimaxes and rearrangements of doubtful value.

This is a dangerous illusion on several counts.

1. It obscures the fact that the Thomist system, like all theological constructs, needs to "humble" itself before the Gospel and the faith, which form the one permanent source of revelation and dominate all theological derivations. Therefore we need to avoid at all costs the possibility of any system, however perfect, standing between the believer—even the theologian—and the Word of God. This is in fact St. Thomas's own explicit opinion, evidenced by his placing faith in Christ, under the light of the Holy Spirit and in union with the Gospel, at the origin of theology and moral action. We can freely affirm that in order to understand St. Thomas in depth we must first detach ourselves from him and follow only the higher light of faith in Christ and his word. Here, and nowhere else, will we discover the pristine source of all authentic theology and the gateway to the profound thought of St. Thomas. The Gospel leads us back to him, as it were, so that we return to him with a viewpoint transformed.

2. The riches of the mystery of Christ contained in the seed of the Gospel have born fruit in the Church from one age to the next, and they surpass anything that the most complete system of thought might have to offer. This living richness needs to be dispensed through a diversity of theological works, each one of which has its own characteristics and traces out a certain pathway to Christ. One suits some, another suits others, according to the variety of spiritual families and intellectual orientations. Experience shows that the disciple of St. Thomas loses nothing by reading St. Augustine, the Greek Fathers, or even the humble Desert Fathers. St. Thomas delighted in these, as he perused Cassian's *Conferences*. In so doing, the disciple will acquire a better understanding of St. Thomas's text and will more clearly perceive its dimensions and background.

3. Finally, to limit oneself to studying St. Thomas, in moral theory or in any field, would be contrary to the spirit of the Angelic Doctor. He was eager for the truth, wherever he might find it, and careful to take it into account. We should consider his work a guide to those authors whom he has exploited, and to the whole truth, of which they, too, were interpreters, rather than a complete, self-contained manual which renders them superfluous. This is the ever-ambivalent feature of systematic

thought: it can be either open or closed in upon itself. Coming to understand how the Thomistic system opens out to the Gospel of Christ, as well as to other works of Christian faith and human thought, depends in large part on the reader himself.

Note on the Thomist School

The heritage of St. Thomas was rapidly taken up by his order. It had to defend him after Stephen Tempier's condemnation of certain propositions in his works in 1277, and Franciscan attacks, among others the famous *Corrections* of William de la Mare. The latter declared 117 propositions taught by St. Thomas to be contrary to the truth and to Franciscan teaching. After 1279 the general chapter of the Dominicans held in Paris prohibited all attacks on the doctrine of Brother Thomas Aquinas. Finally, in 1313, the general chapter of Metz decreed that his doctrine should be taught throughout the Order of Preachers.[5]

The Thomist school developed gradually. It was formed chiefly by numerous commentators on the works of the Master, especially on the *Summa theologiae*. They set out to defend, explain, and circulate his doctrine, particularly after the nominalist crisis of the fourteenth and fifteenth centuries and during the effort for theological renewal that took place in the sixteenth century.

The principal commentators were John Capreolus (+1444), who merited the title "prince of Thomists"; Thomas of Vio, called Cajetan (1469–1534), considered the main commentator on St. Thomas and whose notes are inserted in the Leonine edition of the *Summa theologiae*; and Sylvester of Ferrara (1474–1526) who wrote a beautiful commentary on the *Summa contra Gentiles*.

Spain experienced a remarkable Thomistic renewal in the sixteenth century at the school of Salamanca. Outstanding in this work were Francisco de Vitoria (1480–1546) who is considered the founder of international law, Melchior Cano (1509–60), author of *Loci theologici*, a study of theology's foundations in revelation, and one of the principal theologians at the Council of Trent, and Dominic Banez (1528–1604), celebrated for his controversies with the Jesuits over the theology of grace. In the seventeenth century we should also mention the Carmelite School of Salamanca, called the *Salmanticences,* who composed a *Cur-*

5. For details of this story, cf. J. A. Weisheipl, *Friar Thomas d'Aquino* (Oxford, 1974; Washington, D.C., 1983), 331ff.

sus theologicus summam divi Thomae complectens, and John of St. Thomas (1589–1644), who wrote a *Cursus theologicus* at Alcala in Portugal and a beautiful treatise on the gifts of the Holy Spirit. Finally, in the eighteenth century, there was the Frenchman, Charles R. Billuart (1685–1757), who possessed the art of clear, precise, and succinct exposition and became a principal source for later manuals of Thomistic inspiration.

It is clear that St. Thomas's posterity was numerous. His work produced a school that has known renewals in different periods up to our own day, when it is called Neothomism. Following recent historical studies, however, a problem of fidelity and authenticity has arisen, particularly in connection with moral theory. Does the presentation of moral theology that we find in manuals and commentaries written "according to the thought of Thomas" really correspond accurately with his thought? In recent times, the difference between St. Thomas's teaching and that of his school has been so obvious that a new term has been created, especially in Germany. "Thomanisch" or "thomasisch" has been coined, and in France, "thomasien," to replace "thomiste" which translates into our English "Thomist." We cannot go into a detailed comparison here, but shall speak only of the fundamental question of method.

The traditional method of the Thomistic school was inherited from scholasticism and may be described as speculative. It began with texts from various works of St. Thomas and studied, explained, and commented on them by way of dialectic reasoning. Thus it appeared to be in the direct tradition of the scholastic method used by St. Thomas himself.

We should note, however, that the basis for teaching—the "authorities" and the texts used—was greatly reduced. The commentators confined themselves to the actual works of St. Thomas, while he himself had always taken the greatest care to broaden the range of his sources as far as possible in all areas. Moreover, modern rationalism influenced scholasticism in favor of abstract reasoning and logic, in keeping with an intellectualism separated from concrete experience.

St. Thomas's work was clearly speculative, as is any theology. It could not be understood and explained without speculative reflection. Yet an historical study of the Angelic Doctor's texts and thinking gradually opens to us many perspectives that a purely speculative study cannot grasp. The historical approach facilitates a re-reading that is renewed, more precise, and vastly richer—a great advantage to theological reflection. Here are a few capital points:

1. Simple research into the sources briefly indicated by St. Thomas leads us to fairly long passages from St. Augustine, St. Gregory, Aristotle and other ancient authors. These give a breadth and fulness to his texts that could not otherwise be perceived, because of the extraordinary conciseness of St. Thomas's thought and language. Behind his rigorous reasoning we discover a rich human and Christian experience, selected, clarified, and exposed with extraordinary simplicity.

2. Knowledge of the historical, theological and social setting of the thirteenth century provides us with many points of reference, enabling us to acquire a deeper and more accurate view of St. Thomas's doctrine. To know the theologians contemporary with him, the state of doctrine, the adversaries he had to contend with, and the causes he defended— all this is indispensable if we are to achieve a true and nuanced interpretation in order to grasp the perspectives of his thought and avoid misconceptions.

3. We also need to take into account, far more than the commentators have done, the historical sequence of St. Thomas's work. Something written during his youth, such as his *Commentary on the Sentences,* is not to be ranked with his *Summa theologiae.* A difference in viewpoint is at work here. The speculative student looks for similarities between texts on the same subject, so as to establish St. Thomas's teaching firmly. The historian, on the other hand, is on the lookout for differences, which signal an evolution, a progress in thought and expression. The historical viewpoint enables us to retrace the genesis and maturation of St. Thomas's teaching and to enter into it more profoundly and more exactly. Behind the texts we see more clearly the life and the work unfolding. In the end we understand it all better.

4. Historical study is one method of approach for the theologian. The author under consideration becomes more and more familiar by repeated reading, and a fruitful dialogue can then be initiated and pursued, leading to debates over the most interesting problems. Paradoxically, however, the nearer we wish to come to an author of the past, the greater the gap to be bridged. Once we have learned how to weigh and measure St. Thomas's texts and thoughts, we begin to see with increasing clarity how different they are from the modern interpretations offered by his commentators and disciples. We discover the historical conditioning that has influenced the moderns as they read their master: the debate centering around nominalism, for example (of which we shall speak later), which turned the theological world of the Middle Ages upside down. After that came the Protestant crisis and rationalism. These major historical events in Western thought erected a kind of screen be-

tween the Thomistic school and its master, through the unconscious introduction of problematics, categories and subtly different concepts that were often impoverished and shrunken, especially in the moral domain.

It seems indispensable today, therefore, to combine the historical and speculative methods in the study of St. Thomas, thus restoring the tradition. Our object is not purely historical: as exact a reproduction of a great Master's thought as possible. It is mainly theological and perhaps quite timely. St. Thomas's synthesis is one of those classic masterpieces to which we must return again and again, as to one of the great models of theological thought. These possess a hidden power to shape minds in every age and make them fruitful, if the needed time is allowed for the acquisition of a vital knowledge of them. In-depth understanding of St. Thomas, as of the Fathers, is one of the conditions for an authentic renewal of theology today. It will enhance our rich heritage; it will forestall its loss. Nowhere is this truer than in the case of moral theology.

10

Moral Theology in the Late Middle Ages:
The Nominalist Revolution

The Franciscan and Dominican Schools

Moral theology undoubtedly reached its high point with the Second Part of St. Thomas's *Summa*. This crowning achievement should not make us forget, however, the importance and richness of the Franciscan school—exemplified by Alexander of Hales, St. Bonaventure, and Duns Scotus—which was the self-styled guardian of the Augustinian tradition. The Dominican school took shape and grew in self-awareness for two reasons. First it had to respond to the attacks launched against St. Thomas's theology by the Franciscans, who considered him innovative. Next it had to reply to the condemnation of certain Thomist theses by Stephen Tempier, bishop of Paris, who was supported by the Franciscans and even by some Dominican masters, such as Robert Kilwardby of Oxford. The Franciscans reacted against St. Thomas's Aristotelianism, which they thought exaggerated and dangerous, even though they themselves made use of Aristotle to some extent. The split went deep. Regarding the central point of Christian moral theory, the Franciscans and Dominicans took opposite stands. Where St. Thomas affirmed the primacy of the intellect, defining the first and formal element of beatitude in terms of this faculty, as the vision of God, the Franciscans maintained the primacy of the will and made love the essential element of beatitude.

These struggles between the two schools, prolonged for several centuries, should not, however, obscure the positive side of the common theological research that was being carried on. The theological works produced represented the attempts of Christian minds to express the riches of the mystery of salvation, which surpass all understanding in this life and admit of multiple approaches. These schools could be compared to mighty branches issuing from the one trunk of scholasticism in its creative age, united in their origin and spreading out in opposite directions. We should note, too, that the struggle was not limited to two particular religious families, to a struggle between chapels and forts. It turned on the concept of theology as a whole and concerned the entire Church, in which at the time these orders played a predominant role. It was the Christian mind that was at work, that was in question.

Clearly we cannot go into all the details of the debate here. We shall focus on a decisive stage in the development of moral theology in the fourteenthth century, the appearance of nominalism.

The Destiny of William of Ockham

The Franciscan William of Ockham knew a strange fate. An Englishman studying at Oxford, he never received his master's degree in theology because the chancellor, John Lutterell, accused him of holding dangerous doctrines. He remained a bachelor of theology all his life and was therefore commonly referred to as "the Venerable Inceptor." Summoned to the court of Avignon by Pope John XXII, he arrived there in 1324, one year after the solemn canonization of St. Thomas. Another arrival at the same period was Meister Eckhart, the German Dominican, who died shortly before the condemnation of theses drawn from his works and preaching. Ockham, seeing that his cause was overly compromised, fled to Germany and entered the service of the emperor, Louis of Bavaria, in his struggle with the pope. Ockham is credited with these words to his protector: "Defend me with the sword, and I will defend you with words." He extolled the separation of church and state and denied all temporal power to the pope, thus shattering medieval Christianity's ideal of unity. He also separated faith and reason. In answering him, John XXII drew upon the works of St. Thomas.

Ockham's doctrines were widely diffused and gave birth to nominalism, which was to influence Western thought profoundly at the close of the Middle Ages. While adhering to scholastic tradition externally, nominalism marked a decisive break with the era of the Fathers and great scholastics. It was the direct preparation for the advent of a new period, and this seems particularly apparent in the case of moral theology.

Unfortunately Ockham's moral theories have not been studied extensively. He himself wrote nothing in this field comparable to the Second Part of St. Thomas's *Summa theologiae*. However, the parts of his work that were completed and continued by his disciples suffice to show us his principal ideas and reveal the extent of his influence. I shall not describe Ockham's moral teaching here, with its nuances, subtleties, and occasional contradictions. My chief purpose is to highlight those elements in his work that gave rise to a new structuring of moral doctrine.

The Nominalist Explosion

The comparison I am about to make is perhaps bold, but it is easily verifiable. With Ockham we witness the first atomic explosion of the modern era. The atom he split was obviously not physical but psychic. It was the nadir of the human soul, with its faculties, which was broken apart by a new concept of freedom. This produced successive aftershocks, which destroyed the unity of theology and Western thought. With Ockham, freedom, by means of the claim to radical autonomy that defined it, was separated from all that was foreign to it: reason, sensibility, natural inclinations, and all external factors. Further separations followed: freedom was separated from nature, law, and grace; moral doctrine from mysticism; reason from faith; the individual from society. Later I shall devote a chapter to the study of this concept of freedom, but it seems opportune to discuss it briefly here.

Freedom of Indifference

According to nominalism, only individual realities exist. They are unique in their singular existence. Universals are simply convenient labels, having no reality in themselves and only nominal value. Within the moral domain, reality lies in the individual decision of the free will. For Ockham, freedom meant essentially the power to choose between contraries, independently of all other causes except freedom, or the will itself—whence the term *freedom of indifference.* "What I mean by freedom is the power I have to produce various effects, indifferently and in a contingent manner, in such a way that I can either cause an effect or not cause it without any change being produced outside of this power" (*Quodl.* I, q 16). As Garvens wrote: "According to Ockham, the will is purely indeterminate in the placing of its first act. This first act can be determined by nothing—neither by an external object nor on the basis of an habitual determination. It is itself the basis of its own free activity, and determines itself in opposition to the intellect, which is conditioned by something else, that is, by the will, to posit determined acts. Ockham characterizes freedom of will as something indifferent and contingent, 'quaedam indifferentia et contingentia.' . . . On the basis of this freedom the will maintains complete indifference in the face of individual contraries."[1]

Ockham thus interpreted with a new stringency Peter Lombard's classical definition of freedom: freedom of will is the power to reason and to will ("Liberum arbitrium est facultas rationis et voluntatis"). According to a previously mentioned explanation given by St. Bonaventure (II *Sent.*, dist. 25, a 1, q 2), freedom does not proceed from reason and will, as St. Thomas said, but precedes them and moves them to act; a person can choose whether or not to know and to will. Ockham tended to identify freedom with the will, which he considered the essential human faculty.

The Breaking Down of Action

For Ockham all moral reality was concentrated in free choice thus defined. The free act springs forth instantaneously from a decision that has no other cause than the power of self-determination enjoyed by the will. From this it followed that each of our voluntary acts becomes a single reality, isolated in time by the very power that enables us to choose between contraries. We could not be bound by a past action or obliged to a future one without losing the radical freedom that is ours at each moment. Thus human conduct became a succession of individual actions, drawn as it were with perforated lines, the dots being the unrelated moral atoms. Any connection between them would remain outside the sphere of freedom and dependent upon its decision.

Consequently, the notion of finality lost much of its relevance. For St. Thomas it had been the basic element of voluntary action, which he defined as the properly human power to act in view of an end. This is why the study of moral theology in the *Summa* began with a treatise on our last end, presented as the principle of the unity of all our actions. This was extended potentially to all persons and even to all creatures. Ock-

---

1. A. Garvens, "Die Grundlagen der Ethik Wilhelm von Ockham," *Franziskanische Studien* 21 (1934): 256–57.

ham did not accept these views, which gave a universal significance to finality. In his concept of human action, separation was more important than unity. He did attach real importance to the end, which he called the principal object of the free act. But he considered that the end existed within the individual act and could not therefore establish essential bonds with other acts. In the case of a person willing a thing in view of an end willed for its own sake, he saw two perfectly distinct actions. The act directed to the thing would have as its end a "partial object" and would be distinct from the act that directly sought the end and grasped it as a "total object."[2]

Human action then would be made up of a succession of free decisions or independent acts—cases of conscience as they would later be called— having only superficial relation to one another. Each would have to be studied in isolation. Like each individual person, each act became a kind of absolute, like a small island. Hence the note of insularity that has been attributed to Ockham's thought and that evokes his English background. With his concept of freedom and of the human act he laid the *casuistry* foundations of what was to become casuistry.

The Rejection of Natural Inclinations

A significant feature of Ockham's critique of the Thomist conception of freedom was his rejection of natural inclinations outside the kernel of the free act. Notably, he rejected the inclination to happiness, which pervades the moral doctrine of the *Summa theologiae* and, in keeping with all previous tradition, forms its initial moral question.

Indubitably, the inclination to happiness exists within us, but according to Ockham we remain entirely free to choose it or not, even as we are free in regard to our ultimate end or to our existence itself. We can follow these inclinations or reject them. "I say that the will in this state can choose not to will its ultimate end, either in a general or a particular sense. Here is my proof. We can reject what the intellect orders us to reject. That is obvious. But the intellect may believe that we have no ultimate end or happiness, and consequently it can order us to reject such an end or happiness. Secondly, whoever is able to reject the antecedent can reject the consequent. Now a person can reject his existence. He can therefore also reject the happiness believes follows upon his existence. I say further that if the intellect judges a certain thing to be an

2. I *Sent.* dist. 1, q 1 N, quoted by Garvens in "Grundlagen," 392.

ultimate end, the will can reject this end. My proof runs as follows: because the free power is capable of contrary acts, it can determine itself in any one direction or another. The will, as a free power, can will or not will any object whatsoever. If, therefore, it is capable of choosing God, by the same token it can reject God."[3]

For St. Thomas the natural inclinations to goodness, happiness, being, and truth were the very source of freedom. They formed the will and intellect, whose union produced free will. According to him we are free not in spite of our natural inclinations, but because of them. For Ockham, on the contrary, freedom dominated the natural inclinations and preceded them, because of its radical indetermination and its ability to choose contraries in their regard. From this point of view, it could be said that freedom is more apparent when it resists natural inclinations. In his rejection of all natural inclination outside of the will, Ockham outstripped his master, Duns Scotus, and was led to a stronger form of indeterminism, as Garvens notes (*Ethik von Ockham*, 256).

As a consequence, natural inclinations, no longer included within the voluntary act, were something short of freedom and were relegated to a lower level in the moral world, to the order of instinct, sensibility, or to a biological ambience. Ockham and his followers could no longer understand that in the human person there was a higher natural spontaneity, of a spiritual order, inspiring freedom itself.

Deemphasizing the Virtues

As with natural inclinations and the concept of finality, the free action of *habitus* and virtues, seen as stable dispositions for acting in a determined way, also had to be toned down. *Habitus* and virtues could doubtless help to facilitate the execution of a free decision and overcome obstacles. But if these dispositions were determining, they would di-

---

3. Sed ultra dicta ibi dico quod voluntas pro statu isto potest nolle ultimum finem sive ostendatur in generali sive in particulari. Quod probatur sic. Illud potest esse nolitum quod intellectus potest dictare esse nolendum. (Hoc patet de se.) Sed intellectus potest credere nullum esse finem ultimum sive beatitudinem, et per consequens dictare finem untimum sive beatitudinem esse nolendum. Secundo sic. Quicumque potest nolle antecedens potest nolle et consequens. Sed aliquis poatest velle non esse. Igitur potest beatitudinem nolle quam credit consequi ad suum esse.—Secundo dico quod intellectu iudicante hoc esse finem ultimum, potest voluntas illam finem nolle: quod probatur. Quia potentia libera est receptiva actuum contrariorum: qua ratione potest in unum et in reliquum. Sed voluntas tamquam potentia libera est receptiva nolle et velle respectu cuiuscumque objecti. Si igitur potest in velle respectu Dei: eadem ratione potest in nolle Dei . . ." (IV *Sent.* q. 14 D).

minish the power to choose between contraries, which was the very definition of freedom. An act performed under the impulse of a *habitus* seemed less free than if it had proceeded from a purely voluntary decision. *Habitus* and virtues came to be ranked below freedom and were considered tendencies of which freedom could make use or not, at will. They thus lost their proper moral value and became simply psychological mechanisms, or habits in the contemporary sense. As Father Vereecke has written: "Freedom means total indetermination. For an action to be good and meritorious, the will must have absolute freedom to respond to the obligation or not. Anything that can restrict our freedom—bodily dispositions, sensible inclinations, or psychic dispositions, restricts the scope of morality also. Nominalist moral doctrine will not be a moral theory of being that adapts itself more and more to the good [which is precisely the role of virtue, I would add], but a moral theory of action, freedom assuming at each instant the obligation being imposed upon it" (*De Guillaume d'Ockham à saint Alphonse de Liguori*, 134–35).

I should add that Ockham did subscribe to the teaching on virtue that was held unanimously in scholastic tradition. But he interpreted it in his own way. He recognized virtue only in the action of the will. "The *habitus* of the will alone is the seat of virtue, properly speaking," he affirmed (III *Sent.*, q 10, D). Acts arising from the sensible powers or, in the case of prudence, from the intellect, could be called virtues only in an extraneous sense, by extension. In any case, for him the inclination to virtue was neither a *habitus* nor an act but a simple potency, as matter is to form. In his opinion the act absolutely outweighed any inclination or *habitus*. As can be seen, if Ockham made use of the traditional teaching on virtues, he reinterpreted it within the context of his conceptions of voluntary action and the freedom of indifference, which is to say that he did away with virtue's central role in moral theory as the necessary determination for assuring the perfection of human acts.

God's Omnipotent Freedom

Ockham contrasted human freedom with the freedom of God. His thought was dominated by the idea of the divine omnipotence, which enabled him to carry his idea of freedom to an absolute degree. For him, the divine will was totally free; it governed moral law itself and all the laws of creation. What God willed was necessarily just and good precisely because he willed it. Law, and all moral value or qualification, flowed from this will. Determined in the establishment of good and evil by nothing other than itself, the divine will could at any instant change what we considered to be permitted or forbidden according to the commandments, notably the Decalogue. God could even change the first commandment, and, for example, pushing it to the limit, command a person to hate him, in such a way that this act of hatred would become good. "Every will can conform to the divine precepts; but God can command the created will to hate him, and the created will can do this (thereby refusing its own happiness and ultimate end). Furthermore, any act that is righteous in this world can also be righteous in the next, the fatherland; just as hatred of God can be a good act in this world, so can it be in the next."[4]

Similarly, hatred of our neighbor, theft, and adultery could become meritorious if God commanded them. Ockham did not recognize in human nature any law or order whatsoever that might determine the divine freedom and omnipotence. Undoubtedly there was a customary order of things, "communis cursus rerum," in morality and in nature, and this developed conformably with the laws we know. This fact enabled Ockham to find some meaning in classical expressions such as the natural law, but he believed we had no guarantee that the divine will might not change tomorrow.

Moral Obligation

Thus divine and human freedom were conceived as two absolutes, but with this difference: God was omnipotent in regard to his creatures and could, consequently, impose his will upon us. Having removed from both divine and human wills all dependence upon their respective natures, Ockham could no longer find any links between man and God, as with other freedoms, except those issuing from the divine will and power: such would be the law, the expression of the divine will, acting with the force of obligation. Law and obligation thus held the central position in Ocham's moral theory; they became its inmost core. Obligation was for him the very essence of morality. "The significance of goodness and malice is that an agent is obliged to a given action or to its contrary."[5] The concept of morality implied nothing more than a

4. "Preterea omnis voluntas potest se conformare precepto divino: sed Deus potest precipere quod voluntas creata odiat eum, igitur voluntas creata potest hoc facere. Preterea omne quod potest esse actus rectus in via et in patria: sed odire Deum potest esse actus rectus in via ista si precipiatur a Deo: ergo et in patria" (ibid., dictum quintum).

5. Bonitas moralis et malitia connotant, quod agens obligatur ad illud actum vel eius oppositum" (II *Sent.* q. 19 P).

person's obligation to perform a determined action. It was the fact of obligation, not the observance of any real ordinance, that made the difference between moral good and evil (Garvens, *Ethik von Ockham*, 271). To do good meant to carry out one's obligations; to do evil meant to act contrariwise.[6]

Ockham established the idea of obligation at the center of his moral theory so definitively that even charity was subsidiary to it. Love of God no longer had a directly and essentially moral value for him. The famous supposition that God could command one to hate him and to hate one's neighbors, and so make hatred itself meritorious, tells the whole story in this regard. Ockham went so far as to maintain that God could, without impunity, annihilate a person or condemn to damnation one who loved him above all things and tried with all his heart to please him. The reason given was that God could do whatever he willed with his creatures and was answerable to no one (*Sent.*, q 3, Q). These extreme assertions show that the center of morality was no longer love but rather obligation, flowing from God's sheer will and freedom. To put it another way—for Ockham, love tended to be confused with obedience to obligations.

Thus the moral field came to be fenced in by moral obligations. It extended as far as obligations but stopped short with their limitations. What fell outside of obligation or exceeded it—the striving of charity toward perfection, for example—had no place in moral teaching properly so-called.

The Moral Law

Moral obligation was determined and refined by law. Law therefore confronted human freedom in the form of obligations issuing from the divine will and, to some extent, assumed the role of this will.

First came the divine law, communicated to us through revelation in the Bible, particularly the Decalogue and the evangelical precepts. Ockham's disciples then distinguished a series of laws deduced from those directly revealed. These came from the apostles and their successors, or were formed through obvious reasoning, or again were inspired by individuals.

Ockham maintained the existence of natural law (for this was imposed

6. Malum nihil aliud est quam facere aliquid ad cuius oppositum faciendum aliquis obligatur" (II *Sent.* q. 4 and 5 H).

upon him by scholastic tradition), but he reinterpreted it in keeping with his own system. Natural law was no longer based, for him, on human nature and its inclinations, which reason could reveal. It consisted rather in the authority of right reason presenting directly to the human will the orders and obligations that emanated from the divine will, without there being any need whatsoever to justify them, since the justification of law could be found only in the divine will itself.[7]

It followed from this that law would enjoy an increasingly major function in moral theory, for the scopes of the two now coincided. Moral theory soon came to be divided not according to virtues but according to various laws, particularly the commandments of the principal moral law, the Decalogue.

Without doubt Ockham strongly affirmed God's freedom in regard to the moral law and assigned to the latter a fair amount of relativity. He also admitted the validity of moral laws as we know them in the normal course of events. Later ethicists, less daring and more practical, were content to consider law and the commandments as pure and simple expressions of the divine will, which was clearly the source of obligations and the firm foundation of morality. Their moral theory would comprise both obligation and law on an equal basis.

Practical Reason and Prudence as Subjective Guides

Having established the divine will and law as the sources of obligation, Ockham needed to show how the human person might become aware, subjectively, of these objective rules. This would be the work of the practical reason and prudence. Here Ockham was following the terms and categories of Aristotle, which had influenced theology since the time of St. Thomas. He also used the terms 'practical reason' and 'prudence' rather than 'conscience', which was a part of the Christian tradition and later prevailed.

Here again, however, while apparently holding to the classic doctrine, Ockham transformed it and adapted it to his own views.

For Ockham, only the will could have a properly moral value, could be good or evil, and could be called virtuous. All morality thus depended on freedom. Nevertheless, in order to act well the human will had need of right reason, for, in contrast to the divine will, it was not its own final court of appeal nor the adequate source of its own goodness. It had,

7. Cf. L. Vereecke, *De Guillaume d'Ockham à saint Alphonse de Liguori*, 161–62.

then, to conform to a rule external to it. This was why right reason intervened in the action of the will, to make known to it what the divine will was, to apply the moral law to it, and in this way to exercise a partial causality on the voluntary action.

However, according to Ockham it was no part of the practical reason's function to discover, found, or justify moral laws in view of man's and creation's relationship to God. He no longer spoke of a natural *habitus*, of the first principles of the moral law, or of synderesis, as treated in the scholastic tradition. The function of the practical reason was basically to show to the will the commandments of God, as they were expressed chiefly in revelation, and then to apply these commandments to particular, concrete actions by means of deductive reflection aided by experience. This would be the proper work of prudence.

Practical reason and prudence were, then, simply intermediaries between law and free will. Their function was to transmit precepts and obligations. We should also recall here that all this work had value only "stante ordinatione divina, quae nunc est," that is, only so long as the present order of things as willed by God was in effect, it being understood that God could change it all at any moment. Yet in spite of this ever-present mental reservation of Ockham's, right reason was indeed, moment by moment, the interpreter of the demands of the divine will. The will that opposed right reason was by that fact opposing the will of God. The will should normally therefore conform itself to right reason; without this obedience it could not be virtuous.

It is very revealing to see how Ockham defined the relation between right reason and the will. For him, right reason contributed nothing to the value of the voluntary act when presenting it with an object having in itself some moral quality, such as the love of parents, for example. The fact was that right reason itself became the object and cause of the goodness of the voluntary act, insofar as it transmitted the divine will. What happened was this: an action was virtuous when the will tended, through its action, to what reason commanded, precisely because it commanded it and for no other motive such as the pleasure that might accompany it. For an act to be fully virtuous, it had to be dictated by right reason and willed precisely because right reason so dictated.[8]

Such a formula inevitably calls to mind Kant's categorical imperative. It shows, in any case, the extent to which Ockham identified obligation with moral value. For the will to be good, it was not enough for it to

8. "Quia hoc est elicere conformiter rationi rectae: velle dictatum a ratione recta propter hoc quod est dictatum" (III *Sent.*, q. 12 DDD).

act in conformity with the obligation transmitted to it by right reason, for this kind of conformity could be only material. It was further necessary that there be a formal will to act in conformity with right reason, that is, in conformity with the divine command transmitted by it.

Conclusion

Ockham's thought, as disseminated by nominalism, represented a major stage in the history of moral theology. With the "Venerable Inceptor" we witness the advent of the moral theory of obligation and the formation of a new moral structure, inspired by a rigorous logic that was to exert its influence, either directly or indirectly, upon all modern thought.

Ockham was the first to propose the moral theory of obligation, we may say. Up to his time the primary moral question had been that of happiness and the search for it, among philosophers as well as the Fathers of the Church and theologians. For philosophers, the answer to the question centered upon the moral virtues, for theologians, upon the theological and moral virtues, with charity as the chief focus. The question of moral obligation was certainly not absent from classical theology, but it was secondary and was not viewed with the same urgency.

In St. Thomas, as we have seen, each treatise on a virtue concluded with a question on the relevant precept. Thus precept and obligation were placed at the service of the virtues and played an instructive role, especially in the early stages of moral progress. It is clear that Franciscan theologians gave greater emphasis to the commandments and precepts, as we see in the *Summa* of Alexander of Hales, but no one, to my knowledge, had as yet assigned a preponderant place to obligation. We could therefore say that moral theology, up to the beginning of the fourteenth century, was a moral doctrine of happiness and of virtues ordered to charity.

With Ockham the very center of moral doctrine was displaced, and an entirely new organization inaugurated. Although outwardly he adopted all the traditional ideas and doctrines, Ockham reinterpreted them and transformed them profoundly, basing them on the central idea of obligation, which he substituted for that of happiness and virtue. Obligation became the very essence of morality. Thus his structure fully merited the name of a morality of obligation. It was the first in history to be so qualified.

Ockham's influence regarding obligation was to be decisive for subsequent moral theology. Doubtless there were many theologians, among them some Thomists, who would criticize nominalism and reject its extremes, however logical. Among these extremes were, for example, the relativity of the moral law before God and the refusal to base it upon human nature and reality. Nevertheless, there was a near unanimity among ethicists, especially from the seventeenth century onward, that placed obligation at the center of morality, whatever divergencies there might be among them as to the foundation of moral obligation.

The Structure and Logic of the System

It remains for us to show the logic of Ockham's system and the structure of the resulting moral theory, for that logic insured its success. It seems to me that the original tenet of the system, which affected all the rest, was the concept of the freedom of indifference, or freedom's definition as a purely voluntary choice between contraries. Freedom became a kind of absolute in action, implying the rupture, the dissolution, of all bonds of dependence between the will and whatever was external to it, at the very root of action. Ockham defined both man and God in light of this freedom. Using it as a foundation, he established their mutual relationship and reconstructed the moral theory linking them.

God was for Ockham the absolute realization of freedom, because of his omnipotence. God was subject to no law, not even the moral law. His free will was the sole cause and origin of the moral law. Man also enjoyed complete freedom of will. Yet, as a creature, he was subject to the divine power and his freedom came into direct confrontation with the will of God, which acted upon his freedom and limited it by the divine power of obligation. Morality was born from this encounter between divine and human freedom and marked man's dependence upon God. It focused on obligation, which was the only possible meeting place of the two freedoms thus conceived.

The new moral structure arose from this concept. Its two poles, as we have seen, were divine and human freedom. Moral law was a concrete expression of God's will, receiving from him the power to oblige. Man possessed freedom of action, conceived as a series of voluntary, independent decisions. The function of practical reason and prudence, or conscience as later moralists would call it, was to transmit the commands and obligations issuing from the law. We could say that the essential elements of the "atom" of nominalist morality were freedom and law, practical reason or conscience, and free actions or cases of conscience, with obligation at the core. We can recognize here the subjects of the main treatises in later moral manuals. Only sins are missing; these claimed the special attention of ethicists after the Council of Trent, from the pastoral viewpoint of the sacrament of penance.

Other elements of earlier moral theology were treated according to the logic of the system thus constituted. They were either reinterpreted and cut down or passed over and excluded from the moral domain. Ockham had already criticized the theme of man's desire for happiness; his criticism led to the subsequent neglect of the treatise on beatitude. He reduced virtue to the will's conformity to obligations prescribed by practical reason and the law. He subjected charity to obligation and held that even the command to love God was relative. The gifts of the Holy Spirit, defined by St. Thomas as spiritual "instincts," obviously had no place in this moral system. In brief, all the later developments of moral theology, particularly in its casuistic form, were contained in germ in Ockham's morality of obligation.

With nominalism, a chasm was fixed between modern moralists and patristic tradition. Nominalist categories, and in particular what might be called the "obligationist" conception of morality, became so deeply rooted in men's minds that it seemed impossible that things could have been otherwise. Even the adversaries of nominalism frequently came to accept its notions and the problems it posed. In the end, St. Thomas and the Fathers began to be read through "nominalist lenses." The differences that had been established, and their consequences, were no longer perceived.

This was one of the most basic problems facing Christian morality. It had vast historical and systematic repercussions. Nominalism stirred up a veritable revolution in the moral world and its ideological structures. Nothing would ever be the same again.

In particular, morality's relationship to Scripture was subtly modified with the advent of nominalism. Even if Scripture as a whole was considered the expression of God's will, nevertheless, only passages revealing strictly legal obligations were of interest to ethicists, who had a tendency to interpret them quite literally in a materialistic way, as one would interpret juridical texts. Under this influence, the bond between moral theology and Scripture diminished more and more.

Moral Theology in the Modern Era
of the Manuals

We might mark the beginning of the modern period of moral theology with Ockham in the fourteenth century. Nominalism, as we have seen, made a profound break with the previous tradition of moral theory and laid the foundations for the concepts and systems of subsequent centuries, focusing moral theory upon the idea and sense of obligation. But we need first to distinguish a period of preparation—the fifteenth and sixteenth centuries—before considering the elaboration of the moral system which became classic in the manuals of the seventeenth century.

I. MORAL THEOLOGY IN THE FIFTEENTH AND SIXTEENTH CENTURIES

In broad outline, this period was characterized by several upheavals and divisions within theology, which became increasingly evident and shattered the unity it had enjoyed up to the thirteenth century. Theology began to be more and more sharply distinguished and separated from mysticism on the one hand and from pastoral concerns on the other. These divisions, affecting theology as a whole, had a particular impact upon moral theology and were caused in part by the new conception of the latter.

The Cleavage between Scholastic and Mystical Theology

During these two centuries, theology developed in the universities along the lines of an intensification of the rational procedures of scholasticism: a wider use of dialectic and logic, a stress on speculative orientation, and a proliferation of distinctions, questions, and arguments. A technical vocabulary and specialized terminology developed, along with a penchant for abstraction and a growing complexity of problems and discussions. In truth, scholasticism was expanding, the beehive swarming.

A glance at the major scholastic works of the period illustrates this. In a single article we can find as many as twenty favorable arguments marshalled to support a given proposition, and as many again to disprove it. This was followed by a lengthy conclusion, and objections and responses involving some extremely subtle distinctions. The rational, speculative character of theology became increasingly pronounced, matching the rationalism that was to dominate the modern era. Theology was now the preserve of the universities, in the sense that it was from this time on the specialty of clerics who were going on to higher studies.

Yet, theology still kept its vitality—in fact, knew a remarkable renewal. Consider, for example, the Dominican school of Salamanca, illustrious for the name of Francisco de Vitoria (1480–1546). As the basic text for theological teaching, Vitoria replaced Peter Lombard's *Sentences* with the *Summa* of St. Thomas, since its rational structure was far more satisfactory. With Vitoria, the treatise on justice took on an added dimension in response to the contemporary problems of natural and human rights, which had surfaced with the discovery of the New World. This treatise corresponded at the same time to the increasingly juridical character of moral theory. Once again, we indicate the great commentators on St. Thomas, especially Cajetan, who covered the entire *Summa*.

This markedly speculative theology of the universities distanced itself gradually from what came to be known as mystical theology, the great spiritual currents of the period. Spiritual writers began with the experience of the life of faith. They attempted to disclose the divine realities perceived in the interior life and the growth of the believing soul. All this was conveyed in concrete terms, which spoke to the imagination and sensibility as well as the mind and were, in principle, available to everyone. Their thought was always stamped with their personality, in contrast to the abstract nature of scholasticism. Spiritual writers addressed all Christians, all at least who aspired to a Gospel way of life. Their object was essentially practical: to persuade their readers to embark upon a spiritual journey and to aid their progress. On every count, the difference between speculative and mystical theology was apparent.

In the fourteenth century, however, with Meister Eckhart (1260–1327), who was simultaneously a theologian, a spiritual writer, and a director of souls, mysticism remained profoundly linked with scholastic theology. Later the separation became much more decisive, even though Rhineland and Flemish mysticism, with Tauler (1300–1361), Henry Suso (1295?–1366), and Ruysbroeck (1293–1381), possessed its own speculative orientation. The latter issued actually from experience and the light of faith more than from rational research. Spiritual writers, such as Thomas à Kempis in the *Imitation of Christ,* frequently warned their readers against the vanity of theological speculation. Spanish mysticism, continuing into the sixteenth century, harmonized fairly well with theology, but there was the same contrast as far as works were concerned.

St. Francis de Sales (1567–1622) deserves special mention, since he succeeded to some extent in reestablishing in his works the unity between those dimensions which had for too long been separated. Thanks to his literary genius he conveyed theological knowledge, the spiritual experience of God's love, and pastoral concern in a manner that placed his works within the reach of all. He reacted against current opinion, which reserved the spiritual life and the search for perfection to a chosen few belonging to the religious state. He attempted to show how every Christian, even though living in the world, was called to the interior life, and he indicated ways for advancing in it.

Here we are touching upon one of the contributing causes of the deep separation between theology—particularly moral theology—and spiritual experience and mysticism. Nominalism stressed the idea of law and obligation in morality, to the detriment of interior spontaneity and the vitality proper to love—qualities that form the very basis of the spiritual and mystical life. The split between moral theory and mysticism was reinforced when the distinction between precepts and counsels was applied to moral theory in its entirety. Moral theory dealt essentially with precepts, which determined obligations in various sectors of human activity and were imposed on all without distinction. The counsels were supplementary and dealt with superogatory actions left to each individual's free initiative. By this very fact, they were reserved to the chosen few who sought perfection; this was the terrain of asceticism and mysticism.

This distinction meant a veritable separation between morality, based on the constraint of law, and mysticism, seen as an extraordinary phenomenon. The split was accentuated by a mistrust of spontaneity. On the sociological plane as well there was a separation within the Church between ordinary Christians, who were expected to conform merely to ordinary moral standards, and religious, who were dedicated to a higher way of life.

The Separation between Theology and Pastoral Concerns

The same effects were at work in the relationship between theology and the pastoral ministry, with its various functions of preaching, catechesis and the administration of the sacraments, especially penance. The teaching in the universities was inaccessible to the majority of priests because of its high degree of technicality. It had taken on a speculative orientation, which was very far from the demands of ministry to the faithful and from the experience gained in pastoral practice. The advantage of some kind of compromise began to be felt. Priests needed a more concrete, practical training, guidance in their apostolic work, and help with the problems they encountered, particularly in the moral sphere. This need gave rise to numerous summas for confessors, the most important of which was the *Summa theologiae* of St. Antoninus of Florence (1389–1459). St. Antoninus gave ample attention to the study of the virtues and the gifts of the Holy Spirit. This pastoral concern was taken up by the Council of Trent and exerted a determining influence on the new concept of moral theology that would affect the composition of manuals and direct them towards the solving of cases of conscience.

The Theologian, the Spiritual Writer, and the Pastor of Souls

The phenomena just described took very concrete shape. The development of scholasticism in the universities gave rise to a new function in the Church, that of the theology professor. His principal work was teaching and research. He was a theologian in the current sense of the word. Little by little he was distinguished from the spiritual leader and the mystic, and equally from the pastor of souls, whether bishop or priest. The distances among the representatives of these three functions, as among their fields of competence and their types of knowledge and experience, widened progressively from this time on and has come down to our own day. It is reflected in study programs, where different branches of moral theology are distinguished: ascetical, mystical, and finally pastoral. It constitutes one of the major problems of contemporary theology, which faces the difficult task of reestablishing a lost unity, notably after a council that gave priority to pastoral ministry.

The separations among theology, spirituality, and pastoral care have worked to the detriment of each. In cutting itself off from spiritual and pastoral experience, theology has lost its vitality and creative power. It is too far from its primary source, the Gospel, which is not a book of learned speculation but basically a work of preaching and catechesis springing from faith and destined to produce, guide, and nourish faith. Spirituality, for its part, has lost the support of theological reflection and has slipped into religious sentiment. Pastoral practice has been reduced to a popularization of theology, when in fact it could contribute its own experience of the gift of the life of faith, which links it directly with the preaching of the Gospel.

Is there any need to recall that such separations did not exist for the Fathers of the Church, never entered their minds? Many of the Fathers were at one and the same time bishops, preachers, pastors of souls, theologians and spiritual leaders, to say nothing of mystics. They were all these things simultaneously. Each facet of their personality and work interacted with the other dimensions, enriching them, at the heart of a more and more unified human, Christian experience.

The Separation between Theology and Exegesis

Finally we should note one last separation that had its effect on the preceding ones. After the Renaissance, scriptural exegesis was progressively transformed. Literary exegesis took the place of theological interpretation, and this paved the way for the historical method of the nineteenth century. New technical methods and language evolved. Scientific exegesis distanced itself from theological problems and, by the same token, from the mystical interpretation of Scripture. It no longer had a pastoral goal. In the measure in which, priding itself on its discoveries, it established itself more and more as a scientific discipline, modern exegesis experienced a growing temptation to take over Scripture. It thus ran the risk of becoming a stumbling block for those who were not initiated into its methods and who were therefore somehow disqualified. A serious problem is posed today both for theologians and for exegetes who want to reestablish communication between themselves, concerning the method of reading Scripture and the access to its content. In particular, this problem weighs heavily upon those ethicists who cannot be satisfied to receive from exegetes the alms of a few imperative texts taken at random from Scripture.

We shall now see how, in the seventeenth century, a new moral theology was constructed upon the foundations furnished by the theology of the preceding centuries. Finally, a chapter will be devoted to a comparison between Catholic moral teaching and Protestant ethics, which merits special treatment. In doing this, I shall take some liberties with the historical sequence. This anomaly is necessitated by the fact that post-Tridentine Catholic moral theology was not elaborated until after the crisis of the Reformation.

II. THE DEVELOPMENT OF THE "INSTITUTES OF MORAL THEOLOGY"

Period of Preparation

One of the major preoccupations of the Council of Trent was the establishment of seminaries where future priests would receive a formation adapted to their ministerial needs, particularly the administration of the sacrament of penance. This necessitated the working out of appropriate theological courses, especially in the area of moral theology.

In this connection the Society of Jesus, which experienced its first great burgeoning in the second half of the sixteenth century, felt an urgent need to organize studies that would address both the requirements of theology and the pastoral work it had assumed, notably spiritual direction, as well as contemporary ideas and practical questions—among others, the handling of "cases of conscience" then in vogue. In 1586 a Jesuit commission was formed to draw up a syllabus of theological studies, a *"ratio studiorum* of the Society of Jesus." This syllabus, having been submitted to the scrutiny of the foremost theologians of the Company, was reworked, and new redactions appeared in 1591 and 1615.[1]

---

1. This history has been discussed by J. Theiner in his book *Die Entwicklung der Moraltheologie zur eigenstandigen Disziplin* (Regenburg, 1970).

At the same time, other Jesuit theologians proposed projects and plans for the teaching of moral theology. A keen need was felt, at the end of the sixteenth century, for a new method of teaching theology. The manuals were in the making.

In its *ratio studiorum* the Company, in spite of some resistance, adopted St. Thomas's *Summa theologiae* as the foundation of its teaching. Animated, however, by pastoral concerns, the Jesuits distinguished between a major and minor course in moral theology. The major course was designed for more speculative study, while the minor course was more practical, and basically oriented to the formation of the students in treating concrete cases. This distinction led to a redistribution of the material of moral theology. The general elements necessary as a foundation for moral theology were borrowed from speculative theology, and this became fundamental moral theology. The material comprised by moral theology was then exposed in detail, following the order of the commandments, and this became specialized moral theology. In this way, all elements useful for the direct, circumstantial study of cases of conscience were gathered together. Some treatises, such as those on the final end of man and on grace, were considered too speculative and were dropped from specialized moral theology. Those on human acts, the *habitus* and virtues, law, conscience, and sin, were retained. Finally, the commandments of God and of the Church were to be studied, together with the sacraments, from the viewpoint of the obligations regarding their administration. Eventually, obligations proper to certain states of life, such as religious life, were included, and, last of all, canonical censures connected with the sacrament of penance.

The *Institutiones Morales* of Juan Azor

Such was the program, in general outline, on which the Spanish Jesuit Juan Azor (1536–1603), a professor in Rome, embarked in his syllabus of moral theology, formally entitled "Institutionum moralium, in quibus universae quaestiones ad conscientiam recte aut prave factorum pertinentes, breviter tractantur." The first volume appeared in Rome in 1600 and was followed by two posthumous volumes in 1606 and 1611. Clearly the brevity mentioned in the title did not prevent the work from running on at great length, due to the author's intent to include all moral material in support of this conception: that conscience is the point of departure between good and evil.

A New Arrangement of the Subject Matter of
Moral Theology

In his introduction Azor proposed a fourfold division of moral theology:

1. The Ten Commandments of God
2. The seven sacraments
3. Ecclesiastical censures and penalties, indulgences
4. States of life and final ends

This was obviously a new distribution of the subject matter of moral
theology. It replaced the traditional organization according to virtues,
and from this time onward a wholly new approach was envisaged, determined by obligations. These were explicit in the commandments, and
even the sacraments and the states of life were to be studied from the
point of view of the obligations they imposed. We are moving here from
a morality of virtue to a morality of obligation. The virtues were not
forgotten in the new schema—how could they be passed over in silence?—but they were related and subordinated to certain commandments and always discussed within the context of the relevant obligations.

These broad divisions of moral theology were preceded by the study
of seven general topics which Azor declared he had borrowed from St.
Thomas's *prima secundae*.[2] They were:

1. Human acts
2. Their division into good and bad acts, or their morality (Azor introduced a study of conscience here)
3. The passions or affections, which incline us to good or evil
4. *Habitus*
5. Virtues in general
6. Sins in general, seen as infractions of law and rights

---

2. "Caeterum tamquam prima totius operis elementa septem primis libris ea tracto,
quae in Prima Secundae S. Thomas recto ordine disputavit, nimirum de actionibus humanis, de honestate et turpitudine humanarum actionum, de affectibus quibus ad bonum
aut malum saepius incitamur, de habitibus, qui assidua exercitatione comparantur in
nobis, de virtutibus universim, quae nos ad bonum impellunt, de peccatis itidem genera-
tim, quibus leges et iura perfringimus, de legibus humanis, de divina insuper et naturali
lege, de quinque ecclesiae mandatis, quibus tamquam regulis actiones hominum dirigun-
tur."

7. Laws: human, divine, and natural; the five commandments of the Church, seen as rules for human action

Comparing this outline with the order observed in St. Thomas's *prima secundae,* which Azor claimed to follow and of which he wrote that the material was arranged there in the most appropriate order ("recto ordine disputavit"), we immediately see the differences and in particular the major omissions. Without reference or explanation, Azor left out the treatise on beatitude, which introduces the second part and gives it its characteristic tone. He also omitted the questions on the Beatitudes and the gifts and fruits of the Holy Spirit, as well as the treatise on grace.

The Omission of the Treatise on Beatitude

The omission of the treatise on our final end and on beatitude was particularly significant. Its consequences were weighty. Doubtless Azor wanted to conform to the prescription of the *ratio studiorum* of the Jesuits, in which he had collaborated moreover from 1586 onward, and so to set aside questions too speculative for a practical course in moral theology.

But there was a deeper reason beneath this. The question was precisely this: whether the treatise on man's final end and beatitude had come to be considered as purely speculative and thus superfluous to moral theology. How could it be held that the question of happiness, so human and universal in St. Augustine's thought, was neither concrete nor practical? That the search for true happiness in riches, honors, pleasure, knowledge, and the goods of the mind, as described by St. Thomas, held only speculative interest? The real reason for the omission, unclear perhaps to Azor but nonetheless operative in influencing him and his followers, was that he could no longer see the importance of the treatise on beatitude within the context of his conception of a morality of obligation. Thus he was led to relegate this study to the end of moral theology and place it in the section on the ends of man. He had intended to discuss this at the end of his work, but never had the opportunity. In his opinion, the treatise on beatitude was no longer needed for the foundations of the moral edifice. Lacking knowledge of history, he could not know that St. Thomas had followed a precisely inverse order. Constrained by the outline of Peter Lombard's *Sentences* to treat beatitude with the final ends, St. Thomas placed the question of happiness at the beginning of moral theology, considering it to be primary and principal. Azor therefore followed a logic totally contrary to that of St. Thomas.

This logic was operative in all the authors of the manuals. Taking as their model the *Syllabus of Moral Theology,* they disregarded the question of our last end and beatitude, seeing in it no relevance for fundamental moral theology. In the index of the vast *Moral Theology* of St. Alphonsus Liguori, for example, the word *beatitudo* does not occur. This kind of moral theology had no need for the consideration of happiness. Similarly, the consideration of our last end lost the role of supreme criterion given it by St. Thomas. Finality no longer held a preponderant place in this system. The end, henceforth, was only one element of a moral action—one among others.

The Omission of the Treatise on the Gifts of the Holy Spirit

Did Azor also consider the questions of the Beatitudes and the gifts and fruits of the Holy Spirit too speculative? Yet they played an important part in Christian experience, according to spiritual writers of Azor's period, including Jesuits. Doubtless we can see in this omission an effect of opposition to mysticism, which prevailed toward the end of the sixteenth century. However this may be, the ultimate reason that led all subsequent ethicists to ban the gifts of the Holy Spirit from moral theology is to be found in the logic of the system of morality of obligation. Morality was a matter of obligations binding all. The gifts of the Holy Spirit, the Beatitudes, and the spiritual life they animated could obviously not be objects of strict obligation. They therefore pertained not to moral theology but to the order of counsels and a different kind of science. Thus barred from the life of the ordinary faithful, these questions could seem abstract and far from everyday reality. They were assigned to asceticism and mysticism.

Another factor contributed to the deepening of the rift between morality and spirituality in Azor's perspective. J. Theiner remarks that Azor treated of the love of God in connection with the first commandment and love of neighbor with the fourth commandment, thus unduly separating the two great commandments, which were united in the Gospel, while he connected the other commandments with the virtue of justice.[3] This shift of viewpoint is very significant. Love and its movement, as described by spiritual writers and mystics, was no longer primary in Azor's moral theology. It was subordinated to the commandments, and the study of it could be organized in relation to them. The virtue of

3. Theiner, *Entwicklung,* 274.

justice was of special importance to him because it was directly linked to the idea of obligation. Morality became a matter of justice or of obligation between man and God; even charity was to be fitted into this scheme. It is not surprising, therefore, that Azor's work had a strongly juridical and canonical flavor and was preoccupied with questions of law, notably in the second and third parts.

Small wonder, then, that Azor lingered over the study of the Mosaic Law and slighted the treatise on the New Law, which is one of the crowning peaks of St. Thomas's moral theology. All subsequent ethicists followed in his footsteps. The Decalogue, identified with natural law, provided him with the convenient divisions of specialized moral theology, which took the place of the virtues. We should add that the Mosaic Law was interpreted from then on within the particular context of morality of obligation. This was a far cry from Scripture, which subordinates all commandments and, as I understand it, the very notion of commandments, to the love of God manifested in the Covenant and promises.

The Omission of the Treatise on Grace

The omission of the treatise on grace could be justified, at first sight, for the same reason as was given above: its speculative character. Actually, discussions on grace, revived by the Protestant dispute and pursued up to the seventeenth century, were exceedingly complex and could seem very abstract. But this hardly seems an adequate reason for neglecting all study of grace and failing to show its role and relevance for human action, which had been demonstrated in St. Augustine's *Confessions* and in many other accounts of conversions. Here again, it seems to me, the mechanism of the system of obligation was highly developed. Grace, by definition, could not be reduced to obligation; law and its imperatives had no hold on grace. It could have no part in a law-based morality; strictly speaking, it would be useless there. It could intervene only from the outside, in the form of help promised by faith. The study of grace would pertain more to dogmatics than to moral theology, would be speculative rather than practical. It is odd that Azor and his followers did not notice that, in neglecting the teaching of grace in moral theology, they were falling into the traps of legalism on the one hand and natural humanism on the other, to say nothing of the danger of Pelagianism. Their leaving the treatise on grace out of moral theology simply indicates that they completely misunderstood its role in the Christian life and in their own lives—a reduction to the absurd. Yet, they could find no way of including grace in the moral system they had constructed: a serious situation indeed.

The Principal Treatises of Fundamental Moral Theology

Prescinding from the patent and significant omissions in Azor's *Institutiones morales* as compared with St. Thomas's *Summa,* we can take a closer look at the first part of the moral theology presented. Its principal features come into clear focus. The treatise on free human action was highly developed. It even included a detailed analysis of the various parts according to St. Thomas, which might conceivably have been viewed as too speculative, and went on to a study of morality. At this point, Azor introduced a goodly treatise on conscience, not found in St. Thomas; its position here has always posed a problem for those who look for some connection with the *Summa.* In a single book or chapter, Azor ran swiftly through the "affections" of the soul, the *habitus* and virtues contributing to the quality of human action, and original justice. He then tarried over the study of sins and particularly of various laws.

Free human acts, good and bad; conscience; sins and laws: these were the outstanding features of the landscape in Azor's general section. They were precisely the treatises that would make up the fundamental moral theology of succeeding ethicists. The study of passions and affections, and of *habitus* and virtues—still retained because of their obvious importance in traditional theology—were confined to a small section in Book III of the first part: chapters 1–19 for the passions, chapters 20–24 for *habitus,* chapters 25–30 for virtues. These elements played only a secondary role in moral theology, as helps or hindrances to free action.

In specialized moral theology, the commandments were the basis of the division of subject matter from this time on. They were the backbone of the system and determined the orientation of thought. The virtues— even theological—were nothing more than particular topics, categories serving to classify obligations.

The Influence of the *Institutiones Morales*

We have paused over the study and critique of Azor's syllabus because of its historical importance. As a model, it has had a determining influence upon the innumerable manuals that followed. Their main elements were already clearly discernible in it: the essential themes and characteristics of a duty-driven moral theology. The success of the syllabus was doubtless due to the action of the Society of Jesus, to its response to teaching needs, and to contemporary trends such as the interest in cases of conscience. But more profoundly, and in spite of its omissions, the strength of the syllabus lay in the rigorous systemization it introduced into moral theology. This corresponded to the internal logic of a morality of obligation. The concept of moral theology that it proposed became classic. It was adopted without cavil by ethicists of all religious persuasions. So convincing was it that many believed, with Azor, that in it the moral teaching of St. Thomas, the Catholic moral teaching of all times lay revealed. A mere glance at the *Summa theologiae* and the Church Fathers, a smattering of critical sense, would have shown the profound differences. But the new system was so cogent, its appeal to contemporary ideas so direct, that the possibility of any other line of thought had become quite unimaginable.

III. THE MANUALS OF MORAL THEOLOGY

With the seventeenth century, textbooks of moral theology proliferated. Their authors were divided into different schools according to their stand on the question of probabilism. I shall touch later on this prolonged and confused dispute, which has been very well analyzed by Father Deman in his article on probabilism in the *Dictionnaire de Théologie Catholique*. Here I can remark only that we are very far from the theological perspectives of St. Thomas's time, when schools were divided by their stands on questions of vast importance, such as the respective roles of mind and will in moral action, or the place given to Aristotle's philosophy within Christian theology. Seventeenth-century ethicists turned their entire attention to individual cases of conscience, which became the principal subject matter of moral theology. The question of rules for the solution of doubtful cases gave rise to what were called systems of morality and distinguished the different schools: probabilism, the theory of greater probability, equal probability, etc. As we have already remarked, practically no conscience cases are discussed in the whole of St. Thomas's second part. St. Thomas and those whom we call casuists move in two different worlds, with totally different concepts of systemetization and morality, despite the external resemblance the latter tried to maintain and a similar vocabulary. Each tried, in all honesty, to safeguard and transmit the content of Christian morality.

The Core of Morality in the Manuals

I shall now try to describe the internal structure common to all the manuals and to show the logic behind their system, which assured its success.

Regardless of the differences between schools, nearly all moral manuals from the seventeenth to the twentiethth century adopted the same base and structure that appeared in fundamental moral theology. There were four treatises—on human acts, conscience, laws, and sins. These were always included, with minor variations. Some manuals changed their order. Others, in fidelity to St. Thomas, added a treatise on the virtues, attempting to make room for it in the division of moral theology. Some even began with a treatise on man's final end. Most of these additions and reactions have cropped up in our own century. But however praiseworthy, they have effected no essential change in the structure and logic of the moral system which has become classic.

Henceforth the moral teaching of the manuals can be compared to a building resting upon four foundation stones: human or free action, law, conscience, and sin. The columns are the commandments of God and of the Church, and these indicate the obligations, which mark off the boundaries and provide the furnishings of moral theology, so to speak. The overarching roof is justice, the legal virtue, or honesty, as Suarez declared, which crowns the whole edifice and maintains it with the force of obligation.

This is only the outward show, however. It does not express the dynamism animating morality. In order to demonstrate this, I would use a contemporary comparison. At the core of this morality is the primal atom, which controls all the rest. This atom is formed of two contrary poles. The positive pole, or proton, is freedom; the negative, the electron, is law, which restrains freedom and keeps it in a constant state of tension. Freedom and law come into contact through two intermediary elements, kinds of neutrons: conscience, which dictates the law to freedom, and human acts or cases of conscience, which issue from freedom but are subject to law. All the atomic energy resulting from the tension between freedom and law and from their encounter in the realm of conscience and human acts is concentrated in obligation, which thus forms the primal dynamic core characteristic of this concept of morality. Freedom and law, conscience and human acts or cases of conscience, all are concentrated in obligation. This is the essence of the moral theory in the manuals, this forms its atomic core. All morality will develop and be dealt with from this vantage point.

Let us establish the connection existing between the treatises of fundamental moral theology. Freedom was the foundation of the treatise on human acts, for they were essentially free acts. It was viewed as the freedom of indifference, or the power to choose between contraries, especially for or against the law and its prescriptions. Law was studied in the treatise on laws, which dominated all of moral theology and determined its division according to the commandments. Conscience received a special treatise, a period piece, for it had not existed in this form and in this place in previous theology. Conscience replaced the virtue of prudence. Human acts became cases of conscience, with special attention to doubtful cases, where it was hard to discern where law and where freedom entered in. Further special attention was directed to sins, which took on particular importance from the fact that this moral system was oriented to the sacrament of penance. Obligation did not have its own treatise, but enjoyed the force of law in its rule over freedom. No one ever dreamed of questioning either its nature or its role. It formed the primary element of this moral structure and was considered as obvious as an undemonstrable first principle. To touch it, to call it into question, to subordinate it to any other element, would be to threaten the survival of the entire edifice.

An Examination of the Chief Elements of Fundamental Moral Theology in the Manuals

I shall comment briefly on the principal elements of this moral teaching so as to clarify its nature and role and the profound logic animating it. In this way we will have an understanding of its positions, main themes and limitations.

1. Tension between Law and Freedom

The moving force of this moral theory lay in the tension existing between freedom and law as between two contrary poles. According to a comparison suggested by Father L. Lehu,[4] freedom and law confronted each other like two property owners disputing over the field of human

4. L. Lehu, *Philosophia moralis et socialis*, vol. 1 (Paris: Lecoffre, 1914), 279.

acts. As was commonly said, "the law takes over," or "freedom takes over," according to whether an act fell under the law or was left free. What belonged to the one was by that fact taken away from the other.

Freedom was the positive pole, since it was the source of human acts and therefore their first owner. The presumption would always be in favor of freedom, as juridical language expressed it regarding rules for the solution of doubtful cases of conscience. This was the source of human spontaneity.

Law was morality's negative pole, for it set limits to freedom, to restrain it with its commands and prohibitions. The tension law created gave it the appearance of a pressure external to the person, despite all efforts to interiorize and justify it. Obligation's constraint was set over against freedom's spontaneity.

Caught between these two poles, morality, which was bound by its nature and role to interpret law, but was equally desirous not to repress freedom unduly or to show it favor either, was in a perpetual state of imbalance. Sometimes it inclined toward the rigor of the law, sometimes toward freedom and breadth of view. This is why ethicists of our day, having long been austere guardians of the law, frequently take up the cause of personal freedom of conscience and call into question former legal assumptions.

2. Freedom

In the manuals, including Thomist ones, freedom was obviously the freedom of indifference, or the will's self-determining power to act for or against the law, reason, or conscience. This concept tinged all of morality with voluntarism. Because of its opposition to natural or acquired inclinations, it was the real cause of the rejection of the treatise on beatitude. For the same reason virtues were reduced to good habits that facilitated free action, but they no longer provided the interior motivation that would have given the action full value. In the same way, sensible passions were considered obstacles to free action, although according to St. Thomas they had a positive contribution to offer. In fact, this concept of freedom seems to have been the primary origin of the entire new systematization of moral theology.

3. Law

Law was understood from the point of view of freedom of indifference. It issued from another freedom, another will confronting us and possessing the power to impose itself upon us with the force of obligation. Law was no longer the result of the legislator's reason but issued directly from his will and authority. Therefore, law varied according to the legislators: God, the Church, society. The question of their authority, legitimacy, and power to dictate the law became paramount. In this context, the problem of obedience and authority pervaded the moral world, while intelligence was not allowed to intervene. The question of legal form became more important than the basis of the law or any judgment about it.

Moral theology was consequently a matter of law primarily, and of norms and regulations, but understood in a voluntarist sense. A crucial, perhaps insoluble problem from this point of view would be that of the foundation of laws or norms. What could this be, if not a will that had no other reason for its action but itself?

The essential work of moral theology was to determine the exact meaning of the law, the precise limits of what was allowed or forbidden, what was obligatory or prohibited, and what free. What might one do or not do? All moral theology seemed summed up in this question.

Law was the origin of morality. A human act became moral through its relationship to the law. It would be good or evil in the measure in which it conformed to the law or obligation or opposed it; apart from this, a human act could be regarded as indifferent. This view applied to the literal text of the law. The nature of morality was defined solely in respect of the law; one would be tempted to see its relationship to human actions as merely external and accidental.

It comes as no surprise that this moral teaching gave considerable space to law, notably canon law, and to justice. The treatise on the latter was one of the longest, and its influence pervaded moral theology.

Clearly the danger that threatened the system was that it might turn into pure legalism. It could also become minimalistic: the law, necessarily applied to all, could require only the minimum of any one person. And since morality flowed from the law, one could easily believe all moral duties fulfilled, once the law's demands were met. An upward thrust toward perfection and excellence was replaced by a sense of satisfaction in duties done, along with the temptation to reduce all duties to the minimum.

4. Human Acts

Human acts were also viewed and discussed in the context of freedom of indifference, as purely voluntary choices between contraries. One followed another without any interior connection; they were therefore to be studied in isolation. Each human act resembled a monad or atom. The proper subject matter of this moral teaching was the case of conscience, considered individually. It became the typical moral entity, determined primarily in itself, in its essence and in its object as falling under the law, and secondarily through circumstances or accidental elements. Finality, which played a decisive role for St. Thomas by forming an intrinsic bond between multiple acts, was viewed as extrinsic, related in a more or less contingent way to the object of the individual act.

The distinction between interior and exterior acts was blurred. The ethicist lost sight of the interior dimension, for he felt that it was necessary to study only the exterior aspect of human acts as found in the legal ordinances. Interiority was considered subjective, connected with spirituality. The ethicist focused on the material elements covered by the law; for him, this was objectivity. Whence the danger of objectivism, or the reduction of the moral act to its material object as opposed to all that emanated from the agent.

The definition of morality in terms of law reduced the scope of moral theology unduly. A rejoinder might doubtless be that the subject matter of moral theology was human action. But in reality, only those actions falling under law and obligation were considered; actions pertaining to freedom were outside its ambit. Yet these were the richest of acts, the ones in which the person was most deeply involved—those great actions, works, and creations in the spiritual order such as holiness and moral stature. The heart's thrust toward all that is best, toward perfection and excellence, escaped this moral theology.

Furthermore, of all the human acts in which ethicists did take an interest, what most preoccupied them was sins. This focus on sin is explained not only by their concern to clarify the matter of the sacrament of penance. It came from the law itself, which contained more negative precepts than positive, since its role was primarily to guard against faults. It stemmed also from the nature of sin, which errs by excess or defect and is thus multiple in relation to any single good act. This is also the tendency of legalism, which is more interested in infractions of the law than in the less troublesome conformity to it. In fundamental moral theology, therefore, the treatise on sins replaced the one on virtues, which was thought to be of secondary importance.

5. Conscience

The treatise on conscience was a creation of casuist morality, which introduced it into fundamental moral theology and hoisted it to the heights. It was not that the reality of the human conscience had been ignored up to this time. Its role had been filled by the practical reason supported by prudence, by discretion, or by the discernment of monastic tradition; also by faith and the gift of counsel. But from this time forward, conscience was to dominate the entire scene in relation to action, and its role was to be determined by the characteristic structure of casuistic moral theology.

Conscience was no longer a virtue like prudence, formed and perfected through practice. Together with the actions proceeding from it, it was, within the person, comparable to an intermediate faculty placed between law and freedom. Properly speaking, conscience was a judge. In regard to law, it was passive and could not presume to form or change it. It simply received the law, communicated it to freedom, and applied it to freedom's actions. However, since human actions were diverse, changing and individual, according to circumstances and situations, while the law was fixed and general, conscience had to act as an interpreter of the law, so as to determine with precision the line between the allowable and the prohibited. The principal task of moralists was to assist conscience in these functions: to inform it of the law and above all to enlighten it in its work of interpreting and applying the law to human acts.

Doubtful cases were the crucial problem. This was the vortex of the dispute on probabilism: to establish criteria for abandoning the area of doubt and distinguishing the relative merits of contrary opinions. Within this debate, conscience could take its stand not only on internal reasons but also on the external authority of ethicists, who, by giving their opinions, would help to establish a kind of moral jurisprudence.

Thus placed, conscience occupied a central position in the moral world. Although law ruled conscience, law could not be applied without it, nor could law exercise any force beyond it, for a law had no value unless conscience received and communicated it. Thus it was to conscience that freedom appealed to decided between itself and the law. All roads, in the moral world, led to conscience. Ethicists were constrained, too, to distinguish carefully between different states of conscience in view of law and freedom: the firm conscience, the doubtful conscience, the broad conscience, the scrupulous conscience, and so forth. The whole problem of doubt, which had so preoccupied the age of Descartes, was concentrated in conscience.

Moral Theology and the Sacrament of Penance

Observing the makeup of the moral textbooks, we are struck by their similarity to the sacrament that has been called the tribunal of penance, at least at this period. For both, everything breathed the atmosphere of a courtroom, with some adaptations. Both moral theology and the sacrament were dominated by law, which expressed the will of God and determined the morality of actions. Conscience, in moral theology, exercised the role of the judge who applied the law by determining what one could or could not, might or might not, do. In the sacrament of penance, the role of conscience was filled by the confessor in regard to the judgment to be made, while conscience itself played the role of prosecutor in regard to freedom, through the confession of sins. Human acts were the subject matter of moral theology insofar as they came under the law, with special attention to sins, which formed the subject matter of penance. In his role as judge, the confessor concluded his judgment by assigning a penance or satisfaction suited to the gravity of the sin, and this corresponded to the remorse of conscience which punished faults. Morality and the sacrament of penance were thus set in a juridical and legal context. We should add that ethicists and confessors often had a great concern for mercy, taking care not to overburden consciences and seeking to favor freedom wherever possible. Confessors were mindful that penance was above all the sacrament of divine mercy. Nevertheless, the attitudes inculcated by the theology manuals were too juridical to give free scope to mercy, which is so preeminent in the Gospel. It was treated rather as an afterthought, after judgment had been pronounced, and its intervention was often suspect, in moral theology, as possibly opening the door to laxity.

The Dispute over Probabilism

It seems appropriate to say a word about the debate over probabilism that divided ethicists into opposing camps and disturbed the Church in the seventeenth and eighteenth centuries, for it shows us the background against which casuist morality developed. The introduction of probabilism provoked a veritable crisis in Catholic moral thought; the interest, work, and various positions of ethicists centered around this question. It was probabilism that divided ethicsts into what have been called different "systems of morality."[5] The term *system* no longer designated a total organization of theology like the medieval summas, but a different position on the criteria of judgment in doubtful cases, leading to a different way of handling the generality of cases of conscience.

The problem involved doubtful cases. It was a question of doubt applied within the framework of the Catholic moral theology of the time. The roots of the problem could be traced to nominalism. Morality colored human action because of its relationship to law, the source of moral obligation. The moral question centered, therefore, on the dividing line between what fell under the law and what was left free—between law and freedom. It was precisely at this point that doubt came upon the scene; it touched the power of the law over a given particular act. A law affected by doubt, either as to its existence or its application, lost its obligatory force, according to the principle that a law insufficiently promulgated, or insufficiently known, does not oblige. The heart of the problem lay in the discernment of real doubt, which removed an act from the control of law and left it at the disposition of freedom. The question of doubt, which was encountered in all areas, presented a special difficulty in moral theology, which applied general rules to individual actions made up of many variable elements and circumstances. No law could foresee these altogether, no general formulation could determine them in detail. The problem of doubt tended to invade morality, especially where a fundamental tension between the free agent and the law prevailed.

The question of doubt was raised from opposite angles and for contrary reasons, and it had to be judged comparatively. The traditional position, valid moreover in every field, was to tip doubt toward the solution having the best reasons in its favor. Thus a person could be relieved of legal obligation and escape moral fault if his reasons for opposing the application of the law were stronger than their opposites.

Given the juridical and legalistic mentality that prevailed from that time on and helped to set moral questions in a fixed mold, and also in consequence of this morality's orientation to the sacrament of penance—not only a tribunal but also a place of mercy and pardon—this

---

5. For the history of the dispute over probabilism, the best exposition is that of Fr. Th. Deman, "Probabilism," in *Dictionnaire de Théologie Catholique*, vol. 13 (1936), cols. 417–619. Also, but in another sense: E. Dublanchy, "Casuistries," loc. cit., vol. 2 (1905), cols. 1819–1877; J. de Blic, "Jésuites," III: La théologie morale dans la Compagnie de Jésus, loc. cit., vol. 8 (1924), cols. 1069–1092; J. McAvoy, "Saint Alphonsus de Liguori," in the dictionary *Catholicisme*, vol. 1, 352–57; R. Brouillard, "Casuistiques," *Catholicisme*, vol. 2 (1950), 630–37.

position concerning doubt may have appeared too rigorous to be applied to all Christians in all cases. Such were the motives which, in my opinion, gave rise to the concept of probabilism.

The first to express the idea that originated probabilism was a Spanish Dominican, Bartholomew of Medina, who in 1580 wrote: "It seems to me that if an opinion is *probable,* it is lawful to follow it, even if the opposite opinion is *more probable.* [Mihi videtur quod si est opinio *probabilis,* licitum est eam sequi, licet opposita *probabilior* sit]." This idea, which might have been overlooked among so many other opinions, was taken up by the Jesuit ethicists who were working on a new plan of moral theology. Like a spark it leapt from one person to the next and started a conflagration that could be controlled by the Church only with the greatest difficulty. Throughout the century, minds were divided and opposed on the subject; Jesuits—sometimes divided among themselves—Dominicans, Jansenists, theologians and laity all confronted each other over the question.

The idea was simple, if a bit subtle. In weighing reasons in favor of freedom or of law in doubtful cases, it was permissible to follow the opinion in favor of freedom if it was probable and was supported by good reasons, even if the opposite opinion, maintaining a legal obligation, was based on better reasons.

Without fully realizing it, Bartholomew of Medina and his followers had passed the frontier of reason, which naturally favors the opinion with the best reasons behind it. Conscience, as a result, lost its balance; a long time was required to restore it to normalcy.

The entire question turned on determining exactly what a probable opinion was, once the criterion of "more probable" had been abandoned. How many reasons did it take, and what kind, to constitute a probable opinion? Was it not sufficient to have a single reason, if it removed doubt, in order to judge that one was legitimately freed from legal obligation in a given case? Morality edged toward the downward slope to laxity. Those who wanted to defend the demands of the moral law before all else countered this with rigorism.

The problem of discerning between opinions was complicated by the intervention of what were called "external" reasons. Classic theology had based its judgments on the consideration of internal reasons, resting on the nature of things and actions. Nominalism reversed the perspective. It had described morality as affecting actions from without, through their relation to the law and the will of the legislator. Even if an ethicist did not accept nominalism, his attention shifted now from consideration of the nature of acts to consideration of the law in its literal expression, where it was promulgated, and toward possible interpretations of it.

Here we find the "external reasons" that were to play so large a part in the weighing of opinions. They were the views of ethicists, who were looked upon as experts possessing authority to interpret in moral matters. Their judgments were thought to constitute a kind of jurisprudence, as in civil law. The value of an opinion, therefore, was judged by the number of ethicists who held it; at the same time, special weight was attached to the views of certain eminent Doctors whose learning was recognized by the Church. The position of a St. Augustine or a St. Thomas would suffice, for example, to render an opinion probable. Nevertheless the opinion of a few recognized ethicists, if it was in favor of freedom, could hold against that of the Doctors when they pronounced in favor of legal obligation. This was the logic of the system.

Out of this problem arose the principal trends of casuistic moral theology or "systems of morality." I shall enumerate them briefly.

Probabilism: one could follow a probable opinion even if the contrary opinion, in favor of the law, had greater probability. *The theory of greater probability*: one should always follow the opinion that was more probable and was supported by the larger number of reasons. *The theory of the safer reason*: one should always follow the opinion favorable to the law, to avoid the danger of breaking the law. The extremes took the forms of *laxity*, the temptation of probabilism, and *rigor*, its opposite.

In its essentials, the dispute was terminated only at the end of the eighteenth century, with the intervention of St. Alphonsus Liguori (1696–1787). He reasoned totally within the perspective bequeathed to him by casuistry. It is worth our while to follow his reasoning, for it is characteristic.

The principle was that a doubtful law was one that had been insufficiently promulgated and did not bind. Another basic principle was: "melior est conditio possidentis." In case of doubt, that is, the presumption would be in favor of the possessor of the good. One might deduce from this that all was permitted where nothing was formally forbidden by divine or human law. God gave the world to man to rule over, and made him free of everything except certain fruits. Thus freedom anteceded prohibitory law; before the latter's veto could constrain freedom, it had to be clearly expressed. Freedom was "in possession" until some definite law came to evict it.

Yet one could not without disloyalty choose a way of acting that was contrary to the law if one's reasons for doubting the obligation, serious though they might be, were slighter than those in favor of the law. The doubt would no longer be valid in this case, since one's mind was drawn to adhere to the position favoring the law as being the truer position. In order for a doubt to be valid, the arguments in favor of freedom should be at least equal to those in favor of the law. This demand for equality between the pros and cons gave rise to St. Alphonsus's "theory of equal probability."

After all the shifts and variations of ethicists through two centuries—and they were at times extreme—St. Alphonsus' system established a certain balance by its return to considered reason. There followed a measure of calm in regard to the probabilist dispute, and in 1831 the Church confirmed this by declaring that the moral theology of Blessed Alphonsus might be safely taught and used in the confessional. Without going so far as to assert explicitly that his "theory of equal probability" was the best system for moral theology, the Church declared him a Doctor in 1871. Thus Alphonsus became the patron of moralists.

The patronage of St. Alphonsus, which merits our respect and esteem for his achievements, still leaves ethicists free in regard to following his reasoning. They retain this freedom as long as no definite law constrains them. This freedom is all the more necessary as the limitations of casuist morality, of which St. Alphonsus was the most highly authorized representative, have become more apparent in our day. We can now better perceive the fundamental differences in organization and structure as well as in problematics that separate it from the moral theology of St. Thomas and the Fathers of the Church. Incontestably, post-Tridentine moral theology, in concentrating on cases of conscience and the dispute over probabilism, narrowed its horizon. We see now how it contrasts with the breadth of the views on human action and on God that we find in the Fathers and the great scholastics. The link has not been broken, but there has been a shrinkage and a slight distortion.

Conclusion

The moral teaching of the manuals constitutes one of the principal stages in the history of moral theology. It has become classic, and its influence has predominated up to our own day. It has been spread by means of preaching, catechesis, and teaching in all its forms. It has been imposed to such an extent that many imagine that throughout the entire course of Church history, no other concept of moral teaching could have, or ever did, exist. It has even exerted its influence upon the rest of theology and led to a view of dogmas themselves from the vantage point of obligation, as if they were propositions proposed to our faith by the magisterium. This could lead one to wish them reduced to a minimum, as if they shackled reason, though the Fathers regarded dogma as a higher source of light.

The power of the moral teaching of the manuals stemmed from its concentration on the idea and feeling of obligation and from its conformity with the ideas of the times. We find similar conceptions throughout Western thought, among Protestants and philosophers. We could, for example, trace a parallel between the structures of casuistic and Kantian morality, with their poles of attraction to duty and the categorical imperative. We meet the same supremacy of law or the norm, of obligation or duty, notably in the interpretation of the two commandments of love of God and neighbor. There is the same tension between law and freedom, in spite of Kant's attempt to interiorize law at the heart of practical reason. We find a similar suspicion of spontaneity, which they both reduce to the level of sentiment, and a mistrust of the spiritual spontaneity that is capable of creating an experience transcending sense. Finally, in each, legal justice and obedience predominate. Although aptitudes and settings may differ, there is an obvious connection between the underlying ideas. We can also see the moral theology of the manuals typified in the moral concepts of our own era.

Historically, it would be well to take into account the anti-Protestant reaction, which affected post-Tridentine theology, including moral theories. I shall address this in the next chapter.

In order to make a fair judgment of the moral theology in the manuals, we must grant that they filled, in large part, the role that had been assigned to them: to make available to priests and Christian laity the essentials of Christian morality in a system adapted to modern needs and ideas. We also need to recognize the legitimacy of this presentation of morality at the heart of a theological reflection where a plurality of systems had always been admitted, provided that the essential teachings of the faith were safeguarded. We should also add that casuistic morality did not claim to represent the Church's complete thought on Christian life and action. At the start it dealt only with a portion of what was taught in moral theology and always left room for works of spirituality. Several ethicists of renown were at the same time authentic spiritual writers, such as St. Alphonsus Liguori. Nevertheless, this moral teaching was in the end viewed as *the* moral theology of the Church, and it tended to slight Christian teaching on spiritual doctrine, as if the ethicist needed only the essentials.

This being said, we are within our rights in critiquing the moral theology of the manuals, provided we know how to safeguard the essentials of Christian morality that it contains and that have been transmitted to us. This critique is more difficult than would at first appear, if we do not want to limit ourselves to pointing out insufficiencies and deficiencies, but would seek more solid foundations for the construction of moral theology. It is all too easy to say that today the era of the manuals is over and to take an opposite stand, pronouncing ourselves systematically in favor of freedom and conscience as opposed to law and authority. In so doing, we would be caught in the very spiral of the specific categories of moral theology that we wish to critique, notably the opposition between law and freedom. We should only be contributing to the destruction of moral theology and unsettling the foundations which assure its firmness and stability.

The task is rendered still more difficult by the fact that the terms used in moral theology—such as freedom, law, conscience, prudence, virtue, and justice—have seen their meanings deeply modified, deformed, and impoverished in the modern era, while dictionary definitions remain unchanged. Many authors, like Azor, believed in good faith that they were adopting St. Thomas's ideas and positions, not realizing that they were giving them a very different meaning because of the structure of the moral theology in which they placed them.

Today the Christian ethicist faces a vast and complex task, a task that demands reflection that penetrates to the very foundations of moral theology. I believe one good method of succeeding at this is to compare the different systems of moral theology operative through the course of history, notably those of St. Augustine, St. Thomas, and casuistry. A penetrating glance soon observes that a system built on obligation, such as we observe today, is not the only possibility, and that there have been other models of moral theology in the Church. The fact that they are ancient does not prevent them from corresponding better to the profound aspirations of moderns.

St. Augustine, beginning his work on Christian morality with the question of true human happiness, surely stands a better chance of finding an echo in our hearts than the ethicist who can talk of nothing but laws and obligations. And his was not merely a pedagogical pose. The question of happiness, answering to our natural longings for truth and love, with their own demands far surpassing the requirements of obligation, is a decisive question for every person. Handled rightly, it can open up broader moral perspectives than those of casuistry or of modern, duty-driven morality.

12

Catholic Moral Theology and Protestant Ethics

The comparison between the Catholic and Protestant conceptions of moral theory is important from various viewpoints. Issuing from the same Christian trunk, Catholics and Protestants were divided like two opposite branches of a tree in the great crisis of the sixteenth century, and were mutually conditioned. We cannot fully understand Catholic moral theory as it took shape from this time onward without taking into account the anti-Protestant reaction, which influenced the post-Tridentine Church. Several characteristic features can be explained by this opposition. Furthermore, both Catholics and Protestants are influenced by the intellectual climate in which they came into conflict: a theological tradition transformed by nominalism and a confrontation with Renaissance humanism and the problems of the New World just discovered.

At the present time, when ecumenism has become one of the major concerns of Christians, it may be useful to determine in depth some reciprocal positions regarding morality. We shall consider the question from the perspective of Catholic moral theology, which is our present object of study. A study of Protestantism in itself, with its internal divisions, notably Lutheran and Calvinist, will not therefore be our object. Rather, we shall try to identify the logic that governs Protestant positions, beginning with the principle of justification by faith alone. We shall be dealing with the foundations of Christian moral theology rather than with the particular problems that usually come to mind with the mention of morality. In this way, we shall be able to discover points of divergence and possibilities for convergence that may have been overlooked, even though the latter may pertain to more specialized areas. In our research we shall keep in view, as the basis of our comparison, the great Western theological tradition that preceded the crisis of the sixteenth century, a tradition that can be traced through St. Augustine all the way back to the Gospel and to St. Paul in particular. This will put us in touch with points of contact and treasures we have held in common, lately lost to view. History itself invites us to work out this comparison, for the crisis of the Reformation, faced with Renaissance humanism, was the occasion for reopening the great debate between Christianity and Greek humanism already initiated by St. Paul in Corinthians and Romans and continued by the Fathers.

To begin with, we need to clarify our terms. 'Moral' and 'ethical' have been used equivalently up to the modern era. 'Ethical' is derived from the Greek '*ethos*', custom, and was preferred in Latin translations from the Greek, particularly in commentaries on Aristotle. 'Moral' comes from the Latin '*mores*' and was more generally used. Catholic moral teaching of later periods maintained the equivalence and also the preference for 'moral'. 'Moral theology' therefore designated that branch of theology dealing with human action taken as a whole, and could be applied to the study of foundations and principles as well as to the examination of particular problems. Thus St. Thomas spoke of universal and particular moral theology, understanding by the latter the study of the virtues beginning with faith (Ia IIae q 6, prol.). Later the distinction between fundamental and specialized moral teaching prevailed, the latter being oriented to the study of cases of conscience.

'Ethical' was more often used in a philosophical context, but the difference was not clear cut. From the Protestant viewpoint and in modern philosophical language, a distinction is made between ethics, which studies the principles and criteria of moral judgment, and morality, which deals rather with prescriptions about mores permitted in a given era and society. I prefer to use the term 'moral' in its broad sense for the sake of convenience and also because it seems to correspond to a more generous concept of this branch of theology. But I shall refer to Protestant ethics so as to conform to a usage that was meaningful for the Reform. This will explain my title, "Catholic Moral Theology and Protestant Ethics."

I. THE TRADITION OF PROTESTANT ETHICS

Classic Protestant thought was dominated by the idea of justification: a person was justified by faith alone and not by works. This basic tenet, wholly centered on faith in Jesus Christ, included a systematic refusal of any personal participation in justification by way of works or merits and, consequently, the denial of any value to human actions—even though they be conformed to the moral law—through which a person might glorify himself before God. Protestantism was haunted, as it were, by the threat of human pride in human works. Hence the radical separation between the order of faith and the order of works, between Gospel and Law. Protestantism gave evidence of an instinctive mistrust even of works conformed to the Law, because they are so well adapted to fomenting and concealing a pharisaical hypocrisy.

In the order of faith, justification was a pure grace given by Christ, who alone could justify, without any merit on our part. In the order of works and the Law, we had ethics, which established criteria for distinguishing between good and bad acts according to certain principles or rules. For Luther as for Ockham, good and evil had no existence as such in our actions. He did not consider an action good because it conformed to the law. It became truly good only when lifted up for justification by faith and accepted by the grace of God. In the face of the propensity of ethics to define good as something in its own right, Luther accorded faith a great spontaneity and freedom in regard to works and law. Calvin, for his part, insisted on law much more strongly than did Luther, and he developed ethical questions extensively. On this subject they were at loggerheads, to the point of attesting a hidden legalism within the Reform. However this may be, the two reformers agreed on the essential foundation of salvation and the value of our actions in God's sight: justification could come only from our incorporation in Christ through faith. The moral life unfolded as the manifestation of Christ's dwelling within us through his Spirit.

Protestantism thus set up a clear separation, rupture even, between the order of faith and the order of works or ethics. R. Mehl wrote: "The Gospel is not a form of morality; it belongs to another order. The question it raises is one of faith, not morals."[1] This obviously supposes a whittling down of morals in contrast with the Fathers of the Church and

---

1. C. Yannaras, R. Mehl, J.-M. Aubert, *La loi de la liberté. Evangile et morale.* (Paris, Mame, 1972), 65.

St. Thomas. For them, faith was the primary virtue of Christian morality. Many Protestant authors refused to recognize the proper value of ethics. If they had to choose, they would unhesitatingly have sacrificed ethics and works to the primacy of faith.

But the life of the Christian cannot be completely emptied of works. It is not enough merely to believe; one must act in daily life and thereby produce works. A faith that does not lead to any action conformed to God's will would surely be illusory. The problem for the Protestant was, therefore, was to find some place and meaning for the believer's works in view of a justification already acquired through faith.

Luther's answer was that works obviously did not precede faith but followed upon it, out of a kind of internal necessity, as a good tree yields good fruit. He went on to explain that works resulting from faith had no theological value for salvation and were directed not to God but rather to the service of the neighbor. He was very reticent toward the theory of a third use of the law, proposed by Melanchthon: that law might be *indicativa oboedientiae* that is, might indicate to the believer actions conformed to God's will and requiring obedience. This would seem to compromise faith's freedom and somehow reestablish a Law and ethic for the believer. Calvin's answer was different. Good works were the expression of the believer's gratitude for the salvation bestowed beforehand by faith. He openly accepted the "third use" of the Law.

The Protestant position can be summed up under two aspects. It had a positive side: justification by faith and by faith alone. The negative side was its refusal to admit that human works had any value for salvation, regardless of their nature. This refusal extended to whatever might favor or foster the human notion of any work of salvation other than pure faith.

Protestantism thus refused to admit that the grace of Christ and justification could find any foothold or penetrate and abide within the human person in a lasting manner. This led to an avalanche of further rejections.

1. Justice could not operate internally, within us, for in this case we might think of claiming it as our own. It remained external, "forensic." Justice belonged only to Christ, who attributed it to us. Being at once "just and a sinner," the Christian always stood in need of being justified by Christ.

2. There was no such thing as sanctifying grace, touching and transforming us in our souls, in the depths of our being, as St. Thomas had thought. Nor were there any supernatural virtues, conceived as permanent qualities or dispositions, which would ennoble our faculties and

enable us to perform meritorious actions. Protestantism was suspicious of virtue in general, because it connoted a human attempt to achieve moral value.

3. Protestantism even rejected the idea of holiness and sanctification. Luther attacked the scholastic teaching that charity informed faith, because it seemed to downgrade faith, as if it were not adequate by itself to effect justification; but also because he would not accept an interior sanctity that had been produced by charity. There was always a certain rift in Protestantism between faith and charity, justification and sanctification. Christ alone was holy—whence the rejection of the traditional concept of holiness as a quality of the soul, or as an extraordinary and lofty grace given to some Christians, making them worthy of the honors of cult.

4. Mysticism was also regarded as a purely human work, an attempt to attain an eminent knowledge of God, a boast of possessing God through the sheer power of the human intellect, virtue, asceticism, or interior technique.

5. The monastic life and the religious state were ruled out because of their seeming claim to achieve justice and holiness by means of ascetical works, human observances, or contemplation.

6. Finally, theology itself was ranked among human works. It could no longer presume to share in any way in the divine science. It was a work of human reason using its own natural working procedures and applying them to revelation so as to draw some light under the guidance of faith for the benefit of the Christian community. The value of theological constructs remained always very relative. The bond between faith and reason was stretched to the limit, if not broken.

Clearly the Protestant position derived completely from the original affirmation of justification by faith alone. It led to a rejection—or at the least to the reduction to a relative role—not only of ethics in the modern sense of a science of principles or criteria for action, but of all branches of moral theology that had been developed in the Middle Ages. These included the treatises on grace, the virtues, the gifts, spiritual and mystical ideals, and even the theological dimension of moral teaching. In its critique, Protestantism was aided by nominalism, on which it depended for the working out of its doctrine. It had already discarded all the permanent elements of human nature and human faculties, particularly the virtues, from its broad general structure of moral teaching, in order to enhance free action in its unhampered and instantaneous character. We could say that for Protestantism the act of faith was the purest free act, in the sense in which Ockham understood freedom. It rendered a person

free in the very instant in which it was made, cutting through the sur-
rounding warp and woof of ideas and systems, works and laws, tendencies, virtues, and finally ethics. Countering this freedom, Protestantism, again following Ockham, set up law; but instead of going on
to make law the source of moral value, it gave it a merely negative function, that of convicting a person of sin before leading the way to faith.
This was the primary purpose of law, whether theological or rational.

A Thoughtful Critique

In affirming the primacy of faith in Jesus Christ as the first source of
justification and of the Christian life, Protestantism was in the direct
line of St. Paul and the great primitive Christian tradition. It revived St.
Paul's debate with Jewish justice according to the Law and with Greek
wisdom, and confronted Renaissance humanism and the legalism of certain thought patterns in the medieval Church. Its response was unequivocal on this point: faith in Jesus Christ was the source of the justice
and wisdom coming to us from God, and of all moral worth in God's
sight. It constituted the characteristic and chief element of the Christian
response to the moral question. For St. Thomas, too, in his definition
of the evangelical Law, faith in Christ, which communicates the grace
of the Spirit and works through charity, breathed life into the entire
organism of virtues that made up Christian morality.

What separated Protestantism from the theological tradition preceding it was, first, the refusal to integrate human virtues within the heart
of Christian morality through acceptance and assimilation. At each
stage of history, theologians consistently aimed to integrate human virtues with Christian virtues. Frequently the debate manifested a great
seriousness. Given the primacy of faith and charity, the effort at integration is found in St. Paul himself, was developed by the Greek and
Latin Fathers, and was continued during the period of medieval theology, when theologians availed themselves of Aristotle's moral system.
This Catholic enterprise entailed risks, for whereas the transcendence of
faith had to be constantly emphasized, it was also essential to maintain
faith's incarnational aspect, the works of faith.

Consequently, Protestantism was led to mistrust grace's workings in
the heart of the human intelligence through the gift of a new wisdom
wholly conformed to faith, and in the human will through the unfolding
of charity and holiness. Because of its excessive fear of human pride,
Protestantism's reading of Scripture became selective, and especially its

reading of St. Paul, who speaks so often of this kind of wisdom and holiness.

Intent on observing the polemical aspect of the debate between faith and humanism or law, Protestantism created a deep gulf between faith and ethics, so deep that it could not be crossed. It bisected previous Christian morality by isolating faith and rejecting as useless if not dangerous all its teaching on virtues and all else that might fall under ethics or morality, which, since Ockham's time, had appeared in a strikingly legalistic setting.

gulf b/w faith and ethics

Protestantism, and particularly Lutheranism, adopted a difficult position relative to ethical problems. It narrowed the scope of ethics by separating it from the order of faith, and reduced its subject matter to human criteria for action. Within the polemical perspective, it even gave a pejorative slant to ethics and to the entire range of works, which might feed human pride. The link between faith and the necessary accomplishment of certain good works by believers was indeed fragile. Protestantism was loath to strengthen the bond through a rational system of ethical rules or an honest recognition of their validity. This weakness was to be particularly felt in our pluralistic world, where Christians must live with nonbelievers in a society that requires general legislation, and where the only platform for common exchange, dialogue, and collaboration is reason.

In view of this need to find a solid base for dealing with ethical problems common to all in our times, we can see in contemporary Protestant theologians a tendency to favor a reassessment of the value of natural law. They conceive it as a middle ground between faith and action, a necessary foundation on which to build criteria for judging action, and they believe it has a general relevance. The paradox is that, at this very time, Catholic ethicists are abandoning the teaching on natural law, which has traditionally been the primary basis for their moral theology.

II. CATHOLIC MORAL THEOLOGY

1. Which Catholic Moral Theology Are We Considering?

The Catholic moral theology that responded to Protestantism took shape after the Council of Trent. It was the moral teaching contained in the manuals, commonly called casuistry. We have seen how this differed in structure from the moral theology of St. Thomas, even though it was placed under his patronage and often referred to the *Summa theologiae.* Without realizing it, the authors of the manuals were separated from the Angelic Doctor by the nominalist "chasm."

Casuistry does not represent all moral teaching, all Christian life within the Catholic Church today. In its beginnings, casuistry did not claim to cover the whole field of moral theology; it presupposed a more speculative study in this area. Furthermore, the works of the great spiritual writers and saints such as St. John of the Cross, St. Francis de Sales, and many others, in this era and later, contained moral richness that far surpassed anything the manuals could offer. Certain great moralists like St. Alphonsus Liguori, patron of Catholic moral theologians, were at the same time spiritual writers of renown. Catholic moral theology was not reduced, therefore, to the study of the commandments and obligations, as the manuals would have us believe. It even found profound expression in literary works such as those of Pascal and Bernanos.

For all this, a too-marked separation of morality from spirituality, and an overriding concern with practical matters, placed the manuals in the vanguard of moral teaching in the Church during the last few centuries, and favored the identification of Catholic moral teaching with casuistry. In any case, it was casuistic moral teaching that historically confronted Protestantism, in reaction to it.

2. Anti-Protestant Conditioning

The reaction to Protestantism influenced moral theory as it did all branches of Catholic theology after the Council of Trent. Here are some points in modern Catholic moral teaching in which we can discern an anti-Protestant conditioning.

a. The Protestant affirmation of justification by faith alone led Catholic moralists to stress elements attacked by Protestants, such as the meritorious value of works or actions done in conformity with the commandments of God and of the Church, faith and charity obviously being presupposed with grace. In order to establish this value, Catholic moral teaching moved natural law to the forefront. It was accessible to right reason and found its authorized expression in the Decalogue. But at the same time natural law distanced itself from faith in its practical aspect. It sought criteria for moral actions in law rather than in faith. In the manuals, the treatise on faith consisted mainly in an examination of the obligations and sins related to it. From this time on, faith became the preserve of dogmatic theologians, to whom also were relegated the questions of justification and of grace. The virtue of faith then no longer influenced Catholic moral teaching except in a very introductory way, though later, apparently under pressure from Protestant sources, Catholic moral theologians began to talk more about faith. This is not to say that faith was less fervent among Catholics than among Protestants, but the systematization of morality in Catholic manuals reduced the importance attributed to faith and stressed the moral law.

Thus we see Catholics and Protestants moving in contrary directions. As a result, faith was separated from morality or ethics, where before this time they had been intimately joined. Protestants inclined to the side of faith and were prepared to abandon ethics based on law. Catholics favored morality in its relationship to law and weakened its bonds with faith. Casuists even asked, How many times in a lifetime is one bound to make an act of faith?—as if the faith of a Christian should not be active throughout life. One of the principal causes of the breach thus created between faith and morality resided, I believe, in moral theology's concentration on obligation issuing from law—an effect of nominalism. Faith, with the freedom and élan coming to it from God himself, could not be understood by a morality riveted upon obligations. Such a morality would inevitably give rise to the danger of legalism, which threatens faith.

b. The absolute priority given by Protestantism to Scripture, according to its principle of "Scripture alone," "*Scriptura sola,*" and its rejection of tradition, led Catholic theologians to emphasize the teaching of tradition and to keep their distance from Scripture. Mistrusting an individualistic reading of the Bible, they leaned heavily upon the magisterium and upon a tradition that had become, in reality, more philosophical than theological, based mainly on the natural law and identified with the Decalogue.

The manuals, therefore, having become the basis for moral teaching, developed their own tradition. Recourse to Scripture was limited to texts expressing commands, and a search for supporting arguments. The principle of Scripture, seen as the primary source for theology, was retained in doctrine and moral theology, but its application was greatly reduced. Post-Tridentine moralists thus boxed in the Church's moral teaching, which they were trying to transmit in all fidelity, in too small an enclosure, where the theological virtues were constricted and where there was no room for the gifts of the Holy Spirit, grace, and the evangelical Law—the best of the Gospel.

3. The Humanist Plan

Faced with the anti-humanist reaction of Protestantism, Catholic moralists maintained the value of humanism and worked out a moral system open to the universalism flowing from it. Several currents, furthermore, met and combined in the moral teaching of the seventeenth century to give it a humanistic orientation: the scholastic tradition, highly rational in its construction and procedures; the humanism of the Jesuits, which served as a model for Catholic teaching on the ideals of the Renaissance in the Greco-Latin humanities; the discovery of the New World, which broadened horizons and called for a universalism extending to non-Christians; the rationalism of the age of Descartes, which, blotting out the past, sought to build an edifice of thought upon purely rational foundations.

These various currents contributed to the establishment, as the foundation of moral teaching, of a law based upon the very nature of the human person, beyond differences of race and religion, accessible to all who used reason rightly, and consequently universal in its application. This universal, humanistic plan opened up a wide field to moral theory. Catholic theology, notably in Spain with Francisco de Vitoria (considered the founder of international law), was busily involved in this for some time.

It is all the more pity, therefore, that the moralists of the seventeenth century let themselves be drawn into the narrow toils of the dispute over probabilism, squandering their attention and their best efforts on the examination of individual cases of conscience at the very moment when the philosophers of their time were building the foundations of a new organization of society and the world.

4. The Pastoral Plan

In conformity with the prescriptions of the Council of Trent, Catholic moral teaching was also largely determined by the concern to provide priests in seminaries and houses of formation with adequate instruction for a worthy administration of the sacraments—particularly penance, which had become the principal subject matter of moral teaching at that time. The need for practical courses oriented to problems of conscience was keenly felt in the Society of Jesus, which carried on an intense pastoral ministry of spiritual direction and the hearing of confessions. This perfectly legitimate and necessary preoccupation, however, highlighted the distinction between speculative theological teaching and practical studies in moral theology, which focused on cases of conscience. The attention of moralists was oriented to casuistry, and in particular to sin, which was the proper matter of the sacrament of penance.

In contrast to Protestantism, which considered sin rather globally as a rejection of faith, casuistic moral teaching dealt with a multiplicity of sinful acts engendered by disobedience to various commandments. It attached considerable importance to a precise, detailed distinction between sins, a distinction needful in the sacrament of penance. Different kinds of sin, their number and gravity, whether mortal or venial, must be brought before the tribunal.

Having as their pastoral aim the regulation of moral obligations to be imposed upon all Christians, the Catholic moralists—as we have already seen—made wider use of the distinction between precepts and counsels than had medieval theologians, and they applied it to all of moral science in general. Precepts, applied universally, were the proper domain of moral theology. Counsels became an appendage for an elite, made up notably of religious who freely engaged themselves in the pursuit of perfection through the practice of the counsels. The counsels were the specific subject matter of asceticism and mysticism, like a science annexed to moral theology. This might be called moral teaching at two levels, or a double standard of moral teaching.

5. The Nominalist Influence

Moral teaching in the seventeenth century was strongly under the influence of nominalism, in an indirect but very real way, because it received from nominalism the principal elements of fundamental theology, as we have seen in previous chapters. We find a similar influence at work in Protestantism. Let us look at one or two points.

After the advent of nominalism, the moral order was dominated by the idea of law. Human acts were good or bad depending on their relation to law, which determined obligation. Catholic moral teaching adopted this concept and held its validity, while Protestantism rejected it in the name of faith. But from both viewpoints, morality was seen as beginning with law. We note also, on both sides, a separation between the order of faith and the moral order, and equally a tendency toward legalism, quite direct on the Catholic side but tempered by the indulgent concern to refrain from overburdening consciences. We find it also in

Calvinism, but tending toward rigorism. Again, Lutheran mistrust of all positive use of the law may be explained by a voluntarist and nominalist conception of law, which denied all harmonious relations among freedom, grace, and law.

6. The Starting Point of Natural Law

Since the crisis of the Reformation, Catholic and Protestant theological systems have generally chosen opposite starting points. Catholic theology has customarily begun with the human, and has moved from philosophy to theology, from apologetics and rational arguments to faith, from the natural to the supernatural. Protestantism has spontaneously started with faith, Scripture, and the Word of God, and has been somewhat suspicious and critical of the human and of reason. In its view these belong to a different order than that of faith and and may even be antagonistic to it.

These general tendencies are verified in moral theology. The starting point for the reflection and argumentation of Catholic ethicists in recent centuries has generally been natural law, with its authoritative expression in the Decalogue. Natural law had the obvious advantage of being accessible to reason and presenting a solid and universally viable basis for the rational study of moral questions. It also placed moral teaching within the tradition of the ancient Greek and Roman philosophy that had been adopted by scholasticism.

Natural law thus possessed indisputable value for moral theology, and its rational, foundational role seemed irreplaceable. However, in sustaining natural law, there was not sufficient reflection about the changes in the respective positions of freedom and nature and of the human person and nature after the advent of nominalism. Harmony had given way to opposition. To moderns, nature seemed to shackle their freedom; they must conquer and dominate it. Natural law was drawn into this conflict with freedom. Beneath the surface, however, natural law was fragile, because it rested upon the rift that nominalism had created between freedom and law.

In order to give natural law its necessary role in moral theology, the opposition between freedom and nature must be critiqued. We must show that there is in the human heart a nature transcending the physical or biological level of irrational beings. This nature is spiritual, being made up of inclinations toward the true, the good, and love, none of which are opposed to freedom—they are, rather, the source of the most

Kant

personal spontaneity. Natural law's only true solidity rests on the re-establishment of harmony between freedom and human nature.

For Catholic ethicists, the challenge is to avoid being carried away by considerations of reason at the level of natural law, so as to access Gospel teaching in its full and authentic sense at the theological level. Particularly in our times, ethicists are tempted to reduce Christian ethics to the rules of natural reason.

In starting out from natural reason, we shall often have to recall St. Thomas's saying that grace does not destroy nature but perfects it. This could be seen to imply that we should first study and acknowledge natural gifts in human beings and in moral theory, and then move on to grace and the supernatural. This implication is not the only possible one, however; we could as well, perhaps better, conclude that since grace perfects nature, the more we study human nature in the light of faith, the better we will understand its essence and potential. Grace reveals God to man and man to himself. It would be appropriate, therefore, in moral theology to begin with faith and the Gospel, knowing that the true good of man would then be perceived all the more clearly even on the purely human level.

In the *Summa theologiae* St. Thomas always took God, and the things of God, as his starting point, since God was the principle and source of all things in the order of being and truth. He then moved to the order of creation. In his study of virtues, for example, he began with the supernatural virtues, and first with faith. His treatise on laws started with the eternal law, the highest origin of all authentic legislation. This was the theological order demanded even of divine science, conveyed through revelation and addressed to faith. In light of this we can rediscover the universality of the call to faith through the power of the Word of God.

III. SOME ORIENTATIONS FOR CATHOLIC MORAL TEACHING AS IT LOOKS TO RENEWAL

A. Some Points Favorable to a Renewal of Moral Theology

The present situation offers several features favorable to a renewal of moral theology.

1. The Second Vatican Council, which was preceded by extensive biblical renewal, gave Catholics full access to sacred Scripture. The Con-

stitution on Revelation, *Dei Verbum,* proposed the reading, meditation upon, and study of Scripture to all Christians, and especially to theologians, as the primary source of "knowledge of Christ" together with tradition (chap. 6, nn. 21, 24, 25). The decree *Optatam totius,* on the formation of priests, urged particular care regarding courses for seminarians on Scripture, which should be the soul of all theology. "Special attention needs to be given to the development of moral theology. Its scientific exposition should be more thoroughly nourished by scriptural teaching" (chap. 5, n. 16). Such a return of moral theology to Scripture is in full conformity with the great theological tradition of the first centuries.

2. The ecumenical movement approved by the recent council in the decree *Unitatis redintegratio* favored our passing beyond our anti-Protestant reflexes by returning to our common sources and recovering some of the riches of Christian moral teaching that belong to previous theological tradition and have been neglected since the crisis of the sixteenth century. The primacy of faith, the Holy Spirit, and the Word of God in moral theology affords one example.

3. The current perception of the inadequacies of casuistry challenges Catholic ethicists to strive for a renewal that can no longer be limited to partial adaptations, but should lead to a revision of the foundations of this branch of theology. This is not to say that the teaching of the manuals should be discarded as old-fashioned or outmoded. We need to distinguish here between the container and the contents, between a systematization of moral theology that is a period piece and its contents, which include positions and concrete moral laws belonging to revelation and the tradition of the Church. These latter have permanent value.

Certain parts of moral theology at the rational level, such as the teaching on natural law, also have lasting value and may be endorsed by us, even though they require reinterpretation in order to be fully useful. In this delicate work of discernment, I believe a comparison with the best representatives of ancient theological tradition will be very helpful. The critic should endeavor to remain always in the service of the upbuilding and renewal of Christian moral theology.

4. The development of the historical sciences and their application to the study of the Bible, Church Fathers, and great Christian writers offers us a wealth of material and information, far vaster than what the ancients had. In addition, the development of a sense of history gives us a better grasp of an essential dimension of the quest for truth and the unfolding of human action. We can follow more closely the principal stages of the history and the evolution of theology and can study the

works of the great theologians to greater advantage when we add an historical perspective to our speculative reflection. We can also add the contribution of modern sciences to our knowledge of human nature, mentioned here in passing.

B. Faith as a Starting Point

The various conditions favoring a new beginning for Catholic moral theology will be ineffective, I believe, if we do not have the courage to tackle the fundamental methodological question: What is the primary source, and what, therefore, the starting point of moral theology? Is it faith or rational knowledge?

In my opinion, moral theology must have the daring to begin its research once again with an act of faith. Faith is the principal source of light and strength for action. The act of faith submits and opens our minds to the influence of the Word of God, a Word that comes to us exteriorly through Scripture read in church, and interiorly through the action of the Holy Spirit. The theologian is not simply an intellectual, a scholar who chooses the texts of revelation and the life of the Church as the object of study. The theologian is before all else a believer, well aware that for the one who receives the Word of God with a docile mind, it becomes a source of light and life surpassing all human reason and communication.

St. John's Prologue can clearly be applied to theology: "In the beginning was the Word . . . and the Word was God. . . . Through him all things came to be, not one thing had its being but through him. All that came to be had life in him, and that life was the light of men, light that shines in the dark, light that darkness could not overpower. . . . The Word was the true light that enlightens all men; . . . Grace and truth have come through Jesus Christ. No one has ever seen God; it is the only Son, who is nearest to the Father's heart, who has made him known."

These words are addressed to us in our search for God through intellect and free will, in the search for light and life, the struggle with the darkness of sin and death—all this, in order to form faith in the human heart. We can say, therefore, that at the beginning of creation, and also at the beginning of moral theology, was the Word, the Word of God, source of that divine wisdom that comes to us through Jesus Christ and through him alone. It is he who reveals to us the Father and the ways leading to him, he who is the light of our life.

To recapture faith and the Word of God as the starting point and source of Christian moral theology is not to abandon the approach of Catholic theology for that of Protestantism. We are rather aligning ourselves with what has been the great Catholic tradition from the beginning. We are joining St. Paul, the Fathers of the Church, St. Augustine, the best of medieval theology, and St. Thomas Aquinas, among others. The priority given to faith has many consequences. In moral theology the greatest importance will be given to Gospel teaching, notably the Sermon on the Mount as the expression of the New Law; to the action of the Holy Spirit through grace, the theological virtues, and the gifts; to the themes of the imitation of Christ and life in Christ, taught by St. Paul.

The Leap of Faith

In theology, especially in moral theology, we cannot give true primacy to faith without making what might be called "the leap of faith." We shall be engaged in a fundamental debate with the humanism of our times. Faith means a leap in the dark, beyond human wisdom and knowledge. We need to go beyond philosophy, sciences, our own ideas and systems, our feelings, human views and projects, in order to receive the wisdom and knowledge of God, hidden in Jesus Christ. Let us give a name to this audacity. It is faith in faith, faith in the truth that faith's light is higher. Such an act inevitably brings us into confrontation with humanism, or more accurately, with humanism's temptation to make ourselves the principle, center, and end of our own lives, actions, and knowledge—even of the universe. Faith challenges us to find our principle and end outside of ourselves, in God, through Jesus Christ. This happens in the order of action through charity (which is the love of God above all because he first loved us). and in the order of knowledge through our yielding to the Word of God to enlighten and guide us. We do these things at the risk of appearing fools, a scandal in the eyes of the world.

Such is the starting point for Christian theology. Without this initial act of faith there can be no true theology. The struggle with the humanist temptation began with St. Paul's preaching against Greek wisdom. It has continued throughout the Church's history and has occasioned many heresies. It was renewed at the time of the Protestant crisis in the climate of thought and life special to the sixteenth century. We cannot avoid it today, if we wish to give a Christian answer to the primary and decisive moral question: What is the end of human existence, what the definitive criterion for actions and life? Is it to be found in ourselves, or in God? Better still, where shall we put our faith—in humanity, or in God, through Jesus Christ?

The Light of Faith

There is, however, another side to "faith in faith" and the question of humanism. Faith is not simply *credo quia absurdum*, I believe the absurd, as the expression goes. There has been too great an insistence, perhaps, on the obscure character of faith, and as a result too little attention to the light and strength it gives to the mind and will. According to the Augustinian teaching principle, *Credo ut intelligam*, or *Nisi credidero nòn intelligam*, we believe in order to know and understand better. This presupposes that in our initial act of faith itself we have grasped that the Word of God is true, luminous, and good. Faith in faith therefore includes the perception of true light and wisdom in the heart of faith ("But still we have a wisdom to offer," St. Paul says in 1 Cor 2:6), which is manifested to humanism by faith's power of assimilation in regard to human reason and wisdom, that is, when the latter have been freed from the temptation of self-centeredness caused by human pride.

Surely the wisdom of God, working through faith and charity, is capable of purifying the human heart and mind and lifting human wisdom and science into a harmonious, living unity with faith. Indeed, this is the sort of theological wisdom St. Paul was inviting us to attain when he wrote to the Philippians, after wishing that the peace of God, which surpasses all understanding, might keep their minds and hearts in Christ Jesus, "Finally, brothers, fill your minds with everything that is true, everything that is noble, everything that is good and pure, everything that we love and honor, and everything that can be thought virtuous or worthy of praise" (4:8). These words evoke the best of Greek wisdom.

This was precisely the task of Christian theology for centuries, in line with the two principles that form so to speak two stages in the elaboration of theology:

1. To affirm and defend the superiority of the wisdom of God, communicated through faith, over all human knowledge and wisdom, particularly by resisting the autonomy and anthropocentrism they inculcate;

2. To work in the pure light of faith joined to reason, for the forming of a Christian wisdom, which will be the fruit of the believing mind and will witness the truth of the Gospel to all people and all tenets. This is what we may call authentic Christian humanism.

Natural Law

On the level of applying this theological wisdom to human action, the main consideration should be given to natural law. This foundation is indispensable in moral theory for the working out of concrete regulations and judgments. In the light of faith and Christian experience, natural law will be affirmed, strengthened, deepened, and better understood. It will enjoy an exact, supple, and faithful harmony with the action of grace in the human person and will continue to provide a basis for mutual understanding and collaboration with those who do not share the same faith.

Faith Is Universal

Finally, as theologians we should not fear that we shall close ourselves off from others in a sort of Christian ghetto if our starting point of faith distinguishes us from them. Here again, have we the courage to believe in the power of faith and the Holy Spirit who inspires and acts through faith? In truth the grace of the Holy Spirit has a universality stronger and deeper than human reason. It does not contradict it, but assumes and elevates it. St. Paul himself could have feared, humanly speaking, that he might end by merely forming a new religious sect, marginal to Judaism and the Greek world. But he knew that the Gospel, whose herald he was, was animated by a power capable of transcending the limitations and divisions that separated the peoples and cultures of his time.

The question is whether we theologians and Christians, in our turn, will dare to believe in the power of God's grace for all people, and let our minds and our lives be caught up in faith's adventure. Or shall we remain hemmed in by our too-human horizons, fearing to fall victim to ever-greater pride in intellectual feats, yet profoundly shaken and confused by repeated failures to solve the great human questions: the meaning of life, happiness, love, suffering, justice, death—all the proper field of moral teaching. Today's Christian ethicist cannot stop his ears to the question of faith. It cries out from the very heart of moral theology.

13

Moral Theology Today

The history of moral theology over the last two centuries has been shaped by three trends: the ongoing expansion of post-Tridentine ethics in the manuals, the Thomistic renewal, and finally an effort to revitalize moral theology by a return to the Bible and by an exploitation of Gospel themes.

1. Post-Tridentine Tradition in Manuals and the Thomistic Renewal

The history of the presentation of Catholic moral teaching in manuals designed for seminary courses merits a detailed study, for these books have built up an authentic tradition, more varied and vital than we might suppose. It would be well to approach it from the viewpoint of the organization and structure of moral teaching transmitted since the seventeenth century and resumed with the work of St. Alphonsus Liguori for the restoration of seminaries in the nineteenth century, in the aftermath of the Revolution. However, such a study cannot be made here. I will simply give a broad outline, which may serve as a guide for such a research project; it would require considerable refinement.

The classic schema is the one we discussed in the last chapter. Moral theory was divided into fundamental and particular sections. Fundamental moral theology included four chapters, covering human acts, laws, conscience, and sins. Particular moral theology, after a chapter on the theological virtues and their obligations, was generally divided according to the Ten Commandments, to which were added the precepts of the Church and certain canonical prescriptions. The sacraments were studied in light of the obligations required for their administration. We should note the great amount of space given to the questions of justice and marriage.

This schema has perdured with variations, at least as a background that continues to condition problematics and thinking. It is part of the logic of the system of moral obligation; partial improvements have not succeeded in modifying it substantially.

Some important changes were effected in the push for Thomist renewal instigated by Leo XIII. Comparison with St. Thomas's *Summa* showed up major differences, and this inspired the authors of the manuals to rework some parts and reintroduce neglected treatises. This was the case, for example, with D. Prümmer's *Manual of Moral Theology* (Fribourg im Breisgau, 1914) and the *Summa theologiae moralis* of B. H. Merkelbach (Paris, 1919–33).

The main modification promoted by these authors and others was a return to making the theological and moral virtues, in preference to the commandments, the principle of the organization of moral material.[1] This led to a more positive outlook in the treatment of moral problematics. Under fundamental theology a treatise on the virtues was even included. We have to admit, however, that the material itself was not transformed by these improvements. The categories changed, but the content was always shaped by obligations and legal prohibitions. The teaching on the virtues was interesting but remained more theoretical than practical and still suffered from the impoverishment of notions inherited from nominalism. Virtue, prudence, chastity were far from recovering their lost power and dynamism. Several of the virtues mentioned were, in fact, reduced to a congruous role, because there were no obligations attached to them; among these were hope and courage. The virtues most closely connected with law, such as justice because of its nature and chastity because of its subject matter, continued to predominate, as can be seen by the amount of space allotted to them.

Another change: the omission of the treatise on our last end and on beatitude was repaired. St. Thomas had placed this at the beginning of his moral theology. But the authors showed extreme timidity in speaking of happiness; they preferred to stress our final end, which offered reasonable grounds for obligation. In any case, the schema of the virtues

---

1. A. B. Tanquerey, *Synopsis Theologiae moralis et pastoralis* (Tournai, 1902); A. Vermeesch, *Theologiae moralis principia, responsa, consilia* (Rome, 1922–24); A. Van Kol, *Theologia Moralis* (Barcelona, 1968).

was more and more widely adopted and facilitated a certain reconciliation with St. Thomas, but still there was little thought of the patristic
tradition behind him.

The Thomistic renewal was obviously not limited to manuals of moral
theology. It produced a renowned intellectual movement in France
among other countries, led by Father Sertillanges, O.P., Jacques Maritain, and Etienne Gilson. These writers began with the works of St.
Thomas, whose doctrine they studied from the viewpoint of reflection
and history, in direct contact with contemporary thought. They paid
particular attention to Thomist moral theology, giving excellent expositions of it.[2] But their perspective was mainly philosophical; it led to
the debate over Christian philosophy. These writers were thus somewhat
distanced from contemporary ethicists, who thought of them rather as
theorists, philosophers, or historians. Furthermore, their concentrated
attention to the philosophy of St. Thomas prevented them to some extent
from highlighting the properly theological and evangelical dimension of
his work and taking it into account. The questions on the New Law, for
example, remained in shadow.

2. The Return to Biblical Themes

In the effort to renew moral theology, the Germanic countries were
outstanding in the nineteenth century. They possessed university faculties of theology offering clerics a serious intellectual formation and
encouraging them to confront the philosophical ideas of the time as well
as Protestant thought. The movement of the revision of Catholic moral
theology began earlier here therefore, and attained a deeper level of reflection on moral theory.

The sources of this renewal were, first, a return to scriptural themes,
with the object of giving Catholic moral teaching a more fully Christian
character, and second, the Thomistic movement at the turn of the century. From the beginning of the nineteenth century, J. M. Sailer (1751–
1832) in his *Handbuch der Christlichen Moral* (Munich, 1817), and
later J. B. Hirscher (1788–1865) with his *Christliche Moral* (Tübingen,
1835), set the tone, the latter by organizing moral teaching around the
biblical theme of the Kingdom of God. Following this came the publi-

2. A. D. Sertillanges, *La philosophie morale de saint Thomas d'Aquin* (Paris, 1922);
E. Gilson, *St. Thomas d'Aquin,* coll. "Les moralistes chrétiens," Paris 1952; J. Maritain,
Neuf leçons sur les notions premières de la philosophie morale, Paris 1951; id., *La phi-
losophie morale. Examen historique et critiques des grands systèmes.*

cations of the school of Tübingen, notably the *Moraltheologie* (Salzbach, 1852–54) of M. Jocham (1808–93), which focused on the gift of grace in St. John and St. Paul and were based on the concept of the Christian as a child of God, sanctified by the sacraments in the heart of the mystical Body of Christ. They were seeking to overcome in this way the divisions between dogma, morality, asceticism, and mysticism.

The Thomistic renewal developed parallel with these works, also drawing on biblical sources. We owe special mention to the writings of J. Mausbach (1861–1931), with his *Die Katholische Moral, ihre Methoden, Grundsätze und Aufgabe* (Cologne, 1901), *Die Katholische Moral und ihre Gegner* (Cologne, 1921), and also *Die Ethik des hl. Augustinus* (Fribourg, 1929). Mausbach's basic theme was the perfection of being; he used the glory of God as the supreme measure. We might also mention the *Handbuch der Moraltheologie* (Stuttgart, 1922) of O. Schilling, who had without doubt the most penetrating knowledge of St. Thomas. He insisted strongly on charity as the formal principle of moral theology. Finally, the work of F. Tilmann, *Die Idee der Nachfolge Christi* and the volumes directed by him under the title of *Handbucher Katholischer Sittenlehre* (Dusseldorf, 1934–38), in which he stressed the ideal of the following of Christ and the relevance of the Sermon on the Mount for all Christians, were highly noteworthy.

The effort for the renewal of moral theology was continued, after the war, in Father Bernard Häring's book *The Law of Christ,* which has been translated into many languages. This offers the public a manual centering on the theme of dialogue between God and man, or "a moral theology of responsibility in Christ."

The renewal of Catholic moral theology undertaken in Germany was remarkable and considerable. We need to note, however, that the casuist tradition was maintained at the same time, by means of manuals used for clerical formation. One of the most widely used was P. H. Jone's *Théologie morale catholique,* a characteristic representative of casuistry. This tradition was not, therefore, completely curtailed by the attempts at renewal. In fact, except for the narrowness of a problematic of cases of conscience, the moral teaching of the manuals rested on a more solid basis than might be supposed. It was constructed on the heritage of nominalism and the teaching on the natural law, which corrected it. Together with the predominantly rational morality of obligation, it was connatural with the Kantian moral theory of the categorical imperative and duty, which had such a profound influence upon German, and even European, thought. This concept of morality was deeply imprinted upon minds and carried incredible weight. In order to achieve the clarifications and rectifications needed, a revision of the foundations was called for.

3. Vatican II and Moral Theology

Vatican Council II did not often refer to moral theology, but it occasioned a series of official documents, some of which have special interest for us.[3]

Only one sentence in the decree *Optatam totius* on the formation of priests deals explicitly with moral theology: "Special attention needs to be given to the development of moral theology. Its scientific exposition should be more thoroughly nourished by scriptural teaching. It should show the nobility of the Christian vocation of the faithful, and their obligation to bring forth fruit in charity for the life of the world."[4] We can however apply to moral theology the task indicated in the preceding paragraph: "Let [seminarians] learn to search for solutions to human problems with the light of revelation, to apply eternal truths to the changing conditions of human affairs, and to communicate such truths in a manner suited to contemporary man."

At first sight this may seem inconsiderable. Nevertheless, if moral theology is viewed in a broader context than that of casuistry, several other documents will be seen to deal with it directly. An example is *Gaudium et spes,* with its teaching on the human condition and vocation, the dignity of the person, human activity in the world, the dignity of marriage and the family, socioeconomic life, the political community and the safeguarding of peace. All these topics relate to dimensions of Christian

---

3. Noteworthy among the Church documents on teaching moral theology appearing at the time of or since the Second Vatican Council are the following:

Second Vatican Council Decree on Priestly Formation (*Optatam totius*).
Document of the Sacred Congregation for Catholic Education: "The Theological Formation of Future Priests," *Origins* 6 (1976), no. 11, 173–80; no 12, 181–90.
Works of the International Theological Commission, in *Texts and Documents, 1969–1985,* ed. Michael Sharkey (San Francisco: Ignatius Press, 1989): "Nine Theses in Christian Ethics," by Hans Urs von Balthasar, pp. 105–20; "The Question of the Obligatory Character of the Value Judgments and Moral Directives of the New Testament," by H. Schürmann, pp. 121–28.
Letter of the bishops of the United States: "The Pastoral Letter on Moral Values," *Origins* 6 (1976), no. 23, 357–70.
Apostolic Constitution *Sapientia christiana*: "On Ecclesiastical Universities and Faculties," *Origins* 9 (1979), no. 3, 33–45.
  Veritatis splendor.
4. *Optatam totius,* n. 16.

moral theology that have been too much neglected in recent centuries but were very present in the great tradition of theology of former times.

The postconciliar document with the most particular interest in moral theology comes from the Congregation for Catholic Education and deals with the formation of future priests. In the chapter on the orientations of different theological disciplines, the document touches on moral theology after Scripture, patristics, and dogmatics. It acknowledges the narrowness of view and the gaps (legalism, individualism, separation from the sources of revelation) of "a certain moral system." It insists upon the reestablishment of moral theology's close bond with Scripture and tradition, received in faith and interpreted by the magisterium, and on retaining a reference to natural law. The document also points out the need for renewing the connections between moral theory and dogmatics in the tradition of the "one overall plan of systematic theology . . . so well emphasized by St. Thomas Aquinas." The important contribution of the natural and behavioral sciences and the mediation of philosophy must also be taken into account. The ministry of the sacrament of reconciliation and spiritual direction must not be overlooked, as well as pastoral contacts. The document asks that "the internal, spiritual dimension, which demands the full development of the image of God found in each person, and the spiritual progress which ascetic and mystical theology describe" be restored to moral theology. Here, as a little further on in N. 114, where it ranks spiritual theology among the auxiliary disciplines of theology, the document still recognizes the division between moral and ascetical/mystical theology, or spirituality, which can be seen in the plan of studies but which it invites us to transcend.

In my opinion this document is very fine. In line with the biblical, patristic, and spiritual renewal of recent decades, it indicates the most positive and enriching orientations that should guide the current renewal of moral theology. It is in accord with the main inferences we have drawn from our historical research: teachings on recourse to scriptural sources together with philosophical openness within the context of the faith, as evidenced by the Fathers of the Church; systematic reflection, unified and capable of integrating the offerings of philosophy within theology as the great scholastics did; attention to the sciences and adaptation to modern problems as illustrated by the best Renaissance theologians— but here, perhaps, with a more critical, penetrating eye in the name of the Gospel and the faith.

4. The Postconciliar Situation of Catholic Moral Teaching

It is difficult to describe a situation while living in the midst of all its complexity, variety, and novelty. I expect that my remarks will be considered inadequate, lacking in nuance, inflexible. Still, the risk must be taken. I must dare to choose some direction for research and progress that will avoid dead ends and overcome our current temptations.

The postconciliar era has produced a sort of defrosting of Catholic moral teaching as a new wind sweeps over it. But as often happens when the wind gets too strong, things can get turned upside down, and it is not rare to hear people, even priests, wondering aloud if there is still any moral theology to be taught.

In recent centuries the Church has often been in a state of seige in relation to the modern world. It has had to resist the onslaughts of revolutions and the powerful currents of liberal or Marxist thought. It has raised walls and dug trenches to defend the faithful. In the field of moral theology the Church has tried to retain its solid foundation on natural law; it has always upheld law and authority and maintained objectivity in face of a freedom ever ready to affirm itself in an arbitrary and subjective way, or of an absolutist concept of the state tending to demean the human person and religion.

Openness to the modern world may be said to characterize the work of the recent Council. Freedom of conscience, ecumenism, dialogue with other religions, attention to science and politics—all this has produced in many Christians and theologians a strong reaction leading them from one extreme to the other; they have developed an allergy to traditional positions. Obedience to law had at times been servile or infantile; now the priority has become defense of the rights of the subjective conscience. The teaching on natural law has been demolished by ethicists themselves and readily abandoned in the name of science. Sudden openness to modern thought in the areas of philosophy, psychology, sociology, and history has caused an explosion. All moral theology and religion has been subject to rethinking in light of Hegel, Freud, Marx or Nietzsche. The old fixation of ethicists on the problems of the sixth commandment was reversed in favor of sexuality, breaking down the traditional barriers that had repressed it. Clerical taste for political power moved from the right wing to the left, causing political and social involvement to become the criterion of the evangelical authenticity of the Christian life. The Catholic attachment to orthodoxy and theological and dogmatic truth was soft-pedaled in the climate of research, dialogue, and pluralism, open theoretically to all opinions but in fact excluding the orthodox one. Love of truth yielded to a taste for novelty, variety, relativity, adaptation.

In the face of concrete problems, the opinions of a good number of ethicists have also changed. Difficult questions debated in the public forum, such as abortion, contraception, euthanasia, and in a general and more technical way the problem of the existence of intrinsically evil acts, come to mind. Dealing with cases of conscience, ethicists have been led to revise the very principles that would have solved them at the level of fundamental morality. The rock of moral theology has thus been dashed by the powerful waves of the world and of history, which threaten to break and shatter it.

We should beware, however, of black and white pictures and of the extremes of radical choices between, for example, traditionalists and innovators or conservatives and progressives. We should be clear about what we want to keep, what is indispensable for survival. We should know what it is we are trying to progress toward; it may be something mortal, in the process of dissolution. In the course of these debates, often inspired by real generosity (but as often by little lucidity and maturity), in the midst of the clamor of different opinions, it becomes difficult to discover the point at issue beneath all the sound and fury. It lies hidden in the depths of the moral domain.

The deepest center of postconciliar debates, the eye of the tornado, I might say, seems to me to be a resurgence of the question that was put to St. Paul and that has been put to the Church throughout its history, in the confrontation between Gospel and world, between Christian faith and human wisdom, science and culture. The Council's openness to the world suffered from the ambiguity of the word *world,* already used in St. John's Gospel. It opened the door to interpretations and developments of thought and sentiment that took great liberties with the documents and explicit teaching of the Council. It is rather difficult to find an adequate description of this trend. We could call it "social Christianity" because it attempts to introduce a new attitude to the world on the part of Christianity. But the adjective "social" suggests worldliness.[5] We might prefer to call it "secular Christianity," for this movement aims at the adaptation of faith to secular society, if not to the secularization of the Church. This last expression may be the better one, including as it does the anticlerical nuance connoted by the term "secular" in the West.

---

5. Editor's note: The translator employs the word *social* for the French *mondaine*—thus the author's association with "worldliness."

5. Secular Christianity

What then is the nature of this secular or social Christianity? What are its characteristic features?

Radical Openness to the World

Historically, the movement appeared as a would-be radical interpretation of the openness to the world encouraged by the Second Vatican Council. The Church, heretofore on the defensive and in conflict with a hostile world and suspicious of all it might offer or represent, was now to attempt to engage in dialogue with this world. It would begin by listening to the world and recognizing its values: freedom, justice, science, technology, and philosophical ideas—everything, in a word, that makes up the modern world. This opening of the gates of the ecclesiastical "fortress" introduced among Catholics the contemporary principles of thought and action against which they had formerly been warned: liberalism in thinking and education, socialism and Marxism, positivism in the behavioral and historical sciences, idealistic and existential philosophy, phenomenology, and demythologization in exegesis. Dialogue and confrontation between Christian thought and these modern trends was needed and could undeniably be very beneficial. But there was the danger of unpreparedness in many, and of inadequate intellectual formation and rootedness in the faith, especially among the clergy. In practice, the openness was like a hole in a dike. Suddenly the mighty flood poured through. It was irresistible and threatened to sweep everything in its path.

The upheaval was profound and spread rapidly. It affected all areas of Christian life and theology, particularly moral teaching. Some were led to a reinterpretation of the relation of Church to world that modified the tradition radically. The Church no longer opposed the world, even while dialoguing with it and keeping its distance; now it was a Church in the world and for the world, promoting the world's values and assuming the role of servant. Even the relationship of the world to God was reversed. Nietzsche's avowal that God, or at least a God we needed, "was dead," was accepted. The world was declared "adult," capable of solving all its problems alone, with complete autonomy.

Such was the "secular world." No longer should we seek God outside of it, or indeed above and beyond it, but only at the center of human life and in its service. The elimination of all separation between God and the world accompanied the suppression of distance between the world and the Church. We might express the change in this way: primacy was now given to the second commandment, love of neighbor, which drew love of God along after it. Christian generosity now focused on humanity and its service. "Secular Christianity" was clearly a man-centered humanism. We might wonder if this generosity, however real at first, had not been unwisely separated from its principal source, and whether it would find enough nourishment in the human heart to keep it alive in the tempests and setbacks of the modern world.

The Critical Spirit

One of the most characteristic features of the postconciliar movement in the Church is its propensity for criticism. Criticism of the Church first and, in particular, of its hierarchy and teaching. From a Church that was always right, we have moved to one whose flaws are so apparent to us that we are suspicious whenever pronouncements are made. The prejudice used to be strongly in favor of authority, the magisterium and tradition; today the trend is criticism and freedom of thought at all levels.

This criticism is also directed to the world, whose ideas fostered contestation with the Church, and particularly to existing society. Here we have moved from an originally favorable attitude toward existing power, based on a positive social doctrine, to criticism of "the system," "the established order." There is a systematic opposition to it; we support protesters and all kinds of "marginalized" groups. Undoubtedly such positions can be legitimate and well founded in a society and a Church where human imperfections abound. But we would draw attention here to the predominance of the critical spirit over a constructive spirit. It is often a sign of hidden individualism, incapable of adapting adequately and actively to society and authority.

Reinterpretations in Light of Human Values

"Secular Christianity" also led to a widespread reinterpretation of sciences and religious conduct. Human values were recognized not only at their own level, in their autonomy, in order to be integrated with higher Christian values; rather, the latter were to be reinterpreted so as to harmonize with the former.

Thus, in exegesis a new emphasis has been placed on modern historical and linguistic sciences, whose conclusions and hypotheses are accepted at face value. The text of the Bible is subjected to critical study as though it were a human document. At times the intervention of philosophical categories and criteria rounds out this study, while faith is treated parenthetically because of the method being used. Anything in Scripture that seems to run counter to the modern mentality is rejected or "demythologized." This was the case with miracles. Finally, ideological readings of the Bible are essayed.

Dogmatic theology is reviewed with the aid of the history of dogma, starting with the cultural background and the evolution of ideas within the framework of the history of the Church and that of religions. Here again, philosophical or ideological schemas are often used and applied to authentic documents with utter freedom. Anything incompatible with modern ideas is set aside, such as the so-called "substantialist" thought of patristic theology, which is the foundation for conciliar teaching on the Trinity, the person of Christ, and the Eucharist. The defense of pluralism exceeds the limits of theology and addresses the very propositions of faith. It is particularly averse to anything presented as "orthodox."

Moral theology has experienced the repercussions of these reinterpretations in the measure in which it has tried to reestablish ongoing, profound relations with dogmatics and exegesis. It has also lent itself too easily to a humanistic reinterpretation. The manuals, criticized for the individualism and legalism of their teaching, have been discounted. The doctrine of natural law, on which they relied principally as a foundation for universal unchanging laws, has been demolished in the name of the behavioral sciences, the historical evolution of conditions and cultures, and the multiplicity of circumstances and consequences involved in human action.

The weakening of the ties between post-Tridentine moral theology and Scripture and the Christian spiritual tradition has robbed moral theology of its best resources for answering the "humanistic" attack it is sustaining. We could even say that the humanism that marked the Renaissance was a remote preparation for the present crisis.

Moral theology, therefore, is being rewritten from the point of view of sociology, psychology, anthropology and the philosophies in vogue, without sufficient care being taken to discern and to keep what is essential, what cannot be reduced to positive sciences. Christian moral theology is presented more and more as purely human moral teaching, based on human values and ordered to them. Whatever is specifically Christian about it falls under the heading of generous inspiration nourished by charity, which is itself ordered to the promotion of human values. Moral theology is yielding to the "horizontalism" of the new theology; we hear less and less about God.

In such a context, with the reaction against the individualism of casuistic moral teaching and in accord with the collective dimension of current problems and ideas, we can understand why "politics"—in the wide sense of social and world organization—invades moral theology and tends to take over. Not simply moral theology, but the entire field of theology, is being subjected to revision in light of the political "praxis." Political commitment to the people is presented to theology as a condition for authenticity and the chief object of its study. Scripture, even the Gospel itself, is read in light of political or sociological perspectives and submitted to the imperatives of social practice and a preconceived ideology. "Politics" thus claims to take moral teaching and theology under its wing.

The Christian Character Retained

"Secular Christianity" maintains its Christian character by the generous principle that inspires it and is expressed in the priority given to love of neighbor. This is considered the one commandment of Christian moral teaching, along with concern for the poor, oppressed, and underprivileged members of society. The end it proposes is equally Christian: the completion of history's journey and the directing of humanity's effort to the building of a better world, leading at the last to the Kingdom of God, all this, thanks to the promises of Christ, addressed to the Church and through the Church to the world. This is the foundation of a theology of hope. So moral theology, understood as purely human in its values and norms, is given a Christian horizon that orients it.

Nevertheless, within this concept a change in the center and general orientation of theology is at work. It can be described as a passage from God-centeredness to man-centeredness, using as a bridge a Christocentrism that henceforth will stress the Incarnation and Christ's humanity rather than his divinity. The latter, when evoked, is placed at the service of humanization, as an argument to demonstrate the will of God himself. This change is not simply a matter of emphasis or evolution; it is confrontational and rejects traditional theology understood as God-centered and supernatural. The tradition is caricatured as opposing the desired humanization. In moral theology the predominance of human values leads to a humanistic downgrading of the theological virtues. Charity is in danger of being made equivalent to general good will and a universal, philanthropic generosity. Faith can no longer intervene directly in the realm of concrete values and norms; it is rerouted to dogmatic truths, where it must focus on a voluntary and personal option regarding the person of Jesus. Hope looks to the horizon of human history and the eschatalogical promises, which are interpreted as a guarantee of the success of the human enterprise founded on Christ, the symbol of perfect man.

An Attempt at Evaluation according to the Dialectic of Christian Faith

The question posed by "secular Christianity" should be taken seriously, whatever the deviations and exaggerations it has given rise to and the damage it has caused. Behind the question, the Church's position is at stake, in relation to the modern world with its hopes, drama, culture, values and errors. Also, consequently, the Gospel's penetration into this world and its future is at stake. This question concerns all moral theology: Is there a moral theology for the world of today? How can it be this, and still remain completely itself? These are, in fact, the major orientations of the Council, at work in a realm that is essential to both Church and world.

The "Humanist" Stage of Faith

Obviously we cannot make a complete critical examination here of so complex a phenomenon. It would seem helpful, however, to attempt a certain evaluation in light of the elements of Christian moral teaching provided by our historical research and especially by the New Testament.

Our answer cannot be limited to adopting a position pro or con, but should take into account the different aspects presented, or the various stages included, in what we may call the dialectic of faith. Secular Christianity corresponds well to the first stage of faith, which might be called the moment of the Incarnation or of humanism. God's call and his promises take root in human nature and correspond to our aspirations and values. This stage can be illustrated by reviewing the chief events of sacred history.

The promises made to Abraham corresponded exactly to his most natural desire to have a son, an heir. The hope they aroused included all his human longings and far surpassed his expectations: his wife Sarah would bear him a son, he would become the father of a great people, all nations would be blessed because of him. Already in Abraham, human hope reached its universal dimension.

The promise was repeated for Moses in favor of the Hebrew people and corresponded once more in the most precise and concrete way to the hopes of a nation in the making: liberation from slavery, the promulgation of a law, and the setting up of a social and religious organization; the conquest of a fertile country and the establishment of a "homeland." And we know the permanence and the perduring power of this Jewish hope, so human that it still persists, long after faith in God has disappeared.

We rediscover humanity's hope in the New Testament. The Davidic promises recalled to Mary on the day of the Annunciation corresponded to her natural desire for motherhood and explicitly aroused in her the hope of every Jewish woman to be the mother of the Messiah. You shall bear a son; the Lord God will give him the throne of David, his kingdom shall have no end. Simeon would indicate the universal dimension: he will be a light to the nations.

The preaching of Jesus began, according to St. Matthew, with the announcement of the Beatitudes. These echoed all the ancient promises and pointed them to the coming of the Kingdom of Heaven. The Fathers of the Church and St. Thomas understood the Beatitudes as Christ's answer to the question that had initiated and dominated moral teaching and even philosophy: the natural desire for happiness. The spontaneous, universal desire that receives an unhoped-for answer lifts human hope to its highest pitch. We can even see how the call of the apostles signaled the recapture of human hope with the promise, "You shall be fishers of men," as if their fishermen's hopes would be realized in the hopes of the apostolate.

If we apply this to Christians today, it means that God's promises to humanity respond to our own most natural desires: the longing for happiness, freedom, justice, and truth. His promises invite us to share in all the authentic sentiments and hopes of our times, and they awaken in our hearts a secret desire to see and love God, which can draw all our desires into one and direct them to a higher end.

The Gospel promises also affect the Church in the world and build up the Church's solidarity with the world. The Church recognizes all the world's hopes, weaknesses and flaws as its own, and knows it must take on the human condition in its entirety. The Church is called to lift humanity up to God just as it is. Even more, the Gospel reveals to the Church the deepest aspirations of the human heart, easily overlaid in the world by surface attractions and artificial needs: these are chiefly spiritual and moral yearnings. More than all else, the Church must stir up and foster the desire for God in human hearts, which the Word and the action of the Spirit call forth.

It is at this level that the truth of "secular Christianity" operates, by the correspondence between God's promises and the desires, values, and hopes springing up in each person throughout the world. This "humanist" stage of faith gives ample reason for opposing a certain "supernaturalism" which has stretched and almost severed the bonds between human nature and the order of grace, out of fear of compromising grace's gratuity.

The Stage of Solitude and Separation

The shoe pinches, however, when concern for sharing and for solidarity with people becomes a practical identification with the world. This can cause a misunderstanding of the second stage of faith, that of testing and of the Passion. We may be led to refuse to go apart and be alone with God. As we continue our journey, we come upon the St. Paul of Romans and Corinthians, with his penetrating critique of the world of his time and of all times. With him we discover anew human sinfulness, caught and snared in its proud pretensions of achieving its own justice and wisdom. St. Paul goes on to the exaltation of Christ crucified, rejected, cast out—the unique source of the justice and wisdom of God for those who draw near to him in the humility and solitude of faith. Here, coming together from all the nations of the world, we are united once more in the communion of the Church. This is the stage of folly and scandal in the eyes of the world. It must come, in order to displace the center which was humanity and the world, and replace it with God, found through faith in Jesus Christ.

This testing, which may be named the time of solitude before God, is written into the heart of sacred history. There was the testing of Abraham, who accepted the loss of Isaac and the people of the promise who were to issue from him, so as to stand alone before God. There, in obedience, he opened his soul to the dimensions of the very love of God himself. God restored Isaac to him, and taught him to encompass him, together with all the children of the promise, in a wholly new love whose center would forever be God.

Also in the desert, in the solitude of Sinai, the hope of the Hebrew people was put to the test, to see if their hearts sought God and loved him before all else. The desert has thus become the privileged place of the human encounter with God, alone with the Alone in pure faith. The desert symbolizes the testing of faith, but also the forming of a new people.

Jesus' testing, too, began in the desert with the temptation in preparation for his teaching, and culminated in the Passion, especially in the scene of the agony, which uncovered the roots of the conflict. In a solitude carved out by all that was to follow—the flight of the apostles and Peter's denial, condemnation by the Sanhedrin and the Romans, the weight of the cross and of sin—Jesus set aside self-will, the core of human sin, to deliver himself in obedience to the Father's will, enclosing within it, so to speak, all his own will, his life, his death, his whole being. In the depths of darkness and abandonment a door opened, through which God's love could engulf the world and free it from sin, for "God so loved the world, that he gave his only Son that all might be saved."

The disciples received this inescapable warning from Jesus: "If anyone wants to be a follower of mine, let him renounce himself and take up his cross and follow me. For anyone who wants to save his life will lose it; but anyone who loses his life for my sake, and for the sake of the gospel, will save it" (Mark 8:34–35). Even the Beatitudes demanded the necessary testing: poverty, affliction, hunger and thirst, persecution for the sake of Christ in the world, by the world.

The Christian who would be faithful to the Gospel must pass through the testing of his faith and answer these questions: Where is your life centered? In God or in yourself, in Jesus Christ or in the world? What will be the cornerstone of your life? In whom will you place your faith and hope, to whom give your love? The choice is unavoidable and decisive.

When called by God to the desert, the Christian must accept separation from the world, at least interiorly and for a time, to renounce the human values and hopes the world offers, to stand alone before God in the poverty of faith, believing that the path to the greatest depths of human life and history is opening up ahead. Through obedience and renunciation, the Christian can truly take on the suffering and sins of humankind, to lift them up to the divine mercy. The human values that were abandoned in the spirit of faith will now serve as solid bases to strengthen all hearts.

The Church in its turn must pass through the testing of faith, must stand alone before God far from the world, in order to be rooted in Christ, in God. These are the questions asked: will the Church dare to believe in the Word of God, even when it seems to be folly, a scandal, the stupidity of a prescientific age in the eyes of the world's learned ones? Will it have the courage to hope in God when human hope is gone, and renounce human support if need be? Can it love God more than the world and all it offers, more than itself?

This testing, which bears upon the relations of the Christian and the Church to the world, is by no means always placid and untroubled, as might be a voluntary, temporary separation. Involving both spirit and heart, it can provoke profound opposition; it can demand a categorical refusal when the world insists on making certain values, certain ideas— in the end, even the Christian himself—the center of all things. It can lead to persecution. The truly evangelical response, in the very midst of the conflict, will be forgiveness and the prayer that assures the victory of love over evil and should accompany all witness to Jesus. Thus, in the midst of confrontation the Church should continue to love all people, and the world. It will thereby discover with renewed purity and vigor that love of God that seeks, through the Church, to permeate the world with the power of the Holy Spirit. It will come to know how different it is, in its mysterious source, from what we usually intend by the word "love."

By this paradoxical road, the Christian and the Church advance to the third stage of the life of faith, that of the Resurrection, where the action of grace and the Spirit unfold, in the sanctification and wisdom of God, in the work of bringing forth the new Man, of which St. Paul speaks, and in the spread of the Church to all peoples.

The Flaw in "Secular Christianity"

Within the scope of faith we have just outlined briefly, there is a very obvious danger lurking in "secular Christianity": the temptation to adapt to the world and its spirit in the name of sharing its values and hopes. This would lead to a refusal of Gospel renunciations, of self-renunciation. One would not be willing to place at the center of one's life anyone other than self. To use a word that today has become a bit of a scandal, it would mean a refusal of "the supernatural." This sums it up.

The temptation of "secular Christianity" is to "naturalize" Christianity in both senses of the word. We would wish to adapt so thoroughly to the world as to become naturalized, even as we might acquire the nationality of a country whose values and customs we adopt for the sake of credibility. But we discover that, in suppressing the differences, we are left with nothing worth presenting for belief, nothing worthwhile at all. "Naturalization" also implies the way in which the modern world reduces everything to the natural order. Science and technology dominate externals to the point of destroying them. The affirmation of the supremacy of reason and freedom, and the systematic refusal to accept anything beyond them, dominates the "natural" man. All this happens in spite of the notorious failures of rationalism, scientism, and their offspring.

The crucial point in the encounter between Christianity and the modern world is found in the affirmation and audacious preaching of the supernatural, other-worldly character of faith in Jesus Christ. Then, at the heart of the world, by death to one sort of world, the seed of life will be planted and a new dimension given which surpasses humanity and all its natural powers. Faith, hope, and charity, which dominate and must impregnate Christian moral teaching, cannot be reduced to human values, however noble, because they transplant and root the human person, through intellect and heart, in another world, which is properly divine. At the same time they correspond in an amazing way to the most intimate, most authentically natural human aspirations.

In the measure in which it avoids detachment and the transcendence of human values in order to remain bonded to the world, in the measure in which it refuses to "lose its soul," as the Gospel would say, "secular Christianity" loses the opportunity to receive the seed of the life of Christ who died and rose, the new "supernatural" life, as theology rightly calls it. Whatever upheavals, illusions, books it may produce, it is self-condemned to spiritual sterility. It recoils before the cross of Christ.

There is no Christian moral theory, therefore, that can stand firm and resist the assaults of history unless it rests upon theological faith. Its foundation must be the cornerstone laid by God and rejected by all human builders, by "the world." This faith alone makes Christian moral teaching strong and fruitful, even for the world itself. It is the salt of the earth; its savor is the very sharpness of the renunciations demanded, the contradictions assumed.

6. Scripture and Moral Teaching after the Council

We shall close this study of the postconciliar era with a word on moral theology's relationship to Scripture, from which the Council invites us to draw doctrine anew, for Scripture is the first object of faith and the principal source of Christian theology.

The Difficulty in Reading Scripture Today

One of the most important benefits of Vatican Council II is surely that it has given the People of God full access to Scripture. It has affirmed the necessity of a return to the sacred books for a renewal of theology and of the Christian life in all its circumstances.

However, despite the biblical renewal of recent decades, contact with Scripture is not as easy as we might suppose. We have pointed out the difficulty for ethicists: having come to treat moral theology from the viewpoint of commandments and obligations, they are primarily interested in strictly normative texts and imperatives. They do not see how to integrate moral teaching with the rest of the Bible, although there are many other texts far more suited to this purpose.

But there is another more general problem, which concerns all Christians and which is perhaps more fundamental in its implications. I shall formulate it by means of a very simple question: Which should be given priority, a direct and personal reading of Scripture, or the study of exegetical books which comment and give explanations? To be more exact: What is the starting point for a true knowledge of Scripture, which will nourish theology and moral teaching? Again, we can ask, as theologians and Christians, whether we ought to read Scripture directly, as the Fathers did, or be obliged to go through the exegetical sciences. This is an old problem. It was proposed in former times regarding philosophy and theology, especially scholasticism. It comes to us in a new form today, in connection with applying historical sciences to Scripture, and is widespread in the modern Church.

This is one aspect of the humanistic problem posed by "secular Christianity." If sciences, like human values, take priority and determine all else, even the realm of faith, then Scripture is no longer truly available without the intervention of exegesis, which studies the human data of Scripture: authors, language, and cultural, historical, and religious settings. The consequences are serious, for hardly has Scripture been restored to the Christian faithful than it is taken away from them to become the property of specialists. The current, confusing idea is that one can no longer understand Scripture today without having studied exegesis. The situation is still more delicate for ethicists, who have a need for science and are inclined, professionally, to seek the help of those who have made a special study of Scripture. Dialogue on the subject is difficult, however. Both exegetes and ethicists have created their own very different technical languages. Exegetes have shown little interest in the moral teaching of Scripture and are not comfortable with it because of the moral categories they have grown up with. Ethicists are used to appealing to reason rather than Scripture, and are uneasy with divergences among exegetes. Here again the question arises: must the scientific biblical exegete stand between between the moral theologian on the one hand and the inspired author on the other, whether he be prophet or evangelist? Can nothing worthwhile be understood without him?

The problem becomes more acute when we note how many historians, in every area, through scientific concern have delayed examination of all aspects of their subject. We find a number of interesting problems they have never raised, although they are basic ones. How can we enter into the text, and what does it mean? What is the content, so much more important than the wrappings?

In the end we come back to the problem of establishing a priority between the two levels or types of truth we discussed in connection with the relation between moral theology and the positive sciences. On the one hand, there is the truth of the wrappings: the establishment of the text, its author, its ideas, all set in their own time and milieu, so distant from ours. This is what we call "historical," "factual," or positive truth. On the other hand, there is the truth of the contents, answering the questions, What does the text say, what did the author write, is it true? This second kind of truth can be as important for us as for our forebears. We have called it "real" truth, because it shows us the profound reality behind the words, "facts," or phenomena. We could also call it substantial or ontological truth.[6]

[handwritten margin note: historical-factual truth]

[handwritten margin note: substantial ontological truth.]

6. The qualification "real" used here seems to correspond to the definition of the literal or historical sense given by St. Thomas in the first question of the *Summa,* where he discusses the different senses of Scripture (a 10). For him the words of Scripture are signs of the *res* designated by God. *Res* should be translated as "reality" rather than "thing." This reality answers the question "Is it true?" which we ask of the text, today as at the time of its composition. It is basically spiritual, as is all that God intends. The spiritual senses grafted upon it witness to this. Further, the question as to the truth of the text implies the question of faith, for the latter is necessary in order to reach divine realities above human reason. The relationship is similar to that between disciple and master, which St. Thomas uses as fundamental in his analysis of faith (IIaIIae q 2 a 5). Such seems to be the reading of Scripture with faith's understanding. This is at the origin of theology; it makes it a participation in the knowledge of God.

If this is so, we must distinguish the literal sense of which St. Thomas is speaking from the literal sense that is the object of positive exegesis, when it abstracts from the question of the truth of scriptural affirmations or when it claims to respond only through reason. The difference is very clear when we compare the fruitfulness of the literal sense as viewed by St. Thomas and the Fathers with the restricted sense adopted by positive exegesis. In

It is one thing to establish, for example, the text of the Beatitudes or the Sermon on the Mount by tracing its history; it is quite another thing to take it in itself and understand how the poor, the afflicted, and the persecuted can be happy, or again, to recognize that it is vain to hear and study such texts without putting them into practice, as we are told at the end of the Sermon. The study of historical, positive truth demands time-consuming labor on the part of the specialist and can be protracted indefinitely. If this labor were required as indispensable for an authentic reading of Scripture, access to Scripture would be barred for most Christians, pastors as well as laity. Scripture would become the preserve of professional exegetes. Happily, however, the truth contained in Scripture is of another order. It is accessible to anyone who has ears to hear the questions posed by the Sermon on the Mount about happiness, the meaning of life, and the Kingdom, about the new justice and fraternal love, about the heavenly Father and prayer, Christ and his teaching. Thanks to this content of a text, which becomes a question and a living word, Scripture may once more be offered in its totality to the Christian people, through direct reading. This will light up life, feed prayer, and sustain action; exegetical problems need be no hindrance. Much is at stake for the Church in this regard, as well as for ethicists and exegetes.

The Priority of Direct and Personal Reading: Moving from Text to Word

It seems to me indispensable to give honest priority to a direct reading of Scripture over any type of commentary, exegetical, theological, or whatever it may be. In preparation, only absolutely necessary elements would be required: an exact translation, an explanation of terms, a minimum of historical and religious facts, some introduction by a competent person, and an appropriate setting, such as that of private prayer or liturgy.

For any kind of work whatsoever, a play by Racine for example, the

---

the former view, the literal sense produces the three principal spiritual senses of Scripture, beginning with the reality signified. In the latter view, the literal sense is restricted to itself alone or to what the sacred authors of antiquity intended. Undoubtedly we cannot oppose this twofold interpretation of the literal sense, for theological reading can and should include positive reading. But we must recognize the fact that the latter is not sufficient to lead us to scriptural "reality" in its richness, or to arrive at theology.

The question is of the greatest importance; we can only touch on it here. It is decisive for the reestablishment of the bonds between Scripture and moral theology. The latter can renew its vigor only when we discover the moral sense pervading Scripture. It focuses on Christ, who is for us, yesterday, today and forever, the unique source of God's justice and wisdom.

priority of personal reading is a kind of natural working principle. This provides the substance for understanding (if the reader has the capacity); commentaries will refine, expand, and improve it, so as to facilitate a richer and more penetrating re-reading. The commentary is at the service of the immediate reading. If read first, it risks being a screen or a poor substitute—an *ersatz* as that expression was used during the war. Commentaries do not fulfill their role competently or acquire their proper value unless consulted *after* direct reading. They can never replace it. The danger is more insidious than we might think. The temptation of the commentator, whether an historian or some other type of professional, is to believe, and to convince others, that he understands the work even better than the author or that, in any case, we must read his commentary first if we want to acquire a true, scientific understanding of the work.

This principle is even more important in regard to Scripture. Scripture does not merely offer human knowledge and experience, which the reader could reproduce with the aid of the text. Scripture is an instrument used by God to communicate with a human person, to manifest himself as a word spoken, and to produce in the reader's inmost being the experience of an encounter with a Person who is unique. But the text cannot become a word unless the reader approaches it with the appropriate dispositions and accepts being touched personally through it by a concept hitherto unimaginable, which no human being could invent. This obviously calls for personal reading, comparable to an intimate conversation, where one's first care is to listen.

Human Intermediaries in the Reading of Scripture

It may be argued that God chose to use men to speak to us, authors who expressed themselves in particular languages and in historical and cultural settings that we need to know if we are to understand them. Such knowledge is indispensable if we are to grasp what God wished to tell us through the biblical authors. So there is a series of human intermediaries with whom we will constantly be dealing; the uninitiated may easily become entangled and lose their way as they strive to follow.

All this is merely an intellectual mirage. To return to our comparison, even as Racine's *Phaedra* can touch the heart of the simplest reader who pours over this masterpiece while recalling personal experience, in the same way and with greater impact, the Holy Spirit, sometimes with the help of a single verse from the Gospels, can break through all human intermediaries in an instant and communicate to the humblest of Christians an intimate, vital understanding of Scripture that learned scholars might envy. Such was the case with Anthony, father of monks, and so many others whose spiritual wisdom has nourished the life of the Church and theology. When God wishes to speak to someone, who would dare, who could possibly stand in his way, however learned?

God always speaks directly in the depths of an attentive, humble heart. He often uses Scripture, heedless of any exegetical problems that might arise. It is He who speaks the word, as in former times he inspired the text. There is really only one problem: Can God speak to us? All Christian Scripture depends upon an affirmative answer to this question and bears witness in its favor. Unless we believe this, we can neither understand nor interpret it truly, we cannot reach its substance nor render a full exegesis.

I should like to make it clear that there is no question here of extraordinary words or voices, such as those heard by Joan of Arc and other mystics. We are speaking of that "ordinary," even daily word, which the Holy Spirit addresses to every Christian who knows how to listen truly to Scripture, that word whose echo is particularly clear in the Fathers of the Church and in the liturgy.

In adopting this position, we are in harmony with the profound, primary intention of the sacred authors, which would be open to the most positive exegesis. They did not write for the pleasure of being read by posterity, nor to provide material for their commentators and historians. They wrote explicitly and knowingly as servants of the Word of God manifested in Jesus Christ and as instruments of his Spirit. This Spirit alone is capable, in the last analysis, of speaking to human persons in the here and now of their actual lives, in the new present that the Word creates for them. As St. Paul put it, the sacred authors wrote "from faith to faith," in order to stir up our faith in the Word of God.

We are also in agreement with St. Augustine, St. Thomas, and the generality of the Fathers, as well as many Christian exegetes, who would say to us: "Before you read our works, begin with the Gospel, with Scripture. Listen to the Word of God, for here the Master is heard, and he is the principle source of our knowledge. After this, consult our works. They will help you, like faithful servants, to advance in the knowledge of God." All their works, however voluminous, are, when all is said and done, commentaries on the Gospel, which can be reached only through an inner door, faith's hearing.[7]

---

7. As an illustration of this let me quote the penetrating reflection of St. Augustine on reading of Moses: "Let me hear and understand the meaning of the words: In the begin-

When we give priority to a direct and personal reading of Scripture, seen as the place where God's Word dwells—the origin, principal content, and end of Scripture—we need not fear that we are succumbing to a fundamentalist, simplistic, or naive reading of the Bible. Undoubtedly, the reader with little exegetical formation, even if a saint, may be deceived as to interpretation. But no one, including the exegete, is exempt from possible error. The main thing is to allow ourselves to be led and to advance patiently toward the whole Truth, avoiding the chief error, which is no longer to discern the Word of God in Scripture and to treat it as a human book.

Indeed, contrary to our fears, the person who has received, through faith, the spark of an interior understanding of Scripture will all the better appreciate the authentic findings of modern exegesis and profit from them, using the necessary critical discernment and a right ordering of things. The Word of God holds first place, then comes human science, with the relativity that affects its research, especially when dealing with deep realities, human or divine. To return to our example: once captivated by Racine's *Phaedra,* we are all the more eager to read informed and learned commentaries. But we discern, too, the limitations of interpretations and even at times their foolishness when they are not based on personal understanding.

Personal, direct reading of Scripture is necessary in order that the text become a word that introduces us into the substance or interiority of the text and that communicates to us a profound understanding of it. This is every Christian's first right. We could call it a natural, even a

---

ning you made heaven and earth. Moses wrote these words. He wrote them and passed on into your presence, leaving this world where you spoke to him. He is no longer here and I cannot see him face to face. But if he were here, I would lay hold of him and in your name I would beg and beseech him to explain those words to me. I would be all ears to catch the sounds that fell from his lips. If he spoke in Hebrew, his words would strike my ear in vain and none of their meaning would reach my mind. If he spoke in Latin, I should know what he said, but how should I know whether what he said was true? If I knew this too, it could not be from him that I got such knowledge. But deep inside me, in my most intimate thought, Truth, which is neither Hebrew nor Greek nor Latin nor any foreign speech, would speak to me, though not in syllables formed by lips and tongue. It would whisper, 'He speaks the truth.' And at once I should be assured. In all confidence I would say to this man, your servant, 'What you tell me is true.'

"Since, then, I cannot question Moses, whose words were true because you, the Truth, filled him with yourself, I beseech you, my God, to forgive my sins and grant me the grace to understand those words, as you granted him, your servant, the grace to speak them" (*Confessions,* 11.3.5).

This is a text in which we can clearly distinguish the contents from the wrappings, a particular language. "How could I know if it was true?" This goes beyond the question of languages. It refers to an interior word, which goes straight to the heart of every human person.

supernatural right. It is a necessary condition if the Council's fruits are to be produced in all Christians, including theologians and exegetes.

Clearly this kind of reading is demanding, and cannot remain individual. The Word of God calls for meditation and prayer; it must be put into practice, and this is the principal key to profound, sapiential understanding. We may not isolate ourselves in our own personal interpretation. We must broaden our ideas by entering into a communion of mind and faith with the sacred authors and the entire Church. It is, therefore, an ecclesial reading, done in intimate union with the living tradition and the liturgy, that we must practice.

Scripture and Experience

I should like to mention one final condition for the reestablishment of a vital bond between Scripture and theology—particularly moral theology—in our postconciliar era. The role of experience, of praxis, is increasingly insisted upon today as one of theology's principal sources. This stress on experience has its truth. Unfortunately, however, it often happens that it turns our attention away from Scripture. This is due to a certain overly abstract way of considering Scripture, which we have inherited from the theology of recent centuries. We think of Scripture as a collection of propositions guaranteed by divine authority, which tell us what to believe and what to do, and which will thus serve as principles for theology and moral teaching. Scripture is viewed in the guise of abstract and universal principles, from which we try to draw practical applications. In truth, nothing could be more concrete than scriptural language and thought. The promoters of experience are caught in the breach between life and Scripture, experience and abstract principles, theory and praxis, that we have been taught to absorb and that works to the detriment of both. Experience risks being limited to a purely human form, which, by a process of rationalization, results in a hermeneutic criterion of Scripture. Scripture is then ascribed to the human experience of the apostles and sacred authors, and finally reduced to the common level of human experience and the praxis of its contemporary interpreters. We are no longer dealing with the real, historical Gospel, that of Matthew, John, Paul, and the Church. It is a contingent fabrication, in which we can recognize the traits and oddities of the period, person, or group whose work it is.

This is not the way Christians have understood and experienced the word of God. When the word manifested itself to an individual or a people through the scriptural text, it did not adapt to some previous experience that it came to serve and guarantee. It penetrated rather to the depths of the human reality where human reason and conscience could never reach, to produce there the unique experience of the living God within the trauma of conversion. This was the beginning of a history so new that it could henceforth be called, in the expression of St. Paul, the creation of the New Man, renewed every day. Such was the experience at the origin and foundation of the spiritual life as of theology; from it issued the principal light of Christian exegesis.

This is also the source of the "praxis" demanded by moral theology, which can never rejoice in its own light unless continually nourished by the practice of God's Word. This is the primal experience: listening to the Word of God, which leads to practice, to concrete action. Listening is intended in the fullest sense of the word, which includes obedience. Thus Christian experience comes about: in the accomplishment of a faith-filled action, which contains the source of light and of strength that shape moral reflection, in form of wisdom and prudence, of knowledge and of concrete discernment concerning the good and the better. There is no longer a chasm between experience and Scripture, as occurs in ideas and concepts, but an active compenetration in which the human person is involved in a living bond with the Spirit.

This is not to say that we have arrived, and that this experience establishes us in perfect serenity. Far from it: the intervention of the Word of God stirs up within the believer a division and conflict between flesh and spirit, between the old man and the new, between the "world" and the Church.

Moral theology, the work of the believing mind, is destined to throw light on the pilgrimage, the struggle and the history of the Christian people. To perform this function today, after the Council, Christians must—before studying behavioral sciences, before listening to contemporary philosophers, even before any theological and exegetical reading—devote themselves to hearing, meditating, praying, and practicing the word of God as it resounds in Scripture. All other roads, however attractive and promising, are dead ends and quicksand. By contrast, the way of Scripture will lead moral theology to a hidden center, a subterranean crossroads where all human roads meet, roads of science, roads of action: near God. Then will Scripture truly be restored to moral theologians, to all Christians.

PART THREE

FREEDOM AND NATURAL LAW

———

14

Freedom of Indifference: The Origin of Obligational Moral Theory

INTRODUCTION: THE NEED FOR A STUDY OF FREEDOM IN MORAL THEOLOGY; ITS DIFFICULTY; HOW IT IS KNOWN

The Presence and Mystery of Freedom

In the construction or restoration of a building the foundations need to be examined first, so as to guarantee stability and determine on an architectural plan and dimensions. One of the first foundations of moral theory is the concept of freedom, together with some idea of human nature and human powers. St. Thomas's moral theory elaborated in the *Summa* is based on his study of the human person (Ia, qq 75–76), who possesses cognitive (q 79) and appetitive powers (qq 80–83). These powers focus on the exercise of free will. It is in our free will that St. Thomas perceives the true image of God within us, for it is in our mastery over our actions that we show forth his image (Prologue, IaIIae). We may even say that our idea of God and of our relationship with him depends largely on our concept of freedom. This is not to say that we necessarily conceive God in our own image, but our ideas about God and our relationship with him are inevitably influenced by our concept of human freedom. Surely the human person is the best mirror in which to catch a glimpse of God.

Freedom is at the heart of our existence. It is at the core of our experience and is the source of our willing and acting. It is who we are, at our most personal. It would seem that there is nothing about ourselves that we are more aware of. To hear us speak of freedom, to hear us incessantly defending it, it would seem to be quite familiar to all as a birthright and inalienable possession.

And yet, when we question ourselves about the nature of human freedom, when we attempt to grasp, describe, and define it, it always escapes us. We are left clutching at traces and reflections. Freedom is always just beyond the horizon of our thoughts and actions. It is an amazing capacity for innovation and change, but also for destruction and contradiction.

Freedom is, therefore, what we know best, since it is at the heart of our most personal actions. At the same time, freedom is what we know least, for no idea can encompass it, no piling up of concepts reveal it adequately. The only possible definition, if there is one at all, would be to say that freedom always transcends the action it causes or the thought in which it is reflected.

Two Ways of Knowing Freedom

If it is vain to hope for an adequate definition of freedom, which will not fail by excess or by defect, still there are several fairly sure avenues of approach, which will lead us to recognize some of freedom's characteristics clearly enough to be able to use them in shaping moral theory.

The first and principal method is reflection on our actions and feelings, which are the direct results of our freedom. Regardless of cultural background, everyone is led, sooner or later, by experience and life's problems, to reflect on freedom and the moral realities it generates: responsibility, good and evil, virtue and duty, truth and falsehood, reward and punishment, and so forth. A candid glance at our own conduct leads us to the personal interiority where freedom resides. This search is a form of the self-knowledge recommended by Socrates as the very source of moral understanding.

There is, however, another way of discovering freedom, less immediate but very enlightening. It is provided for us by moral science and consists in the analysis of the development and structuring of moral theory from the point of view of a certain concept of freedom. As a tree bears fruit, freedom not only forms our personal actions but has produced through the centuries systems of moral theory which, in their structure, principal features, particularities, logic, and dynamics reveal freedom.

These two methods, reflection on our individual actions and on moral systems, are complementary and mutually enlightening. Books on moral theory express the author's freely formed thought, or that of a given period, together with moral experience, which is, in the end, always personal.

In studying the history of Catholic moral theology, we have observed the two broad types of organization of moral material. Moral theories based on the question of happiness and the virtues are characteristic of the patristic and great scholastic periods, while theories of obligation and commandments predominate in the modern era. In attempting to reconstruct and trace the internal logic animating these theories and ordering their elements, we are inevitably led, as to the tap root, to varying concepts of freedom. For morality of obligation, it is freedom of indifference; for moral systems based on happiness and virtue, it is what we call freedom for excellence. We note here a remarkable convergence of history and systems, indicating that a certain logic is imposed on the reflections of authors and has influenced the historical transmission of works and ideas. Thus it can be said that two different concepts of freedom have given rise to two different systematizations of moral theology.

Historically, the crucial and decisive moment came at the beginning of the fourteenth century when William of Ockham, in critiquing St. Thomas, worked out his new concept of freedom. But we would be wrong to see in this merely an isolated event, an error of far-off times, or a simple dispute between the Franciscan and Dominican schools. In his teaching on freedom and moral theory, St. Thomas was the faithful interpreter of the patristic tradition, which had nourished his thought and the Greek philosophy he exploited. Ockham, on the other hand, was the initiator of a certain concept of freedom and morality that would be adopted by many theologians and philosophers who came after him, even when they opposed or simply ignored nominalism.

The debate cannot be reduced to a confrontation between ancients and moderns, for, beyond ideas and books, the very exercise of freedom and the experience of action have maintained the coexistence of these two great currents of moral thought, one plunging underground when the other appears on the surface. Today we can still find them and recognize them in ourselves, in the depths of our consciousness and memory, if we are able to penetrate within. The present crisis in Christian ethics, with the upheavals it is causing, could actually be a favorable moment for bringing to the fore once again the doctrine of freedom for excellence, which seems to us richer and more adequate than freedom of indifference. Constant study of moralists—St. Thomas, Ockham, and the rest—can be very revealing, offering us guides and models for our research. Ultimately, however, the question of freedom confronts us with a choice here and now that will be a determining factor in the coming renewal of Christian moral theology.

In our study we shall expound the two concepts, freedom of indifference and freedom for excellence, with their characteristic features, and we shall show the logic they engender in the forming of moral systems. We shall use the data provided by our historical research, developing and refining it, with apologies for any inevitable redundancy. But our perspective will be mainly systematic or architectonic: How was freedom conceived? How did the concept influence the elaboration of moral theory? Obviously we are working from our position within the Catholic tradition, but we shall frequently be in touch with modern philosophy, which also and more than we might suspect flows from the ideological currents that developed from the medieval period onward.

We shall begin with a study of freedom of indifference, even though it came later historically, because it is the most widespread concept today. It so fills the horizon of thought and experience that an approach to freedom for excellence necessitates a process of veritable rediscovery. We shall describe freedom of indifference first, therefore, with its characteristics and limitations. This done, we will be in a better position to understand by contrast the nature of freedom for excellence.

Historically our work presents a special difficulty in that neither St. Thomas nor the Fathers of the Church were acquainted with the nominalist concept of freedom, and therefore neither addressed it with the power and precision of a critical confrontation. So it is up to us to explore their concept of freedom for ourselves. Fortunately, human experience, which persists through varying intellectual debates, can provide us with all the data we need.

Two Interpretations of the Definition of Free Will

The line of demarcation between the two concepts of freedom we are studying is determined, historically and systematically, by the interpretation of the first part of the definition of free will bequeathed to Western theology by Peter Lombard: "Free will is that faculty of reason and will whereby one chooses the good with the help of grace, or evil without this help."[1]

The first part of this definition can be given two diametrically opposed interpretations. Basing his thought on the Aristotelian analysis of choice, St. Thomas explained freedom as a faculty *proceeding from* reason and will, which unite to make the act of choice. This act of choice is thus formed by practical judgment and willing. For him, free will was not a prime or originating faculty; it presupposed intelligence and will.[2] It was rooted, therefore, in the inclinations to truth and goodness that constituted these faculties.

Ockham, on the contrary, maintained that free will *preceded* reason and will in such a way as to move them to their acts. "For I can freely choose," he said, "to know or not to know, to will or not to will." For him, free will was the prime faculty, anterior to intelligence and will as well as to their acts.

This interpretation had already been formulated in the Franciscan school. St. Bonaventure reported it as a first opinion on the distinction among free will, reason, and will: "[Free will] is the power that commands the will and reason, rules them and moves them both; its first act is not discernment and willing but a reflective action upon them both, moving and ruling them, that is, the action expressed when we say we wish to discern and we wish to will. This act precedes reason and will, and its power corresponds to the Father, for his is the most powerful of acts and it is primary, not being moved, but moving."[3]

Being primary to such a degree, freedom clearly could not be demonstrated, since any reason advanced to prove it would include elements at least as doubtful and unknown as the conclusion drawn in its favor (Ockham, *Quodl.* I, q 16). Freedom was postulated as a first fact of human experience. It was affirmed that, whatever the decision dictated by reason, the will could follow it or not (*Quodl.* I, q 16).

In view of this experience, how could freedom be described? Freedom

1. "Liberum vero arbitrarium est facultas rationis et voluntatis, qua bonum eligitur gratia assistente, vel malum eadem desistente" (In II *Sent.*, dist. 24 c. 3).

2. Cf. Ia q 83. This question, devoted to free will, is logically preceded by the study of the intellect, of reason (q 79), and of will (q 82).

3. ". . . et est virtus imperans rationi et voluntati et utramque regens et movens, cuius actus primus non est discernere et velle, sed actus reflexus; super haec duo et haec duo movens et regens, ille videlicet quo dicitur quis velle discernere vel velle se velle. Et iste actus praeambulus est ad rationem et voluntatem, et ista potentia correspondet Patri, pro eo quod actus eius maxime potens est et primus est, cum non moveatur,sed moveat" (In II *Sent.*, dist. 25, p 1, a 1, q 2).

lay entirely in the power of the will to choose between contraries, and this power resided in the will alone. It was the power to opt for the *yes* or the *no,* to choose between what reason dictated and its contrary, between willing and not willing, acting and not acting, between what the law prescribed and its contrary. Thus freedom consisted in an indetermination or a radical indifference in the will regarding contraries, in such a way that actions were produced in a wholly contingent way. As Gabriel Biel was to say, freedom was essentially the power to move in two opposite directions. It was qualified by an indifference to the opposites.

Thus understood, freedom was practically identified with the will, as the origin of willing and acting, as a power of self-determination. In this way it came to constitute, in some way, by itself alone, the very being of the person, at the source of all action. It was in this sense that Sartre could write: "My freedom is not an added quality or a property of my nature; it is the very stuff of my being."

The will issued from this interpretation transformed. It was no longer defined as an attraction toward the good, exercised in love and desire, as in St. Thomas and the Fathers. It became a radical indifference, whence proceeded a pure will, actually an imposition of will on itself or others, "a conscious pressure of self upon self," to use E. Mounier's definition. This was to become the modern understanding of will. Spiritual spontaneity was no longer first; it was overshadowed by the claims of freedom, achieved through indifference. As Nietzsche put it, "To will is to command obedience, or at the least apparent obedience."[4] Willing was no longer characterized by love but by the relationship of command (*befehlen*) and obedience (*gehorchen*).

The Break with Natural Inclinations

The most decisive point of Ockham's critique of St. Thomas's teaching on freedom was the breach between freedom and the natural inclinations, which were rejected from the essential core of freedom. According to St. Thomas, freedom was rooted in the soul's spontaneous inclinations to the true and the good. His entire moral doctrine was based on the natural human disposition toward beatitude and the perfection of good, as to an ultimate end. A person can never renounce this natural order

4. "Ein Mensch der Will befiehlt einem Etwas in sich, das gehorcht oder von dem et glaubt, dass es gehorcht." *Beyond Good and Evil,* part n. 19.

of things, nor be prevented from desiring it. For Ockham, the state of being ordered to happiness, however natural and general, was subject to the free and contingent choice of human freedom. This meant that I could freely choose or refuse happiness, either in particular matters presented to me or in general, in the very desire which attracted me to it, owing to the radical indifference of my freedom.[5] Similarly, I could choose to preserve my life or to loathe my existence. All natural inclinations, summed up in the inclination toward good or happiness, were thus subject to choice and to the will's free determination. It was as though they were uprooted from the will's depths, to be placed before it, beneath it, and subjected to its choice. They were no longer a part of the essence of freedom.

This displacement of inclinations contributed to a modification of their nature. Placed below freedom, they came to be regarded as impulses of a lower order, on the psychosomatic plane. In fact, the total concept of nature was being transformed. The harmony between humanity and nature was destroyed by a freedom that claimed to be "indifferent" to nature and defined itself as "non-nature." The consideration of the nature and spiritual spontaneity of the human person was banished from the horizons of thought. It is small wonder that the treatise on human happiness was so often struck out of the manuals of fundamental moral theology, and that this question was frequently omitted in philosophical studies.

We can note, too, the creation of a profound opposition between freedom and natural inclinations in moral systems based on the freedom of indifference, observable in modern thought. These inclinations appeared as the most insidious threat to the freedom and morality of actions, because they were interior and influenced us from within. This is doubtless the origin of the divorce between moral theory and the desire for happiness, which has been effected in our times.

The Break with the Philosophers and the Fathers

The separation effected by Ockham between freedom and natural inclinations touched all of ancient thought in depth, both philosophers and Fathers of the Church, through St. Thomas. This is very apparent when we study the disputes carried on between the great schools of antiquity, as described for example by Cicero in his *De finibus bonorum*

5. See Chapter 10, section "The Nominalist Revolution."

et malorum and his *De officiis.* We can easily discern the two principles that formed the common basis for discussions between Peripatetics, Stoics, Academicians, Epicurians and others.

There was first of all the famous principle *sequi naturam,* or conformity with nature, which must positively not be understood as a biological inclination, for it chiefly concerned rational nature, which was characterized by a longing for the enjoyment of the good, of truth, and of communication with others. All moral research had for its object the determination of what conformed to human nature: pleasure, the fulfillment of needs, various kinds of goods, virtue and so forth. The schools were distinguished by their different answers, depending on their concept of the human person, but all pronounced themselves in favor of the principle *sequi naturam.*

The second principle matched this. All moral discussion revolved around the question of "the happy life": In what did human happiness consist, and how was it to be attained? Happiness was the first desire of human nature as well as its perfection. If one followed nature, it was in order to obtain the happiness that nature itself proposed as the final end of human beings and their crowning achievement. There was no discussion on this point. All the divergencies sprang from the manner in which this universally human question was answered.

The Fathers of the Church were not content with adopting these philosophical principles. They deepened and intensified them in the light of Christian revelation. They saw in nature the direct work of God, the creator of Genesis, and the work of the Word of John's Gospel. To their minds, the following of nature harmonized with the scriptural following of God and of Christ; in this new light it became more personal. Thus we can understand St. Thomas's method, so foreign to us, his marked preference for examples taken from the physical order, even when explaining realities of the spiritual order. For him, God's action was manifested in a particularly luminous way in the movements of beings completely subject to nature, that is, to the divine rule, untroubled as they were by the intervention of an often-deficient freedom. We can therefore find in them our models for human action, providing always that we realize the role played by analogy.

As to the question of happiness, oriented to beatitude, our final end and perfection, it was always, beyond any doubt or discussion, the first moral question for the Fathers. But they found their answer in the Gospel, especially in St. Matthew's Beatitudes, which ordered our longing for happiness to the vision of God, through active faith in the word of Christ. The problematic was to be transformed. Thinking in regard to happiness became more personal and more objective. Happiness no longer consisted, for the Fathers or St. Thomas, in merely human virtue as a subjective quality, but rather in openness to the divine goodness, to the reality of God himself, through love which came to us from God, through Christ.

It was true nonetheless that the entire tradition of the Fathers adopted and fully maintained the two principles of *sequi naturam* and the primal longing for happiness. Indeed, the tradition confirmed them by founding them in God.

It was precisely these basic principles, undisputed up to his time, that Ockham wrested from the heart of freedom and ranked as inferior to the choice of contraries. In so doing, he achieved a veritable rupture in the most profound depths of the human soul, on the level of principles, at the source of action. It should not, therefore, cause surprise that this "revolution" in the depths where activity rises should result in the upheaval of all moral ideas and their systematic organization.

Rejection of Sensibility

The relation between free will and human sensibility were to be similarly transformed. In his remarkable study of the passions (or sentiments), St. Thomas held that they could be good, could acquire a positive moral value. From the viewpoint of freedom of indifference, the passions first appeared as proceeding from a lower order and reducing the scope of freedom open to contraries. They next became a threat or obstacle to freedom. Doubtless, the will might use the impulse of the passions as an aid in performing actions, but it felt them mainly as a diminution of its freedom of choice.

It even seemed that freedom could find no better way of asserting itself than to struggle against sensibility. Indeed, the combat against an excess of passions is inevitable and necessary, but the idea took hold that moral valor could establish itself in no surer, clearer way than by going counter to sensibility. This was rigorism.

Rejection of *Habitus* and Virtues

St. Thomas had worked out a remarkable analysis of *habitus* and built his moral doctrine upon the foundation of the seven great theological and moral virtues. According to him, the virtues developed the natural inclinations and brought them to perfection; they became like a second nature.

It was to be expected that, having banished natural inclinations from the heart of human freedom, nominalism would also dispense with *habitus* and virtues. The very idea of a *habitus* was opposed to freedom of indifference, for in a sense *habitus* took for granted the idea of a stable determination of actions. A *habitus* required the exercise of action in order to be formed, doubtless, but it preceded the actions issuing from it and deprived them of the complete latitude implied by the power to choose between contraries. The stronger a *habitus* grew, the more it influenced actions and the more it seemed to reduce freedom's scope. If total freedom was to be maintained, *habitus* must be removed from the level of freedom and placed below it. They would then become psychological mechanisms of a sort, created by repeated acts—or habitual procedures—which freedom could use as aids to further action. But one must always mistrust them, lest they acquire too much importance in the moral order and so diminish the free quality of actions. In this connection it is very significant that the translators of St. Thomas used *habitude* for *habitus,* without realizing the difference.[6]

Obviously, no Christian moral theory could dispense with giving the virtues their place; too many authorities treat of them. From the viewpoint of freedom of indifference, however, the concept of virtue was to be changed and reduced. For ethicists, virtue became simply a traditional, convenient category for listing moral obligations. Within the domain of freedom of indifference, there was no longer the need for virtue; in fact, the logical thing to do was to remove it. This is what the textbooks of moral theory did when they suppressed the treatise on virtues in fundamental moral theology and divided the subject matter of specialized moral theology according to the commandments rather than the virtues. There must surely have been many virtuous people at the time, but the concept of virtue was practically dead. Only the shadow remained.

The Break with Continuity and Finality; The Atomic Age of Moral Action

In banishing natural inclinations and virtues from the heart of freedom, nominalism broke the bonds that had united them with moral ac-

---

6. Cf. my book *Le Renouveau de la morale,* II, chap. 4,"La vertue est tout autre chose qu'une habitude" (Paris, 1964 and 1979), 144–64.

tion and had established them in a pattern of continuity ordered to finality. St. Thomas had considered human acts within the perspective of a final end, which would crown human happiness, and of the virtues, which would assure progress toward this end. Human acts were thus linked from within (from interior acts), to form an organic, permanent whole, where the present flowed from the past and opened onto the future.

Nominalism shattered this beautiful progression. If freedom consisted wholly in a choice between contraries, and was possessed sovereignly by our will alone, then each of our actions was held fixed in the instant of choice and separated from all the actions preceding or following it. Under pain of losing our freedom of indifference, we could not allow our past actions to determine an action of the present moment, nor could the latter have any bearing upon what we might do in the future. Freedom was thus caught and held captive in the present moment, which it created and cut off from past and future. Continuity was broken up into a succession of instants, like the perforated line made by an unthreaded sewing machine. Each moral action was forever isolated, like an island, an atom, a monad. Moral theology's atomic age was upon us.

Freedom of indifference was conceived as a given, in principle at least, from the first moment of conscious life. It could undoubtedly be limited by obstacles of all kinds, interior or exterior, or hampered in the performance of an action; but it was integral in its voluntary source and demonstrated this by its protest against all limitation. This type of freedom had no need to grow. Any increase that might be mentioned in its regard would refer to the diminution of exterior limitations that it succeeded in overcoming, not to any interior growth.

The vision of human life and moral theory was totally transformed. Free actions followed one upon another in a person's life without any bond of unity to weld them into a basic whole, as the vision of a last end or even personal sentiment might have done. The consideration of one's final end probably played its part as one weighed the morality of an action, but from this time on it was reduced to the dimensions of the one isolated action. The finality was short-term rather than long-term as St. Thomas had seen it. The end was no longer an essential part of the action; it became circumstantial, qualifying it from the outside. Personality, seen as the permanent substance underlying the flow of accidentals that it tended to unify, disappeared behind the aggregate of actions performed in isolated succession.

Let me quote a scholar who specialized in the study of Ockham. "If it is true that the essential note of personality is independence, and that the human person's basic dignity lies in the power to act at any given moment in the way he chooses, then personality is something we cannot grasp. Only the successive, varying actions of the person matter. They are like small, isolated fruits, each with its own value. . . . What we call personality is no more than the laborious reconstruction of a jigsaw puzzle. Actions continue, each with its bizarre, uncoordinated contours. We try to classify them. None of this makes for unity and orientation. Human discontinuity is one of the basic tenets of Ockham's psychology, and this psychology leads directly to a moral system in which only actions are taken into consideration."[7]

The field of moral theory had been disrupted. It no longer dealt with the study of virtues but focused on isolated actions. Henceforth each action was studied in itself, according to the particular circumstances. In the seventeenth century this would be called the study of cases of conscience, whence the name casuistry.

The Passion for Freedom

Make no mistake: the demolition—and the word is chosen with precision—of St. Thomas's moral teaching by Ockham and the nominalists was no unfortunate accident, no regrettable error stemming from weakness of intellect and of moral concepts. We can see in it the direct, clearly deduced, and fully deliberate result of placing humanity in a central position. This was the core of freedom of indifference. Its results and manifestions might be negative, but they flowed from an initial determination to affirm freedom in the face of all else. Personality might disappear behind the disparate actions it generated, but the point of this was to concentrate on itself and to escape, through the very diversity and contrariety of successive actions, the traps they might lay for freedom.

Freedom of indifference was therefore not so neutral and serene as its name might indicate. It was a far cry from the *apatheia* sought by the Stoics and adopted by the Fathers of the Church in their own manner to designate a calm mastery over the passions. Beneath freedom of indifference lay hidden a primitive passion—we dare not call it natural: the human will to self-affirmation, to the assertion of a radical difference between itself and all else that existed.

7. G. de Lagarde, *La naissance de l'esprit laïque au déclin du moyen age,* vol. 6, L'individualisme ockhamiste (Paris, 1946), 46–47.

This was the origin of the force and dynamism of this concept of freedom, regardless of how negative its results might be and how disruptive its manifestations. Freedom of indifference was first a defense of the human power to choose between contraries sheerly by its own volition. This autonomy included the rejection of all dependence whatsoever, and of any norm or law not made by itself. The power was most clearly evidenced in negation, in all its forms: refusal, criticism, contradiction, confrontation.

Such was the first characteristic manifestation of this sort of passion. It could be encapsulated in the formula, "against the positive and for the negative," or, in other words, an insistence on the freedom to take a negative stand, for this was the very heart of freedom. Freedom of indifference also expressed itself in being arbitrary for the sheer pleasure of it.

A sentence in Sartre's *Les Mots* clearly expresses this passion for freedom joined with fragmentation in time: "I become a traitor and I remain one. Useless to put my whole self into my undertakings, to give myself unreservedly to work, to anger, to friendship. The next minute I will deny myself. I know it, I wish it so, and I already betray myself passionately, anticipating my future betrayal with joy." One single passion has driven out all others: the passion for freedom, operating here through "betrayal."

Montherlant's passage in *The Young Girls* also merits quotation: "Costal's humanity did not lie in the fact that he could not feel human sentiments, but that, on the contrary, he could experience them all indifferently, at will, by pressing the appropriate button, so to speak. A limitless capriciousness rules human lives, some struggling in confrontation, others unaware of it. Costals was aware, and rather than suffer the consequences he preferred to worship it." Indifference and caprice are indeed typical notes of this kind of freedom; worship reveals the passion it can arouse.

Freedom of indifference was thus impregnated with a secret passion for self-affirmation, deeper than any of its manifestations and expressions. We might wonder, in this connection, whether Kantian rigorism, with its scrupulous demand for moral disinterestedness, might have been the result of a desperate effort to escape the fundamental self-interest that was the province of this concept of humanity and freedom.

Loyalties Reversed

As the quotation from Sartre would imply, there was a complete shift in loyalties. Loyalty, usually understood as the recognized bond between the will and a good, an ideal, a person, a way of life, an institution or a previous choice, insured the permanence of this will in a determined sense. Now its value shifted. Loyalty became a threat precisely because it was a bond, detrimental to the freedom of choice between contraries. Betrayal became the good thing, because it alone left the field open to the passion of self-affirmation.

Admittedly, things rarely came to such a pass. It would have been impossible to live one's life or to take one's place in society without retaining a minimum of continuity and loyalty. Many would retain interior faithfulness, but they would see it as repetitive, an adaptation renewed day by day, if not minute by minute, of a similar choice. This faithfulness would be only the semblance of continuity, constantly threatened from within by the temptation to affirm one's freedom by breaking away from it. At bottom, the only loyalty compatible with freedom of indifference was loyalty to oneself, expressed by refusing loyalty to everything but this very freedom. Thus loyalty became entirely subjective.

The Break between Freedom and Reason

We have reviewed successive ruptures effected by the concept of freedom of indifference: a breaking away from natural inclinations and sensibility, *habitus* and virtues, finality, continuity, and loyalty. All these ruptures meet in the final break between free will and reason.

For St. Thomas, freedom and will united to make a free choice. The coordination between the practical judgment and the voluntary decision was so intimate that they were scarcely distinguishable.

With Ockham this unity, beautiful and difficult to achieve, was necessarily and completely destroyed. If freedom consisted in the ability to choose between the *yes* and the *no*, it would have to affirm itself primarily against reason, against the "reasons" proposed for determining its choice and requiring of it a *yes*. Before the rigorous flow of reasons, freedom recoiled as if before prison bars. It escaped by way of negations, and it took refuge in the power to choose between contraries residing in pure will. Because of the ruptures mentioned above, reason no longer had a direct hold on freedom; it could not penetrate the will. No longer could it say with any effect, If you wish to be happy, to live well, then be virtuous and loyal; for all the yearnings thus designated had now been subjected to the choice of contraries. Interior bonds of interpenetration between reason and will were no longer possible. Each faculty acted independently and did its own thing. Radical tension succeeded to the former effort toward harmony. Reason began to fabricate a universal determinism which enveloped the human person and led to the negation of freedom, while the will defended itself by setting itself up as the center of the universe, even to the point of pure caprice if need be. Freedom of indifference gave birth to twin forces forever at enmity, voluntarism and rationalism, which simultaneously attracted and repelled each other. From this time onward, authors, theologians, and philosophers would be either voluntarists or rationalists, particularly in moral theology.

It is true that the power to say *no* to reason had always been recognized as a part of human freedom. In question 6 of his *De malo,* dealing with freedom, St. Thomas had even admitted, at risk of a determinism through rational motives that provoked some objections to his theory, that the human person remained free to refuse beatitude, in general as well as in particular. But for him this was a weakness of human nature, like the possibility of demeaning oneself and falling captive to sin. According to the doctrine of freedom of indifference, on the contrary, the power to say no to reason itself was essential to freedom. Herein lay its force.

We should note here several important consequences for the concept of moral theology that stem from the divorce between reason and free will. Since morality is the proper domain of freedom, its main elements would be taken over by the will and would be ordered according to their relationships of power over various desires. Law, commandments, obedience, all that determined moral action, would flow henceforth from the will alone. The rational content of precepts would have no interest for us; we would be concerned no longer with understanding them, but only with knowing that they had been promulgated by an authority empowered to do so. Reason's role would be progressively limited to declaring that a precept existed in a given instance; no longer would it extend to research and comprehension. We would begin to distrust a reason which sought the why and wherefore of laws and commands.

The Absolute Freedom of God

We are familiar with freedom of indifference as a fact and a postulate of our human existence. For the nominalist theologian, however, it was in God that it achieved its fullest realization. Only in the creator was freedom joined to omnipotence, to become absolute. Thus the very image of God and his work was changed. Reflection on him would focus henceforth on his free and sovereign will far more than on his wisdom, truth, and goodness. A foreshadowing of this can be seen in the Franciscan opinion formulated by St. Bonaventure, that freedom preceded intelligence and will and was attributed to the Father, the origin of the Trinity (*In II Sent.*, d. 24, p. 1, a 1, q 2).

We shall rediscover in the nominalist teaching on God all the characteristics of freedom of indifference. They take on a special, marked emphasis in Ockham, who had the lucidity and audacity to push the logic of his system to its extreme consequences.

God's freedom was sovereign, absolute, and identified, so to speak, with his being. For God, it was one thing to be and to be free. Nothing could limit this freedom except the principle of contradiction. Nothing, and especially not any nature. God being creator through the sheer power of his will, there could not exist in creation, or even within man, any nature or natural inclination that might impose on God or restrain or orient his action. Furthermore, one could not speak of a nature or natural qualities in God which would call for our respect, since freedom was his supreme quality.

God's freedom was expressed most particularly in relation to the moral law, and this in two ways: the moral law was the manifestation of God's will; but also, God remained perfectly free in regard to this law and its precepts.

MORAL LAW, THE EXPRESSION OF GOD'S WILL AND THE SOURCE OF OBLIGATION

St. Thomas had defined law as an *ordinatio rationis ad bonum commune*, that is, the work of the wisdom of the lawgiver, human or divine, together with an impulse of the will. It was effected with authority but was done in an ordered manner. For Ockham, all legislative work proceeded from the will, and first from the will of God, the author of law and source of moral obligation.

The rupture of the natural bonds linking man and God placed them in confrontation, like two freedoms fixed in radical isolation, "indifferent" to each other. To this division was added the chasm separating divine transcendence from the contingency of creatures drawn from nothingness and always needing to be sustained in existence. As G. de Lagarde writes: "For Ockham, there was an absolute separation between God and the world. God created the world, but remained alien to it. There was no symbiosis between the world and God. The two realities were isolated in their respective being. This was no more than the result of the radical insularity of all beings."[8]

In this situation, man had absolutely no natural way of reaching God or of knowing his will. Yet the radical dependence of the creature gave rise to the only possible bond between man and God.

Human freedom was total, granted; but the condition of creaturehood subjected it to the omnipotence of the divine will. God's sovereign power over man created the moral bond. This bond had no other source than God's will, manifested with the force of obligation. A higher will thus exerted pressure and constraint upon a lower one. The expression of God's will imposed itself upon human freedom as an obligation and a limitation. Moral teaching expressed essentially, therefore, a relationship of the will. It focused on the idea and sentiment of obligation, which was henceforth to be the fundamental assumption of moral theory. Freedom of indifference, law, and obligation became inseparable.

Let us note in passing that this introduced a profound transformation and rigidity into the understanding of the word *law* and related terms such as *commandment, precept,* and *order.* This was true regarding not only St. Thomas but also Scripture and the Fathers, where these expressions took on a sapiential connotation and were far richer in content.

This concept of law was to dominate the entire field of moral teaching. It no longer required any reference to natural inclinations, *habitus,* or virtues. On the contrary, it judged them and accorded them value if they conformed to it. Moral law had no other foundation than the pure will of God, from which it issued. From this time on, the law would mark the limits of the scope of moral theology according to its obligations and would divide the material according to the commandments it included. These would be mainly the commandments of God, the Decalogue. We shall see later how God's will and precepts might be known by us.

Since morality drew its origin from the divine will alone, human actions, considered in isolation as we have seen, would be evaluated morally only and precisely as they related to law. In themselves they could be called indifferent, like the freedom that formed them. They became

8. Ibid., 56.

moral through the intervention of the law: good if they conformed to it, bad if contrary to it. Morality thus studied actions from the outside. As the nominalists were to say, the relationship was accidental.

The relationship between freedom of indifference and law was not as peaceful as the abstract discussions of scholastics would lead us to believe. In reality, the tension between them resulted in freedom's being limited and constrained by obligations. This tension was irreducible, regardless of all attempts to lessen it. It often led to the reduction of obligations to a minimum so as not to overburden consciences; but it also happened at times that demands were pushed to the limit, insisting on formal as well as material conformity of actions to the law. They must be performed with a sole, pure motive of respect for the law, for submission to obligations, for duty. In Ockham's time there were already formulas corresponding to Kant's categorical imperative. In any case, the tension between freedom and law never disappeared, whether the law was drawn from pure reason or from revelation.

God's Freedom in Relation to Moral Law

Such was the human view of the moral law. It appeared as a divine, all-powerful absolute, standing over against human freedom. However, when considered from God's point of view, its aspect changed completely. It became extremely relative. Moral law, being dependent upon God's will, could in no way restrict his freedom. God transcended the law and the moral order he had established for man. Morality was for man's sake, not God's. He could freely modify the moral order and even command what was diametrically opposed to his precepts. On this subject, Ockham was very clear in the examples he gave, and he did not hesitate to push his conclusions to the limit. According to him, God could even command the contrary of the first commandment: that a human being should hate him. Such hatred would be good in this case, being an act of obedience to God's will.

It is clear from this that obedience to the law outweighed even love of self. Consequently, legal obedience replaced charity and became the true "form of all the virtues," to use the traditional expression. Like law, obedience became "voluntaristic."

Obviously, the same logic could be applied to the other commandments regarding love of neighbor, murder, adultery, and the rest. A generalized relativism was in place, since every precept, however explicit, was always subject to divine caprice. Moral law was like a suspension bridge over the abyss of divine freedom; it might collapse at any moment. Relativism would be the besetting temptation of every moral system based on freedom of indifference. There was only one fixed point, only one absolute: conformity to the divine will or to sheer obligation. The question would be how to determine this imperative in the concrete situation. No law was capable in itself of supplying sure and definitive direction.

In actual fact, a position such as this would be untenable. Human experience would give it the lie, as would the tradition of the Church, which a theologian would have to take into account. Ockham had too great a sense of concrete reality and too much intellectual ingenuity to stop here. He clarified his position by means of a twofold distinction. What he had affirmed about God's freedom in regard to the moral law was valid in light of "the absolute power of God" (*de potentia Dei absoluta*). But God ordinarily exercised his freedom according to his "ordered power" (*potentia Dei ordinata*). The latter, without suppressing the former, guaranteed the permanence of the divine will in conformity with the precepts of the moral law. This led to a complementary distinction between the *cursus ordinarius rerum,* or ordinary course of things, where the precepts of the law retained their validity, and the *cursus extraordinarius rerum,* the extraordinary state of affairs where, in a totally unpredictable way, the divine arbitrariness could operate. Now the bridge over the abyss was strong enough to answer to the needs of ordinary Christian conduct. Clearly, however, its radical fragility perdured.

Freedom of indifference on one side, and the law, as the expression of the divine will, on the other; between them, isolated human actions carried out under the aegis of obligation: here we have all the elements of moral theory that were to serve as the basis for moral treatises in the centuries to follow. Only the treatise on conscience is lacking; we shall examine its origin in our study of the question of knowledge of God's will. Very logically, therefore, beginning with freedom of indifference, obligational or duty-driven moral theory was formed and began to develop.

Knowledge of the Divine Will

1. Knowledge through Revelation

If all morality depends solely upon the will of God, the problem of knowing his will takes on a decisive importance. Nominalism made this particularly difficult because it denied the possibility of discovering God's will through human nature or through knowledge of God. And yet it presented two means of knowing the divine will: scriptural revelation and—surprisingly—human reason. These two sources were traditional, but the important thing to be grasped is the manner in which this communication was made, since the entire history of modern theology was to be determined largely by nominalist positions.

We shall not go into the details and nuances of Ockham's response to the question of knowing the divine will with the help of Scripture. For this, I refer the reader to G. de Lagarde's presentation,[9] which shows the occasionally contrasting aspects of his thought. Briefly, it ran as follows: "Divine law is the aggregate of stable and *universal* precepts that God has *expressly promulgated*, of rules *implicitly contained* therein, and of the consequences that *logically follow from them*.[10] Scripture alone was true and infallible and manifested God's will directly through his precepts. This revelation needed, however, to be developed through explanations and deduction. The work could be done in two ways: on the one hand, there were laws deduced by the apostles and their successors, or again, regulations and interpretations inspired by Christians endowed with the spirit of prophecy; on the other hand, there were the deductions of clear reasoning.

We shall note some characteristics that seem to follow from the logic of the nominalist system concerning the ethicist's reading of Scripture. These were to have notable consequences in the future. The ethicist's scriptural reading focused on "the divine law" and was limited to searching for those "stable and universal precepts" that might be found in Scripture. These were sources of strict obligation for all—today we would call them imperatives. Thus the ethicist could ignore whole books of Scripture not containing such precepts, in contrast to the Fathers of the Church, who found a moral sense pervading all of Scripture. The passages that were retained, moreover, were understood in a predominantly juridical sense consonant with morality of obligation. This often gave them a rigid, impoverished quality.

Special stress was laid on the literal meaning of the text, as in the promulgation of a law, for everything depended on the expression of the divine lawgiver's will. "[Divine law] presupposed an *express* manifestation. Doubtess the expression could be presented in the most diverse forms: direct revelation, oral tradition, or codified prescriptions. But

9. Ibid., 124ff. See also L. Vereecke, "Loi et Evangile selon Guillaume d'Ockham," in *Loi et Evangile* (Geneva, 1981).

10. Italics are those of G. de Lagarde.

most often, if not always, they took the form of a text. In the strict sense of the word, divine law remained a *written* law, as opposed to the kind of law that might precede any written formulation (*naturaliter notus notus*)."[11] This clinging to the literal sense of the text, and the special attention to the question of the promulgation of the law, would reappear in casuistry.

An important role was also assigned to reason, for deduction was required to make explicit the content of Scripture. The texts chosen were to be set within the context of the logical reasoning of scholasticism and would be viewed as universal and relatively abstract principles, from which a succession of conclusions could be deduced. These were then applied to concrete actions. Scripture, however, did not lend itself well to this role, for its language was of quite a different kind. It was concrete, experiential, and many-faceted, and its thought followed the logic of lived reality rather than that of deductive reasoning.

The result of these several characteristics was to distance ethicists from Scripture or, at the least, to limit their access to it and their interest. It was as if duty-driven morality, stemming from freedom of indifference, operated as a filter and screen separating ethicists from Scripture.

2. Knowledge of God's Will through Reason

We have seen the rupture between the will and reason effected by the doctrine of freedom of indifference. The mind, with its logical ability to tie reasons to reasons as one would braid the knots of an immense net, seemed to be the most direct and forceful opponent to the will. In order to safeguard the will's freedom, there seemed no other option than a violent break with the reasoning process. This was achieved by affirming as a given the power of contraries, the ability to say yes or no regardless of all reason.

One might think from the foregoing that reason and will would fly apart like a divorced couple—that the will would take over the moral field while reason ruled the sciences. But this would be too simplistic. Ockham, in spite of what we might call his voluntarism in moral theory, had already given reason a considerable role in moral judgment, precisely for the discovery of the will of God, which was the foundation of morality.

We have just seen that reason had a part to play in deducing moral laws from scriptural texts, contributing the certitude that is clear rea-

---

11. G. de Lagarde, *La naissance,* 127.

soning's gift. Yet it possessed a still more direct and fundamental role in moral theory. The will of God was manifested to human reason itself, in the form of a clear moral obligation, before it confronted the free will. All human beings have a spontaneous feeling, when we come down to it, that certain actions merit praise or blame. This is a primal experience indissociably linking freedom to the law transmitted by reason. Right reason or conscience is a privileged place, the nearest and most natural where the moral law is revealed to us. Ockham, too, saw in reason the foundation of natural law. For him, a first principle of moral theory would be the duty of acting in conformity with the dictates of reason, even should reason occasionally err. "God wills that we should always follow the dictates of reason, even if, due to some inevitable error, it leads us astray."[12] For Ockham, an action done in conformity with an erroneous conscience was in itself good and meritorious.

It is surprising to see reason recapturing so important a function in moral theory after all its skirmishes with the will. But this is more understandable when we realize that reason's role had changed profoundly. It no longer proposed reasons drawn from the nature of things, of human beings, of God, which would lead to enlightened action. It was content to deliver commands, proclaim precepts, and make known obligations that expressed the divine will. Reason's imperatives needed no support from reasoning; they were imposed just as they stood. Thus G. de Lagarde could define natural law, according to Ockham, as *"reason's categorical imperative."* It included the sum total of precepts, which obliged every rational human being with "a blinding evidence, and which formed the foundation of the moral life." And he added this paradoxical yet totally typical note: *"The chief characteristic* of this imperative is to be *irrational.* I say *irrational* advisedly, even though we are dealing with 'an imperative of reason.' For the reason that gives commands is incapable of justifying them. One must accept them as indemonstrable postulates, analagous to those we find at the threshold of any science."[13]

The change was profound. Moral reason no longer weighed the content of precepts in order to justify them and make them understood. It limited itself to making the existence of the obligatory precept known, and it crowned its work by showing that the precept ought to be observed for its own sake, out of pure obedience to the obligation: as a categorical imperative. The very ideas and formulas of Ockham presaged those of Kant. We are dealing with a "rationalism," at the foun-

12. Ibid., 66.
13. Ibid., 143–44.

dation of moral law, that is perfectly compatible with voluntarism joined to freedom of indifference.

But if reason sufficed to establish all the imperatives that constituted natural or moral law, as Ockham thought, some surprising consequences would follow. We began with a concept, called "heteronomous" by contemporary ethicists, in which God's will, apart from man, was the sole source of law and obligation. If this will expressed itself clearly enough to moral reason, which was natural and common to everyone, it would be valid even for those who did not know God or who denied his existence. We could conclude from this that it would have retained its value even if God had not existed. "After having appeared to sum up all morality in the arbitrary will of God, [Ockham] urged us to believe that, even if God had not existed, the category of morality would have obligated the human person, who always experienced interiorly the coexistence of the two elements that made up morality: reason, asserting categorical imperatives, and a will free to submit or rebel."[14]

The separation between humanity and God created by freedom of indifference had repercussions in moral theory. The latter could be worked out independently of God, and all the more easily in that the moral domain had no relevance for God, according to Ockham. Reason of itself could suffice to pronounce the imperatives that shaped morality. These views were to reappear later in philosophy as well as theology. It is not difficult to recognize the elements that go to make up various modern theories of autonomy and secular ethics.

This manner of thinking prepared the way for humanity's grasp on the power that theology had formerly attributed to God by affirming that his will alone was the foundation of morality. Soon, in the name of reason, human will would be substituted for God's as the source of law: the will of the individual and of conscience, the will of society, of authority, of the state, or of the people.

A SIGNIFICANT TENSION RESULTING FROM FREEDOM OF INDIFFERENCE

The theory of freedom of indifference, which was at the heart of nominalism, together with nominalism itself, influenced all Western thought. It was found almost everywhere, even among those who scarcely knew

14. Ibid., 66.

its name. It did not remain at the level of ideas and doctrines; it penetrated life and its deepest experiences.

One of the surest signs of the active presence of freedom of indifference was the tension it engendered, tension that posed problems of a disjunctive sort, expressed by the "either . . . or" formula. A few samplings of this characteristic disconnectedness follow.

—Either freedom or law. This opposition dominated casuistry and found expression in the comparison of freedom and law to two landowners disputing the field of human actions. Ethicists would say, this action pertains to law, that to freedom.

—Either freedom or reason. Reason opposed law just as the determinism it engendered opposed voluntary choice, or again, as the law it proclaimed opposed freedom of action and limited it.

—Either freedom or nature. Freedom was defined as opposed to nature. It was non-nature. It sought to dominate and exploit nature, understood as subrational or irrational, blind and enslaved to its impulses.

—Either freedom or grace. In theology, freedom and grace were opposed in the manner of the two landowners disputing over human actions. What was ascribed to grace seemed by that very fact taken away from freedom; what was attributed to freedom as merit seemed to diminish grace.

—Either man was free, or God. This opposition led to and culminated in the relationship between God and humanity. From now on, a choice had to be made: one could not exalt man without slighting God, nor exalt God without diminishing man. As E. Borne writes, "Contemporary atheism seeks a total affirmation of man by negating God. . . . Whence the presupposition that belief in God dehumanizes man."[15]

—Either subject or object. These basic terms came to signify on the one hand the person, changeable in will and feelings to the point of caprice, and on the other hand the external world, an apersonal reality with its firm, hard, opaque quality. The worst failure in regard to the person was to treat him as a thing; the greatest danger in science was subjectivity. Subjectivism ended in solipsism; objectivism became materialism.

—Either freedom or sensibility. Freedom became indifferent in order to fulfill itself, and it stiffened against sensibility; or else it identified with the passions and claimed total freedom for them.

—Either my freedom or the freedom of others. The freedom of others appeared as a limitation and a threat, since my idea of freedom was self-

15. E. Borne, "God Is Not Dead," in *Foi vivante* (Paris, 1974), 36.

affirmation in the face of all others. From this issued a struggle with everyone; this was at the root of the dialectic between master and slave.

—Either the individual or society. Freedom of indifference created individualism. It severed the bonds between individuals in the same way in which it had isolated human acts from each other. Society was no longer anything more than an artificial creation and a constraint. Henceforth the individual and society would be opposed and would engage in a struggle for power, in a dialectic of domination. The two poles were individual freedom to the point of anarchy and state control to the point of despotism.

It is clear that the influence of freedom of indifference was very far-reaching. It affected all areas of human action and all the problematics to be encountered in moral theory. It even reshaped the questions; they became disjunctive, where in the case of freedom for excellence they would be synthesized, as we shall see. Wherever it appeared, freedom of indifference seemed to be a force for division and separation, for an opposition engendering an interminable dialectical struggle.

FREEDOM OF INDIFFERENCE AFTER OCKHAM

A lengthy study would be needed to describe the influence and development of freedom of indifference in the modern era, in philosophy as well as theology. I shall merely mention a few instances of it.

Descartes was very familiar with this concept of freedom. In spite of his prudence in speaking of it, it could well have been his preference. In his *Principia philosophiae* he wrote: "We are aware of freedom of indifference within us to such a point that nothing is more obvious or more perfect."[16]

The idea reappears with others in philosophical dictionaries. In Lalande: "[in contrast with determinism] . . . the power to act with no other cause than the power itself, that is, without any reason bearing on the content of the action. . . . The indeterminacy of the will relative to its object under this particular form is generally called *freedom of indifference*."

The dictionary of Foulquié and Saint-Jean proposes under "free will": "Distinguished today from freedom (the power of self-determination

16. "Libertatis autem et indifferentiae, quae in nobis est, nos ita conscios esse, ut nihil sit quod evidentius et perfectius comprehendamus."

through motivation) and close to freedom of indifference (the ability to take decisions independently of motives), in so far as it is viewed as the power to choose between contraries." A quotation from Henri Bergson is added: "Free will, in the ordinary sense of the term, implies that contraries may be equally open to being chosen."

In scholastic theology, the reaction against nominalism was especially strong in the Thomistic school, among commentators on St. Thomas. The outstanding feature of moral theory that was opposed to it was the teaching on natural law, written in every human heart and attainable by reason. Through this, knowledge of the Creator's will was made clear and available to all. Moral obligations could be firmly based on natural law, free from the uncertainties inherent in the notion of divine caprice. It was thought that the nominalist tide, together with the profound relativism it engendered, could be checked in this way.

Yet we can question whether this foundation rested on solid enough ground. Even among Thomists, freedom of indifference was accepted, though it had caused the relativism against which they were fighting. As we have seen, freedom of indifference was at the root of nominalism and the logic behind it. The surest sign of the adoption of freedom of indifference—beyond definitions and discussions—was concentration on the morality of obligation, which was admitted even by ethicists who, following St. Thomas, continued to use the order of the virtues rather than that of the commandments.

Here again, a patient historical study is needed in order to show the evolution of ideas abut freedom in the scholastic tradition. We shall call upon only one witness, Billuart, who has played the role of classical author for the manuals of the last two centuries and is a good interpreter of the tradition he represents.[17]

Billuart enumerated five definitions or five types of freedom. The first three he took from the Fathers of the Church: freedom from suffering, from sin, and from law. These applied principally to God, who had no superior and was himself the law and rule. (Already we hear the echo of nominalism.) Then came the two basic definitions that were at the heart of the lengthy discussion carried on against Jansenism:

—The first kind of freedom was freedom from violence and coercion (*a violentia seu coactione*). It was called the freedom of spontaneity. It was freedom from external force, and also from interior inclinations that could be compelling. This was the freedom with which the blessed loved

17. *Cursus theologiae. Tractatus de actibus humanis.* Dissertatio II (Paris, 1895), vol. 4.

God in heaven, and loved happiness in this life, and with which God loved himself and produced the Holy Spirit. This freedom could be extended to animals and even inanimate objects; we speak of the spontaneity of a bubbling spring or a rock's free fall.

—The second kind of freedom was freedom from all necessity, including every natural instinct and all determination to any "one thing," which would cancel the power to choose between contraries. It was freedom to will and not to will, to will this or that. It was called the freedom of indifference because it was applied to contraries (*est ad opposita*).[18] This was the definition of freedom chosen by Billuart. For him, to ask if man enjoyed free will was equivalent to asking if he possessed freedom of indifference. It was therefore on freedom of indifference that Billuart depended in his attack on the roots of Jansenism (which was, for its part, based on a freedom of spontaneity).

Apparently it did not occur to Billuart to wonder how St. Thomas could place the natural inclination to the good and to happiness at the very source of human freedom, as the inclination that wins us our final end and engenders all our choices. For St. Thomas, there was no opposition between nature—here read *spiritual*—and human freedom, but rather a profound harmony, like the harmony between the spring and the brook it feeds. But with St. Thomas, we envision a totally different concept of freedom. We are in another world.

18. "Quinta libertas est a necessitate; et est immunitas non solum a coactione seu violentia, sed etiam a naturali instinctu et determinatione ad unum sine potentia ad oppositum: qua libertate gaudet qui potest velle vel non velle, hoc vel illud velle. Dicitur libertas indifferentiae, quia est ad opposita."

15

Freedom for Excellence

We are so accustomed to thinking of freedom as the power to choose between contraries that we can hardly imagine any other concept of it. We need, therefore, to embark on a real rediscovery of freedom if we wish to shake off the notion of freedom of indifference.

In this research we shall begin with the concrete experience of certain external activities in which our freedom is at work and can be observed. These examples will help us to discern how our freedom operates in more the interior actions of the moral order. As we combine various characteristic features of this freedom in a harmonious whole, a freedom will emerge that is utterly different from freedom of indifference. Finally, we shall verify the affinity of this new freedom with the teaching of St. Thomas.

I. EXAMPLES

We shall begin with two examples from the realm of art as understood by the ancients: the study of music and of a foreign language. Such activities engage a person sufficiently to provide a number of analogies with moral action, and will serve as an introduction to our study of human freedom.

We all know how music is taught to a child—piano, for instance. In the first place, the child must have certain predispositions. Without some attraction to music and an ear for it, lessons are a waste of time.

But if the child is gifted, it is well worth the effort to find a music teacher who will explain the rules of the art and develop the talent by dint of regular exercises. In the beginning the child, despite a desire to learn, will often feel that the lessons and exercises as a constraint imposed on freedom and the attractions of the moment. There are times when practice has to be insisted upon. But with effort and perseverance, the gifted child will soon make notable progress and will come to play with accuracy and good rhythm, and with a certain ease—even the more difficult pieces. Taste and talent are developing. Soon the child is no longer satisfied with the assigned exercises but will delight in improvising. In this way, playing becomes more personal. The child who is truly gifted and able to keep up these musical studies may become an artist, capable of executing with mastery whatever may be suggested, playing with precision and originality, delighting all who hear. Further, this artist will compose new works, whose quality will manifest the full flowering of talent and musical personality.

In this very simple example, we can clearly see a new kind of freedom. Of course anyone is free to bang out notes haphazardly on the piano, as the fancy strikes him. But this is a rudimentary, savage sort of freedom. It cloaks an incapacity to play even the simplest pieces accurately and well. On the other hand, the person who really possesses the art of playing the piano has acquired a new freedom. He can play whatever he chooses, and also compose new pieces. His musical freedom could be described as the gradually acquired ability to execute works of his choice with perfection. It is based on natural dispositions and a talent developed and stabilized by means of regular, progressive exercises, or properly speaking, a *habitus*.

Let us look now at the study of a foreign language. Undoubtedly the best method is to begin by taking courses in grammar and vocabulary, and then to add a visit to a country or an area where only the new language is spoken. Here again, a minimum of predisposition is needed in the beginning, and then perseverance in our efforts to follow the rules that are the very constraints of a language. Little by little, we will succeed in expressing ourselves correctly and in understanding better what we hear and read. Soon we will feel at ease; we will enjoy speaking the language. In the end we will be able to understand and say whatever we wish, with facility and precision.

Once again, we have seen a new kind of freedom, very different from the choice between contraries; we are free to choose whatever words we wish to form our sentences. It is a freedom subject to the constraint of grammatical rules, of course, but it is far more real and is supported by the rules as it develops. It is not to be confused with the freedom to make mistakes, which is implied by the choice of contraries, but lies rather in the ability to avoid them, without conscious effort. This we call freedom for excellence, for it enables us to understand and speak with perfection.

The Example of Courage

Now we are ready to take an example in the moral order such as the forming of a virtue like courage.

Whatever our temperament, we all have a certain understanding of courage, and we esteem it. In a child, however, courage is more imaginary than real. The child spontaneously identifies with persons who appeal to his imagination—great men, fictional heroes; they must never be cowards, even in the direst situations. He himself however is easily frightened by a trifle, shrinks before a shadow, and is afraid to go to bed in the dark.

The development of courage is progressive. It is acquired far more through small victories of self-conquest, repeated day after day, than through dreams of great actions. It grows with the dogged effort to study, to finish a task, render a service, or overcome laziness or some other fault. There will also be battles to fight, trials to encounter, small and great sufferings to endure, reaching their pitch in the illness and death of loved ones.

There is no course in courage, like courses in music or the other arts. Its best school is the family, where we learn from our parents' example, wise discipline, and the encouragement we receive to make personal efforts and persevere in them. Courage, like any virtue, calls for educators rather than professors.

Courage, which the Romans considered as the highest of virtues, is a characteristic of the morally mature person. It is indispensable for complete moral freedom. Gradually formed in us through life's discipline, first given, then personally appropriated, courage enables us to undertake worthwhile projects of high value to ourselves and others, regardless of all interior and exterior resistance, obstacles, and opposition. We act when and how we wish, to the point of exploiting the very setbacks that might have weakened our resolve and checked our plans. The person of little courage can indeed boast that he is free to do what he wants, and can affirm himself along with the crowd in rebelling against rules and laws. In reality, despite all his talk, his freedom is very weak and he is near to being a slave, for he does not know how to form a firm, lasting determination strong enough to rescue him from the pressure of circumstances or feelings so as to master them as he ought.

Courage presupposes a mature personality, formed by difficulties and trials and capable of initiating and achieving the worthwhile actions that are life's fruits. Once again we are looking at a courageous freedom with qualities far different from those of freedom of indifference.

We could choose many more examples from the other virtues: temperance (the patiently acquired mastery over the body), justice (the consistent desire to give all persons their due), generosity (which gives of itself to the limit), or prudent discernment (the fruit of much experience). All these examples would combine to demonstrate the internal harmony of the virtues. True courage is worth little without wise discernment as to what should be done, and without self-control, justice, and generosity.

The examples we have considered suffice to show us the main characteristics of freedom for excellence and to describe it in general. We shall now examine the origin ŏf this freedom more closely, before tracing its development.

II. THE ROOT OF FREEDOM

We have seen that freedom of indifference opposed natural inclinations in order to dominate them. Here, on the contrary, we find a freedom that presupposes natural inclinations and takes root in them so as to draw forth the strength needed for their development.

Initially, moral freedom is given to us through a specific spontaneity issuing from our spiritual nature as human persons, and is comparable to the dispositions required for engaging in the arts or other professions. There is this difference however: every person possesses basic moral inclinations and a primal moral sense that no corruption due to sin can completely destroy, whereas artistic gifts are bestowed on us individually in varying degrees. Some, for example, see in music nothing but "expensive noise."

The natural root of freedom develops in us principally through a sense of the true and the good, of uprightness and love, and through a desire for knowledge and happiness. Or again, by what the ancients called *semina virtutum,* the seeds of virtue, which give rise to these natural dispositions—the sense of justice, of courage, truth, friendship, and generosity—which cause us to give spontaneous praise to acts so conformed and to condemn their absence, at least in a general way. Such dispositions project a certain ideal of life, which gives direction to our desires and forms and influences our moral judgments.

Far from lessening our freedom, such dispositions are its foundation. We are free, not in spite of them, but because of them. The more we develop them, the more we grow in freedom. In this we discover the true, specifically moral meaning of the famous principle of ancient philosophy, *sequi naturam,* "follow nature," so frankly adopted and christianized by the Fathers of the Church. This "nature" does not restrain human freedom; it is essentially liberating. It produces a spontaneity in the spiritual order that is very different, in its relationship to freedom, from the spontaneity of the senses or external nature. This is why St. Thomas could speak of an *instinctus rationis* or rational instinct, in reference to our natural moral sense linked to reason, and could with marked predilection use the expression *instinctus Spiritus Sancti* to describe the action of the Holy Spirit through his gifts at the heart of the Christian life (IaIIae, q 68). There is obviously nothing blind about such an instinct, nor is it opposed to freedom. It exists at the very source of the light and spontaneity that make for freedom.[1]

1. To illustrate this concept of freedom and show that it is indeed that of the Fathers as well as St. Thomas, here are two quotations from St. Maximus the Confessor, which express very clearly human freedom's rootedness in the spiritual nature of man. The perfection of our free will consists in its conformity to our nature, created by God, and finds its fulfillment in our participation in the divine nature through grace and the Spirit. The quotations are taken from a commentary on the Our Father and in particular on the petition for the forgiveness of our trespasses.

"[God] has clearly shown that when our free will is united to the principle (logos) of nature, our free choices will not be in disagreement with God, since there is absolutely nothing unreasonable in the principle of nature—which is also natural and divine law—when the movement of free choice conforms with the principle of nature. And if there is nothing unreasonable in the principle of nature, our free will, moved according to the principle of nature, is very likely to produce actions wholly in accord with God. This will be due to an efficacious disposition, produced by the grace of the One who is good by nature, to produce virtuous acts" (A. Riou, *Le Monde et l'Eglise selon Maxime le Confesseur* [Paris, 1973], 235, PG vol. 90, col. 901 D).

"In consistently downplaying nature in favor of the passions, [man] has ignored the principle of nature out of his ardor for the latter. In the movement of this principle, we need to know the law of nature and that of the passions (whose tyranny prevails through a choice made by free will and not by nature). Nature's law must also be preserved by actions in conformity with nature, and throw off the rule of the passions which is so far from freedom. Through reason we must safeguard nature, which is pure and innocent in itself, without hatred and dissension; we must unite free will with nature and do only what is indicated by the principle of nature, rejecting all hatred and dissension towards the One in whose image we are made. . . .

"[Christ] gives us as our weapons the law of the commandments. According to this law

Thus founded on a natural sense of goodness and truth, freedom is no longer characterized by indifference, but rather by the spontaneous attraction and interest experienced in regard to all that is true and good, or at least to whatever seems so to us. The morality issuing from this freedom is a morality of attraction, not obligation.

As with the arts and professions, however, experience quickly reveals a considerable distance between our fine plans and our capacities, our intentions and their realization. At the beginning of the moral life we are like children, full of desires and plans, but weak-willed and quick to seek refuge in the imaginary. In this painful struggle between the ideal and the real, we discover how far our freedom is enslaved by our weaknesses and faults, how inappreciable still in the face of life and its demands.

Experience thus shows us our need for an education at the moral level comparable to an apprenticeship in the world of art. We need to learn what it is to be human, through education in freedom. While freedom of indifference is presented whole and entire at the outset of the moral life, at least in principle (for it has no degrees; it exists or does not exist at each instant), freedom for excellence requires the slow, patient work of moral education in order to develop. We shall now outline the principal stages of its growth.

III. DISCIPLINE

There are three basic stages of education in freedom, comparable to the three stages of human life. Childhood corresponds to what we shall call the stage of discipline, adolescence to the stage of progress, and adulthood to the stage of maturity or the perfection of freedom.

Learning an art begins with the study and practice of its rules, under the guidance of a teacher. Similarly, learning freedom requires exercise in the principal rules of moral life, with the help of appropriate teachers,

---

we must overcome our passions; thus nature is bound to the law through charity. It arouses in us an insatiatiable desire for itself, for it is the bread of life, of wisdom, knowledge, justice. Through the accomplishment of the Father's will it makes us like to the angels in their adoration, we who imitate and show forth heavenly joy in our way of life. And it leads us on high to supreme realities, to the Father of lights. It causes us to communicate in the divine nature through the participation in the grace of the Spirit, by which we are called children of God. We are wholly clothed, without spot or stain, in the One who himself gives us this grace and who is by nature the Son of God . . ." (ibid., 237, PG vol. 90, col. 905).

beginning with one's parents. Moral education begins with the acceptance of what may be called the discipline of life, based on rules, which are the moral laws.

We should at once clarify the nature of this discipline, for the word has a harsh connotation in our day, due to the intervention of freedom of indifference. In its original sense, discipline refers to the relationship of a disciple to the teacher who is to impart the principles and rules of some art or science, and particularly that art of living that is morality or wisdom. Discipline involves the communication of knowledge and the formation of mind and will, within the context of a growing harmony between disciple and teacher according to the criterion of excellence. Discipline does not seek a union of wills controlled by a binding authority. The wide difference between the two concepts can be seen in the fact that true discipline appeals to natural dispositions, to a spontaneous sense of truth and goodness, and to the conscience of the child or disciple. It ministers to growth through the rules that correspond to all these in depth. In the case of freedom of indifference, on the contrary, discipline with its laws always appears as the work of an alien will, restrictive if not hostile. The theory of freedom of indifference robs discipline and education of the profound, intimate rootedness they require. Education becomes a battle; it can no longer be service or collaboration.

Nevertheless, as a child deplores the lengthy exercises needed in order to acquire skill at the piano, so moral discipline is often resented in this first stage of education. It is viewed as a painful limitation to one's freedom to act as one pleases, becauses it presents prohibitions, the negative side of law—the side first experienced. After an initial period of easy docility, a kind of dialectical debate ensues between child and teacher, disciple and master, personal freedom and the law.

This is a crucial moment in the work of education. The goal of education is to lead the child to understand (and the educator must first understand this himself) that discipline, law, and rules are not meant to destroy his freedom, still less to crush or enslave him. Their purpose is rather to develop his ability to perform actions of real excellence by removing dangerous excesses, which can proliferate in the human person like weeds stifling good grain, and by guarding him against unhealthy errors that could turn him aside and jeopardize his interior freedom. Ultimately, the achievement of harmony between freedom and law must be the work of the individual himself. He needs to reestablish certain defense zones within his own conscience, where the opposition between freedom and certain laws and precepts is resolved. No one can do this essential work for him, this intimate clarification, which achieves harmony between freedom and law in view of progress toward really worth-while action.[2]

Still, the educator's view of his task is of tremendous importance. It will itself be determined by a dialectical debate between a too-liberal concept (currently called nondirective), which stresses individual freedom exclusively, and an authoritarian concept, which would mold freedom like soft clay. Father Laberthonnière has described this debate very clearly in connection with Catholic education. What he wrote sixty years ago is still relevant, and has to do with the formation of the freedom for excellence we are discussing, "the freedom that does not give into self, but conquers self. . . . One becomes free only by becoming better."

The Catholic educator would betray his title and mission if he were to lose sight of contemporary conditions and follow a "laissez faire" policy under any pretext whatsoever, exerting no influence in the lives of the students entrusted to him. But he would be equally false to his title and mission if, losing sight of the sublime ideal of Christian salvation, he were to form spineless robots who could think and act only upon orders from others. There are better things for him to do than simply pay respect to freedom of conscience; better things than to dominate individuals, forcefully or cleverly imposing ideas and beliefs upon them. His task is infinitely more delicate, more noble. He must work to form free consciences, so that the ideas and beliefs he inspires may develop within them like living fruits, becoming a part of their own being.[3]

This illustrates the moral law's pedagogical role. It first appears as something external, proposed to us by teachers and presented as the expression of a higher, divine will. We experience its external quality especially through its demands and constraints. Yet if we have ears to

2. Nietzsche himself testified to this general experience: the need for rules and restraint in order to develop creative freedom in the arts and in moral life. "The essential thing in all moral theory, a thing of inestimable value, is on-going, continual restraint. To understand Stoicism, or Port Royal, or Puritanism, we need to remember that it has always been through restraint that any language reached the height of its power and freedom, metrical restraint tyrannising over rhyme and rhythm. What pains have been taken by poets and orators of all nations, and also some prose writers of our day, to meet the inexorable demands of the human ear! This is all done 'out of pure folly' according to utilitarian rustics who think they are clever; 'out of servility to arbitrary laws', say anarchists who flatter themselves that they are 'free' and even 'free thinkers'. But strange as it may seem, everything that exists or ever did exist in this world, of freedom, finesse, audacity, dance or statesmanship, everything in the realm of art and morality, of thought, government, eloquence or persuasion, in the arts or in moral life, could never have flourished without the tyranny of these 'arbitrary laws'. And I say this in all seriousness: as far as I can see it is restraint that is 'nature', is 'natural'—not 'freedom to do your own thing'" (*Beyond Good and Evil* [Chicago, 1955], 93).

3. L. Laberthonnnière, *Théorie de l'éducation*, 9th ed. (Paris, 1935), 64–65.

hear, this law resonates within us, revealing a hidden, vigorous harmony with our intimate sense of truth and goodness at the root of our freedom. Thus the law leads us to the discovery of a deeper freedom beyond the external, superficial kind we enjoy. It opens us to an interior voice, which enlightens and attracts us as no other can. The education that began externally has thus finished by exerting an interior influence that alone can unite moral law and freedom, so as to give the latter a running start.

The Decalogue

Moral law is expressed mainly in the Decalogue, which applies particularly to this first stage of moral life. It formulates basic commands and prohibitions; without respect for these, no worthwhile moral life or true freedom is possible. It is appropriate, however, to stress the two commandments of love of God and neighbor from the very beginning; this has not always been done. They are the living seed of the moral law and give inspiration and positive meaning to the other commandments. The child needs to experience God's love and the love of his teachers, even though they may be strict and demanding, if his formation is to be successful and fruitful.

Moral theories of obligation during recent centuries take their value from the teaching of the Decalogue, which they have chosen as their essential foundation. They are therefore particularly appropriate for this first stage of apprenticeship to basic moral rules. However, we can regret their having terminated moral formation with this stage, considering later stages as irrelevant to the generality of students, as if the search for further perfection would be of interest to very few. I believe the reason for this position is to be found in freedom of indifference, which blocks the rapport between law and freedom in an opposition that works to the detriment of freedom's development. We are no longer dealing with a freedom that grows like a living organism, but with an assertive freedom, capable of a yes or no at each instant.

"Beginners" in the Order of Charity

This first stage in moral education corresponds, in St. Thomas, to the first degree in the formation of charity (IIaIIae, q 24 a 9). This is the stage of *incipientes,* beginners, whose main concern is to avoid sins and to fight inclinations opposed to charity. The negative precepts of the Decalogue are especially appropriate during this early stage of the moral life, when the seed of love of God and neighbor implanted in our hearts needs protection for future growth. Clearly, when charity is beginning to be formed, the prohibitions of the moral law can sometimes appear a hindrance to freedom and the spontaneity of love. Yet they are necessary if our sentiments are to acquire uprightness and truthfulness, so as to harmonize with a deep, spiritual spontaneity.

This first stage may also be related to the categories used by the mystics to describe progress in the spiritual life under the impulse of the Spirit. The stage of discipline corresponds to the purgative way, in which the soul undergoes the purifications needed in order that God may act in it and reveal himself to it.

IV. THE SECOND STAGE OF MORAL EDUCATION: PERSONAL PROGRESS AND THE DEVELOPMENT OF VIRTUE

The second stage in the formation of freedom and the moral personality is comparable to young adulthood, at the end of the crisis of adolescence. It is characterized by taking one's own moral life in hand, by a predominance of initiative and personal effort, by the development of an appreciation and taste for moral quality, and the deepening of an active interiority. It is the stage of progress when virtues are formed, together with a consistent personal intention to act in accord with excellence. Little by little, sensible pleasure is put aside, together with the desire for reward and the fear of punishment. These things formerly served as supporting motives in the first stage; now they yield to love of virtue for its own sake, and to love of others for themselves, which is friendship.

Thus a person learns to carry out a task with care, to practice justice, act honestly, seek the truth, and love sincerely, even though such actions may require sacrifice or may be unnoticed by others. It is an apprenticeship in work well done, in daily courage, patience, and perseverance and, in the end, the discovery of a joy very different from pleasure, because it is the result of our actions and character rather than of external events.

To understand what happens in this second stage of moral formation, we need to rediscover, through experience and ideas, the essence of true virtue, for freedom of indifference has completely emptied this notion of content and force.

Virtue is not a habitual way of acting, formed by the repetition of material acts and engendering in us a psychological mechanism. It is a personal capacity for action, the fruit of a series of fine actions, a power for progress and perfection. In the tradition of Aristotle, it is termed a *habitus*. Unfortunately the term *habitus* is not found in modern languages, though it designates a specifically human disposition for action.

At the same time, virtue is contained within a timespan and within the action performed, in a certain sense. Within the timespan, virtue develops the person and his actions; it transforms the passing moment. While freedom of indifference holds us fixed within the instant, moral progress requires our perseverance in the active intention that orients our life toward a goal, a higher reality that gives it its full value. No progress can be made without the ongoing, patient, and courageous effort that directs all our successive actions in one direction, the goal we long for and love supremely through all inevitable obstacles and fluctuations.

Freedom for excellence, like our personality itself, needs permanence if it is to grow, flower, and lead us to the adult stage where it will produce the noblest actions. At the heart of continuity and in its perfection, through the power of virtue, a man achieves works bearing the stamp of his unique quality as a moral person.

With virtue we rediscover true fidelity. Fidelity is not limited to defending and maintaining ideas, observances, institutions, and ancient and revered ways of judging and living, which form tradition. This is only virtue's husk, which could stifle it if hardened. The chief object of real fidelity is that seed of the spiritual life, true and good, which has taken root and appears in a doctrine and institutions, but whose soul is vivified by virtues. We may call it a conserving fidelity, if you will. But as applied to a life principle it is in reality vivifying and dynamic, like the continuity and progress we spoke of above. Fidelity is necessary for virtue's growth, and shares its power of renewal. In sum, it is freedom's fidelity to itself, to its qualitative source, the natural sense of truth and goodness.

Fidelity is primarily spiritual, but it cannot exist without material fidelities. Since we are body and soul we need both, as a support and as concrete material for the exercise of various virtues and progress in them. Moral fidelity will therefore incorporate the more material fidelities and integrate them. At the same time, it will give them that suppleness of movement and adaptation to reality which our soul imparts to our bodily organs.

"Progressives" in the Order of Charity and the Sermon on the Mount

The second stage of moral education, characterized by progress in virtue, is called by St. Thomas the degree of "progressives." Their chief concern is to grow and advance in the exercise of various virtues and especially in the practice of charity.

The Sermon on the Mount is a text admirably suited to this stage. Several aspects of the Lord's Sermon harmonize with our analysis. The Sermon criticizes the legalism of the Pharisees, linked as it is to the negative precepts of the Decalogue. It insists on our moving to a higher kind of justice, on our progress in the qualities of the heart, or virtues, which culminate in active charity. The change is a qualitative one. We move from a limited moral theory to one of progress, based on a generosity that always exceeds the demand with the spontaneity of true love.

In the interpretation of the Fathers of the Church, the Sermon's precepts go beyond external actions to penetrate to the level of the "heart," in the evangelical sense of the word; there where our sentiments and actions are rooted, and where we discover, too, in secret, the qualities that make for justice in God's eyes and that are wrought in us by him.

For St. Thomas, the Sermon is also the text of the New Law, which he calls a law of freedom, among other reasons because it has the unique capacity for opening up to us a vast field of freedom. This is indicated by the counsels, and is offered to our initiative through the inspiration of charity.

Thus the Sermon on the Mount is particularly appropriate for this second stage of moral freedom's progress, as was the Decalogue for the first. Between the one law and the other, there is at once an essential continuity and a profound difference, as between the imperfect and the perfect, or the seed that sends forth its first shoots, tender and needing protection, and the plant that grows tall and strong.

The second stage may be said to correspond with the illuminative way of the mystics. This refers to the soul's ongoing journey in the contemplative life and the practice of virtues through the Holy Spirit's enlightenment and attraction. Faith is seen as the light bearer, illuminating God, oneself, Christ, the world, Scripture, the Church. It infuses wisdom and strength into the soul; these direct the mind's attention and the heart's impulse ever more powerfully to God, the source of Truth and Beauty. At the same time, our attraction to our neighbors is deepened by an effective, pure love.

V. THE THIRD STAGE OF MORAL EDUCATION: MATURITY OF AGE AND FREEDOM

The third stage of moral education brings freedom to maturity. It is the age of adulthood at the moral and spiritual levels.

We can characterize this stage by two features: mastery of excellent actions and creative fruitfulness. Due to the gradual development of his faculties, the human person is now capable of viewing his life in its entirety. He performs his actions personally according to a plan, a higher goal which will profit himself and others. This leads him, through patient acceptance of all trials and obstacles, to the fulfillment of a life project which gives meaning, value and fruitfulness to existence. The perfection of moral freedom is shown by the response to a vocation, by devotion to a great cause, however humble it may appear to be, or the accomplishment of important tasks in the service of one's community, family, city, or Church.

This is the freedom St. Thomas speaks of at the beginning of the *prima secundae,* where he sees in man's mastery over his actions an imaging of God. This self-mastery presupposes moral education and the gradual formation of virtues within us. They are like a sheaf of interior energies bound together by our persevering efforts to follow our vocation and grace. Self-mastery draws together our faculties, ideas, desires, and feelings, directing them all to the higher end we are pursuing. In this way, our personality is integrated and acquires autonomy in regard to external events. We use these to further our plans, drawing profit even from the opposition and trials they occasion. A profound interiority is developing within us. It does not isolate us, but becomes the needed pivot for our ongoing, fruitful exchange with the outer world. Thus our actions can slowly take shape and ripen into life's true fruits, the authentic outgrowth of our freedom.

We need to stress here the paradoxical character of this moral mastery which leads to the development of moral freedom. It unites two dimensions which are ordinarily opposed: the profoundly personal character of excellent action and its vast openness to others.

A symbol of this is a fruiting tree. The Gospel tells us that we know a tree by its fruit. The fruit is so much a part of the tree that it reveals both species and quality. At the same time, the tree offers each of its ripe fruits freely, flushed with color, delicious to the taste. They have been formed by the long exchanges between roots and nourishing earth, leaves, air and sun, through the drift of the seasons. In the same way, our free actions are all the more personal as they result from a greater moral self-mastery, guaranteeing our autonomy and interiority. Like all actions of high quality in the arts and professions, our moral actions are stamped with our personality. Often they have matured in long solitude and trial. If they are carried out in faith, they will issue from the invisible center of our being where we stand alone before the Father's gaze, hidden from all others. Yet those who have eyes to see will perceive their source and will praise the Father. Nothing is so irreducibly personal, arcane, and solitary in its roots and source as moral action.

Yet out of this hidden center of freedom comes openness to others, without which there can be no excellent action, no fruitfulness. Rooted in our hearts are those virtues that benefit others, such as justice (which is the firm resolve to give others their due), generosity, friendship, and many others. This is especially true of charity, which passes from intimacy with God to intimacy with others, through the grace of the Holy Spirit, and becomes for believers the seed, bond, and perfection of all truly moral qualities. Our freedom reaches maturity precisely with our capacity to balance the twofold dimension of personality and openness to others, interiority and outreach, living "for self" and "for others." We should note here that only the concept of freedom for excellence, based on the natural sense of the true and the good, enables us to be aware of this association, so vital for moral theory. The theory of freedom of indifference not only fails to explain it but actually destroys it, breaking it down into contraries.

We rediscover this union of personality and openness to others at the level of works accomplished. The work of excellence, the moral achievement perfect in its ordering, is so personal that it reflects its author in the depths of his being: he is recognized as good, just, generous, upright, charitable. He is known through his actions, somewhat as a great artist is recognized in his works, which need no signature. Works win a wide audience and touch those who know them most profoundly, for a work possesses the savor and perfection of a ripe fruit offered to the individual. In the same way, an excellent moral action is presented to another as a fruit intended for that person, a fertile seed to be received, a model to inspire, and an attractive example to imitate. Here it is appropriate to recall the Aristotelian definition of virtue: it renders good not only the act and the one who performs it but still more those who profit by it and who may, in their turn, become fruitful because of it.

"The Perfect" in the Order of Charity

St. Thomas calls the third stage of progress in charity the age of the *perfecti,* "the perfect," those whose chief concern is to be united to God and to find all their joy in him. He applies to them the expression of St. Paul to the Philippians: their longing is "to be gone and be with Christ" (Phil 1:23).

A word of clarification is needed here. The terms *perfect* and *perfection* should be understood in a human sense, which is always relative in our present condition. In this sense we say a man has reached the perfection of his age, his growth, or his personality, meaning the maturity characteristic of an adult. St. Paul takes up this idea when he invites Christians to "become the perfect Man, fully mature with the fulness of Christ himself" (Eph 4:13). It is a perfection very different from that which is sometimes evoked by the word "virtue" when we say, for instance, that nothing could be more boring and more irritating than the perfect person who possesses every virtue. This perfection is not merely the reproduction of a model or the application of a theory, soulless and artificial. It is, on the contrary, a dynamic perfection, flowering from the heart; it is characteristic of the person who has reached the fulness of his active powers.

St. Thomas characterizes spiritual maturity by the perfection of love of God and Christ, which is the principal dimension of charity, as also of the contemplative life oriented to the vision of God (IIaIIae, q 180 a 4). It might be well to complete this description of the adult Christian with the following passage from Philippians quoted above, where St. Paul concludes: "and yet for your sake to stay alive in this body is a more urgent need. This much I know for certain . . ." (1:24). The perfection of charity sees the "urgency" of being ready to renounce even the fulfillment of the desire to be with Christ, for the sake of the neighbor's good. The tension between the desire for Christ and the good of one's neighbor, which St. Paul describes as a dilemma, shows the power of life and the fruitful strength that exist in perfect charity.

The New Law

We can relate this teaching about the adult stage of the Christian to the Thomistic definition of the New Law, whose chief element is the grace of the Holy Spirit working within us through faith and charity, and also to the teaching about the action of the Holy Spirit through his gifts. Taking his cue from St. Augustine, who had linked the Gospel Beatitudes with the gifts of the Holy Spirit listed in Isaiah's chapter 11, St. Thomas distinguishes a twofold realization of the Beatitudes, through the virtues and the gifts (IaIIae, q 69 a 3). The proper work of the gifts, penetrating the virtues in the form of inspirations, is to enable us to perform perfect actions transcending simple reason and our own initiative, in conformity with the generous upsurge of faith and charity.

Such is the lofty perfection taught us in the Sermon on the Mount, which we are to seek under the direct impulse of the Holy Spirit, our chief teacher. It alone can lead us to the full ripening of charity.

This work of the Holy Spirit corresponds exactly to the flowering of our freedom, as St. Thomas explains in a very beautiful passage in the *Summa contra Gentiles* (4.22), where he describes how the Holy Spirit moves man toward God in the mode of friendship. It happens in the context of a relationship that, humanly speaking, is based wholly on freedom and presupposes a personality matured by virtue. It is well worth our while to reread this extremely interesting passage based on the concept of freedom for excellence, informed by the natural inclination to the truly good.

For all that, one must bear in mind that the sons of God are driven not as slaves, but as free men. For since, according to Aristotle, that person is free who acts on his own, we do freely that which we do of our very selves. This is what we do by our own will; what we do against our will is not done freely but by force, whether the violence brought to bear upon us is absolute, as when "the entire principle of the action is extrinsic, with the subject contributing nothing"—for example, a person is pushed into motion—or whether the violence is combined with a certain voluntariness—for example, one wishes to do or endure what is less contrary to his will in order to avoid what is more contrary to it. But the Holy Spirit moves us to act in such a way that he causes us to act voluntarily, in that he makes us lovers of God. Therefore the sons of God are moved by the Holy Spirit freely, out of love, not slavishly out of fear. Hence the Apostle says, "What you received was not the spirit of slavery to bring you back into fear; you received the spirit of adoption" (Rom 8:15).

The will, of course, is ordered to that which is truly good. But if by reason of passion or some evil habit or disposition a man is turned away from that which is truly good, he acts slavishly, in that he is diverted by some extraneous thing, if we consider the natural orientation of the will. But if we consider the act of the will as inclined to an apparent good, a person is acting freely in following passion or a corrupt habit. He acts slavishly, of course, if while his will remains so fixed, he—out of fear of a law to the contrary—refrains from doing what he wills. Therefore, since the Holy Spirit inclines the will to the good through love—the good to which the will is naturally ordered—he removes both the servitude whereby a man, infected by sin, follows his passion and acts contrary to the natural ordering of his will, and the slavery whereby he acts in accordance with the law but against his will, being the law's slave, not its friend. This is why the Apostle says, "Where the Spirit of the Lord is, there is freedom" (2 Cor 3:17); and, "When you are led by the Spirit, you are not under the Law" (Gal 5:18).

In his commentary on chapter 44 of Isaiah concerning the outpouring of the Spirit, St. Thomas had already used St. Paul's words, "Where the Spirit of the Lord is, there is freedom," to describe "the perfect," whose initial gift is freedom.

In the language of the mystics, the unitive way corresponds to the age of maturity or of "the perfect." This explains the search for union with Christ of which St. Thomas speaks, expressed in the theme of spiritual marriage. The action of the Holy Spirit predominates here.

It is well to remember in this connection, however, that the teaching of the Sermon on the Mount on the gifts of the Holy Spirit was intended, according to St. Thomas and the Fathers, for all Christians. It was a call to commitment to one single way, along which one might advance as far as possible according to one's vocation, with the help of grace. The three stages we have been discussing describe the progress and flowering of freedom for excellence by means of all the virtues, centered, for the Christian, in charity, which binds them together, enlivens them, and brings them to their perfection. The action of the Holy Spirit is at work from the beginning of the Christian life, in the call to faith and through the gift of charity. It is at work in every heart, like sap, which, hidden at first, is later revealed in all its power in the season of fruits, the time of maturity. For every Christian, as for the Church, Pentecost is the harvest feast. In our lives it has been prepared for by the season of sowing—often childhood—when the small grain of the Word was welcomed with faith in the simplicity of our hearts, as if on a day of a very personal annunciation.

The interpretation that would see in the Sermon and the gifts of the Holy Spirit an esoteric doctrine inaccessible to ordinary people is a logical result of the concept of freedom of indifference, which, by means of obligation, checked the principal use of moral freedom at its initial stage, where law and freedom came into conflict. Since all freedom came to a standstill there, it could hardly grow. Moral theory itself remained at this level. It was no longer necessary to offer to all a perfection that transcended legal obligation.

According to St. Thomas, on the other hand, the Sermon on the Mount was addressed to every Christian, with the grace of the Holy Spirit. Each person could aspire, in heart and prayer, to the realization of the central precept of the Sermon: "You must therefore set no bounds to your love, just as your heavenly Father sets none to his" (Mt 5:48). This commandment, "impossible" in the eyes of men, the learned and the clever, becomes accessible to the little ones, the humble whom no one would think of as an elite, precisely because they are more aware of their weakness and better disposed to allow themselves to be led by the Spirit in faith and hope.

VI. SOME REMARKS ON PROGRESS IN THE DEVELOPMENT OF MORAL FREEDOM

1. Continuity in Developing Freedom

The three stages in the formation of freedom for excellence that we have distinguished are not always separated in reality. As in biological growth, the first stage continues in the second and the second in the third, because of the positive quality of each and the weaknesses that sometimes perdure. Our childhood is with us to the day of our death, revealing some of our deepest traits. At life's decline, many feel the need to reawaken memories of their youth, as if to plunge once more into the source of their origin.

If we can characterize the first stage of moral education by the acceptance of discipline and the struggle against sin, this is not to say that as "proficients" or "perfect," where the freedom of initiative is greater, we no longer have to fight against our faults and we can throw off all discipline. The need for a rule of life persists to the end, but with maturity it is assumed personally, and thenceforward based on our own interior urging.

Similarly, if it is true that humility, according to the teaching of the Fathers, constitutes the first stage of the Christian's spiritual journey, it does not follow that those who have reached the stage of wisdom need have no more concern for this virtue. They need to be all the more on their guard against pride, which threatens them more than others. It is said that with the increase of the wisdom that comes from God, humility, rooted in truth, grows all the deeper. We find this illustrated in great masters such as St. Augustine and St. Thomas. In the full maturity of their genius they set themselves, in all devotion and humility, to minister to others, one serving his people through preaching and direction, the other helping beginners in theology, to whom he dedicated his *Summa*. Thus maturity promotes a healthy circulation in moral and intellectual affairs; it is at the end of the journey that one is most inclined to turn to beginners with encouragement and guidance, and to communicate to them all one has learned. This is a far cry from the famous dialectic of master and slave. It is fruitful and leads to care for the weakest, not to constrain them but to lead them toward freedom and maturity.

2. Progress by Contrasting Stages

The progress we have been describing, even though continuous, is not linear. Its stages are often in contrast. Natural spontaneity is countered by the need for discipline imposed by educators. Next, in the stage where virtue is growing strong, the line of progress moves from externals to the interior. In this way, movements continue to contrast with one another, for we can never acquire the balance of virtue without the experience of going from one extreme to the other. Gradually we approach the characteristic "mean" where our efforts adjust to the precise line of moral growth. The line of progress is continuous, therefore, but angular, or better still, spiral. The person who is aiming at courage must fight both fear and audacity, fear and anger. He will often yield too far to one or the other before finally reaching that stage of perfection of virtue that adjusts to different situations and persons.

3. The Problem of Education

The progress in freedom for excellence which we are describing unfolds according to a certain dialectic, which has its extremities and contrasts but whose basic direction is constructive. This leads to a characteristic way of envisaging and posing problems of education. The method will be conjunctive, not disjunctive as in freedom of indifference. It will not be a question of choosing between a liberal or an authoritarian education, but of harmonizing freedom and authority in education and of discerning the stages and seasons when it is best to emphasize authority or to favor initiative. It will be the same with other choices: not between voluntarism and intellectualism, but a choice for the collaboration of reason and will. The connection between freedom and nature must be sought, between freedom and grace, the individual and society, the person and the community. All the great problems concerning freedom will be affected by this difference in viewpoint and method.

4. Involvement of All the Faculties

The length and complexity of moral education stem from the fact that freedom for excellence calls for the collaboration of all the human faculties and requires the patient work of coordinating them, which is achieved through exercise and experience. This work also requires acceptance of the help of educators and a dynamic openness to contributions and exchanges encountered in society, in a spirit of justice and friendship. Here again the task is a lengthy one. Yet it is well worth the effort, for it provides freedom with the material and nourishment necessary for growth, and strengthens and guarantees the quality of its works. We can apply to freedom St. Paul's words about everything working together for the good of those who love God (Rom 8:28). Once we are free, we can profit by everything that happens, within and without, whether it comes from God or man, including contradictions and persecutions.

5. Progress without End

We should not be misled by terminology. The final stage of moral progress in no way designates an end, where all mobility and action cease. The age of adulthood is indeed the end of growth, but it is marked by the height of our powers. At the moral level, mature freedom develops within us an energy that, of itself, need fear no decline. Thus the perfection of virtue is simultaneously an end and a beginning. It marks the end of education but enables us to undertake works of highest excellence, bringing them to a successful outcome. In the same way, spiritual perfection does not put an end to our efforts. It is an interior energy, ever urging us forward to the best manner of acting, without ever wearying.

This is what St. Augustine describes so magnificently in his meditation on the Sabbath rest. The Sabbath has no evening, for it brings us into the creative rest of God, who is our "end without end."

After this sixth age, God will rest as on the seventh day, in the sense that he will make us, who are to be this seventh day, rest in him. . . . I say that this seventh age will be our Sabbath, and that it will end in no evening, but only in the Lord's day, an eternal and eighth day, so to speak. Sunday, made glorious by Christ's resurrection, prefigures the eternal rest of spirit and body. There, we shall rest and we shall see, we shall see and we shall love, we shall love and we shall give praise. This is what shall be in the end without end. And what other end could there be for us, but to enter the Kingdom that has no end? (*City of God*, 22.30.5)

Words cannot contain the realities of the life of the spirit. We speak in paradoxes, trying to describe God as resting and active, trying to depict our rest in him as an end without end, a repose in which we exercise our highest powers to the full, our knowledge in vision, our will in love.

Together with the temptation to pride, the "perfect" may be lured into thinking, some day, that they have "arrived," have reached the summit where at last they can settle down. But true spiritual progress leads us, so to speak, from beginning to beginning, ever deepening our awareness of our origin, our sources of energy, and our end. The further we advance in things moral, the more strongly we are impelled by the wisdom and love that inspire freedom, to undertakings of the highest quality. Thus our freedom participates in the creative freedom of God.

VII. COMPARATIVE TABLE OF THE TWO FREEDOMS AND THEIR RELATION TO MORAL THEORY

Our analyses of freedom of indifference and freedom for excellence will be summarized in the accompanying comparative table. Commenting on this table, I shall add only two remarks, on the first and last points of comparison.

The Freedom to Sin

Because it is defined as a choice between contraries, freedom of indifference implies the power to choose between good and evil as a first form of choice. The choice between good and evil appears to be the essence of this freedom. This is why theologians like Billuart had to work out subtle distinctions in order to explain the difference between the moral freedom we enjoy in this world and that of the blessed in heaven and of God, who cannot sin. This said, we wonder if man is finally led to renounce an essential part of his freedom on approaching God.

Freedom of Indifference	Freedom for Excellence
Definition: The power to choose between contraries. (The choice between good and evil is essential to freedom.) Freedom resides in the will alone.	Definition: The power to act freely with excellence and perfection. (The choice of evil is a lack of freedom.) Freedom resides in reason and will together.
1. *Excludes natural inclinations* from the free act; they are subject to choice. In regard to these inclinations, freedom is indifferent.	1. *It is rooted in the natural inclinations to the good and true,* to what has quality and perfection. It springs from an attraction to what appears true and good, and from an interest in it.
2. *It is entire from the first moment.* No stages of formation and progress are required. There is no middle ground between being free and not being free.	2. *It is bestowed in embryo* at the beginning of moral life; *it must be developed* through education and exercised, with discipline, through successive stages. Growth is essential to freedom.
3. *It is entire in each free choice,* in theory: each act is independent, isolated from other acts, and is performed at the instant of decision.	3. *It integrates actions* in view of an end, which unites them interiorly and insures continuity.
4. *It has no need of virtue,* which becomes a freely used habitude, *or of finality,* which becomes one circumstance of actions.	4. *Virtue is a dynamic quality essential to freedom,* a *habitus* necessary for its development. *Finality is a principal element* of free action.
5. *Law appears as an external restraint and a limitation* of freedom; it creates an irreducible tension with it.	5. *Law is a necessary external aid* to the development of freedom, *together with the attraction to the true and good,* which is a note of inner freedom. Law is especially necessary in the first stage of education. It is progressively interiorized through the virtues of justice and charity.
6. *Freedom is locked within self-assertion,* causing the will to be separated from the other faculties and the individual to be separated from other freedoms.	6. *Freedom is open* to allowing all human powers to make their contribution to its action, and to collaboration with others for the common good and the growth of society.
7. *It creates a moral theory focused on obligation and law; its relationship to Scripture is limited* to texts imposing strict obligations.	7. *Its foundation is the attraction to the true and the good,* and the desire for happiness, *focusing on the virtues* and oriented to quality and perfection, lending itself to a relationship with *all of Scripture.*

In freedom for excellence on the other hand, the ability to commit faults in our moral life as well as in the arts is a lack of freedom, lessened if not eliminated by progress. The ability to sin is accidental to freedom, even though it is a part of the human condition in this world. The greatest freedom is God's. He, being impeccable, is fully creative; his power has no interior limitations. The nearer man approaches to God through the moral progress that weakens his inclination to sin, the more he grows in full freedom, sharing in the divine freedom itself. The blessed have therefore lost none of their freedom; rather, they have become supremely free as God is free, through the grace of Christ and the work of the Holy Spirit. They are free as to truth and goodness and enjoy perfect knowledge and a very pure love, which they express in praise of the works of divine grace in the world and in humanity. We could hardly, for all that, say that their knowledge and love lessens their freedom.

Freedom and the Moral Life

The foregoing table brings us easily and clearly to the conclusion of our research by comparing, in the seventh and last point, freedom of indifference and duty-driven morality, on the one hand, with freedom for excellence and a moral theory based on virtue and happiness on the other.

In freedom of indifference, we note the fundamental features of morality of obligation as it took shape after the nominalist dispute and the humanism of the Renaissance. Freedom of indifference was commonly accepted by ethicists at that time, even by Thomists, and became for them the source of moral theory. The moral foundation rested on the two opposed bases of freedom and law, and it focused on the idea of obligation, which became the sole link, the sole conceivable point of agreement between the two. The subject matter of moral teaching comprised individual human actions, isolated by free decision and by cases of conscience that were studied as realities in themselves, together with the circumstances that particularized them. The consideration of finality faded into the background, and all that was left was the study of finality as sought by a person in some particular action; it was viewed as a secondary, purely circumstantial element. The study of virtue disappeared from fundamental moral theology, yielding to the commandments as the principle of the organization of subject matter. That all these characteristics derived directly and logically from the concept of freedom of indifference shows how close was its bond with the moral theories of obligation that followed nominalism.

We have added the relationship to Scripture, which has been reduced rather effectively during the last four centuries in Catholic textbooks of ethics. This situation can be explained on several counts, such as the anti-Protestant reaction, but certainly not least was the concentration of moral theory on obligation. This caused ethicists to lose interest in scriptural passages that contained no moral imperatives and did not correspond to the problems and the legalizing categories that meant so much to them. If it is true that freedom of indifference was at the origin of duty-driven morality, we are led to believe that it was responsible for this distancing from Scripture and was not perfectly in accord with it. Given freedom of indifference, it is difficult to see how one could explain God's teaching about the chosen people and about believers, presented as a progressive liberation from the sin which had held them in bondage, and as a gradual formation in living by faith, in love of God and neighbor, and in the hope, too, that holds out to us the Kingdom and the Beatitudes as our end. The concept of freedom for excellence seems to me far better adapted to a theology of freedom in conformity with Scripture.

Freedom for excellence harmonizes well with the moral theories of happiness and virtue whose models we have seen in ancient philosophy, in the Fathers, and in the works of St. Thomas. This concept offers moral theory the spiritual spontaneity it needs in order to develop: the natural inclination toward the true, the good, happiness. These tendencies develop through the progressive practice of the virtues, with the help of education, law, and grace. In this tradition, all human faculties and all the elements making up moral action are linked: intelligence, will, sensibility, freedom, with law and grace, virtue and discipline. They tend to join forces in the production of excellent actions, as personality and life are progressively unified through lasting agreement between intentions and actions. It is the same at the societal level: the natural inclination to live in society will be developed by justice and friendship, with a flowering of freedom and the gradual building of dynamic harmony between the members of the city in view of their common good and common tasks.

It seems that such a concept offers a far better foundation for receiving revelation and grace, particularly through freedom's natural openness to the true and the good. Here we can discern the image of God, written indelibly in the human heart.

Furthermore, the example of the Fathers shows what close and constant contact can be established between all of Scripture and an ethics based on the attraction of happiness, truth, and the virtues. The agreement between revelation and moral philosophy was undoubtedly not established without in-depth debates, as we have seen with St. Paul, for example. But the outcome has been a remarkable harmony, attested by the great works of Christian theological wisdom, which flow directly from the wisdom of God and the knowledge of the mystery of Christ of which the Apostle speaks.

16

Human Freedom according to

St. Thomas Aquinas

Having described freedom for excellence, we have only to consider freedom in St. Thomas's texts so as to verify their agreement with this concept.[1] We shall not present a complete study of freedom in St. Thomas, but will attempt a broad outline, with the clarifications needed to distinguish his concept of freedom from freedom of indifference.

In this debate we need to keep in mind the fact that St. Thomas could not confront the theory of freedom of indifference directly, in the form it took after his time. Yet his writings are sufficiently explicit to give us a clear picture of his ideas on the subject. Happily for us, moreover, he was forced to treat the problem of freedom in depth because of the disputes raging at the University of Paris in his day. There he encountered opinions that already anticipated freedom of indifference. The vast number of views on human freedom discussed in his commentary on the Sentences of Peter Lombard shows that it was a topic of great interest in the mid-thirteenth century.

We also need to remember that with St. Thomas we are dealing with an author who gathered together the major currents of thought on freedom that were known in his day: Greek philosophy, particularly Aristotle and his commentators, and the Fathers of the Church, notably St. Augustine. St. Thomas, therefore, was not simply speaking on his own;

1. St. Thomas uses the expression *free will* to designate the faculty, the free will. I shall generally use the term *freedom,* which can designate both the faculty and its mode of exercise.

he was the interpreter of the soundest teachings that had preceded him. It would be very interesting to make an in-depth study of his sources, which would reveal the richness of his teaching on freedom and his fidelity to the best traditions, as well as his originality.

Freedom was foundational in St. Thomas's moral theology. It was in man's freedom, in his control over his own actions, that he imaged God (prologue of the second part). Nonetheless, in the arrangement of the second part, the study of freedom followed that of beatitude and human acts, being placed among the interior principles of action, the human faculties. Actually, these last had already been studied in the first part with the works of God, among the active powers conferred upon the human creature. Freedom, like the other powers, was thus situated at the point of contact between the action of God in man and properly human action. It had two aspects, one in relation to God, whose work it was, and the other in relation to man with his own works.

In the first part, the study of "free will" followed that of the intellectual faculties (q 79). It was introduced by a preamble on sense knowledge (q 78), and placed among questions on the appetitive powers: the sensible appetite (q 81) as a preamble, then the will (q 82), and finally free will (q 83). From this arrangement we can already see clearly the dependency of free will in relation to intellect and will.

Since faculties are revealed through their actions, it was appropriate to extend the study of them with a discussion of the human act, in the *prima secundae*. Here we find the same arrangement of topics: first, the acts of the will, desire, intention, and fruition; then, the acts wherein free will is exercised, particularly choice (q 13). It is the analysis of choice that enables us to establish, as early as the first part (q 83, a 3), the nature of free will.

Among St. Thomas's other works we shall make special use of the famous disputed question *De malo,* q 6, occasioned by discussions in Paris on free will and by the attacks launched against St. Thomas's concept, which was deemed too rationalistic.[2]

---

2. Principal texts: II *Sentences* dist. 24 and 25; *De veritate,* qq 22 and 24 in the context of the study of the will in God and in man; commentary on the *Nichomachean Ethics,* 3.1.5–9, following the study of the voluntary.

I. THE NATURE OF HUMAN FREEDOM

1. Freedom Proceeds from Intelligence and Will

Peter Lombard's classical definition of free will ran thus: "Free will is a faculty of reason and will whereby the good is chosen, with the help of grace, or evil rejected with the same help [Liberum arbitrium est facultas rationis et voluntatis qua bonum eligitur gratia assistente, vel malum eadem desistente]." From the time of his *Commentary on the Sentences,* St. Thomas took a clear stand on this. Contrary to the opinion of some who asserted that free will was a special faculty having the power of judgment over all the other faculties—an anticipation of Ockham's position—St. Thomas placed freedom after the intellect and will, the latter having as its chief object the good seen as end.[3] Freedom was placed at the conjunction of the intellect, which judged, and the will, which willed, loved, and desired. From them it received the light and strength that were united within choice.

Lombard's definition meant, therefore, that freedom was a power deriving from reason and will and that it combined them in its action. St. Thomas further clarified, in opposition to certain opinions, that free will was not a faculty distinct from reason and will. It was the prolongation of each. It united and clarified them in order to produce a concrete action, just as conclusions derive from principles.[4] This rootedness of freedom in mind and will determined the actual plan of studying the faculties in St. Thomas's works, especially in the *Summa theologiae,* as we have seen above.[5] Thus freedom was the outcome of the mind's inclination to truth and the will's inclination to goodness.

---

3. As we have already mentioned, St. Bonaventure is more explicit on this opinion: free will, in the proper sense of the term, is a faculty distinct from intellect and will and precedes them, for its action is distinguished from discernment and from willing as the power to reflect upon them and, consequently, to command them, as the will to discern and the will to will. Thus free will is likened to the Father, whose act is most powerful and prime, for he moves without being moved (II *Sent.,* dist 25, 1, art 1, q 2).

4. II *Sent.,* dist. 24, q 1 ad 3.

5. "Radix libertatis est voluntas sicut subiectum; sed sicut causa, est ratio. Ex hoc enim voluntas libere potest ad diversa ferri, quia ratio potest habere diversas conceptiones bone." Ia q 17 a 1 ad 2.

2. Free Choice Is an Act of the Will "Informed" by the Intellect

The analysis of choice is one of the most difficult questions in ethics. Yet it is decisive. St. Thomas always began with Book Six of Aristotle's *Nicomachean Ethics,* in which the Philosopher showed how choice included a judgment and a desire so closely linked that they were inseparable. He therefore defined choice in a twofold formula that gave them equal importance. Choice was *intellectus appetivus vel appetitus intellectivus,* which might be rendered "appetitive knowledge or intellectual appetite."[6] He added that this beginning was the essence of man, indicating the importance of choice in human understanding and action. Choice thus comprised so close a union of reason and will that Aristotle could not or would not attribute this action more to one than the other.

For St. Thomas, therefore, choice meant a practical judgment, which concluded deliberation or counsel, and a certain willing. But he did not stop there. He needed to ascribe choice to one of the two spiritual human faculties. He therefore set out to cut this formidable Gordian knot. In his opinion choice should be substantially attributed to the will, since its direct object was some good ordered to a willed end, which could be called a useful good (*bonum utile*). St. Thomas found a text in Aristotle that concurred with this; choice was qualified as *desiderium consiliabile* or "a well-considered desire," following upon deliberation.[7] Choice was governed by reasonable research and judgment, which were essential elements of its formation.

To qualify this union, St. Thomas applied to choice the relationship between matter and form. The matter of choice was an act of the will, its form an act of reason. He also invoked Nemesius's comparison (in his *De natura hominis,* attributed to St. Gregory) with the human composite of body and soul. In his analysis of choice we rediscover the vital, substantial union between body and soul held by St. Thomas, applied here in the intimate association between intellect and will.[8]

Our experience of choice shows us clearly the compenetration of appetite and judgment. Let us take a concrete example. The choice of a

6. See VI *Ethics,* ch 2, 1139b, 4–5.

7. III *Eth.* 1113a, 10–11: "Choice is a deliberated desire concerning what depends on us."

8. Cf. Ia q 83 a 3 and IaIIae q 13 a 1: "Sic igitur ille actus quo voluntas tendit in aliquid quod proponitur ut bonum, ex eo quod per rationem est ordinatum ad finem, materialiter quidem est voluntatis, formaliter autem rationis."

dinner from a restaurant menu is basically directed by our appetite, for we are trying to satisfy our hunger, which cannot be done unless we have an appetite. But the comparison of various menu offerings is the work of deliberation, involving many factors such as our taste, memories, prices, the friend with whom we are dining, considerations of health, diet, and so forth. All this is directed by our reason, joined directly to our sensible appetite and will. Truly, as Aristotle says, the simplest of choices engages the whole man, with all his complexity.

The same is true for choices involving a deeper commitment such as a religious vocation. The study of various active and contemplative orders open to our choice entails both rational inquiry and the will's assessment in order to reach the decision that a given order corresponds best to our vocation and desire.

St. Thomas's analysis of choice was unique in that it united and maintained in close relationship two dimensions that were later to be separated as a consequence of nominalism. One dimension related to the intellect: the dimension of essence or specification, in regard to the object (the choice of this or that). The other dimension applied mainly to the will: the dimension of existence or the order of execution, in regard to the subject (choosing to act or not to act). These two dimensions together constituted freedom and its exercise. Later on, theories of choice would be styled existential, intellectual, or rational depending upon the emphasis: some would stress practical judgment to the point of considering the execution of an action as a simple application or consequence, a pure act of obedience on the part of the will.

Choice issued essentially from the will, from the effort of the person who was attracted and moved by a good. This was the existential aspect of the choice and action. Thus, theories in which choice depended chiefly if not solely upon free will could be called existential.

St. Thomas's analysis was distinguished, therefore, by the joining and interaction of intellect and will in free choice, of judgment and willing, essence and existence, object and subject, all of which made up human action as matter and form or body and soul.[9]

Undoubtedly the primacy that St. Thomas assigned to reason as the criterion of morality in the *Summa* has inclined his modern commentators to rational intellectualism. They were misled by a subsequent po-

---

9. See my study on choice in the analysis of the human act, in vol. 1 in *Les Actes humains de la Somme des Jeunes* (Paris, 1962), particularly notes 52 and 88, as well as *Les Renseignements techniques*, 422–34. The distinction between the order of specification and the order of exercise will form the principal support for the argumentation in q 6 of *De malo*.

sition taken on the problem, which caused them to choose between reason and will, whereas St. Thomas's whole effort had been to join these two and to analyze their reciprocal contributions.

3. The Parallel between Intelligence and Reason, Will and Freedom

St. Thomas continued his analysis of freedom by relating it to the will, in which it is rooted, in light of the relationship existing between intelligence and reason. He thus established a very enlightening parallel between our spiritual faculties and their use (Ia, q 83, a 4). Just as reason had its source in the intellect and by reasoning worked upon the first principles furnished by it, so freedom depended on the will, and, by choosing the means to the end the will proposed, put it into action. In the relation between our two spiritual faculties, free will corresponded to reason and collaborated with it to produce the action that bespoke the whole person, an action combining practical judgment and free choice.

Let us study this in greater detail, considering first the intellect in its practical function. The intellectual life has its source in an act so simple and profound that it has the same name as the faculty: intelligence, which is the practical reason's direct knowledge of first principles. Theology was to discern a natural habit in this primordial, stable knowledge and to call it *synderesis*.[10] It was the primordial perception of the good proper to man. We can put it this way: it is good to be alive, to eat, to know the truth, to love. Ordinarily it was expressed by the principle, "Bonum est faciendum, malum est vitandum," which may be translated, "The good is desirable; we should do it. Evil is detestable, and to be avoided." We shall return to this traditional formula, which has too often been interpreted in the light of modern obligational theories. Intuitive knowledge of this kind exists before being expressed and perdures in spite of misinterpretation.

Since the human person is not a pure spirit, wholly intuitive like the angels, the intellect needs the help of the reasoning powers in order to grow and progress in the knowledge of the true and the good. Reason works by way of research and comparison; these take the form of reasoning and judgment. At the level of action, this means deliberation,

10. Cf Ia q 79 a 12. On the origins of this term, cf. Ph. Delhaye, *La conscience morale du chrétien* (Tournai, 1964), 87ff.

which terminates in a practical judgment as its conclusion. Its object is the realization of the natural perceptions of synderesis: Which nourishment is better, material or spiritual? Where are truth and beauty in this concrete situation, where is the evil in such and such an action? Precisely which ways and roads lead to true happiness?

Practical reason's work is very comprehensive. It produces moral science, which we find in part two of the *Summa theologiae*, but it must always deal with concrete, individual action, the realm of personal prudence. Its work will continue unendingly, so long as there are human beings to reflect on their actions.

From the point of view of the will, the source of energy resides in the simple willing of the end, such as goodness and happiness. This initial will indicates the primordial, profound spontaneity of the human person, corresponding to his intuitive knowledge of first principles. We could call it an "original" will, compounded of love and desire. It is also a final will, since it determines the goal and object of this movement. Such is the bodily hunger that drives us to choose and seek food. And again, such is the spiritual hunger that impels us toward truth, love, and goodness. It is the fundamental desire, the spiritual instinct (*instinctus rationis,* as St. Thomas says) that underlies all choices.

But here too, simple willing is not enough. The exercise of freedom is needed to choose ways and means of reaching the goals of the primordial will. This work will be every bit as extensive and demanding as that of practical reason, for it goes on throughout life and engages our entire personality. We must choose a vocation, a friend, or a life companion, choose virtues and values that will give meaning to life. There are the choices of useful means for meeting our needs; daily, repeated choices that make for a good or bad experience. By such successive choices our moral personality is shaped in relation to others.

Seen thus, freedom does not constitute a faculty separate from the will. As we can see from the way it operates, it is a special function of the will, ordered to the fulfillment of our basic desires, which are oriented to supreme goodness or beatitude.

For St. Thomas, free choice was a decisive act but not a primary one. It received its power from the spiritual energy rooted in the will to achieve the final goal, and its enlightenment from reason, which discerned the ways and means of attaining this goal. Choice was concentrated at the point where the will's energy and reason's enlightenment met and mingled, like a matrix wherein action was conceived, formed, and brought to birth. It bore within itself all the wealth and poverty of our faculties and personality. Yet it was only in and through choice that

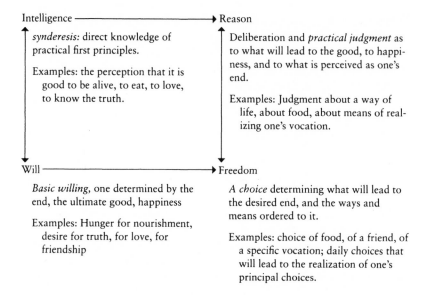

we could find fulfillment in action, come to being, and renew ourselves. (See the accompanying chart, which illustrates this analysis.)

4. Choice Has for Its Object Ways and Means Leading to the Goal

In the *prima secundae,* at question 13, a 3, St. Thomas established with all possible clarity that the matter of choice was not the final end as such; its object was, rather, the ways and means of attaining the final end. These he described broadly as *ea quae sunt ad finem* ("those things that are ordered to the end"). This was at once the result and the direct manifestation of freedom's dependence in relation to intellect and will. He added a very useful clarification. What is an end in one order, as for example health for a physician, may be ordered to a higher end, thereby becoming the object of choice. One might sacrifice health, or life, for a spiritual end such as the preaching of the Gospel, as did St. Paul. Nevertheless, as had been shown in the study of finality (q 1, a 4), the hierarchy of willed ends must necessarily lead to an ultimate end, willed purely and simply, and this was comparable to the first principles of the practical intellect, known naturally. Such was the natural inclination to happiness, studied in the treatise on beatitude. In itself the final end could not be the object of choice, for it was the primordial energy of the will which caused and directed all choices. The proper matter of choice was therefore all that was ordered to the final end, beatitude. Freedom could not affect the natural willing of one's final end, which was freedom's very root and which ordered it to happiness.

The assertion was categorical: "Ultimus finis nullo modo sub electione cadit." We could not find a more radical opposition to the freedom of indifference, which Ockham was to define as the power to choose between contraries precisely in the face of the inclination to happiness and other natural inclinations.

A note of capital importance should be added at once. Influenced as we still are by the concept of freedom of indifference and by its opposition to nature, we run the risk of misunderstanding St. Thomas's position. In asserting that choice cannot have a final end as its object, he seems to be limiting freedom and positing at its origin a constraining natural will, which would be a profound contradiction to free spontaneity.

In reality this apparent limitation is not a lessening of freedom but its very root in the spiritual nature of man. It is precisely because we cannot help aspiring to goodness and truth that we possess limitless freedom, at least potentially, opening onto infinite truth and goodness. We have to struggle here with the weakness of our human language and the images we use to convey spiritual realities. We can speak only in paradoxes, attempting to express the infinite in finite terms—that is, the capacity for truth and goodness, which is the essence of our freedom. We are obviously dealing with a totally different kind of freedom here. We have called it freedom for excellence precisely because it issues from our spontaneous attraction for the highest truth and goodness. We shall return to this point.

We should emphasize once again the interaction and complementarity of our two intellectual faculties regarding both end and choice of means. There can be no perception of goodness, no practical judgment, without the will's attraction and commitment to the good. Nor can there be any inclination to the good or to voluntary choice without knowledge to inform and guide them. The acts of intellect and will are compenetrating. The intellect knows the will in its thrust toward the good and directs it from within. The will in its turn loves truth as its highest good, and moves the intellect toward this truth.

As St. Thomas puts it so well, "The good, insofar as it is a knowable form, is contained within the true as a certain particular truth; the true, insofar as it is an end for our intellectual activity, is contained within the good as a certain particular good. If, therefore, we consider the movement of these faculties of the soul from the viewpoint of the object which specifies the act, the first principle of this movement will be found in the intellect; thus, the good that is known moves the will itself. But if we consider the movement of the soul's faculties from the viewpoint of the execution of the act, then the principle will be found in the will" (*De malo,* q 6).

We should not be misled by the analytical character of St. Thomas's thought as he dealt with the human faculties one by one and distinguished their essences, objects and acts with such keen precision. One of the chief features of his thought regarding the movements of our human faculties was the synthetic unity and dynamic harmony he established between these powers, comparable to the unity and harmony between body and soul in human nature. In concrete action, and particularly in our voluntary choices, all our faculties work together, as in an organism like the human body, where each member contributes to the good of the whole and can do nothing without the other members. This remarkable unity, in which free choice was the pivotal point of concentration, was to be sundered in the following century. It never appeared again in Western thought.

5. Freedom to Choose between Good and Evil

The rootedness of freedom in the intellect and will gave it an orientation toward the highest truth and goodness. This was essential to it and determined its finality. The possibility of doing evil, which was contrary to this finality, did not, according to St. Thomas, belong to the nature of freedom, but was merely a sign of freedom and resulted from a deficiency. St. Thomas had affirmed this in his *Commentary on the Sentences*: "To be indeterminate in regard to good and evil is not an essential note (*ratio*) of free will, since free will is by its nature ordered to the good, and tends to evil only by defect" (II *Sent.*, dist. 25, q 1, a 1, ad 2). He repeated this in his *De veritate* (q 22, a 6), where he added to indetermination regarding the object (specification) and action (execution) an indetermination relative to the end, proceeding from a deficiency in the realization of the latter. Evil consisted in this. (See also q 24, a 9, c and ad 1.) He returned to this point in the *Summa* in connection with the freedom of the angels. "The ability of free will to choose between various things in conformity with the end shows the perfection of freedom; but to choose something not ordered to the end, that is, to sin, evinces a defect of freedom. Therefore the angels, who cannot sin, enjoy greater freedom of choice than do we, who can" (Ia, q 62 a 8, ad 3).

It could not be demonstrated more clearly that the orientation to the highest is what constitutes freedom. Here we are dealing with what we have called freedom for excellence. We are touching a radical point of difference between this freedom and freedom of indifference. The latter, defined as the ability to choose between contraries, includes essentially the power to choose between good and evil, to be for or against the highest good. It is precisely here that freedom of indifference manifests itself by preference, in utmost protest.

6. Some Observations

In order to interpret St. Thomas correctly we need to verify our understanding of his terms, because their meaning has been subtly modified in modern times, particularly by the widespread influence of nominalism. We will therefore look at some of his most ordinary terms.

a. The Will

In current usage the term *will* has taken on the voluntaristic sense of a forceful pressure exerted upon oneself or others, a command calling for pure obedience. The will places constraint upon the spontaneity of the human person subjected to it.

For St. Thomas, the will was primarily the faculty of love and desire. These were its first two acts, according to the treatise on the passions.[11] At the origin of the voluntary movement there existed a spiritual spontaneity, an attraction to the good. Only following this did the will act upon itself and move itself to will those ways and means leading to the good it loved. This was effected precisely by an act of choice. One could speak of the will as imposing itself only in the case of some resistance

---

11. "Now what must come first in such an agent is an attachment to the goal in question as being an attractive one, for nothing sets itself an end which it does not find in some way attractive or appropriate; second, it moves toward the goal; third, it comes to rest in the goal once it has been attained. The aptitude or proportion of the appetite in regard to the good is love, which is none other than complaisence in the good; the movement toward the good is desire or 'concupiscence'; repose in the good is enjoyment or pleasure. According to this order, love therefore preceeds desire and desire preceeds pleasure" (IaIIae q 25 a 2).

to be overcome. This could be interior, issuing from our sensibility, or exterior, on the part of others. In every case the spontaneity of love and desire was primary and animated the will's other acts. The will was therefore not a "pressure," but it gave rise to an "impression" of goodness, which caused the attraction.

The outcome of the voluntary movement would be the pleasure or joy resulting from union with the good. Its fulness was happiness. The will was therefore not domineering by nature but unitive.

b. The Good

In the dictionary the good is defined as "that which moral theory prescribes." Gradually goodness has come to be almost identified with ethical rules of conduct. Also, it is distinguished from the idea of happiness—which would have seemed strange to St. Thomas—for it would seem impossible to do good authentically if the thought of happiness should occur. The rift thus created between moral good and the desire for happiness has had vast repercussions.

For St. Thomas, as for all the ancients, the good was defined by its effect: it was the cause of love and desire, giving promise of pleasure or joy, and in the end, happiness. The good thus signified both excellence and happiness. It might be expressed by the word *good* in the sense in which the Latins understood the word *bonum*,[12] and in which, in Genesis, the work of the six days was declared good and very good.

Clearly we need to distinguish various kinds of goods. St. Thomas adopted the three classical categories of goods, which corresponded to the three kinds of friendship or love. There were the useful goods and the "delectable" goods (paired with friendship based either on utility or

12. Here, according to St. Augustine, is the way of "the good" which leads to God. "Behold, and again see if you can. Certainly you love only the good, because the earth is good by the height of its mountains, the moderate elevation of its hills, and the evenness of its fields; and good is the farm that is pleasant and fertile; and good is the house that is arranged throughout in symmetrical proportions and is spacious and bright; and good are the animals, animate bodies; and good is the mild and salubrious air; and good is health without pains and weariness; and good is the countenance of man with regular features, a cheerful expression, and a glowing color; and good is the soul of a friend with the sweetness of concord and the fidelity of love; and good is the just man; and good are riches because they readily assist us; and good is the heaven with its own sun, moon and stars; and good are the angels by their holy obedience; and good is the lecture that graciously instructs and suitably admonishes the listener; and good is the poem with its measured rhythm and the seriousness of its thoughts.

"But why should I add still more? This good and that good; take away this and that, and see good itself if you can; so you will see God who is good not by another good, but is the good of every good" (*De trinitate*, 8.3.4 [Fathers of the Church, vol. 45]).

on agreement or pleasure), and finally the "honest" good, which corresponded to friendship based on virtue.

Here terminology has fallen upon hard times; the words conceal rather than reveal realities in the moral order. "Honest" good is the good that is loved for its own sake with the love of friendship, beyond all consideration of utility or pleasure. Clearly this kind of good can only be a person, or a personal quality. This is "good" in the full sense of the word, a preeminently moral excellence, very different from the useful or the pleasurable, which are only relative goods. The expression *honesty,* as used to qualify the highest good, has little to do with the respectability claimed by the person who has never fallen foul of the law. It designates a good that has the power to inspire love in the purest and strongest sense of the word.

c. Means

According to St. Thomas, the proper object of choice is *ea quae sint ad finem,* which is usually translated *means.* This translation has a serious drawback. We are accustomed to thinking of finality in a technological context, where means are merely instruments for attaining a proposed goal. Seen thus, the object of every choice we make, whether person or thing, would be reduced to the level of a tool, and all moral theory would risk becoming purely utilitarian. Now it is impossible for us to think of a friend, a spouse, a vocation, truth or justice, even God himself, simply as means for attaining our ends.

St. Thomas's expression *ea quae sint ad finem* is broader than the term *means* as we generally use it. It can certainly designate useful things such as nourishment or pleasant ones such as wine; but it can also qualify human persons, insofar as they are ordered to God as their final end, as well as personal qualities such as virtues, which are our interior approaches to God. These realities transcend the useful and technological order; they must be loved for themselves, with the love of friendship. We can no longer talk about means without leaving ourselves open to misunderstanding. For this reason I prefer to use the term *ways* to an end.

In truth, the finality St. Thomas was discussing belonged properly to the moral order rather than the technical; it applied to those personal qualities he called virtues. In his view these were at once the inspirations and the principal objects of moral choice, elevating it above mere utility and pleasure.

We need also to understand what St. Thomas meant by *useful.* In connection with the appetitive nature of free will, he wrote that the object of choice was *illud quod est ad finem,* that is, whatever would in itself be useful,[13] while the *bonum honestum* would be useful in view of some end. Would we have to say, then, that a friend, or a virtue such as justice or charity, are not *bona honesta,* honest goods, because they are the objects of our choice?

Here again, we need to interpret St. Thomas not from the technical viewpoint of finality, which has become prevalent today to a degree which he could never have imagined, but within the cultural setting of his time, where the moral dimension prevailed. This found expression, for example, in Cicero as transmitted and commented on by St. Ambrose. In the *De officiis* of these two authors, a central point of the discussion was the demonstration that utility should not be separated from moral excellence or virtue, since for man virtue alone was truly useful. These authors bent every effort to reunite usefulness and moral virtue— an effort diametrically opposed to what moderns are trying to do.

In keeping with the tradition he had received, St. Thomas interpreted the useful in a broad sense. He discussed material utility, as found in the goods that serve our needs and are exchanged in commerce, as well as moral and spiritual usefulness found in virtue or friendship. The latter goods were most useful to us in reality, but could be attained only if we preferred them to all other useful goods, even to the point of sacrifice, and loved them for their own sake.

"*Ea quae sunt ad finem,*" "*bonum utile*": these qualifications regarding the object of our choice require of us clarifications St. Thomas could not make because he was never confronted with the utilitarianism and the technological aspirations of our age.

II. BASIS OF FREEDOM: THE UNIVERSALITY OF TRUTH AND GOOD

The Knowledge of Good in Its Universality as the Foundation of Freedom

In the *Summa,* in connection with free will (Ia, q 83 a 1) and choice (IaIIae, q 13 a 6), St. Thomas based freedom on reason, which the will

---

13. ". . . quia proprium obiectum electionis est illud quod est ad finem; hoc autem, in quantum huiusmodi, habet rationem boni quod dicitur utile . . ." (Ia q 83 a 3; cf. also *De veritate,* q 22 a 15 and q 24 a 6).

followed. Its apprehension could not be determined by any particular and contingent good. Man possessed free will from the very fact of being reasonable. In question 6 of *De malo,* the study deepened and showed more clearly, on the one hand, the difference between the universality of our apprehension of the good and the unique character of our actions and, on the other hand, the interaction between intellect and will. We shall not explore all the details of this masterful exposition, but shall select the themes essential to our purpose.

St. Thomas began with the analogy between natural and voluntary action. He saw a certain similarity between them. Voluntary action, like natural action, proceeded from a certain apprehension of the good, which produced an inclination in the will. From the two, action was born. But the essential note of voluntary action consisted in this: that the intellect's apprehension of the good was universal in character, engendering in the will an inclination to the good in all its universality, while the action itself was singular and individual. The result was that the inclination of the will was directed to a number of goods and could not be determined in its choices and individual actions.

Thus freedom was based on the very nature of our spiritual faculties. Their inclination to universal truth and goodness created an opening upon the infinite. This freed the will in regard to all finite, particular goods, among which could be included the act of choice itself. This, emanating from the person, was contingent and individual.

Let us note that the analogy between natural and voluntary action should be maintained in spite of the limp, for voluntary action also proceeds from a certain nature, like an inclination following an apprehension of the good. But this nature is different, in that it is capable of knowing and willing the universal and therefore of engendering a free act, while nonrational nature is determined by the particular character of the perception of good, as in the case of animal instinct and sense perception.

Let us clarify this freedom. It is rooted in our natural inclination to universal truth and good, which constitute our intellect and will. We are not dealing therefore with freedom of indifference, for the will thus viewed, thus animated by the desire for the good, cannot remain indifferent in the presence of any good. All goods that it encounters touch it, draw it, win its interest. Precisely its extreme sensitivity to the good makes it free. Every particular good, all the goods we observe directly in this world, present contrasting aspects. On the one hand they are good and they attract us, but on the other hand they are limited and imperfect, and they disappoint us. It is our reason's ability to survey all these goods, discerning their nature and excellence, that allows us to perceive their limitations and frees us from the attraction they exercise over us.

Freedom is a capacity given to us; it must become an effective power. It could well happen that we might cling to certain goods—money or pleasure come to mind—to the point of becoming enslaved to them and losing our freedom in their regard. Freedom therefore is a power to be developed by the very way we use goods. It grows and becomes apparent in a twofold attitude of attachment and detachment: attachment and appreciation of the good, but also detachment because of its limitations and above all in order to advance toward perfect good. Freedom demands of us an apprenticeship in the handling of goods, within the dynamic perspective of our desire for the good and our progress toward it. Here the virtues intervene, in freedom's service.

The orientation of intellect and will to the universal is not so abstract as the formula might seem to indicate. This is clear from concrete experience. We can call it a thirst for the infinite. It can be seen in every passion: in the miser whom no profit can satisfy, the gambler who cannot stop playing, whether he wins or loses. It is best expressed in St. Augustine's famous formula at the beginning of his life history: "Our hearts are restless, until they rest in you." This desire for happiness, when pursued to the end in truth, frees every human person. It is at work in the smallest, humblest voluntary action, carrying us toward the infinite, as Maurice Blondel has shown in *L'Action*. It is even at work in those who know nothing about it, or who deny it in their theories— so deeply is it rooted in human nature.

A Difficulty: Does Perfect Good Force the Will?

St. Thomas developed his study of freedom by turning his attention to its exercise when the will predominated, and its specification by the ruling intellect; from the viewpoint of the subject, which gave the action its existence, and the object, which conferred on it its essence. Here we come to what looks like the main objection to the Thomist theory of freedom. A person was free in regard to all particular goods, since his intellect and will were open to universal good, as to the infinite. But would he still be free if his intellect grasped something that was purely good in itself, having no limit or imperfection and thus responding completely to the longing of his will for the good? This was not pure hypothesis; indeed, it was the idea of happiness corresponding to the natural desire of all human beings. Boethius had defined it as a state wherein all goods were combined in the fulness of perfection.

St. Thomas answered unhesitatingly: faced with the idea of this full and perfect good, the will could not help desiring it and would be determined by it. It was not free in the presence of such a good. Such a conclusion was inevitable if the primary basis of freedom, the will's desire for the good and for happiness, was to be maintained. St. Thomas never drew back from his affirmation that the will was not free to will happiness.[14] Did this impose a choice between freedom and its foundation?

The difficulty could be compounded by the intervention of some manifestation of God—in revelation, for example, since he was in truth the universal good, as even philosophy would come to discover. Placed before God in this way, would a person not lose his freedom?

The difficulty could be carried still further. It might be proved, through a series of reasons, that a certain concrete action was necessary for the attainment of happiness or the possession of God. Thus the entire range of freedom could be imperiled by reason itself, ending in complete determinism.

Response: Even in Regard to Perfect Good, We Remain Free to Act or Not to Act

St. Thomas responded to the problem by considering it from the viewpoint of an action in which the will of the agent dominated. Though it was true that the will could not relinquish its desire for happiness, and that it could encounter an "object" fulfilling this desire, still the acts of intellect and will, emanating from a human agent, were particular and limited. As such, they could not restrain the will in its desire for full, unlimited good. As St. Thomas wrote in the body of question 6 of *De malo*, if we could apprehend a good that contained in itself all possible particular goods, our will would necessarily be moved by it, that is, "according to the determination [or specification] of the action, because it could not will the contrary; but this is not true of the exercise of the action, since we could, at the moment, will not to think of happiness; for the acts of intellect and will are particular."

He returned to the point in his response to the seventh objection:

14. "Only the perfect good, which is happiness, cannot be apprehended by the reason as evil or defective. Consequently man wills happiness of necessity; he cannot will not to be happy, or to be unhappy" (Iallae, q 13 a 6).

"Since the will is in potentiality in regard to universal good, no good other than this can prevail over it or impel its movement. Perfect good, or beatitude, is of such a nature that the will cannot refrain from willing it, in the sense of willing its contrary. It can, however, refrain from willing it in act, because it is able to turn away from the thought of happiness in the measure in which it might move the intellect to action. Hence, it does not necessarily will even beatitude."

The distinction made here between the objective and subjective aspect of the voluntary act corresponds clearly to the distinction between our objective last end (the reality that is the object of our desire for happiness) and our subjective last end (the possession of this reality). It enabled St. Thomas to show that human happiness did not consist in some good of the soul—science, wisdom, or virtue for example—as most of the ancient philosophers thought. "The human appetite, the will, is directed to universal good. But all the goods of the soul are participated goods, and consequently particular. Therefore it is impossible for any one of them to be man's last end" (IaIIae, q 2 a 7).

Let us carefully note that the two dimensions distinguished by St. Thomas were not separated by him. They were two aspects of voluntary action, involving intellect and will in interaction. It was precisely the intellect's power to reflect on its own act and that of the will, seen as goods, together with what we might call its self-awareness, that provided it with an escape, so to speak, from the grasp of the perfect good. From this subjective, self-regarding viewpoint, the will could withdraw into itself and set limits on the very consideration of happiness and the perfect good.

Indeed, the good could present itself to us as the most attractive, most noble reality in itself; no more would be needed on our part than the effort to consider and grasp it. Yet this effort, and the pain involved, could, from our viewpoint, place limitations on even the most perfect good. The effort required was not minimal, for with the intellect and will it engaged the entire personality. In addition, the good required of us what was undoubtedly most painful: to go out of ourselves and surrender to the good. The higher the good, the stronger the attraction, but on the other hand, the greater would be the demands and the more arduous the efforts required, especially because of sin, which held us back. The Christian experience witnesses abundantly to the strange suffering we endure in committing ourselves to follow the way of promised beatitude and to follow the inspirations of God. St. Thomas's affirmation that we are capable of not wishing to think about beatitude, or of turning away from the thought of it, reveals a profound many-faceted human reality: our difficulty in consenting to the effort required of us by the good, even the highest good.

We are therefore free regarding even the thought of happiness and of the most perfect good, by reason of our subjectivity, which enters into our effort to act, as well as to will truly. Let us note nevertheless that the argument takes its starting point from the will's being ordered to happiness, and this principle is always maintained, because the same good, objectively most perfect, carries with it a demand that is painful to us. In our view it does not completely coincide with our idea of happiness, and we are able to turn our attention and our desire away from the consideration of it. The highest good can thus assume an appearance of imperfection in our eyes.

St. Thomas therefore concluded: "The will is moved necessarily to certain things [beatitude] from the viewpoint of its object, but from the viewpoint of the exercise of the action, it is not necessarily moved." Since the concrete action unites these two dimensions, ruled conjointly by intellect and will, we can say that no voluntary concrete action is necessary.

We must not be misled here. The introduction of the subjective factors of human freedom that we have just observed did not render this freedom any less perfect or noble in St. Thomas's view. Our power to elude somehow the claim of happiness and the attraction of the highest good came in reality from a defect in our spiritual faculties. Our intellect could be deceived, and project an appearance of evil upon happiness and supreme goodness. Our will could weaken in the face of the needed effort. Our power to sin gave us this appearance of freedom, which sprang from error and led to woe. As we have seen, for St. Thomas freedom did not consist in a choice between good and evil; such a choice was accidental, a weakness of human freedom. True freedom was the power to act in truth, in quest of the highest good. It reached its supreme perfection in those who could no longer sin.

We should add, too, that beyond the inclination to evil due to original or habitual sin, our ability to say *yes* to the true and the good, and to God who calls us, goes necessarily hand in hand—because of our condition as creatures—with the possibility of our saying *no* and leaning in the direction of lies and nonbeing. From this obscure foundation of the possibility of falling away and sinning rises our *yes* to the truth, which places us in the light and sets us on the way of authentic freedom.

In contrast to the refusal of faith and life stands the Johannine promise: "The truth shall set you free."

About the Perfect Good

One more word on the perfect good. The idea of the most perfect good easily provokes a reaction of distrust in us, as if it threatened our freedom, for we cannot resist it, or the deductions drawn from it, cannot do other than follow the path to perfection that it demands of us. So the proposal of a perfect good would seem to hold our freedom captive.

But this is a mirage, a play of appearances created by an idea and its subjective representation. We project an idea of the perfect good as something immense, fixed, bedazzling—hypnotizing us by the power of its attraction. Yet a bit of experience and perspicacity reveals a reality that is quite different. The nearer we draw to truth and goodness the more we realize that they increase, rather than diminish, our freedom and mobility. Even as freedom is rooted in the intellect and will, so it grows in truth and goodness as it advances toward perfection. Our freedom will achieve its fulness when it shares unreservedly in the creative freedom of perfect goodness.

Again, everything depends on our concept of freedom. To freedom of indifference, the idea of perfect goodness presents an overwhelming threat to our ability to choose the contrary. To freedom for excellence, tending with all its spiritual energy toward what is highest, the perfect good reveals itself as an infinite source of freedom. It surpasses all the intellectual or imaginative representations that might in some way render it static in our eyes. Only experience, growing out of an assent to truth and goodness, can understand these things.

Perfect good thus envisaged in no way lends itself to a logical deduction of loss of freedom. In fact, as both theology and experience show, the divine goodness—for it is God of whom we are speaking—escapes all human concepts. It can be designated only by the interplay of affirmation, transcendence and negation, through which its higher freedom shines. We have no reason to fear the reality of perfect goodness, but only the imperfection of our ideas of it.

Conclusion

As we conclude this study we can see clearly that freedom, according to St. Thomas, is indeed freedom for excellence, and differs profoundly from the idea proposed by nominalism. In St. Thomas we find the principal characteristics and the points of differentiation that mark freedom for excellence. It proceeds from intellect and will, with their natural inclination to the highest truth and goodness. Its foundation, as freedom, is the universality of truth and goodness; its object, the ways and means leading us to our end. It is thus wholly oriented to finality. Since it is human, it can swerve from its movement toward the end, truth and goodness. Yet this possibility is not essential to it and does not deprive it of its natural inclination to happiness.

In all this, we recognize the principal characteristics underlying St. Thomas's moral teaching. His is a theory based on the ultimate end of man, which unifies human action, rather than a theory of isolated actions and cases of conscience. His focus is happiness rather than obligation; the virtues, which develop our natural inclinations to goodness and truth, rather than commandments and sin. His theory is based on wisdom, fostering the intimate collaboration of intellect and will, rather than on voluntary obedience.

The harmony between St. Thomas's concept of freedom and his design of moral theology stands out in bold relief. This harmony is very profound, for all moral theory implies a certain idea of freedom, even before it has been articulated. There is interaction here: the concept of freedom leads to a certain kind of moral theory, and it is within the theory, which regulates the use of freedom, that this freedom is formed and comes to light.

We can understand from this why the modern commentators on St. Thomas who have adopted the widespread theory of freedom of indifference run into difficulties in interpreting the Master's views on freedom, human acts, and the whole field of moral theology. Despite recourse to subtle distinctions, they have found the difficulties insurmountable.

It now remains for us to study in greater detail the natural inclinations, which are at the origin of human freedom and which accompany its development.

17

———

Natural Inclinations at the Source of
Freedom and Morality

The place and function attributed to natural inclinations mark a decisive split between the two concepts of freedom we have been studying, as well as between the types of morality they produce. In contrast to freedom of indifference, freedom for excellence has its source and foundation in the chief natural human inclinations. These therefore call for our more detailed study. They form the basis of natural law and the source of energy that broadens and develops in the virtues.

I. NATURAL INCLINATION AND FREEDOM

It is difficult to speak of natural inclinations today because of the subtle modifications of ideas and associations that have been caused by nominalism. Nominalist categories are so deeply fixed in our minds that they seem self-evident. They influence our reactions to words and ideas. We need therefore to weigh our concepts critically and in depth, so that we may retreive, at the heart of our experience, the pristine sense of a nature capable of developing in freedom.

Our chief difficulty is caused by our habit of considering nature and freedom as contraries. If we think of freedom as something dependent only on our voluntary decision, and totally indeterminate before we take that decision, then we will be led to think of the natural as something necessarily predetermined. In this view, it is hard to see how we can reconcile the natural and the free. We will see the natural inclinations of both intellect and will as tendencies both blind and coercive.

By way of illustration, here are two quotations from Jacques Leclerq, which describe the situation clearly.

"Natural love, then, is a blind inclination. I repeat that it is regrettable that St. Thomas calls it love, even as he calls the inclination toward the good the natural will; but here again he is following the Greek tradition" (translated from *La philosophie morale de saint Thomas* [Louvain, 1955], 300).

"Metaphysics' affirmation that every being tends toward its own good has little relevance for ethics, for here it is a question of a blind, coercive tendency linked with the idea of goodness and perfection, and the field of ethics deals with free, reflective action. The problem of love is therefore one of intention and thought, a psychological problem. It is not a question of knowing whether man necessarily seeks self-fulfillment or whatever makes him more completely human, but rather of knowing whether he ought to think of himself or of others. These are two different problems, and to confuse them is to understand neither metaphysics nor psychology, and to make any understanding of ethics impossible" (translated from *L'enseignement de la morale* [Paris, 1950], 189).

Without referring explicitly to St. Thomas, the second quotation also has some bearing upon him. The reflection is based on an a priori category that opposes the natural to the free and determines the relations among metaphysics, psychology, and ethics. This last is the domain of freedom and consequently eludes the power of nature. But how, then, are we to interpret St. Thomas, who bases his moral theory on natural inclinations? The reference to Greek influence is merely an excuse, not an explanation. Moreover, it only shifts the problem to a new setting. For how could Aristotle and so many Greek and Latin Fathers, who accepted "nature" as the foundation of morality, all have fallen together into so grave an error?

Apparently, Jacques Leclerq has not perceived the analogical significance of St. Thomas's use of the terms *nature* and *natural* in passing from the physical or biological level to that of the spiritual. In the physical or animal world, nature, whatever its variations, determines the movements it produces in their entirety. Spiritual nature, on the other hand, is such that the inclinations proceeding from it, far from opposing its freedom by setting limits on it, cause and increase its freedom as a source, providing it with principles of truth and goodness. As we have shown, we are free not in spite of our natural inclinations but because of them.

The following quotation from the treatise on the passions shows clearly the analogical use of the term *natural*. It is about the pleasure or "delight" that serves to define beatitude.

Nature in man can be understood in two ways. First, insofar as intellect and will are the chief constituents of human nature, for it is by reason of them that man is constituted as a species. From this point of view, the pleasures man experiences in regard to his intellect can be called natural: thus it is natural for a man to delight in the contemplation of truth and in the practice of virtue.

In another sense, nature in man can be understood as what differs from reason, that is, what he has in common with other beings and above all what is not subject to reason. In this way, those things relating to the preservation of the body, such as food, drink and sleep, and those related to the preservation of the species, such as sexual activity, may be said to give a man natural pleasure. (IaIIae, q 31 a 7)

We should note that this distinction in no way sets up an opposition. In fact, the subject matter of the virtue of temperance, for example, consists in natural pleasures inferior to reason, and it moderates them so as to subject them to reason.

Our problem goes beyond the textual interpretation of St. Thomas. It involves the rediscovery of a spiritual nature, which does not oppose human freedom but lies at its origin and forms it. Of such a nature, clearly, are the human inclinations to truth and goodness.

The natural inclination to truth, which is at the source of the contemplative life, of philosophy and the sciences, obviously cannot be a blind tendency, for darkness does not engender light. Because it exists at the origin of the intellect's life and provides it with its first principles, it should rather be called a radiant splendor, a sort of alpha ray of the mind allowing us to share in the divine Light. It is in itself so dazzling that our reason cannot contemplate it directly. It is as though it were always behind us, as in the Platonic myth of the cave. Do we say the sun is blind because we cannot look straight at it without being blinded?

Similarly, our natural inclination to the good is not a compulsive tendency preceding the moral order or being structured within it. It is in reality the deepest source of that spontaneity which shapes our willing, a primitive élan and attraction that carries us toward the good and empowers us to choose among lesser and greater goods. Here we are at the very origin and principle of morality; this inclination should be described as higher than morality and supremely free, even a sharing in the freedom, goodness, and spontaneity of God.

Verifying This in the Language of Today

Current language can be of great help here. When we speak of a thirst for truth or happiness we are spontaneously using an analogy that describes spiritual desire in terms borrowed from a biological desire. The latter can certainly become an obstacle to freedom by its heaviness and excess, but we are quite aware that this does not apply to the desire for truth. The better we know the truth, the more capable we are of parrying physical constraints and acting freely. As St. Thomas said, man is distinguished from animals precisely in his knowledge of how his actions are formed; this is what enables him to act freely.

Similarly, no one would imagine that an artist's natural gifts were an obstacle to his freedom or that they set limits to it. Rather, the ideal, in the arts, is to achieve the natural. We do not appreciate a work that seems contrived and artificial and is not inspired by a natural sense of beauty. Condillac wrote, "The natural . . . is art become habitual. The poet and dancer are each natural when they achieve that degree of perfection where their conformity to the rules of art appears effortless." And again, "Natural means everything that is not inhibited, strained, artificial, pretentious." Stephen Zweig, speaking of Romain Rolland, remarked, "Nature is art's only rule."

This was the "natural" that the ancients saw as the source of morality and of the arts, and that they proposed to the wise as an ideal. Cicero said that "since all our 'duties' proceed from natural principles, so too should wisdom." To demonstrate this he used the comparison of medicine and dancing, while bringing out the difference: only wisdom exists wholly in each of its acts (*De finibus bonorum et malorum*, 1.3, 7).[1]

We must therefore regain at any cost the sense of this spiritual "naturalness" inherent in our earliest inclinations. Our entire conception of morality depends on this question.

"Inclination" and "Determination"

The term *inclination* also needs to be clarified. It contains a certain orientation that seems contrary to the indetermination of freedom, or

---

1. "Cum autem omnia officia a principiis naturae profiscantur, ab iisdem necesse est proficisci ipsam sapientiam. . . . Sola sapientia in se tota conversa est, quod idem in ceteris artibus non fit."

its "indifference." Here, once again, an analogy is at work. A biological inclination such as hunger or thirst directs the appetite in a determined and compelling way. Yet we would hesitate to say that it is contrary to freedom, since by eating we are achieving the physical strength needed for action. Spiritual inclinations in no way limit freedom but rather incite and develop it. Anyone drawn to a person, a virtue, a science, or an art realizes that his freedom increases through the love he feels and is not diminished by its determination.

As for the inclination to truth and happiness, this empowers us to surmount all limitations and directs us to complete freedom. Spiritual inclinations are intimate determinations that liberate us. The term *determination* we have just used is also analogous, depending on whether the will is determined by something exterior or interior. The will's interior determination shows its power, its ability to impose itself and to endure. It is a sign of great freedom.

We can see from the foregoing how delicate is the use of words when we are dealing with freedom. Our concept, whether of freedom of indifference or of freedom for excellence, imperceptibly modifies the meaning of all the other terms we use in discussing it.

Natural inclinations, which we are about to study, constitute the human person's spiritual spontaneity. They are at the source of voluntary free action and, consequently, of morality. They form what St. Thomas occasionally referred to as the *instinctus rationis,* the rational instinct, which, with Aristotle, he likened to the higher instinct, inspired genius. Here the action of the Holy Spirit intervenes with his gifts, which St. Thomas did not hesitate to call the instinct of the Holy Spirit, *instinctus Spiritus Sancti* (IaIIae, q 68 a 1). Our instinct for truth and goodness, which is at bottom an instinct for God, thus enjoys a relationship with freedom quite different from the animal instinct that first comes to mind. It creates freedom, which can neither exist nor develop without it.

Natural Inclinations and Natural Law

We also have difficulty in forming an idea of the relation between natural inclinations and natural law, because we are used to seeing opposition between law, an external principle, and inclinations, which are interior. Can inclination and law harmonize? Does this not run counter to the requirements of law and morality? How, then, can we claim to base moral law on inclinations, natural though they may be?

Yet this is what St. Thomas did, and apparently he found it no great problem. For him, natural law was the expression, in the form of precepts, of our natural inclinations, which were guided by our inclinations to goodness and truth. Thus natural law, imposed externally when taught, was in reality written in the human heart—that is, in the very nature of our human faculties of reason and will, at the root of free action. This teaching on natural inclinations was fundamental for St. Thomas. It established natural law and provided the basis for morality. Inclinations developed into virtues, which received their beginnings from them and would provide morality with its main categories.

We should add that, in St. Thomas's view, inclinations, like the natural law, were God's most precious work in the human person, a direct, unique participation in his own wisdom, goodness, and freedom and the emanation of the eternal law. St. Thomas's entire moral theology was based largely on his teaching on natural inclinations and on the freedom for the good that activated them.

In separating freedom from natural inclinations and in creating opposition between them with his concept of freedom of indifference, Ockham demolished what we might call the capstone of St. Thomas's doctrinal edifice and completely overturned the structure of moral theology. The demolition extended to the relations and proportions of its elements, and even to the basic concept of what they were. According to Ockham, freedom stood alone in opposition to nature, while law and inclinations were separated and left the virtues marginalized and lifeless. All had to be reconstructed anew.

II. TABLE OF NATURAL INCLINATIONS

In the *prima secundae* there is a remarkable synthesis of the first principles of natural law, beginning with natural inclinations and based on the essential components of human nature (at q 92, a 2). I know of no other work on the subject, either in St. Thomas himself or in contemporary studies, that can parallel the table of inclinations found there. This is not to say that the teaching was innovative; St. Thomas's table adopts and arranges elements provided by Aristotelian and Stoic traditions. Its origin merits a special historical study. Suffice it to say here that it had already been proposed by Cicero in his *De officiis* (1.4), and so clearly that St. Thomas's work might have been an adaptation of it, although he made no mention of the Latin philosopher. The passage is well worth re-reading, for it shows the antiquity and permanence of the teaching proposed by St. Thomas.

Cicero began with the natural tendency to self-preservation found in every living being, the tendency to avoid the harmful and seek all that was needed for life: food, shelter, and so forth. Next came the inclination common to men and animals, leading to sexual union in view of generation and the rearing of offspring. But Cicero immediately pointed out the difference between men and animals. Man, possessing reason, had a sense of past and future; he could use foresight to establish relations between causes. Thus he was better able to provide for the needs, not only of his own family, but of the wider community of language and life formed with others. This was the natural inclination to life in society, of which Cicero was to speak at greater length, and magnificently, in his *De finibus bonorum et malorum* (3.19): "Thus we are disposed by nature to form groups, assemblies, cities. The world . . . is somewhat like a city or commonwealth shared by men and gods, and each one of us is a part of this world."[2]

Another basic inclination was the search for truth, without which there could be no happy life. So truthfulness, simplicity, and sincerity were particularly appropriate to man. Finally, reason conferred upon man the privilege of a sense of order, of fitness, of measure in action and speech, and of beauty. These things together formed *honestas*, the moral quality whose range was divided into four parts: prudence, justice, courage, and temperance. Clearly, this text of Cicero provides the best possible introduction to the teaching of the Angelic Doctor on natural inclinations.

In setting out to describe the precepts of the natural law, St. Thomas was well aware that he was laying the very foundations of moral theory. This was for him the first, and at the same time the most difficult, task of the ethicist. He was at pains therefore to relate these precepts to the first principles of the life of the spirit. As the life of the mind was ruled by its grasp of being, expressed in the speculative intellect by the basic principle that a thing could not simultaneously be affirmed and denied, or even be and not be, so the life of the will was ruled by its perception of the good, which was its end, and was expressed in the principle of the practical reason: "The good is to be done and sought; evil is to be avoided" (Bonum est faciendum et prosequendum, et malum vitandum). This was the foundational principle of natural law, at the base of all other laws. The latter would determine and spell out the specific human good,

2. "Ita que natura sumus apti ad coetus, concilia, civitates. Mundum autem censent . . . esse quasi communem urbem et civitatem hominum et deorum, et unumquemque nostrum eius mundi esse partem."

according to the intrinsic qualities of human nature and the inclinations they engendered.

First came an inclination common to man and to all beings insofar as they were substances: the inclination to self-preservation according to each one's nature, that is, to preserve life and avoid death.

In the second place was a more particular inclination, common to men and animals: that of sexual union between male and female and the rearing of offspring.

Thirdly, man possessed two inclinations proper to his rational nature: the inclination to know the truth about God and the inclination to live in society.

To sum up, we can distinguish five natural inclinations:

1. The inclination to the good
2. The inclination to self-preservation
3. The inclination to sexual union and the rearing of offspring
4. The inclination to the knowledge of truth
5. The inclination to live in society.

These inclinations, serving as principles for the practical reason, were comparable to the first principles of speculative reason. According to St. Thomas they were self-evident to all human beings, before any research and formulation had taken place; they were known intuitively, as it were. They served as premises, on which all reasonings and questionings about human good were based. Doubtless not everyone managed to formulate these principles explicitly; some might even deny the propositions they expressed. Nonetheless, the inclinations existed and were active even when denied, for their profound influence was unaffected by the surface agitation of ideas.

Before moving on to a detailed study of natural inclinations, I will note briefly how this theory was inserted within the context of the *Summa theologiae*.

Although the content of natural law was taken from philosophers such as Aristotle and Cicero, it was built into the setting and structure of a theological work. Here natural law was considered a participation in the eternal law of God and in direct relation to the law revealed in Moses and the Gospels; grace, which completed this law, was included. The movement of the will, naturally tending toward the good, had been carefully studied in the *prima secundae*, in questions 6–10, particularly in question 10, which discussed its natural and free character. The movement of the will was to be developed then through the virtues, among which the principal ones would correspond to the natural inclinations, as Cicero had already pointed out. However, St. Thomas's moral teaching was shaped by the theological virtues, which alone could win happiness for man, that is, the complete fulfillment of his natural inclinations. Notable among these was the desire to see God, which combined the desires for truth and for happiness.

The extreme compression of St. Thomas's exposition of natural inclinations presupposes and requires complementary developments, which can be found in other parts of his work.

III. THE NATURAL INCLINATION TO THE GOOD

We cannot make a complete study of the nature of the good here, but some rectifications of the notion of "the good" are indispensable if we are to regain the dynamic, rich quality of the concept, which was lost with the advent of moral theories of obligation.

1. Definition of "The Good"

Under the influence of modern ethical theories, we have come to think of the good as whatever conforms to moral law and its precepts, and evil as the contrary. Moral law being viewed as a series of imperatives dictated by a will external to ourselves, the concept of good reflects the concept of moral obligation. It tends to become equally static and extrinsic. The notion of the good shrinks, hardens, and is impoverished. Being separated from the notion of happiness and even opposed to it, the good loses one of its chief dimensions. It is as if we must reject the idea of happiness in order to do good. These profound modifications in a fundamental moral concept have been introduced little by little, almost unnoticed by ethicists. Today it is absolutely necessary for us to try to retrieve something of the rich significance that the term "good" held for the ancients. In this way, they will be helping us to rediscover our own profound nature.

The Good Is What Every Being, Every Human Person, Desires

St. Thomas, like Aristotle, did not define the good, for he saw it as a primary notion. Preceding other notions, it could not be defined by them. Or if you will, the perception of the good was a primordial experience; no other could explain it. The good, therefore, could be described only in terms of its effects. Here is St. Thomas's explanation: "Prime realities cannot be expressed by any preceding realities but only in terms of realities that succeed them, as causes are explained by their effects. Since the good moves the appetite, we describe it in terms of the appetite's movement. Hence [Aristotle] says that philosophers stated this well in saying that the good is that which all desire."[3]

This is a far cry from moral theories of obligation. For them, law, the expression of the will of the lawgiver, is in reality the prime notion, determining good and evil. Here good is defined in terms of the attraction it exercises, the love and desire it arouses. The good is the lovable, the desirable.

The Philosopher's definition has universal, metaphysical resonance. Good is what all desire, for it attracts all beings. But we cannot conclude from this, with Leclerq, that this love is blind (as in beings that do not possess intelligence) and has nothing to do with morality. Aristotle set this definition at the beginning of his *Ethics* as the capstone of his work. He was dealing principally with man, since our power to know makes of us the knowing, willing point of convergence for universal good. In this world, man is the receiver of metaphysical good. Through his actions he transforms it, as it were, into moral good. Thus the universal definition of the good applies perfectly to moral good; it even acquires a richer meaning from it, which it does not possess in regard to beings deprived of intelligence: it is now the good known, loved, and willed. In man, therefore, as in all spiritual beings, the notion of good, as of love and desire, is fully realized, being expressed in the general formula *quod omnia appetunt*. It is as if the desire and the good of all beings were concentrated in man, but in a specific, spiritual mode.

We can now move from the universal or metaphysical good to the good that is properly human or moral. Aristotle and St. Thomas could rightly place the definition of universal good at the beginning of their moral teaching. It applied to God in an eminent way, and it was realized in man and in all spiritual beings in a particular manner, as they were the focus of good. The break between metaphysics and ethics was a direct effect of nominalism. Caught up in the current of a moral system

---

3. "Prima autem non possunt notificari per aliqua priora, sed notificantur per posteriora, sicut causae per proprios effectus. Cum autem bonum proprie sit motivum appetitus, describitur bonum per motum appetitus, sicut solet manifestari vis motiva per motum. Et ideo dicit, quod philosophi bene enunciaverunt, bonum esse id quod omnia appetunt" (I *Ethics,* lect. 1).

based on individual freedom, the notion of the good was henceforth confined within the limits of the dispute between freedom and law fixed by the theory of obligation.

To describe the moral dimension of the definition of the good, we may legitimately modify it and say: the good is what all men desire, or again, it is what causes love and desire in every human being, or finally, it is what we desire in all our willing.

Such a formulation may come as a surprise, for at first sight it seems to make all human desires lawful and to blur the distinction between good and evil. Our concept of desire has become so self-centered and subjective that it is difficult for us to use the word in a definition of the good.

The thinking of Aristotle and St. Thomas was more objective than ours. Their definition of the good must be understood in this way: the good is a reality capable of winning the love and desire of all. Thus the good is seen as a reality having universal power over the human heart. This definition is closely linked to the desire for happiness, the first and principal question of moral theory raised in the *Nicomachean Ethics* and the *Summa theologiae*. It is the desire of every heart, as St. Augustine says: "Indeed we all desire the happy life, and everyone would agree with this, almost before the words are out of my mouth" (*De moribus* 3.4). The desire for happiness is like the radiance of the good in all hearts. For Augustine the term *good* meant both goodness and happiness, somewhat as our adjective *good* can designate something good in itself and, at the same time, something that causes pleasure and joy. Clearly, the question of how to discern true good and real happiness still stands. This will be the principal object of the study of beatitude.

The Universality of the Good

We should stress the universal dimension of the desire for the good: the good is what *all* beings, or *all* persons, desire. Because of this universality, the desire for the good is distinguished from particular desires, which are limited to one human dimension or one group of people. The good, in the full sense of the word, applies to everyone and surpasses the limits of other desires. We have here a principle of distinction among goods and desires. We might deduce from this universality a moral rule, as Kant did: the good is what pleases everyone, as contrasted with what pleases just one or a few. However, we cannot oppose the universal will and particular desires, with Kant. The good, by its very universality, can include limited desires while imposing a just measure upon them through reason and the virtues. The good can also attract and engage the entire person, and in this it can clearly be seen as "that which all desire."

The greatest difficulty in speaking of realities such as these comes from the limitations of our experience. We cannot encounter universal good directly, or the love and desire it arouses. No more can we adequately express it. We are driven to the most abstract terms, and these say least to us. In order to understand the definition of the good, we need to start with limited goods we can experience directly, and with the attraction they have for us. Through these various experiences—and sometimes one is enough, if we are keen—we can perceive what the good is and, along with it, what desire and love for the good are.[4] After even one deep, personal experience, we may be able to grasp the definition of the good that we are discussing. This is the reality that gives rise to our total desire and love, in a universal dimension.

The good is a pristine concept and reality, powerful enough to produce the most profound, strong attraction in us, utterly personal and open. It corresponds to truth, which is also endemic in our experience. Appreciation of the good, like taste, is never defined; nor is the vision of light. Yet in the depths of every person there is a sense of the good and the true. These perceptions are inevitably at work within, through all our willings and actions, even if, as in the case of evil and deceit,

---

4. We can reread and complete here the text where St. Augustine shows the way to "the good": "Behold, and again see if you can. Certainly you love only the good, because the earth is good by the height of its mountains, the moderate elevation of its hills, and the evenness of its fields; and good is the farm that is pleasant and fertile; and good is the house that is arranged throughout in symmetrical proportions and is spacious and bright; and good are the animals, animate bodies; and good is the mild and salubrious air; and good is health without pains and weariness; and good is the countenance of man with regular features, a cheerful expression, and a glowing color; and good is the soul of a friend with the sweetness of concord and the fidelity of love; and good is the just man; and good are riches because they readily assist us; and good is the heaven with its own sun, moon and stars; and good are the angels by their holy obedience; and good is the lecture that graciously instructs and suitably admonishes the listener; and good is the poem with its measured rhythm and the seriousness of its thoughts.

"But why should I add still more? This good and that good; take away this and that, and see good itself if you can; so you will see God who is good not by another good, but is the good of every good. For in all these good things, either those which I have enumerated, or any others which are seen or thought, we would be unable to call one better than the other, if we judge in accordance with the truth, if the idea of good itself had not been impressed upon us, according to which we approve of something as good, and also prefer one good to another. Thus God is to be loved, not as this or that good, but as good itself. For the good of the soul that is to be sought is not that over which one flies by judging, but that to which one adheres by loving, and what is this but God? Not the good soul, nor the good angel, nor the good heaven, but the good good" (*De trinitate* 8.3.4 [Fathers of the Church, vol. 45]).

they run contrary to them. They are truly the essential elements of our spiritual nature. We must return to them, however great the difficulty, if we would lay a solid foundation for moral theory.

2. The Notion of Good: Perfection, Happiness, Attainment of the Goal

The Good Considered as Perfection and Happiness

The notion of the good is a rich one. Its first characteristic is perfection, for, as St. Thomas says on defining the good in general, "To be is to desire perfection."[5] The good cannot be reduced to the mean, still less to the minimum that a legal obligation might require. The very notion of the good implies the idea of perfection, of an excellence that attracts; from this comes a desire for the perfection of the one so drawn. Naturally, perfection will vary as beings differ. The perfection of a plant or animal is one thing; that of a person is another matter, although the person may also possess perfection in the biological order—health or vigor, for example. The perfection proper to the human person comes from the intellect and will, from the power to love and will the good as such, to know it and be open to it in its universality. We could therefore define the human person as a being aspiring to perfection and the plenitude of goodness. In this person, the notion of the good and of perfection is realized in a unique way, corresponding exactly to his condition of being free, for an essential feature of freedom is the thrust toward excellence. In the human person the perfection of the good coincides with the fulness of freedom.

We should note, however, that when the term *perfection* is applied to human beings, there is always a certain relativity. This is the result of the limitations of the human condition and the length of time required to attain perfection. Human action is never completely perfect in this life.

The plenitude of goodness was expressed in Boethius's somewhat materialistic concept of the perfect state, which consisted in the accumulation (*aggregatio*) of all goods. For St. Thomas there was no separation between the ideas of the good and of happiness, but rather a reciprocal

---

5. "Ratio enim boni in hoc consistit quod aliquid sit appetibile; unde Philosophus in I Eth., dicit quod 'bonum est quod omnia appetunt'. Manifestum est autem quod unumquodque est appetibile secundum quod est perfectum, nam omnia appetunt suam perfectionem" (I q 5 a 1).

implication: the good was the cause of happiness, and happiness was the plenitude of the good. Yet they could be distinguished by a certain nuance: the good resided in the objective reality, while happiness subsisted in the subject who experienced the good. This distinction could be made, however, only on condition that the opposition of a later age—between subject and object—not be introduced here; for St. Thomas's overriding view was of the coordination that united them.

An ethical view of the good understood in this light would be strongly oriented toward perfection as well as the search for happiness. Perfection and happiness were two aspects of the one object of morality, *bonum,* the good. In theology this concept doubtless drew its inspiration from the Genesis account of creation, where the Vulgate text was quoted: "God saw that it was good . . . God saw all that he had made, and indeed it was very good" (Gen 1:25, 31).

The separation between the idea of moral good and the notions of perfection and happiness was without doubt one of the most serious events in the history of Western ethics. It would have been unimaginable for St. Thomas and the Fathers of the Church. The entire structure of morality was to feel the effects.

The Good as an End

Since the good has been defined as "that which every being desires," it is also viewed as an end for any creature loving and desiring it (compare the analysis of the good as a final cause in Ia, q 5 a 4). This is particularly true of man, whose ability to know the good, as well as his own orientation to it, gives him control over his actions. We might also define man as one who acts in view of the good (even when he sins), or as one who acts in view of an end.

Similarly, moral action will essentially be action performed with some end in view. This is what St. Thomas clearly affirms in his study of finality, which he placed at the beginning of his moral theology: "The object of the will is the end and the good. Therefore all human actions are done with an end in view" (IaIIae, q 1 a 1). He confirms this by saying, "It is a property of rational nature to tend to an end, moving toward it of its own accord" (a 2). The moral order, too, will be dominated by finality: "Actions are called human insofar as they proceed from deliberation and will. Now the object of the will is the good and the end. It is therefore clear that the principle of human actions, insofar as they are human, is the end. And this is likewise their termination. . . . And since, as Ambrose says in his commentary on Luke, 'Morality is a properly human thing,' moral acts are properly specified by their end; for moral acts and human acts are one and the same thing" (a 3).

Finality will also serve to define the voluntary character of human actions: "Since man (in contrast with plants and animals) is one who knows best [*maxime*] the object of his work and moves toward it of his own accord, the voluntary is found chiefly in human actions" (q 6, a 1). It could not be put more explicitly: after the good, finality is the first essential element of human or moral action—these two are one for St. Thomas. Like the attractiveness of the good, this finality is not abstract or purely metaphysical. It has to do with the nature of a person's desire and love, of which he is very conscious. The analysis of finality is continued in the study of happiness, and of the variety of goods which arouse love and desire.

Furthermore the idea of finality, like that of the good, will acquire a universal dimension. It will regulate all of a person's actions and give rise to a hierarchy of interrelated ends dominated by one ultimate end. Finality transcends the individual to give direction to communities and even to all humanity in seeking a common, ultimate end. It may further draw together all other creatures, each according to its own nature (IaIIae, q 1 a 6–8).

St. Thomas's morality may thus be called a morality of finality and of the last end, as well as a morality of the good. In this it is profoundly human as well as divine, for finality thus conceived relates us directly to God. It makes us sharers in divine goodness and freedom, in a work wholly finalized by the good. Once again we rediscover the freedom for excellence, whose development is determined by the excellence of the good, its end and perfection.

The contrast between this moral theory, wholly directed to the good as its end, and the moral theory of the modern manuals, is great indeed. The latter's finality is limited to the subjective intention of the agent and plays only a secondary role in the moral quality of actions; the study of our ultimate end is either suppressed altogether or at least dissociated from the search for happiness.

A brief but important note should be added here. Finality, like the good, corresponds to love and desire, and it will vary according to the nature of the love. St. Thomas distinguishes two kinds of love. There is the love of concupiscence or desire, which consists in loving a good for some other reason than itself alone. For example, I may love some good for my own sake. This is the way I love wine. Then there is the love of friendship, which consists in loving a good, a person in fact, in himself and for his own sake. The love of friendship is love in the proper sense.

Love of concupiscence is ordered to it. The idea of the end is clearly linked with desire, as being its object. But as a good and perfection, the end is also the object of the love of friendship, and this aspect is primary. The end is the term of voluntary intention and desire precisely because it points to a good that is lovable in itself and for itself. This is why the intention of the one who loves cannot and will not go further and consider this good as a means to some other end. This is true particularly of our last end, which is our last end because it is the object of our absolute love. The end is therefore the object of love and desire, and of the love of friendship, but of the latter primarily because it is the good, properly so-called.

Here we encounter a new breach. After St. Thomas a separation was made between desire on the part of the subject and the love of friendship which is open to the object. Finality toppled over, so to speak, into the field of subjective desire and lost much of its objective force. From this came the danger of subjectivism, which gives rise today to a questioning of the value of finality in ethics, and any emphasis on desire and love. But at the same time finality has acquired a rigid objectivity when applied to the external world; this can be seen in modern technology, which is entirely geared to utility. The sense of properly moral finality, the sense that is determined by human excellence, by all that merits the love of friendship, has been lost.

The "Honest," "Useful," and "Delightful" Good

In his *prima pars*, question 5, a 6, St. Thomas concludes his study of the good by introducing a distinction, which applies primarily to human or moral good, and which receives a general treatment here. It is the classic distinction between the "honest," "useful," and "delightful" good. In the *De officiis*, the discussion initiated by Cicero begins with a criticism of Epicureanism, which identifies the good with the voluptuous or pleasurable, that is, the "delightful" good. The discussion reaches its climax with the establishment of the primacy of the "honest" good over the "useful": only the "honest" good is truly useful. The "honest" good is the good that deserves to be loved for its own sake, beyond all interested or utilitarian considerations. It is identified with virtue.[6] For St. Thomas, too, the "honest" good means moral excellence at its highest, in conformity with man's rational nature. The notion of

6. Cf. in *De finibus bonorum et malorum* (5.22–23), the presentation of "honestas" as the essence of moral excellence, formed by the concurrence of all the virtues.

good finds its proper and principal realization in the "honest" good, and only secondarily in the "useful" or "delightful" good.

We should note, however, that St. Thomas gives new meaning to this last. It need not refer only to the sensual pleasure with which Epicureans identified the good; it can also signify delight, the repose of the appetite or the joy found in the possession of the honest good. Understood thus, this concept could be used in the definition of beatitude as the enjoyment flowing from the vision of God. This threefold division of goods corresponds exactly to the three kinds of friendship distinguished by Aristotle: friendship based on pleasure, usefulness, and virtue.

The "honest" good, being sought in itself and for its own sake, has the character of an end in relation to intention and desire. It engenders love in the true sense of the word—friendship. The "useful" good has the character of a means or way of attaining the "honest" good. It arouses the love of concupiscence or desire. The "honest" good is the culmination of goodness. The concept is taken from the moral order, proper to man, but it can also be applied in general to God and the angels directly, and to other beings by analogy. We might say that for St. Thomas, and in the best tradition of the ancients, the "honest" good is at the center of the moral, and even the universal, order of goodness.

We note that St. Thomas gives a particularly realistic and objective quality to the "honest" good. It designates the reality, loved for its own sake, toward which the will moves. "Sicut quaedam res in quam per se appetitus tendit, vocatur honestum, quia honestum dicitur quod per se desideratur." The subjective dimension of the "honest" good is called the repose of the appetite in the thing loved ("quies in re desiderata est delectatio"). This emphasis on the realistic and objective aspect of the "honest" good is, I believe, special to Christian thought in its adaptation of the ideas and teachings of the thought of antiquity.

In speaking of the good, I felt I had to use quotation marks for the word *honest* because of the complete devaluation of this term in modern languages. Behind this a radical drama has been played out in the world of ethics. For both Cicero and St. Thomas, "honesty" or "the honest good" conveyed the idea of moral excellence. "Honesty" meant the best, it was the quality proper to man; it gave meaning to his life and value to his actions.

Now the term *honesty* has been so reduced and disqualified that translators hardly dare use it today, and they search in vain for a replacement. The reason is that in modern textbooks of ethics, honesty has been reduced to a simple respect for law. It means keeping on the right side of the law, keeping out of trouble. It has been child's play for philosophical and literary critics to unmask the hypocrisy behind this legalism, faulting it for weakness and constraint. More is the pity: honesty, once demolished, has not been replaced. We no longer have adequate terms to designate moral excellence as such. Happily, popular language—which is often more faithful and closer to human experience—has preserved a certain understanding of the word honesty and an esteem for it. There is a concern for personal honesty, honesty in business and in human relations, and this gives us something of an idea of the strength and excellence which the term "honesty" connotes. It is well worth the effort to recapture this; we shall once more understand that honesty is not simply keeping the law, but is at the roots of the most authentic human values.

The Good Is Generous, Fruitful

In order to reach an adequate understanding of the good, we need to consider the generosity this concept implies. It can be seen in the Neoplatonic adage "Goodness is diffusive of itself" (*diffusivum sui*). Goodness radiates; it is communicative, active, generous. This quality of goodness is best shown in the divine work of creation and providence. The closer we come to this diffusive, communicative goodness, the more we share in its power of radiance and gift. The term *bounty* applied to the human sphere has retained this nuance of generosity, of the inclination to give without expecting a return. This quality incites love and friendship more than any other, but it has been relegated excessively to the psychological plane. It indicates an essential note of moral goodness and goodness in general—its propensity for communication.

The "generosity" of goodness should also be understood in the sense of fruitfulness. In the Gospel parables, goodness is likened to a seed sown in the human heart, communicating its life-giving power. It grows until the harvest, that is, until we have become capable of producing many works useful to others. The good diffuses itself as a source of life, making us fruitful when we are open to it, while evil renders us sterile.

The generosity and fruitfulness of the good correspond perfectly to freedom for excellence, for this freedom develops, after a lengthy period of maturation, by forming and producing works comparable to savory, nourishing fruits offered to all.

Once again we note the contrast with ethical systems of obligation, in which the good has become immobile and stiff, like all the legal commands and prohibitions. It has been set in opposition to freedom, like a challenge or a hedge. It no longer bespeaks the generosity that spontaneously transcends limitations, but rather evokes the duties which maintain them. Generosity and fruitfulness are refugees, along with freedom; there is no room for them in duty-driven ethics.

3. The Good Proper to Man Is the Known Good

The good of a being lies in the perfection proper to its nature. Human good will be a good conformed to the human intellect, as grasped by our distinctive faculty. This is "the known good" (*bonum apprehensum*).

More precisely, we are dealing here with the practical reason, which grasps the good in view of action and which shares in working it out up to its final execution. This is not the abstract reason, which functions at the level of ideas or is content to tell the will what ought to be done, as it is written in the law and in textbooks of ethics, eventually refining it with the help of a syllogism deduced from principles. Such a reason, no matter how practical we declare it to be, still remains outside the sphere of moral action. It is confined too much to judgment and leaves execution to the will.

St. Thomas was dealing with a reason that really took part in the action because of its close, vital collaboration with the "appetite" and its movements, with the will, and with the human inclinations to the good. Choice, too, the essence of moral action, would be inseparable from the work of reason, which assessed the appropriate good, and of the will, which perceived and experienced this good as suitable. Similarly, the virtue of prudence could not function or even exist without courage, temperance, and justice.

As it sets about its work of research, the practical reason receives a certain perception of the good and a feeling for it from the natural inclination we are discussing. This inclination accompanies the practical reason throughout its work of research. With moral progress in virtue this pristine moral sense develops a clearer knowledge and a clearer taste for the good. Thus there is formed within us what St. Thomas calls a "connaturality" for the good, a special capacity conferred by each virtue in its own setting, which allows us to discern and esteem the good with swift, sure judgment, often more penetrating than the reasonings of the learned.

The known good is not to be confused with knowledge conveyed to the conscience by way of commands. It brings a deeper perception of the harmony between the good indicated by reason and the will that experiences it as such, between this particular good and the person who knows and loves it, who judges and chooses it in this concrete action undertaken in an individual way.

Despite their difference, we should not separate the moral knowledge of the learned and the concrete judgment of the virtuous person, for all moral knowledge is ordered to the formation of prudent judgment and attains its own perfection therein. There is a reciprocal influence between the prudential judgment, with the ensuing good action, and the wisdom and reflection of the scholar, owing to the knowledge of the good experienced and the perfecting of both reason and will. We understand better, and in a different way, the good we have accomplished.

The known good includes, therefore, all the knowledge of goodness that we can gain through study, education, reflection, perception, and, above all, personal experience.

Real and Apparent Good

In spite of the various sources of moral knowledge at our disposal, it can happen that our assessment of the good does not coincide with the real good, and may even oppose it. We can mistake evil for good and good for evil. The causes of our error may be as many as the elements that go to make up our judgment and practical choices. There are the limitations of a mind, which can go astray in its reasoning about moral matters as well as other things, because of limited vision, inattention, lack of penetration or inexperience. Then, too, there are the dispositions of the will and emotions. We judge things from where we are; passions such as anger influence our perception of the good and cause hasty, agitated judgments. Our will itself can be perverted by an excessive attachment such as avarice or by a strong dislike of anything that opposes it, as in the case of jealousy or of hatred.

The gap between the known good and the real good is at the root of sin and can be expressed by the distinction between the "real" and "apparent" good. To earn money and amass a fortune unjustly is an apparent good. It has a certain feel of reality and a strong appeal to the human heart, but in truth it is actually more real as an evil because injustice corrupts the heart while money can never satisfy it. The entire force of temptation lies precisely in the appearance of good with which it captivates the mind and heart. Evil action reinforces the illusion—this is its greatest threat—and we end by thinking as we have acted. Repeated acts of injustice deform the judgment even as they corrupt the will.

Nonetheless, however we may sin, in the depths of our hearts there will always be an inclination to goodness and truth. Without this, the appearance of good—which evil has to wear in order to attract and deceive us—could not be formed. Thus, at the center of the sinful will, a division and an inescapable contradiction is set up between the attraction of the good (which is a part of its very nature) and the evil that it does, between the sense of truth that comes from reason and the play of appearances that captivate the will. It knows no peace.

In spite of all the complexity of the problem of sin and the attraction for evil which can engender passion and vice, it still remains true that the human reason and will are profoundly oriented to the true good and can never be satisfied without it. The "known good," therefore, which is proper to man, is always ordered to the real good, however deeply it may be hidden beneath layers of evil. In this context, a moral choice is not made between good and evil, seen as contraries according to the determination of the law, as in the theory of freedom of indifference. Rather, it is a choice between two goods, the one real and the other apparent. A moral choice requires a judgment about the reality and truth of the good presented, while evil enters only through lying and duplicity. The law intervenes here to enlighten the reason as to the nature and character of things.

Finally we should note that the affirmation that the proper good of man is the good insofar as it is known should not be understood in a subjective sense, as if the good were to be identified with our ideas, feelings, or opinions about it. According to St. Thomas, this would be directly contrary to the very notion of truth, which designates the reality of being grasped in itself by reason. It would also run counter to the love of friendship, which inclines us to love something in itself and for its own sake. The human subject makes and creates neither truth nor goodness; it comes to the fulness of its own being by opening itself to the truth through reason and to goodness through an upright love. A subjective notion of truth and goodness is without any doubt one of the most subtle, insidious temptations of the mind. It imprisons and binds the spirit, often in the name of reason, in a world of mere appearances.

4. "Bonum Est Faciendum, Malum Est Vitandum"

According to St. Thomas, the natural inclination to the good is expressed in the proposition that good is to be done and evil avoided. This proposition was handed down by tradition as the first principle of moral life. He therefore made of it the first principle of the practical reason, corresponding to that of the speculative reason.

The translation and interpretation of this principle seem obvious. Under the influence of schools of duty-driven morality, however, it is usually thought of as the expression of duty seen as the basic impulse, and is translated in this sense: we must do good and avoid evil, that is to say, we have an obligation to do good and avoid evil.

Now for St. Thomas the feeling of obligation did not come first. It was rooted in the natural inclinations toward truth and goodness and was based on the attraction and behest of the true good. Therefore we should attribute a different meaning to the proposition "Bonum est faciendum, malum est vitandum," if we want it to be truly a first principle, the expression of what is most fundamental in moral life.

Our interpretation will be made at two levels, that of the natural inclination to the good, which is at the source of all moral action, and that of the concrete choice, where the moral action takes place.

a. At the level of the natural inclination to the good, the principle "bonum est faciendum, malum est vitandum" is a direct expression of this inclination, and means: everyone spontaneously desires what appears as good and spontaneously avoids what appears as evil; our natural tendency is to do the one and avoid the other. It is the expression of a primordial spiritual instinct, the basic sense of good and evil. This principle applies at all levels of human life, in our reactions to good and evil, happiness and suffering, in all situations, but it is chiefly verified at the moral level. In fact, it is by its very essence a law we cannot break. We cannot help aspiring to the good and fleeing from evil as we see and experience them.

b. At the level of concrete choice, the principle "bonum est faciendum, malum est vitandum" is ordered to concrete action. It is at this level that the moral question of choice is posed: the discernment of the real and apparent good, the real and apparent evil. I may make my fortune by unjust means or renounce wealth in favor of justice. Now our principle is going to express the pressure and demands of the true good and right reason upon our will. Spelled out in practical terms, it means: the true good is to be done in spite of the evil appearance it presents to me (I lose the opportunity to make a fortune); the true evil is to be avoided in spite of the appearance of good it offers and the attraction it exercises over me. The power, the deep-rooted pressure exerted by the sense of truth and goodness within my reason and conscience is at the origin of my sense of moral obligation, but the latter does not exhaust its content, since this inclination carries me beyond it, toward a growth in love for the good and knowledge of the truth.

Such is the moral sense that the virtues strengthen—particularly justice, which is a will, a firm and constant love for what is just. In the distinction between the real and apparent good, which directs the application of the principle "bonum est faciendum, malum est vitandum," the principal role is that of prudence, the virtue of moral discernment: not a prudence intimidated by fear of the law and sin, but a far-seeing and courageous virtue, enterprising, too, for its object is to have us do as well as we can.

The General Influence of the Inclination to the Good

The natural inclination to goodness comes first, at the beginning of the moral order. Its influence is general, for it is the primordial movement of the will that affects the entire field of morality. An action is moral in the measure in which it is voluntary and relates to the good. The natural inclinations observed in the other human faculties and powers are included under the inclination to the good and constitute various kinds of goods, which awaken our desire and love.

In explaining natural inclinations, St. Thomas is careful to point out their rootedness in human nature at its principal levels. The human person is a microcosm. There is one part held in common with all substances, be they animate, such as plants, or inanimate, such as rocks; this is called the physical, chemical, and biological level. Another part is shared with the animals—the psychic level. Finally, there is the part proper to beings endowed with reason; this is the rational or spiritual level.

We should not be misled by this division. These parts are not separated within the person as they are in nature. They are joined together in a natural unity comparable to the unity of the members of the body, to use the classic analogy. The rational part encompasses the biological and psychical parts, giving them a new dimension and capacities. St. Thomas gives strong emphasis to this association when he discusses the substantial unity of the human composite.

We shall look at the chief natural inclinations that actualize the inclination to the good, keeping in mind at the same time their integration within the human person. They are, first, the inclination to self-preservation, common to human beings and all substances; next, the inclination to sexual union, shared by human beings and animals; finally, the two spiritual inclinations: to truth, and to life in society.

We shall change the order, placing the inclination to sexual union last, for it seems useful to discuss the human dimension of this at greater length and to see how the other inclinations work together with it.

IV. THE NATURAL INCLINATION
TO SELF-PRESERVATION

The first human inclination toward the good is common to all "substances": self-preservation in accordance with the nature of each, and the avoidance of all that is harmful to this.

This inclination is basic. It concerns our very being and lies at the root of all our feelings and actions. The universality of the inclination shows its primordial character. It is a substantial part of us and assures our continuance in existence.

Substance and Person

The term *substance* calls for some explanation. Substance can be defined as what is permanent in a being subject to change. The word comes from the Latin *substare,* to stand under. Again, it is that which exists of itself; finally, substance refers to what is essential to a thought or discourse. As we reflect on this, we observe that this notion is best realized not in inanimate beings, as we might easily suppose, but in spiritual beings such as the human person, precisely as person. Actually, *person* designates the subject that subsists within us and develops through all the changes in life and action. It is the center of unity in a multiplicity of lived experiences. At the same time, because we have the power to act freely, of our own accord, we show that we possess being in our own right and that we are, therefore, substances insofar as we are persons. In us, substance designates our being, our existence and our essence.

It is absolutely necessary to understand this analogical dimension of the meaning of "substance" when we apply it to human nature and its inclinations. The term can have a minimum of meaning, as in the case of inanimate beings, which are merely substances (if indeed they are substances strictly speaking), and a maximum of content when we are considering a spiritual, personal nature. Here it reaches its peak.

The Desire to Be and to Live

It follows that the natural inclination to self-preservation that results from our being a substance is not blind and totally unconscious, like the instincts of natural beings or chemical bodies, nor is it determining as are physical laws. Indeed, this inclination is so profound that we are often not clearly aware of it, but it is at work within us as the very source of all our free and conscious willing. It produces our spontaneous desire to be and to live. This desire cannot be commanded, yet it does not constrain us. It does not run counter to our freedom, but rather causes and inspires it. The inclination to self-preservation is at the source of life and action. It carries us toward the primary good of existence according to our proper nature, as living beings, rational and free.

The Natural Love of Self

Ethicists see in the inclination to self-preservation the foundation for the right to legitimate self-defense. We can also see in it the basis for the duty to respect the life of others, expressed in the precept "You shall not kill." But this inclination is richer and more positive than such a utilization would imply, true though it is.

The inclination to be is the direct source of our spontaneous, natural love of self.[7] It forms within us our desire for the most natural goods, such as life and health. It leads us to seek everything we need for subsistence—food, clothing, and shelter. It spurs us on to action, persuades us to find rest in sleep. Through its promptings we make progress in acquiring and using these goods in proper measure.

We are particularly conscious of this inclination when something happens to contradict it. We notice it in our spontaneous reaction to sickness, sorrow, injury and death, hunger and privation, fear and suffering. Like the desire to be and to live, it is impaired by the temptation to despair and suicide, by our vertigo at the brink of nothingness.

However, we cannot limit the inclination to self-preservation to the physical plane, where it first appears. It is more radically operative on the spiritual level, where it tends to coincide with our natural sense of the good. It forms within us the primary love of self on which love of neighbor is based, prior to any egotistic reaction. It is the source of our

7. See, for example, Cicero's beautiful pages on the subject in *De finibus bonorum et malorum* (5.9ff).

need to love. This spiritual inclination, often overlaid with superficial desires, can predominate over all the others when it gains strength, even over love of health and bodily life. We see this in people who endure privation and suffering to the point of giving their lives for those they love, or for the truth, for justice, or for their faith. In doing this, they love themselves in a nobler way, as Aristotle remarked.

A Dynamic Inclination

Contrary to what might be implied by the expression *self-preservation,* this natural inclination is not "conservative" as opposed to "progressive." The conservation of a living being is by its very nature dynamic. It engenders progress and envisions perfection in all areas of human activity, at the material as well as intellectual and spiritual levels. In particular, it is found at the source of the slow progress of freedom we have discussed; this freedom leads it gradually, through education, to maturity.

Furthermore, the inclination to self-preservation and development, when it belongs to a spiritual nature, is capable of redoubling its potential in the human person, owing to the love of friendship, which provides its highest perfection. When we love others as ourself, we begin to seek their preservation and well-being as our own, even while remaining distinct from them. The negative commandments, "You shall not kill, you shall not covet your neighbor's goods," give way to positive and dynamic precepts: "You shall love your neighbor as yourself," and the golden rule, which sums up the Law and the Prophets in the Sermon on the Mount.[8]

8. In *De finibus bonorum et malorum* (5.9, 23), Cicero shows how the inclination to self-preservation and love of self lead finally to the "caritas generis humani" which is expressed in the virtue of justice. In regard to natural love of self a comparison of the thought of St. Thomas with that of Rousseau may also be insightful.

For Rousseau, the concrete individual is naturally good; it is society that corrupts him. Prophet of natural goodness, Rousseau will always stand by his personal conscience, as Diderot maliciously observes, and will refuse to submit to the judgment of anyone, even God who alone can ratify the judgment of his conscience. For St. Thomas, the individual man is a mixture of natural good, coming from God, and sin, caused by human deficiency. Love of self is good in its beginning, but is vitiated by self-love, which is a turning back upon self, the opposite of openness to God and others. Concrete love of self needs to be purified, and this begins with the submission of one's judgment to God and to the light of his truth, and with the admission of fault, which brings about conversion under the action of grace.

Society, too, is a mixed reality. It originates in a good natural inclination tending to

Seen thus, the natural inclination to self-preservation is a certain participation in the love with which God loves himself in his own essence and in his works, causing him to will the conservation and perfection of all beings, loved by him. It gives us the foundation of our share in the freedom of God.

A person's natural inclination to be is developed and strengthened by the virtues. This is especially true of hope (first natural, then supernatural), which kindles the joy of living, and courage, which sustains and fosters hope in the presence of dangers and obstacles. But these virtues cannot be maintained without others, notably justice, which bears directly upon the inclination to life in society. In the context of justice, the natural inclination to be will supply the foundation for a series of rights belonging to everyone: the right to preserve being and life, to obtain the necessary means of subsistence, as well as whatever would serve to promote a certain degree of material, intellectual, and moral development.

Being fundamental, the inclination to be and to live is found in a certain sense at the root of the other inclinations and develops in collaboration with them. The same is true of the various virtues related to these inclinations.

V. THE NATURAL INCLINATION TO KNOWLEDGE OF THE TRUTH

The Desire to Know

The human inclination to know the truth is so natural that it constitutes, so to speak, human intelligence. It coincides with the definition of man as a "rational animal." Love of truth is, in this sense, the most human of all desires. It is at the origin of science in every field. We see it in the simple curiosity, so ingrained in all of us and particularly in children that we might almost be defined as curious animals. We are forever attracted by novelty, like the Athenians in the time of St. Paul, or the readers of today's papers.

---

create friendship between people, but is in fact vitiated by human sin, which tends to proliferate as more and more relationships are formed. Society too, therefore, needs conversion and purification.

The work of grace does not consist in destroying the natural love of self and of life in society, on account of sin, but in restoring these to their original goodness, by pointing them to a love and a goodness that transcend the human. Charity is the perfect fulfillment of love of self and neighbor.

Aristotle declared that the desire to know was at the origin of philosophy. "All men have a natural desire to know. This can be seen in the way we use our senses. We love to use our senses, even more than we need, and especially our eyes. Even when there is nothing to do, we delight in looking around. The reason for this is that sight is the sense most closely linked with knowledge; it enables us to see the difference between things most clearly" (*Metaphysics* 1.1). It was because of their astonishment and admiration for the wonders of the natural world that men first began to philosophize (cf. *Metaphysics* 1, 982 b. 11; St. Thomas, lect. 3).[9]

Curiosity at the sense level develops into intellectual curiosity, resulting in the formation of the various sciences—first the physical ones, then the philosophical. This curiosity is activated by the desire to get back to first causes, the sources of being and truth, first in the world and then in humankind. Socrates focused his search for truth on man, with his famous axiom "Know thyself!" Thus the search for truth took on its human dimension and called for sincerity, uprightness, candor. St. Augustine adopted the Socratic principle and deepened it in the light of Christian experience: "Would that I might know myself, that I might know Thee!" The discovery of divine light reveals us to ourselves. "I shall enter within, I shall gaze with the eye of my soul, and beyond this inward vision, beyond understanding, I shall look upon unchanging light. . . . It is beyond me, because it made me, and I am beneath it because I was made by it. Whoever knows the truth knows this light, and knowing it, knows eternity. Love knows it" (*Confessions* 7.10.16). St. Augustine's entire life, recounted in the *Confessions,* was inspired by a thirst for truth. Truth lit up man's path to God: "Understand, if you can, that God is truth (Wisdom 9:15). For it is written that 'God is light' (1 Jn 1:5), not the light you see with your eyes but the light your heart sees, when you hear the words 'This is the truth'" (*De trinitate* 8.2.3).

Love of truth leads to the contemplative life, where our principal occupation consists in seeking, considering, and enjoying the truth. This was already characteristic of philosophers such as Plato, Aristotle, and Cicero. It took on new intensity and vigor in the Christian tradition. The *Summa theologiae* was inspired by a supreme love of truth. First and foremost a contemplative work, it verified the Augustinian definition of beatitude as delight in the truth, *gaudium de veritate.*

9. Cicero writes: "Man's search for truth and his pursuit of it is primordial. Once freed from the busy cares of life, we give ourselves up to the desire to see, understand, learn. We believe that we must know things hidden or wonderful, if we would enjoy the happy life" (*De Officiis,* 1.4).

Rediscovering the Truth

A challenging task faces us today: to get in touch with our natural desire for truth and to restore to the word "truth" its pristine force. Under the influence of nominalism, truth in philosophy has become abstract and conceptual; in the sciences, depersonalized and constricted. We have confused it with the ideas, formulas, and words we use to express it, and which we think encapsulate it. We are left with mere reflections and imitations.

This is extremely regrettable, especially in ethics. Since it is ordered to action, ethics cannot exist or function if it brackets the human subject, the person who acts. The human dimension of moral truth must therefore be retrieved.

Through personal experience we once more see the principal intellectual virtues as human qualities needed for our grasp and enjoyment of truth. Such are wisdom, the capacity for universal, synthetic judgment; understanding, the ability to penetrate to the heart of things; and knowledge, the power of comprehension and discovery in the various fields of study.

The ethicist, and everyone else as well, will have a special interest in the virtue of prudence, which cries out for rediscovery perhaps more than any other. Prudence is a quality, a perfection of the practical reason and the will together; it combines a penetrating discernment, sharpened by active experience, with the decisiveness of the courageous, disciplined person.

When faith intervenes, these virtues receive a new dimension, something like an instinct for divine truth, enhanced by the gifts of the Holy Spirit, which perfects the intellectual gifts of wisdom, understanding, knowledge, and counsel.

Rights and Duties in Regard to Truth

The inclination to truth lays the natural foundation for our right to receive all we need in developing our minds—instruction, provided by our family or society. Corresponding to this right is our basic responsibility to seek the truth and to cultivate our minds, particularly in the realm of ethics, which concerns people more directly. The obligation to seek the truth is an interior one. It is one aspect of our desire for truth and shows its claim on us. Part of the necessary "discipline" needed if the virtues culminating in prudence are to be formed within us, it requires us to learn moral precepts, to consider carefully the circumstances of our actions, and to maintain our understanding and love of truth. We might wonder whether, over recent centuries, the development of a love for truth and knowledge has been neglected. Perhaps we have been satisfied with mere information on the text and tenor of the law.

As we saw with regard to our sense of the good, our inclination to truth carries us beyond the question of rights and responsibilities to a steady progress in our knowledge of the truth, particularly at the moral and spiritual level. Concern for this should be stronger than ever among Christians and in theology, under the impulse of faith, which seeks to comprehend the object of its love. The Augustinian formula "faith seeking understanding" (*fides quaerens intellectum*) is at the origin of sacred science. This progress does not consist so much in the accumulation of learning and information as in the deepening of fundamental truths and in the enrichment and maturation of the mind, which give it its power and breadth.

The Question of Truth Today

The question of truth is not merely philosophic or scientific. It has a history and has assumed new forms, which affect ordinary people as well as scholars.

Paradoxically, the development of modern sciences, which has extended human knowledge beyond all imagination, has boomeranged in a general relativism in all areas of learning and even in the perception of truth. The temptation to determinism in regard to scientific truth has been followed by the temptation to relativity in all branches of science and truth. Truth has become dependent on the thinker. It is bound up with his history, milieu, culture, interests, and social or political pressures. We say, therefore, "To each his truth," which amounts to a frank admission that there is no truth any more.

The issue is intensified and becomes dramatic when we see a political regime based on an ideology identifying truth with political or economic expediency, imposing upon an entire people a network of lies, which enmeshes their lives and all their activities. Russian dissidents understood this clearly when they proposed as a first rule in their struggle for freedom never to lie to themselves and never to become part of the logic of the system by consenting to its lies, even in trifling matters.[10]

10. See further, in testimony of Soljenitzyn's truth and justice, Vaclaw Havel's book, *Il potere dei senza potere* (CSEO 1979), extolling "life in the truth" as opposed to "post-capitalist" dictatorship. He shows that the simple act of advertising propaganda in a store front leads to "a life of lies."

The problem of truth is not restricted to Eastern regimes. We find it in sometimes more insidious forms in the West, in the measure in which our society allows itself to be dominated by considerations of utility and technology, in the fascination with production, in consumerism. Again, there is the pressure of public opinion and popular thought patterns, as Solzhenitsin mentioned in his lecture at Harvard.[11]

Even Catholic ethicists have sometimes yielded too far to the utilitarian and technological mentality of our age. It seems to me this is the case with so-called "proportionalism" or "consequentialism." The moral quality of an action is evaluated on the basis of the comparison or proportion of its "pre-moral" advantages and disadvantages and its good or evil consequences, immediate or ultimate. Obviously such a comparison must be made in the evaluation of an action, but it remains external. It does not penetrate to the moral level, the interior of the human person, where the demands of truth and goodness prevail with their universal dimension. Such a concept of morality runs the risk of reducing the good to what is calculated as most useful. We are on the downward slope, heading for the diminution of our sense of truth. Losing this, we shall lose the essence of human integrity and morality.[12]

Love of Truth for Its Own Sake, and Objectivity

The fact that love of truth carries us beyond the realm of the useful or of material interests such as pleasure is decisive. Truth insists on being loved, sought and served for its own sake, to the point of setting aside self-interest, even risking life itself if need be.[13] Its nature is therefore

---

11. "In the West there is no censorship, but there is a sly selectiveness at work, separating ideas which are 'in' from those which are not. Although the latter are not directly quashed, they can find no authentic medium of expression in the press, in books, or in university courses. Legally, the spirit of your research is indeed free, but it is restricted on all sides by popular opinion" (Le déclin du courage [Seuil, 1978], 30).

12. See my article on "La question des actes intrinsèquement mauvais" in La Revue Thomiste 82 (1982) 181–212; 84 (1984) 618–24.

13. Here again we can quote Cicero: "And those [the Epicureans] who claim that intellectual pleasure is the motive for the pursuit of the studies I have mentioned [philosophy], do not understand that what makes this kind of study desirable is the fact that no utilitarian advantages are mixed with the joy accruing to the mind and that it is the sheer knowledge itself which delights, even though disagreements may have their place" (De finibus bonorum et malorum, 5.19).

And further on: "From these observations of mine (and I did not develop them at length as I might have, for they are obvious), from these observations, I say, it is quite clear that all the virtues, including 'honestas' (moral excellence) which springs from them and belongs to them, should be sought for their own sake."—"et virtutes omnes et honestum illud quod ex iis oritur et in iis haeret per se esse expetendum" (ibid., 5.23).

disinterested; yet it interests us in the highest degree and attracts us powerfully, for there is no true good without it. Love of truth is an integral part of the human personality and assures its dignity. As persons we are beings-for-the-truth; if the spirit of lying takes possession of us, we suffer an interior wound. We are no longer free if in our hearts we do not love and seek the truth. Inevitably, we become the slaves of causes, passions, or ideas which lead us to deceitfulness. Without love of truth, we lose our last foothold, the foundation on which to build a personal life.

Love of truth goes hand in hand with a sense of objectivity. Not the cold, impersonal objectivity of the positivist sciences, but the human sense of the reality of persons and things, which opens the door of their interiority to us. Once we accept their difference from ourselves, objectivity lays the foundation for the love of friendship. Through this profound objectivity, truth reveals itself to love.

Love and truth are thus naturally linked in the most personal action and encounter each other at the heart of freedom. Education in freedom will be at the same time education in truth and love. Thus all the moral values and virtues will be illumined and penetrated by our love of truth.

Contemplative Dimension and Universality

The truth understood in this way is by its very nature contemplative—which in no way prevents it from being strongly active and practical. This is why theology, which is the work of truth, will be chiefly contemplative, according to St. Thomas. Yet this contemplation contains within itself all the force of love, which it feeds by showing it its chief Object. Love is strengthened by knowledge of the beloved and therefore seeks to know it better. So theology is oriented to the vision of God, in which perfect happiness is found, according to revelation. St. Thomas indicates this succinctly when he refers to "the natural inclination to the truth about God." Here the desire for truth coincides with the desire for God, who is the source and end of all truth.

The natural inclination to truth has therefore a universal bearing on morality, as it has in all areas of knowledge. We could even say that it forms the very sense of the universal in us. Thus all truth, even the humblest, possesses as it were a halo, a radiation of universality. The universality of moral laws is based precisely on their truth, in conformity with human nature, which, in respect to its understanding, was created for truth. In this connection, it is indispensable to restore to morality its contemplative dimension.

VI. THE NATURAL INCLINATION TO LIVE IN SOCIETY

The Origin of Society

Aristotle discusses the inclination to the social life at the beginning of the *Politics*, where man is described as a "political animal." St. Thomas translates this "social and political animal." We could say that man is by nature sociable. Here is Aristotle's text: "This is how we know that man is a social [political] animal, more so even than the bees and all other gregarious animals. For nature does nothing in vain. Now among all living creatures, man alone possesses the power of speech. Whereas the cry [voice, *phone*], indicates pleasure and pain, the power of speech is intended to point out the useful and harmful, or the just and unjust. For it is a property of man that he alone, among all the animals, has a sense of good and evil, the just and unjust, and other like things. Having these things in common [community, *koinonia*] is what constitutes the family and the state" (I *Politics*, 1253, a 7–18; St. Thomas *On the Politics*, lect. I, n 36–37).[14]

Many reasons of utility can be advanced to explain the human inclination to life in society. St. Thomas does this at the beginning of *De regimini principum*. Unlike the animals directly provided for by nature, man has only reason and his hands to meet his natural needs for food, clothing, shelter, and self-defense. He also needs other people to help him procure these things. The animals also have a natural instinct for what is useful for life and health. Man has only a general idea of this, which has to be refined through reasoning and experience. Here, too, he needs other men (1.11; ed. Marietti, nn. 741–42).

The Inclination to Friendship

Important and obvious as it is, material usefulness is not the only, or even the chief, reason for our human inclination toward life in society. We need to seek a deeper reason in our spiritual nature. This is the

---

14. We find the same teaching in Cicero, evidently inspired by Aristotle: "The same nature, by means of reason, unites one man to another in view of forming a community of language and life; it inspires him with love for his offspring and prompts him to organize gatherings and assemblies and to take part in them . . ."—"Eadem natura vi rationis hominem conciliat homini et ad orationis et ad vitae societatem, ingeneratque in primis praecipuum quemdam amorem in eos qui procreati sunt, impellitque, ut hominum coetus, et celebrationes, et esse, et a se obiri velit . . ." (*De officiis*, 1.4). See also the formation of "caritas generis humani" and justice in *De finibus bonorum et malorum*, 5.23.

meaning of Aristotle's sign—language—which is one of our human properties. Speech is the direct work of reason. (In Greek the word *logos* means both reason and speech; in English the word *reason* signifies both the power to reason and the argument we use.) Essentially it serves communication. It is a distinct aspect of human nature, insofar as we are rational and social beings.[15]

The deepest foundation for our inclination to life in society lies in our human need for friendship, affection, or love. According to Aristotle, on whom St. Thomas comments, of all the goods that are useful to us friendship is the highest and most desirable, for "without friends, who would want to live, even though all other goods were present?" (*Ethics* 8.1, 1155). It can be shown that friendship is useful for the young as well as the old, but especially for those in the prime of life, so that they may accomplish good and achieve works of high quality in the intellectual order of contemplation. Friendship facilitates external accomplishments too, where more direct help can be supplied. We may conclude, therefore, that friendship is the most necessary of all goods (cf. St. Thomas, *In VIII Eth.*, lect. 1; ed. Marietti, nn. 1539–1540). Friendship, like virtue, clearly transcends the order of material usefulness.

Within the theme of friendship, the radical relationship of one person to another is intended, so as to fulfill the commandment "You shall love your neighbor as yourself." Because of our spiritual nature, we are inclined to unite with one another in love or friendship. It is a primordial desire, at the source of every community and society.

It can be demonstrated that this inclination finds its first realization in family affection, extends to other communities, and finally gives birth

---

15. One might object, in the Bergsonian tradition, that human language is utilitarian by nature, and this is certainly true in common usage. This explains the fact that words receive meaning from sensible experience, in which the consideration of the useful predominates. They cannot therefore acquire a meaning which transcends the useful without a certain elaboration of meaning, on the part of the hearer as well as the speaker, if communication is to be successful at this level. I would rather say that language and words are ambivalent, in this sense: for the person who considers everything from a utilitarian viewpoint, all words and ideas are oriented to the useful, including the most generous words, where reflection is likely, as in the teaching of the Sermon on the Mount on alms being given for the Father's sake; we are told that the Father sees what is hidden, and that he will reward the gift of alms.

On the other hand, for the person who has discovered the detached, generous nature of moral excellence, words and language receive a wholly different orientation. The very expression, "useful," is now directed toward what transcends utility in the ordinary sense of the word, and we can maintain with Cicero and St. Ambrose after him that what embodies the greatest utility for man is virtue, loved for its own sake. But such realities often need to be expressed in paradoxes, as in Christ's words, "Anyone who loves his life, loses it; anyone who hates his life in this world will keep it for eternal life" (Jn 12:25).

to the love of the human race, the *caritas generis humani* of which Cicero speaks (*De finibus bonorum et malorum* 5.23). Thus society, which is based on the incontestable natural bond that joins man and woman and prolongs and perfects their union, is itself natural. Its similarity to the family appears notably in the fact that the chief relationships within society, within forms of government, for example, are typified by the various relationships formed within the family. This is in agreement with psychological principles as well.

Justice and Friendship

The inclination to life in society, which comes naturally to us because of our intellect and will and the satisfaction of our needs, is strengthened and developed by the virtues, particularly justice. A firm, constant will to give everyone their due as our equals, justice is the virtue proper to life in society. It acquires from this fact a general influence among the other virtues in the measure in which our personal moral life is integrated within the framework of society.

Justice does not reach its perfection, however, until it succeeds in creating friendship at various levels of society, ranging from personal and familial friendship to friendship in the political and social spheres. According to Aristotle and St. Thomas, the goal of civil law is the formation of friendship among citizens, a friendship solidly based on justice and the other virtues, and not something vague and sentimental.

Such a concept prepares the way well for the understanding and acceptance of love, which renews and enriches mutual relationships at community and individual levels. We can observe this in the formation of the apostolic community in Jerusalem, where all had but one heart and soul and held all their goods in common (Acts 4, 32). Henceforth, fraternal love is rooted in the love of God himself and takes on an ecclesial dimension, extending to all in desire and intention.

Society: Natural Development or Artificial Creation?

The once general and apparently solid teaching that society is based on a natural human inclination has become in our day one of the most radical points of divergence with the advent of modern concepts of society stemming from nominalism. From the moment that man defines himself by insisting on his freedom against the same freedom of others, the natural bond with others, henceforth subjected to a choice between contraries, is twisted into antagonism and broken. No longer do we enjoy natural links with relatives and friends; we become adversaries. It is the well-known *homo homini lupus,* man the devourer of man; it is as common in families as in society. Or, if the idea is not pushed to its logical conclusion, at least it is maintained that society is a human creation, an artificial reality, based on convention or some sort of contract, which will preserve us from mutual destruction, so that instead we may help each other to satisfy our needs. The only natural human inclination is to the satisfaction of our desires; but in the end this is subjected to the affirmation of freedom. The natural, which is still recognized, is strongly individual, and its spontaneity turns into a defense of freedom in regard to social rules. Nature is henceforth oriented to the individual self by a freedom that is placed above nature. Moral rules that limit freedom and threaten spontaneity will be attributed to society and will share its artificial character.

Different Interpretations of the Two Great Commandments

Significant factors are at stake in this debate. It involves our relationship to others and the interpretation of the second commandment, which is the cornerstone of morality. If our bond with others, which is at the origin of society, is a natural bond, then the cornerstone is firmly laid; the moral structure can rest squarely on it and share its natural character. On the other hand, if our relationship with others is artificial, if the human reality is totally individual, then the cornerstone of the second commandment is broken. It will need an additional foundation to support it, as will morality. This new foundation will be the concept of obligation, which will regulate love itself and every other natural inclination. The ethical principle in regard to others will then be the imperative of the second commandment rather than the bond of love it embodies.

The interpretation of the first commandment will also be affected by this divergency, since there is a certain kind of society between human beings and God. For St. Thomas, as for the Fathers, the relationships nature has established between us and other creatures are an extension and a participation in the supernatural ties that unite us to God at the source of our nature and being, through creative wisdom and love. We experience a natural love for God and a desire to know him so primordial that they are even stronger than our spontaneous love of self, if we exclude the influence of sin. The first commandment therefore corresponds to a supremely natural inclination within the human heart and spirit. Charity, far from supplanting these aspirations, takes hold of them, disengages them from sin, and makes them its own, so that they may acquire a fulfillment which surpasses created nature. Charity forms bonds between us and God that are more supremely natural, through direct participation in the spontaneity and wisdom of the Holy Spirit.

These relationships are completely destroyed by nominalism. There is no longer any natural bond between human freedom and the freedom of God, but only a play of power: the moral obligation imposed upon us by divine omnipotence. The essence of the first commandment is no longer love but the absolute imperative of the divine will. This will's power over love is so free that God can command a person to hate him, according to Ockham's famous hypothesis. Charity itself can no longer form natural bonds between us and God. Any society uniting us will be basically artificial, like a contract or an alliance which depends upon the free decision of the free parties engaged. It will always be juridical in character. The first commandment will become a kind of principle of divine right: the affirmation of the divine will be seen as the source of all human obligations in respect to God and to civil or ecclesiasial society. In one sense this will be a very solid foundation, because of the divine omnipotence. At the same time it will be very fragile, because of the arbitrariness which characterizes divine freedom.

Another Concept of Justice

Consequently, the notion of justice will be transformed. Having lost its foundation in nature, justice becomes the creature of society. It issues wholly from the pressure of society upon the individual, unless the individual takes things into his own hands and identifies it with the subjective rights he claims from society. Here the struggle between the individual and society is carried over into the very heart of justice. As for justice in regard to God, it will fluctuate between legalism, which flaunts its observance of the law, and antilegalism, which rejects observance in the name of grace and faith.

The theme of friendship has, for all practical purposes, now vanished from the realm of ethics. It obviously cannot be fitted into the scheme of obligation, but the main thing is that friendship, even more than justice, by its nature and in our experience, is a direct witness to the natural bonds that can unite us to one another. Friendship cannot exist without a profound, slowly maturing spontaneity, which brings out all that is best in human nature, our natural capacity for communion and communication, which lies at the very heart of freedom.

A Number of Results

The inclination to live in society affects our lives at many levels. In civil society there is an exchange of goods of all kinds, material and cultural; in personal friendship, the communication is even more profound and rich. At the level of charity, communion depends upon Christ and upon the divine gift. Here it acquires a universal influence, gathering together under the aegis of justice, friendship, or charity all the other natural inclinations, which it helps to develop. Justice is considered a general virtue in its social or political dimensions. Charity becomes the form of all the virtues, breathing life into all of Christian morality.

Friendship is the special type of love that befits moral excellence, the love of friendship, which consists in loving another person or loving the good in itself and for its own sake. No words can adequately describe it; only through experience do we really understand it.

VII. INCLINATION TO SEXUALITY

A. Human Sexuality

St. Thomas relates the sexual inclination to the nature we share with other animals, which promotes the union of the sexes and the generation and rearing of offspring. "There is a human inclination which is more special [than self-preservation], which is shared with the animals. In regard to this it has been said (by Vulpius in the third century and in Justinian's *Digest* of 533) that the natural law covers 'all that nature has taught the animals,' such as the union of the sexes, the rearing of offspring, etc." (IaIIae, q 94 a 2).

Some clarifications are needed in order to understand this. Let us note first of all that the term "animal" has no pejorative or disparaging nuance in St. Thomas any more than in the Roman jurists. The moral depreciation of animality came out of seventeenth-century rationalism, which separated pure thought from the body and sensibilities and gave rise to a certain contempt for the latter. For St. Thomas, the term *animal* was as morally neutral as that of *pasison*, which designated feelings. It referred to creatures endowed with life and sense knowledge. St. Thomas saw in this nature the work of God; as such it was therefore good.

In the same sense we could cite Cicero: "It is something we hold in common with all animals, this desire to be united for the purpose of procreation, and this care of the beings we have been able to engender."[16] But Cicero at once shows the difference between man and animals: thanks to reason, the former can foresee the future and provide better for the needs of his family. Family affection will thus be at the origin of human society.

There is another misconception against which we should be on our guard. Following the Latin tradition, St. Thomas, as we have just seen, situated sexuality at the level of animal nature. Incontestably, sexuality includes a bodily and biological dimension essential to it, in contrast with our spiritual inclinations. We can therefore characterize it by this dimension common to man and animals. But this is not to say that for St. Thomas human sexuality was limited to the animal level. Quite the contrary; it was realized in man in a different and far richer way than in animals, being integrated in the totality of human nature, particularly through its coordination with spiritual inclinations. We shall try to show this further on. Here again St. Thomas's teaching on the substantial unity of human nature was at work. Man was not composed of three souls as the Augustinians of the thirteenth century thought—vegetative, animal, and spiritual—but of one single soul functioning vitally at these three levels as an interior principle of unification and convergence. Thus human sexuality, despite its natural similarity to animal sexuality, would have other dimensions.

A New Doctrine

St. Thomas's teaching on sexuality was relatively new in comparison to the Augustinian tradition and the Franciscan school. Basing his opinion on the texts of St. Paul and St. Augustine, who considered sexuality in the concrete, in experiences affected by "concupiscence" resulting from original sin, Peter Lombard had already proposed the theory of "excuses" for marriage.[17] Because of concupiscence and the uncon-

---

16. "Commune autem animantium omnium est coniunctionis appetitus procreandi causa et cura quaedam eorum quae procreata sunt" (De officiis, 1.4).

17. This expression comes from the text of 1 Cor 7:6, where St. Paul tells the Christians who have abstained from exercising their marriage rights so as to devote themselves to prayer to return to their wives in order to avoid the occasion for incontinence that might ensue. "You must not deprive each other. . . . I am telling you this as a concession, not an order." The Latin reads, "Hod autem dico secundum indulgentiam, non secundum imperium." The need for "indulgence" (the Greek suggnome means indulgence or concession) has been extended to the general use of marriage. The term itself was explained as

trolled desire exercised in sexuality, the use of marriage needed to be restored to its original goodness by certain goods to which it was ordered—that is, procreation, fidelity, the sacrament. It was not a case of deprecating the use of sexuality in marriage, but only of rectifying it because of the carnal concupiscence involved. Moreover, we find some very beautiful texts in St. Augustine and St. Bonaventure on the mutual support, love, and friendship of husbands and wives.

In his commentary on the *Sentences*, St. Thomas, following the thought of St. Albert, adopted a new point of view based on the teaching on natural inclinations.[18] Sexuality had originated in a primordial inclination of human nature. As such it was the work of the Creator, according to the Genesis account of the creation of man and woman. Therefore, whatever might be the deficiencies caused in the individual person by sin and concupiscence, the seat of unbridled desires, sexuality was recognized as something basically good and a source of moral excellence.[19] St. Thomas gave greater consideration to the nature of things than to psychological experience.

This change of perspective had repercussions. Natural inclination provided a solid bedrock for the formation of virtue. Thus sexuality, with the sensibility it included, could be the foundation for the virtue of temperance in the form of chastity. The latter would not then consist in a constraint imposed on sexuality from without, as limiting as possible, but would rather be reason's interior mastery, which would integrate sexuality within the human person better than anything else could and would place it at the service of true love. All of this presupposed a gradual education and maturation. Chastity was a necessary aspect of authentic human love. Thus rectified as far as possible, the use of sexuality within marriage could become meritorious under the influence of charity and could contribute positively to the work of salvation.

St. Thomas also brought out the intervention of the virtue of justice in rendering the matrimonial due, and of religion which is concerned with the spread of divine worship, in the increase of the number of children of God.[20] He differed from the Franciscans in placing virtues such

---

a permission to use a minor good, the matrimonial bond formed by the consent of the spouses, so as to avoid a minor (venial) evil, carnal union under the impulse of concupiscence. The affirmation of the goodness of marriage is firmly maintained, and also the condemnation of those who find fault with it.

18. IV *Sent.*, dist. 26–42. The text is taken up in the Supplement to the *Summa theologiae* q 41 a 68, with some additional questions. St. Thomas unfortunately did not finish his treatment of the sacraments in the *Summa*, but his teaching had already been worked out clearly in the *Sentences*.

19. Supplement, dist. 41, a 3.

20. Ibid., q 41 a 4.

as temperance and chastity in the sensible appetite, in accordance with its capacity to participate in the work of reason (IaIIae, q 56 a 4), and in giving a meritorious character to the right use of marriage.[21] Sexuality could thus be actively integrated into the Christian's personality and life.

The Moral Combat

This positive teaching on sexuality does not eliminate the need for the particularly difficult struggle against the disturbances of the sexual instinct aroused by "concupiscence," which tends to throw one's personal life off balance, corrupt the mutual love of man and woman, and upset social life. Because of its power and its function, the sexual instinct exerts its influence on the entire life of the person; its disorders can place all the virtues in peril. Although St. Paul's categories are broader, it was in this sense that he could describe the moral combat as an opposition between life according to the flesh, where sexual vices were paramount, and life according to the Spirit, with charity, self-control, and chastity, according to the Vulgate. Such is the Christian experience, in keeping with human experience. It would be naive to ignore it.

It is particularly important to establish a close link between control of the sexual instinct, which is chastity, and human love, which perfects charity. Chastity ensures the rectitude of the appetite, without which there can be no true and lasting love, no progress or maturity at the personal level.

The Dualist Interpretation

In connection with this teaching on sexuality and marriage, we need to be on our guard against a dualist concept of the human person. This originated in the rationalism of recent centuries far more than in Platonism, as is often thought. Dualism was radical in Descartes, who defined man as pure thought and who considered animals, and therefore sensibility and the body, simply as mechanisms. Thus the physical and biological were completely separated from reason and the moral order. Descartes was the interpreter of the mentality of an era in which the exaltation of reason led to contempt for the body as bestial. The temptation then was to reduce sexuality to animality, to treat it as a biological function.

---

21. On this teaching, see my study, "Ce que le Moyen Age pensait du mariage," Supplément de la Vie Spirituelle (Sept. 1967), 413–40.

Such a reduction comes about in ethics when the use of sexuality within marriage is seen as an essentially biological process having its own proper laws. If these are observed, the moral quality of this activity is assured. This point of view does indeed take into account a certain fundamental aspect of sexuality, but it is defective because it ignores the fact that in the human person the biological dimension is vitally integrated in a spiritual nature.

We come across a similar tendency to reduction, perhaps in a still stronger form, in the practice of the sciences, where biology, physiology, and psychology are rigorously distinguished, and where the yen for specialization often outweighs a concern for synthesis. Attention will focus on the biological processes of sexuality, allowing for the elaboration of techniques to improve this activity and its results. The predominant criterion for judging sexual behavior will then be health, which remains chiefly in the biological order.

Not only is this perspective false, but it is too restricted to take sufficient account of sexuality as a part of the human person, an activity that ought to serve moral progress. Sexuality should be subject to properly moral criteria, all the more since it normally involves relationships between persons and profoundly affects society.

In order to establish a moral teaching on marriage, it is indispensable to rediscover a sense of the profound unity that joins the biological, psychological, moral, and spiritual dimensions within the human person, and establishes communication among these dimensions without confusing them. Human sexuality has a psychological, moral, and even spiritual aspect. This is apparent in the Bible, where the love of God borrows images and comparisons from human love, at times very concrete. At the same time, the life of the spirit permeates sexuality in order to regulate it. We could even say that without the participation of the body, the human spirit could never find complete fulfillment. We could then show how the natural processes of sexuality (yet to be clarified) have a vital connection with the deep relationships between man and woman, and how the orientation of sexuality to fruitfulness is intimately connected with the demand for fruitfulness which precedes what we might call the law of giving, written at the heart of every love. If it does not know how to give, if it is not fruitful, love will sooner or later die. It is therefore because of the interior demand of love that marriage tends toward physical and spiritual fruitfulness in generation and education.

We are not far now from the problem of freedom. Sexuality cannot be given a real rootedness in the human personality unless we accept the fact that natural inclinations penetrate to the heart of our free will and stand at the origin of our actions. Only freedom for excellence proves to us that we are free not in spite of our sexuality but because of it, since through sexuality the inclination toward the other, which provides the human and moral dimension of sexuality, is exercised in a special way. Thus sexuality can constitute the primary cell of human society. Here the commandment of love of neighbor is fulfilled in a unique way, that commandment which expresses one of the principles of our free, spiritual fruitfulness.

B. Our Other Natural Inclinations Converge with the Inclination to Marriage

The richness of human sexuality is revealed when we consider how our other natural inclinations find their fulfillment in marriage. I shall indicate this briefly from the point of view of the partners and of the children.

The inclination to the good is fulfilled specifically in conjugal love, which finds in the person of the beloved, and in the lifelong union of bodies and souls, the greatest possible human good and happiness. This epitome of excellence is expressed in the bridal theme that is used throughout revelation to exemplify the relationship of love—and of infidelity—between God and his people, between Christ and his Church, between Christ and every believer.

The inclination to self-preservation is reinforced in marriage, for the spouses become "two in one flesh"—one being, if you will, in the words of Genesis. In this union they experience a strengthening of their essential nature and of their confidence in facing life's challenges. They realize that together they are enabled to give existence to other beings like themselves, and through mutual support their capacity for action and their concern for self-defense grow and intensify.

The inclination to truth receives a special dimension within marriage through the wholly personal knowledge that is gained. Through love, each partner's knowledge of the other renews and deepens self-knowledge and is fulfilled in a unique way because of the difference and complementarity of the sexes and their psychology.

The inclination to life in society finds its first, most natural, and in a sense most complete realization in marriage. In the mutual relationship of the spouses and the bonds between parents and children we can discern the primitive types of relationships formed within society, and various types of government. According to Aristotle monarchy corresponded to the relationship of father to children, aristocracy to that of husband and wife, and democracy to that between siblings. These correspondences are so profound that we can see in them true paradigms.

From the point of view of the children, it is in the home that they first experience existence, basic to all the later experiences of life. The security of home gives them that personal self-assurance which will vitalize and support their activities in society. By the same token, insecurity bred in childhood by division within the family can have serious repercussions and prevent children from developing a courageous attitude toward life, so necessary for the forming of personality.

Children gain their first experience of love and happiness at home, together with the different kinds of affection they have for father, mother, brothers, and sisters. Home is where they learn, first and foremost. In the heart of the family, children come to know the difference between good and evil and receive their first moral and religious formation. Here, too, they may encounter suffering, dissension, and unhappiness at an extremely intimate level.

In the family, children acquire their earliest knowledge at a particularly impressionable age. They learn their mother tongue, become familiar with concrete objects, they are taught the truths of religion, form their first ideas, and learn how to use them. Their earliest teaching, especially regarding morals, comes from their parents, and that formation in virtue which we have seen to be so necessary for the development of freedom for excellence. Because of this, deficiencies in home education can be particularly damaging.

In the family, children have their original experience of social relationships and they apprehend the diversity of those relationships as they learn to differentiate between their rapport with parents and with other family members. They bring these first relationships with them as they enter into the wider social setting and the heart of the Church. Even their relationship with God will be influenced, for example, by their relationship with their father. Again, it is at home that children first become aware of authority, and learn to relate to it through personal obedience.

The Unique Relationship with God

These brief indications are enough to show us how human sexuality is naturally linked with our other inclinations, even the most spiritual, and is in fact necessary if the latter are to find true fulfillment in the realities of life.

We should add, however—and this is of capital importance for Christian ethics—that the contribution of the family, however natural and basic, is not enough in itself to produce and explain the nature and development of those inclinations to truth, goodness, and happiness which make the human person. At the very heart of family relationships, precisely in the sense of truth, goodness, and happiness, there is the higher and wholly personal relationship of each human being with God. This forms what we today call self-consciousness, that intimate center which St. Paul called the human spirit, inaccessible to all others, saving only the individual person himself. Christians have called this the soul, and they see in it God's image. This is an essential element of personhood; it is the seed of moral and spiritual life sown in each of us. Inevitably it links the second commandment to the first; love of neighbor is united with love of God as its source and term. This intimate relationship with God, at the level of truth and goodness, can be seen very early in children, as Newman shows us in his memories of his childhood. In its power and attraction it outweighs all other relationships, despite its hidden quality and the demands and obstacles the world throws in its way.

In this spiritual center, at moments of inner lucidity we perceive mysteriously but with certainty the very source and perfection of our natural inclinations; we know our true freedom. No solid morality, above all no Christian morality, can be built except on the foundation of this personal relationship to God, however inadequate our expression of it may be.

The psychological study of family relationships, as well as sociology, are therefore not enough to serve as a base for morality. They cannot explain human behavior at its deepest and most personal, even though their contribution is valuable and necessary for the formation of adequate moral judgments. Here again, we should not oppose sciences to ethics, any more than family or social relationships to our personal relationship with God. These different types of knowledge and levels of being should converge, enabling us to know ourselves in our living, active wholeness. Our relationship to God is not something external, but operates within family and social relationships and is fulfilled through them. Yet the love of God will manifest itself, in its specific and supreme character, in certain choices it may impose, such as the option for virginity, or the renunciation of marriage, of which we shall speak later.

C. The Two Ends of Marriage

The interpretation of the teaching on the two ends of marriage has been profoundly affected by the nominalist conception of freedom and relationship to others. Within the problematic, these ends—procreation and mutual support—have become rivals, the problem being to determine which is stronger. One stands for nature, with its biological force and the moral obligations it imposes. The other is on the side of the person's freedom and sentiment of love, and also on the side of reason, which claims to rule nature through knowledge. Until recent times, ethicists have maintained the classical position, which taught that procreation was the primary end of marriage. This provided them with a solid, objective basis for establishing the obligations of marriage. Currently, a widespread reversal has been initiated in favor of mutual support—of love and its expression—as an autonomous if not overriding end. This calls into question the very institution of marriage, because of the subjective, individual nature of the emotion of love.

In St. Thomas as in Aristotle, the teaching on the two ends of marriage comes through in a very different thought context, where the ends are seen not as conflicting but rather as converging.

Aristotle discusses the relationship of man and woman in marriage in his study on friendship.[22] He sees conjugal affection as a special form of friendship. It is based on nature, that is, the inclination to reproduction found in all animals, but is realized in a higher way, for it includes all the tasks of family life which the man and woman share together. The conjugal relationship may also be based on virtue and become friendship in the full sense of the word. Aristotle also observes that children are a bond uniting the spouses and that they render the marriage more solid. Finally, the community established by marriage, being the source of a natural relationship, is prior to the political society, in which the natural human inclination to societal life is fulfilled. Clearly, his context is in no wise predominantly "biological" but profoundly human, owing to the theme of friendship. Procreation and mutual support, which manifest the friendship of the spouses, correspond to one another.

St. Thomas speaks out of the same perspective.[23] Taking up the question of marriage as a natural institution, he begins by clarifying the sense in which it is called natural: not in the sense of a compelling force, but rather in the sense of an inclination realized with the help of free will. Already we are beyond the biological and moving into the human and moral plane, which includes the biological. St. Thomas then discusses the two natural ends of marriage, insisting on what is properly human

---

22. *Nicomachean Ethics*, 8.12, 1162a 6–8; St. Thomas, *In VIII Eth.*, lect. 12, nn. 1719–1725. Friendship is understood in a broader sense than ours. Its extension equals that of love, of which it is a higher form.

23. Supplement, q 41 a 1.

in them. Beyond the generation of children, the end will be their instruction and education until adulthood, and their acquisition of virtues. Here again the parents collaborate in their complementary tasks, in friendship and conjugal love.

St. Thomas does not explain why procreation is the principal end of marriage, but he clarifies its formula: we are dealing with the *bonum prolis,* the good of the child, with all that this includes, especially education, not merely the *generatio prolis,* or generation. That children are the direct and primary end of the union of man and woman was a classical teaching. To question it would be unimaginable. Did not physiology itself testify on its behalf? It was so natural that even the word *nature* came from it, for in both Greek and Latin the primary meaning of the word was "to be born."

We note that the development of the thought, in Aristotle and Cicero as in St. Thomas, took the form of an addition and clarification of what properly pertained to human generation: the education of the children and the mutual support of the spouses, the latter being so important as to constitute a distinct end of marriage, second but in no sense secondary. This end is also natural, consonant with the integral human person, body and soul. Its purpose is to form between the husband and wife a friendship or affection of a unique kind, which has full moral value when it is based on the qualities or virtues of each.

To build a moral theory of marriage, therefore, we need not oppose the two ends to each other, nor set them up as rivals. They should be joined and bonded. The principal end, especially the education of the children, cannot be attained without the mutual collaboration of the spouses, their friendship and affection. Here it is seen as a natural requirement for familial education.

On the other hand, the denial of the first end of marriage leads almost necessarily to the failure of the second. The child is the proper, natural fruit of conjugal love. Spouses who refuse to have children condemn their love to sterility, even on the affective level, and pave the way for its eventual extinction. At every level, love tends naturally to fruitfulness. It is, as it were, a law of generosity inscribed on the soul as well as the body of every man and woman. To infringe upon this law is to compromise the very life of love in its truth and depth.

It is therefore extremely important, in teaching about marriage, to take into account the interdependence and interaction of the two ends of marriage, for they are inseparable. This is the logic of the human reality, deeper and more powerful than all ideas, opinions, feelings, and passions.

We should also note the influence of individualism on the relationship between man and woman. The propensity for defending individual freedom (understood as freedom of indifference) leads to viewing woman's natural destiny to motherhood and her specific share in education as constraints, rather than qualities designed to complement the gifts of the man. In this view the distinction between the sexes engenders rivalry, as well as the hopeless pursuit of the suppression of all differences, which is equally damaging to both. Only the frank, positive acceptance of these differences as complementary aptitudes will allow the reestablishment of collaboration between man and woman. This will result in a balance based on each's recognition of the other, and through their mutual support it will favor the flowering of freedom for excellence. Obviously there will be variations in these natural differences, according to social and cultural backgrounds and conditions. They will lead to dynamic, personal equality, always developing like life itself, and not to be confused with a materialistic, defensive equality.

D. Marriage and Virginity

Virginity Is in Keeping with Human Nature

The natural inclination to marriage is universal. Every human person has it, and it is the basis of an inalienable right. It is also the basis of natural law, but its concrete realization depends upon a number of determinations and conditions in the social, psychological, and physiological order.

The universality of this inclination is however less demanding than that of other natural inclinations. We cannot legitimately renounce our existence, the pursuit of truth and goodness, or any share in human society. Yet some may be called to renounce marriage and the exercise of sexuality.

The problem is obviously raised by the ideal of virginity or perfect chastity, which has spread within Christianity and been actualized in the religious state as well as in priestly celibacy. In the Christian world, the renunciation of marriage is not exceptional as it was in ancient times. It has become institutionalized, thus posing an important problem—that of the legitimacy of this ideal and these institutions—as well as the question of the reasons and spirit that should guide those who have entered upon this seemingly unnatural way of life.

In answering this question which interested him particularly as a religious, St. Thomas did not make his task easier by placing a natural inclination at the foundation of his teaching on marriage, rather than the experience of "concupiscence" tainted by sin, as the Augustinian tradition had done. If this inclination was natural, and as such the work of God, was it not a duty to marry and have children, and a sin to refuse to assume such a noble task? The question is frankly presented in the *Summa*: Is virginity unlawful?[24] He was calling into question, in the name of human nature, a way of life that had been characteristic of Christianity from its beginnings. The problem is still relevant today.

In contrast with some Fathers of the Church, who considered the cessation of generation as a sort of good (for they saw in it the hastening of the end of the world), St. Thomas maintained stoutly the natural character of this work of procreation. He interpreted the words of Genesis, "Increase and multiply," as a precept that enjoined upon humanity the natural duty of fecundity, of perpetuating themselves by bringing children into the world.

St. Thomas observed, however, that this precept was not limited to the bodily sphere; it also had to do with the spiritual growth and fruitfulness of humanity. Hence a division of functions could be arranged, as in an army or any organized community. To insure humanity's physical increase, it was enough for a certain number of people to marry—and indeed this would always be the majority—while others might devote themselves in a special way to humanity's spiritual growth by renouncing marriage for the sake of the contemplation of divine realities. Contemplation was thus the principal motive for religious celibacy. But we should notice that for St. Thomas contemplation included the active life, which was oriented to it, and apostolic preaching, which ensured its diffusion and communication, each of these modes of life being animated by charity.

Thus the ideal of virginity received its legitimate status from nature itself, not indeed from the inclination toward generation but from the yearning for knowledge of divine truth, seen as humanity's highest good. The choice of virginity or perfect chastity was therefore not opposed to the task of marriage, since it was motivated by the fulfillment of another task, which we might say was even more natural: progress in the knowledge of truth and goodness for the benefit of all society. Indeed, the great "contemplative" work of such men as St. Augustine and St. Thomas himself have clearly profited humanity.

The ideal of virginity fulfills the precept "Increase and multiply" in

24. IIaIIae q 152 a 2.

its own way, through spiritual fruitfulness. It is one of the principal factors in the Church's growth and in all the renewals she has known through the ages. In spite of appearances, there is no opposition, but rather a deep harmony between marriage and perfect chastity, if we consider human nature and human society from the viewpoint of all our natural inclinations, particularly those that are spiritual. Our tasks are not opposed but complementary.

The Supernatural Aspect of Virginity and the Religious Life

The cogency of St. Thomas's answer lies in his basing the legitimacy and motivation of the Christian ideal of virginity on the nature of the human person. At the same time he laid solid theological and psychological foundations for a life consecrated to seeking God in the renunciation of marriage. This could be called supremely natural.

In our day, however, this argument lends itself to a misconception. We might think at first glance that a solid foundation and purely natural reasoning would be enough to establish and explain the ideal of virginity and hence of the religious state. Its most explicit sources can be found in the New Testament teaching, together with the basis for the vows of poverty and obedience. Influenced, however, by modern humanistic thought patterns, which revolve around human relationships and easily become "horizontal," there is the temptation to explain the religious renunciation of marriage in terms of purely natural motives. It could be due to the desire for a more all-embracing devotion and consecration of life to the good of mankind, spent in charitable, social, cultural, or even political work. Supernatural motives, always significant in traditional teaching, would thus be ignored. They can have no real part in a theology subject to the influence of current sciences and philosophies. The end result would therefore be a "humanistic" and seemingly rational reinterpretation of a religious phenomenon that is not easily reducible to such terms.

St. Thomas can certainly not be invoked in support of such an interpretation. The virginity he discusses and defends is none other than the virginity for the sake of Christ that was proposed by St. Paul (1 Cor 7:25–35), whose argument he cites in the *secunda secundae,* question 152 a 2. This was the specifically Christian ideal that was to inspire all forms of traditional religious life, and particularly the great renewal set afoot by the mendicant orders in the thirteenth century. Within the new theological elaboration St. Thomas gave to the religious state, the latter became one of the characteristic notes of the evangelical Law as the "law of freedom" (IaIIae, q 108 a 4). It was to be understood, according to the definition of this Law, as "the grace of the Holy Spirit given through faith in Christ and operating in charity," in conjunction with the Sermon on the Mount and the sacraments, as secondary elements.

The problem of virginity's relation to natural inclinations obviously surfaced because of the Christian fact of religious life. It would have posed no question in a purely philosophical, natural setting such as that of antiquity, where the choice of virginity was too exceptional and furthermore risked the appearance of a fault. This is clear in St. Thomas's answer to the third objection, where Plato is cited. He, according to St. Augustine, gave up his opinion in favor of abstention from sexual pleasure in order to appease the perversity of his fellow citizens. The ideal and the frequent practice of virginity were one of the clearest and surest signs of the intervention of a higher reality, the supernatural, in human life.

Actually St. Thomas's concept of the interaction of human nature and supernatural realities differs from that of modern theologians. For him, our nature is open to the gift of God through our inclinations to truth and goodness, which form our natural desire to see God. Hence the more natural a reality is, the better will it be disposed for the supernatural gift.

Such is the case with virginity. Because it provides freedom from "the concerns of the flesh" it is in harmony with the desire for truth and goodness, and this renders it particularly apt for contributing to a Christian contemplation nourished by the Gospel. The matter of virginity is natural, as it stems from temperance, but it becomes supernatural through its motivation and the new character it receives from the Holy Spirit as a special disposition for the contemplative life. In demonstrating how fitting virginity is to human nature, St. Thomas has no intention of reducing it to a purely human level. He intends rather to give it the firmest foundation possible, and the most precise position for the welcoming of grace's work, where it may serve as grace's chosen instrument.

We for our part have grown used to separating the natural from the supernatural in terms of an "either—or" dialectic inherited from nominalism. In this view, when the natural character and motivations for virginity or the religious life are advanced, there is always the risk of ignoring their supernatural and specifically Christian dimension. Reacting to the excessive supernaturalism of former times, we tend to a naturalism that would reduce everything to the level of man and human relationships.

As far as the ideal of virginity is concerned, I believe this attempt is doomed to failure. Granted, the renunciation of marriage out of devotion is good and beautiful on paper, in theory. But it is very doubtful that abstention from sexual relations for purely human motives will work out over the long haul. The logic of the human reality obviously operates in the opposite direction. We might even wonder if, remaining at the level of pure nature, marriage would not be preferable. Husband and wife could mutually aid each other in the search for higher values such as truth, love, and devotion in all its forms. If we remained at this level it would be impossible to find a foundation for the legitimacy and inspiration of an ideal of virginity or celibacy in theory, still less to ensure its realization and human success in actual practice. In this context we could not hope for the intervention of a new reality, possessing a higher, supernatural power of attraction and support, which would harmonize perfectly with our spiritual nature.

The Complementarity of Marriage and Virginity in the Church and in Christian Life

According to St. Thomas, there is a complementarity between marriage and contemplative virginity, seen as two functions serving the beauty and salvation of humanity. This view is realized at the heart of the Church. Of course at first sight, the use of marriage and abstention from it seem to be quite mutually contrary, as also the formation of this primary cell of society and the solitude of the celibate. But the opposition is transcended by the consideration of the nature of the human person, ordered to truth and goodness beyond sexual differences. This complementarity can be realized and lead to active collaboration, however, only through the intervention of the charity of Christ, the supreme intensity of love, which is capable of conferring a new dimension upon conjugal affection and inspiring the vocation to virginity. Through this virtue, which overflows in divine contemplation and in service of our neighbor, a dynamic bond is established between these so different modes of life, each vocation being empowered to further the progress of the other.

The intervention of charity and grace is all the more necessary in that human nature has been affected by sin, particularly in its sexuality, which needs healing and guidance so that differences may not lead to rivalry and conflicts. St. Thomas stepped back from this aspect of things when he explained the natural fittingness of virginity, but he was well aware that sin was a particularly strong obstacle here. This consideration makes any attempt to build religious life on purely natural motivation all the more chancy and uncertain.

The power of the Gospel ideal of virginity enlivened by the charity of Christ is manifested notably by its ability to call forth new types of communities, consecrated to the evangelical life through renunciation, contemplation, and devotion. It is the proof, founded on facts and a long history, of the supernatural fruitfulness of Christian virginity.

Conclusion

Coordination of Inclinations, Natural Law, and Virtues

If we cast a glance over all the natural human inclinations, we see that they form a sheaf of closely linked yearnings and energies. We do indeed have to distinguish them, for the sake of analysis and clear perception, but we must never forget to regroup them again in a dynamic synthesis, for they act only together, as members of an organism. This coordination of our faculties and inclinations is characteristic of freedom for excellence, as contrasted with freedom of indifference, which divides our faculties and separates our inclinations from each other.

Thus understood, natural inclinations form natural law, which serves as a foundation for our human rights, and they provide the "seeds" of the excellence that will grow out of the virtues. Before going into further detail, I would like to clarify somewhat the relations that link the inclinations to natural law, to human laws, and to the virtues.

When set forth in terms of precepts, natural law is presented to us externally and communicates to our reason and conscience moral demands that restrict our freedom with the force of obligation. But make no mistake: this law is not the work of a will external and foreign to us. Precisely because it is the expression of our natural inclinations, especially the spiritual ones, this law penetrates to the heart of our freedom and personality to show us the demands of truth and goodness. These guide us in the development of freedom through actions of excellence. Thus natural law is an inner law. It is the direct work of the One who has created us to image him in our spiritual nature and our free, rational will. The exigencies of natural law have their source both in God and in our human nature.

Natural law is the foundation of human rights, as it roots them in our personal nature. Thus these rights are, in their source, universal and inalienable. We need to emphasize that they should not be understood in a purely subjective sense, as the individual's defense against the encroachment of others and of society. Rather, they should be seen objectively as rights belonging to everyone. They call forth each one's respect and benevolence in keeping with the virtue of justice, which is a firm determination to give everyone their due. Natural law, like the virtue of justice, is primarily oriented to others, while always including the agent who is also a member of society. This is why rights and duties go together.

Thus understood, the law and our natural rights correspond with precision to personal qualities, or virtues. The latter are not simply dispositions answering to an external law, habitual responses of conformity to commands. Through their exercise, a person's natural inclinations are developed and strengthened, and a profound harmony is established with the inner law inscribed in the "heart." Thus for every inclination we can find corresponding precepts of the natural law, and virtues.

For St. Thomas, virtues were more important than precepts, since they constituted the end and perfection of the inclinations. Furthermore, through the exercise of virtues there came about, at the center of free will, a personal conformity to inclinations and natural law. Thus there was a profound continuity between our inclinations, natural law, and the virtues, within personal, free action. There was no break separating inclinations from freedom or law from virtues, as happens in casuistical ethics.

In this way the natural foundation is solidly laid for the work of grace in us. We are dealing with a concept of the human person naturally open to receive the divine action because of a desire for happiness and a yearning for truth. As spiritual beings, we are capable of receiving God, *capax Dei*, even though this capacity is wholly passive and receptive. The grace of the Holy Spirit touches us in our "substance," in our personal being, and acts even at the level of our natural inclinations. The Gospel law, which perfects natural law, is for St. Thomas equally interior in its principal element, and still more in the measure in which the law of Christ, expressed in the Sermon on the Mount, regulates our interior actions. The precepts of the Decalogue, by contrast, affected only external actions. Through the New Law, our inwardness opens to the mystery of divine inwardness, under the action of the Holy Spirit.

Finally, the supernatural virtues are closely linked to the natural virtues, not by way of juxtaposition but by "infusion." They inspire, animate, and direct them from within, transforming them also by giving them greater intensity and new strength.

Detailed Points of Correspondence

We shall conclude with a detailed schema of the correspondence between inclinations, precepts of the natural law, and virtues that we have just indicated.

1. The inclination to goodness and happiness, which includes all other inclinations, is expressed in the first principle of natural law, "Good is to be done and evil avoided," which was explained above. Now since good is defined as that which causes love and desire, we can relate to this inclination the two fundamental precepts of love of God and neighbor, which are the most profoundly natural according to St. Thomas, and sum up the whole Law, according to the Gospel. They show clearly the primacy of the inclination and attraction to the good.

Although the terms *right* and *duty* are not altogether adequate at this level, these precepts establish for every person a certain right to education in goodness and to moral formation in the broadest sense. We can even speak of a right to happiness, affection, and love, providing that we add the corresponding duties, for at this level we cannot receive if we do not know how to give.

The inclination to goodness is perfected first by the virtue of justice, understood in the general sense in which it regulates our relationships with God and neighbor. We can evoke here the biblical idea of justice, which focuses upon our relationship with God, even though St. Thomas considers this as having a metaphorical sense. This justice is developed in friendship based on virtue, which establishes the most free, most personal relationships between people. Charity, defined precisely as the friendship that unites the divine *agape* and love of neighbor inseparably, is the supernatural perfection of our inclination to goodness. Like the latter, charity influences all inclinations and virtues.

2. The inclination to self-preservation engenders our love of existence and life, a love of self so natural that it needs no command to arouse it; we find it within the second commandment, "You shall love your neighbor as yourself," as well as in the golden rule, "Do unto others as you would have them do unto you."

This inclination is the basis for the fifth commandment, "You shall not kill," which inculcates respect for the life of others and with all the more reason for our own. Included here is respect for the goods of others.

The association of law with inclination, dynamic in nature, invites us to transcend the negative and limiting aspect of the commandment. The prohibition is necessary in order to insure our progress and development in the love of neighbor, which is placed at the head of the Law. This holds for all the other negative precepts.

The right to the legitimate defense of our existence and goods is founded in this way, together wih all that is necessary for the development of life. Nonetheless the concrete, precise implementation of these rights should always take into account our duties toward others and the societal context in which we exercise them. From this flows our natural duty to develop our life in fruitfulness.

The virtue of fortitude, which is the courage to be and the courage to live in spite of difficulties and obstacles, develops our inclination to existence while affirming the natural hope it fosters. The supernatural virtue of hope is grafted onto this inclination, or rather, it takes hold of its very roots to direct it, through confidence in God's omnipotence, to a beatitude transcending nature. At the same time hope maintains us in the daily effort of humility and in our human weakness, so often put to the test.

3. The sexual inclination, which calls forth the love of man and woman and the affection of parents for their children, is regulated by the sixth and ninth commandments of the Decalogue, to which we may add the fourth, concerning filial affection. The object of these precepts is control of our sexuality and the ordering of it to marriage, where it finds complete fulfillment. It is important to understand them as being at the service of conjugal love and its fruitfulness and as a unique, particularly natural realization of love of neighbor.

The sexual inclination is at the basis of each person's right to marry, and the duty to assume the complementary tasks of marriage: mutual support, the education of the children, and respect for the marriage of others.

The virtue of chastity insures control of our sexuality in view of the growth of affection within the family. Chastity infuses human love with a new dimension, like the loving union of Christ and the Church, according to St. Paul's teaching, and at the same time is realized within marriage in a particular way. This natural symbolism is so profound that it points to the bonding of conjugal and filial love to love for God.

Justice, too, has its part in the building of this primary cell of human society. But it is not sovereign here, and cannot be applied with same rigor and type of equality as is found in juridical relationships.

4. The natural inclination to the truth is referred to in the eighth commandment, which forbids lying. This obviously includes far more than mere abstention from lying, as we see from the Sermon on the Mount: "Let your yes be yes and your no, no." Truthfulness in speech implies

truthfulness in our actions and our hearts. It forms a love of truth, and that intellectual curiosity which is at the origin of all human knowledge.

This inclination lays the foundation for every person's right to acquire human culture according to circumstances and ability. It imposes, too, the duty of cultivating our minds, seeking the truth and maintaining it within our hearts, our words, and our life.

The virtues that perfect our inclination to truth are many, because of the breadth of truth's object: wisdom, understanding, and knowledge on the theoretical plane, prudence in practical affairs. The virtue of faith communicates an inchoate understanding of divine truth, with the help of revelation and the articles of faith. Theological wisdom, in which the understanding of faith is at work, takes hold of philosophical wisdom and orders it to the vision of God seen as the plenitude of Truth.

5. Finally, the inclination to life in society relates to the commandment to love our neighbor, from the aspect of justice and respect for the rights of others in the setting of the city. It is expressed in the seventh commandment, which deals with the possessions of others and theft. It is the basis for everyone's right to be accepted as a person by the human community, and imposes on all the duty of consenting to this.

The inclination to life in society is developed by the virtue of justice and culminates in friendship, which is its term and highest achievement. It receives its supernatural dimension in fraternal charity, which forms the Church and is the cement of all truly Christian communities, and also in the love for God which, viewed as friendship, establishes a wondrous and mysterious "society" between man and God

We see in all this a remarkable moral edifice. Natural inclinations are the foundation, destined one day to receive the cornerstone, Christ. The structure is enhanced by the theological virtues and, together with them, all the others. We can never overlook the gifts of the Holy Spirit, which St. Thomas associates with each virtue. If they have not been mentioned in the course of this discussion, it was only to avoid undue complication in our schema. In the thought of St. Thomas, without the help of the Holy Spirit no virtue could reach its full perfection.

Conclusion

As we come to the end of this book, it is good to look back over the road we have travelled. We began by asking in Chapter 1 what Christian ethics is. After looking at several definitions based on the criterion of the principal judgment used, we chose as our preferred definition the one that oriented Christian ethics to the loving vision of God seen as the final end and true bliss of man. We then surveyed the scope of Christian ethics, discussing briefly some of the basic questions it involves, and we noted in Chapter 2 that Christian ethics cannot be limited, as has all too often been attempted, to the question of obligation.

PART ONE: A HUMAN AND CHRISTIAN ETHICS

In Chapter 3 we approached the subject matter of Christian ethics—human actions—and considered this under its two basic aspects, human and Christian. We studied its human character first, observable in the relation of ethics to the sciences, arts, and techniques, which are equally concerned with human action and behavior. We established differences according to the methods used, reflexive for ethics and positivist in the behavioral sciences, and deduced from this the collaboration that could and should be engaged in between the two. We noted as well some current dangers to be forestalled, such as abdication on the part of ethicists and high-handedness on the part of scholars and technicians, both of which would be to the detriment of all concerned. Finally we showed that in ethics "the human" designates the concrete, individual person, and opens out to the divine through a life experience, which has its own proper excellence.

The Christian character of ethics merited a more lengthy study, since today its very existence and uniqueness is being challenged. Furthermore, it is absolutely necessary to reestablish a communication that is broad and solid between Christian ethics and its principal sources, Scripture and living tradition, which have built theology. In Chapter 4 we presented a contemporary response to the question of the existence of a Christian ethics, and we critiqued that response because of its ambiguity and the regrettable conclusions that could be drawn from it. We next questioned the major witnesses for Christian morality, devoting Chapter 5 to St. Paul, Chapter 6 to St. Matthew and St. Augustine on the Sermon on the Mount, and Chapter 7 to St. Thomas Aquinas.

As we questioned St. Paul on Christian ethics, two clarifications regarding the manner of posing the question were needed. The results are less than satisfying if we look only for obligations and imperatives in St. Paul, following the method we have described as residual or fragmented: When Christian documents are compared with Jewish or pagan ones, are there some commandments and imperatives, a residue of fragments, to be found only in the Christian texts? On the other hand, if we approach moral theory from the point of view of the question of happiness and salvation, and if we use a "total" method to question St. Paul, his answer will be as comprehensive as we could wish. In contrast to Jewish morality, dominated by the appeal to justice, and Greek moral thought focused on the search for wisdom, the Apostle, within the dramatic experience of his preaching, depicts Christian ethics from the viewpoint of faith in Christ, who is the justice of God and the wisdom of God for every person. We showed how, for St. Paul, all Christian ethics flowed from faith in Jesus; this formed in the believer the new man, living according to the Spirit, in Christ and in imitation of him. Faith makes possible the crowning gift of charity, which invigorates life and builds the ecclesial community.

The Apostle marked off two main stages in morality. First there was the break with Jewish justice and Greek wisdom, both vitiated by human pride, in order to lay a solid foundation of faith and the humble following of Christ. Then all that was true and good in human wisdom and virtue was taken up and integrated within the new moral organism, under the benevolent rule of faith, hope, and charity.

The Sermon on the Mount is accepted, on a simple reading, as one of the principal sources of Christian ethics. It is presented as a summary of the teachings of Jesus about justice and gives the Beatitudes and the loftier precepts that are to shape the life of his disciples and form them ethically. Such was the intention of the Evangelist in reporting this discourse. But modern theology and exegesis have found the Sermon on the Mount a stumbling block. They draw back because of the difficulty experienced in trying to put it into practice; for them the difficulty is insurmountable, because they see the Sermon as a collection of legal obligations. From the Catholic viewpoint, this difficulty is solved by removing the Sermon from the field of morality and assigning it to that of spirituality. As for Protestants, they have ranged the Sermon on the side of the Law, and in confrontation with the Gospel and St. Paul's teaching in Romans. From all this we have to conclude that in the West we have lost the key to the Sermon on the Mount.

To help us to rediscover this great text, we addressed St. Augustine, who was its most penetrating and most influential commentator at the beginning of the Western tradition which culminated with St. Thomas's *Summa theologiae*. For Augustine, the Sermon of the Lord, destined for everyone, was the charter of the Christian life, conceived as a life lived in accordance with the Beatitudes, which marked out its course, a life lived in the Spirit who gives us his gifts, and finally, a life conformed to the Lord's Prayer. In this interpretation, the teachings of St. Matthew, St. Paul, and the prophets, including Isaiah, all converged. It inspired the response of the Fathers to the objection that the Sermon was impracticable: its teaching is made accessible to us through the grace of Christ and the work of the Holy Spirit.

Part two of the *Summa* of St. Thomas was the culmination and the most finely wrought theological expression of the moral reflection of the Fathers. Yet all too soon St. Thomas was faulted for being more Aristotelian than Christian. It even happened, by a strange misreading of his text, that some of his most faithful commentators overlooked the most specifically Christian parts of his work. This was true notably of his questions treating of the New Law, which, within the structure of the *Summa,* are placed at the peak of the study of law and form the veritable capstone of the entire edifice. It is indispensable that we reevaluate this treatise, which can play an outstanding role in the effort to renew Christian ethics. By associating St. Paul's teaching on faith, which vivifies and justifies us in the Spirit, with the Sermon of the Lord as a specific text and with the sacraments as instruments of grace, this study shows clearly the Christian dimension of St. Thomas's moral teaching. In it, his use of Aristotle is placed at the service of the Gospel. In moral theology, the masterpiece of the Angelic Doctor was the building of a complete organism of virtues and gifts, ruled by the theological virtues and assuming and elevating human virtues so as to direct them effectively to the divine vision proposed to us by the revelation of Christ. Thus St. Thomas was the authentic witness of the apostolic evangelism of his own time and the trustworthy theologian of evangelism for all times.

PART TWO: THE HISTORY OF CHRISTIAN ETHICS

Having firmly established the existence and nature of Christian ethics with the help of the great works of revelation and theology, we then traced the principal stages of its history so as to grasp its teachings and understand better the doctrinal heritage bequeathed to us and the moral problems we face. This was covered in Chapters 8 to 13. Not content simply with a history of facts and documents, we tried to penetrate the depths of ethical reflection where syntheses have been worked out and the systematic structure of moral material supplied by revelation progressively elaborated with the help of philosophy and experience.

The patristic period covered in Chapter 8, running roughly to the rise of scholasticism, showed us the extent to which the moral teaching of the Fathers was nourished by constant contact with Scripture. We can see in all their works how they meditated on it and lived it in a spirit of faith. Here we also noted how the Fathers, in the tradition of St. Paul, did not hesitate to exploit the contributions of Greco-Latin philosophy, often critiquing and transforming them so as to show how the Gospel teaching responded better than any other, and in an unhoped for way, to the great questions of morality and the yearnings of the human heart. We also observed the close bond between the moral teaching of the Fathers and the great spiritual currents of the first centuries: the ideal of martyrdom, the ideal of virginity, the call to contemplation, and to monastic life.

The twelfth century inaugurated a new period with the advent of scholasticism, the use of the dialectic method associated with the reading of Scripture, patristics, and philosophy, and the founding of great universities where theological work was organized. From the Fathers to the scholastics, there was no break, but considerable renewal in the manner of treating theological material. This resulted in those great syntheses, the summas, comparable to the cathedrals of the period. That of St. Thomas was incontestably the finest and most widely known, and highly original in its moral section. We described the vast yet simple structure that the Angelic Doctor gave to Christian ethics. It has become classic.

In order to bring this out in bold relief and prepare the way for the remainder of our historical research, we then compared the plan of the second part of the *Summa* with what was followed later in the manuals of moral theology, which claimed to be following St. Thomas's order. We also discussed briefly a method for studying the Angelic Doctor, in which the relation of history to theological reflection would be taken into account; this differs from the purely speculative method of his classic commentators.

The fourteenth century had a surprise in store for us. It was the theater of a veritable revolution in the concepts of ethics and theology, with the arrival of nominalism. In Chapter 10, studying Ockham, we were present at the birth of a new system, that might be called the morality of obligation or duty-driven ethics. Here the idea and sense of obligation were substituted for virtue, and they moved from the periphery to the center of morality, where henceforth they were to set the limits of its scope, and this indirect opposition to St. Thomas. All classical moral notions were thereby affected and subtly transformed, taking on a voluntaristic and rationalistic tone. The nominalistic concept of moral theory had repercussions in theology as well as in philosophy.

The modern era, studied in Chapter 11, built on the new foundations laid by nominalism. The breakup of human faculties produced by Ockham's freedom of indifference gradually permeated all of theology, which consequently lost the unity it had enjoyed in the patristic period. Speculative theology was little by little separated from mystical, pastoral, and finally exegetical theology. The seventeenth century opened with the publication of the *Institutiones morales,* which was to serve as a role model for all subsequent ethicists. Oriented to the administration of the sacrament of penance and the solution of cases of conscience, moral textbooks relied on a simplified presentation of fundamental moral theology that in reality introduced a new systematization. The treatises on law, human acts, conscience (read "cases of conscience"), and sins, formed the foundation; legal obligation was central. The Ten Commandments and the precepts of the Church provided the divisions of special moral theory. Decisions between the claims of law and of freedom, especially in doubtful cases, became the principal work of ethicists. The dispute over probabilism took up their entire attention and split them into factions according to the criteria they adopted for the solution of cases of conscience or systems of morality. In spite of their initially modest aims and their frequent references to St. Thomas, the manuals inaugurated and spread abroad a very different concept and organization of moral material, well adapted moreover to the spirit of the times.

In order to understand the post-Tridentine moral theory presented in the manuals, we found a comparison with Protestant ethics helpful, for the crisis of the Reformation gave rise to a reciprocal conditioning in the relationship between Catholics and Protestants. This we undertook in Chapter 12. Roughly speaking we might say that since the disputes of the sixteenth century we have shared the riches of our Christian heritage between us. One side has stressed only faith and Scripture; the other, meritorious actions, tradition, the ecclesial magisterium, humanism, and natural law. The present climate, which encourages ecumenism and is profiting from biblical, patristic, and liturgical renewal, is certainly a favorable one for setting aside the antagonisms of former days. But this calls for a lucid, in-depth investigation of positions, particularly in the moral field. We need to rediscover the audacity of faith and to place it once more at the foundation of Christian ethics. We should see faith not merely as a simple act of the will but as a source of understanding drawn from the Word of God which enlightens the Christian even in the concrete details of action.

We completed our historical survey in Chapter 13, with a glance at the contemporary scene, beginning with the efforts for renewal that were made in Germany in the last century in light of Gospel themes, and the still more recent Thomist renewal. We studied texts inspired by the Council, inviting theologians to reestablish the bonds of ethics with Scripture and patristics, with spirituality and pastoral theology. We gave special attention to the phenomenon that we call "secular Christianity," considering it in the perspective of the stages of faith. Finally, we touched on the problem of the interpretation of Scripture today, urging the sort of reading that would once more feed moral theology, as in the age of the Fathers.

Our historical study shed light on many points. After the great wellsprings of the New Testament we were given the example of the Fathers of the Church, working out theology and ethics through constant contact with Scripture and a critical use of philosophy. Our study provided us with the model of the systematic construct achieved by St. Thomas. It revealed to us the great split in the fourteenth century and the rise of a particular conception of ethics—no longer a moral theory based on beatitude and the virtues, but a morality of obligation and commandments, more rational than scriptural. We were thus confronted with the need for a decisive choice in solving the present day crisis of moral theology, one of whose effects is to marginalize moral theories of obligation. Should we try to reestablish the latter, for better or for worse, on purely rational foundations, which are increasingly threatened by the incessant debate between law and freedom, or should we reconnect with the great Christian moral tradition founded directly upon the Word of the Lord welcomed in faith, like a light for the mind and strength for the will?

PART THREE: FREEDOM AND NATURAL LAW

Before building a solid edifice, we have to examine the land site. The foundations of the moral life lie within us, and they reside precisely in our freedom. We have already discerned that a certain concept of freedom underlay the morality of obligation promoted by nominalism. In Chapter 14 we made a special study of freedom of indifference, whose origins could be traced directly to Ockham's criticism of St. Thomas. This theory was the most widespread and inspired many currents of modern thought. We showed how, logically and historically, it gave rise to moral systems based on duty and obligation.

In this way we were ready in Chapter 15 to rediscover, by way of contrast, another concept of freedom, formerly a common holding of Christian theology, and one that, happily, still exists today. It is like a subterranean stream flowing beneath the many new ideas. This we called freedom for excellence, because it springs from our natural thrust toward truth and goodness. Given to us in the form of a spiritual seed, this freedom has need of education in order to grow and gradually come to maturity through the power conferred by virtue, so that we may act with excellence for ourselves and others. This is the freedom that develops within the Christian moral system of virtues, whose principle is charity, associated with the gifts of the Holy Spirit. The comparative table illustrating these two concepts of freedom shows how they differ and the consequences they have for morality.

Next, it was appropriate in Chapter 16 to study St. Thomas's teaching on freedom in order to verify his correspondence with freedom for excellence and to profit from our study of the Angelic Doctor's precise analogies. These helped us to reestablish, in the moral field, the harmonious interplay of mind and will, and to rectify the most basic ideas, such as those of the will and the good.

Our research on freedom gave us a means of reopening the lines of communication between human freedom and natural inclinations, which had been broken by nominalism. It made clear to us that we are free because of these inclinations, not in spite of them. We thus rediscovered our spiritual nature with its inclinations to truth, goodness, and life with others, as a source that emanates from God and returns to him. We found once more the principle of following nature, *sequi naturam,* which had been adopted by the Fathers and transformed in light of our creation in the image of God. This led us to a reinterpretation of natural law as something written in the human heart, at the very origin of our freedom; a dynamic interior law, not a limiting and external law that constrains us. We verified this point of view by examining each of the major human inclinations distinguished by St. Thomas: the inclination to the good, to self-preservation, to truth, to life in society, and to marriage.

Thanks to these inclinations, which make up our spiritual nature, we have a firm basis, anchored in freedom itself, for undertaking the construction of a moral system. We are able to show how we can welcome the Word of God and the work of grace in all openness, for they form the New Law, and it is chiefly from them that Christian ethics proceeds. Thus from this human pole, natural law, we are carried to the divine pole revealed to us in the teaching of Christ. This is why Christian theology must begin with faith and the Gospel, which reveal to us, beyond sin, our heart and our true nature, such as they were in the beginning and as they shall once more become through the grace of Christ.

Christian Ethics and Sin

Perhaps someone may object at this point that in our view of morality we have not given enough attention to sin, which occupies so important a place in salvation history and in the preoccupation of ethicists. Did Christ not come to save the people from their sins?

In the face of the casuist morality of former times, which might be called a morality of sin, we have deliberately set out to reestablish in all its fulness the primacy of grace, which is more powerful than sin, and the primacy of our spiritual nature, which renders us "capable of God" and at the same time is that which sin erodes. For us, in spite of its gravity, sin remains a parasite which attacks and opposes the work of God in creation and redemption, without ever being able to destroy it. If it is true that, like grace, sin remains an impenetrable mystery beyond our theories, it is nonetheless useful to situate it as well as we can.

This is where the concept of freedom we adopted intervenes once more. Freedom to sin is essential to the theory of freedom of indifference, but this conception of freedom works to the detriment of grace and nature, which are here placed in opposition to freedom. In the case of freedom for excellence, on the other hand, the ability to sin is a weakness linked with our condition as creatures, for we cannot, alone and unaided, give ourselves being or moral perfection. In this case the fulness of freedom consists in impeccability, which is the negative expression of perfection and confirms one in the love of goodness. This perfection belongs to God as the primary source of all good and all freedom. Only this concept of freedom, in my opinion, enables us to discern as best we can the depths of evil as contrasted with the richness of the good and the work of God's power and mercy. Sin not only affects the human person, as if it were something man had freely created and could take pleasure in as his own construct; it aims at God as well in that it seeks to vitiate his crowning work, who is made in his own image.

Kindliness and Spiritual Spontaneity

The study of natural inclinations, which we undertook in our final chapter, concentrated, following St. Thomas, on the first among them—the natural inclination to goodness, which is at the same time the inclination to happiness (if it is true that authentic happiness consists in the fulfillment of our love for the true good, and the enjoyment it gives us). In the tradition of St. Thomas and the Fathers of the Church, we were then confronted with the first great question of the moral life, that of happiness, which stands out in boldest relief when contrasted with evil and suffering, as the Gospel Beatitudes suggest. The study of this fundamental question obviously calls for its own book. Yet it seemed necessary to me to say a few words about it in concluding this present work because of the deeply rooted prejudices that persist in our minds against all concepts of morality that take the form of kindliness or warmth of heart.

The basic objection to all moral systems espousing the search for happiness is that they lead to an individualistic and self-serving concept of morality (characterized, for example, by an overriding concern for one's personal salvation) and that they lead logically to a generalized egocentricism in which others, and God himself, will be seen as means, the end being our own happiness. This is clearly contrary to the teaching of the Gospel.[1] This idea seems to be so self-evident that one would hardly dream of questioning it. Have ethicists not given up examining such problems since the treatise on beatitude was removed from the moral field? The prejudice is more deeply rooted than a theoretical question: it seems to be based on a profound feeling, capable of arousing almost instinctive reactions.

In responding to this objection we began with a discussion of two concepts of freedom, which we said produce two concepts of morality.

---

1. Cf. Häring, B., *The Law of Christ* (Westminster, Md.: 1961), where a pedagogical role, in the form of an initiation into conversion and support for moral life, is recognized in the desire for happiness; this function, however, is purely subsidiary.

They also result in two contrasting ideas of happiness. Freedom of indifference lies at the origin of modern individualism and centers everything on the human subject, who stands over against the world as the epitome of independent freedom. A freedom such as this is in opposition to the desire for happiness, and all other natural desires as well, yet it penetrates inward so as to shape the person to its exigencies. Thus the desire for happiness, clothed in freedom of indifference, is now as individualistic and self-centered as that same freedom. It is no longer fit to carry out its function in the moral sphere. Henceforth, it can base itself only on law, which restricts freedom with the sense of obligation or duty. A fundamental opposition ensues between the desire for happiness, turned totally subjective, and the sense of obligation. This explains the utilitarian character of modern ethical systems of happiness and their deficiency in establishing moral excellence. From this, too, derives the serious phenomenon of the split between duty-driven morality and the desire for happiness.

On the other hand, freedom for excellence is rooted in a desire for happiness which proceeds principally from a sense of truth and goodness, together with the inclination to life in society. Such a desire, spiritual in its origin, empowers us to conceive the love of friendship, which leads us to love truth and goodness, God and others, in their reality, in themselves and for their own sake. This desire, in contrast to sensible needs, can bring about within us that openness and unique bonding between our own happiness and the happiness of others that culminates in true love and is manifested by joy.

Yet the desire for happiness raises a question, and everything depends on the way we answer it. We must, in a free choice, agree to love that which possesses the quality of goodness, beyond all consideration of utility and sensible pleasure, and often to their detriment, if we wish to find the true answer and perceive through our own experience that our freedom and happiness increase in the measure of our generous love of truth and goodness. We cannot place just any desire whatsoever for happiness at the source of morality; but in the depths of our being there is a certain sense of happiness that is identified with our sense of true goodness. This comes from God and draws us to him. It is imperative for us to rediscover this. It is this desire which awakens in us the message of the Gospel Beatitudes and makes them resound within us. They must once more become the foundation of Christian morality. This desire for happiness is capable of opening itself to charity, being ordered to it, and accepting it as its very foundation—if it is true that charity is, as St. Thomas affirmed, friendship with God based on communion with his beatitude. In fact, ordinary human experience proves that the desire for happiness cannot be separated from love; for how can we love another without wanting their happiness, and how can we help feeling joy when we can contribute to it? We can note, too, that moral systems based on obligation slight love as well as the desire for happiness, subjecting them both to the constraint of obligations.

The rediscovery of the spiritual desire for happiness at the very source of freedom for excellence calls, however, for a profound purification of the human heart, because of sin, which affects it and has its taproot in self-love and pride. One of the major and praiseworthy concerns of duty-driven systems such as that of Kant is certainly to purify the moral intention and eliminate all contamination brought on by sensible and selfish desires. But can we ever shield the man of duty against the secret pride that convinces him that he has acted rightly by his own power each time he strives to act purely out of a sense of duty? Can anyone ever purify himself?

The spiritual desire for happiness, when it is inspired and guided by the Word of God, sets us upon a long journey marked by various trials, which progressively purify our hearts in regard to our principal instincts. Poverty detaches us from the instinct of possessiveness, sweetness tempers aggressiveness, affliction sobers our thirst for pleasure, and so forth. Scripture compares this to the work of dyeing cloth or the purifying of gold and silver, and the Fathers well understood how the Beatitudes combine to effect the cleanness of heart needed for seeing God and sharing his bliss.

Such a work in us must needs be the work of another, the Spirit of Christ, who alone can establish the Kingdom within us and effect a purification that strikes even at the roots of self-love. We cannot take the first step on such a road until we pass through the narrow gate of humility and renunciation for the Lord, and we cannot advance without a continual awareness of our insufficiency, together with a joyous confidence in the power of grace. In thus yielding to the action of the Spirit, we can rest assured that the work of our cleansing will be carried forward far better than if it were undertaken by the most exacting man of duty. Instead of destroying our desire of happiness or continually restraining it, the Spirit knows how to heal and rectify it at its very source, and finally fulfill it.

This is why the Beatitudes and the Sermon on the Mount promise us joy and rewards, without a shadow of hesitation. When in the end it is purified, the desire for happiness will have changed its nature, so to speak; it will spring henceforth from true charity, which God alone can form, and no longer from a desire limited by self-interest. Behind the simple words of the Gospel we must uncover the new realities it proclaims and forms in the hearts of believers.

Clearly, the entire question turns on reestablishing full contact between Christian ethics and its wellsprings, which we have sought throughout this book. The two external sources are Scripture, transmitted by the Church, with the magisterium, and the wisdom of those enlightened by the Word. But above all there are the two interior sources, which give these impetus and life: the grace of the Holy Spirit with the gifts and virtues, and natural law, the sense of truth and goodness and the yearning for God. Through these "higher" instincts, as St. Thomas calls them, Christian ethics, too narrowly confined and become stagnant, can once more become water flowing from the wellsprings to quench our thirst.

Select Bibliography

This select bibliography includes all sources cited in the notes, all English-language entries in the bibliography of the original French edition, and English translations of other entries insofar as they could be located in library catalogs. For an exhaustive listing of other sources, the reader is referred to the full bibliography in the original French edition.

Adams, R. M. "Autonomy and Theological Studies." *Religious Studies* 15 (1979), no. 2, 191–94.

Adler, Alfred. *Understanding Human Nature.* Trans. Wolfe. New York: Greenberg, 1946.

Alexander of Hales. *Summa theologica.*

Alfaro, J. *Theology of Justice in the World.* Vatican City: Pontifical Commission on Justice and Peace, 1973.

Aquinas, Saint Thomas. *De malo.*

———. *De officiis.*

———. *De regimini principium.*

———. *De veritate.*

———. *Scriptum super libros Sententiarum.*

———. *Sententia libri Politicorum.*

———. *Summa theologiae.*

Aristotle. *Nicomachean Ethics.*

———. *Politics.*

Augustine, Saint. *Confessiones.*

———. *De civitate Dei.*

———. *De moribus Ecclesiae catholicae.*

———. *De trinitate.*

Bahnsen, G. L. *Theonomy in Christian Ethics.* Nutley, 1977.

Basil, Saint. *Moralia.*

———. *Regulae fusius tractae.*

Bergson, Henri. *The Two Sources of Morality and Religion.* Notre Dame: University of Notre Dame Press, 1977.

Billuart. *Cursus theologiae. Tractatus de actibus humanis.* Dissertatio II. Vol. 4. Paris, 1895.

Böckle, Franz. *Fundamental Moral Theology.* Trans. N. D. Smith. New York: Pueblo, 1980.

Bonaventure, Saint. *Works.*

Borne, E. "God Is Not Dead." In *Foi vivante*. Paris, 1974.

Bourke, V. J. "Right Reason in Contemporary Ethics." *Thomist* 38 (1974): 106–24.

———."Moral Philosophy without Revelation?" *Thomist* 40 (1976): 555–70.

Bouyer, Louis. *The Meaning of the Monastic Life.* Trans. Kathleen Pond. New York: P. J. Kenedy, 1955.

———. *The Spirit and Forms of Protestantism.* Cleveland: World, 1964.

———. *The Spirituality of the New Testament and the Fathers.* Trans. Mary D. Ryan. New York: Desclee, 1964.

Boyle, L. E. *The Setting of the Summa theologiae of St. Thomas.* Toronto: Pontifical Institute of Mediaeval Studies, 1982.

Brouillard, R. "Casuistique." In *Catholicisme, hier, aujourd'hui, demain*. Vol. 2, 1950.

Brown, O. J. *Natural Rectitude and Divine Law in Aquinas. An Approach to an Intergal Interpretation of the Thomistic Doctrine of Law.* Toronto, 1981.

Bucceroni, J. *Institutiones theologiae moralis.* 4 vols. Rome, 1913.

Burch, R. "Objective Values and Divine Command Theory." *New Scholasticism* 54 (1980): 279–304.

Buzy, Denis, S.C.J. "Beatitudes." In *Dictionnaire de Spiritualité* (1961).

Capone, D. *Introduzione alla teologica morale.* Brescia, 1972.

Castiello, J. "The Psychology of Habit in St. Thomas." *Modern Schoolman* 14 (1936): 9–12.

Cerfaux, L. *Christ in the Theology of St. Paul.* Trans. Geoffrey Webb and Adrian Walker. New York: Herder and Herder, 1959.

———. *The Church in the Theology of St. Paul.* Trans. Geoffrey Webb and Adrian Walker. New York: Herder and Herder, 1959.

———. *The Christian in the Theology of St. Paul.* Trans. Lilian Soiron. London: G. Chapman, 1967.

———. *The Spiritual Journey of St. Paul.* Trans. John C. Guinness. New York: Sheed and Ward, 1968.

Cessario, Romanus, O.P. *The Moral Virtues and Theological Ethics.* Notre Dame/London: University of Notre Dame Press, 1991.

Chenu, M.-D. *St. Thomas d'Aquin et la théologie.* Paris, 1952.

———. *Toward Understanding St. Thomas.* Trans. A. M. Landry, O.P., and D. Hughes, O.P. Chicago: Regnery, 1964.

———. *Nature, Man, and Society in the Twelfth Century; Essays on New Theological Perspectives in the Latin West.* Chicago: University of Chicago Press, 1968.

Cicero. *De finibus bonorum et malorum.*

———. *Disputationes Tusculanes.*

Connery, J. R. "Morality of Consequences. A Critical Approach." *Theological Studies* 34 (1973): 396–414.

———. "Catholic Ethics: Has the Norm for Rulemaking Changed?" *Theological Studies* 42 (1981): 232–50.

Connolly, J. L. *John Gerson, Reformer and Mystic.* Louvain, 1928.

Crotty, N. "Biblical Perspectives in Moral Theology." *Theological Studies* 26 (1965) 574–95.

———. "Conscience and Conflict." *Theological Studies* 32 (1971): 208–32.

Crowe, M. B. "St. Thomas and Ulpian's Natural Law." *St. Thomas Aquinas, 1274–1974.* Toronto, 1974.

———. "The Pursuit of the Natural Law." *Irish Theological Quarterly* 44 (1977): 3–29.

Curran, Charles E. *Absolutes in Moral Theology?* Washington, 1968.

———. *A New Look at Christian Morality.* Notre Dame, 1968.

———. *Catholic Moral Theology in Dialogue.* Notre Dame, 1972.

———. *New Perspectives in Moral Theology.* Notre Dame, 1974.

———. *Ongoing Revision: Studies in Moral Theology.* Notre Dame, 1976.

———. "Utilitarianism and Contemporary Moral Theology: Situating the Debates." *Louvain Studies* 6 (1977): 256–72.

———. "Method in Moral Theology. An Overview from an American Perspective." *Studia Moralia* 18 (1980): 107–27.

Curran, Charles E., and Richard A. McCormick. *Moral Norms and Catholic Tradition.* New York, 1979.

———. *Themes in Fundamental Moral Theology.* Notre Dame, 1979.

———. *The Distinctiveness of Christian Ethics.* Paulist Press, 1980.

D'Annibale, J. *Summula theologiae moralis.* 3 vols. Rome, 1908.

Davies, William David. *The Sermon on the Mount.* Cambridge: Cambridge University Press, 1966.

Deferrari, R. J., and Sister M. Inviolata Barry. *A Complete Index of the Summa Theologica of St. Thomas Aquinas.* Washington, 1956.

De Finance, Joseph. *Essai sur l'agir humain.* Rome, 1959.

———. "Devoir et amour." *Gregorianum* 64 (1983): 243–72.

———. *An Ethical Inquiry.* Trans. and adap. Michael O'Brien. Rome: Editrice Pontificia Universita Gregoriana, 1991.

Degnan, D. A. "Two Models of Positive Law in Aquinas: A Study of the Relationship of Positive Law and Natural Law." *Thomist* 46 (1982): 1–32.

Delhaye, Philippe. *La conscience morale du chrétien.* Tournai, 1964.

———. "La mise en cause de las spécificité de la morale chrétienne." *Revue Théologique de Louvain* 4 (1973).

Deman, Th. "Probabilisme." In *Dictionnaire de Théologie Catholique* 13 (1936).

Dibelius, M. *The Sermon on the Mount.* New York, 1940.

Dodd, Charles Harold. *About the Gospels.* Cambridge: Cambridge University Press, 1950.

Dubay, T. "The State of Moral Theology: A Critical Appraisal." *Theological Studies* 35 (1974): 482–506.

Dublanchy, E. "Casuistique." In *Dictionnaire de Théologie Catholique* 2 (1905).

———. "Charité." In *Dictionnaire de Théologie Catholique* 2 (1905).

Durchow, U. "Der Aufbau von Augustinius Schriften Confessiones und De Trinitate." *Zeitschrift für Theologie und Kirche* 62 (1965).

Eschmann, I. T. "A Catalogue of St. Thomas's Works; Bibliographical Notes." In E. Gilson, *The Christian Philosophy.* New York, 1956, pp. 381–430.

Farugi, I. R. *Christian Ethics. A Historical and Systematic Analysis of Its Dominant Ideas.* Montreal, 1968.

Feinburg, J. *Moral Concepts*. London: Oxford, 1969.

Flannery, Austin, ed. *Vatican Council II. The Conciliar and Post Conciliar Documents*. Northport, NY: Costello, 1975.

Fonck, A. "Prière." In *Dictionnaire de Théologie Catholique* 13 (1936).

Ford, C. I., and G. Kelly. *Contemporary Moral Theology*. Westminister, 1959. Vol. I: *Questions in Fundamental Moral Theology*. Vol. II: *Marriage Questions*.

Forell, G. W. *Ethics of Decision. An Introduction to Christian Ethics*. Philadelphia, 1955.

Fuchs, Josef. *Theologica moralis generalis*. Rome, 1963.

———. "The Absoluteness of Moral Terms." *Doing Evil to Achieve Good*. Chicago (1978), 145–64.

———. "The 'Sin of the World' and Normative Morality." *Gregorianum* 61 (1980): 51–76.

———. *Le désir et la tendresse*. Geneva, 1982.

———. *Personal Responsibility and Christian Morality*. Washington, D.C.: Georgetown University Press, 1983.

Gardeil, A. "Béatitude." In *Dictionnaire de Théologie Catholique* 2 (1905).

———. "Béatitudes évangéliques." In *Dictionnaire de Théologie Catholique* 2 (1905).

———. "Bonheur." In *Dictionnaire de Théologie Catholique* 2 (1905).

Garvens, A. "Die Grundlagen der Ethik Wilhelm von Ockham." *Franziskanische Studien* 21 (1934).

Geisler, N. L. *Ethics: Alternatives and Issues*. Grand Rapids, 1971.

Génicot, E., and J. Salsmans. *Institutiones theologiae moralis*. 17th ed. Brussels, 1951.

Gibson, A. "Visions of the Future." *Concilium* 86 (June 1973).

Gilleman, Gérard. *The Primacy of Charity in Moral Theology*. Trans. William F. Ryan, S.J., and André Vachon, S.J. Westminster, MD: Newman Press, 1959.

Gilson, E. *Saint Thomas Aquinas*. London: Milford, 1935.

———. "Les moralistes chrétiens." In M.-D. Chenu, *St. Thomas d'Aquin et la théologie*. Paris, 1952.

———. *The Christian Philosophy of St. Thomas Aquinas. With Catalogue of St. Thomas's Works*. Trans. L. K. Shook, C.S.B. New York: Random House, 1956.

Girard, R. *Violence and the Sacred*. Baltimore: Johns Hopkins University Press, 1977.

———. *Things Hidden since the Foundation of the World*. Stanford: Stanford University Press, 1987.

Grabman, M. *The Interior Life of St. Thomas Aquinas Presented from His Works and the Acts of His Canonization Process*. Trans. Nicholas Ashenbrener. Milwaukee: Bruce, 1951.

Granel, G. "The Obliteration of the Subject in Contemporary Philosophy." *Concilium* 86 (June 1973): 64–72.

Greenwood, D. "Moral Obiligation in the Sermon on the Mount." *Theological Studies* 31 (1970): 301–9.

Gregory of Nyssa. *The Beatitudes*. (Westminster, MD: Newman Press, 1954).

Grisez, G. *The Way of the Lord Jesus.* Vol. 1. *Christian Moral Principles.* Chicago, 1983.

Grunston, M. *Freedom, a New Analysis.* London, 1953.

Gustafason, J. M. *Christ and the Moral Life.* New York, 1968.

———. *Christian Ethics and the Community.* Philadelphia, 1971.

———. "The Relationship of Empirical Science to Moral Thought." *Proceedings of the Catholic Theological Society of America* 26 (1971): 192–207.

———. *Can Ethics Be Christian?* Chicago, 1975.

———. *Protestant and Roman Catholic Ethics.* Chicago, 1978.

Hamman, A. G. *Explication du Sermon.* Paris, 1978.

Häring, Bernard. *The Law of Christ.* Trans. Kaiser. Paramus, NJ: Newman Press, 1961.

———. "The Normative Value of the Sermon on the Mount." *Catholic Biblical Quarterly* 29 (1967): 375–85.

Hare, R. M. *Moral Thinking. Its Levels, Method and Point.* Oxford 1981.

Harnack, A. von. *What Is Christianity?* New York: Harper, 1957.

Helm, P. *Divine Commands and Morality.* Oxford, 1981.

Herms, E. "Virtue: A Neglected Concept in Protestant Ethics." *Scottish Journal of Theology* 35 (1982): 481–95.

Hughes, G. J. "Infallibility in Morals." *Theological Studies* 34 (1973): 415–28.

Janssen, A. Review of J. Tonneau's *Absolu et obligation en morale* in *Ephemerides Theologicae Lovanienses* 41 (1965).

Janssens, L. "Ontic Evil and Moral Evil." *Louvain Studies* 4 (1972): 115–56.

———. "Norms and Priorities in a Love Ethics." *Louvain Studies* 6 (1977) 207–28.

Jeremias, Joachim. *The Sermon on the Mount.* Trans. Norman Perrin. Philadelphia: Fortress Press, 1963.

John of St. Thomas. *The Gifts of the Holy Ghost.* New York: Sheed and Ward, 1951.

John Paul II. *Encyclical Redemptor hominis.* London: Catholic Truth Society, 1979.

———. *On Human Work: Encyclical Laborem exercens.* Washington, DC: United States Catholic Conference, 1981.

———. *On the Family: Apostolic Exhortation Familiaris Consortio.* Washington, DC: United States Catholic Conference, 1982.

Kaufman, G. W. "A Problem of Theology: The Concept of Nature." *Harvard Theological Review* 65 (1972): 337–66.

Keane, P. S. "The Objective Moral Order: Reflections on Recent Research." *Theological Studies* 43 (1982): 260–78.

Kelly, D. F. "Aspects of Sin in Today's Theology." In *Louvain Studies* 9 (1982–83): 191–97.

Kiely, B. M. *Psychology and Moral Thought: Lines of Convergence.* Rome, 1980.

King, J. C. "The Inadequacy of Situation Ethics." *Thomist* 34 (1970): 423–37.

Kissinger, W. S. *The Sermon on the Mount.* Metuchen, NJ, 1975.

Kühn, U. *Via caritatis. Theologie des Gesetzes bei Thomas von Aquin.* Göttingen, 1965.

Laberthonnière, L. *Théorie de l'éducation.* 9th ed. Paris, 1935.

Lacroix, J. *Vocation personnelle et tradition nationale.* Paris, 1942.

Lagarde, G. de, *La naissance de l'esprit laïque au déclin du moyen age.* Vol. 6. L'individualisme ockhamiste. Paris, 1946.

Lee, P. "Permanence of the Ten Commandments: St. Thomas and His Modern Commentators." *Theological Studies* 42 (1981): 422–43.

Leff, G. *William of Ockham.* Manchester, 1975.

Lehmkuhl, A. *Theologia moralis,* 2 vols. 11th ed., Freiburg im Breisgau, 1910.

Lehu, L. *Philosophia moralis et socialis.* Vol. 1. Paris: Lecoffre, 1914.

Le Senne, R. *Le devoir.* Paris, 1931.

———. *Traité de morale générale.* Paris 1942.

Leclerq, Jacques. *L'enseignement de la théologie morale.* Paris, 1950.

———. *La philosophie morale de saint Thomas.* Louvain, 1955.

Linwood, U. "William of Ockham's Theological Ethics." *Franciscan Studies* 11 (1973): 310–50.

Lombardi, J. L. "The Theological Justification of Morality." *New Scholasticism* 52 (1978), no. 4, 569–74.

Lyonnet, Stanislas. *The Christian Lives by the Spirit.* Trans. John Moriss. Staten Island: Alba House, 1971.

McAvoy, J. "Saint Alphonse de Liguori." In *Catholicisme.* Vol. 1. 1950.

McClendon, J. W. "Three Strands of Christian Ethics." *Journal of Religious Ethics* (Spring 1978): 54–80.

McCormick, R. A. "Morality and Magisterium." *Theological Studies* 29 (1968): 707–18.

———. "Specificity of Christian Morality." *Theological Studies* 32 (1971): 71–78.

———. "Norms, Experience, and the Behavioral Sciences." *Theological Studies* 33 (1972): 86–90.

———. *Ambiguity in Moral Choice.* Milwaukee, 1973.

———. *Notes on Moral Theology: 1965 through 1980.* Washington, 1981.

McDonagh, E. "Morality and Spirituality." *Studia Moralia* 15 (1977): 121–37.

———. *Doing the Truth. The Quest for Moral Theology.* Dublin 1979.

McInerny, R. "Naturalism and Thomist Ethics." *Thomist* 40 (1976): 222–24.

MacIntyre, A. *After Virtue.* Notre Dame, 1981.

McHenry, F. "Natural Morality of Christian Living?" *Irish Ecclesiastical Record* 1 (1968): 14–54.

McNamara, L. J. *Direct and Indirect. A Study in the Principle of Double Effect in Roman Catholic Theology.* Oxford, 1981.

McNamara, V. "Religion and Morality." *Irish Theological Quarterly* 44 (1977): 105–16; 175–91.

Macquarrie, J. *A Dictionary of Christian Ethics.* London 1967.

Maguire, D. C. *The Moral Choice.* Garden City, 1978.

Malloy, E. A. "Natural Law Theory and Catholic Moral Theology." *American Ecclesticial Review* 169 (1975): 456–70.

———. "The Christian Ethicist in the Community of Faith." *Theological Studies* 43 (1982): 379–98.

Manning, F. "Bonhoeffer's Ethical Concepts." *Louvain Studies* 2 (1969): 315–28.

Manson, T. W. *Ethics and the Gospels.* London, 1960.

Maritain, Jacques. *St. Thomas, Angel of the Schools.* London: Sheed and Ward, 1931.

———. *The Degrees of Knowledge*. Trans. Bernard Wall and Margot R. Adamson. London: Century Press, 1937.

———. *Neuf leçons sur les notions premières de la philosophie morale*. Paris, 1951.

———. *The Education of Man: Educational Philosophy*. Trans. Don Arthur Gallagher and Idella Gallagher. Garden City, NY: Doubleday, 1962.

———. *Moral Philosophy, an Historical and Critical Survey of the Great Systems*. New York: Scribner, 1964.

Marshall, G. J. "Human Nature Changes." *New Scholasticism* 54 (1980): 168–91.

Matsagouras, E. G. "Moral Development and Education: Educational Implications of the Early Greek Patristic Anthropology and Their Relation to Modern Theories of Moral Education." *Theologia* 52 (1981): 361–89; 550–70.

Mehl, R. *Les attitudes morales*. Paris, 1971.

Metz, Johannes Baptist. *Theology of the World*. London: Burns and Oates, 1969.

Michel, A. "Vérité, Véracité." In *Dictionnaire de Théologie Catholique* 15 (1950).

Midgley, L. C. "Beyond Human Nature. Natural Law and Contemporary Moral Theology." In *Contemporary Problems in Moral Theology*. Notre Dame, 1970.

Milhaven, J. C. "Towards an Epistemology of Ethics." *Theological Studies* 27 (1966): 228–41.

Miller, J. "Ethics within an Ecclesial Context." *Angelicum* 57 (1980): 32–44.

Mitchell, B. *Morality: Religious and Secular. The Dilemma of the Traditional Conscience*. Oxford, 1980.

Murphy, F. X. "The Foundations of Tertullian's Moral Teaching." *Thomistica Morum Principia*. Vol. 2. Rome, 1960.

———. "The Background to a History of Patristical Moral Thought." *Studia Moralia* 1 (1962).

———. *Moral Teaching in the Primitive Church*. New York, 1968.

Nierynck, F. *The Sermon on the Mount in the Gospel Synopsis*. Louvain, 1976.

Newman, John Henry, Cardinal. *Essay in aid of a Grammar of Assent*. New York: Longmans, Green and Co., 1906.

———. "Personal Influence, the Means of Propagating the Truth." In *Newman: Fifteen Sermons Preached before the University of Oxford*. London, 1906.

Niebuhr, R. *An Interpretation of Christian Ethics*. New York, 1979.

Nietzsche, F. *Beyond Good and Evil*. Chicago, 1955.

O'Callaghan, D. "Moral Principles and Exception." *The Furrow* 22 (1971): 686–96.

O'Connell, T. E. "The Search for Christian Moral Norms." *Chicago Studies* 11 (1972): 89–99.

———. *Principles for a New Christian Morality*. New York, 1978.

O'Donovan, O. *The Problem of Self-Love in St. Augustine*. New Haven/London, 1980.

Omoregbe, J. *Ethics. A Systematic and Historical Study*. London, 1979.

Oraison, Marc. *Morality for Our Time*. Garden City, NY: Doubleday, 1968.

———. *Morality for Moderns*. Trans. J. F. Bernard. Garden City, NY: Doubleday, 1972.

O'Riordan, S. "The Teaching of the Papal Encyclicals as a Source and Norm of

Moral Theology: A Historical and Anayltic Survey." *Studia Moralia* 14 (1976).

Osborn, E. *Ethical Patterns in Early Christian Thought*. Cambridge, 1976.

Pannenberg, Wolfhart. *Ethics*. Philadelphia: Westminster Press, 1981.

Pesch, Otto Herman. *The God Question in Thomas Aquinas and Martin Luther*. Trans. Gottfried G. Krodel. Philadelphia: Fortress Press, 1972.

Peschke, C. H. *Christian Ethics*. Vol. I: *A Presentation of General Moral Theology in Light of Vatican II*; Vol. II: *A Presentation of Special Moral Theology in Light of Vatican II*. Dublin, 1975–78.

Pinckaers, S. "Une morale sans péché." *Evangéliser* 10 (1955).

———. "Le Dr. Hesnard et la morale sans péché." *Revue génerale belge* (1956).

———. "La vertu est tout autre chose qu'une habitude." *Nouvelle revue théologique* 80 (1960): 387–403.

———. "Der Sinn für die Freundschaftsliebe als Urtatsache der thomistischen Ethik." *Sein und Ethos* (Mainz) (1963): 228–35.

———. *The Renewal of Morality*. Tournai/Paris, 1964, 1979.

———. "Lecture positive et lecture 'réelle' de la bible." *Sources* 3 (1977).

———. "La violence, le sacré et le christianisme." *Nova et Vetera* (1979).

———. "Amour de Dieu, amour unique." *Sources* 5 (1979): 105–17.

———. "L'encyclique *Dives in misericordia*." *Sources* 7 (1981): 59–67.

———. "La question des actes intrinsèquement mauvais." *Revue Thomiste* 82 (1982); 84 (1984).

———. "Le cas du Dr Augoyard." *Sources* 9 (1983): 193–200.

———. "Suivre sa conscience." *Sources* 9 (1983): 97–102.

Piper, O. *Christian Ethics*. London, 1970.

Plé, Albert. *Duty or Pleasure? A New Appraisal of Christian Ethics*. New York: Paragon House, 1987.

Prat, F., et alia. "Charité." In *Dictionnaire de Spiritualité* 2 (1953).

Prümmer, D. *Handbook of Moral Theology*. New York: P. J. Kenedy, 1957.

Rahner, Karl. *Do You Believe in God?* Trans. R. Strachen. New York: Newman Press, 1969.

Ratzinger, Joseph. *Principles of Christian Morality*. Trans. Graham Hamson. San Francisco: Ignatius Press, 1986.

Ricoeur, Paul. *Philosophy of the Will*. Chicago: Regnery, 1965.

Riou, A. *Le monde et l'Eglise selon Maxime le Confesseur*. Paris, 1973.

Robinson, John A. T. *Christian Morals Today*. Philadelphia: Westminster Press, 1964.

Robinson, N. H. G. *The Groundwork of Christian Ethics*. London, 1971.

Rollero, P. "Commentary on *Expositio in Lucam*." In *Augustinus Magister*. Vol. 1. Paris, 1954.

Rosenstock, G. G. *Towards Our New Morality*. New York, 1967.

Scheler, Max Ferdinand. *The Nature of Sympathy*. Trans. Peter Heath. London: Routledge and Kegan Paul, 1954.

———. *Formalism in Ethics and Non-formal Ethics of Values: A New Attempt toward the Foundation of an Ethical Personalism*. Trans. Manfred S. Frings and Roger L. Funk. Evanston: Northwestern University Press, 1973.

Schnackenburg, Rudolf. *The Moral Teaching of the New Testament*. Trans. J. Holland Smith and W. S. O'Hara. New York: Herder and Herder, 1967.

Sertillanges, A. D. "Dicussions. La morale ancienne et la morale moderna." *Revue philosophique* 51 (1901): 280–92.

———. *La philosophie morale de saint Thomas d'Aquin*. Paris, 1942.
———. *Saint Thomas Aquinas and His Work*. Trans. Godfrey Anstruther, O.P. London: Burns, Oates, and Washburne, 1933.
Simon, V. *Freedom of Choice*. Ed. Peter Wolff. New York: Fordham University Press, 1969.
Smalley, B. *The Study of the Bible in the Middle Ages*. 3d ed. Oxford, 1952–83.
Spaemann, R. "A quoi sert la morale?" *Communio* 7 (1977): 47–56.
Spicq, Ceslaus. *Agapé in the New Testament*. Vol. 3. Trans. Marie Aquinas McNamara, O.P., and Mary Honoria Richter, O.P. St. Louis: Herder, 1966.
———. *Theological Lexicon of the New Testament*. Vols. 1–3. Hendrickson, 1994.
Suárez, Francisco. *Opera*. Ed. Vivès. Paris, 1856–78.
Tanquerey, A. B. *Synopsis Theologiae moralis et pastoralis*. Tournai, 1902.
Theiner, J. *Die Entwicklung der Moraltheologie zur eigenständigen Disziplin*. Regensburg, 1970.
Thielicke, Helmut. *Theological Ethics*. Ed. William H. Lazareth. Philadelphia: Fortress Press, 1966.
Tierney, B. "Infallibility in Morals: A Response." *Theological Studies* 35 (1974): 507.
Tonneau, J. "Devoir." In *Dictionnaire de Spiritualité* (1957).
Van den Marck, W. "Ethics as a Key to Aquinas Theology." *Thomist* 40 (1976): 535–54.
Van Kol, A. *Theologia Moralis*. Barcelona, 1968.
Vereecke, L. "Loi et Evangile selon Guillaume d'Ockham." In *Law and Gospel*. Geneva, 1981.
———. *De Guillaume d'Ockham à St. Alphonse de Liguori*.
Vermeesch, A. *Theologiae moralis principia, responsa, consilia*. Rome, 1922–24.
Vignaux, P. *Philosophy in the Middle Ages*. Trans. E. C. Hall. New York: Meridian Books, 1959.
Vittrant, J. B. *Théologie Morale*. 19th ed. Paris, 1948.
Waddann, H. *A New Introduction in Moral Theology*. London 1982.
Walter, J. J. "Christian Ethics: Distinctive and Specific?" *American Ecclesiastical Review* 169 (1975): 470–89.
———. "The Dependence of Christian Morality on Faith. A Critical Assessment." *Eglise et théologie* 12 (1981): 237–77.
Ward, K. *Ethics and Christianity*. New York, 1970.
Weisheipl, J. A. *Friar Thomas d'Aquino. His Life, Thought, and Works*. Oxford, 1975/Washington, DC, 1983.
Yannaras, C., R. Mehl, and J.-M. Aubert. *La loi de la liberté. Evangile et morale*. Paris: Mame, 1972.

Index

The Sources of Christian Ethics was composed in Sabon by Brevis Press, Bethany, Connecticut; printed and bound by Braun-Brumfield, Inc., Ann Arbor, Michigan; and designed and produced by Kachergis Book Design, Pittsboro, North Carolina.